# Corporate Purpose, CSR, and ESG

# Corporate Purpose, CSR, and ESG

*A Trans-Atlantic Perspective*

Edited by
JENS-HINRICH BINDER, KLAUS J. HOPT, AND
THILO KUNTZ

Great Clarendon Street, Oxford, OX2 6DP,
United Kingdom

Oxford University Press is a department of the University of Oxford.
It furthers the University's objective of excellence in research, scholarship,
and education by publishing worldwide. Oxford is a registered trade mark of
Oxford University Press in the UK and in certain other countries

© Jens-Hinrich Binder, Klaus J. Hopt, and Thilo Kuntz 2024

The moral rights of the authors have been asserted

All rights reserved. No part of this publication may be reproduced, stored in
a retrieval system, or transmitted, in any form or by any means, without the
prior permission in writing of Oxford University Press, or as expressly permitted
by law, by licence or under terms agreed with the appropriate reprographics
rights organization. Enquiries concerning reproduction outside the scope of the
above should be sent to the Rights Department, Oxford University Press, at the
address above

You must not circulate this work in any other form
and you must impose this same condition on any acquirer

Public sector information reproduced under Open Government Licence v3.0
(https://www.nationalarchives.gov.uk/doc/open-government-licence)

Published in the United States of America by Oxford University Press
198 Madison Avenue, New York, NY 10016, United States of America

British Library Cataloguing in Publication Data
Data available

Library of Congress Control Number: 2024939135

ISBN 978–0–19–891257–6

DOI: 10.1093/oso/9780198912576.001.0001

Printed and bound by
CPI Group (UK) Ltd, Croydon, CR0 4YY

# Contents

*Table of Cases*     ix
*Table of Legislation*     xi
*List of Abbreviations*     xxi
*List of Contributors*     xxiii
*About the Authors*     xxv

1. Corporate Purpose, Corporate Social Responsibility, and ESG: An Introduction to the Trans-Atlantic Dialogue     1
   *Jens-Hinrich Binder, Klaus J. Hopt, and Thilo Kuntz*
   I. Introduction     1
   II. Thematic Overview     5

2. Corporate Purpose and Stakeholder Value: Historical, Economic, and Comparative Law Remarks on the Current Debate, Legislative Options, and Enforcement Problems     17
   *Klaus J. Hopt*
   I. The Current Debate on Corporate Purpose, Stakeholder Participation, and ESG     17
   II. Current Economic, Social Science, and Policy Arguments, and Legislative Options     25
   III. Making Stakeholder Governance Work: Enforcement Problems     39
   IV. Conclusions and Theses     51

3. Corporate Purpose: Theoretical and Empirical Foundations/Confusions     55
   *Holger Spamann and Jacob Fisher*
   I. Introduction     55
   II. Theory of Purpose     57
   III. Empirics of Purpose     72
   IV. Conclusion     81

4. US ESG Regulation in Transnational Context     83
   *Virginia Harper Ho*
   I. Introduction     83
   II. The Transnational Context of ESG Regulation     84
   III. US ESG Regulation: An Overview     87
   IV. The US Institutional Context for ESG Regulation     95
   V. Conclusion     102

5. Stakeholder Governance Models and Corporate Interests: Experiences from Germany     105
   *Rüdiger Veil*
   I. Introduction     105
   II. The Trustee Model of Stakeholder Governance: Enterprise Accountability of the Board in Germany     106

|     |     |
| --- | --- |
| III. The Representative Model | 119 |
| IV. Conclusion | 125 |

6. Corporate Purpose: The US Discussion and the Restatement of the Law of Corporate Governance — 127
   *Edward B. Rock*
   I. Introduction — 127
   II. The Restatement of Corporate Governance's Description of the 'Objective' of a Corporation — 129
   III. What Is 'Corporate Purpose'? — 132
   IV. The Link between the 'Objective of a Corporation' and 'Corporate Purpose' — 133
   V. The US Discussion of Corporate Purpose — 135
   VI. Shareholder-driven ESG Activism — 136
   VII. The Golden Thread: Corporate Law's Single Firm Focus — 137
   VIII. Conclusion — 139

7. ESG Regulation, CSR, and Corporate Purpose: A UK Perspective — 141
   *Irene-marié Esser and Iain MacNeil*
   I. Introduction — 141
   II. UK Regulatory Position — 142
   III. Aligning ESG with UK Corporate Law: An Entity Model of ESG — 153
   IV. Conclusion — 159

8. ESG and the Ethical Dimension — 161
   *Christine Osterloh-Konrad*
   I. Introduction — 161
   II. Corporations as Moral Agents? — 162
   III. Moral Behaviour and Fiduciary Duties — 165
   IV. Mandatory ESG Reporting and the Law-Morality Divide — 167
   V. Brave New World — 170
   VI. Concluding Remarks — 170

9. Corporate Purpose in the United States 1800–2000 — 173
   *Harwell Wells*
   I. Introduction — 173
   II. Purpose in the Nineteenth Century — 174
   III. The Origins of the Modern Debate — 177
   IV. Corporate Purpose at Mid-century — 182
   V. Back to Shareholders — 189
   VI. Conclusion — 194

10. Corporate Purpose and the Blurred Boundaries of Internal and External Governance — 195
    *Ann M. Lipton*
    I. Introduction — 195
    II. The Great Debate — 196
    III. Corporations Are Designed to Benefit Multiple Constituencies — 200

IV. Shareholder Primacy Is One Option for a Governmentally
   Mandated Design to Benefit All Stakeholders 203
V. The Stakeholderist Side of the Coin 212
VI. Rethinking the Form 215
VII. Conclusion 216

11. Leading Wherever They Want? CSR, ESG, and Directors' Duties 217
   *Jens-Hinrich Binder*
   I. Introduction 217
   II. Stakeholderism versus Shareholderism: The Backdrop in
      Traditional Corporate Law Doctrine 222
   III. Which Duties? Emerging Obligations in the Light of Statutory
      Frameworks and International Standards—A European Perspective
      on a Global Trend 233
   IV. How Will They Respond? The Reorientation of Directors' Duties
      and Their Implications in the Real World 241
   V. Conclusions 244

12. Stewardship and ESG in Europe 247
   *Guido Ferrarini and Michele Siri*
   I. Introduction 247
   II. Main Legal Strategies 249
   III. Investment Activities and ESG 258
   IV. Engagement Activities and ESG 269
   V. Concluding Remarks 273

13. The French 'Duty of Vigilance' and the European Proposal on
   Companies' Due Diligence Duties 275
   *Alain Pietrancosta*
   I. Introduction 275
   II. The Genesis of the French 'Duty of Vigilance' and the Proposed
      European Generalization of 'Due Diligence Requirements' 284
   III. The French Vigilance and the European Diligence Compared 288

14. Green Bonds and Their New Regulation in the EU 301
   *Christoph Kumpan*
   I. Introduction 301
   II. Green Bonds 302
   III. Self-regulation of Green Bonds 307
   IV. EU Approach to Regulating Green Bonds 309
   V. Summary 316

15. ESG Demand-side Regulation—Governing the Shareholders 319
   *Thilo Kuntz*
   I. Introduction 319
   II. Demand-side Regulation and Its Place in Corporate Governance 322
   III. Direct Demand-side Regulation 334
   IV. Indirect Demand-side Regulation 348
   V. Conclusion 355

16. Sustainability and Competition Law                                    357
    *Stefan Thomas*
        I. Introduction                                                   357
        II. The Externality Problem in Competition Law                    359
        III. Integrating Externalities into the Consumer Welfare Paradigm 361
        IV. Reducing Externalities beyond the Consumer Welfare Paradigm   365
        V. Conclusions                                                    368

*Index*                                                                   371

# Table of Cases

## UNITED KINGDOM

BTI 2014 LLC v Sequana SA & Ors [2022] UKSC 25 .......................... 143–44, 144n.12
McGaughey v USSL [2022] EWHC 1233 (Ch) and on appeal [2023] EWCA Civ 873 ........ 143n.11
Richmond Pharmacology Ltd v Chester Overseas Ltd [2014] EWHC 2692 (Ch). ............ 143n.8
Southern Countries Fresh Foods Ltd, Re [2008] EWHC 2810 (Ch) ....................... 143n.8
West Coast Capital (Lios) Ltd, Re [2008] CSOH 72 ...................................... 143n.8

## EUROPEAN UNION

### Commission Decisions

Case COMP/34.493 et al., DSD, Commission Decision 2001/837/EC [2001] OJ L319/1 .... 358n.11
Case COMP/39579, Consumer Detergents, Commission Decision C(2011) 2528 final. ..... 358n.11
Case IV/34.252, Philips-Osram, Commission Decision 94/986/EC [1994] OJ L378/37. ..... 358n.11
Case IV.F.1/36.718, CECED, Commission Decision 2000/475/EC [1999] OJ L187/47 ...... 358n.11
Case M.8084, Bayer/Monsanto, Commission Decision C(2018) 1709 final ................ 358n.11

### Court of Justice

Case 56 and 58/64 Consten and Grundig v Commission ECLI:EU:C:1966:41 ............. 366n.45
Case C-67/96 Albany International BV v Stichting Bedrijfspensioenfonds
    Textielindustrie ECLI:EU:C:1999:430 ........................................ 367, 367n.48
Case C-309/99 Wouters and others v Algemene Raad van de Nederlandse Orde
    van Advocaten ECLI:EU:C:2002:98 ....................................367, 367n.47, 369
Case C-381/98 Ingmar, Rec p I-9305, EU:C:2000:605 .................................. 289n.69

### General Court

Case T-29/92, Vereniging van Samenwerkende Prijsregelende Organisaties in
    de Bouwnijverheid and others v Commission ECLI:EU:T:1995:34 .................... 366n.45
Case T-328/03 O2 (Germany) v Commission ECLI:EU:T:2006:116 ...................... 366n.45

## NATIONAL COURTS

### Australia

McVeigh v Retail Employees Superannuation Pty Ltd [2019] FCA 14. ....... 340, 340n.125, 340n.126

### Georgia

Cherokee Iron Co v Jones 52 Ga 276 (1874) ............................................. 176n.20

### Germany

BVerfG [1979]: 1 BvR 532/77, 1 BvR 533/77, 1 BvR 419/78, 1 BvL 21/78, BVerfGE 50 ...... 123n.108
BVerfG, Order of the First Senate of 24 March 2021; 1 BvR 2656/18 ...................... 278n.24
German Bundesgerichtshof decision of 28 July 2021; 1 StR 519/20, NJW 2022 ............. 41n.158

### Netherlands

Vereniging Milieudefensie and Others v Royal Dutch Shell plc, Rechtsbank Den Haag,
    case No C/09/571932/HA ZA 19-379 (26 May 2021). .................... 4n.15, 50–51, 51n.227

## TABLE OF CASES

**United States**

Alliance for Fair Board Recruitment v SEC No 21-60626 (5th Cir 2023) .................... 92n.73
AP Smith Manufacturing Co v Barlow 98 A2d 581 (NJ 1953) ..................... 179n.40, 185n.79
Blackmore Partners LP v Link Energy LLC 864 A2d 80 (Del Ch 2004) ............. 69n.57, 69n.59
Braun v Walsh 23-cv-00234 (E Dist Wisconsin 2023) ...................................... 93n.81
Burwell v Hobby Lobby Stores Inc 573 US 682 (2014) ...................................... 29n.78
Business Roundtable v SEC 647 F3d 1144 (DC Cir 2011) ................. 96n.96, 97n.100, 97n.101
Calloway v Clark 32 Mo 305 (1862) ....................................................... 176n.21
Chevron USA Inc v Natural Resources Defense Council Inc 467 US 837 (1984) ............. 93n.81
Dodge v Ford Motor Co. 170 NW 668 (Mich 1919) .................. 29n.76, 179, 179n.38, 181, 187
eBay Domestic Holdings Inc v Newmark 16 A3d 1 (Del Ch 2010) ............... 29n.76, 68, 68n.53, 192n.122, 324n.23
Faragher v City of Boca Raton 524 US 775 (1998) ........................................ 201n.43
Fifth Third Bancorp v Dudenhoeffer 134 S Ct 2459 (2014) ................................ 90n.53
Freeman v Sea View Hotel Co 40 A219 (NJ Ch 1898) ...................................... 176n.19
Guth et al v Loft Inc 5 A2d 503 (Del 1939) .............................................. 68n.50
Hobby Lobby Stores Inc 573 US 682 (2014) .............................................. 164n.21
Kahn v Sullivan 594 A2d 48 (Del 1991) ........................................... 66n.41, 69n.57
Marchand v Barnhill 212 A2d 805 (Del 2019) ............................................. 203n.56
Massey Energy Co, In re WL 2176479 (Del Ch 2011) ...................................... 203n.57
National Association of Manufacturers v SEC (NAM II) 800 F3d 518
    (DC Cir 2015) ............................................................. 97n.102, 97–98n.104
National Federation of Independent Business v Department of Labor 595 US 109,
    142 SCt 661 (2022) ...................................................................... 98n.106
North American Catholic Educational Programming Foundation Inc v Gheewalla
    930 A2d 92 (Del 2007) ............................................................... 68n.50, 69
Paramount Communications, Inc. v Time Inc 571 A2d 1140 (Del 1989) ........... 21n.40, 192n.121
People ex rel Attorney General v Utica Insurance Co 15 Johns 358 (NY 1818) .............. 176n.15
Quadrant Structured Prods Co Ltd v Vertin 102 A3d 155 (Del Ch 2014) ................. 69, 69n.60
Revlon Inc v MacAndrews & Forbes Holdings Inc 506 A2d 173 (Del 1986) ... 29n.79, 69–70, 69n.57, 69n.61, 131, 138, 138n.33, 191–92, 192n.120, 324n.24
Robin Crest and Ors v Alex Padilla (Padilla I) 19-STCV-27561 (LA Super Ct 13 May 2022) .... 92n.72
Robin Crest and Ors v Alex Padilla (Padilla II) 20-STCV-37513 (LA Super Ct 1 April 2022) .... 92n.72
Shlensky v Wright 237 NE2d 776 (Ill App 1968) ......................................... 179n.40
Simeone v The Walt Disney Co WL 4208481 (Del Ch 2023) 1 ...................... 66n.41, 69n.58
State of Utah and Ors v Walsh and Ors WL 6205926 (ND Tex 2023) ....................... 93n.81
State v Standard Oil Co 30 NE 279 (Ohio 1892) .......................................... 176n.22
Trados Inc Shareholder Litigation, In re 73 A3d 17 (Del Ch 2013) ...................... 68n.52, 69, 69n.57, 69n.59, 324n.23
Unitrin Inc v American General Corp 651 A2d 1361 (1995) ............................... 203n.59
Unocal Corp v Mesa Petroleum Co 493 A2d 946 (Del 1985) ...................... 68n.51, 69–70, 70n.63, 191–92, 191n.119
Water Island Event-Driven Fund v Tribune Media Co 39 F 4th 402 (7th Cir 2022) .......... 206n.77
West Virginia v Environmental Protection Agency 142 S Ct 2587 (2022) ........... 97–98, 98n.107, 100n.121, 214n.132
Youngstown Sheet & Tube v Sawyer 343 US 579 (1952) ................................... 183n.66

# Table of Legislation

## INTERNATIONAL INSTRUMENTS, TREATIES AND CONVENTIONS

European Social Charter, and the Charter of Fundamental Rights of the European Union . . . . . . . . . . . 236n.70
European Convention for the protection of Human Rights and Fundamental Freedoms . . . . . . . . . . . . . . . . . . . . . . . 236n.70
International Labour Organization's Declaration on Fundamental Principles and Rights at Work and the fundamental conventions of the International Labour Organization . . . . . . . . . . . . . . 236n.70
Paris Agreement to the United Nations Framework Convention on Climate Change (12 December 2015) . . . . . . . . . 256, 261n.82, 287–88, 309n.69
Art 2(1)(c) . . . . . . . . . . . . . . . . . . 83n.3, 309n.70
Art 9(3) . . . . . . . . . . . . . . . . . . . . . . . . . . . 261n.82
Treaty on the Functioning of the European Union (TFEU)
Art 101 . . . . . . . . . . . . . . . . . . . . . . . . 16, 366–67
Art 101(1) . . . . . . . . . . . . . . . . . . . . . . . . . . . . . 367
Art 101(3) . . . . . . . . . . . . . . . . . . . . 360, 366–67
UN Convention on the Rights of Persons with Disabilities . . . . . . . . . . 236n.70
UN Declaration on the Rights of Indigenous Peoples . . . . . . . . . . . . . . 236n.70

## EUROPEAN UNION

### Directives

Commission Delegated Directive (EU) 2021/1269 of 21 April 2021 amending Delegated Directive (EU) 2017/593 as regards the integration of sustainability factors into the product governance obligations [2021] OJ L277/137 (2 August 2021) . . . . . . . . . . . . . . . . . 267n.104
Commission Delegated Directive (EU) 2021/1270 of 21 April 2021 amending Directive 2010/43/EU (Text with EEA relevance) as regards the sustainability risks and sustainability factors to be taken into account for Undertakings for Collective Investment in Transferable Securities (UCITS) [2021] OJ L277/141 (2 August 2021) . . . 255n.57, 266n.96, 268–69
Art 1 . . . . . . . . . . . . . . . . . . . . . . . . . . . . . . . . . . 266
Art 5a . . . . . . . . . . . . . . . . . . . . . . . . . . . . . . . . 266
Council of the European Union, Proposal for a Directive of the European Parliament and of the Council on Corporate Sustainability Due Diligence and amending Directive (EU) 2019/1937, Brussels (30 November 2022) (OR. en) 15024/1/22 Rev 1 (CS3D) (Corporate Sustainability Due Diligence Directive) . . . . . . . . . . . 4n.14, 5–6, 33, 36–39, 36n.130, 45–46, 47–48, 49, 49n.212, 52, 116n.68, 142n.4, 229n.42, 237n.73, 240–42, 243, 275n.2, 280n.31, 284, 287, 292–94, 297–98
Annex 1 . . . . . . . . . . . . . . . . . . . . . . . . . . . 239n.89
Pt I . . . . . . . . . . . . . . . . . . . . . . . . . . . . . . . . . . . 292
Pt II . . . . . . . . . . . . . . . . . . . . . . . . . . . . . . . . . . 292
Art 2(1)(a) . . . . . . . . . . . . . . . . . 25n.59, 37n.138
Art 2(1)(b) . . . . . . . . . . . . . . . . . 25n.59, 37n.138
Art 2(2)(a) . . . . . . . . . . . . . . . . . . . . . . . . . 37n.139
Art 2(2)(b) . . . . . . . . . . . . . . . . . . . . . . . . . 37n.139
Art 2(4) . . . . . . . . . . . . . . . . . . . . . . . . . . . 298n.116
Art 3(a) . . . . . . . . . . . . . . . . . . . . . . . . 237–38n.76
Art 3(a)(iv) . . . . . . . . . . . . . . . . . . . . . . . . . . 25n.57
Art 3(b) . . . . . . . . . . . . . . . . . . . . . . . . . . . . 292n.81
Art 3(c) . . . . . . . . . . . . . . . . . . . . . . . . . . . . 292n.83
Art 3(e) . . . . . . . . . . . . . . . . . . . . . . . . . . . . 293n.88
Art 3(f) . . . . . . . . . . . . . . . . . . . . . . . . . . . . 293n.89
Art 3(g) . . . . . . . . . . . . . . . . . . . . . . . . . . . . 292n.85
Art 3(l) . . . . . . . . . . . . . . . . . . . . . . . . . . . . 292n.84
Art 4 . . . . . . . . . . . . . . . . . . . . . . . . . . . . . . . 37n.141
Art 4a . . . . . . . . . . . . . . . . . . . . . . . . . . . . . . 37n.141
Arts 5–11 . . . . . . . . . . . . . . . . . . . . . . . . . . 37n.141
Art 5(1) . . . . . . . . . . . . . . . . . . . . . . . . . . . . 238n.77
Art 6(1) . . . . . . . . . . . . . . . . . . . . . . . . . . . . 238n.78
Art 6(4) . . . . . . . . . . . . . . . . . . . . . . . . . . . . 238n.79
Art 7(1) . . . . . . . . . . . . . . . . . . . . . . . . . . . . 238n.80
Art 7(2)(a) . . . . . . . . . . . . . . . . . . . . . . . . . 293n.90
Art 7(2)(b) . . . . . . . . . . . . . . . 38n.143, 45n.190
Art 7(3) . . . . . . . . . . . . . . . . . . . . . . . . . . . . 38n.143
Art 7(5)(b) . . . . . . . . . . . . . . . . . . . . . . . . . 38n.144
Art 8 . . . . . . . . . . . . . . . . . . . . . . . . . . . . . . . 238n.81
Art 8(3)(b) . . . . . . . . . . . . . . . . . . . . . . . . . 293n.90
Art 8(6)(b) . . . . . . . . . . . . . . . . . . . . . . . . . 38n.144

## TABLE OF LEGISLATION

Art 9 . . . . . . . . . . . . . . . . . . . . . . . . . . . . 238n.82
Art 10 . . . . . . . . . . . . . . . . . . . . . . . . . . . 238n.83
Art 11 . . . . . . . . . . . . . . . . . . . . . . . . . . . 238n.84
Art 12 . . . . . . . . . . . . . . . . . . . . . . . . . . . . 38n.147
Art 13 . . . . . . . . . . . . . . . . . . . . . . . . . . . . 38n.147
Art 15 . . . . . . . . . . . . . . . . . . . 37n.142, 292n.82
Art 15(3) . . . . . . . . . . . . . . . . . 48n.209, 297n.107
Arts 17–19 . . . . . . . . . . . . . . . . . . . . . . . 238n.85
Art 17 . . . . . . . . . . . . . . . . . . . . 49n.212, 297n.106
Art 17(2) . . . . . . . . . . . . . . . . . . . . . . . . 298n.115
Art 17(3) . . . . . . . . . . . . . . . . . . . . . . . . 298n.117
Art 18 . . . . . . . . . . . . . . . . . . . . . . . . . . . . 49n.212
Art 18(1) . . . . . . . . . . . . . . . . . . . . . . . . 297n.108
Art 18(4) . . . . . . . . . . . . . . . . . . . . . . . . 297n.110
Art 18(7) . . . . . . . . . . . . . . . . . . . . . . . . 297n.113
Art 19 . . . . . . . . . . . . . . . . . . . . . . . . . . . 297n.109
Art 20 . . . . . . . . . . 238n.86, 297n.111, 297n.112
Art 20(3) . . . . . . . . . . . . . . . . . . . . . . . . . 49n.213
Art 20(4) . . . . . . . . . . . . . . . . . . . . . . . . . 49n.214
Art 21 . . . . . . . . . . . . . . . . . . . . . . . . . . . . 49n.215
Art 22 . . . . . . . . . . . . 38n.145, 38n.146, 45n.190,
238n.87, 298n.118
Art 22(2) . . . . . . . . . . . . . . . . . . . . . . . . 299n.121
Art 22(3) . . . . . . . . . . . . . . . . . . . . . . . . 299n.120
Art 22(4) . . . . . . . . . . . . . . . . . . . . . . . . 299n.123
Art 22(5) . . . . . . . . . . . . . . . . . . . . . . . . 299n.124
Art 24 . . . . . . . . . . . . . . . . . . . . . . . . . . . 298n.114
Art 25 . . . . . . . . . . . . . . . . . . . . . . . . . . 239, 282
Art 25(1) . . . . . . . . . . . . . . . . . . . . . . . . . . . . 4–5
Art 25(2) . . . . . . . . . . . . . . . . . . . . . . . . . 47n.198
Art 26 . . . . . . . . . . . . . . . . 38n.146, 47n.198, 239
Art 29 . . . . . . . . . . . . . . . . . . . . . . . . . . . . 38n.148
Directive 78/660/EEC of 25 July 1978
on the annual accounts of certain
types of companies [1978] OJ L222/11
(14 August 1978)
Art 46 . . . . . . . . . . . . . . . . . . . . . . . . . . . 233n.54
Directive 83/349/EEC of 13 June 1983
based on Article 54(3)(g) of the
Treaty on consolidated accounts
[1983] OJ L193/1 (18 July 1983)
Art 36(1) . . . . . . . . . . . . . . . . . . . . . . . . 233n.54
Directive 2003/51/EC of the European
Parliament and of the Council of
18 June 2003 amending Directives
78/660/EEC, 83/349/EEC, 86/635/
EEC and 91/674/EEC on the annual
and consolidated accounts of certain
types of companies, banks and other
financial institutions and insurance
undertakings [2003] OJ L178/16
(17 July 2003) . . . . . . . . . . . . . . . . . . . 276n.13
Recital 9 . . . . . . . . . . . . . . . . . . . . . . . . . 233n.54
Art 1(14) . . . . . . . . . . . . . . . . . . . . . . . . . 233n.54
Art 2(10) . . . . . . . . . . . . . . . . . . . . . . . . . 233n.54
Directive 2007/36/EC of the European
Parliament and of the Council of 11
July 2007 on the exercise of certain
rights of shareholders in listed
companies, [2007] OJ L184/17
(14 July 2007) . . . . . . . . . . 269n.116, 337n.99
Directive 2009/65/EC . . . . . . . . . . . . . . . 256n.64
Art 3g(1) . . . . . . . . . . . . . . . . . . . . . . . . . . . . 337
Art 3g(1)(a) . . . . . . . . . . . . . . . . . . . . . 337n.100
Art 3g(1)(b) . . . . . . . . . . . . . . . . . . . . . 337n.101
Art 12(1) . . . . . . . . . . . . . . . . . . . . . . . . 271n.123
Art 14(1) . . . . . . . . . . . . . . . . . . . . . . . . 271n.123
Directive 2009/138/EC of the European
Parliament and of the Council of 25
November 2009 on the takingup and
pursuit of the business of Insurance
and Reinsurance (Solvency II) [2009]
OJ L335/1 (17 December 2009) . . . 256n.64
Art 132 . . . . . . . . . . . . . . . . . . . . . . . . . . 266n.101
Directive 2010/43/EU on UCITS
Art 4(1) . . . . . . . . . . . . . . . . . . . . . . . . . . . . . 266
Directive 2011/61/EU . . . . . . . . . . . . . . . 256n.64
Directive 2013/34/EU of the European
Parliament and of the Council of 26
June 2013 on the annual financial
statements, consolidated financial
statements and related reports of
certain types of undertakings [2013]
OJ L182/19 (29 June 2013)
Art 1 . . . . . . . . . . . . . . . . . . . . . . . . . . . . 234n.56
Art 1(2)(17) . . . . . . . . . . . . . . . . . . . . . . 235n.67
Art 2(1) . . . . . . . . . . . . . . . . . . . . . . . . . . 234n.56
Art 3(4) . . . . . . . . . . . . . . . . . . . . . . . . . . 234n.56
Art 19(1)(3) . . . . . . . . . . . . . . . . . . . . . . 234n.55
Art 19a . . . . . . . . . . . . . . . . . . . . . . 235n.66, 264
Art 19a(1) . . . . . . . . . . . . . . . . . . . . . . . . 234n.56
Art 19a(1)(1) . . . . . . . . . . . . . . . . . . . . . 234n.57
Art 19a(1)(5) . . . . . . . . . . . . . . . . . . . . . 234n.58
Annex . . . . . . . . . . . . . . . . . . . . . . . . . . . 234n.56
Directive 2013/36/EU . . . . . . . . . . . . . . . 256n.64
Directive 2014/65/EU of the European
Parliament and of the Council of 15
May 2014 on markets in financial
instruments and amending Directive
2002/92/EC and Directive 2011/61/
EU [2014] OJ L173/349 (12 June 2014)
(MiFiD II) . . . . . . . . . . 256n.64, 349, 349n.189
Art 14 . . . . . . . . . . . . . . . . . . . . . . . . . . . 271n.123
Art 23 . . . . . . . . . . . . . . . . . . . . . . . . . . . 271n.123
Art 24(1) . . . . . . . . . . . . . . . . . . . . . . . . 349n.190
Art 25(2) . . . . . . . . . . . . . . . . . . . . . . . . 349n.191
Directive 2014/95/EU of the European
Parliament and of the Council
of 22 October 2014 amending
Directive 2013/34/EU as regards
disclosure of non-financial and
diversity information by certain large
undertakings and groups [2014] OJ
L330/1 . . . . . . . . . . . . . 2n.3, 13–14, 44n.180,
112n.46, 145n.18, 233n.52, 234n.56,
264n.90, 277–78, 277n.14

Directive 2016/97/EU ............... 256n.64
Directive 2016/2341/EU .............. 256n.64
Directive 2017/828/EU of the European
 Parliament and of the Council
 amending Directive 2007/36/EC as
 regards the encouragement of
 long-term shareholder engagement
 [2017] OJ L132/60 .......... 252n.34, 269,
  269–70n.117, 270, 270n.120
  Art 1(1) ........................... 269–70
  Art 3g. ............................... 271
  Art 3g(1) ............................. 271
  Art 3g(2) ......................... 271n.123
Directive 2022/2464/EU of the European
 Parliament and of the Council of 14
 December 2022 amending Regulation
 (EU) No 537/2014, Directive
 2004/109/EC, Directive 2006/43/EC
 and Directive 2013/34/EU, as regards
 corporate sustainability reporting
 [2022] OJ L322 (16 December 2022)
 (CSRD)....... 2n.5, 44n.179, 84n.8, 85n.16,
  99n.116, 113n.48, 116n.69, 117, 118,
  124, 126, 167n.27, 235n.65, 235n.67,
  264n.90, 265, 277, 277n.16, 287–88
  Recital 3 ......................... 113n.47
  Recital 9 .............. 44n.181, 234–35n.59
  Recital 25 ........................... 3n.6
  Recital 29 ....................... 44n.182
  Art 1(1) ................... 234n.57, 234n.58
  Art 1(3) .................... 234–35n.59
  Art 2............................... 235
  Art 15............................ 287–88
  Art 19a(2)(a)(iii)–(v).............. 118n.75
  Art 19(a)(4) ........................ 265
  Art 26a............................ 235n.69
  Art 27a............................ 235n.69
  Art 28a............................ 235n.69
  Art 29a............................ 235n.60
  Art 29b ...................... 235n.68, 265
  Art 29b(2)........................ 236n.70
  Art 29c............................ 235n.68
  Art 30............................. 37n.137
  Art 36a............................ 235n.69

## REGULATIONS

Commission Delegated Regulation
 (EU) 2015/35 of 10 October 2014
 supplementing Directive 2009/138/
 EC of the European Parliament and
 of the Council on the taking-up and
 pursuit of the business of Insurance
 and Reinsurance (Solvency II) [2015]
 OJ L12/1 (17 January 2015)...... 266n.103
Commission Delegated Regulation (EU)
 2017/2358 of 21 September 2017
 supplementing Directive (EU) 2016/97
 of the European Parliament and of
 the Council with regard to product
 oversight and governance requirements
 for insurance undertakings and
 insurance distributors [2017] OJ
 L341/1 (20 December 2017)....... 268n.115
Commission Delegated Regulation (EU)
 2017/2359 of 21 September 2017
 supplementing Directive (EU)
 2016/97 of the European Parliament
 and of the Council with regard
 to information requirements and
 conduct of business rules applicable
 to the distribution of insurance-
 based investment products [2017] OJ
 L341/8 (20 December 2017) ..... 268n.115
Commission Delegated Regulation
 (EU) 2021/1253 of 21 April 2021
 amending Delegated Regulation
 (EU) 2017/565 as regards the
 integration of sustainability factors,
 risks and preferences into certain
 organisational requirements and
 operating conditions for investment
 firms [2021] OJ L277/1 (2 August
 2021)....... 267n.104, 349n.192, 349n.194,
  349n.198, 350n.200
  Art 1............................ 349n.197
Commission Delegated Regulation (EU)
 2021/1255 amending Delegated
 Regulation (EU) No 231/2013 as
 regards the sustainability risks and
 sustainability factors to be taken into
 account by Alternative Investment
 Fund Managers (AIFMs) [2021] OJ
 L277/11 (2 August 2021). .256n.59, 266n.97
Commission Delegated Regulation (EU)
 2021/1256 of 21 April 2021 amending
 Delegated Regulation (EU) No
 231/2013 as regards the integration of
 sustainability risks in the governance of
 insurance and reinsurance undertakings
 [2021] OJ L277/14 (2 August 2021)... 255n.58,
  256n.60, 266n.102, 268
Commission Delegated Regulation (EU)
 2021/1257 of 21 April 2021 amending
 Delegated Regulations (EU) 2017/2358
 and (EU) 2017/2359 as regards the
 integration of sustainability factors,
 risks and preferences into the product
 oversight and governance requirements
 for insurance undertakings and
 insurance distributors and into the
 rules on conduct of business and
 investment advice for insurance-
 based investment products [2021] OJ
 L277/18 (2 August 2021) ........... 255n.58,
  256n.60, 268n.111, 349n.193

Commission Delegated Regulation (EU) 2021/2139 of 4 June 2021 supplementing Regulation (EU) 2020/852 of the European Parliament and of the Council by establishing the technical screening criteria for determining the conditions under which an economic activity qualifies as contributing substantially to climate change mitigation or climate change adaptation and for determining whether that economic activity causes no significant harm to any of the other environmental objectives [2021] OJ L442/1 (9 December 2021)...278n.20, 311n.88

Commission Delegated Regulation (EU) 2021/2178 of 6 July 2021 supplementing Regulation (EU) 2020/852 of the European Parliament and of the Council by specifying the content and presentation of information to be disclosed by undertakings subject to Articles 19a or 29a of Directive 2013/34/EU concerning environmentally sustainable economic activities, and specifying the methodology to comply with that disclosure obligation [2021] OJ L 443/9 (10 December 2021).......278n.19, 311n.89, 341n.131, 341n.133
    Annex 1..............................313

Commission Delegated Regulation (EU) 2022/1214 of 9 March 2022 amending Delegated Regulation (EU) 2021/2139 as regards economic activities in certain energy sectors and Delegated Regulation (EU) 2021/2178 as regards specific public disclosures for those economic activities [2022] OJ L188/1........311n.90

Commission Delegated Regulation (EU) 2022/1288 of 6 April 2022 supplementing Regulation (EU) 2019/2088 of the European Parliament and of the Council with regard to regulatory technical standards specifying the details of the content and presentation of the information in relation to the principle of 'do no significant harm', specifying the content, methodologies and presentation of information in relation to sustainability indicators and adverse sustainability impacts, and the content and presentation of the information in relation to the promotion of environmental or social characteristics and sustainable investment objectives in pre-contractual documents, on websites and in periodic reports [2022] OJ L196/1 .......... 271, 310n.78, 336n.95
    Recital 16 ..........................310n.80
    Recital 17 sentence 1 ...............310n.79
    Art 35..........................337n.102
    Art 38..........................337n.102
    Annex III .......................337n.96

Commission Delegated Regulation (EU) 2023/2486 of 27 June 2023 supplementing Regulation (EU) 2020/852 of the European Parliament and of the Council by establishing the technical screening criteria for determining the conditions under which an economic activity qualifies as contributing substantially to the sustainable use and protection of water and marine resources, to the transition to a circular economy, to pollution prevention and control, or to the protection and restoration of biodiversity and ecosystems and for determining whether that economic activity causes no significant harm to any of the other environmental objectives and amending Delegated Regulation (EU) 2021/2178 as regards specific public disclosures for those economic activities [2023] OJ L2023/2485 .....................311–12n.91

Commission Delegated Regulation (EU) 2023/2772 of 31 July 2023 supplementing Directive 2013/34/EU of the European Parliament and of the Council as regards sustainability reporting standards ........84n.8, 265n.91

Regulation (EC) 864/2007 of the European Parliament and of the Council of 11 July 2007 on the law applicable to non-contractual obligations (Rome II) ............295n.97
    Art 4..........................300n.125
    Art 7..........................300n.125

Regulation (EU) 345/2013 ............256n.64
    Art 14..........................259n.76

Regulation (EU) 346/2013 ............256n.64
    Art 15..........................259n.76

Regulation (EU) 1308/2013 of 17 December 2013 establishing a common organisation of the markets in agricultural products and repealing Council Regulations (EEC) No 922/72, (EEC) No 234/79, (EC) No 1037/2001 and (EC) No 1234/2007, OJ L347/671
    Art 210a.................. 366–67, 366n.42

## TABLE OF LEGISLATION xv

Regulation (EU) 2016/1011 of the European Parliament and of the Council.....261n.82
Regulation (EU) 2017/1129 of the European Parliament and of the Council of 14 June 2017 on the prospectus to be published when securities are offered to the public or admitted to trading on a regulated market, and repealing Directive 2003/71/EC [2017] OJ L168/12 ...314n.103
  Recital 54, sentence 4.....................316
  Art 22....................................316
Regulation (EU) 2018/842 of the European Parliament and of the Council of 30 May 2018 on binding annual greenhouse gas emission reductions by Member States from 2021 to 2030 contributing to climate action to meet commitments under the Paris Agreement and amending Regulation (EU) No 525/2013 [2018] OJ L156/26 (19 June 2018).........282n.43
Regulation (EU) 2019/2033 of the European Parliament and of the Council and Directive (EU) 2019/2034 of the European Parliament and of the Council contains provisions concerning the introduction of an ESG risk dimension in the Supervisory Review and Evaluation Process (SREP) by competent authorities, and contains ESG risk disclosure requirements for investment firms.............. 334–35n.83
Regulation (EU) 2019/2088 of the European Parliament and of the Council of 27 November 2019 on Sustainability-Related Disclosures in the Financial Services Sector [2019] OJ L317/1 (SFDR)............ 3n.6, 13–15, 44n.180, 85n.13, 89n.48, 91n.60, 94–95, 154n.39, 248–49, 255n.55, 256–57, 256n.61, 256n.62, 258–62, 266, 269, 271n.124, 310, 310n.77, 334n.81, 337, 338–39, 349
  Recital 5 ..........................341n.132
  Recital 9 ..........................310n.80
  Recital 10 .........................310n.79
  Recital 11 .........................311n.84
  Art 2..............................335n.91
  Art 2(1)...........................259n.76
  Art 2(17).................. 261, 267, 336n.94
  Art 2(22)......................... 259–60
  Art 3(1).............................259
  Art 4............................. 259–60
  Art 4(1).............................336
  Art 4(1)(b) .........................336
  Art 5 ff............................311n.83
  Art 6...... 261n.82, 336–37, 338–39, 353, 355
  Art 6(1)................. 259, 261n.80, 336
  Art 6(3)......... 261n.80, 263n.89, 336n.92
  Art 7.............................336n.92
  Art 7(1).....................336, 336n.92
  Art 8.............. 260–62, 263–64, 336–37, 337n.103, 338–39, 353, 355
  Art 8(1)....... 260–61, 263n.89, 271, 336–37
  Art 8(2)................... 261n.80, 340 41
  Arts 8–11........................340n.130
  Art 9..................... 260–62, 263–64, 336–37, 339n.118, 355
  Art 9(1)....................... 261, 336–37
  Art 9(3)......................... 261–62
  Art 11(2).........................263n.89
  Annex II, Art 8.....................336n.95
Regulation (EU) 2020/852 on the establishment of a framework to facilitate sustainable investment [2020] OJ L198/13 (Taxonomy Regulation) ........13–14, 84n.9, 154n.38, 255n.56, 257–58, 257n.69, 257n.70, 257n.71, 258n.72, 258n.73, 267, 277n.18, 310, 311, 311n.81, 311n.85, 313, 315, 334n.82, 336–37, 338–39, 340–41
  Recital 11 .........................307n.48
  Art 1...............................336n.93
  Art 1(1)............................311n.82
  Art 3....................261n.81, 313n.100
  Art 5..................... 263n.89, 336–37
  Art 5(1)(b) .......................337n.98
  Art 6..................... 263n.89, 336–37
  Art 7.................................336
  Art 9...............................261n.81
  Arts 10–16 ........................261n.81
  Art 10(3)..........................261n.81
  Art 11(3)..........................261n.81
  Art 12(2)..........................261n.81
  Art 13(2)..........................261n.81
  Art 14(2)....................261n.81, 316
  Art 15(2)..........................261n.81
  Art 17.............................261n.81
  Art 18.............................261n.81
  Art 19.............................311n.87
Regulation (EU) 2021/1119 of the European Parliament and of the Council of 30 June 2021 establishing the framework for achieving climate neutrality and amending Regulations (EC) No 401/2009 and (EU) 2018/1999 (European Climate Law) [2021] OJ L243/1 (9 July 2021) ....282n.43
Regulation (EU) 2023/2631 of the European Parliament and of the Council of 22 November 2023 on European Green Bonds and optional

xvi  TABLE OF LEGISLATION

disclosures for bonds marketed as environmentally sustainable and for sustainability-linked bonds [2023] OJ L2023/2631 (30 November 2023) .............. 302n.6, 309, 312–14, 312n.97, 315, 316, 317
Recital 11 ........................ 313n.100
Art 1................................. 313
Art 2(3) ........................ 313n.100
Art 4................................. 313
Art 4(1)(b) ......................... 314
Art 4(1)(c) ......................... 314
Art 4(2) ............................. 313
Art 5(1) ............................. 313
Art 5(2) ............................. 313
Art 6................................. 313
Art 7................................. 314
Art 8(1) ............................. 314
Art 8(2) ........................ 314n.101
Art 10 ............................... 314
Art 11 ............................... 314
Art 12 ............................... 314
Art 14(1) ........................... 314
Art 14(3) ........................... 314
Art 15(1) ........................... 314
Arts 16–19 ......................... 314
Arts 20–21 ......................... 314
Art 22–43 .......................... 314
Annex I ............................. 314

## COMMUNICATIONS AND PROPOSALS

European Commission and High Representative of the Union for Foreign Affairs and Security Policy, 'Joint Communication to the European Parliament and the Council: EU Action Plan on Human Rights and Democracy 2020-2024' (25 March 2020), JOIN(2020) 5 final ......... 235n.64
European Commission, 'Communication from the Commission: Guidelines on non-financial reporting: Methodology for non-financial reporting' (2017/C/215/01) [2017] OJ C215/1 (5 July 2017) .......... 235n.61
European Commission, 'Communication from the Commission: Guidelines on non-financial reporting: Supplement on reporting climate-related information' (2019/C 209/01) [2019] OJ C209/1 (20 June 2019) .......... 235n.62
European Commission, 'Communication from the Commission to the European Parliament, the Council, the European Economic and Social Committee and the Committee of the Regions: A renewed EU strategy 2011-14 for Corporate Social Responsibility, COM(2011) 681 final (25 October 2011) .............. 235n.64
Communication from the Commission to the European Parliament, the European Council, the Council, the European Central Bank, the European Economic and Social Committee and the Committee of the Regions, Action Plan: Financing Sustainable Growth, COM (2018) 97 final (3 August 2018) ...... 86n.23, 257n.68
European Commission, Communication from the Commission to the European Parliament, the European Council, the Council, the European Central Bank, the European Economic and Social Committee and the Committee of the Regions, Action Plan, Financing Sustainable Growth COM(2018) 97 final (Brussels, 8 March 2018) .......... 309n.71, 310n.72
European Commission, Communication from the Commission to the European Parliament, the European Council, the Council, the European Economic and Social Committee and the Committee of the Regions, Strategy for Financing the Transition to a Sustainable Economy COM(2021) 390 final 1 (Strasbourg, 6 July 2021) ..................... 310n.76
European Commission, Communication from the Commission to the European Parliament, the European Council, the Council, the European Economic and Social Committee and the Committee of the Regions, Sustainable European Investment Plan, European Green Deal Investment Plan COM(2020) 21 final (Brussels 14 January 2020) ........ 312n.94
European Commission, Communication from the Commission to the European Parliament, the European Council, the Council, the European Economic and Social Committee and the Committee of the Regions, 'The European Green Deal' COM/2019/640 final (Brussels, 11 December 2019) ..... 3n.7, 310n.73, 319n.5
European Commission, 'Proposal for a Directive of the European Parliament and of the Council amending Directive 2013/34/EU, Directive 2004/109/EC, Directive 2006/43/EC

and Regulation (EU) No 537/2014, as regards corporate sustainability reporting' COM(2021) 189 final (21 April 2021) .................235n.63
European Commission, 'Proposal for a Regulation of the European Parliament and of the Council on European green bonds' COM(2021) 391 final (6 July 2021) ...........312n.95
   Recital 5 .........................312n.99
   Recital 6 ................312n.98, 312n.99
   Recital 7 .........................312n.99

## NATIONAL LEGISLATION

**Austria**

Austrian Cartel Act
   Art 2(1)(2) .........................357n.5

**Canada**

Business Corporations Act 1985
   s 238(d) ..........................50n.223

**Denmark**

Danish Code .............13–14, 251, 252–53

**France**

Civil Code
   Art 1833 .................. 34–35, 114n.54
   Art 1833(2) ....................323–24n.18
   Art 1835 .............. 31, 34–35, 114n.55
Code de Commerce
   Art L. 22-10-35 ....................276n.12
   Art L. 210-10 ......................33n.105
   Art L. 210-11 ......................33n.105
   Art L. 210-12 ......................33n.105
   Art L. 225-35 .......................34–35
   Art L. 225-102-4 s 3.................34n.114
   Art L. 225-102-4 s 5.................34n.115
   Art L. 225-102-4 s 6.................34n.115
   Art L. 225-102-5 ...................34n.115
Code de l'environnement
   Art L. 229-25 ......................276n.11
Law of 15 May 2001 on new economic regulations (NREs) .............. 276–77
   Art 116..........................279n.25
   Art 116(1).......................345n.157
Law no 2012-1559 of 31 December 2012 on the creation of the Public Investment Bank
   Art 4.............................291n.77
Law no 2017-399 du 27 mars 2017 relative au devoir de vigilance [2017] OJ 1–99 (Duty of Vigilance Law) .......5–6, 33–35, 33n.109, 50–51, 52
Law no 2019-486 du 22 mai 2019 relative à la croissance et la transformation des entreprises [2019] OJ 2–152........ 33–35, 36n.131, 52, 284
   Art 169............31n.96, 33n.109, 33n.110
Law no 2021-1104 of 22 August 2021......................34n.113, 295
   Art 35(V) .........................295n.94
Public Procurement Code
   Art L2141-7-1 .....................295n.94

**Germany**

Co-Determination Act of 1976......... 109–10
Commercial Act
   § 267..............................25n.58
Constitution (Grundgesetz)...............113
   Art 14............................113n.52
Corporate Act of 1937, § 70 s 1 ..........30n.84
Corporate Governance Code 2022 ........... 41–42, 112n.41, 125
   Recommendation A1 ...............30n.84
   Recommendation C.1 .............122n.97
Corporate Governance Code 2019
   Art 4.1.1.........................112n.43
General German Commercial Code of 1861 .........................106–7
Stock Corporation Act 1937 .... 107–9, 114–15, 119, 125–26, 231–32
   § 70.....................108n.17, 108n.19
   § 90..............................121n.91
   § 93..............................50n.218
   § 93(1) sentence 2 ..........110n.32, 224n.23
   § 111(4) sentence 2 ........110n.28, 121n.90
   § 111l1............................120n.89
   § 116..............................50n.218
   § 161(1)...........................112n.41
   § 147(1)...........................50n.220
Stock Corporation Act of 1965...... 106–9, 113
Supply Chain Due Diligence Act of 2021 (Gesetz über die unternehmerischen Sorgfaltspflichten in Lieferketten of 16 July 2021, Official Gazette 2021 I 2959)......... 5–6, 35–36, 35n.121, 36n.132, 46n.191, 52
   § 2 s 1............................35n.122
   § 2 s 2............................35n.123
   § 2 s 8.............................45–46
   §§ 3–10 ..........................35n.124
   s 3...............................35n.123
   § 3 para 1 sentence 2 no 8 ..........45n.190
   § 3 s 3............................36n.127
   s 6...............................35n.124
   § 9..........................36n.126, 45n.190
   § 11..............................50n.225
   § 22.......................36n.128, 49n.217
   Annexes 1–11......................35n.122

xviii    TABLE OF LEGISLATION

## Italy

Corporate Governance Code .......... 254n.49
Stewardship code ................... 253–54
    Principle 3 ....................... 253–54

## Netherlands

Civil Code .......................... 252–53
    Art 2:135a(2) ..................... 252n.35
Corporate Governance Code .......... 253n.37
Stewardship Code 2018 .............. 252n.32

## Switzerland

Stewardship Code ................... 255n.52

## United Kingdom

Companies Act 1937 ..................... 108
Companies Act 2006 (CA 2006) (c 46) ... 43, 143,
    144, 145n.19, 147, 228–29
    s 6 .............................. 33n.106
    s 171 ................................ 143
    s 172 ......... 9–10, 48n.210, 143–44, 143n.7,
        143n.8, 143n.9, 143n.11,
        145–46, 149, 151, 152
    s 172(1) ......... 43n.174, 43n.176, 144, 225,
        229n.39, 242n.100, 323n.17
    s 172(1)(a)–(f) .................... 43n.176
    s 414A(1) .......................... 145n.19
    s 414A(2) .......................... 145n.19
    s 414CZA ........................... 43n.176
Companies (Audit, Investigations and
    Community Enterprise) Act 2004
    Pt 2 ............................. 33n.106
Consolidated Law on Finance (Testo
    Unico della Finanza, Legislative
    Decree 24 February 1998
    Art 124-quinquies ................. 254n.48
    Art 147-ter ....................... 254n.47
Corporate Governance Code 2018 ... 19, 30n.85,
    42n.162, 42n.166, 142–43, 144,
    144n.16, 147, 148–49, 156–57
    Provision 5 .............. 9–10, 147, 148–49
Stewardship Code 2020 ......... 13–14, 30n.85,
    42n.166, 144, 249–50, 250n.17, 250n.20,
    251, 252–55, 255n.53, 269, 319–20, 334,
    346–47, 346n.166, 346n.168
    Principle 4 ....................... 346n.171
    Principle 5 ....................... 346n.170
    Principle 7 ....................... 259n.75
    Principle 11 .......................... 346
Takeover Code 2021 ................. 42n.167

## United States

16 CFR § 802.9 ...................... 211n.114
17 CFR § 229.101 (2020) .............. 89n.40
17 CFR § 229.1502–§ 223.1506 ......... 88n.36
17 CFR § 229.1504 .................... 88n.37
17 CFR § 230.507 .................... 199n.29
15 USC §§ 18, 19 .................... 202n.52
42 CFR § 1001.601 ................... 199n.29
42 USC § 2000e-2 .................... 202n.51
Accountable Capitalism Act, 115th
    Cong (2018) ........ 128n.4, 212–13n.123
    s 3348 ........................... 194n.136
California Transparency in Supply
    Chains Act of 2010, SB 657, Civ
    Code S1714.43 (2010) ............. 92n.71
Climate Corporate Data Accountability
    Act of 2023, Cal SB 253 ch 382
    (7 October 2023) .................. 92n.68
Del Code Ann (2022)
    § 102(a)(4) ....................... 200n.32
    § 141 ............................. 200n.33
    § 154 ............................. 202n.55
    § 160 ............................. 202n.55
    § 174 ............................. 202n.55
    § 203 ............................. 192n.123
    § 211 ............................. 200n.32
    § 251 ............................. 200n.32
    § 275 ............................. 200n.32
Delaware General Corporation Law
    § 102(b)(7)(ii) ..................... 65n.37
    § 122(9) ........................... 68n.49
    § 362 ..................... 131n.16, 131n.17
Dodd-Frank Wall Street Reform
    and Consumer Protection Act,
    Pub L No 111-203, 124 Stat 1374
    (2010) ............................ 96n.96
Employee Retirement and Income
    Security Act of 1974, Pub L No
    93-406, 88 Stat 829 (ERISA) .... 90, 209–10
29 USC, §§ 1001–1461 ................ 90n.52
29 USC § 110(a)(1)(A)(i)–(ii) ........ 90n.53
Internal Revenue Code
    s 401(k) .......................... 209–10
Investment Company Act of 1940 ...... 319–20
    15 USC § 80a-2(c) (2018) .......... 97n.100
Model Benefit Corporation Legislation
    § 301 ............................. 131n.16
    § 104 ............................. 131n.17
National Securities Markets Improvement
    Act of 1996, Public Law 104-290
    (NSMIA) ............................... 96
Pa Cons Stat (2022)
    § 15.515(b) ....................... 192n.125
Restatement of the Law of Corporate
    Governance of the American
    Law Institute ...... 29–30, 131–32n.18, 135
    § 1.23 ............................ 130n.15
    § 2.01 ............ 30n.83, 129, 129n.14, 136
    § 2.01(a) .......................... 29n.77
    § 2.01(a)(1) .......................... 130
    § 2.01(a)(2) .......................... 131

Securities Act of 1933, 15 USC .......... 218n.3
 § 77b(b) (2018) .................... 97n.100
 § 77g(a)(1) (2018). ................. 97n.100
 § 77s(a) .......................... 97n.100
Securities Exchange Act of 1934,
   15 USC ................... 96–97, 218n.3
 § 2................................ 97n.99
§ 3(f) ............................. 97n.100
§ 78(c)(f) ......................... 97n.100
§ 78w(a)(2) (2018) ................ 97n.100
Sherman Act of 1890....................... 24
Voluntary Carbon Market Disclosures
   Act (VCMDA) Cal SB 390
   (7 October 2023). ................ 93n.74

# Abbreviations

| | |
|---|---|
| AIFMs | alternative investment fund managers |
| ALI | American Law Institute |
| BAFA | German Federal Office of Economics and Export Control |
| BBA | Better Business Act |
| BIS | Bank for International Settlements |
| CA 2006 | Companies Act 2006 (UK) |
| CapEx | capital expenditure |
| CDP | Carbon Disclosure Project |
| CDSB | Climate Disclosure Standards Board |
| CEOs | chief executive officers |
| CS3D | Directive on Corporate Sustainability Due Diligence |
| CSR | corporate social responsibility |
| CSRD | Corporate Sustainability Reporting Directive |
| DEI | diversity, equity, and inclusion |
| EBA | European Banking Authority |
| ECB | European Central Bank |
| EESG | employee, environmental, social, and governance |
| EMS model | entity maximization and sustainability model |
| ERISA | Employee Retirement and Income Security Act 1974 |
| ESG | environmental, social, and governance |
| ESMA | European Securities and Markets Authority |
| ESRS | European Sustainability Reporting Standards |
| FRC | Financial Reporting Council |
| FSOC | Financial Stability Oversight Council |
| GAR | green asset ratio |
| GFANZ | Glasgow Financial Alliance for Net Zero |
| GHG | greenhouse gas |
| GRI | Global Reporting Initiative |
| ICMA | International Capital Market Association |
| IFRS | International Financial Reporting Standards |
| IOSCO | International Organization of Securities Commissions |
| IIRC | International Integrated Reporting Council |
| ISSB | International Sustainability Standards Board |
| KPIs | key performance indicators |
| LLC | limited liability company |
| LLP | limited liability partnership |
| MiFiD II | Markets for Financial Instruments Directive |
| MPs | members of Parliament |
| NREs | new economic regulations |
| NFRD | Non-Financial Reporting Directive |
| NGOs | non-governmental organizations |

| | |
|---|---|
| NSMIA | National Securities Markets Improvement Act of 1996 |
| PBC | public benefit corporation |
| PIEs | public interest entities |
| SASB | Sustainability Accounting Standards Board |
| SDGs | sustainable development goals |
| SEC | US Securities and Exchange Commission |
| SFDR | Sustainability Finance Disclosure Regulation |
| SMEs | small and medium-sized enterprises |
| SRD II | Shareholder Rights Directive II |
| SRIs | socially responsible investments |
| TCFD | Task Force for Climate-related Financial Disclosure |
| TFEU | Treaty on the Functioning of the European Union |
| UCITS | Undertakings for Collective Investment in Transferable Securities |
| UKSC | UK Stewardship Code |
| UNGPs | United Nations Guiding Principles on Business and Human Rights |
| UNPRI | United Nations Principles for Responsible Investment |
| WTO | World Trade Organization |
| WTP | willingness to pay |

# Contributors

**Jens-Hinrich Binder** has been Professor of Private Law, Corporate, Banking, and Securities Law at Eberhard-Karls-University Tübingen since 2013.

**Klaus J. Hopt** is a Professor and Director (Emeritus) at the Max-Planck-Institute for Comparative and International Private Law, Hamburg.

**Thilo Kuntz** is Professor (chair) in Private Law, Commercial and Corporate Law, and Managing Director of the Institute of Corporate Law at Heinrich-Heine-University Düsseldorf, Germany.

**Holger Spamann** is the Lawrence R. Grove Professor at Harvard Law School, where he teaches corporate law, corporate finance, and a course on private funds.

**Jacob Fisher** is a JD candidate at Stanford Law School, as well as a PhD candidate in Finance at the Cornell Johnson Graduate School of Management.

**Virginia Harper Ho** is a Professor of Law at City University of Hong Kong School of Law and was formerly the Associate Dean for International & Comparative Law at the University of Kansas School of Law (USA).

Professor Dr **Rüdiger Veil** holds the Chair for Civil Law and Business Law at the Ludwig-Maximilians-University (LMU), Munich/Germany.

**Edward B. Rock** is the Martin Lipton Professor of Law at New York University School of Law.

Professor **Irene-marié Esser** is a Professor of Corporate Law and Governance and Dean of the Graduate School, College of Social Sciences.

**Iain MacNeil** is the Alexander Stone Professor of Commercial Law at the University of Glasgow.

**Christine Osterloh-Konrad** holds the Chair in Private Law, Commercial and Corporate Law, Tax Law, and Legal Philosophy at Tübingen University.

**Harwell Wells** is the Richard H. Walker Professor of Law at Temple University's James E. Beasley School of Law.

**Ann M. Lipton** is the Michael M. Fleishman Professor in Business Law and Entrepreneurship and an affiliate of Tulane's Murphy Institute.

**Guido Ferrarini** is Emeritus Professor of Business Law at the University of Genoa in Italy.

**Michele Siri** is Professor of Business Law at the University of Genoa (Italy) and Director of the Jean Monnet Centre of Excellence EUSFIL, European Union Sustainable Finance and Law.

**Alain Pietrancosta** is Professor of Law and Director of the Masters in Financial Law programme at the Sorbonne Law School (University of Paris).

Professor Dr **Christoph Kumpan**, LL.M. (University of Chicago), Attorney at Law (New York) is the Dr Harald Hack Professor of Private Law, Company Law, and Capital Markets Law at the Bucerius Law School, Hamburg, Germany

**Stefan Thomas** has been a professor of Private Law, Commercial Law, Competition and Insurance Law at Eberhard-Karls-University Tuebingen since 2009.

# About the Authors

**Jens-Hinrich Binder** has been Professor of Private Law, Corporate, Banking, and Securities Law at Eberhard-Karls-University Tübingen since 2013. He is also Visiting Professor at Università Cattolica del Sacro Cuore, Milan, and a member of the Academic Board of the European Banking Institute. He has written extensively in the areas of corporate and financial law, and has advised numerous German and European institutions in these fields. He is co-editor and serves on the editorial board of two leading German banking law journals.

**Klaus J. Hopt** is Professor and Director (Emeritus) at the Max-Planck-Institute for Comparative and International Private Law, Hamburg. He holds honorary doctoral degrees by the Universities of Brussels, Louvain, Paris, Athens, and Tiflis. He is a member of the National Academy of Sciences Leopoldina. Professor Hopt held visiting professorships at the Universities of Chicago, Columbia, Harvard, NYU, Paris, Rome, Vienna, Kyodai, and Todai. From 1981 to 1985, he served as Judge at the Court of Appeals Stuttgart; from 2002 to 2008, he was Vice-president of the German Research Foundation; and from 2011 to 2014, he was a member of the International Advisory Board of the Alexander von Humboldt-Foundation. His publications deal with European corporate, capital market and financial law, eg 'Comparative Corporate Governance' 59 (2011) 1–73 and 'Corporate Boards in Europe' 61 (2013) 301–75 (with Davies) in The American Journal of Comparative Law, and *The Anatomy of Corporate Law* (with Kraakman and others, 3rd edn, OUP 2017).

**Thilo Kuntz** is Professor (Chair) in Private Law, Commercial and Corporate Law, and Managing Director of the Institute of Corporate Law at the Heinrich-Heine-University Düsseldorf, Germany. He has held visiting positions at Notre Dame Law School and UCLA School of Law. His research focuses on fiduciary law, corporate law, and legal theory. Kuntz has edited and co-edited several books on Transnational Fiduciary Law, ESG, and, with OUP, Methodology in Private Law Theory (2024).

**Holger Spamann** is the Lawrence R. Grove Professor at Harvard Law School, where he teaches corporate law, corporate finance, and a course on private funds. His research focuses on the law and economics of corporate governance and financial markets, judicial behaviour, and comparative law. Before embarking on his academic career, he practised M&A law with Debevoise & Plimpton in New York and clerked for two years in Europe. He holds law degrees from France, Germany, and the United States, and a Ph.D. in economics from Harvard University. He is fellow of the ECGI and editor-in-chief of the *Journal of Legal Analysis*.

**Jacob Fisher** is a JD candidate at Stanford Law School, as well as a PhD candidate in Finance at the Cornell Johnson Graduate School of Management, where he assisted with courses on corporate governance and financial markets and institutions. His research focuses on corporate law and governance, banking, and financial regulation.

**Virginia Harper Ho** is a Professor of Law at City University of Hong Kong School of Law and was formerly the Associate Dean for International & Comparative Law at the University of Kansas School of Law (USA). Her scholarship focuses on the intersections of corporate governance, securities regulation, sustainability, and finance from a comparative perspective. She is a Research Member of the European Corporate Governance Institute (ECGI) and serves on the Executive Committee of the American Society of Comparative Law. She holds a JD from Harvard Law School (with honours) and a B.A. and M.A. from Indiana University (Bloomington) (USA).

Professor Dr **Rüdiger Veil** holds the chair for civil law and business law at the Ludwig-Maximilians-University (LMU), Munich/Germany. He graduated at the Humboldt University, Berlin in 1995 with a doctoral thesis on 'Conversion of a Stock Corporation'. In 2002, he obtained his habilitation at the Humboldt University with a book on 'Intercompany Agreements'. Rüdiger Veil has published books on 'European Capital Markets Law' (3rd edn, Hart Publishing 2022) and on 'The Law of Corporations' (6th edn, C.H. Beck 2015) and more than 100 articles in top ranked journals and research handbooks on corporate law and financial markets regulation. Rüdiger Veil was a member of the ESMA Securities and Markets Stakeholder Group (SMSG) from 2014 to 2018; from 2016 to 2018, he was Chair of the SMSG. Since 2012, Rüdiger Veil has been advising the German Federal Ministry of Finance on reforms of EU financial markets regulation. He has acted as an expert for the German, European, Chinese, and Russian Parliaments on draft laws on corporate law and capital markets law. ESMA has appointed him as an Alternate Member of the ESA Joint Board of Appeal in 2021.

**Edward B. Rock** is the Martin Lipton Professor of Law at New York University School of Law. His main areas of teaching and research are corporate law and corporate governance. He has written about institutional investors, systemic stewardship, shareholder activism, corporate voting, poison pills, politics and corporate law, proxy access, corporate federalism, and mergers and acquisitions, among other things. In addition to teaching and research, Rock is co-director of NYU's Institute for Corporate Governance & Finance and the Reporter for the American Law Institute's Restatement of the Law of Corporate Governance.

Professor **Irene-marié Esser** is a Professor of Corporate Law and Governance and Dean of the Graduate School, College of Social Sciences. Since 2020 she has been an Extraordinary Professor at Stellenbosch University, South Africa. She was admitted as an Attorney of the High Court of South Africa in 2005. She was the Company Law Convener for the Society of Legal Scholars of the UK and Ireland for three years until

2021. She currently teaches Corporate Governance and Company Law. Her research spans doctrinal and empirical approaches, covering the UK, the EU, and South Africa.

**Iain MacNeil** is the Alexander Stone Professor of Commercial Law at the University of Glasgow. He began his academic career after a decade working in investment banking in the City of London. He has undertaken research and collaborated with colleagues in Australia, Canada, China, Hong Kong, and the United States. He is a Trustee of the British Institute of International and Comparative Law and Chair of the International Securities Regulation Committee of the International Law Association. He has acted as Senior Adviser on several projects examining national compliance with EU financial sector Directives.

**Christine Osterloh-Konrad** holds the Chair in Private Law, Commercial and Corporate Law, Tax Law, and Legal Philosophy at Tübingen University. Previously, she was a Senior Research Fellow at the Max Planck Institute for Tax Law and Public Finance, where she completed both her SJD *summa cum laude* (several prizes) and her postdoctoral studies with an award-winning thesis on comparative and theoretical perspectives on tax avoidance. Drawing from her comparative expertise, she has advised German, Norwegian, and US institutions on the design of various legal instruments counteracting tax avoidance strategies and on the taxation of pass-through entities.

**Ann M. Lipton** is the Michael M. Fleishman Professor in Business Law and Entrepreneurship and an affiliate of Tulane's Murphy Institute. Prior to entering academia, Professor Lipton practised for over ten years as a securities litigator in New York, and served as a law clerk to Chief Judge Edward R. Becker of the Third Circuit Court of Appeals, and Associate Justice David H. Souter of the United States Supreme Court.

**Harwell Wells** is the Richard H. Walker Professor of Law at Temple University's James E. Beasley School of Law. He has written widely in both corporate law and business history and holds a PhD in history from the University of Virginia, as well as a law degree from Vanderbilt University Law School.

**Guido Ferrarini** is Emeritus Professor of Business Law at the University of Genoa in Italy. He is a founder and fellow of the European Corporate Governance Institute (ECGI), a member of the European Company Law Experts (ECLE) Group, an Academic member of the Jean Monnet Centre of Excellence on Sustainable Finance and Law (EUSFiL), and an Academic Member of the European Banking Institute. He was chairman and founder of an alternative finance platform and is board member of a private bank.

**Michele Siri** is Professor of Business Law at the University of Genoa (Italy) and Director of the Jean Monnet Centre of Excellence EUSFIL, European Union Sustainable Finance and Law. He has held a Jean Monnet Chair on the regulation of financial and insurance markets in the European Union. Since 2018, he has been a member of the Joint Board of Appeal of the European Supervisory Authorities, which he has been appointed to chair in 2021. He is a regular lecturer at the LLM programme of Luigi Bocconi University and at the Frankfurt School of Finance and Management.

**Alain Pietrancosta** is Professor of Law and Director of the Masters in Financial Law programme at the Sorbonne Law School (University of Paris). He is a member of the Legal High Committee for Financial Markets of Paris; the Corporate governance committee of the MEDEF; the ParisEuroplace legal committee on financial law; the European Company Law Experts Group (ECLE). He is also founder of the Corporate Finance and Capital Markets Law Review and Research Associate of the ECGI. Professor Pietrancosta has developed a practice as a law consultant and expert for the last twenty-five years.

Professor Dr **Christoph Kumpan**, LL.M. (University of Chicago), Attorney at Law (New York) is the Dr Harald Hack Professor of Private Law, Company Law, and Capital Markets Law at the Bucerius Law School, Hamburg, Germany. He counsels the German Ministry of Finance on matters regarding capital markets regulation and has advised the Turkish Capital Markets Board on takeover law. Before joining the Bucerius Law School he was a professor at the University of Halle-Wittenberg and at the Humboldt University Berlin and was a senior research fellow at the Max Planck Institute for Comparative and International Private Law in Hamburg.

**Stefan Thomas** is a full professor at the Law Faculty of the University of Tübingen, Germany. He is a director at CZS Institute for Artificial Intelligence and Law, and at the Tübingen Institute on the Determinants of Economic Activity (TRIDEA). Stefan specializes in European and German antitrust law. He is a Member of the International Advisory Board of the Institute for Global Law, Economics, and Finance, Queen Mary University of London, and he was a fellow at the Center for Advanced Studies on the Foundations of Law and Finance at the Goethe University Frankfurt.

# 1
# Corporate Purpose, Corporate Social Responsibility, and ESG

An Introduction to the Trans-Atlantic Dialogue

*Jens-Hinrich Binder, Klaus J. Hopt, and Thilo Kuntz**

## I. Introduction

Ever since their invention as vehicles for the funding of colonial trade in the seventeenth century, corporations have oscillated between the private interests of the shareholders, who invest in the corporation and seek a return in the form of dividends, and public interests, which have inspired and driven both the recognition of limited liability entities in the first place *and* the imposition of regulatory requirements on their formation and ongoing operation. During the greater part of the twentieth century, corporation laws on both sides of the Atlantic had come to be dominated by the view that corporations should, by and large, serve their shareholders' interests, and that directors' (fiduciary) duties ought to be interpreted accordingly. Over the last twenty years or so, however, this understanding has met with increasing criticism. Reflecting a growing concern about ecological and social externalities caused by the economic activities (particularly of large, listed corporations), a growing number of scholars and policy-makers have been asking and, indeed, questioning the overarching social and economic functions especially of the large public corporation and ensuing normative implications for their business activity. 'Corporate purpose', 'corporate social responsibility' and 'ESG' (for environmental, social, and governance implications of corporate behaviour) are the relevant catchwords. Most recently, claims supporting a fundamental reinterpretation of the 'corporate purpose'—in the sense of a fundamental shift from *private* to public interests as the guiding paradigm of corporate law and corporate behaviour—have been advanced particularly in the United States and in the UK.[1] This debate centres on whether—at least—public companies of a certain size should be qualified 'public' in a double sense, that is, as a company open for a large

---

* All internet sources were last accessed on 10 January 2024.
[1] Exemplarily and programmatically see Colin Mayer, *Prosperity* (OUP 2018); see also Colin Mayer, 'The Future of the Corporation and the Economics of Purpose' (2021) 58 Journal of Management Studies 887; Alex Edmans, *Grow the Pie* (CUP 2020); cf also the earlier contribution of Andrew Keay, *The Corporate Objective* (Edward Elgar Publishing 2011) 173–230.

Jens-Hinrich Binder, Klaus J. Hopt, and Thilo Kuntz, *Corporate Purpose, Corporate Social Responsibility, and ESG* In: *Corporate Purpose, CSR, and ESG*. Edited by: Jens-Hinrich Binder, Klaus J. Hopt, and Thilo Kuntz, Oxford University Press.
© Jens-Hinrich Binder, Klaus J. Hopt, and Thilo Kuntz 2024. DOI: 10.1093/oso/9780198912576.003.0001

ıber of shareholders with shares traded on anonymous markets and as an institution serving an additional purpose beyond maximizing monetary profit, obligated to pursue external political goals, namely social and/or ecological objectives. Adherents maintain that all they want is nothing more than a return to the historical 'normal' and raise the—highly dubious—claim that, historically, the business corporation and the business company were subject to a set of far-reaching duties towards the public,[2] not only in specific areas of the law such as for example antitrust, but also and already in corporate and company law. Critics, by contrast, question not just the underlying policy considerations (the notion that business associations could and should effectively be turned into 'good corporate citizens'), but highlight also potential implications for the effectiveness of existing corporate governance structures.

The present volume, prepared by an academic conference organized by the editors at Eberhard Karls University Tübingen in the summer of 2022, presents the first trans-Atlantic analysis of the developments summarized above. Bringing together analyses by both US and European legal scholars, it presents a broad range of different views on the relevant issues and highlights not just common features between the academic debates on CSR, ESG and 'corporate purpose' on both sides of the Atlantic Ocean. It also reveals fundamental differences in terms of the *operationalization* of these concepts in US corporate laws on the one hand and within the EU on the other hand, facilitating a better (and perhaps more realistic) understanding of substantial conceptual differences underpinning the academic debates in both systems.

Significantly, as will be discussed in greater detail in several chapters below, the notion of corporate social responsibility and ESG, in the US corporate law domain, has to be regarded, to a large extent to date, as a market-driven phenomenon, triggered and fuelled by growing investor and consumer demand and societal pressure. In the EU, by contrast, the increasing role of public-interest considerations as a paradigm for corporate behaviour has been largely a regulatory matter. A first (if tentative) step in this regard was the introduction of CSR disclosure requirements with the 2014 Non-Financial Reporting Directive (NFRD).[3] In the United States, by contrast, initiatives for non-financial reporting and disclosure obligations like the US Securities and Exchange Commission's proposal on climate-change disclosure[4] have not yet been adopted. Within the EU, a second, far more comprehensive step was then made with the enactment of the Corporate Sustainability Reporting Directive (CSRD)[5] in 2023,

---

[2] See eg Mayer(n 1) 63–83.
[3] Directive 2014/95/EU of the European Parliament and of the Council of 22 October 2014 amending Directive 2013/34/EU as regards disclosure of non-financial and diversity information by certain large undertakings and groups [2014] OJ L330/1.
[4] Proposed Rule: 'The Enhancement and Standardization of Climate–related Disclosures for Investors' https://www.sec.gov/rules/proposed/2022/33-11042.pdf. For an analysis see Lisa Fairfax, 'A Green Victory in the Midst of Potential Defeat? Concern and Optimism about the Impact of the SEC's Climate-Related Disclosure Rule' in Thilo Kuntz (ed), *Research Handbook on Environmental, Social, and Corporate Governance* (Edward Elgar Publishing 2024) ch 13.
[5] Directive (EU) 2022/2464 of the European Parliament and of the Council of 14 December 2022 amending Regulation (EU) No 537/2014, Directive 2004/109/EC, Directive 2006/43/EC and Directive 2013/34/EU, as regards corporate sustainability reporting [2022] OJ L322/15.

which introduced an elaborate scheme of detailed disclosure duties, interwoven with one of the EU's major pillars of sustainability regulation, the Sustainability Finance Disclosure Regulation (SFDR).[6] Coupled with other legislative acts growing out of the EU Commission's 'Green Deal'[7] and its ambition to transform the economy as a whole,[8] these developments reveals a much bolder—again, regulatory—attempt at strapping companies onto a large-scale normative programme oriented towards CSR and ESG. Indeed, an Ernst & Young study written on behalf of and emphatically endorsed by the EU Commission unequivocally recommends a large-scale reform of corporate governance structures towards sustainability, which met with strong criticism.[9] In the UK, the British Academy engages in a research project on the 'Future of the Corporation',[10] embracing the idea of corporate purpose, and has published reports on a reorientation of the purpose of public companies in 2018 and 2019.[11] These initiatives—and, indeed, the substantial criticism they provoked—will be discussed in more detail in several chapters of the book.

From the perspective of the history of ideas, it may be tempting to interpret the concept of corporate purpose merely as a concept emerging from the earlier classical debate setting 'shareholder value' and 'stakeholder value' against each other, with the former centring on shareholder-value maximization as primary duty and the latter including the interests of others, especially creditors and employees. An illustrative example, in this respect, is the statement of the US 'Business Roundtable'.[12] On closer inspection, however, as suggested in a number of chapters below, both academic arguments supporting the notion of a fundamental reorientation of the objective of corporations (and, correspondingly, directors' duties) *and* the growing body of regulatory interference with corporate behaviour within the EU go much further than a mere organic evolution of existing concepts and amount to no less than a novel concept with distinct characteristics that deviate from, and indeed conflict with, established foundations of corporate law and corporate governance. Proponents argue that the economic power wielded by public corporations comes with a special responsibility for social and ecological interests. The consequences are unclear, however. While new requirements and obligations have been addressed to corporations in a wide range of fields ranging from environmental law to due diligence requirements in value chains, the implications for the orientation of directors' duties—including their fundamental fiduciary duties to the corporation—remain far from settled. It is particularly in this regard that the debate

---

[6] Regulation (EU) 2019/2088 of the European Parliament and of the Council of 27 November 2019 on sustainability-related disclosures in the financial services sector [2019] OJ L317/1 (9 December 2019). On the connection between CSDR and SFDR see recital 28 of the CSDR (n 4).

[7] European Commission, Communication from the Commission to the European Parliament, the European Council, the Council, the European Economic and Social Committee and the Committee of the Regions, 'The European Green Deal' COM/2019/640 final (11 December 2019).

[8] ibid 2.

[9] European Commission, *Study on Directors' Duties and Sustainable Corporate Governance: Final Report* (2020) https://data.europa.eu/doi/10.2838/472901. For further analysis see Klaus J. Hopt, Chapter 2 of this volume.

[10] See https://www.thebritishacademy.ac.uk/programmes/future-of-the-corporation/.

[11] ibid.

[12] See https://www.businessroundtable.org/business-roundtable-redefines-the-purpose-of-a-corporation-to-promote-an-economy-that-serves-all-americans. For further discussion see chs 2, 6, and 8 of this volume.

on 'corporate purpose' significantly overlaps with the general discourse on CSR and the social and ecological responsibility of business.[13]

Irrespective of scholarly disagreement on which elements of the debate are actually new and which are old, one trend is undisputably new—the intensity of legislative action as well as court decisions especially in Continental Europe, but also in the United States and the UK. Contrary to what was the case twenty years ago, legislators, other norm-setting bodies, and courts have come to establish and refine relevant normative frameworks in a well-oiled production line. In Europe, the 2022 proposal for a Corporate Sustainability Due Diligence Directive aimed at covering the whole value chain[14] and was adopted in 2024. The Corporate Sustainability Due Diligence Directive proposal contained not only extensive duties and responsibilities of the corporation, but also a far-reaching provision in Article 25(1), establishing a corporate duty of care requiring 'directors of companies ... to take into account the consequences of their decisions for sustainability matters, including, where applicable, human rights, climate change and environmental consequences'. Even though this provision is not part of the final version, it still can serve as a showcase for the perspective of the European Commission concerning fiduciary duties of board members. In the *Shell* case, a Dutch Court relied on Dutch tort law and the tort duty of care to hold Royal Dutch Shell responsible for climate change mitigation.[15] Other regulatory playing-fields relate to institutional investors and financial intermediaries in general and their role in 'green finance'. On the other side of the Atlantic, the US Securities and Exchange Commission has published a proposal on climate change disclosure mentioned above[16] and enacted rules requiring institutional investors to include ESG-related information in their proxy voting reports.[17] California promulgated its own set of climate disclosure rules,[18] and similar regulatory requirements have made their way into the legislative frameworks of EU Member States. As a counter-movement, several US states led by Republican governments chose to enact 'anti-ESG legislation'.[19] In sum, corporate purpose, CSR, and ESG pose difficult problems not only for corporate law

---

[13] cf Cynthia Williams, 'Corporate Social Responsibility and Corporate Governance' in Jeffrey Gordon and Wolf-Georg Ringe (eds), *Oxford Handbook of Corporate Law and Governance* (OUP 2018) 634.

[14] EU Commission, Proposal for a directive of the European Parliament and of the Council on Corporate Sustainability Due Diligence and amending Directive (EU) 2019/1937, COM/2022/71 final https://eur-lex.europa.eu/legal-content/EN/TXT/?uri=CELEX%3A52022PC0071. For a report on the current status of the legislative proceedings, see https://www.europarl.europa.eu/legislative-train/theme-an-economy-that-works-for-people/file-legislative-proposal-on-sustainable-corporate-governance.

[15] Vereniging Milieudefensie, in Amsterdam, and others, versus Royal Dutch Shell plc in The Hague, The Hague District Court, Judgment of 26 May 2021, case number C/09/571932/HA ZA 19-379 (English version), ECLI:NL:RBDHA:2021:5339 https://uitspraken.rechtspraak.nl/inziendocument?id=ECLI:NL:RBDHA:2021:5339.

[16] See n 4 above.

[17] SEC Release Nos 33-11131; 34-96206; IC-34745; File No S7-11-21, RIN 3235-AK67 https://www.sec.gov/news/press-release/2022-198.

[18] AB-1305 Voluntary carbon market disclosures https://leginfo.legislature.ca.gov/faces/billTextClient.xhtml?bill_id=202320240AB1305; SB-253 Climate Corporate Data Accountability Act https://leginfo.legislature.ca.gov/faces/billTextClient.xhtml?bill_id=202320240SB253; SB-261 Greenhouse gases: climate-related financial risk https://leginfo.legislature.ca.gov/faces/billTextClient.xhtml?bill_id=202320240SB261.

[19] For a short survey and an inquiry to what extent ESG is a European problem only see Thilo Kuntz, 'How ESG Is Weakening the Business Judgment Rule' in Thilo Kuntz (ed), *Research Handbook on Environmental, Social, and Corporate Governance* (Edward Elgar Publishing 2024) s IV.

scholars and traditional avenues of theoretical inquiry, but also for corporate practice, with enormous economic implications. Additionally, the ramifications of the various normative frameworks in the EU and in the United States will not stay confined to national borders. US corporations doing business in Europe will have to comply with EU laws and vice versa.

This latter aspect drives the composition of this book. While it is certainly true that purpose, CSR, and ESG are not only European, US, or even Western topics,[20] the normative thrust and the number of regulatory initiatives is highest in Europe (including the UK) and the United States. Astonishingly, the conversation appears to be stuck in regional pockets. Intense in the respective jurisdictions, there is a lack of trans-Atlantic debates and an integration of the various strands of the discussions of core ideas and normative movements, at least to the mind of this volume's editors. Consequently, it is high time to start a dialogue and provide trans-Atlantic perspectives.

## II. Thematic Overview

### 1. General Report

Chapter 2 presents a general report on 'Corporate Purpose and Stakeholder Value' (which opened up also the proceedings at Tübingen conference in 2022). In this chapter, Klaus Hopt presents an historical, economic, and comparative law analysis of the current trans-Atlantic debate and critically discusses the available legislative options and enforcement problems. In the first part of the chapter, he recounts the current debate on corporate purpose, stakeholder participation and ESG. The new promise is that the purpose of the corporation will solve the problem and decide the battle between shareholder value and stakeholder interests. Yet Hopt shows that this reform, supposedly 'an embarrassingly simple policy', is anything but simple and effective. Common practice shows that, if the choice of purpose is left to the shareholders, corporate purpose clauses will often be too generic with little use for stakeholders, and they are difficult to monitor. Yet extending mandatory public purposes to companies in non-regulated industries would require a fundamental reconsideration of the relationship between the state and entrepreneurial endeavour. Hopt then looks into history. In the nineteenth century, state concessions for corporations were granted only if a public utility could be established. Yet the concession system faded away, and the targeted pursuit of general interests was assigned no longer to stock corporations under stock corporation law, but to antitrust law, securities regulation, and other laws. With the ESG movement, this historical development seems to be reversing.

In the second part, Hopt then discusses the current economic, social science and policy arguments and legislative options. Prevailing economic theory defends the primacy of the shareholder as 'the most efficient operating principle'; profit maximization

---

[20] For in ESG in Asia see the chapters on China, India, common law Asia, and Japan in Kuntz (n 19).

'leads to value creation for all stakeholders of the company'; 'in addition tax and transfer systems can be used to redistribute economic value to non-shareholders'. This leads to various individual arguments and rejoinders. From the side of behavioural economics and the social sciences, the main criticism is the externalization of costs and damages as projected onto stakeholders other than the company and the shareholders. Legislators have various options for regulating ESG, corporate sustainability diligence, and climate change. Prominent examples can be found in France with the Duty of Vigilance Law of 2017 and the Loi Pacte of 2019, and in Germany with the Supply Chain Due Diligence Act of 2021. The most recent movement in the direction of stakeholderism is the controversial European Directive on Corporate Sustainability Due Diligence (CS3D), adopted in 2024. In the third part, Hopt then takes a closer look at enforcement problems. Not only the setting of rules that is important; rather, it is the enforcement and enforceability of such rules that is perhaps of even greater significance. In this context, a whole arsenal of regulatory or legislative options with different possible effects as well as drawbacks emerges: What counts is making stakeholder governance work. Hopt identifies various possibilities: (1) market discipline and self-regulation; (2) the code movement: comply and explain; (3) disclosure and auditing; (4) enterprise law with outside and inside requirements, in particular: duties of the enterprise and rights, duties and organization of the corporate organs; (5) public enforcement: state agencies, public procurement, the attorney general; and (6) private enforcement by shareholders and stakeholders. Each of these enforcement options has its pros and cons. The task, as Hopt concludes, is to find the right mix, a challenge for the legislator which is anything but simple, but which is also unavoidable.

## 2. National and Transnational perspectives

In Chapter 3 on 'Corporate Purpose: Theoretical and Empirical Foundations/Confusions', Holger Spamann and Jacob Fisher argue that 'corporate purpose' may mean many things, will make relatively little difference in theory, and is virtually not supported by data. Starting out with the theoretical underpinnings of corporate purpose and the difference between choosing the social good and monetary profit maximization, Spamann and Fisher construe corporate purpose as an ex ante commitment to a decision criterion where private profit and social good diverge. After delineating the basic opposites, they emphasize the importance of substitution effects which may undermine boycotts and preferential treatment of pro-social actions in markets because, for example, new buyers will be attracted by lower prices, taking the place of those dispensing with certain products. Exploring their construal of corporate purpose as commitment, they maintain that a broader corporate purpose may indeed increase profits, due to contractual incompleteness and the resulting inability of stakeholders like employees to gain full protection through private bargaining. Spamann and Fisher hasten to add, however, that the constituency with the weakest ability to contract for protection is the shareholder, given that an equity investment is not a contractual claim, but defined by the absence of contractual claims to payment. Turning to the institutional underpinnings of corporate purpose, Spamann and Fisher underscore that external regulation remains the most important instrument, constraining what corporate purpose can be. Concerning corporate fiduciary duties, they point out that the line between shareholder profit and stakeholder well-being is blurred and the distinction not enforceable under US corporate law. Parsing extant Delaware case law, Spamann and Fisher hold that even those cases explicitly putting shareholder interests centre stage rest on specific sets of facts, making it hard to extract a general shareholder primacy rule. They describe how instruments of structural governance, for example, board elections and executive pay could help foster stakeholder concerns. Moving on to the empirics of purpose, the authors express scepticism about empirical studies, pointing to endogeneity problems like reverse causation and omitted variables, limited empirical variation, and noise as issues affecting the literature. Moreover, given the lack of a clear definition of corporate purpose, empirical studies suffer from a lack of a concept which could be studied as a phenomenon of its own. Spamann and Fisher also think that empirical studies on the effects of the adoption of state constituency statutes on fiduciary duties are without merit, given that most corporations never experience such a change in the applicable law and that the most important corporate state, Delaware, never enacted such a statute. They also discard organizational structure and different types of owners as significant factors and explain that studies on the real-world effects of sustainable investing are inconclusive. Spamann and Fisher conclude with scepticism whether corporate purpose 'can live up to the hype'.

Chapter 4, by Virginia Harper Ho, then puts the US debate into a 'transnational context'. Harper Ho leads into her chapter by exploring the transnational context of ESG regulation. She describes how current ESG regulation evolved out of a mixture of international frameworks promulgated by non-governmental organizations, older voluntary standards, guidance, and other soft law sources. Considering this chequered map of ESG norms, Harper Ho deems full international alignment of ESG standards unlikely. Segueing into US ESG regulation, she first provides an overview of federal and state regulation. Harper Ho illustrates how the Biden administration's government-wide strategy to respond to climate-related risk plays out on the federal level. On the corporate level, the most important element is the SEC proposal on climate change disclosure rules, which is, Harper Ho maintains, more flexible and less demanding than comparative frameworks such as those enacted in the EU. On the investor level, current and proposed SEC disclosure rules cover investment advisers and investment companies, in addition to state and federal regulation on fiduciary duties, information disclosure, and compliance obligations, informing the ability to integrate ESG factors into investment analysis. On the investment product level, standards for sustainable investment products are voluntary; there is no US equivalent to the EU Taxonomy Regulation. For large financial institutions, the Federal Reserve Board, together with other financial regulators, have issued principles for climate-related financial risk management. With respect to the state level, Harper Ho draws a picture of the division between ESG-oriented regulation in states like California and 'anti-ESG' legislation in several other states, especially those with Republican governments. Taking a step back, Harper Ho elucidates the US institutional context for ESG regulation. She emphasizes a unique feature of the United States, that is, the division of responsibility between the federal and state governments with regard to corporate law and securities regulation. Corporate law's nature as state law in the United States and its enabling character makes it a more difficult subject matter to implement ESG regulation. Moreover, several limitations to its rule-making power constrain the SEC in promulgating comprehensive ESG norms and standards on the federal level. Furthermore, Harper Ho delineates concerns and criticism in the United States resulting from considerations of regulatory costs and the perils of a shrinking capital market as a result of firms going private due to rising compliance burdens. Another layer, in Harper Ho's mind, is US politics and opposite views along the political spectrum relating to the legitimacy of government intervention.

In Chapter 5 ('Stakeholder Governance Models and Corporate Interests: Experiences from Germany'), Rüdiger Veil then follows up on Klaus Hopt's Chapter 2 and 'examines whether it makes sense to include regulations on the objectives and purpose of a company in the law or in the articles of association … or whether the company's interest should be determined by other areas of law, such as labour law, accounting law, etc.' Basing his reflections on German stock corporation law (*Aktienrecht*), he begins with enterprise accountability of the board in Germany and what he describes as a trustee model of stakeholder governance. Veil explains that the debate about the *Unternehmen an sich* (corporation per se) and the proposal to protect large corporations against individual shareholders was the starting point of the German discourse on whether the public corporation should also serve the interests of the general public. The important 1937 reform of the German stock corporation introduced the so-called 'common good clause', obliging directors to pursue, inter alia, the 'welfare of the company and its employees and the common benefit of the people'. It remained in place until the major overhaul of 1965, which abolished the text. However, many observers believed it remained just as self-evident. Additionally, with the introduction of the post-war co-determination laws, the legislature enshrined employee interests in corporate fiduciary law. Veil describes how the pendulum of the German debate swung towards a more shareholder-friendly view akin to US vantage points in the 1990s and back to stakeholderism in the wake of the financial crisis 2007. The EU CSR and ESG regulation continues to gain influence. Against this background, Veil states that currently, 'it does not make sense to regulate the purpose in German stock corporations'. He tentatively concludes that ESG concerns are likely to be reflected in an adjusted definition of the corporate goal in Germany, which, in his mind, leads to a significant limitation of the management's entrepreneurial discretion. Veil cautions against a legal reform he considers to be ineffective. Concerning employee co-determination, he explores how co-determination rules allow labour representatives as members of the supervisory board to influence corporate policy. He thinks that, on the one hand, employee participation ensures better decision-making practices on the board level and helps with long-term workforce affiliation. On the other hand, Veil cites several disadvantages, among them the danger of conflicts of interests and a negative impact on corporate governance. Referring to these disadvantages, he positions himself against including additional stakeholder representatives as board members.

In Chapter 6 ('Corporate Purpose: The US Discussion and the Restatement of the Law of Corporate Governance') Edward Rock reports from the engine room of the American Law Institute and his work as a reporter on the relevant Restatement. He describes how traditional jurisdictions like Delaware do not explicitly define the objective of the corporation. Rock emphasizes, however, that there are several ways in which the priority of shareholder interests emerges. After touching on stakeholder or 'constituency' statutes enacted in the 1980s, he mentions that despite their importance for understanding the full range of alternative enterprise forms, the Restatement will not 'restate' them, due to their recent vintage. Rock then turns to the definition of corporate purpose and distinguishes corporate purpose as a claim about how best to manage businesses (and not about the law) and a more normative usage of purpose which, in his mind, is akin to CSR. After clarifying his background assumptions, Rock deals with the link between the corporate objective and corporate purpose. Beginning with what he coins a 'public law' approach, he thinks that any attempt at requiring corporations to set out a specific corporate purpose in their constitutive documents were misconceived, pointing, inter alia, to a lack of evidence for superior performance following from such a statement. The 'private law' approach appears more interesting to Rock, allowing for opening up the question of what the best organizational form for purpose-oriented firms in light of the legal menu. Rock maintains that there is value to the traditional version of contract and corporate law, according to which restricting the law to a narrow set of goals and not overloading either subject matter with additional demands will fail to advance those goals while undermining their traditional usefulness. In Rock's mind, conflating purpose and performance bars one from asking whether superior performance requires a shareholder- or stakeholder-oriented organizational form. Building on this premise, he holds that the task of the Restatement should be accurately to describe the characteristics of the corporate form as it exists in traditional jurisdictions like Delaware and as it has been modified in states with 'constituency' statutes, an exercise he regards as technocratic rather than normative. Rock thinks that efforts of proponents of corporate purpose and shareholder driven ESG activism to prioritize social goals over promoting the value of individual firms run counter to an important feature of corporate law, namely the 'single firm focus'; that is, the focus on shareholders as a whole and not on the interests of individual actual stockholders. In his mind, the advantage of this vantage point is that it reduces heterogeneity of interests and thus avoids higher decision costs. Rock concludes that the traditional corporate law rules, as reflected in the Restatement, do not preclude boards from pursuing the social good at the expense of firm value, but certainly make it more difficult.

Irene-marié Esser and Iain MacNeil write Chapter 7 on 'ESG Regulation, CSR, and Corporate Purpose: A UK Perspective' and discuss directors' duties, non-financial reporting (NFR), and stakeholder engagement. They start out with the UK regulatory position and UK directors' duties. Esser and MacNeil state that section 172 of the UK

Companies Act 2006 (CA 2006) embeds some form of stakeholder protection without changing shareholder primacy as the main duty. Nevertheless, they maintain that NFR quality in the UK is relatively high, even amounting to super or over-compliance with NFR requirements. With respect to stakeholder engagement, the UK Corporate Governance Code 2018 introduced workforce engagement tools in Provision 5. Esser and MacNeil view Provision 5 as a key stage in the evolution of the UK Corporate Governance Code in terms of integrating stakeholder interests into board decision-making. While the outcome of board decision-making is defined by section 172 CA 2006, Esser and MacNeil maintain that the Corporate Governance Code now mandates a specific process of the integration of stakeholder interests. They add that this, in their minds, also represents a move away from the reliance on NFR disclosures as the primary regulatory technique of protecting stakeholders. To Esser and MacNeil, corporate purpose has been revitalized as a concept by reference to sustainability considerations, encompassing stakeholder interests. While they deem the latter to dominate contemporary discourse, they point out two other instantiations, namely the division between commercially and socially oriented entities and the protection of shareholders and creditors against directors in transactional contexts. Sympathizing with corporate purpose as a vantage point indirectly to adjust capital, profit, and governance in commercial entities, they also discuss the possibility of a direct recalibration of purpose through the adjustment of a company's articles of association. After sketching out this framework, Esser and MacNeil ponder how ESG and UK corporate law can be aligned by employing an enterprise approach. After distinguishing between ESG as a financial model and CSR as a concept focusing on ethical responsibility and accountability, they argue that the transmission channel for ESG and CSR differs. CSR, according to Esser and MacNeil, depends on corporate entities and their boards implementing CSR policies, whereas ESG piggybacked on finance as the main driver of change. Esser and MacNeil propose an entity model of ESG as a move away from a financial model, encompassing corporate purpose in the transition to sustainability. They define corporate purpose as 'the articulation of how a company's business model links to its environmental and social responsibilities'. The authors assert this entity view would not require reform of directors' duties or an adjustment of the articles of association. They outline how it could be facilitated by reforms in the governance process and due diligence.

## 3. Philosophical and Historical Foundations

Shifting towards a more theoretical perspective, Chapter 8 by Christine Osterloh-Konrad then examines the 'ethical dimension' of ESG. The first part of the chapter critically examines the rationale for the treatment of corporations as moral agents in the way that humans are. In this regard, the author emphasizes that corporations are not autonomous, responsible actors but mere instruments in the hands of individuals and serve their aims—and that, despite the intuitive appeal of the concept of viewing corporations as moral agents, their treatment as such reflects a fundamental misconception. As Osterloh-Konrad shows, on the one hand this reasoning should not be confused with a primitive concept of shareholder value, whereby corporate behaviour would be treated as legitimate entirely irrespective of externalities for stakeholders, society, or the environment. Modern legal systems, she argues, should always (and do) leave room for individual moral behaviour. Even shareholder-oriented jurisdictions thus do not impose a duty on managers to maximize profits in the interest of shareholders at all costs. On the other hand, the dependence of responsibility on autonomy makes any attempt to institutionalize ethics in companies through legal interventions and detailed guidelines highly questionable. The third part of the chapter finally explores the law-and-morality divide, and argues that the strict separation of law and morality is an important achievement of modern liberal thought that should not easily be abandoned, for example, by mandatory ESG reporting which, in the author's view, tends to obscure the line between the two realms. Osterloh-Konrad then demonstrates that behind some of the corporate purpose rhetoric there is a fundamental desire for unanimity, which she finds deeply problematic. While a world where all conflicts of interests may have been a vision of political philosophers at all times, it is, she argues, a dangerous vision, as it can lead to anyone who denies the possibility of converging interests being considered problematic, and it tends to turn into totalitarianism. Against this backdrop, Osterloh-Konrad sees a potentially helpful role of corporate purpose as a voluntary tool, but criticizes the current development of regulatory requirements which, in her view, obscure rather than clarify public expectations vis-à-vis the corporation and, ultimately, the obligations of firms and their directors in law.

Harwell Wells then explores 'Corporate Purpose in the United States 1800–2000' in Chapter 9. He observes that the question of corporate purpose is old and that Americans have considered and reconsidered the purposes for which corporations can be created and the ends they should pursue over the last two centuries. Wells states that corporate purpose has always been questioned and in dispute. Wells explains that already in the first half of the nineteenth century, many business corporations pursued private profit, despite being dependent on a state charter. He finds that the corporation's purpose was empowering in that it justified its legal creation and was the source of its powers, but at the same time limited the corporation to only those activities fulfilling its stated purpose. After enforcement had been public and left to a state's attorney general, private enforcement arose via the ultra vires doctrine. Wells describes how ultra vires litigation faded by the end of the nineteenth century, due to abuse of related claims by corporations themselves and reflecting changing views of the corporation. He then delineates how the purpose debate shifted, following a worry about the newly emerged large corporations possessing significant political, social, and economic powers and overwhelming communities and legal controls. Corporations, Wells tells us, reacted by refashioning themselves as institutions with a human face imbued with ethical purpose, instead of being just money-making machines. The advent of dispersed ownership in the 1920s and 1930s and the ensuing separation of ownership and control combined with power shifting to management sounded the bell for the modern debates over corporate purpose in the United States. Wells sketches out the Dodd-Berle debate centring on whether the directors' duty should be owed to the corporation itself and not the shareholders (Dodd) or if, to the contrary, the loosening of shareholder control over management should justify a more stringent set of directorial fiduciary duties towards the stockholders (Berle). In the middle of the twentieth century, Wells reports that Berle admitted to having been wrong and now siding with Dodd, with Dodd's view having become commonplace as a consequence of changing economic and social circumstances, including strong unions and workers and the so-called 'managerial capitalism'. After a short period of activism for CSR in the 1960s and 1970s, the 1980s rang the bell for the next round of purpose debates. With a once again rapidly evolving and transforming economic and social environment, the tide turned back to shareholders, gaining momentum through a developing market for corporate control and takeover battles. Shareholder value was the emerging consensus view. Wells concludes with ESG and various policy initiatives as signs of a renewing debate over corporate purpose.

## 4. The Implications for Corporate Law and Corporate Governance

In Chapter 10, the first chapter taking a closer look at specific implications of the debate for corporate law and corporate governance, Ann M. Lipton investigates 'Corporate Purpose and the Blurred Boundaries of Internal and External Governance'. As a foil for her chapter, she emphasizes that internal views on the aims of corporate governance and external demands of society vis-à-vis corporations are, to her mind, two sides of the same coin and thus must be viewed as a whole. Lipton argues that whatever side of the shareholder-stakeholder debate one takes, corporate law is necessarily deployed in service of societal interests more broadly. According to Lipton, a wide swathe of regulation regarded as external operates not merely by dictating permissible corporate behaviour, but by altering the corporate decision-making process, for example, by establishing specific inspection and production schemes or by creating internal procedures for preventing and remedying misbehaviour. She counts corporate law rules such as restrictions on dividend payments to the benefit of creditors as examples of state regulation protecting the interests of third parties. Lipton underlines that in order for shareholder primacy to work as governmentally-mandated design to benefit all stakeholders, the corporation must incur penalties for antisocial behaviour, investors must receive disclosure so that they can make informed decisions, and investor power must be checked to avoid distortions in the corporate governance architecture. She thinks that investors' preferences and capital allocation decisions are not natural features, but shaped by regulatory choices, implying that the shareholder primacist view depends on governmental intervention regarding shareholder power and motivations. Lipton then turns to stakeholderist vantage points and describes how relevant proposals rely on shareholders and thus not only on a reconceived version of shareholder primacy, but also on stockholders as the 'capital class' to make determinations as to the best interest of society as a whole without being representative of the broader society.

Summing up, Lipton claims that it is impossible to preserve corporate governance as a purely investor-oriented space because the rest of society inevitably intrudes.

Chapter 10 ('Leading Wherever They Want? CSR, ESG, and Directors' Duties') by Jens-Hinrich Binder then examines the implications of new regulatory requirements and claims for a fundamental redefinition of the 'corporate purpose' on directors' (fiduciary) duties. Binder first recounts the regulatory status quo within the United States and the EU, as well as incoming regulatory initiatives on both sides of the Atlantic. He then examines if and to what extent positive, prescriptive obligations for directors to address stakeholder considerations can be reconciled with established concepts of shareholder supremacy on the one hand and stakeholder-orientation as a paradigm of corporate law on the other hand, arguing that, while both regimes have been tolerant of directors' pursuit of stakeholder interests to some extent, neither would have permitted the subordination of the corporation's interest to remain profitable to stakeholder interests. Following a closer examination of the more recent regulatory initiatives within the European Union, the chapter argues that these initiatives amount to no less than a shift in the fundamental paradigm, and explores potential implications. Given the vaguely defined obligations in both existing and incoming regulation, Binder remains sceptical as far as the tangible benefits to stakeholders are concerned. Rather than facilitating a more effective protection for the respective stakeholder interests, he expects such regulation to actually incentivize directors to exploit their discretion to self-serving ends—and to weaken the established checks and balances in the corporate governance systems on both sides of the Atlantic.

Guido Ferrarini and Michele Siri take up 'Stewardship and ESG in Europe' in Chapter 12. They analyse the role of soft law and hard law in promoting ESG stewardship by institutional investors and asset managers. Ferrarini and Siri begin by examining the rules and incentives that stimulate institutional investors to integrate sustainability risks of investee companies in portfolio management, monitor their evolution, and engage with companies when needed. Explaining how stewardship codes originated in the UK and describing the UK Stewardship Code as the prototype for stewardship codes around the world, they turn to ESG in stewardship codes. Whereas the Danish code refers to CSR and the Dutch version explicitly mentions ESG factors, the Italian code remains silent in this respect. Yet, Ferrarini and Siri maintain that, in Italy, institutional investors are expected to engage with investee companies concerning ESG issues. The UK code includes ESG since its 2020 iteration, the Swiss code refers to sustainability. Ferrarini and Siri explain how the EU approach to stewardship in ESG matters relies on regulation rather than voluntary codes. They provide an overview of the EU SFDR and the EU Taxonomy Regulation. In the second part of their chapter, Ferrarini and Siri scrutinize the rules and incentives leading institutional investors and intermediaries to identify their clients' ESG preferences and to tailor their financial products offering accordingly. They describe the requirements of the SFDR and its ambit, covering both ESG and impact investing. Building on this background, Ferrarini and Siri outline investment criteria and processes used by institutional investors. Providing examples for diverging approaches in defining ESG, they explain that ESG risk integration follows international best practices and the EU SFDR (if applicable). Sketching out issuer disclosure duties pursuant to the NFRD, they show which information companies must produce and how it can be used by institutional investors. Additionally, Ferrarini and Siri show how EU regulation requires the integration of sustainability factors in product governance and rules of conduct. In the third part of their chapter, Ferrarini and Siri first demonstrate how the Shareholder Rights Directive as amended in 2017 and the SFDR enforce engagement disclosure. They then point out several limits of engagement. Firstly, they maintain that returns do not necessarily depend on engagement with investee companies. Secondly, the costs of engagement are borne only by those engaging, while the benefits are enjoyed by all shareholders. Thirdly, fees do not depend on engagement, but on assets under management. These points, in addition to other impediments, are reasons for Ferrarini and Siri to remain cautious concerning the effectiveness of ESG engagement by institutional investors.

In Chapter 13 ('The French "Duty of Vigilance" and the European Proposal on Companies' Due Diligence Duties'), Alain Pietrancosta follows up on the previous chapter with an analysis of the incoming corporate social responsibility due diligence obligations to be established by the EU CSDDD in the light of experiences with earlier French legislation that also informed the incoming EU model. Specifically, Pietrancosta examines the introduction of a so-called 'duty of vigilance' on large French corporations in 2017: a legally binding obligation to implement a proactive plan to prevent serious adverse impact resulting from company, subsidiary, supplier and subcontractor activities throughout the world, to human rights and fundamental freedoms, human health and safety, and the environment. He also discusses the 2019 'PACTE law', a law applicable to all companies registered in France, regardless of their form or size, which imposes a broadly defined duty to take into consideration the social and environmental impacts of their activities. As Pietrancosta demonstrates, both laws can be regarded as conceptual blueprints for the use and exploitation of company law for CSR purposes, the consequent politicisation of the role of companies, and the consequent 'mix of genres' or confusion introduced between public interest and private interest goals. With a comparison of the French and EU texts, Pietrancosta shows that while the general inspiration and orientation are common, significant differences between the two models exist in terms of scope, content of the obligations and enforcement. He also reveals a number of policy choices different than those in the French law. These include its application to a larger array of companies, including non-EU companies operating in Europe, its provisions on climate change, and its imposition of a general directors' duty of care on various social and environmental matters—aspects which, as the author predicts, are likely to raise strong national opposition.

Christoph Kumpan provides a survey on 'Green Bonds and Their (Envisaged) Regulation in the EU' in Chapter 14. Taking his cue from the growing economic impact of green bonds, Kumpan sketches out the market development. He explains the benefits observers see in green bonds, for example, a stronger focus on green investment and the chance for issuers to promote green projects. With respect to the challenges of green bonds, Kumpan mentions the problem of competing standards and ensuing investor confusion, limitations in assessing the sustainability of projects, greenwashing, and moral hazard due to a lack of control of how the money is actually spent by the issuer. Kumpan proceeds to describe two important voluntary standards, the Green Bond Principles of the International Market Association and the Climate Bonds Standard established by the Climate Bonds Initiative. Moving on to the EU, Kumpan situates green bond regulation in the general normative framework of the EU Action Plan 2018, the 'Green Deal', and the SFDR and Taxonomy. Setting out the draft for an EU green bond standard, Kumpan explains the worry over a market fragmentation as a main source of the EU Commission's regulatory drive and then provides an overview of the draft regulation. He describes the tie-in with the EU Taxonomy and the extent to which the draft regulation grants flexibility to issuers to use the investment. Kumpan welcomes the intended voluntary nature of the EU standard, but doubts whether it can hold up against more developed and already established bond regulation in other parts of the world. He also cautions that there is no real reason for a regulatory intervention by the EU and that smaller issues will shy away from green bonds as a financing instrument because of the prospectus requirement they might find becoming too onerous. Kumpan also points out that there is no supervision by state authorities.

In Chapter 15, Thilo Kuntz tackles ESG demand-side regulation. He proposes a novel vantage point and presents demand-side regulation as a new regulatory concept. He claims that if a regulator wants to implement ESG-oriented decision-making in the structure of corporate governance, the regulatory strategy must include the shareholders and investors. When stockholders have to abide by norms mirroring those operating on the level of the corporate board, at least in theory, the incentives and investment aims of corporate directors and shareholders should align. Kuntz argues that as long as shareholders measure return on their investment in monetary terms, regulating directors' fiduciary duties towards supplying ESG-oriented decision-making lacks teeth. Therefore, Kuntz argues that instead of focusing on the side offering managerial services in the interests of others, regulators aiming at implementing ESG factors in corporate governance should concentrate on the demand side. According to Kuntz, governing the shareholders holds the promise to change the incentive structure reigning over managerial decision-making. He starts out by explaining how demand-side regulation fits into the general scheme of corporate governance and explores basic strategies of demand-side regulation and draws a distinction between direct and indirect demand-side regulation. Whereas the first type addresses shareholders and investors directly through ESG disclosure rules and requirements to commit to ESG, the second targets retail investors as a group and tweaks their revealed preferences towards ESG. In the EU, indirect demand-side regulation comes in the form of the rules on investment nudging retail investors into ESG products. Instead of narrowing down the number of eligible voting outcomes, it aims at letting only those into the corporate arena who subscribe to ESG in the first place. If both institutional and retail investors lean towards ESG and disclose related information, it becomes easier for boards of directors to discern their stockholders' preferences and to adapt corporate management accordingly. Moreover, ESG-friendly shareholders should find it easier to coordinate. Kuntz attests direct demand-side regulation to hold promise, but ultimately remains doubtful. Considering the broad variety of sometimes diverging values and perspectives subsumed under the ESG rubric, navigating shareholders and investors towards this regulatory goal does not in itself alleviate the coordination problems within that group. Consequently, Kuntz maintains, balancing and coordination problems remain. He comes to similar conclusions for indirect demand-side regulation. Surveying and analysing investors' preferences, according to recent EU regulation, falls to investment advisers. Asking for ESG preferences exploits the social desirability bias, that is, the tendency to act in conformity with prevailing legal and social norms, and nudges retail investors into the direction desired by the regulator. Kuntz cautions, however, that many empirical studies show that even those opting for an ESG product more often than not prefer pecuniary benefits once the investment is made. Consequently, the largest group of shareholders will still judge directors based on monetary gains.

Stefan Thomas explores the connection between 'sustainability and competition law' in Chapter 16. Thomas states that industry faces increasing pressure to consider sustainability agreements and to share competitively sensitive data relevant for sustainability goals. Competition supervision authorities do not follow diverging approaches. The question facing them and the enforcement of competition law more generally is, Thomas points out, whether consumers should be allowed to prefer their own benefits in a competitive market at the expense of the environment and future generations or whether firms may agree to counter such externalities. He stresses the importance of distinguishing between a scenario in which an increase in price due to a sustainability agreement is offset by a rising willingness to pay (WTP) and one in which WTP does not rise or at least not sufficiently in order to offset the higher price. Thomas emphasizes that only the second case entails a conflict between consumer benefit and the mitigation of externalities through sustainability agreements. After cautioning against a 'multi-goals' strategy according to which competition law should prefer the mitigation of environmental externalities over the protection of competition, he explains ways to integrate externalities into the consumer welfare paradigm. Whereas it may seem feasible to measure WTP with an eye to sustainability preferences, Thomas delineates several issues impairing the established approach focusing on revealed preferences and proposes a novel vantage point, drawing from marketing science. He adds that it is important to add the dimension of time when considering consumers' WTP for sustainability, that is, a possible change in a future generation WTP. Moreover, the mitigation of externalities may affect a group larger than those of the relevant consumers. Thomas then reflects on possibilities to reduce externalities beyond the consumer welfare paradigm, acknowledging that consumer welfare analysis is fraught with difficulties. He mentions several obstacles, however, posing problems especially in the EU. The basis for European competition law is enshrined in Article 101 of the Treaty on the Functioning of the European Union, making it difficult to open European competition law through national or agency action in light of EU primary law's primacy.

# 2

# Corporate Purpose and Stakeholder Value

Historical, Economic, and Comparative Law Remarks on the Current Debate, Legislative Options, and Enforcement Problems

*Klaus J. Hopt\**

## I. The Current Debate on Corporate Purpose, Stakeholder Participation, and ESG

### 1. Corporate Purpose: Mandatory or Optional?

'One of the oldest corporate law issues—for whom is the corporation managed?—has become one of the hottest public policy issues.' With these words, Edward B. Rock, the designated rapporteur of the forthcoming new US Restatement of the Law of Corporate Governance,[1] began his reflections for the first Munich Lecture on Securities Regulation and Corporate Governance at the University of Munich.[2] The current protagonist of corporate purpose, with numerous widely acclaimed publications,[3] is the British economist Colin Mayer, who teaches at Oxford and, together with the British Academy,[4] has initiated a discussion that has spread far into the sphere of economy, society, and politics,

---

\* The chapter refers back to the general report at the international conference on 'The Public Corporation and Its Environment: How Public Is It?', held on 16 and 17 June 2022, organized at the University of Tübingen by Jens-Hinrich Binder (Tübingen), Klaus J Hopt, and Thilo Kuntz (Hamburg). The chapter corresponds to Part I of the general report prepared by Hopt. Part II was presented by Rüdiger Veil (Munich) and constitutes a separate article: 'Two Models of Stakeholder Governance: The Trustee Model and the Representative Model; Experiences from Germany (and Europe)'. Rüdiger Veil is professor and director of the Munich Centre for Capital Markets Law (MuCCML), Munich University. The chapter here draws on an earlier study presented by both authors at the University of Florence on 5 November 2019 and later published in Italian: Klaus J Hopt and Rüdiger Veil, 'Gli stakeholders nel diritto azionario tedesco: il concetto e l'applicazione. Spunti comparatistici di diritto europeo e statunitense' (2020) 65 Rivista delle Società 921. As to the enforcement problems see Klaus J Hopt, 'Le regard du comparatiste' in France Drummond and Louis d'Avout (eds), *Les transformations européennes du droit des sociétés* (Éditions Panthéon-Assas 2023) 195. All internet sources were last accessed on 10 January 2024.

[1] Edward B Rock, *American Law Institute, Restatement of the Law, Corporate Governance* (New York University Press 2023).

[2] Edward B Rock, 'For Whom Is the Corporation Managed in 2020? The Debate over Corporate Purpose' (2021) 76 Business Law 363.

[3] Colin Mayer, *Prosperity: Better Business Makes the Greater Good* (OUP 2018); Colin Mayer, 'The Future of the Corporation and the Economics of Purpose' (2021) 58 Journal of Management Studies 887; Colin Mayer, 'The Governance of Corporate Purpose' in Ronald J Gilson and others (eds), *Festskrift till Rolf Skog* (Norstedts Juridik 2021) 913, also available as an ECGI Law Working Paper No 609/2021 https://ssrn.com/abstract=3928613.

[4] British Academy, Research Project 'Future of the Corporation' <https://thebritishacademy.ac.uk/programmes/future-of-the-corporation/>; British Academy, *Policy & Practice for Purposeful Business: Final Report of the Future of the Corporation Programme* (September 2021).

although corporate purpose is by no means a new topic.[5] Mayer opposes the prevailing idea, especially in the United States, of profit generation for shareholders (shareholder value) and the associated externalization of negative effects by companies. This leads him to a new conception of profit, a corresponding method of accounting and the corporate goal: 'The purpose of companies is to produce solutions to problems of people and planet and in the process to produce profits, but profits are not per se the purpose of companies. They are derivative from purpose.'[6] Mayer is not in favour of regulation; rather, companies should set themselves a corporate purpose in their articles of association. However, this is precisely what the legislature should prescribe for them,[7] and at least insofar it is mandatory. The corporate bodies and functionaries must then act in a fiduciary capacity according to this corporate purpose.[8] At the same time, the legislature should make various legal forms with different corporate purposes available to companies,[9] including the legal form of a benefit corporation.[10] In this context, Mayer mentions foundations that support industrial companies such as Germany's Bosch and Bertelsmann and others.[11] But he is also thinking of alternative legal forms that give employees and other stakeholders or even certain shareholders stronger control rights.[12]

Similar ideas can be found in Alex Edmans, who uses the metaphor of a pie and calls his theory 'pieconomics'.[13] The pie represents the value an enterprise creates for society, ie value not only for shareholders and investors, but also for other stakeholders such as employees, customers, suppliers, the environment, and governments. The aim is to increase the size of this pie (pie-growing), instead of distributing it differently (pie-splitting), as according to him has been the case in the past. Andrew Keay[14] has already presented his 'entity maximisation and sustainability model (EMS)' and placed special emphasis on the enforcement[15] of this model. But he has been well aware of the difficulty of combining managerial discretion and accountability.[16]

---

[5] Elizabeth Pollman and Robert B Thompson (eds), *Research Handbook on Corporate Purpose and Personhood* (Edward Elgar Publishing 2021); Jens-Hinrich Binder, Klaus J Hopt, and Thilo Kuntz (eds), *Corporate Purpose, CSR and ESG: A Transatlantic Perspective* (OUP 2024); Brian R Cheffins, 'The Past, Present and Future of Corporate Purpose' (June 2023) ECGI Law Working Paper No 713/2023 https://ssrn.com/abstract=4420800. In September 2023, there was an ECGI conference on corporate purpose in Copenhagen. Thilo Kuntz, 'Corporate Purpose, konzeptionelle Grundlagen, rechtshistorische und rechtsdogmatische Aspekte' (2022) 186 Zeitschrift fur das gesamte Handelsrecht und Wirtschaftsrecht 652, 653 attributes the large impact of the book to the fact that Mayer's ideas are, with the help of the British Academy, marketed (*vermarktet*) internationally with an apocalyptic campaign trumpeting a transformation of capitalism. For details on corporate purpose legislation see section II3 below.

[6] Mayer, *Prosperity* (n 3) 109.

[7] ibid 22, 24, 225, 232; British Academy, *Final Report* (n 4) 22: 'Legislation would require companies to adopt purposes that aim to benefit people and planet as well as shareholders, and report on their success in so doing.' In several later articles, Colin Mayer has nuanced his position, in particular in response to the fundamental criticism by Paul L Davies; see n 90 below.

[8] Ira Milstein and others, 'Session I: Corporate Purpose and Governance' (2019) 31(3) Journal of Applied Corporate Finance 10.

[9] Mayer, *Prosperity* (n 3) 201.

[10] On benefit corporations see n 104 below.

[11] Mayer, *Prosperity* (n 3) 40–41.

[12] ibid 157.

[13] Alex Edmans, *Grow the Pie: How Great Companies Deliver Both Purpose and Profit* (CUP 2020); see also Parajon Skinner, 'Cancelling Capitalism?' (2021) 97 Notre Dame Law Review 417.

[14] Andrew Keay, *The Corporate Objective* (Edward Elgar Publishing 2011).

[15] ibid 233, 240–75.

[16] ibid 302. Keay states that the ten accountability mechanisms are: markets, boards, investors, courts, contract, regulators, social norms, regulation, codes, and auditing.

But what could or should be the appearance of such corporate objectives? The UK Financial Reporting Council has included the following principle in the revised UK Corporate Governance Code 2018: '[T]he board should establish the company's purpose, values and strategies, and satisfy itself that these and its culture are aligned.'[17] In corporate practice, there are numerous examples of how such freely chosen corporate objectives can look. Some of them can be found in the charter, others only on the websites of the companies. Traditionally, they simply lay out a broad field for corporate activity, such as the objective set by DowDuPont in the United States.[18] Often they also define a corporate mission and vision, as done, for example, by Adidas, Europe's largest sportswear manufacturer: 'Through sports we can change lives'; by the French tyre manufacturer Michelin: 'Offering a better way forward'; or by Google: 'To organize the world's information and make it universally accessible and useful.'[19] Danone, a French food and beverage company, ambitiously defines its corporate goal as building a balanced, profitable, and sustainable growth model.[20]

## 2. Shareholders versus Stakeholders or Shareholders and Stakeholders?

a) The classical shareholder value concept

The Statement on the Purpose of a Corporation issued by the Business Roundtable on 19 August 2019 caused quite a stir among the international public and experts. This statement was signed by 181 chief executive officers (CEOs) from the United States, led by Jamie Dimon, chairman and CEO of JPMorgan Chase & Co.[21] According to the statement, these CEOs 'commit to lead[ing] their companies for the benefit of all stakeholders—customers, employees, suppliers, communities and shareholders'.[22] This is a break with the conventional belief in shareholder value, which is firmly established in the United States and which has paid little heed to the continental European ideas of

---

[17] Financial Reporting Council, *The UK Corporate Governance Code* (2018) https://frc.org.uk/directors/corporate-governance-and-stewardship/uk-corporate-governance-code >.
[18] Jill E Fisch and Steven Davidoff Solomon, 'Should Corporations Have a Purpose?' (2021) 99 Texas Law Review 1309, 1316–17: 'The purpose of the Company is to engage in any lawful act or activity for which a corporation may now or hereafter be organized under the General Corporation Law of the State of Delaware.'
[19] For examples of corporate purpose statements from Germany, France, and the United States see Holger Fleischer, 'Corporate Purpose: A Management Concept and Its Implications for Company Law' (2021) European Company and Financial Law Review 161, 170, 173, 178.
[20] Guido Ferrarini, *'Redefining Corporate Purpose: Sustainability as a Game Changer'* in Danny Busch, Guido Ferrarini, and Seraina Grünewald (eds), *Sustainable Finance in Europe: Corporate Governance, Financial Stability and Financial Markets* (Springer 2021) 85, 91–94: Danone, Vodafone, Enel, Electrolux https://doi.org/10.1007/978-3-030-71834-3_4.
[21] Business Roundtable, 'Statement on the Purpose of a Corporation' (19 August 2019) https://opportunity.businessroundtable.org/ourcommitment/.
[22] Press Release of the Business Roundtable (August 2019). Similarly, based on interviews see Stavros Gadinis and Amelia Miazad, 'Corporate Law and Social Risk' (2020) 73(5) Vanderbilt Law Review 1401 https://ssrn.com/abstract=3441375.

taking stakeholder interests into account.[23] The classic formulation comes from Milton Friedman in 1970: 'There is one and only one social responsibility of business—to use its resources and engage in activities designed to increase its profits so long as it stays within the rules of the game.'[24] Almost five decades later, US economists Oliver Hart and Luigi Zingales similarly stated: '[C]ompanies should maximize shareholder welfare not market value.'[25]

b) Stakeholder value theories

The reversal made by the Business Roundtable with its statement of 19 August 2019 was thus all the more astonishing.[26] The first reaction in the United States was correspondingly sizeable and in part enthusiastic. In any case, the statement was seen as 'tremendous news', according to Darren Walker, president of the Ford Foundation.[27] The new ordering of stakeholders in the statement was also surprising. Shareholders are mentioned last. However, the pronouncement says that every stakeholder is important, and it promises to create value for all stakeholders.[28] The Davos Manifesto 2020 took this up and propagated 'stakeholder capitalism'.[29] Such stakeholder value concepts had been advocated long before.[30] They belong to different theories. One can distinguish between the stakeholder theory, the shared value theory, the team production theory, and others.[31] These theories are considered by some to be part of conventional corporate

---

[23] See eg Klaus J Hopt, 'Comparative Corporate Governance: The State of the Art and International Regulation' (2011) 59 American Journal of Comparative Law 1, 28–30.

[24] Milton Friedman, 'The Social Responsibility of Business Is to Increase Its Profits' *The New York Times Magazine* (13 September 1970) 126; Milton Friedman, *Capitalism and Freedom* (UCP 1962). See also Alfred Rappaport, *Creating Shareholder Value* (The Free Press 1986); Henry Hansmann and Reinier Kraakman, 'The End of History for Corporate Law' (2001) 89 Georgetown Law Journal 439, 440–43; Michael C Jensen, 'Corporate Control and the Economics of Finance' (2001) 14(3) Journal of Applied Corporate Finance 8; Henry Hansmann and Reinier Kraakman, 'Value Maximization, Stakeholder Theory, and the Corporate Objective Function' (2002) 12(2) Business Ethics Quarterly 235, regarding enlightened value maximization, ie 'the maximization of shareholder valuations subject to safeguarding its reputational capital in the eyes of all stakeholders'. From Germany see eg Peter Mülbert, 'Shareholder Value aus rechtlicher Sicht' (1997) 26(2) Zeitschrift für Unternehmens- und Gesellschaftsrecht 129; Peter Mülbert, 'Marktwertmaximierung als Unternehmensziel der Aktiengesellschaft' *Festschrift für Röhricht* (Otto Schmidt 2005) 421, 424–41.

[25] Oliver Hart and Luigi Zingales, 'Companies Should Maximize Shareholder Welfare Not Market Value' (July 2017) ECGI Finance Working Paper No 521/2017 https://ssrn.com/abstract=3004794. In the same vein see Oliver Hart and Luigi Zingales, 'The New Corporate Governance' (April 2022) ECGI Law Working Paper No 640/2022 https://ssrn.com/abstract_id=4087738.

[26] Business Roundtable (n 21).

[27] Business Roundtable press release (n 22) with numerous comments on the statement.

[28] Business Roundtable (n 21) last sentence.

[29] 'The purpose of a company is to engage all its stakeholders in shared and sustained value creation. In creating such value, a company serves not only its shareholders, but all its stakeholders—employees, customers, suppliers, local communities and society at large.' Klaus Schwab, 'Davos Manifesto 2020: The Universal Purpose of a Company in the Fourth Industrial Revolution' (2 December 2019) World Economic Forum, The Davos Manifesto https://weforum.org/agenda/2019/12/davos-manifesto-2020-the-universal-purpose-of-a-company-in-the-fourth-industrial-revolution/.

[30] Edward Freeman, *Strategic Management: A Stakeholder Approach* (Pitman Publishing 1984); Lynn Stout, *The Shareholder Value Myth* (Berret-Koehler 2012); Kent Greenfield, *The Failure of Corporate Law* (UCP 2010) 123–24, 127–30, 142–46; Keay (n 14) 197–230.

[31] See also Eli Bukspan, 'Corporate Purpose and Stakeholder Fairness Through the Lens of Behavioral Economics: Legal Implications' (28 November 2021) 6–13 https://ssrn.com/abstract=3972970: on law see behavioural economics and fairness.

social responsibility (CSR),[32] but the representatives of the new movement explicitly reject this.[33] Their theses also go beyond mere management concepts.[34] It is about a shift in mindset; the task is legally framing the corporate purpose based on stakeholderism.[35]

c) Compromising views: pursuit of both shareholder and stakeholder interests

In response to this discussion, legal and economic mainstream thinkers, especially in the United States, have defended the shareholder value principle in detail, as done very resolutely by Lucian Bebchuk and Roberto Tallarita[36] and more subtly by Edward Rock.[37] While it is correctly noted that there is no binary choice between shareholders and stakeholders,[38] Rock points out and criticizes a common misunderstanding that shareholder primacy is equated with 'short-term share-price maximisation' during the day-to-day management of the company.[39] The Delaware Supreme Court has clarified that: '[t]he question of "long-term" versus "short-term" results is largely irrelevant because directors, generally, are obliged to chart a course for a corporation which is in its best interests without regard to a fixed investment horizon'.[40]

It is also clear in the United States that the Business Roundtable's statement and adherence to it by business leaders is not a legally binding commitment, and the initial enthusiasm soon ebbed[41] and there was even a good deal of

---

[32] See Elizabeth Pollman, 'Corporate Social Responsibility, ESG, and Compliance' in Benjamin Van Rooij and D Daniel Sokol (eds), *The Cambridge Handbook of Compliance* (CUP 2021) 662; Cynthia A Williams, 'Comparative and Transnational Developments in Corporate Social Responsibility' in Afra Afsharipour and Martin Gelter (eds), *Comparative Corporate Governance* (Edward Elgar Publishing 2021) 92; Barnali Choudhury and Martin Petrin, *Corporate Duties to the Public* (CUP 2019); Onyeka K Osuij, Franklin N Ngwu, and Gary Lynch-Wood, *Corporate Social Responsibility Across the Globe* (CUP 2022).

[33] Mayer, *Prosperity* (n 3) 117: 'This is not corporate social responsibility (CSR) as meritorious philanthropy; it is poverty alleviation and environmental protection as core corporate activities'; Edmans (n 13) 27: 'pieconomics' is more, specifically '[t]o create profits only through creating value for society'.

[34] See Fleischer (n 19).

[35] Bukspan (n 31) 19–24, 27; cf recently Christopher M Bruner, 'Corporate Governance Reform and the Sustainability Imperative' (2022) 131 Yale Law Journal 1217.

[36] Lucian A Bebchuk and Roberto Tallarita, 'The Illusory Promise of Stakeholder Governance' (2020) 106 Cornell Law Review 91; cf also Lucian A Bebchuk, Kobi Kastiel, and Roberto Tallarita, 'Does Enlightened Shareholder Value Add Value?' (2022) 77 The Business Lawyer 731; Lucian A Bebchuk, Kobi Kastiel, and Roberto Tallarita, 'For Whom Corporate Leaders Bargain' (2021) 94 Southern California Law Review 1467; Book Review of Stephen Bainbridge, *The Profit Motive: Defending Shareholder Value Maximization* (CUP 2023) by Ann M. Lipton in (2024) 137 Harvard Law Review 1584. But see also the rebuttal by Colin Mayer, 'Shareholderism versus Stakeholderism: A Misconceived Contradiction' (4 June 2020) ECGI Law Working Paper No 522/2020 https://ssrn.com/abstract_id=3617847.

[37] Rock (n 2) 391–95. See also Columbia Law School Symposium, 'Corporate Governance "Counter-Narratives": On Corporate Purpose and Shareholder Value(s)' (2019) 31(3) Journal of Applied Corporate Finance 10; Columbia Law School Roundtable, 'The Future of Capitalism' (2020) 32(2) Journal of Applied Corporate Finance 42; Stephen Bainbridge, 'A Critique of the American Law Institute's Draft Restatement of the Corporate Objective' (2022) 2 The University of Chicago Business Law Review 1.

[38] British Academy, *Final Report* (n 4) 21, contending that the debate of shareholder versus stakeholder is a 'sterile debate'; Bruner (n 35) 1237–41.

[39] Rock (n 2) 379. On the distinction between short-termism and sustainability see Eckart Bueren, 'Sustainable Finance' (2019) 48(5) Zeitschrift für Unternehmens- und Gesellschaftsrecht 813, 819–20; Eckart Bueren, *Short-termism im Aktien- und Kapitalmarktrecht* (Mohr Siebeck 2022).

[40] *Paramount Communications Inc v Time Inc* 571 A2d 1140, 1150 (Del 1989). On the controversial debate as to short-termism see eg Martin Petrin and Barnali Choudhury, 'Corporate Purpose and Short-Termism' in Afra Afsharipour and Martin Gelter (eds), *Comparative Corporate Governance* (Edward Elgar Publishing 2021) 73.

[41] Blackrock, 'Reply to the Attorneys General Letter dated 4 August 2022' (6 September 2022) https://www.blackrock.com/us/individual/literature/press-release/blackrock-response-attorneys-general.pdf; cf also Patrick

'greenwashing'.[42] Suggestions for reform have come from the pen of Leo E. Strine, Jr., former Chief Justice of the Delaware Supreme Court and now an affiliate of Harvard and the University of Pennsylvania. In a long article entitled 'Toward Fair and Sustainable Capitalism', he argues for 'a system of enlightened capitalism' with more sustainability for the American economy and attention paid to ESG (environmental, social, and governance) factors as well as workers' interests (EESG—employee, environmental, social, and governance).[43] Among his numerous reform proposals, the following are particularly interesting for the topic here: more disclosure, the establishment by the board of a committee for employee concerns in large companies (annual sales of US$1 billion or more), and easier formation of, and reorganization into, a benefit corporation.[44] But the 'corporate governance machine' in the United States with its many mighty players—in particular institutional investors, but also investor associations, proxy advisers, the stock exchanges with their stock indices, and the rating agencies—is so well established that the prognosis is convincing that stakeholderism may gain ground only by shaping the meaning of shareholder primacy to encompass stakeholder interests.[45]

d) The special case of financial institutions and other regulated companies

The debates described above are about public limited companies and other companies that do not constitute regulated companies, such as financial institutions or insurance companies. This is important to mention precisely because proponents of ESG and climate protection are making statements and legal policy demands that amount to a blurring of a fundamental difference which is central for our economic system. In the case of regulated companies, such as financial institutions, corporate governance is quite different. Typical of this is the clear statement of the Basel Committee on Banking Supervision in its Corporate Governance Principles for Banks of July 2015: 'The primary objective of corporate governance should be safeguarding stakeholders' interest in conformity with public interest on a sustainable basis. Among stakeholders, particularly with respect to retail banks, shareholders' interest would be secondary to

---

Bernau and Roland Lindner, 'Nicht mehr ganz so heilig' *Frankfurter Allgemeine Sonntagszeitung* (18 September 2022) No 37, 17.

[42] See Miriam A Cherry and Judd F Sneirson, 'Beyond Profit: Rethinking Corporate Social Responsibility and Greenwashing After the BP Oil Disaster' (2011) 85 Tulane Law Review 983.

[43] Leo E Strine Jr, 'Toward Fair and Sustainable Capitalism' (1 October 2019) University of Pennsylvania Law School ILE Research Paper No 13-39 https://ssrn.com/abstract=3461924. Strine uses EESG as described in the text, but in other contexts the first 'E' in EESG stands for 'economic' and sometimes also for 'ethical'. See also Milstein and others (n 8). For the history and the main uses and a critique of the term ESG and its consequences see Elizabeth Pollman, 'The Making and Meaning of ESG' (October 2022) ECGI Law Working Paper No 659/2022 https://ssrn.com/abstract=4219857.

[44] As to benefit corporations see n 104 below.

[45] Dorothy S Lund and Elizabeth Pollman, 'The Corporate Governance Machine' (2021) 121 Columbia Law Review 2563, 2634; the authors also mention the Delaware courts, the US Congress, the Securities and Exchange Commission, and the Department of Labor (at 2579–88); Robert P Bartlett and Ryan Bubb, 'Corporate Social Responsibility through shareholder governance' (February 2023) ECGI Law Working Paper No 682/2023 https://ecgi.global/content/working-papers. All this is different for small-cap corporations, for which the private-ordering mechanisms of corporate governance fail. See Kobi Kastiel and Yaron Nili, 'The Corporate Governance Gap' (2022) 131 Yale Law Journal 782.

depositors' interest.'[46] This is even more remarkable since, at that time, there was no talk of ESG.

In banking supervisory law and in the law of other regulated companies, this view is concretized more precisely—in what some see as an infatuation with detail—by regulations for the companies and their bodies.[47] As one sees in Germany, this can tempt the civil courts to make use of this legal arsenal and to subject non-regulated companies to these provisions by analogy. However, this is rightly regarded as very problematic because in this way the courts, instead of the legislature being called upon to do so, disregard the fundamental difference between regulated and non-regulated companies. An analogy can therefore be only an exception and justified only in exceptional cases under special conditions.

## 3. The 'Public' or the 'Private' Corporation?

a) The 'public' corporation in the first half of the nineteenth century and the separation of corporate law, antitrust, securities regulation, and other public laws

In the debate about the iconic turn from shareholder value to CSR, ESG, and stakeholder value, there is often a recalling of the early days of the public limited company.[48] The state concession of the joint stock company and its predecessors played a decisive role in this period. In England, the English crown and Parliament began to grant corporate charters to joint stock companies in the early seventeenth century. These were granted only if a public utility could be established. This concession system was also adopted in the United States. Here we are talking about the 'Public Service Origins of the American Business Corporation'.[49] In the case of the Dutch East India Company (VOC), for example, the preamble stated how important shipping and trade commerce were for the 'prosperity of the United Netherlands'.[50] According to the Ministerial Instruction on the Licensing of Joint Stock Companies in Prussia of 1845,[51]

---

[46] Basel Committee on Banking Supervision, *Guidelines: Corporate Governance Principles for Banks*, Bank for International Settlements (BIZ) (July 2015) 3, Introduction No 2. cf Klaus J Hopt, 'Corporate Governance of Banks and Financial Institutions: Economic Theory, Supervisory Practice, Evidence and Policy' (2021) 22 European Business Organization Law Review 13; Sarah E Light and Christina P Skinner, 'Banks and Climate Governance' (2021) 121 Columbia Law Review 1895.

[47] cf Klaus J Hopt, Jens Binder, and Hans-Joachim Böcking (eds), *Handbuch Corporate Governance von Banken und Versicherungen* (2nd edn, C.H. Beck 2020).

[48] See eg Elizabeth Pollman, 'The History and Revival of the Corporate Purpose Clause' (2021) 99 Texas Law Review 1423; see also Fisch and Davidoff Solomon (n 18) 1313–15, mentioning English companies of the sixteenth and seventeenth centuries; Fleischer (n 19) 164–65, looking back to the medieval companies of Northern Italy in the Trecento, and at 167–69 mentioning early German stock corporations in the nineteenth century.

[49] Ronald E Seavoy, 'The Public Service Origins of the American Business Corporation' (1978) 52 Business History Review 30.

[50] 'This was considered by us, the States General, and given due weight in recognising how much importance to the united provinces and the good residents thereof was thereto attached that this shipping trade and commerce be maintained.' See Pollman (n 48) 1430.

[51] *Instruktion, die Grundsätze in Ansehung der Konzessionierung von Aktiengesellschaften betreffend, vom 22.4.1845, Ministerial-Blatt für die gesamte innere Verwaltung in den Königlich Preußischen Staaten 1845*, 121; Klaus J Hopt, 'Ideelle und wirtschaftliche Grundlagen der Aktien-, Bank- und Börsenrechtsentwicklung im 19. Jahrhundert' in Helmut Coing and Walter Wilhelm (eds), *Wissenschaft und Kodifikation des Privatrechts im 19. Jahrhundert, vol. V Geld und Banken* (Klostermann 1980) 128, 144.

what mattered was whether the promotion of the branch of industry or business to which the company belonged was desirable in the general interest, whether the form of the joint stock company was necessary because of the amount of capital required or the nature of the business, and, finally, whether the public was sufficiently protected from harm in personal and financial terms. In addition to investor, consumer, and creditor protection, the issue was the danger of monopolization and a corruption of the political process.[52] A recent study penned by Thilo Kuntz, however, specifies that a distinction must be made between the concepts of the general public benefit and the public purpose of the public limited company and that, from a legal, historical, and comparative law perspective, the concession requirement cannot be used as a general basis for the public purpose character of public limited companies.[53]

As is well known, the concession system first eroded in most countries in the second half of the nineteenth century and was then changed in favour of the normative system that is generally applicable today.[54] The targeted pursuit of general interests was no longer assigned to stock corporations under stock corporation law. Instead, it became the task of antitrust law (first and foremost in the United States with the Sherman Act of 1890) and securities regulation (since the 1930s and again first in the United States). This occurred both times with a worldwide following. This was later succeeded by numerous other special areas of public law, such as environmental law in particular.[55]

b) Return of the 'public' corporation?

With the ESG movement, this historical development seems to be reversing. This is facilitated by the fact that the state has become increasingly influential in response to the various major crises of the twenty-first century. This is immediately evident in the extent to which the state participates in the economy. It is not only in Romance countries, such as France, Italy, or Spain, that public enterprises (in the sense of companies that the state controls or companies in which the state has a significant stake) have traditionally played a central role; rather, state-owned enterprises and state participation are also very common and important in countries with a strong market economy, such as Germany. As a result of the Covid-19 pandemic, but also as occurred in earlier financial crises, this state influence through corporate participation has increased even

---

[52] On the political aims of the concession system, cf Bernhard Grossfeld, 'Die rechtspolitische Beurteilung der Aktiengesellschaft im 19. Jahrhundert' in Helmut Coing and Walter Wilhelm (eds), *Wissenschaft und Kodifikation des Privatrechts im 19. Jahrhundert, vol. IV Eigentum und industrielle Entwicklung. Wettbewerbsordnung und Wettbewerbsrecht* (Klostermann 1979) 236, 239–40.

[53] Kuntz (n 5).

[54] Stephan Harbarth, 'Die Aktiengesellschaft im Wandel der Zeit zwischen Wirtschaftlichkeit und Gemeinwohl' (2022) 51(4–5) Zeitschrift für Unternehmens- und Gesellschaftsrecht 533.

[55] Norbert Horn and Jürgen Kocka (eds), *Recht und Entwicklung der Großunternehmen im 19. und frühen 20. Jahrhundert/Law and the Formation of the Big Enterprises in the 19th and Early 20th Centuries* (Vandenhoeck und Ruprecht 1979); William R Cornish, 'Legal Control over Cartels and Monopolization 1880–1914: A Comparison' in Norbert Horn and Jürgen Kocka (eds), *Recht und Entwicklung der Großunternehmen im 19. und frühen 20. Jahrhundert/Law and the Formation of the Big Enterprises in the 19th and Early 20th Centuries* (Vandenhoeck und Ruprecht 1979) 280; Morton Keller, 'Public Policy and Large Enterprise: Comparative Historical Perspectives' in Norbert Horn and Jürgen Kocka (eds), *Recht und Entwicklung der Großunternehmen im 19. und frühen 20. Jahrhundert/Law and the Formation of the Big Enterprises in the 19th and Early 20th Centuries* (Vandenhoeck und Ruprecht 1979) 515.

further and more significantly.[56] It is true that these companies basically operate on the market like other private companies, unless they have a special legal form such as foundations, savings banks, or, in some cases, cooperatives. But state influence is unmistakable, although it is by no means oriented only towards the common good, sometimes being even quite to the contrary, as is the case with other private enterprises.

In addition, there is the enhanced regulation of important companies, and not only the so-called regulated companies such as financial institutions and insurance companies.[57] In this context, different concepts of 'public companies' must be distinguished, for each of which special groups of legal rules apply. First of all, one speaks of public companies if the company is listed on the stock exchange (eg the CAC 40 in France or the recent DAX 40 in Germany) or is otherwise active on the capital market. For these companies, a separate 'stock exchange company law' (*Börsengesellschaftsrecht*) has developed over and above the public stock exchange law, as evidenced in Germany, Switzerland, and Austria. In accounting law, especially European accounting law, as well as capital market law there are the so-called public interest entities (PIEs). These are defined with the help of a triad of criteria (balance sheet total, turnover, and number of employees).[58] In the new European supply chain legislation, the companies are covered in terms of their number of employees and global turnover.[59] Such European legislation and the corresponding national ESG and supply chain laws, as in France and Germany, blur the traditional lines between unregulated and regulated companies in a critical way.

## II. Current Economic, Social Science, and Policy Arguments, and Legislative Options

### 1. Economic Arguments versus Social Science and Policy Arguments

The debate on corporate purpose and stakeholder value described under (I) occurs mostly on a very abstract level. Factual statements, socio-political postulates, and values are not always clearly distinguished. Edward Rock is right when he criticizes the fact that four different debates on corporate governance are conflated: the legal debate, the academic finance and economics debate, the management debate, and the political debate.[60] The classical basic statement, which clearly prevails among economists and lawyers, especially in the United States, can be summed up as follows: 'Economic theory defends the primacy of the shareholder as the most efficient operating principle', profit

---

[56] Ferrarini (n 20) 94–96: corporate purpose movement and Covid-19.
[57] See the notion of 'regulated financial undertaking, regardless of its legal form' in EU Corporate Sustainability Due Diligence Directive, art 3(1)(a)(iii) (24 April 2024), see section II4c) below.
[58] See eg, for Germany, § 267 of the Commercial Act: balance sheet EUR 6 million; turnover EUR 12 million; number of employees 50.
[59] EU Corporate Sustainability Due Diligence Directive, art 2(1)(a), (b) (24 April 2024): more than 1,000 employees and worldwide turnover of more than EUR 450 million. See section II4c) below.
[60] Rock (n 2) 369; see also Ferrarini (n 20) 138–39, describing the multiple uses of corporate purpose.

maximization 'leads to value creation for all stakeholders of the company', and 'tax and transfer systems can be used to redistribute economic value to nonshareholders'.[61] This leads to various individual arguments and rejoinders. In what follows, the arguments and counterarguments used explicitly or implicitly in these debates will be summarized briefly. In part, they overlap.

a) The shareholders as ultimate risk-bearers versus impacts on and contributions of stakeholders

The starting point of the economic argument is the conviction that shareholders are the ultimate risk-bearers, and, as such, their interests deserve priority as residual claimants of the firm. This is indeed reflected in all insolvency laws, as the shareholder group is the last to be satisfied, with priority given to all creditors.

By contrast, it is argued that both capital and labour contribute to the generation of profit. This is used to justify worker participation in the boardroom, for example. Insofar as the generation of profit is associated with costs and damages for other stakeholders, such as the environment and the climate, externalization to the detriment of the latter is criticized and reinternalization is demanded.[62] This is propagated in the ESG movement. Yet there is a clear tension in ESG between 'E' on the one side and 'S' and 'G' on the other side, with the regulatory initiatives concentrating solely on 'E', while neglecting 'S' and particularly 'G'. This has become particularly obvious in Germany, with its two-tier board system and labour co-determination in the supervisory board, where there is no place for a third party beyond shareholders and labour.

b) Principal–agent theory and stakeholder interests

According to the principal–agent theory that is established in the current law and economics debate, shareholders are seen as the principals of the directors, who are their agents. If directors are allowed, or even required, to take into account the interests of other stakeholders, this necessarily has the effect of insulating the directors to some extent from the influence and control of the shareholders. Most company laws therefore see shareholders as the primary controllers of directors, a control which today is increasingly exercised outside the general assembly. Michael Jensen had already concluded in 2002 that stakeholder theory cannot specify the relationship between the various interests[63] and therefore only leads to top managers being able to determine this for themselves and thus run their companies in the company's interest.[64] In addition,

---

[61] Fisch and Davidoff Solomon (n 18) 1319, with further arguments at 1320–22.
[62] On the shareholders as residual claimants see Reinier Kraakman and others, *The Anatomy of Corporate Law: A Comparative and Functional Approach* (3rd edn, OUP 2017) 79–108, discussing the protection of minority shareholders, employees, and external constituencies.
[63] In Germany, these stakeholder interests are considered to be equal. See Gerald Spindler in Gerald Spindler and Eberhard Stilz (eds), *Beck-OGK Aktiengesetz* (C.H. Beck 2022) § 116 comment 31.
[64] Jensen (n 24) argues for enlightened value maximization, ie the maximization of shareholder valuations subject to safeguarding its reputational capital in the eyes of all stakeholders. See similarly Vikas Mehrotra and Randall Morck, 'Governance and Stakeholders' (May 2017) ECGI Finance Working Paper No 507/2017 https://ssrn.com/abstract=2971943.

shareholder value can be measured by share price, even if it is generally agreed that this is only an imperfect yardstick.[65]

However, the influence of institutional investors—but also of other stakeholders such as large debtholders—who press for ESG to be taken into account[66] is pointed out, and it is proposed to strengthen their rights and make directors legally responsible for stakeholder concerns as well. Some control is also possible through transparency, as, for instance, shown by the far-reaching ESG regulations of the European Union.[67] Share prices also reflect both the reputational risks in terms of ESG and the pressure from institutional investors on companies and directors in this regard. Finally, there is social performance measurement. While it is still difficult, it is no longer in its infancy.[68]

c) The problem of divergent interests of shareholders and of stakeholders

It is true that the interests of the various shareholders, namely major and minor shareholders, are by no means always the same. This is already evident from the fact that the protection of minority shareholders from controlling shareholders is traditionally considered the core problem of company law. Nevertheless, these shareholders' interests are more uniform than those of the various stakeholders, who are heterogeneous and present directors with difficult choices and a balancing act.

In various European countries, however, laws on employee participation in the workplace and on the board specifically take into account the interest of employees. There is an extensive, but mixed, experience with this topic, for example in Germany.[69] In some countries there are also so-called public interest representatives on the board. But even without such institutional anchoring, the legal system can oblige directors to take stakeholder concerns into account and require that they are selected in conformity with certain criteria, such as, for example, diversity or even ESG. It is also true that the business judgment rule, which grants directors broad entrepreneurial discretion, is limited by several, sometimes far-reaching requirements. This is laid down by rules in German company law, for example, and it is spelled out extensively in legal commentaries. Legislatures could require that business judgment include ESG concerns as well, but it would be crucial whether the business judgment rule remains an 'open norm' or whether its ambit would be restricted by an actual legal ESG duty.[70]

---

[65] cf Keay (n 14) 47–52, 72, considering metrics and the role of share price.
[66] Gerard Hertig, 'Governance by Institutional Investors in a Stakeholder World' in Jeffrey N Gordon and Wolf-Georg Ringe (eds), *Oxford Handbook on Corporate Law and Governance* (OUP 2018) 109.
[67] See section II4 below.
[68] cf John Armour, Luca Enriques, and Thom Wetzer, 'Mandatory Corporate Climate Disclosures: Now, But How?' (2021) 3 Columbia Business Law Review 1086. On measurement see British Academy, *Final Report* (n 4) 35–41; Sanjai Bhagat and Glenn Hubbard, 'Rule of Law and Purpose of the Corporation' (2022) 30 Corporate Governance International Review 10, 20–21, on measuring and understanding a company's ESG policy, ESG ratings and the impact on corporate performance; Andreas Engert, 'ESG Ratings: Guiding a Movement in Search for Itself' (31 July 2023) ECGI Law Working Paper No 727/2023 https://ssrn.com/abstract=4525932.
[69] Kraakman and others, *The Anatomy of Corporate Law* (n 62) 105–107.
[70] For the Netherlands on an open duty see Manuel Lokin and Jeroen Veldman, 'The Potential of the Dutch Corporate Governance Model for Sustainable Governance and Long Term Stakeholder Value' (2019) 4 Erasmus Law Review 50 https://ssrn.com/abstract=3759767; similarly as to climate change see Gregor Bachmann, 'Zielsetzung und Governance von Unternehmen im Lichte der Klimaverantwortung' (2023) 187 Zeitschrift fur das gesamte Handelsrecht und Wirtschaftsrecht 166. For a legal ESG duty see Thilo Kuntz, 'ESG and the Weakening Business Judgment Rule' (2023) https://ssrn.com/abstract=4395003; Marc-Philippe Weller and Tim

### d) Solving social and environmental problems: who can contribute?

Directors and managers, it is argued, are ill-equipped to solve social problems. Their skills and experiences are different, and they are also not democratically legitimized. Social and general economic problems such as unemployment or inflation cannot be solved in isolation by individual companies. Here, the legislative and executive branches are in a very different position in terms of identifying such problems across sectors and weighing solutions.[71] They have the help of experts and interdisciplinary inquiries.

However, such skills and experience can be taken into account also at the time of selecting directors and managers. Accordingly, what becomes important is the profile of these individuals and whether this profile is made transparent to shareholders and investors. The legislature can also hold companies accountable for their contribution to solving these problems.

### e) Economic and social problems: responsibility of the state versus engaging private enterprises

Finally, it is considered possible that the choice of shareholder value or stakeholder interests may have wider economic consequences, such as a reduction in innovation.[72] However, this and many other possible economic and political consequences and side-effects of such decisions should and must be empirically substantiated. This also applies to the advantages and disadvantages of employee participation in the supervisory board or the (one-tier) board.

From the side of behavioural economics and the social sciences, the main argument in favour of rethinking is the externalization of costs and damages as projected onto stakeholders other than the company and the shareholders.[73] According to authors in these fields, the future of humanity and the planet is ultimately at stake.[74] Private companies should be obliged to make their contribution towards protecting such interests, or at least have the company and its shareholders (re)internalize costs and damages.

---

Fischer, 'ESG-Geschäftsleiterpflichten' (2022) Zeitschrift für Wirtschaftsrecht 2253; Timo Fest, 'Nachhaltige Unternehmensführung: Die Perspektive des Vorstands unter besonderer Berücksichtigung von Art. 25 CSDDD-E' *Die Aktiengesellschaft* (20 October 2023) 713, 720–21. On the actual German business judgment rule see Klaus J Hopt and Markus 'Roth in Heribert Hirte, Peter Mülber, and Markus Roth (eds), *Großkommentar zum Aktiengesetz* (5th edn, De Gruyter 2015) § 93, comments 69–71, 73–115.

[71] cf Company Law Review Steering Group, *Company Law Review, Modern Company Law for a Competitive Economy: Developing the Framework* (DTI 2000) para 2.12: '[w]ould impose a distributive economic role on directors'.

[72] Skinner (n 13) 429–30. For a survey of the literature in economics, finance, organization behaviour and management strategy as regards organizational higher purpose and for the empirical pros and cons see Anjan Thakor, 'Higher Purpose, the Greater Good and Finance' (April 2022) Finance Working Paper No 824/2022 http://ssrn.com/abstract_id=4097198.

[73] Bukspan (n 31).

[74] British Academy, *Final Report* (n 4) 22; Beate Sjåfjell, 'Reforming EU Company Law to Secure the Future of Corporate Business' (2021) European Company and Financial Law Review 190; Beate Sjåfjell and Jukka Mähönen, 'Corporate Purpose and the Misleading Shareholder vs Stakeholder Dichotomy' (2022) 34(2) Bond Law Review 69 https://ssrn.com/abstract=4039565, taking sides against Kraakman and others (n 62): Corporate purpose as 'the core overarching issue of company law … (is) not something that should be framed within path-dependent Anglo-American inspired law and economics'; see also Bruner (n 35) 1250–53: 'Re-envisioning the corporate form and corporate law.'

Yet the questions remain how this contribution should be made (directly or indirectly, economically efficient, or just and 'fair'?[75]) and by what standards this issue should be judged in each case.

In the text that follows, we shall consider the experiences that several countries have faced when including stakeholder interests into corporate law and also the practice of corporations.

## 2. Legislative Options: Shareholder Value, Constituency Statutes, and Balancing of Interests

a) Pure or enlightened shareholder value systems

The classic fiefdom of shareholder value is Delaware, featuring the traditionally most attractive legal system for the incorporation of American companies. According to Chancellor William Chandler of the Delaware Chancery Court, the 'objective' of the corporation is 'to promote the value of the corporation for the benefit of the shareholders'.[76] The American Law Institute (ALI), in its Principles of Corporate Governance of 1984, clearly stated that: 'A corporation ... should have as its objective the conduct of business activities with a view to enhancing corporate profit and shareholder gain.'[77] However, the US Supreme Court clarified in 2014: 'While it is certainly true that a central objective of for-profit corporations is to make money, modern corporate law does not require for-profit corporations to pursue profit at the expense of everything else, and many do not do so.'[78] This is also true in Delaware, although—after the famous *Revlon* case—with the exception that when a company is sold for cash, all shareholders must participate and the board's duty is to obtain the highest possible amount for the shareholders. In this 'end game', a balancing with other stakeholder interests is not permissible.[79] Incidentally, however, shareholder primacy must not be equated with 'short-term share-price maximization'; under Delaware law, the question of 'long-term' versus 'short-term' is largely irrelevant.[80]

b) Constituency statutes and balancing of interests

By contrast, numerous individual US states have been so-called constituency states since as far back as the 1980s.[81] The relevant Pennsylvania statute, for example,

---

[75] cf Bukspan (n 31) 10–13, 19–24; Thilo Kuntz (ed), *Research Handbook on Environmental, Social, and Corporate Governance* (Edward Elgar Publishing 2024).

[76] *eBay Domestic Holdings Inc v Newmark* 16 A3d 1, 34 (Del Ch 2010). See the earlier ruling of *Dodge v Ford Motor Corporation* 170 NW 668, 684 (Mich 1919), but this was in the company's charter, and it was a close corporation rather than a public corporation. On Delaware case law see Rock (n 2) 371–74; Fisch and Davidoff Solomon (n 18) 1324–27.

[77] 1994 Principles of Corporate Governance of the American Law Institute (ALI), vol I § 2.01(a).

[78] *Burwell v Hobby Lobby Stores Inc* 573 US 682, 711–12 (2014) (citations omitted).

[79] *Revlon Inc v MacAndrews & Forbes Holdings Inc* 506 A2d 173, 182 (Del 1958). For detailed comments see Rock (n 2) 372–73, 380.

[80] Rock (n 2) 379 n 53: '(D)irectors, generally, are obliged to chart a course for a corporation which is in its best interests without regard to a fixed investment horizon.'

[81] See Rock (n 2) 371–72: at present in 41 US states.

explicitly rejects shareholder primacy and allows directors to consider all relevant interests and, in the event of a conflict, to put the interests of shareholders aside.[82] The forthcoming, newly drafted US Principles of Corporate Governance will probably also provide for such an opening.[83] This corresponds to the traditional legal situation in many European countries, such as Germany.[84] Similar determinations are made on the question of enlightened shareholder value, as is the case in the United Kingdom (UK), for example.[85] However, it is an open question whether and to what extent this actually benefits stakeholder interests.[86] This, in turn, depends on how much discretion the formulation of the business judgment rule affords directors, on whether directors are required to 'balance' the interest of the members with those of the stakeholders (required in Germany but not required in the UK)[87] and on the associated legal preconditions; but it also depends on the degree of pressure exerted by institutional investors or otherwise outside the law.[88]

---

[82] ibid 371–72 on the very detailed '§ 1715 Exercise of power generally'.

[83] Restatement of the Law Corporate Governance, Tentative Draft No 2 (March 2024) :

§ 2.01. The Objective of a Corporation (T.D. No. 1) (approved 2022)
(a) The objective of a corporation is to enhance the economic value of the corporation, within the boundaries of the law;
  (1) in common law jurisdictions: for the benefit of the corporation's shareholders. In doing so, a corporation may consider:
    (a) the interests of the corporation's employees;
    (b) the desirability of fostering the corporation's business relationships with suppliers, customers, and others;
    (c) the impact of the corporation's operations on the community and the environment; and
    (d) ethical considerations related to the responsible conduct of business;
  (2) in stakeholder jurisdictions: for the benefit of the corporation's shareholders and/or, to the extent permitted by state law, for the benefit of employees, suppliers, customers, communities, or any other constituencies.
(b) A corporation, in the conduct of its business, may devote a reasonable amount of resources to public-welfare, humanitarian, educational, and philanthropic purposes, whether or not doing so enhances the economic value of the corporation.

[84] Jens Koch, *Aktiengesetz* (18th edn, C.H. Beck 2024) § 76 comments 60–113, discussing the interpluralistic purpose concept, explicitly in German Corporate Act of 1937, § 70 s 1; Mathias Habersack, 'Gemeinwohlbindung und Unternehmensrecht' (2020) 220 Archiv für die civilistische Praxis 594; Klaus J Hopt, 'Aktionärskreis und Vorstandsneutralität' (1993) 22(4) Zeitschrift für Unternehmens- und Gesellschaftsrecht 534, 536–37; Anne-Christin Mittwoch, *Nachhaltigkeit und Unternehmensrecht* (Mohr Siebeck 2022), chs 9, 10. cf also German Corporate Governance Code (28 April 2022) Recommendation A1; Gregor Bachmann, 'Nachhaltiger Kodex?' (2022) 186 Zeitschrift fur das gesamte Handelsrecht und Wirtschaftsrecht 641.

[85] Paul L Davies, Susan Worthington, and Christopher Hare, *Gower's Principles of Modern Company Law* (11th edn, Sweet & Maxwell 2021), marginal notes 10-026–10-039 on s 172, and marginal notes 9-016–9-020 on the UK Corporate Governance Code; David Kershaw and Edmund-Philipp Schuster, 'The Purposive Transformation of Company Law' (2021) 69 American Journal of Comparative Law 478 https://ssrn.com/abstract=3363267. On the UK Corporate Governance Code 2018 and on the UK Stewardship Code 2020, cf Ferrarini (n 20) 91. cf also Fleischer (n 19) 174–75.

[86] Fisch and Davidoff Solomon (n 18) 1338. For a view unlikely to change behaviour but offering similar assessments for the United States (largely ineffective) and the UK (even more shareholder-centric than the United States) see Petrin and Choudhury (n 40) 78–80. For a more positive evaluation see Vanessa Knapp, 'Sustainable Corporate Governance: A Way Forward?' (2021) European Company and Financial Law Review 218.

[87] Davies/Worthington/Hare (n 85), marginal note 10-027.

[88] For an earlier articulation of this idea, see section I2 above on the Business Roundtable Statement (n 21), at the end; see also A Johnston and others, 'Corporate Governance for Sustainability' https://ssrn.com/abstract=3502101. As to the growing role of institutional investors see Zohar Goshen and Sharon Hannes, 'The Death of Corporate Law' (2019) 94 New York University Law Review 263.

## 3. Corporate Purpose Legislation

### a) Options for the shareholders and the board

In the meantime, as already mentioned at the outset, there is a growing demand to oblige companies to state their own purpose as a legal requirement. It would then be the duty of the directors to manage the company according to this purpose.[89] Unfortunately, this reform, supposedly 'an embarrassingly simple policy', is anything but simple and effective.[90] This starts with the terminology itself, which is used and applied very differently in the various disciplines.[91] But of even greater relevance is that, while many companies today announce their own purpose,[92] by far not all companies do this, and if they do, then usually this is not explicitly stated in the articles of association and appears only very exceptionally in a manner oriented towards public welfare interests beyond the specific field of business.[93] With a purpose such as that chosen by the Danish brewery company Carlsberg—our purpose is to brew better beers[94]—nothing is gained for ESG. To prescribe by law a common good purpose for all companies can necessarily be done only in a very general and unspecific way. The advocates of a legally prescribed choice of a purpose acknowledge this and only seek to prescribe the choice as such, but not the content.[95] For the same reason the French Loi Pacte of 2019[96] introduced only a non-mandatory option, ie a kind of enabling provision for the company, in Article 1835 of the Code Civil it was stated that: 'The Articles of Association may specify a raison d'être, consisting of the principles which the company sets out to uphold and for which it intends to allocate resources in order to carry out its activity.'[97]

---

[89] The British Academy, *Principles for Purposeful Business: How to Deliver the Framework for the Future of the Corporation* (2019). See n 4. cf Johnston and others (n 87). See also Mayer, *Prosperity* (n 3); Edmans (n 13).

[90] Paul L Davies, 'Shareholder Voice and Corporate Purpose: The Purposeless of Mandatory Corporate Purpose Statements' (November 2022) ECGI Law Working Paper No 666/2022 7, 38 https://ssrn.com/abstract=4285770. Responding to the fundamental criticism see Colin Mayer, 'The Purpose of Corporate Purpose Statements: A Response to "Shareholder Voice and Corporate Purpose: The Purposeless of Mandatory Corporate Purpose Statements" by Paul Davies' (March 2023) ECGI Law Working Paper No 694/2023 http://ssrn.com/abstract_id=4397435 and the short rejoinder by Paul L Davies in a postscript to his above-mentioned article (ibid 40–42); for a shift in mindset see eg Bukspan (n 31); Petrin and Choudhury (n 40); Ferrarini (n 20) 137–42, offering a holistic view of corporate purpose; Fisch and Davidoff Solomon (n 18) 1328–44, although corporate purpose sceptics, the authors favour an instrumental view of corporate purpose; Fleischer (n 19) 182–88; Pollman (n 48) 1423; see also IESE, 'ECGI Conference on Corporate Purpose October 28–30' (2020) 33 Journal of Applied Corporate Finance 41. From Germany see Mathias Habersack, 'Corporate Purpose' in *Festschrift für Windbichler* (De Gruyter 2020) 707; see also the earlier work of Wolfgang Schön, 'Der Zweck der Aktiengesellschaft: geprägt durch europäisches Gesellschaftsrecht?' (2016) 180 Zeitschrift fur das gesamte Handelsrecht und Wirtschaftsrecht 279.

[91] Rock (n 2); see also Ferrarini (n 20) 138–39, discussing the multiple uses of corporate purpose.

[92] This purpose must not be confused with the general purpose of the company in a legal sense.

[93] Pollmann (n 48) 1448: 'The vast majority of corporations have adopted broad, boilerplate purpose clauses, or use the "any lawful purpose" language.'

[94] Carlsberg Group, 'Our Purpose' https://carlsberggroup.com/who-we-are/about-the-carlsberg-group/our-purpose/.

[95] Mayer, *Prosperity* (n 3) 22–25, 109–10, 201–202. Against mandatory rules but in favour of flexibility of the law see Kershaw and Schuster (n 85).

[96] Loi Pacte, art 169, Loi no 2019-486 du 22 mai 2019 relative à la croissance et la transformation des entreprises [2019] OJ 2–152; for more on this law in detail see section II4a) below.

[97] Alain Pietrancosta, 'Codification in Company Law of General CSR Requirements: Pioneering Recent French Reforms and EU Perspectives' (July 2022) ECGI Law Working Paper No 639/2022 nos 53–58 https://ssrn.com/abstract=4083398.

## b) Mandatory purpose clauses

But even if the public limited company has chosen a purpose oriented towards the common good, this does not necessarily mean much in terms of entrepreneurial activity—apart from benefit corporations and similar legal forms.[98] For it is indisputable that the board and the management must have broad entrepreneurial discretion in the development of the corporate strategy and even more so in making individual, day-to-day entrepreneurial decisions. If it is to be ensured that these decisions are based on or take into account the common good or individual and concrete common good goals, this cannot be prescribed at the general level of the choice of a purpose; rather, it must occur through a legal requirement governing the entrepreneurial activity of the board or management. As we shall see, this is what the European corporate sustainability due diligence directive of 2024 actually attempts to do.[99] Even then, however, the question is how the board can actually be held accountable for not following the purpose of the company. One option could be to leave this to the institutional investors, who already exert considerable pressure on companies and their directors before and during the general meeting. If one does not trust them and the market, one can give shareholders more say in the corporation itself, for example through a say on environmental matters.[100]

In summary, Paul Davies has rightly said that: '[E]xtending mandatory public purposes to companies in non-regulated industries would require a fundamental reconsideration of the role of companies in society and of the relationship between the state and entrepreneurial endeavour.'[101] If the choice of purpose is left to the shareholders, Marco Ventoruzzo's criticism cannot be dismissed out of hand: corporate purpose is often too generic, and it is difficult to monitor; it just means a move from the business judgment rule to a 'benefit judgment rule'.[102] Holger Fleischer writes succinctly about these efforts in his article entitled 'Corporate Purpose: A Management Concept and Its Implications for Company Law': 'Much ado for little'.[103] Instead of mandatory corporate purpose provisions for all companies, shareholders should be able to decide on their own, which is already possible in many legal systems, including the choice of a

---

[98] See nn 103–105 below.
[99] See section II4c) below.
[100] See section III4b) below at the end.
[101] Paul L Davies, *Introduction to Company Law* (3rd edn, OUP 2020) 332–39; for more detail see Paul L Davies, *Shareholder Voice and Corporate Purpose* (n 90); the paper concludes that 'the mandatory, broad purpose requirement will either be (largely) ineffective or (largely) unnecessary', 38. From the perspective of behavioural ethics with concrete reform proposals see Yuval Feldman, Adi Libson, and Gideon Parchomovsky, 'Corporate Law for Good People' (2021)115 Northwestern University Law Review 1125.
[102] Marco Ventoruzzo, 'Brief Remarks on "Prosperity" by Colin Mayer and the Often Misunderstood Notion of Corporate Purpose' (2020) 65 Rivista delle società 43, 46; Ferrarini (n 20) 123–24. See also Guido Ferrarini, 'An Alternative View of Corporate Purpose: Colin Mayer on Prosperity' (2020) 65 Rivista delle Società 27. cf Hopt (n 84) 540–42, describing corporate purpose as too generic and hard to concretize, and seeing the better option as having directors as trustees.
[103] Holger Fleischer, 'Gesetzliche Unternehmenszielbestimmungen im Aktienrecht: Eine vergleichende Bestandsaufnahme' (2017) 46(4) Zeitschrift für Unternehmens- und Gesellschaftsrecht 411, 425. Even more critical is Rock (n 2) 393: 'Here, Mayer's lack of legal background gives him an optimism for legal solutions that few corporate lawyers would share.' See also Holger Spamann and Jacob Fisher, 'Corporate Purpose: Theoretical and Empirical Foundations/Confusions' (November 2022) ECGI Law Working Paper No 664/2022 https://ecgi.global/content/working-papers: II. Empirics of Purpose and at 24: sceptical that corporate purpose 'can live up the hype'. See also the hard critique from an Asian viewpoint by Dan W Puchniak, 'No Need for Asia to be Woke: Contextualizing Anglo-America's "Discovery" of Corporate Purpose' (July 2022) ECGI Law Working Paper No 646/2022 http://ssrn.com/abstract_id=4122483.

special legal form such as the US benefit corporation,[104] the French *société à mission*,[105] and the British community interest company.[106]

## 4. ESG, Corporate Sustainability Due Diligence, and Climate Change Legislation: Examples from France, Germany, and the European Union

While corporate purpose legislation may change much less than its advocates promise, other more focused legislative options are proposed. Indeed ESG, corporate sustainability due diligence, and climate change legislation, together with climate change litigation (globally far more than 2,000 cases) is proliferating.[107] In what follows, just three examples are spelt out: the French legislation because it was setting the example in 2017 and 2019, the German legislation which followed this example in 2021, and, most recently, the European Directive (CSDDD) of 2024.

a) The French Duty of Vigilance Law of 2017 and the Loi Pacte of 2019
The dilemma which has been described above[108] is confirmed when we first look at the French Duty of Vigilance Law of 2017[109] and the French Law Pacte of 2019.[110] With both laws the French legislators set international examples for ESG regulation.

---

[104] See Frederick H Alexander, *Benefit Corporation and Governance* (Berret-Koehler Publishers 2018); Livia Ventura, 'Philanthropy and the For-profit Corporation: The Benefit Corporation as the New Form of Firm Altruism' (2022) 23 European Business Organization Law Review 603. See also Rock (n 2) 374; William M Klimon, 'Beyond the Board: Alternatives in Nonprofit Corporate Governance' (2019) 9 Harvard Business Law Review 1; Holger Fleischer, 'Benefit Corporation zwischen Gewinn- und Gemeinwohlorientierung: Eine rechtsvergleichende Skizze' in *Festschrift für Seibert* (Otto Schmidt 2019) 219; Birgit Weitemeyer, 'Alternative Organisationsformen auf dem Vormarsch: Unternehmensstiftung, gemeinnützige GmbH, Benefit Corporation' (2022) 51(4–5) Zeitschrift für Unternehmens- und Gesellschaftsrecht 627.
[105] Code de Commerce, arts L 210-10, 210-11, 210-12; on the five conditions to acquire the label of *société à mission* see Pietrancosta (n 97) Pt II B no 59.
[106] Companies Act 2006, s 6; Companies (Audit, Investigations and Community Enterprise) Act 2004, Pt 2.
[107] European Commission, *Study on Due Diligence Requirements through the Supply Chain* (January 2020) 40–42, 170–75, with a list of countries where such laws have been adopted or discussed; Anne Lafarre, 'The Proposed Corporate Sustainability Due Diligence Directive: Corporate Liability Design for Social Harms' (2023) 34 European Business Law Review 213, 226: table on due diligence initiatives in France, the Netherlands, Germany, Norway, and others; Mathias Habersack and Peter Zickgraf, 'Sorgfaltspflichten und Haftung in der Lieferkette als Regelungsmodell' (2023) 87 Rabels Zeitschrift für ausländisches und internationales Privatrecht 532, 546-66.
As to climate change litigation see Sabin Centre for Climate Change Law, Columbia Law School and Arnold&Porter, *Databases* <http://climatecasechart.com/>: US Climate Change Litigation, 1,669 cases found; Global Climate Change Litigation, 723 suits against governments listed, 196 suits against corporations and individuals; 53 cases in Germany (last visited 29 October 2023). See also Grantham Research Institute on climate change and the environment (London School of Economics and Political Science), 5th Annual Report: Global trends in climate change litigation: 2023 snapshot: 2,341 cases, outcome of more than 50 per cent of climate cases understood as favourable to climate action. See also Deutsche Umwelthilfe, DUHwelt 3/2021, 9–11, Klagen fürs Klima <https://duh.de/publikationen/duhwelt/>; European Coalition for Corporate Justice (ECCJ), 'Suing Goliath' Brussels (September 2021): Collection of civil actions for damages and for injunctive relief and other proceedings <https://corporatejustice.org/publications/suing-goliath/>.
For a recent overview see Livia Ventura, 'Corporate Sustainability Due Diligence and the New Boundaries of the Firms in the European Union' (2023) 34 European Business Law Review 239; Jens Koch, 'ESG: Zündstufen zum Megatrend' *Die Aktiengesellschaft* (1 August 2023) 553.
[108] See section II3b below at the end.
[109] The French Duty of Vigilance Law: Loi no 2017-399 du 27 mars 2017 relative au devoir de vigilance [2017] OJ 1–99. See the very detailed information in Pietrancosta (n 97) Pt I, nos 11–34; as to the many criticisms see ibid no 15.
[110] Loi Pacte (n 96) art 169. See the very detailed information in Pietrancosta (n 97) Pt II, nos 35–60. See also Fleischer (n 19) 171–73.

The Duty of Vigilance Law of 2017 was the first law which imposed a general mandatory due diligence requirement for human rights and environmental impact and therefore received very broad attention.[111] The law is very brief; it contains only three articles that are included in the French Commercial Code (Article 225-102-4 and Article 225-102-5). The law applies to French companies and to their French subsidiaries having at least 5,000 employees or to French companies having subsidiaries in and outside France with a total of at least 10,000 employees.[112] The main obligation for these companies is to establish a vigilance plan.[113] The plan shall include reasonable vigilance measures which should identify risks and prevent serious infringements of human rights and fundamental freedoms, the health and safety of persons, and the environment, if these infringements result from the activities of the company and its directly or indirectly controlled subsidiaries.[114] This obligation is enforced by fines, public injunction, public disclosure, and civil liability at the request of any interested party.[115] The notion of interested party is defined very broadly and includes all kinds of affected people and communities. With this the enforcement threat goes far beyond what has been provided for in other European countries.[116] It is hardly surprising that the law has met with doubts and criticisms.[117] Ultimately, the law was somewhat softened, the envisaged presumption of wrongdoing in the event of harm was dropped, and the penalties of EUR 10–30 million were declared unconstitutional by the French Constitutional Court.[118]

The Loi Pacte amended Article 1833 of the Code Civil, which applies to all French companies. The former Article 1833 provided that a company must have a lawful purpose and be formed in the common interest of its members. The new article retains this but adds further: 'The company shall be managed in the corporate interest, taking into account the social and environmental concerns linked to its activity.' The Code of Commerce Article L. 225-35 provides that: '[t]he board of directors shall determine

---

[111] See the long list of publications in French in Pietrancosta (n 97) no 12 n 75.
[112] It has been estimated that this affects around 250 companies. See Pietrancosta (n 97) no 20 n 109.
[113] Among other elements, the plan includes: a mapping of the risks with procedures for regular assessment of the risk situation of the subsidiaries, subcontractors, or suppliers who are subject to the provision; appropriate measures to mitigate risks or prevent serious harm; an alert mechanism which is established in consultation with the representative trade union in the company; and a mechanism for monitoring the measures implemented and evaluating their effectiveness. The requirements for the plan were extended for certain companies in view of 'combating climate change and strengthening resilience' by Law no 202-1104 of 22 August 2021, Pietrancosta (n 97) no 22. The serious harms envisaged may come not only from the company and its subsidiaries but also from suppliers and subcontractors, though only in respect of those with whom there is an 'established business relationship'. As to the doubt whether the latter extends to cascade partners, idem no 22.
[114] French Commercial Code, art L225-102-4 s 3.
[115] For details see ibid art L225-102-4 ss 5, 6 and art L225-102-5.
[116] Axel Marx and others, 'Corporate Accountability Mechanisms in EU Member States for Human Rights Abuses in Third Countries' in Philip Czech and others (eds), *European Yearbook on Human Rights 2019* (CUP 2019) 157 https://ssrn.com/abstract=3524499.
[117] For example, Pietrancosta (n 97) no 15, identifying considerable and ill-defined obligations, distortion of international competition, and problems for SMEs; he sees all this without achieving the objectives of the law, since companies might turn to less risky global suppliers, to the detriment of local businesses.
[118] Conseil Constitutionnel, decision no 2017-750 of 23 March 2017. As of the end of 2022, the Law has not yet led to any fines or penalties. However, on 28 September 2022 nine leading food manufacturers and distributors were given formal notice from non-profit groups to reduce their use of plastic and three NGOs have initiated court proceedings against one of the ten biggest plastic polluters in the world. They requested the court to order the company to publish a new more ambitious vigilance plan.

the direction of the company's activities and shall ensure that they are carried out in accordance with the company's interest, taking into account the social, environmental, cultural, and sporting concerns connected with its activities. It shall also take into account, where appropriate, the raison d'être of the company within the meaning of Article 1835 of the Code Civil'. This amendment has been widely debated in France and raises many doubts, but it is understood that the law increases the directors' scope for decision-making.[119] However, it has been noted that this law does not instil pluralistic stakeholder theory as the firm's profitability should remain the priority.[120]

b) The German Supply Chain Due Diligence Act of 2021

The German Supply Chain Due Diligence Act of 2021[121] is intended to implement the United Nations Guiding Principles for Business and Human Rights of 2011 and a number of other international conventions listed in the appendix to the Act.[122] The law applies to enterprises, regardless of their legal form, which have their head office or seat in Germany and generally employ at least 3,000 employees. Foreign companies that have a branch in Germany and at least 3,000 employees are also covered. From 2024 onwards, the threshold will be lowered to 1,000 employees. This means that from then on around 4,800 companies will be covered. The law primarily aims to prevent human rights violations that are sufficiently likely to occur on the basis of factual circumstances, but it also seeks to prevent some particularly serious environmental risks. Which human rights violations are recorded is defined in detail in the law. This also applies to environmental risks.[123] The core of the law is the duties of care, which are spelt out in detail in the Act.[124]

In view of the stricter European law,[125] it is important to note that the law distinguishes between direct and indirect suppliers. In the case of the latter, the company has to intervene only if it has factual indications that make a violation of a human

---

[119] See in detail Pietrancosta (n 97) nos 37–46, raising the fear that this may add to managerial entrenchment. See also ibid no 43.

[120] Veronique Magnier and Yves Paclot, 'Le clair-obsur de la loi pacte: vers un nouveau paradigme de la gouvernance?' (Mélanges Alain Couret 2020) 121; François-Xavier Lucas and Didier Poracchia, 'La prise en considération des enjeux sociaux et environnementaux de l'activité de la société' (Mélanges Alain Couret 2020) 89; Pietrancosta (n 97) nos 44.

[121] Gesetz über die unternehmerischen Sorgfaltspflichten in Lieferketten of 16 July 2021, Official Gazette 2021 I 2959 (German Supply Chain Due Diligence Act). See the first comments on the many problems that the application of the law entails in respect to corporate groups by Patrick C Leyens in Klaus J Hopt (ed), *Handelsgesetzbuch (Commercial Law Commentary)*, vol 2 Lieferkettensorgfaltspflichtengesetz (43rd edn, C.H. Beck 2024); for more detail see Holger Fleischer and Peter Mankowski (eds), *Lieferkettensorgfaltspflichtengesetz* (C.H. Beck 2023); Markus Kaltenborn and others (eds), *#Lieferkettensorgfaltspflichtenrecht* (C.H. Beck 2023); and in several new commentaries and handbooks on the new law.

[122] See German Act, § 2 s 1with annexes Nos 1–11.

[123] German Act, § 2 ss 2 and 3.

[124] According to §§ 3–10 of the Act, these due diligence obligations include, among other obligations, the establishment of risk management, the performance of regular risk analyses, the issuing of a policy statement, the anchoring of preventive measures in the company's own business area and vis-à-vis direct suppliers, and the implementation of risk due diligence obligations for indirect suppliers. The company's own business area includes all activities for the manufacture and exploitation of products and the provision of services, regardless of whether they are carried out at a location in Germany or abroad. In affiliated companies, the parent company's own business area includes a company belonging to the group if the parent company exercises decisive influence over the company belonging to the group (§ 2 s 6 of the Act).

[125] See section II4c) below.

rights-related or environmental obligation by indirect suppliers appear possible (substantial knowledge).[126] It is also significant that the law expressly states that a breach of the obligations under this law does not give rise to civil liability. Civil liability established independently of the act remains unaffected.[127] The law is controlled and enforced by the competent national authority. This supervision is the responsibility of the German Federal Office of Economics and Export Control (BAFA). Apart from fines, there is also a risk of being excluded from the awarding of public contracts.[128] In the meantime, BAFA has considerably increased the number of its employees and has begun to carry out a comprehensive risk assessment. There are already numerous articles, commentaries, and books on the new law, which point out the very considerable requirements for companies and many remaining uncertainties in the law.[129]

c) The European Corporate Sustainability Due Diligence Directive of 2024

On 23 February 2022, the European Commission presented the draft of a directive of the European Parliament and of the Council on Corporate Sustainability Due Diligence (CSDDD) that, after bitter controversies, has been adopted in a highly controversial compromised version on 13 June 2024 and went into force on 5 July 2024.[130] This is the latest example of extensive ESG legislation. As mentioned above, it had been preceded by due diligence legislation in France in 2017[131] and in Germany in 2021.[132] Other Member States, in particular the Netherlands,[133] have followed or are expected to follow in the near future. The wording of the draft was deemed to be difficult to comprehend and sometimes controversial. The European Commission did not follow its

---

[126] German Act, § 9.
[127] ibid § 3 s 3.
[128] ibid § 22.
[129] See the list in Leyens (n 121), before the introduction.
[130] Directive (EU) 2024/1760 of the European Parliament and of the Council of 13 June 2024 on corporate sustainability due diligence and amending Directive (EU) 2019/1937 and Regulation (EU) 2023/2859, OJ L2024/1760, 5 July 2024. The original proposal was: Council of the European Union, Proposal for a Directive of the European Parliament and of the Council on Corporate Sustainability Due Diligence and amending Directive (EU) 2019/1937, Brussels (30 November 2022) (OR. en) 15024/1/22 Rev 1 (CSDDD). The original proposal of the European Commission was far more ambitious, Proposal for a Directive of the European Parliament and of the Council on Corporate Sustainability Due Diligence and amending Directive (EU) 2019/1937 (23 February 2022) COM(2022) 71 final (Corporate Sustainability Due Diligence Directive). Among the many reactions in academia, cf eg Paul Davies, 'Corporate Liability for Wrongdoing within (Foreign) Subsidiaries: Mechanisms from Corporate Law, Tort and Regulation' (January 2023) https://ssrn.com/abstract=4345589; Leonhard Hübner, Victor Habrich, and Marc-Philippe Weller, 'Corporate Sustainability Due Diligence' (2022) Neue Zeitschrift für Gesellschaftsrecht 644. For a comparison of the European law and the German law, cf Sebastian Lutz-Bachmann, Kristin Vorbeck, and Lenard Wengenroth, 'Nachhaltigkeitsbezogene Sorgfaltspflichten in Geschäftsbeziehungen: zum Entwurf der EU-Kommission für eine "Lieferkettenrichtlinie"' Betriebs-Berater (2022). In industry and parts of academia also the final version of the directive is harshly criticised, cf Alexander Schall, 'The CSDDD: Good Law or Bad Law?' (2024) 21(3) European Company Law Journal 56, 58: 'overreaching compliance monster'; Jessica Schmidt, '"Patchwork-Kompromiss" zur EU-Lieferketten-RL (CSDDD)' (2024) 10 Neue Zeitschrift für Gesellschaftsrecht 417: actual significant progress for the protection of people and the environment is 'extremely doubtful'.
[131] See French Duty of Vigilance Law (n 109).
[132] German Supply Chain Due Diligence Act (n 121).
[133] The Netherlands has introduced a more specialized law on child labour: Wet van 24 oktober 2019 houdende de invoering van een zorgplicht ter voorkoming van de levering van goederen en diensten die met behulp van kinderarbeid tot stand zijn gekomen (Wet zorgplicht kinderarbeid) Staatsblad (2019) 401. As to the proliferating climate change litigation, see n 107.

own principles of good regulation and was criticized from inside[134] and outside[135] as being biased. In view of the clear reservations of the Member States, in particular from the Scandinavian countries,[136] and after various controversial versions in the legislative process, a compromise was found, and the Directive has been agreed upon and enacted on 5 July 2024, but it allows for a generous transposition time.[137] The Directive includes a number of interesting legislative options, and therefore a brief look at it may be useful.

The Directive foresees obligations for companies regarding actual and potential adverse human rights impacts and adverse environmental impacts, as well as liability for violations by the company itself, its subsidiaries, and within its value chain. It applies to companies with more than 1,000 employees on the average and a net worldwide turnover of more than EUR 450 million.[138] In an attempt to create an equal playing field, it also applies to third-country companies having a turnover of more than EUR 450 million within the European Union.[139] The Commission estimates that about 13,000 EU companies and 4,000 third-country companies will be covered.[140] These companies are expected to conduct human rights and environmental due diligence by carrying out various actions such as integrating due diligence into their policies and risk management systems, identifying and assessing actual or potential adverse impacts and, where necessary, prioritizing actual and potential adverse impacts, preventing and mitigating potential adverse impacts, and bringing actual adverse impacts to an end and minimizing their extent.[141] This includes remediation, meaningful engagement with stakeholders, a notification mechanism and a complaints procedure, monitoring, and public communication. A special article deals with combating climate change.[142] The value chain responsibilities of the company extend beyond the business partners with whom the company has a direct relationship to partners of these business partners ('direct business partners' and 'indirect business partners'), this to be achieved

---

[134] The Regulatory Scrutiny Board of the European Commission twice issued an overall negative opinion.

[135] See the detailed comment by Patricia Sarah Stöbener de Mora and Paul Noll, 'Noch grenzenlosere Sorgfalt?' (2023) Europäischer Zeitschrift für Wirtschaftsrecht 14. As to the risks for companies under the Directive see Sophie Burchardi, 'Lieferkettensorgfaltspflichten: Risiken für die Unternehmensleitung' (2022) Neue Zeitschrift für Gesellschaftsrecht 1467.

[136] cf Ernst & Young, *Study on Directors' Duties and Sustainable Corporate Governance, Final Report by Ernst & Young for the European Commission DG Justice and Consumers* (July 2020) 157 with two Annexes, Annex I (branches), Annex II (country fiches of the 12 selected Member States). This study has been severely criticized, eg by the European Company Law Experts (ECLE) Comment (July 2020) https://europeancompanylawexperts.wordpress.com/publications and by Edmans, one of the protagonists of ESG (n 13); see response of Edmans (1 January 2021), contending the evidence was 'very one-sided and low-quality'.

[137] Corporate Sustainability Due Diligence Directive, art 37 Transposition, two years from the entry into force, see n 130.

[138] ibid art 2(1)(a), (b). cf Rachel Chambers and David Birchall, 'How European Human Rights Law Will Reshape U.S. Business' (2024) 20 Hastings Business Law Journal 3.

[139] ibid art 2(2)(a), (b), (c).

[140] Proposal for a Directive (n 130) Explanatory Memorandum, 16.

[141] See art 5 on due diligence, art 5(1)(a)–(c) mentioned supra in the text, in addition art 5(1)(d)–(h); spelt out in detail in arts 7–16. Art 6 deals extensively with due diligence at a group level. cf the definitions in art 3(1)(b)–(d) of 'adverse environmental impact', 'adverse human rights impact', and 'adverse impact'.

[142] According to art 22, the companies are to adopt and put into effect a transition plan for climate change mitigation which aims to ensure, through best efforts, that the business model and strategy of the company are compatible with the transition to a sustainable economy and with the limiting of global warming to 1.5°C in line with the Paris Agreement.

by a contractual cascade of assurances, yet without making clear how this could be put into practice nor what economic consequences it would have for international trade.[143] This is in sharp contrast to the German value chain legislation, which encompasses only contractual suppliers and which is, unsurprisingly, highly controversial both in practice and in theory. As a last resort, if the actual adverse impact is severe, the company may even be obliged to terminate its business relationship with the partner in question.[144] Under certain conditions, where a company has caused or jointly caused an actual adverse impact, the company must provide remediation, and it can be held liable for damages caused to a natural or legal person, provided that it intentionally or negligently failed to comply with its obligations, and this liability is to be of overriding mandatory application in cases where the law applicable to claims to that effect is not the national law of a Member State.[145] The Directive retained a provision according to which directors had to set up and oversee due diligence and could be personally liable for breach of their duties; however, this was no longer included in the final version of the Directive.[146] In view of all these controversies and remaining uncertainties,[147] it is important that the Directive foresees a report by the European Commission after two years.[148]

In summary, the European Directive must be transposed into the national law of the Member States, and less strict national legislation, such as the German value chain responsibility laws, will have to be tightened up. The enterprises affected as well as the national supervisory agencies must live with the far-reaching demands and many uncertainties of the Directive and will have to adapt themselves to it. Yet the effects of these new laws will be considerable. In order to meet the requirements, enterprises will have to alter their value chains considerably. The result of this process may very well be that certain developing countries—and their suppliers—not meeting the new standards will be left out of these chains entirely. One must realize that not only those enterprises for which the Directive is directly applicable will be affected since these enterprises will also require their suppliers and their buyers, irrespective of their size, to meet the prescribed standards. Small and medium-sized companies will in effect carry the burden. The effects on international competition are also open, even though the Directive reaches out to non-EU enterprises. In view of this, it will be important that

---

[143] ibid art 8(1): adverse impacts arising from their own operations or those of their subsidiaries and, where related to their chains of activities, those of their buseinss partners. 'Business partner (direct and indirect)' is defined in art 3(1)(f) and 'chain of activities (upstream and downstream)' in art 3(1)(g).

[144] ibid art 11. Bringing actual adverse impacts to an end, art 11(7)(b), as a last resort, allows termination of the business relationship. cf John Armour in ECGI-Symposium (29 March 2022) https://ecgi.global/content/corporate-sustainability-due-diligence.

[145] Corporate Sustainability Due Diligence Directive art 12 as to remediation and art 29 as to civil liability of companies and the right to full compensation. As to the conflict of law provision see art 29(7). Art 29(3)(a) deals with limitation periods and art 29(3)(d) with the authorization of a trade union or non-governmental organization to bring actions. The regulation of the burden of proof is left to national law, Recital (81), but according to art 29(3)(e), under certain circumstances courts are able to order disclosure of evidence by the company.

[146] Proposal of a Directive (n 130) arts 25, 26 have been deleted in the final version.

[147] But see the Directive art 18, which foresees model contractual clauses, and art 19, with forthcoming guidelines by the Commission. See also art 21, Single helpdesk.

[148] ibid art 36, Review and reporting. Further reports after six years and every three years afterwards.

enterprises are not left unsupported and that the Member States live up to their own responsibilities regarding human rights, climate change, and ESG.

## III. Making Stakeholder Governance Work: Enforcement Problems

As shown at the beginning of this chapter, the debate on the corporate goal and on shareholder or stakeholder value is based on basic economic and ethical convictions that are difficult to reconcile. The economic, sociological, and legal policy arguments discussed in section II and the options available to legislatures thereafter have been and still are constantly confronted with arguments for and against them. In the following section, an attempt is made to bring the debate down from the top level of general theories and fundamental convictions to a more realistic level, without getting lost in the details of the individual arguments, especially since these are mostly without empirical support.[149] In this attempt, genuine possibilities of an actual realization and implementation of stakeholder governance are to be examined. In our opinion, it is not only the setting of rules that is important; rather, it is the enforcement and enforceability of such rules that is also relevant and perhaps of even greater significance. In this context, a whole arsenal of regulatory or legislative options emerges. These options must be graded according to the intensity of the interference with personal freedom and the market, and a strict principle of proportionality must apply to such interventions. This is already stipulated by the constitutions of many countries.

### 1. Market Discipline and Self-regulation

In business, it is already the case today that many companies—and not only the large and internationally active ones—are aware of the challenges of realizing more sustainable business beyond mere profit maximization, and they are changing course accordingly.[150] This transformation process is now strongly driven by institutional investors, societal expectations, and reputational risk, but—as should be acknowledged in view of the growing general ideological condemnation of capitalism—also by a true sense of entrepreneurial responsibility and employee motivation. According to a German survey of CFOs and supervisory board chairs of 160 listed companies from October 2021,[151] 76 per cent of the respondents already have a sustainability strategy in place.

---

[149] Dirk A Zetzsche and Linn Anker-Sorensen, 'Regulating Sustainable Finance in the Dark' (2022) 23 European Business Organization Law Review 47, 82, fearing a 'quack regulation'.
[150] cf the empirical data in Allen Ferrell, Hao Liang, and Luc Renneboog, 'Socially Responsible Firms' (2016) 122 Journal of Financial Economics 585; see also Pollman (n 32) 666–67 on the difficulties of interpreting the empirical data.
[151] Hengeler Mueller and Deutsches Aktieninstitut, *Unternehmen im Transformationsprozess* (Deutsches Aktieninstitut e.V. 2021). The survey covered 310 people, of whom 20 per cent answered. Among the factors

These companies set concrete ESG targets and use ratings, benchmarking, and key performance indicators (KPIs). More than half of the respondents report that their company already has a corporate sustainability board consisting of board members and executives from different divisions. Six out of ten respondents already take ESG objectives into account in board compensation, and this number increases to nine out of ten when including companies planning such a step. The number of ESG committees is projected to more than triple. Risk management has been expanded with regard to ESG at 74 per cent of the respondent companies. Empirical studies also show that well-managed companies have higher CSRs and that CSR is perfectly compatible with corporate value and shareholder returns.[152] Above all, however, there is a very considerable influence of institutional investors and hedge fund activists on companies in the market and increasingly also in general meetings.[153]

This does not, however, rule out the insight that market regulation and self-discipline alone are insufficient. This is not limited to a few 'black sheep' among many 'white' ones. Greenwashing remains a problem. An empirical study from the United States has shown that the signatories of the Business Roundtable's 2019 Statement[154] have indeed not noticeably changed their entrepreneurial decisions since that time.[155] Moreover, it is easy to measure profits but very difficult to capture consideration of stakeholder interests and ESG. The role of manipulation and deception in the corporate world and in the markets has been impressively demonstrated by Nobel Prize winners George A. Akerlof and Robert J. Shiller.[156] The results of a 2019 empirical study suggest that in many companies unethical behaviour is tolerated to some degree; indeed, 'a quarter of managers tend to set aside moral views and act in an ethically questionable manner in certain situations'.[157] The ruthless exploitation of the formal text and lacunae in the applicable legislation is illustrated by the huge and outrageous German tax scandal that

---

identified as motivating more sustainable action, the results were: reputation (8 per cent), feeling of responsibility (87 per cent), expectation of the investors (85 per cent), ESG risk (78 per cent) and potential of innovation (78 per cent).

[152] See Ferrell, Liang, and Renneboog (n 150) 605: '[c]orporate social responsibility ... can be consistent with a core value of capitalism, generating more returns to investors, through enhancing firm value and shareholder wealth'. cf also Felix Mormann and Milica Mormann, 'The Case for Corporate Climate Ratings: Nudging Financial Markets' (28 April 2022) https://ssrn.com/abstract=3952018.

[153] James D Cox and Randall S Thomas, 'A Revised Monitoring Model Confronts Today's Movement Toward Managerialism' (2021) 99 Texas Law Review 1275; cf also Williams (n 32) 97–100, 114, noting, however, that CSR is hardly sufficient. On ESG investing and in favour of a market-led approach see Wolf-Georg Ringe, 'Investor-Led Sustainability in Corporate Governance' (10 November 2021) ECGI Law Working Paper No 615/2021 https://ecgi.global/content/working-papers; Iain MacNeil and Irene-Marie Esser, 'From a Financial to an Entity Model of ESG' (2022) 23 European Business Organization Law Review 9.

[154] See n 21 above.

[155] Lucian A Bebchuk and Roberto Tallarita, 'Will Corporations Deliver Value to All Stakeholders?' (2022) 75 Vanderbilt Law Review 1031 https://ssrn.com/abstract=3899421. None of the twenty companies reviewed amended its corporate governance guidelines to incorporate stakeholder welfare as an independent aim of the corporation; to the contrary, in many of them the guidelines kept a strong statement of the shareholder primacy principle. See also Ferrarini (n 20) 142–44.

[156] George A Akerlof and Robert J Shiller, *Phishing for Phools: The Economics of Manipulation and Deception* (Princeton UP 2015).

[157] See Wertekommission and TUM School of Management der Technischen Universität München, *Führungskräftebefragung* (2019) 22, 30. See also similar results for the financial sector in Alain Cohn, Ernst Fehr, and Michel André Maréchal, 'Business Culture and Dishonesty in the Banking Industry' (2014) 516 Nature 86.

featured the illegal issuance of multiple dividend refunds by tax authorities who had been deceived on the basis of an alleged lacuna in tax law (the so-called cum/cum and cum/ex affair), which is now before the courts and has been clearly described by them as illegal.[158] The temptation to gain an edge over competitors in this way is particularly strong when a company is struggling in the market. So when it comes to restoring the legitimacy of the capitalist structures, market discipline and self-regulation certainly make an important contribution that is unjustly underestimated by the public. But they are not enough. From the other point of view, it is not enough immediately to call for regulation. Empirical studies indicate that, apart from compensation, the behaviour of managers is determined less by regulation than by being decisively influenced by their values and corporate culture.[159] This is a broad field not only for practice but also for the law. Furthermore, the increasing influence of institutional investors may bring about decisive changes in the market and in companies.

## 2. The Code Movement: Comply and Explain

In recent decades, the movement of corporate governance codes has gained great importance not only in the European Union and its Member States, but internationally as well. Most industrially developed countries now have such codes, which are usually enforced by declarations of compliance—'comply or disclose' or the stronger 'comply or explain'—and some are even required by law.[160] These codes require corporate leaders, although usually only those of listed companies, to comply not only with laws and regulations (the vast field of legal compliance) but also with business ethics, and they encourage the setting of a corporate goal. The German Corporate Governance Code refers back to the model of the 'honourable merchant', which first appeared among the Italian merchants of the Renaissance and, as far as Germany is concerned, dates back to the times of the North German Hanseatic League in the sixteenth century.[161]

---

[158] The punishability of such business practices has now been confirmed by the Federal Court of Justice. See the German Bundesgerichtshof decision of 28 July 2021 1 StR 519/20, NJW 2022, 90; many penal court cases are still pending. A Hamburg top banker was recently sentenced to five-and-a-half years in prison.

[159] Renée Adams, *ECGI-Symposium* (29 March 2022) https://ecgi.global/content/corporate-sustainability-due-diligence. For reforms in viewing corporate governance through the lens of behavioural ethics see Feldman, Libson, and Parchomovsky (n 101) 1130–35, 1144–82. See also Amir Licht, 'Culture and Law in Corporate Governance' in Jeffrey N Gordon and Wolf-Georg Ringe (eds), *Oxford Handbook on Corporate Law and Governance* (OUP 2018) 129. As to compensation see Raghuram Rajan, Pietro Ramella, and Luigi Zingales, 'What Purpose Do Corporations Purport? Evidence from Letters to Shareholders' (March 2023) 37 https://ssrn.com/abstract=4405063: executive compensation remains overwhelmingly focused on shareholder value, increase of the use of environmental and social metrics, but magnitude is still small.

[160] See the collection of such codes by the European Corporate Governance Institute (ECGI) https://ecgi.global/content/codes. For international standards, such as the UN Global Compact see Ferrarini (n 20) 140; OECD Guidelines for Multinational Enterprises on Responsible Business Conduct (Paris 2023).

[161] Daniel Klink, 'Der Ehrbare Kaufmann: Das ursprüngliche Leitbild der Betriebswirtschaftslehre und individuelle Grundlage für die CSR-Forschung' in Joachim Schwalbach (ed), *Corporate Social Responsibility* ZfB-Special Issue 3/2008, 57 61–72; Joachim Schwalbach, 'Ehrbare Kaufleute als Leitbild verantwortungsvoller Unternehmensführung: Geschichte und Perspektiven' (2016) 17(2) Zeitschrift für Wirtschafts- und Unternehmensethik 216.; Michael Hüther, 'Ordnungspolitischer Einspruch, Moral als Unternehmenswert' (2008) 103 Handelsblatt 8. More generally on codes of conduct/ethics see CalPERS, 'Governance & Sustainability Principles' (18 June 2018) 31, https://calpers.ca.gov/docs/forms-publications/governa

The UK Corporate Governance Code of July 2018 states: 'The board should establish the company's purpose, values and strategy, and satisfy itself that these and its culture are aligned.'[162] For some time now, these codes have increasingly focused on sustainability and the long-term pursuit of stakeholder interests,[163] for example in the Netherlands[164] and most recently also in Germany.[165] There is even talk of these codes becoming 'green', and in some cases the codes explicitly integrate climate protection, such as the UK Stewardship Code 2020.[166]

The effectiveness of such codes has always been debatable. The experience with them—in the UK, for example, and there especially in the financial sector and in the context of corporate takeovers[167]—has in some cases been quite impressive, but in other countries experiences are mixed.[168] At present, the contribution of such codes to the improvement of corporate governance of companies must certainly be regarded as important. This is especially true if there is appropriate transparency. Today, this is largely achieved through a legal or regulatory principle of comply or explain. However, there is clearly a lack of empirical evidence that non-compliance with code recommendations really has an impact on the price of the corresponding shares.[169] The only certainty is that company managers actually shy away from explaining non-compliance. This is also shown by the high compliance rates. So, ultimately, codes are simply regulation in the shadow of the law,[170] motivated also by the desire to maintain low levels of state regulation.[171]

---

nce-and-sustainability-principles.pdf. But voicing doubts see Holger Fleischer, 'Ehrbarer Kaufmann: Grundsätze der Geschäftsmoral: Reputationsmanagement: Zur "Moralisierung" des Vorstandsrechts und ihren Grenzen, Der Betrieb' (2017) 2015, 2016. cf also Jennifer Milinovic, *Der ehrbare Kaufmann im deutschen Recht* (Peter Lang 2019). See more generally G20/OECD Principles of Corporate Governance (OECD) 2023.

[162] UK Corporate Governance Code as of July 2018, in its opening section: 'Board Leadership and Company Purpose', Principle B. cf Fleischer (n 19) 173–75.
[163] Michele Siri and Shanshan Zhu, 'Integrating Sustainability in EU Corporate Governance Codes' in Danny Busch, Guido Ferrarini, and Seraina Grünewald (eds), *Sustainable Finance in Europe: Corporate Governance, Financial Stability and Financial Markets* (Springer 2021) 175; Maria Lucia Passador, 'Stewardship or Trusteeship Codes?' https://ssrn.com/abstract=4029991.
[164] Manuel Lokin and Jeroen Veldman, 'The Potential of the Dutch Corporate Governance Model for Sustainable Governance and Long Term Stakeholder Value' (2019) 4 Erasmus Law Review 50.
[165] German Corporate Governance Code, Rev 2022 (n 84). On the preceding version of 2020 see Klaus J Hopt and Patrick C Leyens, 'Der Deutsche Corporate Governance Kodex 2020: Grundsatz- und Praxisprobleme' (2019) 48(6) Zeitschrift für Unternehmens- und Gesellschaftsrecht 929.
[166] Paul L Davies, 'The UK Stewardship Code 2010–2020: From Saving the Company to Saving the Planet' in Dionysia Katelouzou and Dan W Puchniak (eds), *Global Shareholder Stewardship* (CUP 2022) 44 59–65, discussing ESG (including climate change). See more generally UK Stewardship Code 2020 and UK Corporate Governance Code 2018.
[167] UK Takeover Code (13th edn, 5 July 2021); cf Klaus J Hopt, 'Takeover Defenses in Europe: A Comparative, Theoretical and Policy Analysis' (2014) 20 Columbia Journal of European Law 249, taking sides in favour of the British model against the US model.
[168] In Germany, the experiences with the voluntary Insider Trading Guidelines and the Takeover Guidelines were so bad that the legislature stepped in, although only as a result of European Union pressure.
[169] Patrick C Leyens in Heribert Hirte, Peter Mülbert, and Markus Roth (eds), *Großkommentar zum Aktiengesetz* (5th edn, De Gruyter 2015) § 161, comments 48–51; Klaus J Hopt, 'Self-Regulation in Banking and Finance: Practice and Theory in Germany' in *La Déontologie bancaire et financière/Ethical Standards in Banking & Finance* (Bruylant 1998) 53.
[170] On UK and US law see Ferrarini (n 20) 114–20.
[171] Davies (n 166) 65: 'common concern to keep government regulation of investment intermediation to a minimum'.

## 3. Disclosure and Auditing: Selected Countries and the European Corporate Sustainability Reporting Directive of 2022

Traditionally, mandatory disclosure is considered to be a more appropriate enforcement mechanism than mandatory regulation.[172] The idea behind this is that disclosure obligations turn 'under the table into a duty of conduct' and that (European company) law thus sets in motion 'an ingenious mechanism of action' that unexpectedly changes the purpose of the public limited company and practically enforces this change.[173]

The UK has embraced the enlightened shareholder value principle since the 2006 reforms introduced in the Companies Act 2006. According to these principles, directors have a duty to promote the long-term success of the commercial company, taking into account a non-exhaustive catalogue of stakeholder interests (including those of employees, suppliers, customers, the community, and the environment).[174] However, this was apparently successful only to a limited extent.[175] Consequently, for accounting periods beginning on or after 1 January 2019, UK legislators have prescribed a so-called section 172(1) statement, in which a 'strategic report' must be included in the company's annual report and accounts.[176] In their report, directors must describe how they have taken into account the wider social factors.

For the motherland of shareholder value, the United States, Justice Strine has also suggested a whole series of disclosure requirements,[177] namely annual reports for large, socially important companies as to the impact of their business on workers, consumers, communities, the environment, and the nation. All companies with annual revenues of more than US$1 billion would be covered, including those that are not listed on the stock exchange, so as not to distort competition. The supervisory authorities are to ensure that the reports are standardized so that they can be compared more easily. Where companies issue prospective quarterly reports, not only three-month earnings expectations should be disclosed but also long-term planning. The US Securities and Exchange Commission (SEC) does not only require disclosure of certain material human capital measures or objectives that management focuses on in managing the

---

[172] cf Holger Daske and others, 'Mandatory IFRS Reporting Around the World: Early Evidence on the Economic Consequences' (last revised 19 January 2023) https://ssrn.com/abstract=1024240. On the theory of financial disclosure see SP Kothari, Liandong Zhang, and Luo Zuo, 'Disclosure Regulation: Past, Present, and Future' (March 2023) https://ssrn.com/abstract=4122664; Wolfgang Schön, 'Informationspflichten der Unternehmensleitung zwischen Aktionärsinteresse, Kapitalmarktinformation und sozialer Verantwortung' vol II *Festschrift für Karsten Schmidt* (C.H. Beck 2019) 391; on voluntary versus mandatory enterprise disclosure see ibid 394–96.

[173] Schön (n 90) 283.

[174] Companies Act 2006, s 172(1): duty 'to promote the success of the company for the benefit of its members as a whole, and in doing so to have regard (amongst other matters) to …' For details see Davies, Worthington, and Hare (n 85), marginal notes 10-027–10-032. On enlightened shareholder value see Jensen (n 24) 245–46 (enlightened stakeholder theory).

[175] See also Andrew Keay and Taskin Iqbal, 'The Impact of Enlightened Shareholder Value' [2019] Journal of Business Law 304.

[176] Companies Act 2006, ss 172(1), 414CZA (UK) from 2019, identifying the strategic report as part of the annual report; description of how the directors have had regard for the matters is set out in s 172(1)(a)–(f).

[177] Strine (n 43) 8–13.

business, but has adopted final rules to require registrants to disclose even certain climate-related information in registration statements and annual reports filed with the SEC.[178]

The most recent piece of legislation on mandatory disclosure is the European Corporate Sustainability Reporting Directive of 2022.[179] This Directive goes far beyond the Directive on non-financial reporting of 2014, the CSR Directive.[180] While the latter was intended to strengthen the confidence of investors and consumers via information, the Corporate Sustainability Reporting Directive expressly extends the addressees of information to two primary groups of users, the first being investors, including asset managers, the second being civil society actors, including non-governmental organizations and social partners who wish to improve their hold on undertakings to account for the impact they have on people and the environment.[181] Although the CSR Directive relied on the comply and explain principle, the Corporate Sustainability Reporting Directive goes considerably further. The Directive will cover many more enterprises (an estimated 15,000 enterprises), the mandatory information is greatly expanded, and instead of the comply and explain principle the sustainability report must be audited. The Corporate Sustainability Reporting Directive relies on a so-called double materiality perspective: undertakings are required to report both on the impact of their activities on people and the environment, as well as on how sustainability matters affect the undertaking.[182] Whether this affects the purpose of the corporation is both unclear and disputed.[183]

---

[178] SEC, 'The Enhancement and Standardization of Climate-Related Disclosures' adopted on 6 March 2024: press release and fact sheet. A petition for review has been filed on the same day.

[179] Directive (EU) 2022/2464 of the European Parliament and of the Council of 14 December 2022 as regards corporate sustainability reporting [2022] OJ L322/15, referred to in this chapter as the Corporate Sustainability Reporting Directive (CSRD). cf Eberhard Vetter, 'Sustainable Corporate Governance Reporting, ESG-Berichterstattung' in Peter Hommelhoff, Klaus J Hopt, and Patrick C Leyens (eds), *Unternehmensführung durch Vorstand und Aufsichtsrat* (C.H. Beck 2024) § 42. For a thorough and critical evaluation of the European sustainability disclosure rules see Wolfgang Schön, '"Nachhaltigkeit" in der Unternehmensberichterstattung' (2022) Zeitschrift für die gesamte Privatrechtswissenschaft 207.

[180] Directive 2014/95/EU of the European Parliament and of the Council of 22 October 2014 amending Directive 2013/34/EU as regards disclosure of non-financial and diversity information by certain large undertakings and groups [2014] OJ L330/1 (15 November 2014). See also Regulation (EU) 2019/2088 on sustainability-related disclosures in the financial services sector [2019] OJ L317 (9 December 2019) (Transparency-Regulation); Regulation (EU) 2020/852 on the establishment of a framework to facilitate sustainable investment [2020] OJ L198 (22 June 2020) (Taxonomy-Regulation); on both regulations see eg Chris van Oostrum, 'Sustainability through Transparency and Definitions: A few thoughts on Regulation (EU) 2019/2088 and Regulation (EU) 2020/852' (2021) 18(1) European Company Law Journal 15.

[181] CSRD (n 179) recital (9). The text continues on and states that other stakeholders might also make use of sustainability information disclosed in annual reports, in particular to foster comparability across and within market sectors.

[182] CSRD (n 179) recital (29), ie not only information to the extent necessary for an understanding of the undertaking's development, performance, and position, but also information necessary for an understanding of the impact of the undertaking's activities on environmental, social and employee matters, respect for human rights, anti-corruption, and bribery matters. cf Emirhan Ilhan and others, 'Climate Risk Disclosure and Institutional Investors' (2023) 36 The Review of Financial Studies 2617.

[183] As to this discussion see Stefan Harbarth, 'Nachhaltigkeit im Rahmen unternehmerischer Entscheidungen' in *Festschrift für Ebke* (C.H. Beck 2021), 307, 314–15; Stefan Harbarth, 'Unions- und verfassungsrechtliche Vorgaben der Unternehmensausrichtung an nichtfinanziellen Parametern (ESG)' in Hommelhoff, Hopt, and Leyens (n 179) § 6; Mittwoch (n 84) 145–48; Koch (n 84) § 76, comment 35d; Vetter (n 179).

Even though some international empirical data is already available on the consequences and possible benefits of mandatory disclosure on ESG,[184] many questions about the effectiveness of such disclosure requirements remain unanswered and controversial.[185] Mandatory auditing in particular has been criticized,[186] although it is true that a formal disclosure may still be helpful.[187] Colin Mayer and others go further and advocate a total reform of accounting and reporting which has as its central focus the 'net of the costs of maintaining human, social, and natural as well as physical assets'.[188] While this may well be debatable theoretically, it is hardly realistic.

## 4. Enterprise Law: Outside and Inside Requirements

### a) Outside requirements: duties of the enterprise

Disclosure requirements—as demonstrated by the European Union's accounting law—reflect a seemingly unstoppable trend towards ever increasingly detailed disclosure. This overburdens medium-sized and smaller companies, in particular financially and in terms of personnel, and it puts them at a noticeable disadvantage in international competition. There is thus a case for legislators to impose instead clear, limited conduct requirements on companies, thereby ensuring that the impact of corporate conduct on ESG, climate change, and other stakeholder interests is not externalized but borne rather by the companies themselves. Yet such regulations should be examined in advance as to both their effectiveness and their compliance with the principle of proportionality (by means of a careful, comprehensive cost-benefit analysis); thereafter, they would have to be democratically legitimized. This has not really been done sufficiently in connection with the European Corporate Sustainability Due Diligence Directive.[189] In particular, the cascading rules of the Directive regarding obligations extending beyond the specific contractual relationship are unclear and problematic.[190]

---

[184] Florencio Lopez-de-Silanes, Joseph A McCahery, and Paul C Pudschedl, 'ESG Performance and Disclosure: A Cross-Country Analysis' [2020] Singapore Journal of Legal Studies 217.

[185] Chiara Mosca and Chiara Picciau, 'Making Non-Financial Information Count: Accountability and Materiality in Sustainability Reporting' in Hugues Bouthinon-Dumas, Bénédicte François, and Anne-Catherine Muller (eds), *Finance durable et droit: perspectives compares* (IRJS éditions 2020) 175; Chiara Mosca and Chiara Picciau (6 February 2020) Bocconi Legal Studies Research Paper No 3536460 https://ssrn.com/abstract=3536460; Patrick A Hell, *Offenlegung nichtfinanzieller Informationen* (Mohr Siebeck 2020); cf on the pros and limits of disclosure Kraakman and others (n 62) 245–55.

[186] Joachim Hennrichs, 'Die Grundkonzeption der CSR-Berichterstattung und ausgewählte Problemfelder' (2018) 47(2–3) Zeitschrift für Unternehmens- und Gesellschaftsrecht 206, 229–30, finding the relevant matters 'only externally auditable and justiciable to a limited extent', this with regard both to the accuracy and, above all, to the completeness of the disclosures; the author articulates instead a fear of bureaucratization and instrumentalization for positive self-promotion ('greenwashing').

[187] cf International Accounting Standard Board (IASB), *Effects of Climate-related Matters on Financial Statements* (November 2020) https://ifrs.org/news-and-events/news/2020/11/educational-material-on-the-effects-of-climate-related-matters/. See also British Academy, *Final Report* (n 4) 37.

[188] Mayer, *The Governance of Corporate Purpose* (n 3) 10.

[189] See section II4c) below.

[190] In particular, art 29 of the CSDDD (n 130) on the civil liability of the companies and a right of full compensation. On the elements and legal consequences of this provision (as proposed) see the detailed analysis by Habersack and Zickgraf (n 107) 599–606. Based on a detailed economic analysis the authors come to a positive evaluation because of a reasonable reinternalization of the external effects (n 62 above). See ibid 567–99, 607.

They go much further in terms of content and addressees than the German Supply Chain Responsibility Act, which for its part covers indirect supplier relationships only in exceptional cases, and departs from the established independent contractor rule of the tort law of German and Anglo-American countries (shift of paradigm).[191] A key problem which the directive does not face is how to cope with state complicity in human rights abuses.[192] Also, the effect of a bureaucratization of the value chain and the probable consequences for economic concentration have not been addressed properly.[193] Experience from business practice shows that the corporations are only slowly beginning to adjust to the very significant new requirements.[194]

b) Inside requirements: rights, duties, and organization of the corporate organs
More far-reaching than such externally directed rules of conduct for the companies are the requirements for the internal organization of those companies and, above all, the personal commitment of the corporate bodies and other functionaries in the companies with regard to stakeholder interests, ESG, and climate protection.

In Germany, in particular, there is long experience of requiring board members (in the two-tier system, executive board and supervisory board members) to consider the interests of other stakeholders, namely employees, as well as the common good in their decisions—which therefore reaches beyond specific shareholder interests.[195] The German experience is that this legal rule gives the directors broad entrepreneurial discretion (business judgment rule). But this discretion is by no means a *carte blanche*, instead being limited by a number of preconditions, especially with regard to the required disclosure and conflicts of interests.[196] There is also extensive, well-established strict case law on the limits that the board of directors must observe with regard to corporate donations and other benefits if it does not want to incur liability for damages.[197] The decisive factor under corporate law is that the corporate interest takes precedence over the individual interests of shareholders and stakeholders, which follows from the concept of the corporation as a separate legal entity. This precedence is evident not only, but above all, in a company crisis. The European Commission's Proposal for a Directive had proposed that directors, when acting in the best interests of the company,

---

[191] Habersack and Zickgraf (n 107) 541–66. See the German Supply Chain Due Diligence Act (n 121) § 2 para 8, § 3 para 1 sentence 2 no 8, § 9.
[192] Davies (n 130) 26–30; Davies concludes (at 33): There is a risk of 'exit from host states by companies whose parents are subject to the due diligence obligation rather than any significant alleviation of the position of those abused'.
[193] Moritz Renner, 'Menschenrechts- und umweltbezogene Unternehmensverantwortung zwischen Kapitalmarkt und Lieferkette' (2022) Zeitschrift fur Europaisches Privatrecht 782, 797–803, 818–19.
[194] Michaela Balke, 'Zwischenbefund aus der Praxis zu den organisatorischen Herausforderungen der ESG-Richtlinien für Unternehmen' *Die Aktiengesellschaft* (20 October 2023) 732.
[195] See Rüdiger Veil, 'Stakeholder Governance Models and Corporate Interests Experiences from Germany' ch 5 in this volume.
[196] Hopt and Roth (n 70) § 93, comments 61–65, 90–96, 102–12; § 116 comments 60–62, 142–43; Klaus J Hopt, 'Conflict of Interest, Secrecy and Insider Information of Directors: A Comparative Analysis' (2013) 10(2) European Company and Financial Law Review 167. cf Guido Rossi, *Il conflitto epedemico* (Adelphi Edizioni 2003). On the reach of the business judgment rule see also n 70 above.
[197] Hopt and Roth (n 70) § 93, comments 210–11.

had a duty 'to take into account the consequences of their decisions for sustainability matters, including, where applicable, human rights, climate change and environmental consequences, including in the short, medium and long term'. Accordingly, directors would have been personally liable for such breaches of duty.[198] But such a duty coupled with personal liability met with broad criticism, and, in contrast to duties of the company itself, was ultimately not taken up by the final version of the Directive.[199] Such a duty would have gone beyond the well-established duty of the board concerning ESG risks for the company.[200]

In Europe, there are also many years of experience with corporate co-determination in the supervisory board, which has recently been considered also in the United States.[201] However, these proposals do not go as far as in Germany, with its quasi-parity employee participation in large German companies.[202] While limited employee co-determination on the board is now widely established and accepted in Europe, Germany's much more far-reaching co-determination remains controversial. It has blocked agreement on a relatively modest regime of European company law for decades and is by no means an 'export model', as is claimed by interested parties such as German labour unions and, in part, by the Social Democratic Party. It is far too inflexible and clearly in need of reform.[203]

In international discourse, there are various other model proposals, such as the establishment of special bodies in the company for ESG matters, for example an ESG officer or an ESG committee, or special ESG knowledge and requirements in terms of the composition of the board.[204] Many companies already do this in response to

---

[198] See arts 25(2) and 26 of the draft directive (n 130). They have been dropped. These articles left open the decisive questions of who has a claim (the company, the shareholders, or third parties) and who has standing. See Robert McCorquodale and Stuart Neely, 'Directors' Duties and Human Rights Impacts: A Comparative Approach' (2022) 22 Journal of Corporate Law Studies 605; Guido Ferrarini and others, 'The EU's Proposed Reform of Directors' Duties and the Missing Link to Soft Law' (2024) 25 European Business Organization Law Review 359.
[199] cf ECLE (n 136).
[200] See Norman T Sheehan and others, 'Overseeing the Dynamic Materiality of ESG Risks: The Board's Role' (2023) 35 Journal of Applied Corporate Finance 52. But see also Eva-Maria Kieninger, 'Zivilrechtliche Haftung für Sorgfaltspflichtverletzungen nach Lieferkettengesetz und Sustainability-Richtlinie' (2024) Zeitschrift für Wirtschaftsrecht 1037. Further literature in n 70.
[201] Senator Elizabeth Warren, Accountable Capitalism Act, s 3348, 115th Cong (2018), stating that the Act would be applicable to all firms with more than US$1 billion in sales; employees would elect at least 40 per cent of the directors, and the board must consider the interest of all stakeholders, not just of the shareholders. On the Warren proposal see Rock (n 2) 387–91; Bruner (n 35) 1262–66, but also pointing at the Volkswagen scandal, 1265; Strine (n 43) 9–10, proposing for large companies (with over US$1 billion in annual sales) the formation of a board committee on labour interests; Martin Gelter, 'The Dark Side of Shareholder Influence: Managerial Autonomy and Shareholder Orientation in Comparative Corporate Governance' (2009) 50 Harvard International Law Journal 129. See also the utopia of Kent Greenfield, 'Reclaiming Corporate Law in a New Gilded Age' (2008) 2 Harvard Law and Policy Review 1, 24, finding that all important stakeholders should be represented on the board. Contra Jens Dammann and Horst Eidenmüller, 'Codetermination: A Poor Fit for U.S. Corporations' (2020) 3 Columbia Business Law Review 870. cf also Leo E Strine Jr, Aneil Kovvali, and Oluwatomi O Williams, 'Lifting Labor's Voice: A Principled Path Toward Greater Worker Voice and Power Within American Corporate Governance' (2022) 106 Minnesota Law Review 1325.
[202] For details see Veil (n 195).
[203] See the reform proposals made by interdisciplinary experts 'Arbeitskreis Unternehmerische Mitbestimmung' (2009) Zeitschrift für Wirtschaftsrecht 885.
[204] Strine, Kovvali, and Williams (n 201); Philipp Jaspers, 'Nachhaltigkeits- und ESG-Ausschüsse des Aufsichtsrats' *Die Aktiengesellschaft* (5 May 2022) 309.

the pressure of institutional investors, the financial press, or the public, but also on their own initiative. More problematic is the inclusion of an ESG or stakeholder representative on the board, as requested in the reform discussion. In countries with labour representation on the board—in particular if parity or quasi-parity is required by law, as in Germany,[205] but also in countries with mandatory minority representation as in Italy[206]—this may have unwelcome consequences, such as splitting up the shareholder side of the board excessively. This is even more true regarding pleas to install a debtholder representative or even a public interest representative on the board.[207] By contrast, the consideration of ESG in the variable remuneration of board members is, as mentioned above,[208] already corporate practice in some instances. This is what the proposed European Directive of 2022 had taken up in view of the Paris Agreement, but has not been adopted in the final version.[209] Interesting also are proposals to give shareholders more say in the pursuit of ESG, not only through more information about it and the possibility of discussion and proposals in the general assembly, but through a broader dialogue between the board (including the individual directors) and institutional investors. The latter proposal, however, raises questions of equal treatment of other shareholders. Additionally, a mandatory resolution of the general meeting on ESG (a 'say on climate' parallel to a 'say on pay') could be envisaged.[210] The annual general meeting could even be opened up to certain stakeholder groups.[211]

## 5. Public Enforcement: State Agencies, Public Procurement, and the Attorney General

The actual enforcement of such proposals to take into account stakeholder interests, ESG, and climate protection raises numerous further problems that can only briefly be touched upon here. A basic distinction must be made between enforcement by government bodies and by private parties, although it is now generally agreed that both must be involved and fill their specific roles.

---

[205] See Veil (n 195).

[206] As to minority representation on the board, as required eg in Italy since the reform of 2005 see empirical data provided by Andrea Ciavarella and others, 'Who Looks for Sustainability? Diverging Interests within the Boardroom' (12–13 November 2022) Miami Herbert Business School.

[207] Paul L Davies and Klaus J Hopt, 'Non-Shareholder Voice in Bank Governance: Board Composition, Performance, and Liability' in Danny Busch, Guido Ferrarini, and Gerard van Solinge (eds), *Governance of Financial Institutions* (OUP 2019) 117. A less far-reaching proposal is to install stakeholder bodies in the corporation with an advisory function only, cf Pierre-Henri Conac, 'Le comité des parties prenantes' in Pierre-Henri Conac, *Mélanges en l'honneur d'Isabelle Urbain-Parléani* (Dalloz 2023) 57.

[208] See section III1 above.

[209] Proposed Directive (n 130) art 15(3); section II4c) above.

[210] Edmans (n 13) 206–208; cf ShareAction, 'Fit-for-purpose? The Future of the AGM' (January 2021) and references therein to the Companies Act, s 172. Contra Ferrarini (n 20) 108, because of the collective action problems; Fleischer (n 19) 184–85, identifying 'murky corporate governance clauses in practice' and up to now no 'informed decisions' being possible. See also Jill E Fisch, 'Purpose Proposals' (April 2022) ECGI Law Working Paper No 638/2022 http://ssrn.com/abstract_id=4079135, discussing the problems raised by intermediate stock ownership. For a survey on comparative law see Holger Fleischer and Philipp Hülse, 'Klimaschutz und aktienrechtliche Kompetenzverteilung: Zum Für und Wider eines "Say on Climate"' *Der Betrieb* (2023) 44.

[211] ShareAction (n 210), stating that a core list of stakeholder groups should be given the right to register.

State enforcement is carried out by public authorities. In this respect, the CSDDD provides that each Member State is to entrust one or more supervisory authorities with the task of monitoring compliance with business rules, and it stipulates that these authorities are to be given broad powers, including, for example, the power to investigate and impose sanctions.[212] Sanctions must be effective, proportionate, and dissuasive. Pecuniary sanctions are to be based on the company's worldwide net turnover.[213] Decisions of the supervisory authority imposing sanctions must be published.[214] National supervisory authorities are to cooperate in a European Network of Supervisory Authorities.[215] Corresponding activities on ESG and climate protection can also be seen in actions undertaken by the European Banking Authority (EBA), the European Securities and Markets Authority (ESMA), and the European Central Bank (ECB).[216]

A particularly severe state sanction is exclusion from the awarding of public contracts. This is explicitly provided for in the German Supply Chain Responsibility Act, and has been taken up in a somewhat milder version by the European Directive.[217] It is important that such an administrative exclusion be subject to judicial review.

The European Directive itself does not contain any criminal sanctions. This is partly because to date there is no uniform corporate criminal law in the European Union. However, the Directive foresees national rules on penalties, including pecuniary penalties, that must be effective, proportionate, and dissuasive. Pecuniary penalties shall be based on the company's net worldwide turnover with a maximum limit not less than 5 per cent of this turnover. This is harsh, but it is a provision that is used also in other areas of EU law. It should be remembered that using criminal law against enterprises and organizations as such is controversial and that there is a need for more empirical data regarding the extent and effectiveness of criminal sanctions imposed against directors. In any case, using criminal sanctions should be restricted to grave violations as a last means of enforcement.

## 6. Private Enforcement by Shareholders and Stakeholders

Private enforcement is particularly controversial. This is already true under the conventional shareholder value concept, but it is even more the case for stakeholder suits.

---

[212] CSDDD (n 130) arts 24, 25. On public enforcement of the German Law of 2021 and the CSDDD see Martin Burgi, 'Public Enforcement im Recht der nachhaltigen Unternehmensführung' (2022) 186 Zeitschrift fur das gesamte Handelsrecht und Wirtschaftsrecht 779.
[213] CSDDD (n 130) art 27(4).
[214] ibid art 27(5).
[215] ibid art 28.
[216] cf European Banking Authority, *EBA Report on Management and Supervision of ESG Risks for Credit Institutions and Investment Firms*, EBA/Rep/2021/18; European Banking Authority, *Action Plan on Sustainable Finance* (6 December 2019); ESMA, *Strategy on Sustainable Finance* (6 February 2020); European Central Bank (ECB), *Guide on Climate-related and Environmental Risks, Supervisory Expectations Relating to Risk Management and Disclosure* (November 2020).
[217] German Supply Chain Responsibility Law (n 121) § 22; CSDDD art 31: compliance must be taken into account 'as part of the award criteria for public and concession contracts'.

Under German stock corporation law, for example, executive and supervisory boards not only have entrepreneurial discretion, but they are also personally liable if they exceed it—although in principle only vis-à-vis their own company.[218] Direct liability towards third parties exists only in exceptional cases, namely if a law violated by the corporate body is a protective law for third parties.[219] Whether the latter is the case is rarely explicitly stated in the law in question; it is instead decided on a case-by-case basis with reference to existing court jurisprudence—and not for the act as a whole but for each individual provision which has allegedly been violated. This also means that under German corporate law there is no standing for individual shareholders, let alone all possible stakeholders. However, certain minorities can bring a court action so as to require that the company holds a (management or supervisory) board member liable.[220] The claim—common in foreign literature and sometimes even amongst German academia—that this approach has the consequence that in Germany board members, and especially supervisory board members, are only rarely held liable may have been true in the past, but it is no longer grounded in corporate reality since the various major financial crises. Indeed, it is actually highly inaccurate.[221] While it is indisputable that directors must also be subject to personal liability for their misconduct, the extent of personal liability is regulated very differently internationally, and it is a controversial topic in terms of legal policy, especially with regard to ESG obligations.[222]

Internationally, the situation is partly different. For example, the Canadian Business Corporation Act 1985 provides for shareholder suits by individual shareholders.[223] Most importantly, however, the number of international law suits related to environmental damage, climate change, and human rights is increasing dramatically today.[224] This goes hand in hand with the affirmative standing of non-profit associations, environmental groups, trade unions,[225] and, more recently, even of individual aggrieved stakeholders. According to the French Duty of Vigilance Law, stakeholders even have the right to bring pre-emptive claims.[226] However, such standing for everyone is highly problematic, especially if all possible jurisdictions are open to claimants based on both the place of violation and its effect. There is then a danger that companies will

---

[218] Stock Corporation Act, §§ 93, 116, covering members of the management board and those of the supervisory board.
[219] For details see Hopt and Roth (n 70) § 93, comments 623–34, 648–80.
[220] German Stock Corporation Act, § 147 para 1; Hopt and Roth (n 70) § 93, comment 623.
[221] Klaus J Hopt, 'Die Verantwortlichkeit von Vorstand und Aufsichtsrat: Grundsatz und Praxisprobleme: unter besonderer Berücksichtigung der Banken' (2013) Zeitschrift für Wirtschaftsrecht 1793.
[222] Favouring personal liability see eg John Armour, Jeffrey Gordon, and Geeyoung Min, 'Taking Compliance Seriously'(2020) 37 Yale Journal on Regulation 1; but see also Adams (n 159).
[223] Business Corporations Act 1985 (Can), s 238(d): 'any other person who, in the discretion of a court, is a proper person to make an application under this part'; see PM Vasudev, 'Corporate Stakeholders in Canada: An Overview and Proposal' (2013) 45 Ottawa Law Review 137, 141, 145–49; but this approach has not been followed up by other jurisdictions. See Fleischer (n 103) 425.
[224] Marc-Philippe Weller and Mai-Lan Tran, 'Klimawandelklagen im Rechtsvergleich – private enforcement als weltweiter Trend?' (2021) Zeitschrift fur Europaisches Privatrecht 573, with reports on the United States, Canada, Australia, UK, Italy, France, and the Netherlands; Marc-Philippe Weller and Nina Benz, 'Corporate Governance und Klimaschutz' (2022) 51(4-5) Zeitschrift für Unternehmens- und Gesellschaftsrecht 563. See also OECD, *Climate Change and Corporate Governance* (OECD 2022).
[225] See eg § 11 of the Germany value chain law (n 120).
[226] See section II4a) above, n 114.

be overburdened with years of litigation, even if a claim is unfounded. Even it cannot be excluded that a business niche may emerge for 'predatory E holders', as is the experience in Germany with 'predatory shareholders'. B only standing that is problematic; it is also the role of the courts. The climate change law suit against Shell in the Netherlands, in which a civil court ordered the Shell group to make very specific reductions in its climate-damaging emissions (at least 45 per cent by the end of 2030 relative to 2019 emissions), ordered in response to law suits by private associations and foundations,[227] was an international sensation and met with both vehement approval and vehement criticism. There are now numerous other similar proceedings.[228] On the one hand, in accordance with the view expressed here, it is certainly the case that in such a manner the enforcement of regulations for the protection of the environment, climate, and human rights is considerably promoted. On the other hand, due to the lack of clear and sufficient limits for such law suits, especially in terms of standing, the effort and uncertainties for companies are enormous. Above all, however, it is problematic when courts impose requirements on companies in individual proceedings between individual private parties, as in the *Shell* case. Understood properly, this is a matter for democratically legitimized legislatures, which have very different avenues for undertaking the necessary investigations and which are capable of taking measures across the entire sector and of more generally distributing the costs incurred.

Ultimately it remains to be seen how all these efforts may change the culture of corporate governance. The culture of the players involved in corporate governance—but also of the legislator, the courts, and society—may be the most important factor.[229] It may very well be that the culture in the United States and in Europe becomes more divergent as to shareholderism versus stakeholderism.

## IV. Conclusions and Theses

1. One of the oldest corporate law issues—for whom is the corporation managed?— has become one of the hottest public policy issues. The traditional idea, especially in the United States, is one of profit generation for shareholders (shareholder

---

[227] *Vereniging Milieudefensie and Others v Royal Dutch Shell plc*, Rechtsbank Den Haag (26 May 2021). In the meantime, Shell has changed its seat to the UK, presumably also in reaction to this judgment.

[228] Wolfgang Kahl and Marc-Philippe Weller (eds), *Climate Change Litigation* (C.H. Beck 2021); Holger Fleischer, 'Klimaschutz im Gesellschafts-, Bilanz- und Kapitalmarktrecht' *Der Betrieb* (January 2022) 37; Sarah E Light, 'The Law of the Corporation as Environmental Law' (2019) 71 Stanford Law Review 137; Stefanie Schmahl, 'Internationale Klimaklagen aufgrund von Menschenrechtsverträgen: sinnvoll oder vergeblich?' *Juristen-Zeitung* (24 March 2022) 317. For a collection of environmental law suits internationally see Sabin Centre for Climate Change Law, Columbia Law School and Arnold&Porter (n 107).

[229] cf Oliver E Williamson, 'The New Institutional Economics: Taking Stock, Looking Ahead' (2000) 28 Journal of Economic Literature 595, 596; Peter A Hall and David Soskice, 'Varieties of Capitalism: The Institutional Foundations of Comparative Advantage' in Peter A Hall and David Soskice (eds), *Varieties of Capitalism* (OUP 2001) 1, 13; Lund and Pollman (n 45) 2602–609. On boards and stakeholders and on enforcement see Paul L Davies and others (eds), *Corporate Boards in Law and Practice: A Comparative Analysis in Europe* (OUP 2013) 68–78, 78–79. On employee representation on the board cf also Paul L Davies and Klaus J Hopt, 'Corporate Boards in Europe: Accountability and Convergence' (2013) 61 The American Journal of Comparative Law 301, 339–46.

value). Yet the new trend holds: 'The purpose of companies is to produce solutions to problems of people and planet and in the process to produce profits, but profits are not per se the purpose of companies. They are derivative from purpose …'. Today there is a vivid battle between the shareholder value theory and the stakeholder value theory.

2. For financial institutions and other regulated companies, the regulators see the primary objective of corporate governance as safeguarding stakeholders' interests, in conformity with the public interest on a sustainable basis.

3. Historically, state concessions for corporations were granted only if a public utility could be established. Yet the concession system faded away, and the targeted pursuit of general interests was assigned no longer to stock corporations under stock corporation law, but to antitrust law, securities regulation, and other laws. With the ESG movement, this historical development seems to be reversing.

4. Prevailing economic theory defends the primacy of the shareholder as 'the most efficient operating principle'; profit maximization 'leads to value creation for all stakeholders of the company'; '(i)n addition tax and transfer systems can be used to redistribute economic value to nonshareholders'.[230] This leads to various individual arguments and rejoinders. From the side of behavioural economics and the social sciences, the main criticism is the externalization of costs and damages as projected onto stakeholders other than the company and the shareholders.

5. The classic fiefdom of shareholder value is Delaware. By contrast, numerous individual US states have been so-called constituency states since as early as the 1980s. The forthcoming and newly drafted US Principles of Corporate Governance will probably also provide for such an opening.

6. The corporate purpose movement demands that companies be legally obliged to formulate their purpose. It would then be the duty of the directors to manage the company according to this purpose. Yet this reform, supposedly 'an embarrassingly simple policy', is anything but simple and effective. This dilemma is confirmed when one looks at the French Loi Pacte law of 2019.
Extending mandatory public purposes to companies in non-regulated industries would require a fundamental reconsideration of the relationship between the state and entrepreneurial endeavour. If the choice of purpose is left to the shareholders, corporate purpose clauses are often too generic, and they are difficult to monitor; it may just mean a move from the business judgment rule to the 'benefit judgment rule'.

7. Legislators have various options for regulating ESG, corporate sustainability diligence and climate change. Prominent examples can be found in France with the Duty of Vigilance Law of 2017 and the Loi Pacte of 2019, and in Germany with the Supply Chain Due Diligence Act of 2021. The most recent movement in the direction of stakeholderism is the European Directive on Corporate Sustainability Due Diligence of 2024.

---

[230] Fisch and Davidoff Solomon (n 18) 1319; with further arguments at 1320–22.

8. Yet it is not only the setting of rules that is important; rather, it is the enforcement and enforceability of such rules that is perhaps of even greater significance. In this context, a whole arsenal of regulatory or legislative options with different possible effects as well as drawbacks emerges: (1) market discipline and self-regulation; (2) the code movement: comply and explain; (3) disclosure and auditing; (4) enterprise law with outside and inside requirements, in particular: (a) duties of the enterprise; (b) rights, duties and organization of the corporate organs; (5) public enforcement: state agencies, public procurement, the attorney general; and (6) private enforcement by shareholders and stakeholders.

9. In all of the jurisdictions mentioned, large companies are confronted with new and far-ranging duties of diligence and are effectively treated as vicarious agents for international law obligations that were originally addressed to states. What's more, obligations that are seemingly imposed only on larger companies are passed on by them to their smaller business partners (SMEs, trickle-down effect). The effects of the Directive on national and international competitions will be significant.[231] We can only strongly hope that these laws and policy efforts will have the desired and absolutely essential effects on human rights, the environment, and climate protection. Much will depend on the actual practice of implementation and compliance, in the end, on business culture and society.

---

[231] Mark J Roe, 'Corporate Purpose and Corporate Competition' (19 August 2021) ECGI Law Working Paper No 601/2021 https://ssrn.com/abstract=3817788; Moritz Renner, 'Menschenrechts- und umweltbezogene Unternehmensverantwortung zwischen Kapitalmarkt und Lieferkette' (2022) Zeitschrift für Europäisches Privatrecht 782; Thilo Kuntz, 'ESG: USA gegen Europa' (2024) Zeitschrift für Unternehmens- und Gesellschaftsrecht, forthcoming.

# 3
# Corporate Purpose: Theoretical and Empirical Foundations/Confusions

*Holger Spamann and Jacob Fisher*[*]

## I. Introduction

'Corporate purpose' is the talk of the town.[1] But what does it mean, what difference might it make in theory, and are there any data to support the theory?[2] Our answers are 'many things', 'relatively little', and 'virtually none'.

We mostly focus on corporate decision-makers' ultimate decision criterion, specifically the choice between social values and 'shareholder value', and on attempts to influence it through the law or the corporation's governing documents, be it by explicit mandate or implicitly through the corporation's governance structure.

We begin with the theory in section II. Pursuing social values will sometimes generate better social outcomes than profit maximization. However, the difference may be small. One reason is that individual firms' pro-social actions are often undermined by market substitution and value pluralism. Another reason is that direct regulation of externalities, binding contracts, and market demand constrain profit-maximization to respect most social concerns. The corporation's decision criterion matters only in the gaps left by these constraints. The biggest gap concerns equity investors, ie shareholders. By definition, equity has no legal rights to payment; it depends entirely on a corporate commitment to make at least some decisions, such as dividend payments, in their favour. Commitment is provided by structural governance such as board electorates rather than fiduciary duties, which we show to be not nearly as important or sociopathic as is often assumed.

---

[*] All internet sources were last accessed on 15 January 2024.

[1] cf Elizabeth Pollman and Robert B Thompson, 'Corporate Purpose and Personhood: An Introduction' in Elizabeth Pollman and Robert B Thompson (eds), *Research Handbook on Corporate Purpose and Personhood* (Edward Elgar Publishing 2021) ('Purpose has become the frontline of a wide-ranging debate over shareholder vs. stakeholder primacy and profit maximization vs. broader social purposes').

[2] cf Edward B Rock, 'For Whom Is the Corporation Managed in 2020? The Debate over Corporate Purpose' (2021) 76 Business Lawyer 363; Edward B Rock, 'Business Purpose and the Objective of the Corporation' in Elizabeth Pollman and Robert B Thompson (eds), *Research Handbook on Corporate Purpose and Personhood* (Edward Elgar Publishing 2021) 27 (distinguishing the legal mandate, finance academics' assumptions, the managerial perspective, and a political debate); Robert T Miller, 'Corporate Personality, Purpose, and Liability' in Elizabeth Pollman and Robert B Thompson (eds), *Research Handbook on Corporate Purpose and Personhood* (Edward Elgar Publishing 2021) 222 (distinguishing different philosophical and legal perspectives).

We then discuss the empirical evidence, or rather the lack of (good) evidence, in section III. The challenges to obtaining good evidence in this area are formidable: plausible effects are subtle and arguably systemic, and thus hard or even impossible to detect with convincing causal inference. What good evidence we have suggests at most modest immediate effects even of policies that many consider radical, such as employee co-determination.

Our reason to focus on corporations' ultimate decision criterion is that this is what policy makers possibly could and should influence.[3] In the empirical section III.1, we briefly touch upon other ways of understanding purpose that would be germane for management but not regulators. Businesses—legal or not—may operate more successfully if they develop and maintain a coherent organizational identity.[4] But if this is the case, corporate leaders and investors have strong incentives to create such an identity; regulatory intervention is unnecessary.

We briefly dispense with fallacious arguments denying a real choice between social values and 'shareholder value'.

On the 'shareholder value' side, an argument often associated with Michael Jensen is that a corporation—more specifically, its decision-makers—must have one single purpose because '[i]t is logically impossible to maximize in more than one dimension at the same time'.[5] The argument is correct as far as it goes (leaving aside the cognitive-behavioural question whether humans truly maximize in complex situations, whatever their avowed goal). It does not follow, however, that corporate decision-makers can only care about a single constituency such as shareholders. Mathematically, secondary goals can be specified as constraints in a constrained maximization problem, and multiple goals can be transformed into a single maximand by means of an aggregation/weighting function such as a social welfare function. Social welfare is hard to maximize, but so is shareholder value.[6]

---

[3] The stress here is on policy-makers, not on influence. In any understanding, corporate purpose is set by humans, albeit possibly different humans than policy-makers. Even writers who argue that the corporation has an (Aristotelian) purpose of its own accept that this purpose is defined by the corporation's community and thus, ultimately, humans. cf eg Robert C Solomon, 'Aristotle, Ethics and Business Organizations' (2004) 25 Organization Studies 1021.

[4] This is related to, but distinct from 'corporate culture', a set of values such as adaptability and integrity practiced inside the organization, which corporate leaders find very important. See John R Graham and others, 'Corporate Culture: Evidence from the Field' (2022) 146 Journal of Financial Economics 552.

[5] Michael C Jensen, 'Value Maximization, Stakeholder Theory, and the Corporate Objective Function' (2001) 14 Journal of Applied Corporate Finance 8, 10.

[6] At a minimum, maximizing 'shareholder value' involves a prediction of an action's complex consequences, including trade-offs between many intermediate goals (eg customer satisfaction vs. production costs). Perhaps 'shareholder value' is on average easier to maximize than 'social welfare' because the former takes fewer ingredients than the latter (but note that remote effects will get less weight, and may efficiently be disregarded altogether), or because, viewed dynamically as a repeated problem, the former gets some feedback from the stock market. But the additional computational and informational costs of pursuing 'social welfare' may be outweighed by the benefits. cf Dorothy S Lund, 'Enlightened Shareholder Value, Stakeholderism, and the Quest for Managerial Accountability' in Elizabeth Pollman and Robert B Thompson (eds), *Research Handbook on Corporate Purpose and Personhood* (Edward Elgar Publishing 2021) 91 (arguing that various measures other than stock price are already being used to incentivize managerial behaviour). For distributional questions (ie the division of profits ex post), welfare maximization is ill-defined (ie there is no maximum—all divisions are equally good) if one does not consider declining utility of wealth (see Robert T Miller, 'How Would Directors Make Business Decisions Under a Stakeholder Model?' (2022) 77 Business Lawyer 773); see section II.2.b). for a related argument that shareholder primacy is particularly compelling as an ex ante rule for distributions.

On the social values side, asking about 'the' corporate purpose—as if there were only one—suggests the false necessity that a broad 'social purpose' is the normatively right answer everywhere. We take for granted that policy-makers should create and regulate corporations only for the public interest. In ultimate pursuit of the public interest, however, policy-makers may set a different proximate goal for corporate decision-makers. In particular, policy-makers may *instrumentally* condone purely financial corporate objectives in the belief—*à la* Adam Smith—that the private profit motive unwittingly serves the public interest.[7]

Finally, any enthusiasm for well-sounding social purpose slogans should be tempered by the realization that some of the most pathetic companies were (in)famous for slogans exposed as hollow when the companies collapsed.[8]

## II. Theory of Purpose

What difference can the choice between various corporate purposes make, and how is it made?

### 1. Is Corporate Purpose Irrelevant?

Commentators from both sides of the spectrum have argued that, properly understood, there is *ultimately* no difference between pursuing corporate profit and pursuing the social good. (a) From the social side, a common refrain is that corporations and investors 'do well by doing good': doing the right thing ends up being the profitable thing to do.[9] (b) From the other side, Milton Friedman famously argued in 1970: 'The social responsibility of business is to increase its profits'.[10] To be sure, these two arguments are diametrically opposed regarding the *proximate* goal that corporations should pursue. (c) A third argument, however, is that this proximate goal does not even matter: substitution from or to other corporations in markets will offset any individual corporation's choice. All three arguments contain a kernel of truth.

---

[7] cf Adam Smith, *The Wealth of Nations* (MεταLibri 2007) 16 (first published in 1776) ('It is not from the benevolence of the butcher, the brewer, or the baker that we expect our dinner, but from their regard to their own interest').

[8] For a recent example, compare United States Securities and Exchange Commission, 'The We Company, Form S-1 Registration Statement' (draft filed 14 August 2019) 1 perma.cc/M5DK-8YKP> ('We are a community company committed to maximum global impact. Our mission is to elevate the world's consciousness') with Eliot Brown and Maureen Farrell, *The Cult of We* (HarperCollins Publishers 2022) (the company's main mission seemed to be to enrich its egocentric founder, and its main impact was to waste investor money).

[9] cf eg the very title of 'Who Cares Wins: Connecting Financial Markets to a Changing World' (World Bank 2004). This report coined the term 'ESG'. See Elizabeth Pollman, 'The Making and Meaning of ESG' (2022) ECGI Law Working Paper No 659/2022, 11 ff.

[10] Milton Friedman, 'The Social Responsibility of Business Is to Increase Its Profits' *The New York Times Magazine* (13 September 1970) 17.

## a) 'Doing Well by Doing Good'

In a trivial sense, 'doing well by doing good' describes most of what businesses do. To make money legally, businesses generally must offer a useful product and attractive employment.

Even when regulation runs out, such as sourcing inputs from less regulated countries, companies face long-term reputational constraints through consumer and employee choice. Companies vie for customers and employees through 'sustainable sourcing', 'fair trade', 'living wages', and the like. To the extent this is true, profit and welfare maximization coincide.

However, the interesting cases—the reason to debate corporate purpose—are those where private profit and social good diverge. Such cases surely exist. For example, even if pumping oil is socially harmful and frowned upon, a corporation whose sole asset is an oil well will make more money pumping the oil than shutting the well.[11] In general, regulation is incomplete, and it would be miraculous if reputational penalties always exactly offset the potential gain from doing bad. In these cases, the company must do less well by doing good—except to the extent *ex ante commitment* to doing good buys it valuable cooperation from others.[12]

To be sure, people make mistakes. If businesses underestimate the financial promise of 'good' products and technologies, then 'doing good' will do financially well because it offsets this mistake. There is no reason to suspect that people systematically make this mistake, however: they might just as well be mistaken in the opposite direction.

## b) Friedman's legitimacy argument

Charitably reconstructed, Friedman's argument was that conflicts between competing social goods or groups pose trade-offs, that these trade-offs are democratically decided through regulation, and that corporate executives illegitimately override this decision if, going beyond the regulation, they shift costs onto others such as shareholders (through reduced profits) or consumers (through higher prices).[13] In this view,

---

[11] It could sell the well, but the only profit-minded buyer for the well would be one who pumps the oil.

[12] See section II.2.a) below. The commitment caveat is specific to operating companies, which are our topic; it does not hold for investors' capital allocation. For capital, commitment is generally provided by binding contract, and the exceptions including relationship banking are irrelevant for standard portfolio investment. Investors thus must do (financially) worse by doing (social) good with their money, ie preferentially funding 'good' businesses. Indeed, reducing 'good' businesses' cost of capital tends to be the point of 'good' investment. Businesses' cost of capital and investors' return are two sides of the same coin, however: if one goes down, so does the other. See Cliff Asness, 'Virtue Is Its Own Reward: Or, One Man's Ceiling Is Another Man's Floor' *AQR* (18 May 2017) www.aqr.com/Insights/Perspectives/Virtue-is-its-Own-Reward-Or-One-Mans-Ceiling-is-Another-Mans-Floor>; Ľuboš Pástor, Robert F Stambaugh, and Lucian A Taylor, 'Sustainable Investing in Equilibrium' (2021) 142 Journal of Financial Economics 550; Lasse Heje Pedersen, Shaun Fitzgibbons, and Lukasz Pomorski, 'Responsible Investing: The ESG-Efficient Frontier' (2021) 142 Journal of Financial Economics 572, 573 ('restricting portfolios to have any ESG score other than that of the [mean-variance efficient] tangency portfolio must yield a lower maximum [Sharpe ratio]').

[13] Friedman framed most of his argument in terms of the 'property' right of the 'owners of the business', by which he meant the shareholders. But he also wrote: 'Insofar as his [ie the manager's] actions in accord with his 'social responsibility' reduce returns to stockholders, he is spending their money. Insofar as his actions raise the price to customers, he is spending the customers' money. Insofar as his actions lower the wages of some employees, he is spending their money ... But if he does this, he is in effect imposing taxes, on the one hand, and deciding how the tax proceeds shall be spent ... He becomes in effect a public employee, a civil servant ... If they are to be civil servants, then they must be selected through a political process'. Similarly, Friedman distinguishes the case of sole

deviating from profit maximization for an ostensible social good ends up hurting the true social good, democratically understood.

Friedman's view has become a punching bag. Many think that 'the problems'—especially climate—'are too urgent to wait on the slow course of political processes, that the exercise of social responsibility by businessmen is a quicker and surer way to solve pressing current problems'. Friedman anticipated this objection: the quote is from his 1970 essay. He rejected it because, in his view, 'it amounts to ... an assertion that those who favor the taxes and expenditures in question have failed to persuade a majority of their fellow citizens to be of like mind and that they are seeking to attain by undemocratic procedures what they cannot attain by democratic procedures'. If an overwhelming democratic majority agreed with a policy, then presumably it would already have been adopted. Salient policies left to managers will be the controversial ones.

The common rejoinder is that today's political process is 'broken' or 'dysfunctional', and thus its outcomes are not 'really' democratic. The premise raises deep factual and normative questions. At the very least, its suggested practical implication risks backlash. Consider the main lightning rod for much of the contemporary corporate purpose debate, climate change. Policies to curb it, such as (more aggressive) carbon taxes, have not been adopted because they have not garnered sufficient political support. Those that were adopted often faced serious popular resistance, such as the fuel tax increase that triggered France's yellow vest protests in 2018.[14] Against this background, is it legitimate and sustainable for wealthy corporate CEOs, directors, and shareholders (virtually all shares are owned by the top 1 per cent) to restrict the supply of fossil fuel, or to take other actions that increase product prices? Usually, coordinating—through common shareholder-owners or otherwise—to reduce output would be an illegal cartel. Arguing that (wealth-weighted) investors know better than the (equal-weighted) electorate at large is obviously problematic. Nor is it clear that, if decisions such as the (shadow) cost of carbon were put to investor votes, as some have proposed,[15] these votes would be any less 'dysfunctional' than political votes.[16]

---

proprietors not only on grounds that they spend their own money but also: 'In the process, he, too, may impose costs on employees and customers. However, because he is far less likely than a large corporation or union to have monopolistic power, any such side effects will tend to be minor.' Friedman was particularly concerned with the distribution of corporate profits, on which see section II.2.b) below.

[14] See eg Feargus O'Sullivan, 'Why Drivers Are Leading a Protest Movement Across France' *Bloomberg* (20 November 2018) www.bloomberg.com/news/articles/2018-11-19/-yellow-vests-why-france-is-protesting-new-gas-taxes.

[15] Oliver Hart and Luigi Zingales, 'The New Corporate Governance' (2022) 1 The University of Chicago Business Law Review 195; Eleonora Broccardo, Oliver Hart, and Luigi Zingales, 'Exit vs. Voice' (2022) 130 Journal of Political Economy 3101. They argue that shareholder votes resemble referenda, and that referenda are not as dysfunctional as (bundled) general votes.

[16] Since we wrote this sentence, the first clear signs of political debate migrating to shareholder votes have emerged. cf eg Vivek Ramaswamy, 'Our Letter to Chevron' *Strive* (6 September 2022) https://strive.com/strive-asset-management-letter-to-chevron/. For a proposal to import 'legitimacy-enhancing' procedural devices from administrative law see Stavros Gadinis and Christopher Havasy, 'The Fight for Legitimacy in Corporate Law' (2024) 57 University of California Davis Law Review 1581. It is questionable, however, whether corporate decisions could ever have anything like the legitimacy of public administrative decisions given that corporate decision-makers are privately appointed (even outside committees are ultimately appointed by corporate insiders).

A related criticism of Friedman is that corporate lobbying undermines regulation, such that relying on regulation to fix problems is circular and futile. But if so, then it is surely an inadequate remedy to call on the CEOs orchestrating the noxious lobbying to make social decisions themselves. The only reasonable request to them is to stop lobbying.

Friedman's legitimacy concern has no purchase, however, for the countless decisions that are out of the political spotlight or could not possibly be regulated effectively.[17] In neither case does regulatory inaction equal political endorsement, even in the most idealistic view of the democratic process. Social control of such behaviour is partly by way of moral norms, possibly enforced by social sanctions. Even shareholders probably would and certainly should not want corporations to disregard these norms.[18] Friedman agreed in principle, writing that managers' 'responsibility is to conduct the business in accordance with [shareholders'] desires, which generally will be to make as much money as possible while *conforming to the basic rules of the society*, both those embodied in law and those *embodied in ethical custom*' (emphasis added). However, Friedman also wrote that it was wrong for managers 'to make [corporate] expenditures on reducing pollution beyond the amount that is in the best interests of the corporation or that is required by law in order to contribute to the social objective of improving the environment'. This statement appears too broad. For example, the corporation may know about a novel chemical's toxicity long before any regulator. Should the corporation dump this chemical into the environment until the regulator finds out and prohibits it? From a welfare perspective, this would be inefficient. From a social and psychological perspective, individuals would not or at least should not do this, and probably would not want their corporation to do so either. Of course, this argument is only as strong as the moral norms are widely shared. (For the avoidance of doubt, this section is only concerned with abstract possibilities, not legal mandates and their enforcement, which raise a host of other issues considered below.)

c) Substitution effects

Friedman also touched upon an entirely separate mechanism that limits the effectiveness of individual pro-social actions in markets: substitution effects.[19] The forces of supply and demand work against both boycotts and preferential treatment. If demand for some product or service decreases because some buyers boycott it, its price will go down, attracting other buyers who do not participate in the boycott—and conversely

---

[17] See Einer Elhauge, 'Sacrificing Corporate Profits in the Public Interest' (2005) 80 New York University Law Review 733.

[18] There is psychological evidence that people do not feel responsibility for delegated decisions, and even strategically delegate to avoid responsibility. See eg John R Hamman, George Loewenstein, and Roberto A Weber, 'Self-Interest Through Delegation: An Additional Rationale for the Principal-Agent Relationship' (2010) 100 American Economic Review 1826; Björn Bartling and Urs Fischbacher, 'Shifting the Blame: On Delegation and Responsibility' (2012) 79 Review of Economic Studies 67.

[19] Friedman broached the issue in relation to fighting inflation: 'Will his [the manager's] holding down the price of his product reduce inflationary pressure? Or, by leaving more spending power in the hands of his customers, simply divert it elsewhere? Or, by forcing him to produce less because of the lower price, will it simply contribute to shortages?' See Friedman (n 10).

for preferential treatment. Similarly, if some producers increase production of some product because of its perceived beneficial effects, its price will go down, leading other producers to decrease their production—and conversely if some reduce production of harmful products. In the limit of perfect competition, individual consumption and production decisions have no effect whatsoever.[20]

We do not live in a world of perfect competition. Individual decisions do have consequences, especially those of large corporations with market power or consumer movements with collective market power.[21] In the chemical example above, the world will be better off if the company handles the chemical well—except in the rare case that the company cannot survive in this market if it bears the extra cost.

Another saving grace is that first movers may conjure the help of regulation. They may demonstrate what is possible (eg a clean technology). They have incentives to lobby for more stringent regulation to force competitors to incur similar costs or even exit.

Nevertheless, substitution forces are powerfully at work. For example, many government or privately held oil and gas producers are increasing production as large publicly held ones hold back under pressure from environmentally-minded investors. Truth Media launched as a reaction to Twitter's ban of certain speech (especially Donald Trump's). And so on.

Substitution in production is likely to lead to higher cost and thus reduction in total output. Substitution in *ownership* of productive assets may not even achieve that. If public oil companies 'reduce' *their* carbon footprint by selling their oil-producing assets to private companies, *the industry's* carbon footprint remains constant.[22]

Finally, what we might call substitution in purpose itself means that some purposes are not even well-defined, and hence implementable, at the level of an individual corporation. The prime example is reducing carbon emissions. Even if the world agreed on a percentage target of net emissions reduction (possibly 100 per cent, ie net zero), this would not mean that every individual firm should reduce their net output by this percentage. Some particularly carbon-efficient firms or industries might even have to *increase* their activity and thus emissions to reach this global goal. Individual firms are unlikely to be able to coordinate in this way, whatever their purpose. Even if they tried, they would hardly know how to do so without the guidance of a carbon tax or the prices of traded emissions certificates.[23]

---

[20] This limit is also the basis of the Fisher Separation Theorem that shareholders will unanimously prefer profit maximization regardless of their own consumption preferences and endowments. It holds only if markets are perfectly competitive. See generally Harry DeAngelo, 'Competition and Unanimity' (1981) 71 American Economic Review 18.

[21] Indeed, the price impact of large corporations' decisions was one reason why Friedman thought it illegitimate for them to pursue social issues. See quote at n 13 above.

[22] cf Anjli Raval, 'A $140bn Asset Sale: The Investors Cashing in on Big Oil's Push to Net Zero' Financial Times (6 July 2021) www.ft.com/content/4dee7080-3a1b-479f-a50c-c3641c82c142 (tallying sales of oil and gas assets from public companies to private ones).

[23] See generally Friedrich A Hayek, 'The Use of Knowledge in Society' (1945) 35 American Economic Review 519.

Substitution effects are a major reason why most major environmental and other issues are most effectively addressed through regulation. That said, to the extent substitution happens across national borders, large multinational companies may sometimes have an advantage over a national regulator.[24]

## 2. Corporate Purpose as Commitment

Let us now focus on the situations where corporate decisions do make a difference (no perfect substitution), corporate profits and some competing good are maximized by different actions (doing well and doing good diverge), and sacrificing profit for the competing good is legitimate (*pace* Friedman). Corporate purpose, as defined in section II, is a commitment to a decision criterion. Viewing corporate purpose as commitment shows how a broader corporate purpose may increase profits (a) but nonetheless underlines the importance of 'shareholder value' (b). Commitment is important, but shareholders arguably need it most.

a) Commitment and contractual incompleteness
We are not aware of a single firm that openly and unambiguously states that its only goal is to make money for its equity investors.[25] If one did, it would struggle to attract employees and customers. No doubt some firms are insincere. Even so, the question is why firms bother—why does their audience care?

One reason may be the audience's fear of exploitation. A firm that proclaims not to engage in exploitation will find it legally and psychologically harder to do so. The risk of exploitation arises because customers, employees, suppliers, etc. make firm-specific investments. Creditors hand over money in the expectation of being repaid (with interest) in the future. Employees work in the expectation of being paid at the end of the month. Customers pay the purchase price in the expectation that the product will function as advertised. They would not do this if the firm could not assure them that their expectations will actually be met.

The basic solution is contract. If the firm does not pay, creditors and employees can sue for payment under their credit and employment agreements. If the product is unsafe, customers can sue under their warranty. Contracts allow the firm to commit to honouring expectations in the future.

The problem is that contracts are often unavoidably incomplete.[26] Employees make long-term decisions—relocation, rotation, retention—for careers that cannot be mapped out in detail in the contract ex ante. Customers cannot assess products such as

---

[24] This depends in part on whether national regulators can prevent cross-border substitution through sourcing rules and/or multinational collaboration.
[25] The exceptions are private investment funds, but there the outside investors are better thought of as clients; they have no control whatsoever.
[26] There is an extensive theoretical literature arguing why contracts could possibly be incomplete between fully rational actors. However, nobody seriously doubts that contractual incompleteness exists in the real world.

advice even *after* using them (so-called credence goods). All contractual claims can be impaired in insolvency, the likelihood of which depends on myriad firm choices that cannot all be constrained in the contract. And so on. This requires non-contractual ways to create trust and, to justify the trust, commitment.

Traditionally, economists have located commitment in hard governance rights, including the allocation of residual discretion (ownership rights).[27] For example, financial institutions and hospitals commonly organize as mutuals or non-profits, arguably reassuring their customers that they will not exploit their superior knowledge to sell expensive but unnecessary services.[28] As another example, co-determination may reassure workers that the company will not engage in opportunistic lay-offs in bad times and will honour implicit promises of raises in good times. Perhaps fiduciary duties can create similar commitment through the threat of legal sanctions. We discuss these legal embodiments of purpose in section III.3 below.

Plausibly, commitment can also be generated by a firm's culture, which may in turn be supported by explicit purpose statements.[29] The more deeply engrained a firm's dedication to its customers, employees, creditors, and suppliers, the less likely the firm will be able to exploit them. Employees, including managers, might rebel or quit rather than engage in exploitation. To the extent customers, employees, creditors, and suppliers can distinguish genuine dedication from marketing slogans, better deals can be struck, and the firm may end up making *more* money by credibly committing not to exploit. In this sense—and in this sense only—aiming to do good may do better than aiming to do well, ie the firm may paradoxically maximize profits by not trying to do so.

There are two major caveats to this theory. First, a culture of not pushing customers, etc. beyond the implicit bargain can easily degenerate into a culture of not pushing, ie slack.[30]

### b) Shareholder primacy

Secondly, and relatedly, the constituency whose investment is least protected by hard claims and reputation is shareholders. The contractual claims of creditors, employees, and customers may be imperfect. But at least they are contractual claims. By contrast, equity investment is *defined by* the absence of contractual claims to payment. The whole business point of equity financing is flexibility without a fixed repayment

---

[27] The seminal articles are: Oliver E Williamson, 'The Vertical Integration of Production: Market Failure Considerations' (1971) 61 American Economic Review (Papers & Proceedings) 112; and Sanford J Grossman and Oliver D Hart, 'The Costs and Benefits of Ownership: A Theory of Vertical and Lateral Integration' (1986) 94 Journal of Political Economy 691.

[28] See generally Henry Hansmann, *The Ownership of Enterprise* (HUP 2000).

[29] cf Andrei Shleifer and Lawrence H Summers, 'Breach of Trust in Hostile Takeovers' in Alan J Auerbach (ed), *Corporate Takeovers: Causes and Consequences* (University of Chicago Press 1988) 33, 38–41 (arguing that to generate the trust necessary for long-term implicit contracts, 'shareholders ... seek ... train ... elevate ... and entrench ... managers' to whom 'stakeholder claims, once agreed to, are prior to shareholder claims').

[30] cf Armen A Alchian and Harold Demsetz, 'Production, Information Costs, and Economic Organization' (1972) 62 American Economic Review 777 (arguing that to prevent slacking, control should be vested in a residual claimant—someone who gets what is left over after all contracts have been paid); Lucian A Bebchuk and Roberto Tallarita, 'The Illusory Promise of Stakeholder Governance' (2020) 106 Cornell Law Review 91, 101 (stakeholderism 'would increase managerial slack and agency costs').

horizon. Moreover, equity financing is irregular, and much or all of it may be provided early in the firm's lifetime. By contrast, customers and employees—and to some extent creditors—are protected by the repeat-play of their interactions with the firm. For example, if the firm does not pay wages this month, employees are unlikely to show up next month. Even if, for example, the same customer only buys once from a firm, negative experiences can be shared and will influence the next customer's purchase decision. Not so with equity. Shareholder primacy—as an instrument, not an end-goal—responds to shareholders' predicament.[31]

Commitment to shareholder returns is particularly important for payouts. Given diminishing utility of wealth and the fact that shareholders tend to be wealthy, any dollar of corporate profit could generate higher utility as a donation to the poor than as a dividend to shareholders. However, if this ex post efficient distribution rule were adopted, nobody would invest in shares ex ante, ie corporations would not be able to raise equity financing.

Ex post inefficiencies are an unfortunate but inevitable byproduct of ex ante optimal arrangements in our imperfect, second-best world.[32] In a first-best world, we would eliminate all ex post inefficiencies, which make everyone worse off ex ante. In a second-best world, however, some ex post inefficiency is unavoidable because of agency problems or other reasons why management may not maximize firm value and distribute gains in accordance with expectations not memorialized in hard claims. A commitment to shareholders arguably minimizes these inefficiencies ex ante.[33]

Outside equity financing is an important concern even though much debate explicitly or implicitly foregrounds large existing firms that do not need it.[34] In most of the world, such firms are the norm and outside equity is an unimportant form of financing. Weakening their shareholders may seem to be costless from the perspective of the economy while reducing (large) shareholders' wealth and political power. The obvious counter is that such policies, or their expectation, may be the precise reason why outside equity financing is unavailable, as only powerful insiders are able to protect their equity investment.[35]

---

[31] See eg Oliver Hart, *Firms, Contracts, and Financial Structure* (Clarendon Press 1995) 9; Hart and Zingales (n 15) n 7; Miller (n 6) s A.

[32] cf Grossman and Hart (n 27) 691 ('inevitably creates distortions').

[33] For these reasons, we disagree that '[s]hareholder primacy is illogical'. Frank Partnoy, 'Shareholder Primacy Is Illogical' in Elizabeth Pollman and Robert B Thompson (eds), *Research Handbook on Corporate Purpose and Personhood* (Edward Elgar Publishing 2021) 186. It would be if shareholder primacy meant to maximize firm value ex post. But it does not, as even the term itself suggests.

[34] The treatment of outside equity is only as relevant as outside equity. If founders are sufficiently wealthy and risk-neutral to self-finance or finance with debt, the canonical principal-agent problem between outside investors and the founder/manager simply disappears. cf William H Meckling and Michael C Jensen, 'Theory of the Firm: Managerial Behavior, Agency Costs and Ownership Structure' (1976) 3 Journal of Financial Economics 305 (canonical model predicated on the need for outside financing). There might still be value in lodging control (and residual claims) in a party that has no other role in the enterprise. See Raghuram G Rajan and Luigi Zingales, 'Power in a Theory of the Firm' (1998) 113 The Quarterly Journal of Economics 387; Bengt Holmström, 'Moral Hazard in Teams' (1982) 13 Bell Journal of Economics 324. But see Mukesh Eswaran and Ashok Kotwal, 'The Moral Hazard of Budget-Breaking' (1984) 15 Rand Journal of Economics 578 (pointing out that the third party can be bribed). But this is a secondary concern.

[35] cf Mark J Roe, 'Political Preconditions to Separating Ownership from Corporate Control' (2000) 53 Stanford Law Review 539.

As emphasized above, a corporation serves as a nexus of many purposes. Not all corporate actors must perpetually and exclusively aim to increase shareholder returns. Such a crude incarnation of 'shareholder primacy' as an overarching ideology is not only unnecessary but also impossible to enforce in practice (see section II.3.b.aa) below). However, enabling broad equity investment requires compensating investors for their lack of contractual claims. This will generally require giving shareholders strong governance rights.

## 3. Institutional Underpinnings

Law—but arguably not fiduciary duties—and governance play a big role in shaping corporate purpose.

a) External regulation

External regulation—such as emissions standards, workplace safety rules, and prohibitions of certain drugs—is by far the most important. It constrains what corporate purpose can be. 'Contract killing at its best' or 'heroin for all' are simply not permissible purposes. Elaborate enforcement mechanisms implement such regulation, which has been growing steadily over the last century.

To be sure, regulation is not perfect. Purdue Pharma was prosecuted only long after it had started an opioid epidemic that killed hundreds of thousands, and its controlling shareholders may still walk away with billions. DuPont concealed the negative health effects of its Teflon production for decades and might have made a calculated cost-benefit decision that dumping was worth it given uncertain punishment.[36] Oil companies may never face a legal reckoning for their climate disinformation campaigns. Nonetheless, regulation's impact is profound. Without it, we would be having a very different, much more urgent debate about corporate purpose.

b) Fiduciary duties

Most legal debates around corporate purpose emphasize fiduciary duties, ie legal directives as to how managers and directors are supposed to exercise their discretion left by external regulation.[37] Specifically, the emphasis has been on shareholder primacy versus 'stakeholderism', ie a concern for various constituents beyond shareholders. Within shareholder primacy, a distinction is sometimes made between furthering shareholders' financial pay-offs ('shareholder value') or their overall wellbeing,

---

[36] Roy Shapira and Luigi Zingales, 'Is Pollution Value-Maximizing? The DuPont Case' (2017) National Bureau of Economic Research Working Paper 23866.

[37] For the avoidance of doubt, the law is crystal clear that corporate fiduciaries must comply with external regulation, and that they are liable to the corporation for any damage from non-compliance. cf s 102(b)(7)(ii) of the Delaware General Corporation Law (prohibiting exculpation of corporate claims against their fiduciaries for 'knowing violation of law') and the so-called Caremark doctrine imposing liability on directors for utter failure to maintain and monitor a compliance system (see generally Holger Spamann, Gabriel Rauterberg, and Scott Hirst, *Corporations in 100 Pages* (3rd edn, Self-published 2022) 45–46).

which would include the ethical concerns discussed above ('shareholder welfare').[38] Animating this debate is the fear that a pure norm of shareholder value maximization would force managers and directors to sacrifice potentially unlimited social welfare for infinitesimal shareholder wealth gains.

This emphasis and fear are misplaced. The primary reason is that fiduciary duties are not enforceable with this level of precision, ie the shareholder/stakeholder distinction makes no practical legal difference. Moreover, even the nominal content of existing fiduciary duties—that might matter to conscientious fiduciaries irrespective of enforcement—is far less shareholder-centric than the grotesque shareholder value norm sketched out above. 'Shareholder value' can have the feared nefarious effect only through a vulgar version that may have crept into managerial culture.

Our sole concern here is with duties of *corporate* fiduciaries. Investment trustees are subject to stricter fiduciary duties—notably lacking a 'business judgment rule'—and have less opportunity to justify 'social' acts with the profitability of long-term commitment (see section II.1.a)).[39] Presumably, this is the reason why investment funds and their managers consistently claim to pursue social objectives only instrumentally to manage risk.[40] However, the impact of investment trustees' stricter duties is mitigated by the fact that they do not make operational decisions in their portfolio companies, while the fungibility of money neutralizes most impact of capital allocation decisions (see section II.1.c)).

*aa) The shareholder/stakeholder distinction is not enforceable*

In corporate law, there is not a single case of managers or directors being held personally liable for furthering stakeholder interests over shareholder interests—ever, anywhere. (For *Revlon* injunctions, see section II.3.b).bb) below.) Indeed, we are not aware of a single lawsuit or prosecution even attempting this in recent decades.[41] This is hugely revealing because (aa) companies take pro-stakeholder actions without rhetorically tying them to shareholder returns all the time[42] and (bb) directors and

---

[38] Oliver Hart and Luigi Zingales, 'Companies Should Maximize Shareholder Welfare Not Market Value' (2017) 2 Journal of Law, Finance, and Accounting 247.

[39] See generally Max M Schanzenbach and Robert H Sitkoff, 'Reconciling Fiduciary Duty and Social Conscience: The Law and Economics of ESG Investing by a Trustee' (2020) 72 Stanford Law Review 381.

[40] See Hart and Zingales (n 38) 16.

[41] There have been cases where societal interests were in play, but the allegation was classical self-interest. cf eg *Kahn v Sullivan* 594 A2d 48 (Del 1991) (corporation made a large donation to a museum bearing its CEO's name; plaintiff alleged that directors were beholden to CEO; case settled for some additional conditions on the donation and no contribution by directors). Recently, to investigate a possible lawsuit against Disney's directors, a would-be plaintiff tried to obtain documents from Disney regarding its advocacy against Florida's 2022 'don't say gay' statute—advocacy that may have cost Disney tens of billions of dollars—but the judge flatly denied that request on the grounds that 'Delaware law vests directors with significant discretion to guide corporate strategy—including on social and political issues'. See *Simeone v The Walt Disney Company* WL 4208481 (Del Ch 2023) 1.

[42] For example, Exxon withdrew from Russia after Russia's invasion of Ukraine. Its press release announcing the withdrawal did not say a word about shareholders. See Press Release ExxonMobil, 'ExxonMobil to Discontinue Operations at Sakhalin-1, Make No New Investments in Russia' (1 March 2022) https://corporate.exxonmobil.com/News/Newsroom/News-releases/2022/0301_ExxonMobil-to-discontinue-operations-at-Sakhalin-1_make-no-new-investments-in-Russia. Instead, it talked about Ukraine, employees, and the environment. That said, the evidence suggests companies in general withdrew for PR rather than moral reasons. See Anete Pajuste and Anna Toniolo, 'Corporate Response to the War in Ukraine: Stakeholder Governance or Stakeholder Pressure?' (2022) ECGI Finance Working Paper No 839/2022.

managers are sued all the time for different reasons in the United States.[43] If it were possible to sue managers and directors for being 'too social', somebody would have done so.

But it is not possible, and for good reason. It is a general principle of corporate law that business decisions are not subject to judicial review (except in cases of pecuniary or comparably strong self-interest, which do not concern us here). In the United States, this is explicit in the 'business judgment rule'; elsewhere, it is often implicit in insurmountable procedural hurdles, even though duties may nominally be strict and capacious. This is uncontroversial; even shareholders voluntarily agree to it. As one of us has explained at length elsewhere, judicial review is simply not worth its cost given the tremendous difficulties courts would have in reconstructing the decision environment.[44]

With respect to potential conflicts between profits and stakeholders in particular, the line is usually blurred to the point of being invisible: which social action could not be justified by long-term reputational concerns?[45] Besides, how would a judge trade off ex post costs to one constituency with the need (to make ex ante promises) to give an 'adequate' return to another constituency? (In a second-best world, ex ante efficient arrangements often entail ex post inefficiencies.[46]) From a psychological and institutional point of view, it seems difficult to imagine that a judge would come down hard on a manager or director for furthering the social interest. (We distinguish pure transfers of money—donations—which are welfare-neutral as a first approximation.)

*bb) The nominal content of fiduciary duties in current law*

Even to the extent they are not enforced, fiduciary duties might exert influence because faithful fiduciaries do what they are told, or because they foster a culture. If so, the nominal content of fiduciary duties would matter independent of enforcement. We cannot exclude the possibility that managerial thinking has or had become infused with a vulgar version of 'shareholder primacy' that would have required managers to do great social harm in the name of shareholder profits.[47] We can, however, dispel the myth that anything like this vulgar version is current law.

Fiduciary duties differ by jurisdiction. We focus on Delaware—where most US corporations incorporate—because Delaware most strongly endorses shareholder

---

[43] For example, until recently, virtually every M&A transaction attracted a lawsuit in Delaware, where directors and managers were usually named as co-defendants, and many transactions are still litigated today in other fora. See Matthew D Cain and others, 'Mootness Fees' (2019) 72 Vanderbilt Law Review 1777.
[44] Holger Spamann, 'Monetary Liability for Breach of the Duty of Care?' (2016) 8 Journal of Legal Analysis 337.
[45] See eg Roland Bénabou and Jean Tirole, 'Individual and Corporate Social Responsibility' (2010) 77 Economica 1, 12.
[46] See n 32 and accompanying text.
[47] At least in the cross-section of countries, however, directors' and legal shareholderism are uncorrelated. See Amir N Licht and Renée B Adams, 'Shareholders and Stakeholders Around the World: The Role of Values, Culture, and Law in Directors' Decisions' (2021) LawFin Working Paper No 13, 25.

primacy among major jurisdictions.[48] Nevertheless, even in Delaware, the commitment to shareholder value is rather limited.[49]

Delaware courts routinely assert that managers and directors owe their duties 'to the corporation and its shareholders'.[50] On occasion, Delaware courts have been more explicit, stating that 'directors have a fiduciary duty to act in the best interests of the corporation's stockholders'[51] and even 'to maximize the value of the corporation for the benefit of the common stockholders'.[52] Perhaps most notoriously, in 2010, *eBay v Newmark* seemingly held that '[d]irectors of a for-profit Delaware corporation cannot ... eschew ... stockholder wealth maximization'.[53]

A close read of the relevant opinions, however, paints a much more nuanced picture. The ellipsis in the *eBay* quote stands for 'deploy a rights plan to defend a business strategy that'.[54] Thus, the holding was explicitly limited to use of the 'rights plan' also known as a 'poison pill', a rather peculiar anti-takeover device.[55] What is more, the defendant directors and controlling shareholders, Newmark and Buckmaster, won another count and thus the war because it allowed them to keep eBay off of the company's—craigslist's—board. The Chancellor handed them this win even though he explicitly found that '[f]or most of its history, craigslist has not focused on "monetizing" its site' and that defendants 'did prove that they personally believe craigslist should not be about the business of stockholder wealth maximization, now or in the future'.[56] The Chancellor did not hold that this vitiated defendants' dealings with eBay, who very much did want to 'monetize'. Much less did the Chancellor force defendants to change their and craigslist's ways—and, tellingly, eBay never asked for that. Ultimately, *eBay* thus shows almost the exact opposite of what the case nominally stands for: in the normal course of business, directors are free to pursue social goals.

Other Delaware cases dealing with shareholder primacy all concerned sales of the business, conflicts between shareholders and senior investors (creditors or preferred stockholders), or both, and, with one exception, involved a conflict of interest on the

---

[48] cf ibid at Table 1A (rating only the United States a perfect 10 on 'legal shareholderism'—the perception of law by local law professors—in a sample of eighteen countries comprising most of the world's large economies).

[49] Besides fiduciary duties discussed in the text, cf also s 122(9) of the Delaware General Corporation Law (explicitly granting corporations 'power to ... [m]ake donations for the public welfare or for charitable, scientific or educational purposes, and in time of war or other national emergency in aid thereof').

[50] See eg *Guth et al v Loft Inc* 5 A2d 503, 510 (Del 1939); *North American Catholic Educational Programming Foundation Inc v Gheewalla* 930 A2d 92, 99 (Del 2007). See Leo E Strine, Jr, 'The Dangers of Denial: The Need for a Clear-Eyed Understanding of the Power and Accountability Structure Established by the Delaware General Corporation Law' (2015) 50 Wake Forest Law Review 761, 768.

[51] *Unocal Corp v Mesa Petroleum Co* 493 A2d 946, 955 (Del 1985).

[52] *In re Trados Inc Shareholder Litigation* 73 A3d 17, 62 (Del Ch 2013); see also ibid 41 (same phrase, using 'residual claimants' instead of 'common stockholders').

[53] *eBay Domestic Holdings Inc v Newmark* 16 A3d 1, 35 (Del Ch 2010).

[54] One page earlier, the Chancellor similarly held: 'I cannot accept as valid *for the purposes of implementing the rights plan* a corporate policy that specifically, clearly, and admittedly seeks not to maximize the economic value of a for-profit Delaware corporation for the benefit of its stockholders'. Ibid 34 (emphasis added).

[55] Craigslist's board had unconventionally deployed the pill to prevent its shareholder eBay from selling its block of shares. The Chancellor's general statements—not tied to, albeit in the context of, the rights plan—were much softer: '[t]he corporate form ... is not an appropriate vehicle for purely philanthropic ends' and its 'standards include acting to promote the value of the corporation for the benefit of its stockholders' (emphasis added).

[56] ibid 8, 34, respectively.

board.[57] These details are important. As any lawyer knows, precedents are bound to their facts. The facts where shareholder primacy would be truly worrisome—eg a board deciding whether to pollute for the sake of shareholder profits—have never been decided, presumably for the reasons we laid out above. In the absence of conflicts or sales, Delaware courts routinely repeat that board discretion extends to social and political issues and 'addressing interests of corporate stakeholders'.[58]

In the investor conflict cases, the main concern would be that shareholder primacy, strictly applied, would force boards to 'gamble for resurrection': take inefficient risks in the hope of an upside for shareholders, at the expense of senior investors bearing the downside (since thanks to limited liability, shareholders' pay-off cannot be less than zero). In the *Gheewalla* case, the Delaware Supreme Court let the shareholder-appointed board get away with such a gamble, illustrating the importance of governance rights that we discuss below. But in the *Trados* case, the Delaware Chancery Court let the preferred appointed board get away with *not* taking the gamble.[59] Indeed, in *Quadrant Structured Products*, Vice-Chancellor Laster explicitly held that 'when directors make decisions that appear rationally designed to increase the value of the firm as a whole, Delaware courts do not speculate about whether those decisions might benefit some residual claimants more than others'.[60] No Delaware court has ever forced a board to take the gamble.

This leaves sales. *Revlon* famously held that in a sale, the board's sole duty is to get the highest price and 'concern for non-stockholder interests is inappropriate'.[61] This might force boards to pick among competing bids the one that offers an extra penny for stockholders even at great harm to other constituencies (eg lay-offs).[62] Unlike other fiduciary duty details, this one has practical teeth because bids tend to be easily comparable (the sole, limited uncertainties being closing certainty and, in some deals, valuation of the deal consideration), and courts have indeed enforced *Revlon* through injunctions. Nonetheless, the potential harm is limited, at least relative to the alternative. First, the board does not need to sell. *Unocal* allowed this for reasons including 'the impact on

---

[57] Conflicts, or alleged conflicts, notably existed in *Revlon Inc v MacAndrews & Forbes Holdings* 506 A2d 173 (Del 1986) (directors were afraid of personal liability if they did not help noteholders), *Kahn v Sullivan* (n 41), and *In re Trados Inc Shareholder Litigation* (n 52) (directors were preferred stockholders themselves). The exception is *Blackmore Partners LP v Link Energy LLC* 864 A2d 80 (Del Ch 2004), an LLC case where the board was not alleged to have a conflict in its decision to sell all the assets, turn over all proceeds to the creditors, and dissolve.

[58] See eg *Simeone v The Walt Disney Company* (n 41) 1, 11.

[59] *In re Trados Inc Shareholder Litigation* (n 52) 17. The court reached this result via a valuation that ignored the option value of the gamble for stockholders, ibid at 76–78, even though the court was clearly aware of the concept, ibid at 50 with n 25. The *Blackmore* case, 864 A2d 80, involved a similar situation but not a decision on the merits. On motion to dismiss, the court held: 'that the Defendant Directors approved a sale of substantially all of Link's assets and a resultant distribution of proceeds that went exclusively to the company's creditors raises a reasonable inference of disloyalty or intentional misconduct ... it would appear that no transaction could have been worse for the unit holders and reasonable to infer ... that a properly motivated board of directors would not have agreed to a proposal that wiped out the value of the common equity and surrendered all of that value to the company's creditors'. ibid at 86. It is an open question if the *Blackmore* court would have valued common stock as the *Trados* court did.

[60] *Quadrant Structured Prods Co Ltd v Vertin* 102 A3d 155, 187–88 (Del Ch 2014).

[61] *Revlon Inc v MacAndrews & Forbes Holdings* (n 57) 182.

[62] See Leo E Strine Jr, 'The Social Responsibility of Boards of Directors and Stockholders in Charge of Control Transactions: Is There Any 'There' There?' (2002) 75 Southern California Law Review 1169.

"constituencies" other than shareholders (ie creditors, customers, employees, and perhaps even the community generally).[63] Secondly, if the deal is unpalatable to the point of being repulsive even to shareholders, shareholders can vote it down.[64] Thirdly, shareholders could also vote down the alternative, a constituency-friendly deal for lower shareholder consideration.

c) Structural governance
aa) Board elections
If boards are effectively unconstrained by fiduciary duties, the key question is who appoints boards.[65] To be sure, some corporate decisions may require approval by shareholders or, rarely, by another constituency such as a works council in addition to, or in lieu of, board approval. Direct shareholder votes have been proposed for corporate matters of social concern such as a corporation's shadow cost of carbon for capital allocation purposes.[66] But most corporate decisions are made by the board alone.

Customarily, shareholders appoint the board. Indeed, equity investment without governance rights is unheard of.[67] This is not a coincidence, given our discussion of commitment see section 2.b): Board representation is all that shareholders have to get a return on their money.

That said, the need to give shareholders something does not imply that they need to get everything and be free to choose whomever they want. Most European jurisdictions reserve at least some board seats in some companies to employee representatives (so-called co-determination); there are also various levels of shop-floor representation (so-called works councils).[68] A few US companies, such as United Airlines, also have employee-appointed directors.[69] Commentators have advocated other constituency directors.[70] In addition, the last two decades have witnessed a trend towards mandatory quotas for certain groups, particularly women, on corporate boards, which restricts shareholders' choice. Employee representation explicitly aims to change the goal of the corporation from pure shareholder primacy to broader social goals.[71]

---

[63] *Unocal Corp v Mesa Petroleum Co* (n 51) 955.
[64] Mergers or sales of substantially all assets generally require a shareholder vote.
[65] cf eg Bebchuk and Tallarita (n 30) 139–47 (directors have incentives to favour their electorate, shareholders).
[66] Hart and Zingales (n 38); Broccardo, Hart, and Zingales (n 15). The latter show that voting ('voice') beats divestment ('exit') because it avoids substitution in capital markets (but not in product markets) (see section II.3.c) aa) above). Voting also avoids Friedman's legitimacy critique (see section II.3.a)a) above) as far as shareholder interests are concerned.
[67] Some companies issue non-voting stock, but they also issue voting stock that cannot receive payments unless the non-voting stock receives them too.
[68] See Simon Jäger, Shakked Noy, and Benjamin Schoefer, 'What Does Codetermination Do?' (2022) 75 Industrial and Labor Relations Review 857, 860–62.
[69] See United Airlines Holdings Inc., Amended and Restated Certificate of Incorporation, Part II.8.1 https://www.sec.gov/Archives/edgar/data/100517/000110465919037929/a19-12113_1ex3d1.htm.
[70] cf eg Paul Pfleiderer, 'The Milton Friedman Constraint: A Proposal for Improving Corporate Governance' (2020) Working Paper, Revised 2021 (proposing that one director be held liable for any fines imposed on the company, thus giving that director a strong incentive to prevent corporate wrongdoing).
[71] Mandatory quotas are sometimes advocated in the name of shareholder payoffs. This argument seems dubious: if it were good for shareholders, why wouldn't shareholders do it voluntarily? The argument is more likely a pretext to avoid censure by the US Supreme Court, whose case law allows consideration of group status, if at all, only in the name of diversity, ie to help everyone, not just the favoured group.

Putting competing groups on the board changes board dynamics.[72] Some fear that inevitable conflict on the board will render it dysfunctional. The empirical evidence reviewed below does not bear out the worst of such fears. In any event, any allocation of governance rights involves a trade-off. Frictions may be a price worth paying for better direction.

*bb) Anti-takeover/activist devices*

A frequently heard argument for anti-takeover and anti-activist devices is that they protect non-shareholder constituencies like employees and the environment.[73] The devices' direct effect, however, is merely to shift power from shareholders to boards and managers. The reason is that neither takeovers nor activists could succeed without support from other shareholders (provided minimal protections are in place to prevent 'herding' of shareholders through tactics like two-tiered front-loaded tender offers).[74] It is a priori unclear why this shift should benefit any constituencies other than managers and directors. Concern for constituencies may be pretext.[75] For example, a recent paper on 'Pills in a World of Activism and ESG' proposes to liberalize anti-activist pills generally, untethered from specific ESG concerns.[76]

d) Executive pay

Finally, a very important lever for the direction of the corporation is executive pay. It is generally set by the board.

In recent years, many companies have augmented their stock-based pay with ESG performance metrics.[77] In the preceding decades, executive pay had become heavily focused on the stock price.[78] This strongly oriented executives to the pursuit of shareholder value. To the extent that 'doing well by doing good' holds (see section 1.a)), stock-based compensation is socially, not just privately, optimal. Otherwise, partially or fully replacing stock-based compensation with other metrics can be socially beneficial, for example in countering excessive risk in banks.[79]

---

[72] Katharina Pistor, 'Codetermination: A Sociopolitical Model with Governance Externalities' in Margaret M Blair and Mark J Roe (eds), *Employees and Corporate Governance* (Brookings Institute Press 1999) 163, 191.

[73] cf eg Martin Lipton, 'Takeover Bids in the Target's Boardroom' (1979) 35 Business Lawyer 101, 130 ('The directors should consider the impact of the takeover on employees, customers, suppliers, and the community. National policy is a proper consideration').

[74] See eg Lucian Arye Bebchuk, 'The Case Against Board Veto in Corporate Takeovers' (2002) 69 University of Chicago Law Review 974, 999–1004; Lucian Arye Bebchuk, 'The Case for Increasing Shareholder Power' (2005) 118 Harvard Law Review 833, 883.

[75] See eg Bebchuk, 'The Case Against Board Veto in Corporate Takeovers' (n 73) 1023–25; Bebchuk and Tallarita (n 30).

[76] Caley Petrucci and Guhan Subramanian, 'Pills in a World of Activism and ESG' (2022) 1 The University of Chicago Business Law Review 417.

[77] Lund (n 6); Shira Cohen et al, 'Executive Compensation Tied to ESG Performance: International Evidence' (2022) ECGI Finance Working Paper No 825/2022; Raghuram Rajan and others, 'What Purpose do Corporations Purport? Evidence from Letters to Shareholders' (2023) ECGI Finance Working Paper No 904/2023.

[78] Kevin J Murphy, 'Executive Compensation: Where We Are, and How We Got There' in George Constantinides, Milton Harris, and Rene Stulz (eds), *Handbook of the Economics of Finance*, vol 2A (North Holland 2013) 211. Alex Edmans, Xavier Gabaix, and Dirk Jenter, 'Executive Compensation: A Survey of Theory and Evidence' in Benjamin Hermalin and Michael Weisbach (eds), *Handbook of the Economics of Corporate Governance*, vol 1 (North Holland 2017) 383.

[79] Lucian A Bebchuk and Holger Spamann, 'Regulating Bankers' Pay' (2010) 98 The Georgetown Law Journal 247.

A major problem is that ESG performance metrics are coarse at best. For shareholder value, the stock price is the ultimate object of interest, and the current stock price is at least a very good predictor of the long-term stock price. There are no obvious candidates for such a forward-looking, all-encompassing metric for social welfare or any of its other components.[80] This measurement problem exacerbates the ever-present concern that managers will abuse an ostensible pay-for-performance scheme to line their own pockets without performance.[81]

Nonetheless, ESG concerns should not be dismissed out of hand. An imperfect proxy may be better than no proxy. Only paying for stock price performance is also a weighting scheme: one that puts zero weight on other concerns. This may be the best weighting scheme if other concerns are negligible.[82] If they are large, however, and if sensible metrics for these other concerns cannot be found, then the standard result from the multitasking literature is not to give *any* performance incentives: paying for the one dimension that is measured—stock price—will create perverse incentives to neglect or harm the other dimensions.[83] It is thus fundamentally misguided to conclude from the difficulty of measuring and aggregating multiple dimensions of executive behaviour that one should focus on only one (stock price). It depends on the importance of the other dimensions.

## III. Empirics of Purpose

There is an overwhelming empirical literature about or, mostly, around corporate purpose. And yet, we have disappointingly little empirical knowledge about corporate purpose.[84] The reasons are twofold.

First, empirical studies about corporate purpose are objectively very difficult and often simply impossible. The theoretical predictions we discussed are subtle: they are context specific, concern complex organizations and their environment, more likely to manifest through culture than individual rules and firms, and most likely small. Small effects are hard to pin down (in statistical terms, studies will lack power), 'culture' is difficult to operationalize as an empirical variable, society-wide shifts are difficult to impossible to isolate from other social trends, and lab experiments have virtually no chance of credibly capturing countless, complex interactions between highly specialized actors in very special settings. Even when studies focus on individual companies,

---

[80] For an attempt to translate ESG goals into money see Aneil Kovvali and Yair Listokin, 'Valuing ESG' (2024) 49(3) Brigham Young University Law Review 706.

[81] See generally Lucian A Bebchuk and Jesse M Fried, *Pay Without Performance: The Unfulfilled Promise of Executive Compensation* (HUP 2004).

[82] See Robert P Bartlett and Ryan Bubb, 'Corporate Social Responsibility Through Shareholder Governance' (2023) 97 Southern California Law Review 1, 43.

[83] Bengt Holmström and Paul Milgrom, 'Multitask Principal-Agent Analyses: Incentive Contracts, Asset Ownership, and Job Design' (1991) 7 Journal of Law, Economics, & Organization 24; Lucian A Bebchuk and Roberto Tallarita, 'The Perils and Questionable Promise of ESG-Based Compensation' (2022) 48 Journal of Corporation Law 37, 62–63 attend to this argument only within ESG goals—arguing one should include no ESG goals in pay because one cannot include all—but not between ESG and profit goals.

[84] For a more optimistic take on the evidence see eg Alex Edmans, *Grow the Pie: How Great Companies Deliver Both Purpose and Profit* (CUP 2021).

there are the ever-present problems of endogeneity (reverse causation and omitted variables), limited empirical variation (too few firms change relevant attributes too rarely and too little—another source of low power), and noise.

To be sure, much of the literature is acutely aware of many or all these problems and tries to devise fixes, above all for the endogeneity problem. Not to put too fine a point on it, however, most of these attempts are not credible or answer very limited questions, as we will discuss in examples below. More generally, there is now widespread awareness of a credibility problem in empirical research in the social sciences. Part of the problem is that researchers have enormous flexibility in designing empirical studies in ways that materially affect results: variables, model, sample, statistics, and interpretation. Researchers may not make the right choice if there is one, or fail to reveal the fragility of their results when multiple choices could be justified. The other part of the problem is that the publication process selects for 'results', ie studies confirming rather than disconfirming an effect, leading to massive publication bias. Each part would be a problem on its own, but together they turbocharge each other as researchers consciously or unconsciously try various specifications to 'get a result' (also known as *p*-hacking). These problems have been well known in principle for a long time[85] but have recently (again) caught the attention of the profession,[86] in part thanks to powerful empirical demonstrations of the problem.[87]

For these reasons, making sense of countless, often contradictory results in all areas relevant to corporate purpose would be a fool's errand. The very source of the credibility problems just discussed is the difficulty for outside readers to assess the strength of a paper's evidence and the depth of the 'file drawer' of unpublished negative results. We merely review some papers that we find relatively informative and discuss some issues to sensitize the reader to the problems.

## 1. Corporate Purpose Proper

We start by noting a glaring absence. Prominent publications touting purpose's importance, such as that of the Enacting Purpose Initiative, do not cite any empirical studies of corporate purpose.[88]

---

[85] See eg Edward E Leamer, 'Let's Take the Con Out of Econometrics' (1983) 73 American Economic Review 31.
[86] See eg Garret Christensen and Edward Miguel, 'Transparency, Reproducibility, and the Credibility of Economics Research' (2018) 56 Journal of Economic Literature 920.
[87] See eg Joseph P Simmons, Leif D Nelson and Uri Simonsohn, 'False-Positive Psychology: Undisclosed Flexibility in Data Collection and Analysis Allows Presenting Anything as Significant' (2011) 22 Psychological Science 1359; Annie Franco, Neil Malhotra, and Gabor Simonovits, 'Publication Bias in the Social Sciences: Unlocking the File Drawer' (2014) 345 Science 1502; Wei Jiang, 'Have Instrumental Variables Brought Us Closer to the Truth' (2017) 6 Review of Corporate Finance 127; Raphael Silberzahn and others, 'Many Analysts, One Data Set: Making Transparent How Variations in Analytic Choices Affect Results' (2018) 1 Advances in Methods and Practices in Psychological Science 337; Todd Mitton, 'Methodological Variation in Empirical Corporate Finance' (2022) 35 Review of Financial Studies 527; Albert J Menkveld and others, 'Non-Standard Errors' (2024) 79(3) Journal of Finance 2339; Bernard S Black and others, 'The SEC's Short-Sale Experiment: Evidence on Causal Channels and on the Importance of Specification Choice in Randomized and Natural Experiments' (2022) ECGI Finance Working Paper No 813/2022.
[88] Enacting Purpose Initiative, 'Enacting Purpose Within the Modern Corporation: A Framework for Boards of Directors' (2020) https://enactingpurpose.org/assets/enacting-purpose-initiative---eu-report-august-2020.pdf,

To be sure, it is exceedingly difficult to study corporate purpose proper empirically. To study corporate purpose empirically, one would first need to define the concept, or more to the point, one needs to specify *which concept* one wants to study: a regulatory directive, a motivational slogan, or something else. Once defined, one would have to find empirically observable manifestations of the concept, ie to operationalize it. Easily observable facts will rarely match the concept of interest. For example, a corporation's 'purpose statement' on its website may have nothing to do with its true purpose as understood by its owners, managers, or employees—it may be mere make-believe.[89] Thus, a study of 'purpose statements' is exactly that, not a study of purpose per se. In any event, something like a 'purpose statement' would be completely endogenous. If 'purpose statements' correlate with corporate success, it may be because purpose statements facilitate success, or because success creates room for purpose statements, or because some third factor, such as a thoughtful workforce or management, is responsible for both. And that is assuming one has ruled out chance as an explanation. Finally, even if one could show that purpose or purpose statements *cause* success (or whatever else), the policy implications would be doubly unclear. First, purpose (statements) may only work for the few firms that have (voluntarily) adopted them, and might be useless or counterproductive for other firms and/or if all firms adopted them. (Indeed, forcing all firms to adopt them might destroy the distinguishing value even for the firms that initially adopted them voluntarily.) Secondly, a regulator can only set minimum requirements for mandatory purpose statements, which might end up being different from voluntary purpose statements. (The second problem does not apply to corporate boards contemplating corporate purpose.)

We have found one good paper—by Gartenberg, Prat, and Serafeim—that studies 'Corporate Purpose and Financial Performance' in for-profit corporations.[90] To be more precise, the paper studies one particular conception of corporate purpose, namely whether the corporation's employees perceive a sense of purpose in their work, measured through surveys prepared for Fortune's '100 Best Companies to Work For' competition. The paper finds no association of this measure with ROA (return on assets) or Tobin's Q (market value over book value of equity). The paper then uses 'exploratory factor analysis' to break its purpose measure into four separate parts. One of

---

cites no study whatsoever. A separate 'Bibliography' document on the organization's website, Enacting Purpose Initiative, 'EU Report: References & Further Reading Bibliography' (2020) https://enactingpurpose.org/assets/epi---eu-report-references---bibliography.pdf, lists under the heading 'Purpose' only programmatic books or articles by the project's two academic leaders (Colin Mayer and Robert Eccles), a law firm memo by one of the project's sponsors (Wachtell, Lipton, Rosen, & Katz), a letter from BlackRock's CEO Larry Fink, and a website advocating for corporate purpose (blueprintforbusiness.org). The Business Roundtable's 2019 Statement on the Purpose of a Corporation, Business Roundtable, 'Statement on the Purpose of a Corporation' (19 August 2019), https://opportunity.businessroundtable.org/ourcommitment/, cites no evidence either.

[89] cf Alex Edmans, Caroline Flammer, and Simon Glossner, 'Diversity, Equity, and Inclusion' (2023) ECGI Finance Working Paper No 913/2023 (a measure of diversity, equity, and inclusion constructed from employee survey responses is unrelated to specific initiatives or board level diversity).

[90] Claudine Gartenberg, Andrea Prat, and George Serafeim, 'Corporate Purpose and Financial Performance' (2019) 30 Organization Science 1. For non-profits see Zannie Giraud Voss, Daniel M Cable, and Glenn B Voss, 'Organizational Identity and Firm Performance: What Happens When Leaders Disagree About "Who We Are?"' (2006) 17 Organization Science 741.

these parts—whether management provides clarity—positively covaries with ROA and Q. Whether this association is credible, and if credible, whether it is causal, is an open question.

## 2. Fiduciary Duties

As we mentioned previously, legal debates around corporate purpose have largely centred on fiduciary duties. We expressed theoretical scepticism that the variations of fiduciary duties considered in these debates would make any difference (see section II.3.b.aa)). Ultimately, however, the question is empirical. Answering it convincingly would have immediate policy pay-off because legislators and courts directly control this lever.

One type of company that has more inclusive fiduciary duties than the standard 'shareholder primacy' business corporation (at least in Delaware) is the public benefit corporation (PBC). One might therefore think of comparing the behaviour of PBCs to other corporations. However, such comparison would not be able to identify the effect of fiduciary duties because of selection bias: different types of founders, etc. may select different corporate structures, and any observed difference between structures may be due to differences between the founders, etc. that tend to use them.[91]

To avoid such selection issues, the empirical literature has focused on the adoption of state statutes that change the content of fiduciary duties for all (normal) corporations in a state. Many US states passed so-called 'constituency statutes' allowing or mandating concern for non-shareholder interests in the 1980s or later. Researchers have attempted to trace the effect of these statutes in firm-level panel data, ie data on many firms from different states over time. The statewide statutory change is plausibly exogenous for almost all firms (in particular, there is no selection bias), and firms from states without a statutory change can serve as the control group. Notwithstanding, this literature is plagued by massive and mostly insurmountable methodological problems, in addition to myriad errors in individual studies.[92] The main systematic problem is that most corporations never experience a change in the applicable law. Delaware, home and legislator to more than half of US public corporations, never enacted a constituency statute, and neither did the runners up California and New York. Those that did usually did so in combination with, or at least close temporal proximity to, other related statutes.[93] Even controlling for the other statutes, the paucity of affected states

---

[91] That said, it is unlikely that the rules for PBCs make a meaningful difference. cf Jill E Fisch and Steven Davidoff Solomon, 'The "Value" of a Public Benefit Corporation' in Elizabeth Pollman and Robert B Thompson (eds), *Research Handbook on Corporate Purpose and Personhood* (Edward Elgar Publishing 2021) 68 (PBCs' organizational structure does not meaningfully differ from standard corporations, and most large PBCs' 'purpose statements' are vacuous).
[92] Emiliano M Catan and Marcel Kahan, 'The Law and Finance of Antitakeover Statutes' (2016) 68 Stanford Law Review 629.
[93] Jonathan M Karpoff and Michael D Wittry, 'Institutional and Legal Context in Natural Experiments: The Case of State Antitakeover Laws' (2018) 73 Journal of Finance 657.

creates great difficulty for statistical inference, such that only implausibly large effects would be detectable in the data, ie the studies lack power for small effects.[94] As we argued in the theoretical part, however, we would expect any effects to be small.

Bebchuk, Kastiel, and Tallarita take a different tack and examine deal terms in a sample of M&A deals involving firms from constituency states as sellers.[95] The official justification for adopting constituency statutes was generally to protect employees in such deals. Yet Bebchuk et al. find terms protecting employees in virtually none of the deals. Of course, this leaves open the possibility that boards used their discretion in less visible ways.

### 3. Structure

Unlike fiduciary duties, structure must make a difference, at least if we consider sufficiently strong variation. After all, the organizational differences between for-profits and non-profits, cooperatives and share corporations, etc. seem too large, and the distribution of these organizational forms across the economy too uneven, to think that they are exchangeable.[96]

Within the for-profit corporate form, however, the variation is much smaller, and the effects much less obvious. Short of nationalization, the biggest structural variation is co-determination (see section II.3.c.aa)). Nevertheless, even for co-determination, the best available evidence suggests that it barely makes a difference, if any—neither for shareholder nor for workers.[97] The best, if unsatisfactory, explanation of this surprising null-finding is that co-determination is part of a package of social-democratic policies, none of which is individually determinative.[98]

Until recently, the main live empirical debate regarding corporate structure was about corporations' vulnerability to takeovers and activists, ie anti-takeover provisions. Most of this literature considered the adoption of state anti-takeover statutes

---

[94] Allen Hu and Holger Spamann, 'Inference with Cluster Imbalance: The Case of State Corporate Laws' (revised 2020) ECGI Finance Working Paper No 644/2019.

[95] Lucian A Bebchuk, Kobi Kastiel, and Roberto Tallarita, 'For Whom Corporate Leaders Bargain' (2021) 94 Southern California Law Review 1467.

[96] See generally Hansmann (n 28). For an empirical example see Ryan Bubb and Alex Kaufman, 'Consumer Biases and Mutual Ownership' (2013) 105 Journal of Public Economics 39. That said, even there, differences are not always what one would think. For example, non-profit hospitals are not measurably more charitable than for-profit hospitals according to Ge Bai and others, 'Analysis Suggests Government and Nonprofit Hospitals' Charity Care Is Not Aligned with their Favorable Tax Treatment' (2021) 40 Health Affairs 629; Ge Bai, Hossein Zare, and David A Hyman, 'Evaluation of Unreimbursed Medicaid Costs Among Nonprofit and For-Profit US Hospitals' *JAMA Network Open* (14 February 2022) https://jamanetwork.com/journals/jamanetworkopen/fullarticle/2789009>.

[97] Simon Jäger, Benjamin Schoefer, and Jörg Heining, 'Labor in the Boardroom' (2021) 136 The Quarterly Journal of Economics 669; Christine Blandhol and others, 'Do Employees Benefit from Worker Representation on Corporate Boards?' (2020) National Bureau of Economic Research Working Paper 28269; cf Jäger, Noy, and Schoefer (n 68) 85 ('The conclusion suggested by the evidence [is] that codetermination in its current form has limited consequences for core economic outcomes').

[98] cf Jens Dammann and Horst Eidenmüller, 'Codetermination: A Poor Fit for US Corporations' (2020) 3 Columbia Business Law Review 870 (arguing that co-determination interacts with other policies such as collective bargaining).

and suffered the same methodological problems as the constituency statute literature discussed in the prior section. Some instead considered firm-level provisions such as dual-class and staggered boards, but these are endogenous (ie selected) and hence lead to the same selection bias as PBC status; there were also other problems.[99]

Today's main debate concerns the effects of board diversity. A recent review documents disparate results from dozens of papers.[100] In part, the disparity is explained by the variety of questions studied and not always clearly distinguished—ie by a disparity of effects. A first distinction is between effects on different groups, especially shareholders versus other stakeholders. Another distinction is between the variation and settings studied. It makes a big difference whether diversity is mandated or voluntarily adopted, by how much diversity increases how fast, and from what level (eg going from two to three directors in five years is very different than going from zero to parity in one). Similarly, effects are unlikely to be identical for different diversities (eg gender, race), countries, time-periods, and perhaps industries.

In other parts, the disparity of results is probably attributable not to disparity of effects but to the above-mentioned problems of the research machine. Diversity is a hot topic. Thousands of researchers are looking in all corners of the world whether some outcome occurred more or less often when some measure of some diversity was higher. Even if diversity has no influence on outcomes whatsoever, some outcomes are bound to be unevenly distributed across some measure of diversity by mere chance. Moreover, ideological commitments and (journals') prioritization of papers that 'find' an effect (as opposed to null-findings) will lead many researchers, consciously or unconsciously, to tweak specifications to 'find' an effect, and perhaps some journal editors to be less critical of the methods used. The consequence is randomness masquerading as scientific findings.

To give a sense of possible issues, we briefly discuss one well-known study, Ahern and Dittmar's study of Norway's 2003 gender quota, published in one of the top economics journals.[101] To identify the causal effect of the quota on firm value as measured by stock price changes, Ahern and Dittmar compared firms with varying gender gaps (possibly zero) before the quota: the greater the gap, the greater the required adjustment, ie treatment. Ahern and Dittmar found negative effects in the short-run (event study) and the long-run (fixed effect panel regression using Tobin's Q). An obvious limitation of Ahern and Dittmar is conceptual: if quotas address non-shareholder concerns, share value effects are at most part of the story, whereas if quotas address shareholder

---

[99] Emiliano Catan and Michael Klausner, 'Board Declassification and Firm Value: Have Shareholders and Boards Really Destroyed Billions in Value?' (2017) NYU Law and Economics Research Paper 17–39.

[100] Anzhela Knyazeva, Diana Knyazeva, and Lalitha Naveen, 'Diversity on Corporate Boards' (2021) 13 Annual Review of Financial Economics 301. Beyond diversity, the literature finds surprisingly little or consistent effects of board structure in general. See Bryce C Tingle, 'What Do We Really Know About Corporate Governance: A Review of the Empirical Research Since 2000' (2017) 59 Canadian Business Law Journal 292; Renée B Adams, 'Boards, and the Directors Who Sit on Them' in Benjamin Hermalin and Michael Weisbach (eds), *Handbook of the Economics of Corporate Governance*, vol 1 (North Holland 2017) 291; Ryan Krause and Matthew Semadeni, 'Apprentice, Departure, and Demotion: An Examination of the Three Types of CEO-Board Chair Separation' (2013) 56 Academy of Management Journal 805.

[101] Kenneth R Ahern and Amy K Dittmar, 'The Changing of the Boards: The Impact on Firm Valuation of Mandated Female Board Representation' (2012) 127 The Quarterly Journal of Economics 137.

concerns, the underlying rationale is probably that the market does not understand the value of diversity (or else the quota is arguably unnecessary), such that stock price reactions are simply beside the point. In any event, a careful reanalysis by Eckbo and others showed that Ahern and Dittmar's event study lumped together offsetting events (ie political news regarding the quota), that pre-quota variation in gender representation was correlated with other possible drivers of post-quota returns, and, most importantly, that cross-sectionally correlated errors created more noise than accounted for by Ahern and Dittmar.[102] Correcting these issues, Eckbo and others found neither short- nor long-term valuation effects. This does not necessarily mean that the quota had no effect on valuation—but none large enough to detect in the noisy data. And it may yet have important effects on other concerns, such as gender equality.

## 4. Owners

An evergreen empirical debate is about the effects of different types of owners, particularly financial investors—private equity and activist hedge funds—and, in recent years, 'common' or 'universal' owners that hold a broad portfolio of firms, particularly index funds. We defer 'sustainable investing' to the next section.

Activist hedge funds' main strategy is to purchase a company's stock, agitate for change, and then sell, on the expectation that the change will increase the company's stock price. Unsurprisingly given activists' persistence and success, academic studies confirm that activists do indeed tend to increase targets' stock price.[103] Allegations that this is due to stock-market short-termism presume an implausible degree of market inefficiency and find no support in the data.[104]

The more interesting question is activism's and private equity's effect on non-shareholder constituencies. On the one hand, it would not be surprising if that effect were negative because activists and private equity funds squeeze rents out of creditors, workers, customers, and others. On the other hand, constituencies may benefit from efficiency improvements brought about by activism and private equity. The evidence is mixed and, for private equity, depends on the type of target (private or public).[105] In

---

[102] B Espen Eckbo, Knut Nygaard, and Karin S Thorburn, 'Valuation Effects of Norway's Board Gender-Quota Law Revisited' (2022) 68 Management Science 4112.

[103] See Alon Brav and others, 'Hedge Fund Activism, Corporate Governance, and Firm Performance' (2008) 63 Journal of Finance 1729 (seminal empirical paper); Alon Brav, Wei Jiang, and Rongchen Li, 'Governance by Persuasion: Hedge Fund Activism and Market-Based Shareholder Influence' in Jonathan H Hamilton and others (eds), *Oxford Research Encyclopedia of Economics and Finance* (OUP 2022) (most recent survey).

[104] Null results for long-term stock returns are due to increased noise in long-term returns, not a disappearance of the effect. cf Ed DeHaan, David Larcker, and Charles McClure, 'Long-Term Economic Consequences of Hedge Fund Activist Interventions' (2019) 24 Review of Accounting Studies 536; Andrew C Baker, 'The Effects of Hedge Fund Activism' (2021) https://andrewcbaker.netlify.app/publication/baker_jmp/Baker_JMP.pdf (reporting such null results).

[105] See Brav, Jiang and Li (n 102); Hadiye Aslan, 'A Review of Hedge Fund Activism: Impact on Shareholders vs. Stakeholders' in Douglas Cumming and others (eds), *The Oxford Handbook of Hedge Funds* (OUP 2021) 283; Steven J Davis and others, 'The (Heterogenous) Economic Effects of Private Equity Buyouts' (2021) https://ssrn.com/abstract=3465723; Morten Sorensen and Ayako Yasuda, 'Impact of Private Equity' in Gordon M Phillips and B Espen Eckbo (eds), *Handbook in Economics: Corporate Finance: Private Equity and Entrepreneurial Finance* (North Holland 2023). See also Sophie A Shive and Margaret M Forster, 'Corporate Governance and Pollution

any event, activism's and private equity's effects ought to be evaluated at the economy-wide level, as companies may adjust behaviour to the mere threat of activism or takeovers, and adjustments at many firms may have ripple effects through the economy. Convincing direct empirical evidence of economy-wide effects is, however, virtually impossible to obtain.

Theoretical predictions of the effects of ownership overlap, particularly index fund ownership, are similarly ambiguous. The 'common ownership' literature analyses the malign anti-competitive effect: common owners have incentives to restrict competition between their portfolio firms. By contrast, the 'universal ownership' literature analyses the benign pro-social effect: universal owners have incentives to limit negative externalities.[106] Both literatures recognize that ownership overlap leads to partial internalization of cross-firm externalities, but they differ in the type of externality they emphasize. The empirics of 'common ownership' are hotly contested.[107] The ultimate effects of 'universal ownership' would be even harder to estimate. There is evidence that institutional ownership (most of which is presumably broadly diversified) leads to increases in portfolio firms' sustainability ratings,[108] but whether those ratings mean anything is another matter (see next section).

## 5. Sustainability: Disclosure, Performance, and Returns

Sustainability (or ESG or CSR—we gloss over differences between them[109]) is not the same as corporate purpose. Nevertheless, integrating sustainability into corporate purpose is arguably the main impetus of the purpose debate. There is considerable demand for 'sustainable investment'.[110] According to an industry group, the global sustainable investment industry now has US$35 trillion under management.[111] Institutional

---

Externalities of Public and Private Firms' (2022) 33 Review of Financial Studies 1296 (finding no differences between private equity owned and public firms, although both pollute more than other privately held firms).

[106] See Madison Condon, 'Externalities and the Common Owner' (2020) 95 Washington Law Review 1; Jeffrey N Gordon, 'Systematic Stewardship' (2022) 47 Journal of Corporation Law 627. But see Roberto Tallarita, 'The Limits of Portfolio Primacy' (2023) 76 Vanderbilt Law Review 511; Dhammika Dharmapala and Vikramaditya S Khanna, 'Controlling Externalities: Ownership Structure and Cross-Firm Externalities' (2023) Journal of Corporation Law Studies https://papers.ssrn.com/sol3/papers.cfm?abstract_id=3904316; Marcel Kahan and Edward B Rock, 'Systemic Stewardship with Tradeoffs' (2023) 48 Journal of Corporation Law 497 (questioning the efficacy of 'universal ownership').

[107] For reviews see Martin C Schmalz, 'Common-Ownership Concentration and Corporate Conduct' (2018) 10 Annual Review of Financial Economics 413; Martin C Schmalz, 'Recent Studies on Common Ownership, Firm Behavior, and Market Outcomes' (2021) 66 Antitrust Bulletin 12; Matthew Backus, Christopher Conlon and Michael Sinkinson, 'Empirical Studies of the Effects of Common Ownership' (2021) https://www.dropbox.com/s/cielt8q3uh5vkwe/BCS_ESECO.pdf?dl=0.

[108] Alexander Dyck and others, 'Do Institutional Investors Drive Corporate Social Responsibility? International Evidence' (2019) 131 Journal of Financial Economics 693.

[109] On differences see Pollman (n 9).

[110] See eg Samuel M Hartzmark and Abigail B Sussman, 'Do Investors Value Sustainability? A Natural Experiment Examining Ranking and Fund Flows' (2019) 74 Journal of Finance 2789; Michal Barzuza, Quinn Curtis, and David H Webber, 'Shareholder Value(s): Index Fund ESG Activism and the New Millennial Corporate Governance' (2019) 93 Southern California Law Review 1243.

[111] Global Sustainable Investment Alliance, 'Global Sustainable Investment Review 2020' www.gsi-alliance.org/wp-content/uploads/2021/08/GSIR-20201.pdf.

investors increasingly affirm that they care about issues like climate change,[112] and some have successfully engaged portfolio companies on such matters.[113] This warrants a brief mention of the key empirical debates in the burgeoning literature on sustainability and corporate governance.[114]

An initial problem is how to define and measure sustainability. Researchers have documented enormous divergence between different commercial sustainability ratings.[115] Worse, one popular rating is being rewritten retroactively, and positive associations between returns and ratings only exist in the rewritten data.[116]

Even setting aside measurement issues, interpreting the evidence is difficult, especially for returns. Many studies find that sustainable investments outperformed the market in recent times.[117] Does that mean that sustainable investments are better investments going forward? Not necessarily. First, 'past performance does not necessarily predict future results':[118] it could have been luck. In particular, an unexpected taste transition to 'sustainable investment' will temporarily generate high returns for 'sustainable' assets (see section II.1.a)).[119] Secondly, high expected returns are usually a reward for higher risk—why else would rational investors buy assets with different expected returns?[120]

Theoretical arguments that are legitimate in the abstract can unwittingly become tools to dismiss inconvenient evidence and thus, ultimately, undermine all evidence. As Gillan and others note, 'papers that draw similar overall conclusions ... do so from opposite results. For example, researchers have concluded a positive causal effect of ESG/CSR from results that indicate ESG/CSR produces high values today and low returns going forward. Others conclude a positive effect from results that indicate low values today and

---

[112] See eg Philipp Krueger, Zacharias Sautner, and Laura T Starks, 'The Importance of Climate Risks for Institutional Investors' (2020) 33 Review of Financial Studies 1067.

[113] See eg Elroy Dimson, Oğuzhan Karakaş, and Xi Li, 'Active Ownership' (2015) 28 Review of Financial Studies 3225; Caroline Flammer, Michael W Toffel, and Kala Viswanathan, 'Shareholder Activism and Firms' Voluntary Disclosure of Climate Change Risks' (2021) 42 Strategic Management Journal 1850; S Lakshmi Naaraayanan, Kunal Sachdeva, and Varun Sharma, 'The Real Effects of Environmental Activist Investing' (2021) ECGI Finance Working Paper No 743/2021.

[114] Stuart L Gillan, Andrew Koch, and Laura T Starks, 'Firms and Social Responsibility: A Review of ESG and CSR Research in Corporate Finance' (2021) 66 Journal of Corporate Finance 101889.

[115] Aaron K Chatterji and others, 'Do Ratings of Firms Converge? Implications for Managers, Investors and Strategy Researchers' (2016) 37 Strategic Management Journal 1597; Dane M Christensen, George Serafeim and Anywhere Sikochi, 'Why Is Corporate Virtue in the Eye of the Beholder? The Case of ESG Ratings' (2022) 97 The Accounting Review 147; Florian Berg, Julian F Koelbel, and Roberto Rigobon, 'Aggregate Confusion: The Divergence of ESG Ratings' (2002) 26 Review of Finance 1315; David F Larcker and others, 'ESG Ratings: A Compass Without Direction' (2022) Rock Center for Corporate Governance Working Paper.

[116] Florian Berg, Kornelia Fabisik, and Zacharias Sautner, 'Is History Repeating Itself? The (Un)Predictable Past of ESG Ratings' (2021) ECGI Finance Working Paper 708/2020.

[117] Gillan and others (n 114) 13. But cf the meta-analysis by Lars Hornuf and Gül Yüksel, 'The Performance of Socially Responsible Investments: A Meta-Analysis' (2023) 30 European Financial Management 1012 https://doi.org/10.1111/eufm.12439 (estimates are unstable, better publications find less).

[118] United States Securities and Exchange Commission, 'Mutual Funds, Past Performance' www.investor.gov/introduction-investing/investing-basics/glossary/mutual-funds-past-performance.

[119] See Rajna Gibson, Philipp Krueger, and Shema F Mitali, 'The Sustainability Footprint of Institutional Investors: ESG Driven Price Pressure and Performance' (2020) Swiss Finance Institute Research Paper No 17-05; Ľuboš Pástor, Robert F Stambaugh, and Lucian A Taylor, 'Dissecting Green Returns' (2022) 146 Journal of Financial Economics 403.

[120] Whether, and which, sustainable assets should be low risk or high risk is a surprisingly hard question. Some may appear to be a natural hedge against, eg climate change. However, the inverse is also possible. Certain sustainable assets—think expensive abatement technologies—may be economically viable only if the economy is doing very well and thus has a need for the technology. See generally Stefano Giglio, Bryan Kelly, and Johannes Stroebel, 'Climate Finance' (2021) 13 Annual Review of Financial Economics 15.

high returns going forward'.[121] Indeed, a researcher could insist on 'a positive causal effect of ESG/CSR' even if values were low today *and* returns were low going forward: after all, if the market gets it wrong today, it might get it wrong for a long time. Ultimately, Gillan et al.'s observation illustrates the impossibility of learning from data unless one commits to certain background understandings such as market efficiency (which humans arguably achieve, more or less, by triangulating and insisting on consistency).

On the regulatory side, the main corporate sustainability initiatives have been supply chain monitoring, which is best thought of as an extension of external regulation (see section II.3.a)) and sustainability disclosure.[122] Teasing out the consequences of mandatory disclosure is complicated.[123] As far as investors are concerned, one might think that mandated disclosure must be cost-benefit inefficient because investors—and the founders and managers they interact with—have incentives to pick the optimal disclosure regime, such that regulation can only make matters worse. Sustainability is a different matter, however, because it involves externalities. Some studies have found mandated sustainability disclosure to reduce externalities at the firm or local level[124]—which is encouraging but raises the usual question of whether the offending activities simply migrated to different firms and locations (see section II.1.c)). Christensen, Hail, and Leuz provide a thorough survey.[125]

## IV. Conclusion

Our review of theory (II) and empirics (III) leaves us sceptical that 'corporate purpose' can live up to the hype. If we gave in to the temptation of the follow-up question 'whence the hype', we might hypothesize that 'corporate purpose' is an elaborate decoy orchestrated by CEOs, boards, and their lawyers to relieve pressure from regulators and shareholder activists.[126] But we would have as little evidence for this hypothesis as for the importance of 'corporate purpose'.

---

[121] Gillan and others (n 114) 13.

[122] This is after the defeat of more far-reaching European proposals that were arguably not very sensible. cf Mark Roe and others, 'The Sustainable Corporate Governance Initiative in Europe' (2021) 38 Yale Journal on Regulation Bulletin 133 (critiquing the initial proposals). The US is only considering disclosure so far. cf The Enhancement and Standardization of Climate-Related Disclosures for Investors, Release Nos 33-11042 and 34-94478, 87 Fed Reg 21334 (11 April 2022); cf also Enhanced Disclosures by Certain Investment Advisers and Investment Companies About Environmental, Social, and Governance Investment Practices, Release Nos 33-11068 and 34-94985, 87 Fed Reg 36654 (17 June 2022).

[123] See generally Christian Leuz and Peter D Wysocki, 'The Economics of Disclosure and Financial Reporting Regulation: Evidence and Suggestions for Future Research' (2016) 54 Journal of Accounting Research 525.

[124] Hans B Christensen and others, 'The Real Effects of Mandated Information on Social Responsibility in Financial Reports: Evidence from Mine-Safety Records' (2017) 64 Journal of Accounting and Economics 284; Yi-Chun Chen, Mingyi Hung, and Yongxiang Wang, 'The Effect of Mandatory CSR Disclosure on Firm Profitability and Social Externalities: Evidence from China' (2018) 65 Journal of Accounting and Economics 169; Benedikt Downar and others, 'The Impact of Carbon Disclosure Mandates on Emissions and Financial Operating Performance' (2021) 26 Review of Accounting Studies 1137.

[125] Hans B Christensen, Luzi Hail, and Christian Leuz, 'Mandatory CSR and Sustainability Reporting: Economic Analysis and Literature Review' (2021) 26 Review of Accounting Studies 1176.

[126] cf Joel Bakan, *The New Corporation: How 'Good' Corporations Are Bad for Democracy* (Knopf Doubleday 2020).

# 4
# US ESG Regulation in Transnational Context

*Virginia Harper Ho**

## I. Introduction

Since the mid-2000s, environmental, social, and governance (ESG) concepts have gone mainstream. ESG has also grown beyond its roots in voluntary corporate responsibility initiatives for companies and socially responsible investments (SRIs) by niche investors.[1] Increasing investor demand for ESG-themed investment products has raised greenwashing concerns among regulators[2] at the same time as many governments are working to improve investor access to corporate ESG information so that financing can be directed to reach the goals of the Paris Accord.[3]

Internationally, these ESG regulatory initiatives are wide-ranging in their scope and ambition. They are directed at both the corporate and shareholder levels, including measures targeting asset managers and other financial intermediaries.[4] Still others target specific investment products, funds, and activities.[5] With regard to substance, ESG mandates have generally reflected a 'climate-first' approach, but the range of issues ESG encompasses is, like corporate social responsibility before it, dynamic and potentially broad, raising challenges for companies, investors, and regulators.

These developments push against long-standing regulatory silos and blur the historical dividing lines between 'private' and 'public', 'financial', and 'non-financial'. They have therefore raised questions in the United States and elsewhere about the authority of financial regulators to adopt rules that relate to climate, environmental, or workforce-related matters. In the United States, ESG mainstreaming and the advance of pro-ESG regulation internationally and domestically has sparked intense public debate that has further complicated regulatory efforts at all levels. In some cases, the concerns driving this debate resonate outside the United States, but in many respects, as

---

* All internet sources were last accessed on 15 January 2024.
[1] Sustainable investment accounted for approximately 13 per cent of all US assets under management in 2022. US SIF Foundation, 'Report on US Sustainable Investing Trends' (13 December 2022) www.ussif.org//Files/Trends/2022/Trends%202022%20Executive%20Summary.pdf.
[2] International Organization of Securities Commissions (IOSCO), FR08/21, 'Recommendations on Sustainability-Related Practices, Policies, Procedures and Disclosure in Asset Management 11-14, 28-35' (2021) (discussing greenwashing concerns).
[3] Sustainable capital allocation is a goal of the Paris Agreement. See Paris Agreement to the United Nations Framework Convention on Climate Change, art 2(1)(c) (12 December 2015), TIAS No 16-1104.
[4] IOSCO has published analysis on both the investor and asset manager dimensions. IOSCO, FR04/21, 'Report on Sustainability-Related Issuer Disclosures' (2021); IOSCO (n 2).
[5] Some of these regulations are discussed below in section II.1.

other contributions to this volume make clear, the US debate is being driven by issues that are linked to unique aspects of its domestic legal and political landscape.

This chapter surveys the major ESG and anti-ESG federal and state-level regulatory initiatives in the United States, although given the pace of new developments, it is not possible to do so comprehensively. It aims to explore the division between pro-ESG and anti-ESG regulation in the United States with reference to important features of the US institutional context. From a comparative perspective, this discussion may help explain why US reform efforts to integrate ESG concepts in new or existing legislation lag behind those on the other side of the Atlantic (and indeed the Pacific). Understanding this context may also help clarify where ESG integration can advance in the United States, as well as where it might require more fundamental normative shifts or legislative reform.

## II. The Transnational Context of ESG Regulation

This volume is inspired by the proliferation of ESG regulation worldwide. Indeed, ESG reporting mandates and other measures have now been adopted by over 130 governments worldwide with the support of prominent international organizations including the United Nations, the G20's Financial Stability Board, the Bank for International Settlements (BIS), and the International Organization of Securities Commissions (IOSCO).[6] Key among these developments are the climate and sustainability reporting standards introduced by the International Sustainability Standards Board of the IFRS Foundation (ISSB),[7] and the European Sustainability Reporting Standards (ESRS), which implement the EU's Corporate Sustainability Reporting Directive (CSRD).[8] The EU has also adopted a green taxonomy in order to define sustainability-related activities and products, and is developing a social taxonomy.[9] Many of these disclosure-based reforms directly or indirectly regulate corporate practice by requiring specific

---

[6] Global Reporting Initiative, United Nations Environmental Programme & University of Stellenbosch Business School, 'Carrots and Sticks: Beyond Disclosure in ESG and Sustainability Policy 18' (2023) www.carrotsandsticks.net/.

[7] International Sustainability Standards Board (ISSB), IFRS S1 General Requirements for Disclosure of Sustainability-related Financial Information (June 2023) www.ifrs.org/issued-standards/ifrs-sustainability-standards-navigator/; ISSB, IFRS S2 Climate-Related Disclosures (June 2023) www.ifrs.org/issued-standards/ifrs-sustainability-standards-navigator/.

[8] Directive (EU) 2022/2464 of the European Parliament and of the Council of 14 December 2022 amending Regulation (EU) No 537/2014, Directive 2004/109/EC, Directive 2006/43/EC and Directive 2013/34/EU, as regards corporate sustainability reporting [2022] OJ L322 (16 December 2022) (CSRD). The full suite of ESRS standards includes two general standards and ten separate ESG topical standards. Commission Delegated Regulation Supplementing Directive 2013/34/EU as regards sustainability reporting standards (and Annexes) (31 July 2023) finance.ec.europa.eu/regulation-and-supervision/financial-services-legislation/implementing-and-delegated-acts/corporate-sustainability-reporting-directive_en.

[9] Regulation (EU) 2020/852 of the European Parliament and of the Council of 18 June 2020 on the establishment of a framework to facilitate sustainable investment, and amending Regulation (EU) 2019/2088 [2020] OJ L198/13 (22 June 2020); Platform on Sustainable Finance, 'Final Report on Social Taxonomy' (February 2022) finance.ec.europa.eu/system/files/2022-08/220228-sustainable-finance-platform-finance-report-social-taxonomy_en.pdf.

changes in corporate governance and in the policies and practices of corporate boards and asset managers.[10]

This ESG regulation is not being created out of whole cloth but is often built on earlier voluntary standards, guidance, and soft law sources. In some areas, such as corporate reporting, ESG regulation is emerging in response to the fragmentation, inconsistency, and gaps of these voluntary sources. Voluntary reporting has historically been directed at a broader base of stakeholders than investors alone and is generally based on different materiality and assurance standards than those that companies must use in their annual reports.[11] ESG disclosure mandates are therefore intended to standardize reporting rules, compel companies to identify material ESG information for investors, and reduce greenwashing at the corporate level and in the market for investment products and services.[12] The EU and the UK are among the jurisdictions that have already adopted specific disclosure rules for fund managers and other investment intermediaries,[13] but the effectiveness of these rules depends on the quality of underlying corporate ESG information, and therefore on the success of corporate ESG disclosure reforms.[14]

However, full international alignment of emerging ESG standards, even in the area of disclosure, now appears unlikely, since designing ESG regulation requires critical choices about which firms, investment activities, or financial products will be within its scope, which ESG concepts will be covered by the rules, and how flexible or prescriptive specific regulations will be.[15] Answers to these questions depend upon whether the goals of the reform are focused solely on investor protection, market efficiency, and financial stability concerns, or also include the regulation of corporate operations and the promotion of sustainable finance and development. For example, divergence among jurisdictions has led the ISSB to bound ESG disclosure regulation more narrowly to ESG factors that are financially material to the firm and its investors—a 'single materiality' standard, while the EU, and to some extent, the UK, has adopted a 'double-materiality' standard that considers not only the financial materiality of ESG factors to the firm or investment but also the significance of the firm or investment's own environmental or social impacts on external stakeholders.[16] As I have observed elsewhere, these differences are also informed by how the corporate law of a given jurisdiction

---

[10] On these corporate governance implications see Virginia Harper Ho, 'Climate Risk Disclosure Line-Drawing and Securities Regulation' (2023) University of California Davis Law Review 1875, 1900–901.
[11] Virginia Harper Ho, 'Modernizing ESG Disclosure' [2022] Illinois Law Review 277, 288–95.
[12] IOSCO (n 4) 13–32.
[13] Regulation 2019/2088 of the European Parliament and of the Council of 27 November 2019 on Sustainability-Related Disclosures in the Financial Services Sector [2019] OJ L317/1 (SFDR); see also Financial Conduct Authority (FCA), 'Enhancing Climate-Related Disclosures by Asset Managers, Life Insurers and FCA-Regulated Pension Providers' (2021) www.fca.org.uk/publication/policy/ps21-24.pdf. The UK is also developing product- and entity-level disclosure rules. Financial Conduct Authority, 'Sustainability Disclosure Requirements (SDR) and Investment Labels' PS23/16 (28 November 2023); Extending the SDR Regime to Portfolio Management Consultation Paper CP24/8 (23 April 2024).
[14] See IOSCO (n 2) 6 (noting that 'any firm-level and product-level disclosures made by asset managers relating to sustainability are dependent on the quality, reliability and accuracy of ESG data from disclosures by corporate issuers and third-party data providers').
[15] Harper Ho (n 10) 1885–91; Harper Ho (n 11) 312–24.
[16] CSRD (n 8); FCA (n 13).

defines fiduciary duty and how the fiduciary duties of investor fiduciaries and asset managers are defined'.[17]

Across jurisdictions, there is broad consensus on the narrow view that at least some ESG factors are financially material to risk and return, both for firms and at the portfolio level for investors.[18] From this perspective, ESG disclosure regulation rests on traditional market efficiency and investor protection goals, and draws support from the standard literature on the advantages of mandatory disclosure systems in promoting transparency and creating a level playing field for investors and reporting companies.[19] Globally, ESG transparency mandates at their core focus on risk, which can be defined more narrowly in terms of financial risk to the firm itself or its investors, or more broadly to corporate and portfolio externalities.[20] With respect to climate risk (although not yet for most other ESG risks), an additional economic justification for mandatory ESG reporting is that the failure of financial institutions and other large firms to identify, manage, and possibly mitigate climate risk is itself a potential source of market instability and a systemic risk threat.[21] In the US capital markets, such risks may be exacerbated by the high concentration of institutional ownership and the broad, economy-wide exposure of these investors at the portfolio level.[22]

However, in the EU, sustainability regulation is intended not only to improve transparency around ESG-related financial risks, but also to achieve broader policy goals. These include reducing corporate greenhouse gas (GHG) emissions, climate impacts, and other social and environmental externalities.[23] ESG regulation therefore functions as a form of soft regulation to encourage companies and investors to operate more sustainably and to direct capital in alignment with international sustainable development goals. Whether investors will use ESG information in this manner or will continue to

---

[17] Harper Ho (n 10) 1886 and n 36.

[18] See eg Securities and Exchange Commission (SEC), 'Commission Guidance Regarding Disclosure Related to Climate Change' 75 Fed Reg 6290 (8 February 2010) www.sec.gov/rules/interp/2010/33-9106.pdf. See also Harper Ho (n 11) 280 and n 9 (surveying this literature).

[19] See eg John C Coffee Jr, 'Market Failure and the Economic Case for a Mandatory Disclosure System' (1984) 70 Virginia Law Review 717, 733–34 (discussing the inefficiencies of research in the absence of mandatory disclosure); Frank H Easterbrook and Daniel R Fischel, 'Mandatory Disclosure and the Protection of Investors' (1984) 70 Virginia Law Review 669, 680–85 (emphasizing improved corporate governance as a recognized benefit of mandatory disclosure); Zohar Goshen and Gideon Parchomovsky, 'The Essential Role of Securities Regulation' (2006) 55 Duke Law Journal 711, 718–19 (arguing that mandatory disclosure lowers agency costs).

[20] Virginia Harper Ho, 'Risk-Related Activism: The Business Case for Monitoring Nonfinancial Risk' (2016) 41 Journal of Corporation Law 647, 655–58.

[21] See Commodity Futures Trading Commission (CFTC), 'Managing Climate Risk in the U.S. Financial System 1-11' (2020) www.cftc.gov; Financial Stability Oversight Council (FSOC), 'Report on Climate-Related Financial Risk' (21 October 2021) home.treasury.gov/system/files/261/FSOC-Climate-Report.pdf; Basel Commission on Banking Supervision, 'Principles for the Effective Management and Supervision of Climate-Related Financial Risks' (June 2022) www.bis.org/bcbs/publ/d532.pdf.

[22] See generally John C Coffee Jr, 'The Future of Disclosure: ESG, Common Ownership, and Systematic Risk' (2021) 602 Columbia Business Law Review; Madison Condon, 'Externalities and the Common Owner' (2020) 95 Washington Law Review 1; Harper Ho (n 20) 655–58.

[23] See generally Communication from the Commission to the European Parliament, the European Council, the Council, the European Central Bank, the European Economic and Social Committee and the Committee of the Regions, Action Plan: Financing Sustainable Growth, COM(2018) 97 final (3 August 2018) (EU Action Plan) (noting the foundational role of disclosure in the sustainable finance transition); EU High-Level Expert Group on Sustainable Finance, Financing a Sustainable European Economy 6 (31 January 2018), ec.europa.eu/info/files/180131-sustainable-finance-final-report_en.

invest in environmentally riskier assets that may offer a higher short-term return is an open empirical question.[24]

Scholars have also questioned whether the economic goals of ESG and sustainable finance reforms can be achieved without due consideration for their ultimate effects on the real economy and their impact on the environment and climate change.[25] It is also therefore clear that regardless of whether ESG regulation is motivated only by financial considerations or also by broader climate or sustainability goals, the two are closely connected.[26]

## III. US ESG Regulation: An Overview

At present, major ESG regulation in the United States has been adopted or is pending at both the federal and state levels. These initiatives include ESG disclosure obligations for corporate issuers and for investment advisers, mutual funds, and ESG investment products; rules on the fiduciary duties of federally regulated pension funds; government procurement requirements, and climate risk guidance for banks and other financial institutions. At the same time, ESG has become a political flashpoint, sparking anti-ESG bills in Congress and legislation in many states that in some cases is directly at odds with measures already in force in others.[27] The following discussion surveys this complex regulatory environment. Part III then explores some of the legal constraints and political dividing lines that are behind these developments.

### 1. Federal ESG Regulation

Under the Biden administration, all federal agencies are part of a 'comprehensive, Government-wide strategy' to respond to climate-related risk and consider the level of investment needed to meet US commitments under the Paris Agreement.[28] In this effort, the US Securities and Exchange Commission (SEC), the Federal Reserve, and the Treasury Department, among others, have developed ESG policies or have incorporated ESG considerations into certain rule-making, enforcement, and policy initiatives. In addition, pending changes to the procurement rules for federal agencies would require significant federal contractors to disclose greenhouse gas emissions and climate-related financial risks, and to set science-based emissions reduction targets.[29]

---

[24] See generally Sebastian Steuer and Tobias H Tröger, 'The Role of Disclosure in Green Finance' (2022) 8 J Financial Regulation 1 (surveying the theoretical and empirical support for this expectation).
[25] See eg Iain MacNeil and Irene-marié Esser, 'From a Financial to an Entity Model of ESG' (2022) 23 European Business Organization Law Review 9-45.
[26] See IOSCO (n 4) 24–29 (discussing the relationship between financial and double materiality goals).
[27] Ongoing updates of federal and state initiatives are available at Ropes & Gray, 'Navigating State Regulation of ESG' www.ropesgray.com/en/sites/navigating-state-regulation-of-esg.
[28] Executive Order on Climate-Related Financial Risk, Executive Order 14030 (14 October 2021) www.whitehouse.gov/wp-content/uploads/2021/10/climate-finance-report.pdf.
[29] Federal Acquisition Regulation: Disclosure of Greenhouse Gas Emissions and Climate-Related Financial Risk (proposed), 87 Fed Reg 78910 (23 November 2022). Major contractors (ie those with over US$50 million

### a) Corporate disclosure regulation

At the corporate level, the most prominent federal ESG initiatives are the disclosure rules on climate-related financial risk adopted by the SEC in 2024.[30] In view of the inevitable legal challenges the rules were expected to face from both sides,[31] the SEC's rules explicitly state that their purpose is 'not to address climate-related issues more generally'[32] but instead to improve the 'consistency, comparability, and reliability of climate-related disclosures', in keeping with its core investor protection mission.[33] The rules are based on the framework developed by the Task Force for Climate-related Financial Disclosure of the G20's Financial Stability Board (TCFD), and the Greenhouse Gas Protocol Corporate Standard for GHG emissions reporting,[34] the same frameworks that ground the EU and the ISSB's climate disclosure standards.

However, the US approach is more flexible and generally less demanding than either the EU or the ISSB standards.[35] For example, the rules do not require companies to set climate mitigation targets, adopt climate transition plans or internal carbon prices, or use of scenario analysis, although if they do so they must then provide related disclosures.[36] The US rules limit required disclosure to financially material climate risk to the company itself.[37] In contrast to the EU corporate disclosure rules, they do not extend to corporate climate and environmental impacts. If adopted, the rules will extend more general disclosure requirements in the existing framework for corporate reporting that can elicit climate or ESG information if determined by the reporting company to be material to investors.[38]

In 2023, an SEC advisory panel proposed strengthening current disclosure rules on human capital management and workforce diversity.[39] Such reforms would expand on

---

in contract obligations) would also have to have their reduction targets validated by the Science Based Targets Initiative.

[30] Securities and Exchange Commission, 'Enhancement and Standardization of Climate-Related Disclosures for Investors' 89 Fed Reg 21668 (28 March 2024) (to be codified at 17 CFR pts 210, 229, 239, 249).

[31] At the time of writing, opponents, as well as environmental NGOs seeking stringent disclosure rules have challenged the final SEC rules and their effectiveness has been stayed pending resolution of the litigation. See *National Legal and Policy Center v SEC* No 24-2685 (8th Cir, docketed 1 April 2024).

[32] The SEC's final rules state that 'our objective is limited to advancing the Commission's mission to protect investors, maintain fair, orderly and efficient markets, and promote capital formation … not to address climate-related issues more generally'. See SEC (n 30) 21671.

[33] ibid 21669, 21671, and 21679.

[34] World Business Council for Sustainable Development & World Research Institute, The Greenhouse Gas Protocol: A Corporate Accounting and Reporting Standard (2015) ghgprotocol.org/sites/default/files/standards/ghg-protocol-revised.pdf; Task Force on Climate-Related Fin. Disclosures [TCFD], Final Report: Recommendations of the Task Force on Climate-Related Financial Disclosures (2017) assets.bbhub.io/company/sites/60/2020/10/FINAL-2017-TCFD-Report-11052018.pdf.

[35] SEC (n 30). The SEC's final rules seek to align more closely with the TCFD. See also Harper Ho (n 10) 17–18 (discussing these differences).

[36] SEC (n 30) 21915–18 (proposing 17 CFR § 229.1502–§ 223.1506).

[37] ibid 21914 (defining climate-related risk) and 21916 (proposing GHG emissions disclosure under new 17 CFR § 229.1504).

[38] These include, for instance, the discussion of 'known trends and uncertainties' in Management's Discussion and Analysis, required risk factor disclosures, and board risk oversight disclosure in corporate proxy statements. For detailed discussion of these provisions see SEC (n 18); see also Harper Ho (n 11) 334–40 (discussing these provisions).

[39] Recommendation of the SEC Investor Advisory Committee's Investor-as-Owner Subcommittee Regarding Human Capital Management Disclosure (14 September 2023) https://www.sec.gov/files/20230914-draft-recommendation-regarding-hcm.pdf.

the basic disclosures for material workforce-related information that the SEC introduced in 2020 as part of a broader review of the federal reporting regime.[40] Although not often considered within the scope of ESG reforms, the SEC has also adopted rules on cybersecurity risk management for public companies and has proposed similar rules for investment advisers that, like the climate risk disclosure rules, are intended to tighten corporate reporting on common operational risks and require greater oversight of these risks as a matter of corporate governance.[41]

b) Investor regulation

Several federal ESG measures are already directed at investment advisers and mutual funds, most notably the SEC's 2022 proposed disclosure rules for investment advisers and investment companies (ie mutual funds).[42] The proposed rules are designed to combat greenwashing and give investors 'consistent, comparable, and reliable' information on investment strategies that incorporate ESG factors.[43] If they are adopted, investment advisers would be required to support any claims that a fund, investment process, or investment or engagement strategy considers ESG performance factors or achieves ESG-related goals'.[44] Funds that more extensively integrate ESG factors into their investment strategies, set targets for ESG impacts, or have a particular ESG focus, would be required to provide additional detail to investors about their strategies, metrics, targets, and performance.[45] Those whose strategies include issuer engagement around ESG issues would also be required to provide information about their proxy voting and engagements,[46] and environmentally focused funds would be required to disclose portfolio-level GHG emissions, including carbon intensity measures.[47] In contrast to the EU's Sustainable Financial Disclosure Regulation (SFDR),[48] the proposed measures do not require disclosure on the negative externalities of investment advice and investment products, nor do they obligate asset managers to incorporate climate risk or other ESG assessments into their policies or investment analysis.

Beyond the specific ESG-related measures introduced above, the various federal and state regulations governing the fiduciary duties, information disclosure, and other compliance obligations of fund managers also inform their ability to integrate ESG factors into investment analysis and the exercise of shareholder rights.[49] As the SEC has

---

[40] 17 CFR § 229.101 (2020).

[41] SEC (US), 'Cybersecurity Risk Management, Strategy, Governance, and Incident Disclosure' 88 Fed Reg 51896 (4 August 2023); SEC (US), 'Proposed Rule on Cybersecurity Risk Management for Investment Advisers, Registered Investment Companies, and Business Development Companies' 87 Fed Reg 13524 (9 March 2022).

[42] SEC (US), 'Enhanced Disclosures by Certain Investment Advisers and Investment Companies About Environmental, Social, and Governance Investment Practices' 87 Fed Reg 36654 (17 June 2022) (proposed rule).

[43] ibid 36655, 36658.

[44] ibid 36659–73 (providing higher reporting requirements for funds defined as 'ESG-focused' funds, including those that seek to achieve a specific ESG impact (ie ESG impact funds)).

[45] ibid 36659, 36673–74.

[46] ibid 36673–76.

[47] ibid 36676–36685.

[48] SFDR (n 13).

[49] See generally SEC (US), 'Commission Interpretation Regarding Standard of Conduct for Investment Advisers' 84 Fed Reg 33669 (12 July 2019). See also Max M Schanzenbach and Robert H Sitkoff, 'Reconciling Fiduciary Duty and Social Conscience: The Law and Economics of ESG Investing by a Trustee' (2020) 74 Stanford Law Review 381.

previously clarified, these rules neither encourage nor prohibit them from considering ESG factors in pursuit of the client's objectives. In addition, investment advisers have fiduciary obligations to understand the client's objectives, comply with any client mandates, and act in the best interests of the client when exercising proxy voting rights or making investment decisions.[50] They may therefore be bound to consider ESG factors if directed to do so by the client. In addition, even in the absence of particular rules on ESG disclosure, mutual funds are already under general obligations to disclose their investment policies, voting policies and voting record, as well as relevant policies of proxy advisers and other third parties on which they may rely.[51]

The US Department of Labor (DoL), which has regulatory authority over private pension funds under the Employee Retirement and Income Security Act of 1974 (ERISA),[52] has also had to consider whether pension fund trustees may consider ESG factors bearing on financial risk and return when making investment, voting, and engagement decisions, a question that has bedevilled successive administrations. The US Supreme Court has previously determined that ERISA fiduciaries' obligation to act in the 'sole interest' of beneficiaries refers to beneficiaries' 'financial benefits',[53] but some plan fiduciaries had read the DoL's prior guidance as preventing them from considering ESG factors even on economic grounds.[54] In 2022, the DoL's final rules on 'prudence and loyalty in selecting plan investments and exercising shareholder rights' clarified that financially relevant ESG factors may be taken into account, and that plan fiduciaries may choose economically targeted investments in part for 'collateral benefits' such as ESG considerations where two investments offer equal financial benefits.[55] Notably, the DoL's 2022 rule does not *require* ERISA fiduciaries to consider ESG factors, and the DoL's long-standing position, consistent with the Supreme Court's interpretation, is that ERISA fiduciaries must not take account of ESG factors to achieve non-economic goals, nor may they adopt proxy voting or engagement practices that sacrifice risk-adjusted returns to plan beneficiaries.[56]

c) Investment product regulation and standards

At the level of investment products and services, the EU and in over twenty other jurisdictions, have developed 'taxonomies' to define 'sustainable' or 'green' investment products and activities.[57] In the United States, by contrast, standards for sustainable

---

[50] See SEC (US) (n 49) 33672–74.

[51] SEC (US), 'Disclosure of Proxy Voting Policies and Proxy Voting Records by Registered Management Investment Companies' 68 Fed Reg 6563 (7 February 2003).

[52] Pub L No 93-406, 88 Stat 829 (codified as amended at 29 USC, §§ 1001–1461 and in scattered sections of 5, 18, and 26 USC).

[53] Schanzenbach and Sitkoff (n 49) 403–405 and n 110 (citing *Fifth Third Bancorp v Dudenhoeffer* 134 S Ct 2459, 2468 (2014) for its interpretation of 29 USC § 110(a)(1)(A)(i)–(ii)).

[54] US Department of Labor (DoL), 'Prudence and Loyalty in Selecting Plan Investments and Exercising Shareholder Rights' 87 Fed Reg 73822, 73826–27 (1 December 2022).

[55] ibid 73822, 73827, 73835–37.

[56] ibid 73825–28.

[57] Annex to International Platform on Sustainability Finance (IPSF), Common Ground Taxonomy—Climate Change Mitigation Instruction Report 35–43 (3 June 2022) finance.ec.europa.eu/system/files/2022-06/220603-international-platform-sustainable-finance-common-ground-taxonomy-instruction-report_en.pdf, Annex (identifying these jurisdictions).

investment products, including green bonds, have not been set by regulation but by voluntary standards developed by private industry. These include, for example, the International Capital Market Association (ICMA)'s suite of principles for green bonds and other sustainable investment products,[58] as well as the Global ESG Disclosure Standards for Investment Products, developed by the CFA Institute.[59] However, in contrast to the EU's SFDR, all of these standards are voluntary and are directed solely at investment products, not at the conduct or reporting obligations of issuers or asset managers.[60]

In 2023, the SEC adopted its sole ESG product-level regulation to date, which amends an existing Investment Company Act rule regulating investment fund names.[61] The amendment was prompted in part by the SEC's concerns about greenwashing by funds claiming to adopt ESG strategies or policies and then failing to follow them.[62] In line with US regulators' general deference to market innovation, the amendments do not *require* funds to adopt ESG investment strategies, prohibit any particular fund strategy, nor define what is 'green' or 'sustainable'. In contrast to taxonomy regulations adopted elsewhere, the Names Rule amendments only require that funds whose names include such terms or other terms that suggest an investment focus must disclose to investors in the fund prospectus how such terms are defined and must report quarterly on the value of the holdings considered to satisfy the criteria that justify the funds' name.[63]

d) Systemic risk

Finally, in addition to the SEC's ESG rule-making efforts, the Federal Reserve Board, together with other financial regulators, has issued principles for climate-related financial risk management for the largest financial institutions (ie those with over US$100 billion in assets).[64] The Financial Stability Oversight Council (FSOC), which

---

[58] ICMA, 'The Principles, Guidelines and Handbooks' (2023) www.icmagroup.org/sustainable-finance/the-principles-guidelines-and-handbooks/.

[59] CFA Institute, 'Global ESG Disclosure Standards for Investment Products' (June 2022) www.cfainstitute.org/-/media/documents/ESG-standards/Global-ESG-Disclosure-Standards-for-Investment-Products-Handbook.pdf. These standards are 'global' in the sense that they are intended to apply across all investment vehicles, asset classes, ESG approaches, and investment strategies: ibid vii. Their purpose is to 'facilitate fair representation and full disclosure of an investment product's consideration of ESG issues in [terms of] its objectives, investment process, or stewardship activities'.

[60] The CFA Institute has developed guidance to explain how its standards align with the SFDR. CFA Institute, 'Global ESG Disclosure Standards for Investment Products: Sustainable Finance Disclosure Regulation (SFDR) Cross-Reference' (November 2021) www.cfainstitute.org/-/media/documents/ESG-standards/Global-ESG-Disclosure-Standard-for-Investment-Products---SFDR-Cross-Reference.pdf.

[61] Investment Company Names, 88 Fed Reg 70436 (11 October 2023) (to be codified at 17 CFR pts 230, 232, 239, 270, 274) (amending Rule 35d-1 of the Investment Company Act).

[62] ibid 70438–40. In 2021, the SEC created a Climate and ESG Task Force to examine investment advisers' and funds' disclosure and adherence to their stated ESG strategies. 'SEC Announces Enforcement Task Force Focused on Climate and ESG Issues' (4 March 2021) www.sec.gov/news/press-release/2021-42.

[63] Investment Company Names (n 61) 70440–41.

[64] Federal Reserve Board, Federal Deposit Insurance Corporation, Office of the Comptroller of the Currency, Principles for Climate-Related Financial Risk Management for Large Financial Institutions' (24 October 2023) www.federalreserve.gov/supervisionreg/srletters/SR2309a1.pdf; Remarks by Secretary of the Treasury Janet L Yellen at the First Meeting of the FSOC Climate-related Financial Risk Advisory Committee (7 March 2023) home.treasury.gov/news/press-releases/jy1325 (surveying several of these initiatives).

was formed in 2010 to identify potential threats to financial stability, is coordinating initiatives by federal regulators to mitigate systemic risk threats related to climate change.[65]

## 2. State ESG Investment Regulation

Beyond federal regulation, about one-third of the US states have adopted policies to promote ESG-related investment in some form.[66] These include policies to support decarbonization in investment or regulations requiring state pension funds to consider ESG factors in investment and/or voting policies.[67] State pension funds in California, New York, Illinois, and Connecticut are also among the states whose pension funds regularly lead or back shareholder proposals and other engagement around climate risk disclosure.

The state of California has been a leading adopter of ESG regulation, and in 2023 passed several climate disclosure measures that apply to all public and private companies over a certain size that do business in the state, as well as further measures to prevent climate greenwashing. The first, the Climate Corporate Data Accountability Act (SB 253), will require covered companies to disclose Scopes 1 and 2 greenhouse gas emissions starting in 2026 and Scope 3 in 2027, and to have Scopes 1 and 2 reporting assured.[68] The second, Greenhouse Gases: Climate-Related Financial Risk (SB 261), will require TCFD-based corporate reporting as of 2026 that is similar, but not identical to, the proposed SEC reporting rules.[69] Companies that comply with the ISSB climate disclosure standards would satisfy the California requirements.[70] Other prominent ESG measures introduced in California include supply chain disclosure rules for companies doing business in the state[71] and board diversity quotas for gender and other minorities. The board diversity quotas have been struck down by state and federal courts as being in violation of the Fourteenth Amendment's equal protection clause and parallel provisions in the state constitution,[72] and Nasdaq's rules on board diversity disclosure face a similar challenge in the US Court of Appeals for the Fifth Circuit.[73] In addition to these measures, California has adopted anti-greenwashing disclosure rules that apply

---

[65] Remarks by Secretary Yellen (n 64).
[66] Ropes & Gray (n 27).
[67] ibid.
[68] Climate Corporate Data Accountability Act 2023, Cal SB 253 ch 382 (7 October 2023) (requiring California's State Air Resources Board (CARB) to adopt such regulations). This bill applies to both public and private companies with over US$1 billion in annual revenue.
[69] Greenhouse gases: climate-related financial risk, Cal SB 261 ch 383 (7 October 2023). This bill applies to both public and private companies with over US$500,000 in annual revenue.
[70] ibid.
[71] California Transparency in Supply Chains Act of 2010, SB 657, Civ Code S1714.43 (2010).
[72] *Robin Crest and Ors v Alex Padilla (Padilla I)* 19-STCV-27561 (LA Super Ct 13 May 2022) (finding gender quotas under Senate Bill 826 unconstitutional); *Robin Crest and Ors v Alex Padilla (Padilla II)* 20-STCV-37513 (LA Super Ct 1 April 2022) (finding board diversity quotas for under-represented communities unconstitutional); *Alliance for Fair Board Recruitment v Weber* 2023 WL3481146 (ED Cal 2023) (finding Assembly Bill 979 unconstitutional).
[73] *Alliance for Fair Board Recruitment v SEC* No 21-60626 (5th Cir 2024).

to all companies, public or private, domestic or foreign, that make carbon neutrality or emissions reduction claims to California residents or engage in carbon offset transactions in California.[74] California's climate measures faced immediate legal challenge at the state level on federal pre-emption and constitutional grounds.[75]

## 3. Anti-ESG Backlash and Regulatory Limits on ESG Integration

The 'hardening' of voluntary ESG investment and corporate practices domestically and abroad has sparked an anti-ESG backlash from some sectors of the public, the business community, and law-makers at both the federal and state levels. This opposition was fuelled by the increasingly visible ESG policies and public statements issued by the 'big three' asset managers and proxy advisory firms, who in recent years have included ESG in their voting and investment strategies or recommendations, and who have at times supported investor campaigns advocating corporate board diversity, divestment from fossil fuels, or decarbonization.[76]

a) Federal ESG challenges

At the federal level, numerous anti-ESG bills have been proposed,[77] and major asset managers have faced pressure from conservative politicians in Congress who are concerned that ESG investment strategies are advancing liberal political agendas and that institutional investors may engage in coordinated engagement that could violate antitrust regulations.[78] Opposition to ESG in Congress came to a head in early 2023 when Congress passed a bill to block the implementation of the DoL's amended rule on consideration of ESG factors by ERISA fiduciaries.[79] President Biden ultimately vetoed the measure,[80] and the rule later survived a challenge brought in a federal court by twenty-six states.[81]

---

[74] Voluntary Carbon Market Disclosures Act (VCMDA) Cal AB 1305 (7 October 2023).

[75] *Chamber of Commerce of the United States of America and Ors v California Air Resources Board and Ors* Case No 2:24-cv-00801 (CD Cal, filed 30 January 2024) https://www.uschamber.com/assets/documents/FILED-Chamber-v.-CARB-Complaint.pdf.

[76] See generally Dorothy S Lund, 'Asset Managers as Regulators' (2022) 171 University of Pennsylvania Law Review 77.

[77] See generally Ropes & Gray, 'Federal Initiatives' https://www.ropesgray.com/en/sites/navigating-state-regulation-of-esg/federal-initiatives (tracking these initiatives).

[78] See eg Steven T Dennis, 'House Republicans Probe BlackRock, Vanguard on Their ESG Policies' *Bloomberg* (6 July 2023) www.bloomberg.com/news/articles/2023-07-07/house-republicans-probe-blackrock-vanguard-on-their-esg-policies.Key academic work on the potential anticompetitive effects of common ownership includes José Azar, Martin C Schmalz, and Isabel Tecu, 'Anticompetitive Effects of Common Ownership' (2018) 73(4) Journal of Finance 1513; José Azar and Xavier Vives, 'Revisiting the Anticompetitive Effects of Common Ownership' (15 March 2021) ECGI Working Paper ssrn.com/abstract=3805047; C Scott Hemphill and Marcel Kahan, 'The Strategies of Anticompetitive Common Ownership' (2020) 129 Yale Law Journal 1392.

[79] DoL, Prudence and Loyalty (n 54); 'Biden Uses First Veto to Defend Rule on ESG Investing' *Reuters* (21 March 2023) www.reuters.com/business/sustainable-business/biden-vetoes-resolution-block-labor-dept-rule-esg-investing-2023-03-20/.

[80] ibid.

[81] *State of Utah and Ors v Walsh and Ors* WL 6205926 (ND Tex 2023). The court rejected arguments that the rule exceeded the DoL's authority and was 'arbitrary and capricious' under the standard of review for administrative rulemaking under *Chevron USA Inc v Natural Resources Defense Council Inc* 467 US 837 (1984).

## b) State ESG challenges

Anti-ESG regulation at the state level has become particularly prominent in recent years. Since early ESG legislation in strongly supportive states like California was already in force, the result is a patchwork of state legislation on ESG that corresponds roughly to the division between politically liberal and politically conservative states. For example, at least eight states, including Washington and Illinois, require state pension funds to integrate ESG factors into investment strategies, while twenty-one states, mostly between the coasts, ban them from doing so.[82] Nine states, including California, Nevada, and New York, encourage or require companies incorporated in the state to divest from carbon-intensive sectors, while Texas and West Virginia are among the ten states banning investment in the state from firms that adopt carbon divestment or other pro-ESG policies.[83] As of 2023, at least nineteen states had adopted legislation targeting ESG investment, although most anti-ESG bills introduced have failed to pass in the face of ongoing debates about the financial impact of such bans on pension beneficiaries and on state economies.[84] Companies and major financial institutions alike have found themselves caught between these often incompatible rules.

State anti-ESG legislation adds new barriers for asset managers who already face economic and legal disincentives to engage in or coordinate shareholder activism, including activism targeting portfolio firms with poor climate or ESG risk management. Prior scholarship has observed that most investors are rationally passive, and so shareholder activism in the United States is usually initiated or led by hedge funds,[85] individual corporate 'gadflies',[86] SRI investors,[87] or other 'governance arbitrageurs'.[88] In addition, federal beneficial ownership reporting requirements and other rules that take an aggregate view of fund holdings can discourage large fund managers from engaging in and coordinating activism through managed funds.[89]

All of these factors further limit the potential for US fund managers to exercise investor stewardship in the way that investor stewardship codes,[90] international voluntary regimes like the United Nations Principles for Responsible Investment (UNPRI) and the Glasgow Financial Alliance for Net Zero (GFANZ),[91] and sustainability

---

[82] Karin Rives, 'Some States Backtrack on Anti-ESG Efforts, Citing "Unintended Consequences"' *S&P Global Market Intelligence* (22 February 2023) www.spglobal.com/marketintelligence/en/news-insights/latest-news-headlines/some-states-backtrack-on-anti-esg-efforts-citing-unintended-consequenses-74371958.

[83] ibid. Ropes & Gray (n 27).

[84] Rives (n 81).

[85] Ronald Gilson and Jeffrey Gordon, 'The Agency Costs of Agency Capitalism: Activist Investors and the Revaluation of Governance Rights' (2013) 113 Columbia Law Review 863; Alon Brav and others, 'Hedge Fund Activism, Corporate Governance, and Firm Performance' (2008) 63 Journal of Finance 1729.

[86] Kobi Kastiel and Yaron Nili, 'The Giant Shadow of Corporate Gadflies' (2021) 94 Southern California Law Review 469.

[87] Harper Ho (n 20).

[88] Gilson and Gordon (n 85).

[89] On the chilling effect of these and other rules on shareholder activism see generally JD Morley, 'Too Big to Be Activist' (2019) 92 Southern California Law Review 1407.

[90] See generally Dionysia Katelouzou and Dan Puchniak (eds), *Global Shareholder Stewardship* (CUP 2022) (surveying investor stewardship codes and examining their impact).

[91] 'Glasgow Financial Alliance for Net Zero' www.gfanzero.com/ (creating a coalition of financial institutions to facilitate coalition member efforts to reach net zero targets). Signatories to the UNPRI commit to use their governance rights as shareholders to advance ESG goals to the extent consistent with their fiduciary duties. United

disclosure mandates for asset managers, like the EU's SFDR, contemplate. If regulation outside the United States requires asset managers to monitor and disclose information on ESG performance at the portfolio level or to exercise more active ESG oversight through voting and engagement, divergent compliance obligations between the United States and other jurisdictions will need to be resolved.

## IV. The US Institutional Context for ESG Regulation

As many governments move to mandate GHG reporting and other forms of ESG disclosure and require asset managers to monitor the climate impacts of investment portfolios, the more strongly market-driven US approach, which preferences private ordering and voluntary standards, has become somewhat of an outlier. This is so even in comparison to the UK, which has similar market characteristics and whose corporate and securities laws also have much in common with those of the United States. Some of the reasons for this are political, others have to do with unique features of the US system, while still others relate to some of the basic challenges all jurisdictions confront in pursuing policies to promote sustainable finance and a post-carbon transition. The following discussion starts from the institutional constraints in the US system and then offers a brief perspective on the underlying political debates.

### 1. Federalism and Constitutional Constraints

A key source of divergence between US and continental, or even UK and commonwealth regulatory approaches to ESG, has to do with the rather unique division of responsibility in the United States between federal and state governments with regard to company (or corporate) law and securities regulation. The issue is whether ESG regulation that may require firms to implement corporate governance reforms should be undertaken, if at all, at the state or federal level, and whether the SEC has authority to adopt climate disclosure rules that may affect corporate governance as the TCFD framework contemplates.

Corporate governance matters have historically been determined under state law, but state corporate law may be less well-suited to serve as the site of ESG-related corporate governance and reporting reform compared to company law elsewhere. First and most obviously, one of the goals of emerging ESG mandates is to achieve greater harmonization, but the United States does not have a single national source of corporate law. In addition, state corporate law is generally understood to be facilitative rather than regulatory. Beyond the rules governing the fiduciary duties of corporate directors and officers, it is not directed at incentivizing particular corporate conduct.

---

Nations' Principles for Responsible Investment, 'About Us' www.unpri.org/about-us/what-are-the-principles-for-responsible-investment.

In contrast, securities and the issuance of securities are regulated more comprehensively, although not exclusively, at the federal level. The National Securities Markets Improvement Act of 1996 (NSMIA) pre-empts state power to regulate public offerings, as well as securities offered under certain federal private offering exemptions.[92] As a result, the scope of state securities regulation is relatively limited. State ESG regulations have also been challenged as potentially violating a federal constitutional doctrine known as the 'dormant commerce clause', which prohibits states from adopting regulations that discriminate against interstate commerce.[93]

At the same time, the federalization of corporate governance is a matter of some controversy.[94] When the SEC has adopted disclosure rules that are clearly directed at changing corporate behaviour, such as corporate governance disclosures to encourage the adoption of codes of ethics, director independence standards, and risk oversight and risk management systems, most of these have been done at the direction of Congress.[95] Even with such a mandate, prior SEC disclosure rule-making that touches on corporate governance matters has at times been struck down in the courts,[96] although earlier cases have not squarely considered the SEC's general authority to adopt rule-making that affects corporate governance or may affect corporate behaviour.

## 2. Constraints on the SEC's Rule-making Authority

The authority of the SEC to undertake ESG rule-making is another critical aspect of the US institutional context that explains its relatively narrow approach to climate disclosure. Contention over the validity of the SEC's climate disclosure rules centres in part on whether the adoption of such rules is within the scope of the SEC's statutory authority and whether the SEC has exercised its power in a manner that is consistent with relevant requirements for administrative rule-making. The SEC's climate disclosure rules and other ESG disclosure regulation has also been challenged on several constitutional grounds, including some that have been raised with mixed success in prior litigation against SEC rule-making.[97]

To begin, the SEC has the power to adopt corporate disclosure rules under its general statutory authority to protect investors, maintain fair, orderly, and efficient markets,

---

[92] Public Law 104-290 (1996). State securities laws (ie 'blue sky laws'), continue to apply to private offerings not covered by NSMIA, and state antifraud provisions are not preempted.

[93] *National Pork Producers Council v Ross* 598 US 356 (2023) (affirming the balancing test of *Pike v Bruce Church* 397 US 137, 142 (1970)). The 2023 California climate legislation was challenged on these grounds (n 75 above).

[94] See eg Amanda M Rose, 'A Response to Calls for SEC-Mandated ESG Disclosure' (2021) 98 Washington University Law Review 1821, 1844 (arguing that the use of ESG disclosure to incentivize certain corporate behaviour 'blur[s] the line between the domains of federal securities regulation and state corporate law').

[95] These include a number of reforms introduced under the Dodd-Frank Act and the Sarbanes-Oxley Act. Harper Ho (n 11) 303 (referencing these authorities).

[96] See eg *Business Roundtable v SEC* 647 F3d 1144 (DC Cir 2011) (challenging the SEC's federal proxy access rules undertaken pursuant to the Dodd-Frank Wall Street Reform and Consumer Protection Act, Pub L No 111-203, 124 Stat 1374 (2010)).

[97] *National Legal and Policy Center v SEC* No 24-1685 (8th Cir 2024).

and encourage capital formation.[98] Scholars have also argued that the authority to maintain 'orderly' markets gives the SEC a role in mitigating systemic risk concerns, although the SEC's climate disclosure rules do not rest on this justification.[99] In addition, the Securities Act of 1933 and the Exchange Act of 1934 require that when the SEC 'is engaged in rulemaking and is required to consider whether an action is necessary or appropriate in the public interest, [it] shall also consider, in addition to the protection of investors, whether the action will promote efficiency, competition, and capital formation'.[100] This language implies the power to undertake rule-making in the public interest, although the contours of that authority have not yet been defined by the courts.

Rule-making by US federal agencies is also subject to administrative law principles, and litigation against prior rule-making by the SEC and other federal agencies, as well as some of the many comments submitted to the SEC on its climate disclosure rules, offered early indication of the potential bases for legal challenge that constrain the ambition of SEC rule-making. First, opponents have previously challenged the SEC's rule-making process and its assessment of the potential costs and benefits of new rules as a matter of administrative law, alleging that the rules are 'arbitrary and capricious'.[101] As noted above, earlier cases suggest that the SEC will be more likely to satisfy this standard when 'the SEC can rely on Congress' determination of the governmental interest motivating the rule, where the court concludes that the rule is likely to be effective in achieving that goal, and where the SEC can show that the rule advances the 'economic or investor protection benefits' that the SEC is currently required to consider under its statutory mandate'.[102] However, specific Congressional direction supporting ESG rule-making is unlikely, and the history of the SEC's conflict minerals rules and other 'specialized disclosure' reforms suggests that even Congressional authorization does not insulate new rules from constitutional or administrative challenge.[103]

Opponents have also argued that requiring companies to produce potentially negative disclosures may be invalid as 'compelled' commercial speech in violation of the First Amendment,[104] even though this challenge would, if successful, imperil the

---

[98] See eg Climate Disclosure Release (n 30) 21683 (relying on this authority). See also SEC, Business and Financial Disclosure Required by Regulation S-K: Concept Release, 81 Fed Reg 23916, 23921 (22 April 2016).

[99] Hilary J Allen, 'The SEC as Financial Stability Regulator' (2018) 43 Journal of Corporation Law 715 (observing that the SEC has authority to maintain financial stability under s 2 of the Exchange Act).

[100] Securities Act of 1933, 15 USC § 77b(b), 77g(a)(1) (2018); see also ibid § 77s(a); Securities Exchange Act of 1934, s 3(f), 15 USC, ss 78(c)(f), 78w(a)(2) (2018); see also Investment Company Act of 1940, s 2(c), 15 USC § 80a-2(c) (2018). This language was added in 1996 and was intended to require the SEC to consider economic efficiency in addition to investor protection. See *Business Roundtable v SEC* (n 96) 1148 (quoting 15 USC §§ 78c(f), 80a-2(c)).

[101] The SEC's attempted proxy access rules were struck down on these grounds in 2011 by the DC Circuit. See *Business Roundtable v SEC* (n 94).

[102] Harper Ho (n 11) 346–47 (discussing *National Association of Manufacturers v SEC (NAM II)* 800 F3d 518, 521, 527 (DC Cir 2015), where the court found that the SEC's conflict minerals rules did not advance economic or investor protection benefits and stated that the SEC must demonstrate that its rule would 'in fact alleviate' the stated harms 'to a material degree').

[103] ibid. On the legal challenges to the SEC's conflict minerals disclosure rules see Jeff Schwartz, 'The Conflict Minerals Experiment' (2016) 6 Harvard Business Law Review 129, 140–43.

[104] This argument prevailed against some aspects of the SEC's initial conflict minerals disclosure rules in *National Association of Manufacturers v SEC* 800 F3d 518, 556 (DC Cir 2015) and was raised by 16 state attorneys general in response to the SEC's proposed climate disclosure rules. Letter from Patrick Morrisey, W Va Attorney General and others to Hon Gary Gensler, regarding Climate Change Disclosures (14 June 2021) www.sec.gov/

entire mandatory disclosure regime under the federal securities laws.[105] Finally, recent Supreme Court cases have suggested that agency action may be invalidated if it 'impermissibly take[s] on responsibilities given to other federal agencies',[106] or if it falls foul of the 'major questions doctrine' the Supreme Court articulated in its 2022 decision in *West Virginia v EPA*.[107] Under this doctrine, an agency must identify 'clear congressional authorization' if the agency is using its authority to address a question of major 'economic and political significance'.[108] These decisions raise serious challenges for any new federal regulation, and nearly all of these battles become more difficult for the SEC to win if it does not limit justifications for new rule-making strictly to market- and investor-oriented grounds.

## 3. Regulatory Cost Considerations

In addition to the factors outlined above, there are regulatory cost considerations beyond direct compliance costs that affect how the SEC has approached ESG-related rule-making but that may weigh less heavily for regulators in the UK or Europe.[109] The first is that private enforcement mechanisms are more robust in the United States than they are elsewhere.[110] Expanding mandatory disclosure may therefore spur new shareholder campaigns and increase the risk of private securities fraud litigation, even if, as I have argued elsewhere, liability risk may be remote.[111] In the case of the SEC's climate disclosure rules, litigation safe harbours that apply to forward-looking information extends to disclosures of transition plans, targets and goals, use of internal carbon pricing, and climate resilience analysis that reporting companies may provide.[112]

Another concern that has loomed large in US debates is that expanded compliance costs could drive companies to go private or 'stay dark', impairing capital formation and weakening the competitiveness of the US capital markets and of listed firms.[113] Such an

---

comments/climate-disclosure/cll12-8915606-244835.pdf. On the nature of these First Amendment arguments see generally Sean J Griffith, 'What's "Controversial" About ESG? A Theory of Compelled Commercial Speech Under the First Amendment' Fordham Legal Studies Research Paper No 4118755 (2022) ssrn.com/abstract=4118755.

[105] See Sarah Haan, 'The First Amendment and the SEC's Proposed Climate Risk Disclosure Rule' Working Paper (23 June 2022) ssrn.com/abstract=4138712.

[106] *National Federation of Independent Business v Department of Labor* 595 US 109, 117–18, 142 S Ct 661, 665–66 (2022) (blocking a Covid-19 vaccination policy adopted by the Occupational Safety and Health Administration as a public health measure not within its remit to protect employees).

[107] 142 S Ct 2587 (2022) (deciding that the EPA lacked broad authority to set GHG emissions caps).

[108] ibid 2608–609.

[109] I have considered and responded more fully to these concerns elsewhere. Harper Ho (n 11) 304–309.

[110] On this cross-jurisdictional variation see generally Mathias Reimann, 'Private Enforcement in the United States and in Europe: A Comparative Perspective and Potential Lessons for Asia' in Robin Hui Huang and Nicholas C Howson (eds), *Enforcement of Corporate and Securities Law: China and the World* 14 (CUP 2017).

[111] Harper Ho (n 10) 1908–15.

[112] SEC (n 30) 21773–76. Some commentators had urged that the final rules should go further to include a temporary moratorium on private securities fraud litigation during the initial period after the rules take effect. Harper Ho (n 10) 1916–17. See also Amanda M Rose, Comment Letter on Proposed Rule for the Enhancement and Standardization of Climate-Related Disclosures for Investors (17 June 2022) www.sec.gov/comments/s7-10-22/s71022-20132215-302734.pdf (advancing this proposal).

[113] SEC, Regulation S-K Concept Release (n 98) 23930.

outcome would be incompatible with the SEC's statutory mandate.[114] Of course, as the SEC itself has long recognized, mandatory disclosure enhances 'capital formation and the allocative efficiency of the capital markets, [leading to] more accurate share prices, [and can also] discourage fraud, heighten monitoring of the managers of companies, and increase liquidity'.[115] Moreover, arguments about the effect of ESG disclosure reform on capital formation and competition now arguably cut in favour of some forms of ESG regulation, such as climate risk disclosure. When stronger mandates have been widely adopted elsewhere, the United States' failure to do so may actually hurt the reputation and competitiveness of US capital markets and listed firms, as other markets offer greater climate risk transparency at lower cost to investors.

In addition, most jurisdictions outside the United States have addressed concerns about the uneven burdens of new ESG disclosure on listed firms by extending certain ESG disclosure mandates to all large firms or across the economy.[116] Although some contributors to this volume do not support this approach,[117] it has the advantage of levelling the playing field for large public and privately held firms and reducing the barriers to listing. However, this approach is at odds with Congress' most recent direction to the SEC to streamline disclosure obligations[118] and with earlier reforms that narrowed the scope of non-listed firms that are nonetheless defined as 'public' under the securities laws.[119] There is little appetite in the United States at present to expand the reach of mandatory disclosure to private firms.[120]

## 4. Politics

Reasons for the SEC's more modest approach to mandatory climate risk disclosure and ESG-related rule-making are ultimately rooted in the US political context. The poles of US ESG debates align roughly but imperfectly with divisions over the proper scope of government power that also tend to distinguish political conservatives and liberals in

---

[114] See authorities referenced in n 97 above.
[115] SEC, Regulation S-K Concept Release (n 98) 23919.
[116] See eg the EU's approach under the CSRD (n 8). The UK is introducing mandatory TCFD-compliant climate disclosures across the economy. UK Ministry of Business, Innovation and Employment, Mandatory Climate-related Disclosures (2021) www.gov.uk/government/consultations/mandatory-climate-related-financial-disclosures-by-publicly-quoted-companies-large-private-companies-and-llps.
[117] See eg Hopt, chapter 2, p 22 (arguing that nationally applicable ESG reporting mandates 'and supply chain laws, as in France and Germany, blur the traditional lines between unregulated and regulated companies in a critical way').
[118] The SEC's first proposals to introduce climate disclosure mandates under Regulation S-K came in the context of a decades-long review of the federal reporting system at the direction of Congress, which at that time was particularly concerned about the accretion of reporting obligations for listed companies and their potential burden on smaller issuers. See generally SEC (n 98).
[119] On the scope of 'publicness' see generally Donald C Langevoort and Robert B Thompson, '"Publicness" in Contemporary Securities Regulation After the JOBS Act' (2013) 101 Georgetown Law Journal 337; Hillary A Sale, 'Public Governance' (2013) 81 George Washington Law Review 1012.
[120] Academic views are mixed. Those who have advocated bringing more large firms within the scope of those regulated as 'public' include Langevoort and Thompson (n 116) and Sale (n 116). Among the sceptics are Elizabeth Pollman, 'Private Company Lies' (2020) 109 Georgetown Law Journal 353, 397–98 (arguing the need to expand scaled disclosure to private companies is unclear in view of alternatives).

the United States. Along this spectrum, libertarians and conservatives have historically advocated less (or no) government intervention and greater autonomy for individuals and market forces. These positions have played out in legal challenges to climate regulation in the Supreme Court[121] and in the legal challenges to the DoL's ESG rule.[122] The divide also gives rise to Congressional logjams and inaction on everything from funding the federal government, to climate change, AI, and lesser areas of political debate.

These fundamental differences in individuals' views about the proper role for government regulation, particularly at the federal level, are amplified by lack of public (and academic) consensus about the financial effects of climate change on firms and investors,[123] and by uneven support in Congress and among the public for a national climate change response. Similar differences have polarized debates over gender and racial issues, raising the level of controversy over diversity, equity, and inclusion (DEI) policies in companies and academic institutions, and over proposed regulation that falls within the 'S' or social dimension of ESG.[124]

Many of these objections to ESG regulation, investment, and engagement can be distilled to two fears that may be referred to more colourfully as the ESG Pandora's Box and Trojan Horse.[125] The first worry is that the range of ESG issues is potentially unbounded, like the proverbial Pandora's Box, leaving federal regulators like the SEC and the DoL free to justify broader regulation of an ever-expanding list of ESG matters.[126] The Trojan Horse worry is that ESG is being promoted as essential to effective financial risk management as a cover, but that these economic rationales are in fact an attempt by pro-ESG regulators and asset managers to foist their own social and political values on investors and the capital markets. The international embrace of ESG has also raised fears among more conservative parts of the US polity about the threat of another kind of ESG Trojan Horse—the prospect that international, 'globalist', or socialist policies may extend to US companies without due regard to US sovereignty and national interests. More critically, these policies may be introduced not through the political process but through foreign rules or international soft law that give unelected asset managers

---

[121] West Virginia v EPA, 142 S Ct 2587 (2022).

[122] See cases referenced (n82) above.

[123] Opposing comments were submitted by US corporate and securities law professors on the SEC's proposed rules. See Jill E. Fisch and George S. Georgiev, Comment Letter on Proposed Rule for the Enhancement and Standardization of Climate-Related Disclosures for Investors (6 June 2022) www.sec.gov/comments/s7-10-22/s71022-20130354-297375.pdf (arguing that the rules fall squarely within the SEC's authority). But see Lawrence A Cunningham, Comment Letter on Proposed Rule for the Enhancement and Standardization of Climate-Related Disclosures for Investors (25 April 2022) www.sec.gov/comments/s7-10-22/s71022-20126528-287180.pdf (arguing the contrary).

[124] These issues have been litigated in challenges to Nasdaq's board diversity rule. See *Alliance for Fair Board Recruitment v SEC* (n 73).

[125] I first used these somewhat mixed metaphors in earlier commentary. Virginia Harper Ho, 'Climate Disclosure Line-Drawing—and Why to Take Both Sides in the ESG Debate Seriously' Duke University Financial Economics Center FinReg Blog (20 April 2023) tinyurl.com/2r97uept.

[126] Republican SEC Commissioner Hester M Peirce has been a consistent opponent of ESG disclosure mandates on these grounds. See eg Hester M Peirce, 'Speech by Commissioner Peirce on ESG Disclosure' Harvard Law School Forum on Corporate Governance (21 July 2021) https://corpgov.law.harvard.edu/2021/07/21/speech-by-commissioner-peirce-on-esg-disclosure/.

and proxy advisers power to pressure companies toward environmental and social strategies that may be at odds with the views of other US shareholders and beneficial owners.

As with most arguments among reasonable people, both sides in these debates have a point.[127]

a) Pandora's box: ESG scoping challenges

ESG sceptics are right to be vigilant about the potential for ever-expanding ESG demands from investors and regulators, and so attention to the scope and bounds of ESG regulation is critical as new rules are drafted. The SEC's disclosure rules, for example, do not mandate open-ended ESG disclosure or particular corporate practices but are focused on climate-related financial risk. As discussed above, they also give companies considerable flexibility. At the same time, materiality concepts are dynamic, so ESG advocates must also acknowledge that companies' ESG compliance obligations may increase over time, and that mandatory ESG disclosure rules may also 'move the goalposts' for ESG shareholder activism. Carefully drafted rules that are limited to defined climate and sustainability matters can help address these concerns, as all current and pending ESG regulation attempts to do in some form.[128]

b) The Trojan Horse: fears of an ESG takeover

At the same time, fears of a Pandora's Box or Trojan Horse are overstated. The fact that ESG may simultaneously advance both financial and societal goals does not render financial justifications disingenuous—indeed, the prospect of a 'win-win' for business and society is a normative foundation for defining corporate purpose in terms of shareholder wealth maximization, and is the basis of the business case for voluntary corporate responsibility. In addition, safeguards against politicization and self-interest are already in place under existing law. For example, the current fiduciary obligations of fund managers do not permit them to push client assets toward their own investment agendas in disregard of client directions or the financial interests of fund beneficiaries as the case may be.[129]

Those worried that the real Trojan Horse is a foreign, globalist, or transnational agenda may wish to recall that ESG is a market-driven concept led in large part by US investors and civil society. Nearly fifteen years ago, the SEC led the world as one of the first regulators to adopt guidance on climate risk materiality for listed firms before the topic had attracted much attention abroad.[130] In addition, the TCFD framework,

---

[127] The arguments advanced here build on perspectives I have previously expressed elsewhere. See Harper Ho (n 125).

[128] ESG regulation focused on climate risk management and disclosure nonetheless may require companies to take account of other environmental or sustainability matters, such as resource consumption and biodiversity loss, and climate risk disclosure may also require consideration of whether the company's impact on the environment is an indirect source of financial risk, such as reputational or legal risk. All of these matters are contemplated in the TCFD framework (n 35).

[129] See SEC (n 49) 33675–78 (discussing the scope of the duty of loyalty).

[130] SEC (n 18).

which both the SEC and international climate reporting rules use, was developed with the input of US investors and companies and is based on a wide range of voluntary standards, many designed by US organizations. Indeed, the ISSB had to consider how best to internationalize the sector-specific standards created by the Sustainability Accounting Standards Board (SASB) that its own standards reference—precisely because they were based on the US federal definition of materiality and US industry experience.[131]

All of these debates will continue to shape prospects for US ESG (and anti-ESG) regulation at both the federal and state levels. They will also influence how Congress, state legislatures, and the courts respond to new ESG regulation and will define the space for future climate and sustainability-related reforms in corporate and securities law and in financial regulation as well as in more traditional arenas.

## V. Conclusion

At the core of the US ESG debate is the central governance question of decision-making power—'Whose voice should count?' Is it shareholders or directors? Shareholders or stakeholders? And which shareholders—institutional or retail, short-term or long-term, present, or future? When and how should beneficial owners have a voice? Similarly, which stakeholder concerns matter across sectors—environmental interests, workforce issues, or others? Many of these choices are firm-specific and few of these dichotomies are as stark as current debates seem to assume. But how these questions are answered depends on even more fundamental normative positions about how corporate purpose, board fiduciary duties, and managerial incentives should be understood and reflected in law. In the US context, there are also significant institutional, and even constitutional, questions about which of the above issues are properly resolved at the federal or state levels or left more fully to the market. The political debates discussed above therefore have strong corporate governance implications, as other contributions to this volume make clear.

These questions are not new and are likely to remain subject to necessary contention and debate. Within the United States, corporate policies, regulatory initiatives, and public discourse around this volume's themes—ESG, CSR, and corporate purpose—remain fraught precisely because climate change, DEI matters, and other ESG concerns touch on important values and divides. ESG regulation in the United States must respond to these domestic challenges, while taking account of a rapidly changing transnational regulatory context. And despite clear investor demand for ESG standardization and harmonization, it is not surprising that diverse regulatory approaches to ESG are emerging on both sides of the Atlantic, given the litigation context of new

---

[131] IFRS, Methodology for Enhancing the International Applicability of the SASB Standards and SASB Standards Taxonomy Updates (Exposure Draft) (May 2023) www.ifrs.org/content/dam/ifrs/project/international-applicability-sasb-standards/ed-issb-2023-1-international-applicability-sasb-standards.pdf.

## CONCLUSION 103

regulation in the United States, and the strong head start European governments have in establishing broad green development and green finance frameworks. At the same time, diverse transnational regulatory approaches may well spur on the kind of public and private innovation that is needed to drive better corporate governance, greater transparency, and greater corporate (and investor) accountability around ESG risks and impacts.

# 5
# Stakeholder Governance Models and Corporate Interests

## Experiences from Germany

*Rüdiger Veil*\*

## I. Introduction

In German stock corporation law, the term corporate interests (*Unternehmensinteressen*) captures the interests of a company which are decisive for the actions of the management. In contrast, the term corporate purpose (*Gesellschaftszweck*) refers to the basic purpose of a corporation to generate profits. The shareholders may also assign another purpose to the company, namely a non-profit purpose. In practice, however, this is an exception. The international discussion about the purpose of a corporation concerns—from a German perspective—the question of what interests a corporation has and which its management has to pursue. I will therefore limit myself to discussing the interests of a stock corporation under German law.[1]

Indeed, this is a fundamental issue of corporate law. Should the board of directors manage the company in the interests of the shareholders who had founded the company to run a business and make profits, or should it act (also) in the interest of the employees who work for the company and make it possible for the company to make profits from entrepreneurial activities at all? In addition, it is conceivable that the managers are (also) obliged to serve the interests of the creditors who provide the company with the capital to finance the business. Finally, the board could even be required to take into account the interests of the general public, whose concerns are that producers and service providers comply with environmental standards, respect human rights, and support social projects.

Klaus Hopt has already explained in detail the theories on shareholder versus stakeholder interests. He has also put the debate about a corporate purpose into context and shed light on the impact of recent legislative acts on sustainability on the basics of

---

\* All internet sources were last accessed on 15 January 2024.
[1] This chapter deals with the corporate interests of a company. It also refers to a corporate purpose, in the **sense** of a *raison d'être*, but only marginally, because the concept is not of great importance in German corporate law.

Rüdiger Veil, *Stakeholder Governance Models and Corporate Interests* In: *Corporate Purpose, CSR, and ESG*. Edited by: Jens-Hinrich Binder, Klaus J. Hopt, and Thilo Kuntz, Oxford University Press. © Jens-Hinrich Binder, Klaus J. Hopt, and Thilo Kuntz 2024. DOI: 10.1093/oso/9780198912576.003.0005

corporate law.[2] I follow up on the analyses by Klaus Hopt on the different legislative options[3] and examine whether it makes sense to include regulations on the objectives and purpose of a company in the law or in the articles of association of a company or whether the company's interests should be determined by other areas of law, such as labour law, accounting law, etc.[4] For almost ninety years, politicians and academics in Germany have been discussing which interest it is that a public limited company is committed to and what significance a regulation of the corporate interests has for the company and its board members. This is reflected in a wide range of reforms of stock corporation law, which, among other issues, affect the supervisory board of a company. The supervisory board of a German stock corporation consists of not only shareholder but also employee representatives. This regime of co-determination is unique in the world because it gives workers' representatives a powerful voice. In this way, the board of directors is confronted with the interests of employees and may feel obliged to take their interests into account.

Thus, two approaches can be identified in Germany: on the one hand, the approach of determining the corporate interests (in former times through special provisions, today through interpretation) and thereby providing a guiding principle for the board's actions; and, on the other hand, the approach of giving certain interest groups representation in decision-making bodies of the company. This chapter addresses the question of how legislation and academia have assessed the company's interests and what advantages and disadvantages are associated with a representative model, which also provides a mechanism for certain stakeholders to have a say in the decision-making process.

## II. The Trustee Model of Stakeholder Governance: Enterprise Accountability of the Board in Germany

### 1. From the Early Days of the Stock Corporation until the Stock Corporation Act of 1965

The beginnings of stock corporation law in Germany go as far back as the middle of the nineteenth century.[5] The Kingdom of Prussia[6] had already adopted a company law at that time. According to Prussian stock corporation law, only those companies approved

---

[2] Klaus J Hopt, 'Corporate Purpose and Stakeholder Value: Historical, Economic and Comparative Law Remarks on the Current Debate, Legislative Options and Enforcement Problems' (2023) European Corporate Governance Institute: Law Working Paper No 690 https://papers.ssrn.com/sol3/papers.cfm?abstract_id=4390119.
[3] ibid section II.2.
[4] cf Umberto Tombari, *Corporate Power and Conflicting Interests* (Giuffrè 2021) XI: 'most important issues, whether and to what extent companies can pursue stakeholder interests other than shareholder value; whether this radical reform necessarily requires purposeful legislation … whether corporate law should regulate these issues or they should be left to other areas of law'.
[5] Erik Kießling, 'Das preußische Aktiengesetz von 1843' in Walter Bayer and Mathias Habersack (eds), *Aktienrecht im Wandel der Zeit, Volume I, Entwicklung des Aktienrechts* (Mohr Siebeck 2007) ch 7.
[6] Together with other states, the Kingdom of Prussia founded the German Reich in 1871.

by the state were to have legal capacity that permanently pursued a non-profit purpose.[7] However, the legislator was unable to maintain this restrictive approach. In the discussion on a reform of stock corporation law with the General German Commercial Code of 1861, the understanding prevailed that a public limited company is a legal entity with its own legal personality, irrespective of its purpose.[8] Finally, in 1870, the legislature abolished the concession system.[9]

One of the most prominent scholars at the time was Achilles Renaud, who taught at Heidelberg University. The second edition of his great work on 'The Law of Stock Corporations' from 1875 says nothing about the consideration of stakeholders' interests in a stock corporation. Instead, Achilles Renaud highlighted that the idea behind stock corporations is to operate a company through the joint resources of several people and for their benefit.[10]

a) The debate about the *Unternehmen an sich* and reform legislation influenced by the national socialism

It took more than four decades before a discussion arose as to whether the board of directors of a public limited company should also consider the interests of the general public. In his work on the essence of a stock corporation (*Vom Aktienwesen*), Walter Rathenau argued that large corporations should be protected from the special interests of individual shareholders. It had to be ensured that the living conditions of the companies were maintained for the benefit of society without violating the rights of individuals.[11] Fritz Haussmann then formed the concept of the *Unternehmen an sich*, which can be loosely translated as 'the corporation per se'.[12] For him, large companies operating in the legal form of a stock corporation had to consider their importance and position in general economic life and their managers would be responsible to the general public.[13]

I will not delve into the sophisticated discussion on the *Unternehmen an sich*, which ended with the end of the Weimar Republic.[14] Suffice it to say that the *Unternehmen an sich* played a role in the reform of the Stock Corporation Act.[15] The opponents of democracy in stock corporation law prevailed and managed to ensure that the shareholders' meeting lost its position as the supreme body of a stock corporation.[16] The reform discussion finally led in 1937 to the following regulation in the German Stock

---

[7] Kießling (n 5) ch 7 para 31.
[8] Louis Pahlow, 'Das Allgemeine Deutsche Handelsgesetzbuch von 1861' in Walter Bayer and Mathias Habersack (eds), *Aktienrecht im Wandel der Zeit, Volume I, Entwicklung des Aktienrechts* (Mohr Siebeck 2007) ch 8 para 38.
[9] cf Hopt (n 2) ch 2; for more detail on the introduction of the system of normative provisions seePeter Hommelhoff, 'Eigenkontrolle statt Staatskontrolle' in Werner Schubert and Peter Hommelhoff (eds), *Hundert Jahre modernes Aktienrecht* (de Gruyter 1985) 53, 55.
[10] Achilles Renaud, *Das Recht der Actiengesellschaften* (2nd edn, Tauchnitz 1875) 9.
[11] Walter Rathenau, *Vom Aktienwesen: Eine geschäftliche Betrachtung* (Fischer 1917) 41.
[12] Fritz Haussmann, 'Die Aktiengesellschaft als "Unternehmen an sich"' [1927] Juristische Wochenschrift 2953.
[13] Fritz Haussmann, *Vom Aktienwesen und vom Aktienrecht* (J Bensheimer 1928) 42.
[14] Arndt Riechers, *Das 'Unternehmen an sich'* (Mohr Siebeck 1996) 154.
[15] Mathias Habersack, 'Gemeinwohlbindung und Unternehmensrecht' (2020) 220 Archiv für die civilistische Praxis 594, 606 ff.
[16] Riechers (n 14) 165 ff.

Corporation Act: 'The board of directors shall, on its own responsibility, manage the company in such a manner as the welfare of the company and its employees and the common benefit of the people and the empire require.'[17]

The National Socialist background to this definition of corporate interests—the so-called common good clause—is still disputed today. On the one hand, it is argued that the reform was shaped by social and economic policy ideas that had already prevailed before the National Socialists took power.[18] The aspect of a company's commitment to the common good already played a major role in the discussion of the *Unternehmen an sich*.[19] On the other hand, it is pointed out that the common good clause introduced in 1937 had reflected the ideology of National Socialism. The regulation corresponded to the National Socialist principle of 'common good before self-interest' of the NSDAP party programme from 1920.[20] The 1937 Companies Act was therefore shaped by national socialist ideas.[21] This applies in particular to the regulation on the objectives of a stock corporation.

It is noteworthy that the shareholders are not mentioned in the provision of the Stock Corporation Act on the interests of a company; they are only to be found 'hidden in the legal materials', where it is stated that the welfare of the company also includes the interests of the shareholders.[22] It is also not entirely clear which effect the legislator specifically expected the new provision to have. The legislative materials suggest that the law-maker was concerned with an interpretation maxim for the courts.[23] However, there is no case law on this aspect and the literature at the time did not discuss this issue. Therefore, the question cannot be answered conclusively today.

b) Reforms after the Second World War

The common good clause in the Stock Corporation Act, determined by national socialism, remained in place until 1965. In that year, the 1937 Act was replaced by a new Stock Corporation Act. The reform law pursued the goal of modernizing stock corporation law in Germany.[24] Interestingly, the determination of the company's interests was also the subject of debate. However, the government draft was limited to the regulation that the executive board should manage the company under its own responsibility. The suggested provision no longer stipulated that the board should pursue the welfare of

---

[17] Stock Corporation Act 1937, § 70.
[18] Walter Bayer and Sylvia Engelke, 'Die Revision des Aktienrechts durch das Aktiengesetz von 1937' in Walter Bayer and Mathias Habersack (eds), *Aktienrecht im Wandel der Zeit, Band I, Entwicklung des Aktienrechts* (Mohr Siebeck 2007) ch 15 para 122.
[19] In literature, the provision of § 70 of the Stock Corporation Act 1937 is also understood as a concession by the legislator to the doctrine of the *Unternehmen an sich*. cf Adolf Grossmann, *Unternehmensziele im Aktienrecht. Eine Untersuchung über Handlungsmaßstäbe für Vorstand und Aufsichtsrat* (Carl Heymanns Verlag 1980) 148 ff; Peter Ulmer, *Der Einfluss des Mitbestimmungsgesetzes auf die Struktur von AG und GmbH* (Mueller 1979) 14, 33 ff.
[20] Holger Fleischer, 'Gesetzliche Unternehmenszielbestimmungen im Aktienrecht: Eine vergleichende Bestandsaufnahme' (2017) 46 Zeitschrift für Unternehmens- und Gesellschaftsrecht 411, 421.
[21] Bayer and Engelke (n 18) ch 15 para 122.
[22] Friedrich Klausing, *Gesetz über Aktiengesellschaften und Kommanditgesellschaften auf Aktien (Aktiengesetz) nebst Einführungsgesetz und 'Amtlicher Begründung'* (Carl Heymanns Verlag 1937) 58 ff.
[23] Fleischer (n 20) 411, 413.
[24] Bruno Kropff, *Aktiengesetz 1965, Textausgabe mit Begründung des Regierungsentwurfs* (Institut der Wirtschaftsprüfer 1965) 13.

the company and its employees and the benefit of the general public. Some members of Parliament (MPs) criticized this.[25] In the committees of the *Bundestag*, MPs requested that a separate provision be inserted stating that the company must operate the company with due regard for the welfare of its employees, shareholders, and the general public. The majority of MPs opposed this proposal. They shared the view that every public limited company would be part of the overall economy and should consider the interests of the general public, arguing this would be self-evident in a social market economy and would also result from a multitude of legal provisions. It would therefore be superfluous to supplement corporate law accordingly.

Furthermore, the MPs criticized the vagueness of a norm concerning the goals of a corporation. The suggested provision would have no legal substance and no independent meaning. If it were to be included in the law, there would be a risk that courts would nevertheless give specific interests (shareholders, employees, creditors, the general public) a broader meaning. This risk would be all the greater if the order of enumeration were to lead to the conclusion that, in case of doubt, the welfare of the employees mentioned first would take precedence over the interest of the shareholders and these two in turn over the welfare of the general public, which was mentioned in the MPs' proposal in last place.[26]

Since 1965, therefore, the Stock Corporation Act has no longer included a provision on the corporate objectives of a public limited company. The concern expressed by some politicians in the *Bundestag* that courts would no longer consider that the board of directors should be obliged also to consider the public good and the welfare of the employees as before initially proved to be unfounded. This was also due to the fact that the German legislator, with the co-determination laws, gave great importance to employee interests. In the academic discussion on corporate interests, co-determination in the supervisory board played an important role.

## 2. The Influence of Co-determination Laws

Company co-determination in Germany is governed by a number of laws. In the period following the Second World War, the legislature introduced far-reaching co-determination for companies operating in the coal and steel industry, where the supervisory board was comprised of shareholder and employee representatives in equal parts. In all other companies, only one-third of the supervisory board of a company (stock corporations and limited liability companies) were composed of employee representatives. In 1976, the Co-Determination Act introduced a further co-determination statute for stock corporations and limited liability companies employing at least 2,000 employees. These companies were obliged to have an equal number of shareholder and employee representatives on the supervisory board. The chairperson

---

[25] cf ibid 97 ff.
[26] cf ibid 98.

of the supervisory board is usually the representative of the shareholders and, according to the law, has a double voting right in the event of a casting vote. Therefore, if necessary, the shareholders' representatives can prevail against the workers' representatives. Nevertheless, parity co-determination gives employees a great deal of influence.[27]

The Co-Determination Act involves employees in corporate decision-making processes, because the supervisory board appoints the members of the executive board, supervises them, and can exert influence on business policy decisions taken by the executive board.[28] In the academic discussion, even those who were critical of co-determination recognized the importance of the co-determination law for the interpretation of the corporate objectives. According to Klaus Hopt, 'a pure doctrine that focuses exclusively on the (well-understood) interests of shareholders is difficult to reconcile with the corporate constitution shaped by the Co-Determination Act of 1976'.[29] The law on co-determination is still seen today as evidence of the pluralism of interests in German company law.[30]

## 3. Modernization of German Stock Corporation Law in the 1990s—Towards US–American Doctrines?

At the end of the 1990s, the legislator started to modernize company law. This was the beginning of a permanent reform.[31] The legislator adapted stock corporation law to international models, especially those of the United States. The most significant legal transplant was the business judgment rule, introduced in § 93(1) sentence 2 of the Stock Corporation Act.[32] In addition, the legislator exempted the public limited company from some strict requirements in order to make public finance easier. The Federal Supreme Court also began to 'reshape traditional stock corporation law in light of the reform legislation'.[33] For some legal scholars, this was a turning point; they claimed that German stock corporation law had opened up to the primacy of shareholder value.[34]

A highly controversial discussion arose in which the advocates of market value maximization seemed to gain the upper hand. The shareholder value approach arises from

---

[27] The requirements as well as the pros and cons of the co-determination of employees, which is unique in the world, are set out in detail in the next chapter (and see section III below).
[28] The supervisory board can exert its influence primarily through rights of approval pursuant to § 111(4) sentence 2 of the Stock Corporation Act. For more detail see section III below.
[29] Klaus J Hopt, 'Aktionärskreis und Vorstandsneutralität' (1993) 22 Zeitschrift für Unternehmens- und Gesellschaftsrecht 535, 536.
[30] Jens Koch, *Kommentar zum Aktiengesetz* (17th edn, CH Beck 2023) § 76 para 30.
[31] Wolfgang Zöllner, 'Aktienrechtsreform in Permanenz: Was wird aus den Rechten der Aktionäre?' (1994) 38 Die Aktiengesellschaft 336.
[32] Stock Corporation Act, § 93 provides rules on the duty of the members of the management board to exercise skill and care and specifies liability and responsibilities of the members. The business judgement rule is formulated as follows: 'No dereliction of duties will be given in those instances in which the member of the management board, in taking an entrepreneurial decision, was within their rights to reasonably assume that they were acting on the basis of adequate information and in the best interests of the company.'
[33] Peter O Mülbert, 'Marktwertmaximierung als Unternehmensziel der Aktiengesellschaft' in Georg Crezelius, Heribert Hirte, and Klaus Vieweg (eds), *Festschrift für Volker Röhricht* (Otto Schmidt 2005) 421, 422.
[34] ibid 421, 440; Wolfgang Zöllner, 'Unternehmensinnenrecht: Gibt es das?' (2003) 48 Die Aktiengesellschaft 2, 7 ff; Max Birke, *Das Formalziel der Aktiengesellschaft* (Nomos 2005) 209 ff.

the principal–agent problem.[35] It aims to limit the powers of the board that exist in a stakeholder approach due to the broad discretion of the board in balancing the different interests. Conflicts of interest of the executive board are manifold.[36] Under the shareholder value approach, on the one hand, the board is obliged to promote the welfare of shareholders alone. This monistic interest model promises control cost advantages for shareholders.[37] If, on the other hand, the stakeholder approach is applied, the board has greater discretion, thus making it easier for the board members to pursue their own interests, which do not necessarily coincide with those of the shareholders.

When assessing a specific case, the differences between the shareholder value approach and the stakeholder concept are probably not very great. Indeed, most supporters of the shareholder value approach recognize that the board of directors of a public limited company may in principle also pursue stakeholder interests, provided that in doing so it meets a social expectation and cultivates the reputation of the public limited company as a good corporate citizen.[38] It can have a positive effect on business development if the board also considers the interests of stakeholders. This is why the literature also speaks of an 'enlightened shareholder value' or a 'moderate shareholder value approach'.[39]

The debate on the corporate objectives of a public limited company at the end of the 1990s illustrates how much the interpretation of the corporate objective depends on the decisions taken by the legislature to reform the law or introduce new concepts. The objectives of a public limited company can only be assessed in a larger context, which is determined on the one hand by the constitution (social obligation of property ownership), and on the other hand by the governance of the company, which shapes the purpose of profit-making and the participation of shareholders and stakeholders.

## 4. Financial Crisis

Crises and scandals are usually the reason to rethink fundamental concepts of regulation and revise the regimes.[40] In Germany, it took only two years for the issue of corporate interests to be tackled again under the impact of the financial market crisis, this time not by the legislator but by the *Regierungskommission Deutscher*

---

[35] Holger Fleischer, 'AktG § 76 Leitung der Aktiengesellschaft' in Gerald Spindler and Eberhard Stilz (eds), *Aktienrecht. Band I* (5th edn, CH Beck 2022) para 34.
[36] Klaus J Hopt, 'Übernahmen, Geheimhaltung und Interessenkonflikte: Probleme für Vorstände, Aufsichtsräte und Banken' (2002) 31 Zeitschrift für Unternehmens- und Gesellschaftsrecht 333; Tombari (n 4) 20–27.
[37] Fleischer (n 35) para 34; for a critical view see Gerald Spindler, 'AktG § 76 Leitung der Aktiengesellschaft' in Wulf Goette and Mathias Habersack (eds), *Münchener Kommentar zum Aktiengesetz. Band 2* (6th edn, CH Beck 2023) para 93.
[38] Fleischer (n 35) para 38.
[39] Martin Empt, *Corporate Social Responsibility: Das Ermessen des Managements zur Berücksichtigung von Nichtaktionärsinteressen im US-amerikanischen und deutschen Aktienrecht* (Duncker & Humbolt 2004) 200; Fleischer (n 35) para 38; Spindler (n 37) paras 93 ff.
[40] cf Holger Fleischer, 'Von "bubble laws" und "quack regulation": Zur Kritik kriseninduzierter Reformgesetze im Aktien- und Kapitalmarktrecht' in Peter Hommelhoff (ed), *Festschrift für Hans-Joachim Priester* (Otto Schmidt 2007) 75–94.

*Corporate Governance Kodex*. The German Federal Minister of Justice established the *Regierungskommission* in 2001 and entrusted it with the task of shaping standards of good corporate governance in the Corporate Governance Code.[41] The Commission consists of managing and supervisory board representatives of German listed companies and their stakeholders.

The self-regulation by the *Regierungskommission* consists of principles, recommendations, and suggestions for the executive board and the supervisory board of listed companies that are intended to help ensure that managers act in the best interests of the company. In 2009, the *Regierungskommission* reacted to the criticism of capitalism in the wake of the financial market crisis[42] and reformulated the goals of a stock corporation as follows: 'The management board is responsible for independently managing the enterprise with the objective of sustainable creation of value and in the interest of the enterprise, thus taking into account the interests of the shareholders, its employees and other stakeholders.'[43]

With this statement, the *Regierungskommission* explicitly committed itself to the stakeholder approach. It was an unusual step, as it is not the task of the *Regierungskommission* to comment on academic disputes about fundamental questions of stock corporation law (left open by the legislature), but to develop best practices for the corporate governance of listed companies. The *Regierungskommission* is also not competent to clarify important legal issues due to a lack of democratic legitimacy. However, the *Regierungskommission* had admittedly learned an important lesson from the financial market crisis, which had revealed the disastrous consequences of short-term thinking by managers. Reflecting on the stakeholder approach seemed important to the *Regierungskommission* in order to counteract harmful behaviour by managers. The *Regierungskommission* also implemented these insights through further changes in the Code, for example by developing recommendations for sustainable remuneration systems.[44] To sum up, the financial market crisis has discredited the shareholder value approach.[45] The stakeholder value approach celebrated its resurrection!

## 5. Impact on the ESG Legislature

Finally, the corporate social responsibility (CSR) legislation of the European Union has revived the discussion about corporate interests. The CSR Directive of 22 October 2014[46] is determined by the idea that 'disclosure of non-financial information is vital for

---

[41] The management board and the supervisory board of a listed company are to declare annually that the recommendations of the *Regierungskommission* Corporate Governance Code have been and are being complied with or which of the Code's recommendations have not been applied or are not being applied, with the reasons therefor being provided. cf Stock Corporation Act, § 161(1).
[42] Fleischer (n 20) 416.
[43] cf GCGC 2009, art 4.1.1.
[44] cf ibid 4.2.3.
[45] Fleischer (n 35) para 34.
[46] Directive 2014/95/EU amending Directive 2013/34/EU as regards disclosure of non-financial and diversity information by certain large undertakings and groups [2014] OJ L330/1.

managing change towards a sustainable global economy by combining long-term profitability with social justice and environmental protection. In this context, disclosure of non-financial information helps the measuring, monitoring and managing of undertakings' performance and their impact on society'.[47] The recitals highlight that the business activities of companies have an impact on the climate and the environment. In the more recent ESG legislation of the EU, the aspect of externalizing costs (to the detriment of society) and the interest of stakeholders in access to sustainability information is emphasized much more strongly.[48] Therefore, it should come as no surprise that the CSR disclosure requirements have stimulated the discussion about a statutory regulation of corporate interests in company law.[49]

In Germany, ESG legislation has not yet led to any reforms, but the sustainability movement has influenced the political and academic discussion on a corporate goal. In 2012, MPs of Bündnis 90 and the Green Party proposed that the duties of the board of directors of a public limited company be specified by law.[50] The draft law was intended to ensure that ethically oriented board decisions are in line with the duties of board members, not only in the event when they have a positive impact on the company's returns. The MPs put forward that, according to the current interpretation of the duties under company law, board actions would only be considered lawful if they have a positive impact on the company's assets. However, the legislative proposal was not successful because the MPs were not members of the government coalition.

Finally, in another parliamentary term, MPs of the Social Democratic Party advocated a reform of the corporate goals in 2017.[51] According to their draft bill, the board of directors should be 'obliged to the welfare of the company, the employees, the shareholders and the general public'. The MPs wanted to ensure that the social obligations of property ownership under the German Constitution[52] be expressed in the law of stock corporations. Their proposal is largely in line with the amendments put forward by some members of the Bundestag when the Stock Corporation Act was enacted in 1965. The draft bill did not get a majority in the German Bundestag either, as the MPs were not members of the government coalition.

---

[47] ibid recital 3.

[48] Directive 2022/2462/EU amending Regulation (EU) No 537/2014, Directive 2004/109/EC, Directive 2006/43/EC and Directive 2013/34/EU, as regards corporate sustainability reporting [2022] OJ L322/15 (CSR Directive).

[49] cf Joachim Hennrichs, 'Die Grundkonzeption der CSR-Berichterstattung aus ausgewählte Problemfelder' (2018) 47 Zeitschrift für Unternehmens- und Gesellschaftsrecht 206 ff; Victor Klene, 'Corporate Social Responsibility: Richtlinie, Umsetzung und Konsequenzen' [2018] Wertpapier-Mitteilungen: Zeitschrift für Wirtschafts- und Bankrecht 308 ff; Wolfgang Schön, 'Der Zweck der Aktiengesellschaft – geprägt durch europäisches Gesellschaftsrecht?' (2019) 180 Zeitschrift fur das gesamte Handelsrecht und Wirtschaftsrecht 279 ff.

[50] Draft law of the parliamentary group Bündnis 90/Die Grünen on the amendment of the German Stock Corporation Act, Bundestag printed papers 17/11686 *Deutscher Bundestag* (28 November 2012) https://dserver.bundestag.de/btd/17/116/1711686.pdf; Fleischer (n 20) 417.

[51] Draft law of the parliamentary group of the Social Democratic Party on the adequacy of executive board compensation and the limitation of tax deductibility *Deutscher Bundestag* (20 February 2017) 6 https://www.spdfraktion.de/system/files/documents/gesetzentwurf_manager-verguetungen_spdbt_final.pdf.

[52] Art 14 of the German Constitution provides that property entails obligations and its use shall also serve the public good.

In France, the situation is different. For the past ten years, the French legislator has been trying to anchor the stakeholder approach more firmly in French corporate and financial markets law.[53] In 2019, the French legislator recast the rules on the corporate goal. It is now provided that the company shall be managed in the corporate interest, considering the social and environmental aspects of its activities.[54] In addition, the shareholders have the possibility to specify the company's purpose (*raison d'être*) in the articles of association of the companies.[55]

For Germany, the development in France is of particular interest, because the fundamental question of whether the corporate interests should be regulated in company law is once again hottest game in town. Now it is up for debate whether the board should be obliged to also take ecological and social concerns into account. In 2017, the *Regierungskommission* Corporate Governance made an even stronger commitment to the stakeholder value approach and ESG concerns, emphasizing the social responsibility of the company and its bodies and pointing out that social and environmental factors influence success of a company.[56] The Sustainable Finance Advisory Council has recently advocated for even more far-reaching reform.[57] The outcome of the discussion is open. This will be discussed in more detail in the next section.

In contrast, the French approach to regulating the corporate purpose is not considered to be an effective measure in German company law. It is already difficult to describe precisely what the difference between the purpose and the interests of a company (in the system of German corporate law) should be.[58] If the purpose is understood to be the *raison d'être*, it is a vague concept that does not work as a guideline for the board's actions. This can be illustrated by way of example. The self-proclaimed purpose of RWE is 'Our Energy for a Sustainable Life'.[59] This programmatic statement does not allow any legal conclusions to be drawn.[60] It is also doubtful whether it has a signalling effect, in the sense that the executive board signals to the market that it will meet the expectations addressed to it in terms of corporate management that promotes the common good. For the time being, it remains to be seen whether the concept of a

---

[53] cf Pierre-Henri Conac, 'The reform of articles 1833 and 1835 of the French Civil Code: recognition or revolution?' in Katharina Boele-Woelki and others (eds), *Festschrift für Karsten Schmidt, Band I* (CH Beck 2019) 213, 215.

[54] French Civil Code, art 1833.

[55] ibid art 1835; Conac (n 53) 217.

[56] Foreword to the Code [2017] 2 https://dcgk.de/de/kommission/die-kommission-im-dialog/deteilansicht/kodexaenderungen-2017-beschlossen-vorsitzwechsel-zum-1-maerz.html.

[57] cf Sustainable Finance-Advisory Council of the German government, 'Shifting the Trillions: Ein nachhaltiges Finanzsystem für die Große Transformation' (Sustainable Finance Beirat 2021) 96 https://sustainable-finance-beirat.de/wp-content/uploads/2021/02/210224_SFB_-Abschlussbericht-2021.pdf. The Council suggests that the company should be managed in the long-term interest of the company with due and appropriate consideration of sustainability goals.

[58] Thilo Kuntz, 'Corporate Purpose: konzeptionelle Grundlagen, rechtshistorische und rechtsdogmatische Aspekte' (2022) 186 Zeitschrift fur das gesamte Handelsrecht und Wirtschaftsrecht 652 argues the corporate purpose would affect the corporate purpose (*Gesellschaftszweck*) and the object of the company (*Unternehmensgegenstand*).

[59] See https://www.rwe.com/der-konzern/laender-und-standorte/.

[60] cf Holger Fleischer, 'Corporate Purpose: Ein Management-Konzept und seine gesellschaftsrechtlichen Implikationen' (2021) 18 Zeitschrift für Wirtschaftsrecht 5; Mathias Habersack, 'Corporate Purpose' in Gregor Bachmann and others (eds), *Festschrift für Christine Windbichler* (de Gruyter 2020) 707.

corporate purpose will be given sharper contours in economics and law.[61] According to the current understanding, it does not make sense to regulate the purpose in the German Stock Corporation Act.

## 6. Evaluation and Conclusion

Finally, three questions remain to be assessed: (i) how can the corporate interest of a stock corporation be defined under German company law; (ii) what significance does it have for the decisions and actions of the board of directors; and (iii) is it worth regulating the company's goal/interests by law?

a) The corporate goal: shareholder or stakeholder value?
The answer to the first question has already been sketched out by the previous analyses. The prevailing opinion is (once again) in favour of the stakeholder value approach. In the literature on German corporate law, the shareholder primacy approach is supported up to the present day.[62] However, in its pure form, the primacy of shareholder value is not upheld anymore; instead, it is best captured by the concept of enlightened shareholder value.[63] The discussion on shareholder versus stakeholder interests has so far been dominated by arguments stemming from the principal–agent conflict. If the focus were on shareholder value, the executive board would be provided with clearer operating guidelines.[64] This reduces the risk of the board pursuing its own interests and reduces the shareholders' costs of control.

The ESG era draws attention to an issue that the discussion on company law in general and on the goal of a corporation in particular has so far not considered: the externalization of costs arising from entrepreneurial activity to the public's detriment (inside-out perspective). However, it is addressed in the more recent discussion in corporate law. It is put forward that the dichotomy of shareholder and stakeholder interests would not go far enough adequately to meet modern requirements of corporate governance and corporate law.[65] According to this interpretation, the promotion of sustainability should be reflected in the understanding of the corporate interests.

---

[61] The purpose concept was developed in economics. cf Colin Mayer, *Prosperity: Better Business Makes the Greater Good* (OUP 2019); with a view to the legal aspects of the purpose concept cf Guido Ferrarini, 'Corporate Purpose and Sustainability' [2020] Rivista della Societa 27, 37; Jill E Solomon and Steven Davidoff Solomon, 'Should Corporations Have a Purpose?' (2021) 99 Texas Law Review 1309.

[62] Fleischer (n 35) para 37; Tobias Bürgers, '§ 76 Leitung der Aktiengesellschaft' in Tobias Bürgers, Thorsten Körber, and Jan Lieder (eds), *Heidelberger Kommentar Aktiengesetz* (5th edn, CF Müller 2021) para 13; Christoph Seibt, '§ 76 Leitung der Aktiengesellschaft' in Karsten Schmidt and Marcus Lutter (eds), *AktG Kommentar* (4th edn, Otto Schmidt 2020) para 12.

[63] Of course, the supporters of shareholder value take into account the specificities of the governance of a dualistic stock corporation in which employees have strong representation. However, they do not give much weight to these stakeholder interests.

[64] For a view critical of this argument see Hans-Joachim Mertens and Andreas Cahn, '§ 76 AktG' in Wolfgang Zöller and Ulrich Noack (eds), *Kölner Kommentar zum Aktiengesetz. Band 2/1* (3rd edn, Carl Heymanns Verlag 2010) para 17.

[65] Anne-Christin Mittwoch, *Nachhaltigkeit und Unternehmensrecht* (Mohr Siebeck 2022) 330 ff.

The goal of a corporation should be to create sustainable value within the planetary boundaries.[66]

Looking back at the discussion on the interests of a corporation over ninety years, it seems possible that academia and politics will take up this approach. The understanding of the corporate interests has always been significantly shaped by legislative reforms of company law. Although the European Commission has not proposed harmonizing the interests of a corporation across Europe, as suggested by a report commissioned by it,[67] the most recent EU legislative acts on due diligence obligations for companies and their business managers in the supply chain[68] and reporting obligations for companies on the achievement of climate targets and on climate risks inherent in the business model under the CSR Directive[69] will have an indirect effect on corporate governance. How this will be reflected in the interpretation of the company's interests cannot yet be assessed. The proposal in the literature that the goal of a stock corporation is 'to create sustainable value within the planetary boundaries' does not take into account the legal economic arguments concerning the principal–agent conflict, so it seems unlikely that it will prevail.[70] To some extent, however, ESG concerns are likely to be reflected in an adjusted definition of the corporate goal.

b) Corporate goal and business judgment rule

The company's interests determine business judgments by the board of directors. But how does the stakeholder value approach affect the business judgment rule? Admittedly, key issues are still discussed controversially today, in particular, whether there is a hierarchy of relevant interests. If we accept a pluralism of interests (shareholders, employees, creditors, and contractual partners, as well as the common good), then it is not possible generally to prioritize shareholders' over other stakeholders' interests.[71] Thus, the board of directors acts in accordance with its duties if it takes a decision in the interests of the employees or the public welfare, provided that the board *also* considers the interest of the shareholders.[72] The board must not ignore the interests of shareholders in maximizing the value of the company. The pluralism of interests

---

[66] ibid 381.
[67] The EY Final Report for the European Commission DG Justice and Consumers Study, 'Study on directors' duties and sustainable corporate governance' (EY, July 2020) 73 https://op.europa.eu/en/publication-detail/-/publication/e47928a2-d20b-11ea-adf7-01aa75ed71a1/language-en, which suggested that the Commission should propose a new EU directive 'providing an EU-wide formulation of directors' duties and company's interest', requiring directors to properly balance 'long-term interests of the company (beyond 5–10 years), interests of employees, interest of customers, interest of local and global environment, interest of society at large' and 'identify and mitigate sustainability risks and impacts, both internal and external, connected to the company's business operations and value chain'. The report has been strongly criticized by academics and politicians. The European Commission has therefore not taken up a large part of the proposals, including the one on corporate interest.
[68] The so-called Corporate Sustainability Due Diligence Directive has not yet been adopted. See Proposal of the European Commission for a Directive on Corporate Sustainability Due Diligence COM(2022) 71 final.
[69] CSR Directive (n 48).
[70] The proposal is seen critically by Gregor Bachmann, 'Klimaverantwortung: Zielsetzung und Governance von Unternehmen' (2023) 187 Zeitschrift fur das gesamte Handelsrecht und Wirtschaftsrecht 166, 182.
[71] cf Koch (n 30) § 76 para 31; Karsten Schmidt, *Gesellschaftsrecht* (4th edn, Carl Heymanns Verlag 2002) § 28 II.1.a.
[72] The extent to which the board has to consider the interest of the shareholders is assessed differently. In the literature, the interpretation has prevailed that the board of directors may regularly give priority to the interest in profitability over other interests. cf Koch (n 30) § 76 para 33; Seibt (n 62) para 40.

calls for a balancing of interests, both in the management and supervisory board, as well as between both bodies in determining the corporate strategies.[73]

The corporate interests do not establish any concrete duties to act for the executive board.[74] The board of directors is therefore not required to donate a certain amount of money to social or political projects, nor is it required to invest a certain amount of money in ecologically sustainable financial investments. However, it may do so and then may refer to the business judgment rule if the decision is made in the interests of the public welfare or the employees, even if this reduces the amount that is paid out as profit to the shareholders. The enlightened shareholder value approach advocated in parts of the literature would arrive at a different assessment, because according to this approach, such decisions would only be covered by the business judgment rule if they had a positive impact on the enterprise value, because this improves, for example, the reputation of the company and thus the prospects for profits.

What are the consequences for the corporate discretion of the board of directors if the corporate interests are also shaped by ESG concerns? At first glance, the discretion of the board seems to become greater. If the board is allowed to consider other interests, such as the protection of the oceans or biodiversity, a decision may also be justified which serves these objectives but is disadvantageous for the company. But on closer inspection it is doubtful whether the reference to sustainability goals results in greater entrepreneurial discretion of board members. Rather, the effect of the ESG legislation is to limit discretion. Under the EU Green Deal, the European legislature pursues the goal of transforming the economy. The recent reform acts provide a number of reporting obligations for companies, which have a considerable impact on the duties of management and supervisory board. This can be illustrated by the example of three disclosure requirements under the Corporate Sustainability Reporting Directive (CSR Directive).

The CSR Directive applies to undertakings regardless of their legal form, provided that those undertakings are large undertakings, or small and medium-sized undertakings, which are public-interest entities. These undertakings are to disclose

> [t]he plans of the undertaking, including implementing actions and related financial and investment plans, to ensure that its business model and strategy are compatible with the transition to a sustainable economy and with the limiting of global warming to 1,5 °C in line with the Paris Agreement,

> [h]ow the undertaking's business model and strategy take account of the interests of the undertaking's stakeholders and of the impacts of the undertaking on sustainability matters

> and

---

[73] Thomas Raiser and Rüdiger Veil, *Recht der Kapitalgesellschaften* (6th edn, Vahlen 2015) § 14 para 14; Koch (n 30) § 76 paras 28, 33.
[74] Jochen Vetter, 'Geschäftsleiterpflichten zwischen Legalität und Legitimität: Muss sich Ethik lohnen?' (2018) 47 Zeitschrift für Unternehmens- und Gesellschaftsrecht 338, 342.

[h]ow the undertaking's strategy has been implemented with regard to sustainability matters.[75]

How are these obligations to be classified? First of all, it follows from the wording that the provisions do not provide substantive obligations in the sense that the company must align its business model with the stated objectives. The legislator has only stipulated the obligation to report on a specific aspect (the plan; impact on sustainability matters; implementation of the strategy). However, the wording implies that the company develops a plan how to achieve the environmental objectives, assesses the impacts of the undertaking on sustainability matters and implements its strategy. The company therefore does not fulfil its reporting obligation if it states in the management report that it does not intend to achieve the stated objectives. No comply-or-explain mechanism is provided for, as under the previous CSR Directive. The reporting obligation therefore has a regulating effect on the behaviour of the company. Through the backdoor of the reporting obligations, the company is induced to align its business model with the sustainability goals of the EU. However, this is not enforceable, as the CSR Directive only provides for disclosure rules.

The requirements to report on the transformation plan also apply to the board of directors through the duty of legality.[76] In general, the management board is obliged to its company to fulfil the company's duties.[77] Of course, this also applies to the reporting obligations of the undertaking, which in turn require certain behaviour from the company (to develop a plan, etc.). The board may therefore still be empowered under the business judgment rule to maximize shareholder value, but it is only permitted to do so within the framework of ESG requirements, in particular the obligation under the CSR Directive to develop a transformation plan and a business strategy, which takes account of the interests of the undertaking's stakeholders. The ESG legislation will significantly limit the management's entrepreneurial discretion.[78]

c) Reform agenda

In Germany, all attempts to regulate the corporate interests by law since 1965 have failed. Looking back to 1965, the legislator's decision not to specify the corporate interests that determine the decisions of the management board appears to be wise. The arguments put forward at the time are still convincing today.

Interestingly, the reform proposals made since then have all provided vague concepts (interest of employees, public interest, etc.). It does not help much if the results of interpretation are adopted into law. What would be the added value of such a regulation, especially considering that the stakeholder value approach has prevailed? Secondly, a

---

[75] CSR Directive, art 19a(2)(a)(iii)–(v).
[76] Thilo Kuntz, 'How ESG is Weakening the Business Judgment Rule' in Thilo Kuntz (ed), *Research Handbook on Environmental, Social, and Corporate Governance* (Edward Elgar Publishing 2024) 78: 'The duty vis-à-vis the corporation and its shareholders not to violate any laws and norms the corporation hast to comply with ... works as a transmission belt in the context of fiduciary duties.'
[77] In German corporate law, this is referred to as the duty of legality.
[78] Kuntz (n 76) 78–83, pointing to the supply chain regulation and ESG regulation.

regulation specifying the interests might complicate the balancing processes, as a statutory regulation always raises the question of whether conclusions can be drawn about the importance of the interests to be taken into account from the order in which they are listed. With the inclusion of sustainability concerns in the catalogue of corporate interests, further questions would arise. This concerns not only the understanding of ESG goals, but also conflicting goals, which are becoming larger. Sustainability is multi-faceted; different ecological goals may be in competition with each other.[79]

In the discussion on aligning business activities with the goal of a sustainable economy, a statutory reform of corporate interests is seen by some as an effective regulatory strategy.[80] However, one should not expect too much from a specification in the Stock Corporation Act. First, a consideration of ESG concerns in the concept of corporate interests does not result in any obligations to act in a certain way for the board of directors. To encourage or even urge the board to develop a business strategy that contributes to the transformation of the economy, corporate reporting requirements on the business model and its alignment with sustainability goals[81] are more effective.

Secondly, the introduction of a rule on the interests to be taken into account by the board of directors may have adverse effects. The more abstractly the corporate interests are defined, the greater the risk that the board of directors will make decisions that are not in the interests of the shareholders and stakeholders, but in its own. The wording that the board should operate within 'planetary boundaries'[82] is rightly described as an empty phrase[83] that can be used almost arbitrarily to justify corporate decisions.

## III. The Representative Model

### 1. Labour Co-determination in the Supervisory Board

a) Development of the regimes

Labour co-determination saw the light of day in the period after the Second World War. In view of the winding down of the German war economy by the Allies and the reparations to be paid by Germany, the boards and owners of large companies were open to cooperating with the re-established trade unions and granting workers more extensive co-determination rights in companies.[84] This made it possible to establish a far-reaching co-determination in companies of the coal and steel industry. However, the wind changed quickly. As a result of the rapid recovery of the German economy, the trade unions were not able to push for parity co-determination for all companies in the

---

[79] Bachmann (n 70) 166, 183.
[80] cf Sustainable Finance Advisory Council (n 57); Mittwoch (n 65) 330 ff.
[81] See section III.6.b) above.
[82] Beate Sjåfjell, 'Reforming EU company law to secure the future of European business' (2021) 18 ECFR 190, 210 ff; Mittwoch (n 65) 360.
[83] cf Bachmann (n 70) 166, 182.
[84] Thomas Raiser, *Verhandlungen des 66. Deutschen Juristentages Stuttgart 2006, Band I Gutachten/Teil B: Unternehmensmitbestimmung vor dem Hintergrund europarechtlicher Entwicklungen* (CH Beck 2006) B 13.

political process.[85] The 1952 reform therefore resulted in only one-third employee participation in the supervisory board of corporations. There was no political support for more far-reaching proposals.

This only changed in 1976, when the legislator introduced parity co-determination in the supervisory board of companies employing more than 2,000 workers. The reform was based on recommendations of the so-called Biedenkopf Commission set up by the German Bundestag to evaluate experiences with the existing co-determination. The Biedenkopf Commission explained its recommendations with the 'essence of the democratic and social constitutional state' and the 'protection of human rights' (as provided for under the German constitution), which would require that workers participate in the management of companies because they are significantly affected by their decisions.[86] Interestingly, the proposals received broad support in the Bundestag.[87] The goal of equal co-determination was only softened by the compromise that in the event of a tie, the vote of the chairperson of the supervisory board, who is regularly appointed by the shareholders, is decisive.

Since nothing has changed in this system to this day, German law provides for three co-determination statutes, aiming at representation of employees in the supervisory board of a stock corporation or a limited liability company: (i) one-third participation in companies with more than 500 employees; (ii) quasi-parity co-determination in companies with more than 2,000 employees; (iii) co-determination on equal terms in the coal and steel industry.

b) Impact of labour co-determination on corporate policy

In order to understand the impact of co-determination, it is essential to determine the responsibilities and powers of the supervisory board in the governance of a stock corporation and a limited liability company.[88] The scope of tasks is broadly defined by the law: 'The supervisory board is to supervise the management board.'[89] This task has two dimensions; one is future-, the other past-oriented. On the one hand, the supervisory board advises the executive board on the business strategy (future). Principle 6 of the Corporate Governance Code therefore highlights that the supervisory board has to be involved in decisions with fundamental importance to the enterprise. On the other hand, the supervisory board has to control the executive board with regard to the business activities (past). This includes measures such as the dismissal of the board of directors and the assertion of claims for damages if management violates its duties.

---

[85] ibid. Raiser explains this also by the fact that demands for the socialization of the economy have not been successful.

[86] Mitbestimmungskommission, Bericht der Sachverständigenkommission zur Auswertung der bisherigen Erfahrungen bei der Mitbestimmung, Bundestag printed papers VI/334 *Deutscher Bundestag* (4 February 1970) 18, 56 https://dserver.bundestag.de/btd/06/003/0600334.pdf.

[87] The bill was also supported by the opposition group; only 22 MPs voted against and one abstained. cf Raiser (n 84) B 16.

[88] In principle, a limited liability company does not have a supervisory board. However, if it has more than 500 employees, it must establish one.

[89] cf Stock Corporation Act, § 111I1).

In order to fulfil these tasks, the board is granted important powers. First, the supervisory board has the power to appoint members of the management board, as well as remove them from office. In addition, it is competent to determine the remuneration of the members of the management board. Although measures to be taken by management may not be transferred to the supervisory board, the supervisory board or the by-laws may require that certain types of business transactions may be implemented only with the supervisory board's consent.[90] The management board shall inform the supervisory board periodically and on an ad hoc basis so that the supervisory board can properly perform its duties.[91]

The system of co-determination is based on the idea that representatives of the employees will take into account the interests of the employees in the context of business policy and personnel decisions (appointment and dismissal of members of the management board). However, the members of the supervisory board elected by employees are not representatives of the employees in the legal sense, and in particular not subject to instructions from trade unions or works councils. Rather, according to the interpretations of the Federal Supreme Court, they are independent and only obliged to serve the interests of the company.[92] This does not, however, preclude the members of the supervisory board from taking into account the impact of business policy decisions on employees.

The supervisory board is a powerful body in the governance of a stock corporation or limited liability company. The co-determination of employees in companies established in Germany is unique in Europe. Most EU Member States do not provide for labour participation in the board of directors or supervisory board at all.[93] In some Member States, different labour co-determination statutes do exist. However, the influence of the employees is generally low, as the supervisory board of stock corporations has few powers compared to the German supervisory board.[94] If co-determination in a monistic company takes place in its board of directors, a maximum of one-third of the members are elected by the employees. Indeed, a quasi-parity codetermination only exists in Germany.[95] Finally, representatives of trade unions have a seat on the management or supervisory board in only a few European countries.[96]

c) Experiences

Quasi-parity labour co-determination has existed in Germany for almost fifty years. In order to be able to assess the approach of co-determination, it is important to note at the outset that the tasks and powers of the supervisory board have changed over the

---

[90] cf ibid § 111(4) sentence 2.
[91] cf ibid § 90.
[92] BGH [2006] II ZR 137/05, BGHZ 169, 98 para 18.
[93] In 2006, eleven out of twenty-five EU Member States provided for a labour co-determination in a board; cf Robert Rebhahn, *Verhandlungen des 66. Deutschen Juristentages Stuttgart 2006, Band II/1/Teil M: Unternehmensmitbestimmung vor dem Hintergrund europarechtlicher Entwicklungen – Referat* (CH Beck 2006) M 17–M 19.
[94] ibid M 11.
[95] ibid M 26.
[96] ibid M 14: Czech Republic, Slovenia, and Sweden.

last thirty years. First, the aspect of advising the board on fundamental issues of the corporate policy (future-oriented task) plays a much greater role than it used to. As a consequence, the supervisory board is involved in strategic management decisions at an early stage. In order to shoulder this task, members of the supervisory board must have special expertise. Although it is not yet a legal requirement, the Corporate Governance Code suggests that the supervisory board shall determine specific objectives regarding its composition, and shall prepare a profile of skills and expertise for the entire board, while taking the principle of diversity into account.[97] For supervisory board members elected by employees, special challenges arise from the more numerous and more complex tasks. In large companies it is now common for the employee side to be advised by external experts (investment bankers, lawyers) on major transactions that require the approval of the supervisory board. These costs are usually borne by the company.

More than almost any other topic, labour co-determination is the subject of a highly controversial discussion in company law. Although co-determination is strongly rooted in German economic and social history,[98] it is still perceived by trade associations and shareholder representatives as anti-systemic as it gives trade unions and workers a say in corporate decisions.[99] If we look at it without ideological bias, a number of advantages and disadvantages can be identified.

First, managers, trade-unions, and a wide range of stakeholders appreciate that co-determination in the supervisory board provides both board members and employees with extensive opportunities for information and consultation.[100] In particular, employee representatives improve access to information by representatives of the shareholders in the supervisory board and improve the decision-making practices of the board.[101] Employee representatives often know the company very well from many years of service and are therefore able to assess the impact of business policy decisions. Secondly, empirical studies suggest that strong co-determination facilitates an employment model that aims for long-term workforce affiliation.[102] The reason given is that employees not only have the alternative of leaving the company, but also the possibility of influencing company decisions.[103]

The criticism primarily concerns the impact on corporate governance. It is put forward that labour co-determination in the supervisory board weakens the system of checks and balances. First, co-determination results in a disproportionate size of the supervisory board. In large companies (usually with more than 20,000 employees), the supervisory board consists of twenty people. At this size, it is difficult to work

---

[97] German Corporate Governance Code, Recommendation C.1.
[98] Kommission Mitbestimmung, 'Bericht der Kommission Mitbestimmung: Mitbestimmung und neue Unternehmenskulturen: Bilanz und Perspektiven' *Bertelsmann Stiftung/Hans Böckler-Stiftung* (1998) https://www.boeckler.de/pdf/p_hbs_bertelsmann_kommmb_abschluss1998.pdf.
[99] Zöllner (n 31) 336, 338.
[100] Raiser (n 84) B 53.
[101] Rebhahn (n 93), M 28.
[102] Raiser (n 84) B 51.
[103] ibid B 52.

effectively. The legislator therefore wanted to reduce the number of members in 1998, but the reform failed due to opposition from the trade unions. Secondly, critics argue that co-determination would have the effect of consensus-driven decision-making in the supervisory board, which strengthens management's influence.[104] They claim that the board of directors and employee representatives in the supervisory board would conclude gentlemen's agreements prior to fundamental corporate transactions, which may be to the detriment of the shareholders. Thirdly, co-determination can lead to serious conflicts of interest.[105] This mainly concerns those members who were elected to the supervisory board as trade union representatives.[106] Fourthly, critics doubt that quasi-parity co-determination could be justified today, as a small number of employee representatives would be sufficient to improve the decision-making processes in a supervisory board.[107]

d) Assessment

The German representative model enables stakeholders to participate in corporate policy decisions. To understand this model, it is important to bear in mind that co-determination can only be explained historically. Moreover, quasi-parity co-determination reflects a specific economic policy developed by the legislature,[108] which is still valid today because it reflects the social obligations of property ownership under the German constitution (*Grundgesetz*). According to the Federal Constitutional Court, the quasi-parity co-determination does not violate the fundamental rights of shareholders, as these retain sole responsibility for the basic decisions, which are still adopted by the shareholders' meeting.[109]

Nevertheless, the criticism has not been silenced to this day. While there are no attempts to reduce or abolish co-determination through legislative reforms,[110] the far-reaching co-determination is often a reason for companies to adopt a foreign legal form in order to avoid co-determination or to change to the legal form of the Societas Europaea, which makes it possible that representatives of the employees and the management board negotiate on the co-determination. Finally, the popularity of the limited partnership (*Kommanditgesellschaft*) is also explained by the fact that this legal form is

---

[104] Rebhahn (n 93), M 27. However, consensus building is considered as a positive effect of co-determination by Raiser (n 84) B 53.

[105] cf Peter Ulmer, 'Generalbericht' in Theodor Baums and Peter Ulmer (eds), *Employees' Co-Determination in the Member States of the European Union* (Verlag Recht und Wirtschaft GmbH 2004) 159, 176.

[106] A major controversy was caused by the fact that Frank Bsirkse, chairman of a trade union and member of the supervisory board of Lufthansa AG, called for a strike, which resulted in enormous financial losses for Lufthansa AG. cf Marcus Lutter and Karl-Heinz Quack, 'Mitbestimmung und Schadensabwehr' in Reinhard Damm, Peter W Heermann, and Rüdiger Veil (eds), *Festschrift für Thomas Raiser* (de Gruyter 2005) 259, 270: 'It was not easy for the management board to explain to the shareholders that under current German law, their own supervisory board members are entitled to damage their company, at least passively.'

[107] Rebhahn (n 93), M 32–M 33.

[108] cf BVerfG [1979]: 1 BvR 532/77, 1 BvR 533/77, 1 BvR 419/78, 1 BvL 21/78, BVerfGE 50, 290: Guiding principle 2: 'The legislature may pursue any economic policy it deems appropriate, provided that in doing so it respects the *Grundgesetz*, in particular fundamental rights.'

[109] cf ibid, para 91.

[110] In 2006, the German Jurists' Conference discussed a comprehensive reform of co-determination. The debate was so controversial that no resolutions were passed.

not subject to labour co-determination. Indeed, avoidance of co-determination is often a central reason for transformation of companies.

## 2. Representation as a Model to Integrate ESG in Business Policy

The report prepared for the European Commission by EY argued that the current board composition would not fully support a shift towards sustainability.[111] It would be conceivable to require members of the supervisory board to have special expertise in sustainability issues.[112] In addition, a possible reform proposal could also affect the composition of the supervisory board. If representatives of non-governmental organizations (NGOs) have seats on the supervisory board, they might be able to enforce sustainability concerns within the company. The EY Report points in this direction, suggesting that the European Commission proposes 'a new EU directive laying down rules on board composition of listed companies, including a requirement for companies to consider sustainability criteria in the board nomination process'.[113]

How useful is this approach to reform? One of the reasons for labour co-determination on the supervisory board is that employees are affected by business policy decisions. This is also true for other stakeholders, especially for the general public. As explained above, business activities result in negative impacts on the environment and sustainability matters. The CSR Directive is based on this recognition. In addition, it can be argued that in a governance model of interest pluralism, it is consistent to grant certain stakeholders representation on the supervisory board. Certainly, it is more difficult to determine who might be representative of ESG stakeholders, particularly in light of the fact that environmental concerns are multifaceted and the impact of the company's business activities is difficult to capture precisely. However, the issue can be resolved; similar to employees, shareholders would have the option of electing representatives to the supervisory board proposed by ESG interest groups for one or two seats. Therefore, at first glance, it seems plausible at any rate, to give representatives of environmental interest groups (ie NGOs) a say by granting them seats on supervisory boards.

However, experience with corporate co-determination teaches us that severe conflicts with interests of shareholders and employees would arise. In contrast to employees, representatives of ESG interest groups do no not have any relationship with the company and are not interested at all in maximization of the profits. It could hardly be assumed that they exclusively pursue the company's interests, as required by the Federal Supreme Court to ensure effective corporate governance. Effective control of the management by the supervisory board requires that the members of the supervisory board work together in a confidential manner. This is usually the case in supervisory boards subject to labour co-determination, but is likely to be more difficult if

---

[111] EY Report (n 67) 37, 40, 43, 122.
[112] ibid 130 ff.
[113] ibid Option C5, 130.

ESG representatives were present. Finally, the balance between shareholder representatives on the one hand and employee representatives on the other would no longer be maintained. ESG-representatives do not fit into the governance of a stock corporation.[114] If one wants to achieve that ESG concerns are taken into account in the supervisory board, it can be considered to require a special expertise for (a certain number of) members of the supervisory board.

On a different note, the board of directors is empowered to seek external expertise in ESG matters. We can already see a trend toward this occurring through voluntarily established boards. In Germany, some stock corporations have already established such boards whose task is to advise the management board on diversity and ESG issues. Such advisory boards are not part of the corporate governance of a company and may be established by the board on a contractual basis. Thus, they have no powers vis-à-vis the management board.

## IV. Conclusion

1. In German corporate law, the concept of corporate interests determines the parameters for decisions by the management and supervisory board. The term is to be distinguished from the objective of the company, which is either to make profits or to conduct non-profit activities.
2. In 1937, the German Stock Corporation Act provided a regulation on the corporate interests to be observed by the management board, which goes back to the discussion about the *Unternehmen an sich* during the Weimar Republic, but was significantly motivated by national socialism. Since the regulation was repealed in 1965, the determination of the corporate interests has been the subject of controversial debate.
3. Since the 1970s, the debate on shareholder versus stakeholder approach in Germany has been significantly influenced by reforms of stock corporation law, labour law, and business law. In the academic discussion, the stakeholder value approach has prevailed. Likewise, the Corporate Governance Code states that the management and supervisory board are 'to take into account the interests of the shareholders, the enterprise's workforce and the other groups related to the enterprise (stakeholders) to ensure the continued existence of the enterprise and its sustainable value creation (the enterprise's best interests)'.
4. Proposals to specify the corporate interest in the Stock Corporation Act failed. Indeed, statutory provisions on the corporate interest are typically vague and therefore not suitable for specifying the standard of duty of the board of directors and the supervisory board. In addition, a regulation specifying the interests might complicate the balancing processes, as a statutory regulation always

---

[114] Bachmann (n 70) 166, 194 is more positive, but ultimately rejects the proposal.

raises the question of whether conclusions can be drawn about the importance of the interests to be taken into account from the order in which they are listed.
5. In the ESG discussion, it is suggested that the goal of a company should be regulated by law. It is proposed that the goal of a corporation should be to create sustainable value within the planetary boundaries. However, this clause is not suitable for determining the decision-making behaviour of management in the sense of aligning the business model with transformation goals. Furthermore, the proposed regulation increases the risk that managers will pursue their own interests to the detriment of the company.
6. The EU legislation on sustainability reporting (the CSR Directive) will determine corporate behaviour. The obligation to report on the transformation plan and the company's goals on climate neutrality will have an impact on managers' duties. In order to be able to fulfil the reporting obligation, the management board must take appropriate measures. The disclosure obligations therefore have a regulatory function.
7. To encourage or even urge the management board to develop a business strategy that contributes to the transformation of the economy, corporate reporting requirements on the business model and its alignment with sustainability goals are more effective than a statutory regulation of corporate interests, which includes ESG concerns.
8. Under German stock corporation law, the supervisory board is responsible for monitoring the executive board. In large companies, the supervisory board is composed of equal numbers of shareholder and employee representatives. The quasi-parity co-determination affects the interests of a corporation. It is widely acknowledged that the interests of the company also include the interests of the employees. The board members are obliged to act exclusively in the interests of the company. This also applies to the employee representatives. But employee representatives in the supervisory board have wide-ranging discretion to take employee interests into account when taking part in business policy decisions.
9. The quasi parity co-determination has both advantages and disadvantages. On the one hand, labour co-determination in the supervisory board provides both members of the management board and employees with extensive opportunities for information and consultation. On the other hand, labour co-determination in the supervisory board weakens the system of checks and balances.
10. Experience with co-determination teaches us that severe conflicts with interests of shareholders and employees would arise, if ESG interest groups were given seats on the supervisory board.

# 6
# Corporate Purpose: The US Discussion and the Restatement of the Law of Corporate Governance

*Edward B. Rock\**

## I. Introduction

Everyone is talking about 'corporate purpose', both in the United States, in Europe, and in Asia. What is 'corporate purpose' and how does it relate to corporate law? I am the Reporter for the American Law Institute's new 'Restatement of the Law of Corporate Governance'. In this chapter, I discuss the relationship between the current high profile debate on 'corporate purpose' and the Restatement.

Let us start with the current debate. Discussions of 'corporate purpose' are seemingly everywhere. In the United States, BlackRock CEO Larry Fink made waves with his January 2018 letter to CEOs in which he called for companies to articulate and pursue a 'purpose':

> Society is demanding that companies, both public and private, serve a social purpose. To prosper over time, every company must not only deliver financial performance, but also show how it makes a positive contribution to society. Companies must benefit all of their stakeholders, including shareholders, employees, customers, and the communities in which they operate.[1]

The Business Roundtable, an organization of chief executive officers (CEOs) of America's leading companies, has issued a 'Statement on the Purpose of a Corporation'.[2] This statement, signed by 181 CEO members, set forth a broad and inclusive conception of the corporate purpose:

> While each of our individual companies serves its own corporate purpose, we share a fundamental commitment to all of our stakeholders. We commit to:

---

\* All internet sources were last accessed on 15 January 2024.
[1] Larry Fink, 'A Sense of Purpose' https://corpgov.law.harvard.edu/2018/01/17/a-sense-of-purpose/.
[2] Business Roundtable, 'Statement on the Purpose of a Corporation' (19 August 2019) https://perma.cc/972D-DC42.

- Delivering value to our customers. We will further the tradition of American companies leading the way in meeting or exceeding customer expectations.
- Investing in our employees. This starts with compensating them fairly and providing important benefits. It also includes supporting them through training and education that help develop new skills for a rapidly changing world. We foster diversity and inclusion, dignity and respect.
- Dealing fairly and ethically with our suppliers. We are dedicated to serving as good partners to the other companies, large and small, that help us meet our missions.
- Supporting the communities in which we work. We respect the people in our communities and protect the environment by embracing sustainable practices across our businesses.
- Generating long-term value for shareholders, who provide the capital that allows companies to invest, grow and innovate. We are committed to transparency and effective engagement with shareholders.

Each of our stakeholders is essential. We commit to deliver value to all of them, for the future success of our companies, our communities and our country.[3]

Others have entered the debate. Senators have introduced legislation designed to make corporations more responsive to employees.[4] Similar calls have been heard in Europe.[5] Recently, Professor Colin Mayer, and the British Academy's *Future of the Corporation* project that he led, has called for 'purpose' to be mandatory and legally enforced.[6]

In these various debates, what exactly is meant by 'corporate purpose'? I am not sure that there is a single answer to that question. It can be understood to be 'a concrete goal or objective for the firm that reaches beyond profit maximization.'[7] This is a somewhat more general definition that, nonetheless, is relatively close to the articulation in the British Academy's 'Principles for Purposeful Business' as 'the purpose of business is to solve the problems of people and planet profitably, and not profit from causing problems.'[8]

Let me take as given that Larry Fink's assertion that 'purpose driven' businesses perform better in the long term than pure 'profit maximizing' businesses and the British Academy's assertion that, normatively, businesses with a purpose of profitably solving problems of the people and the planet without profiting from causing problems is a

---

[3] ibid.

[4] See eg Elizabeth Warren's Accountable Capitalism Act 2018.

[5] See eg Klaus Schwab, 'Davos Manifesto 2020: The Universal Purpose of a Company in the Fourth Industrial Revolution' *World Economic Forum* (2 December 2019) https://perma.cc/Q2RP-2NYK.

[6] The British Academy, 'Policy & Practice for Purposeful Business' (2021) 25 https://perma.cc/5BSU-APDY; Colin Mayer, 'The Future of the Corporation and the Economics of Purpose' (2021) 58 Journal of Management Studies 887 ('Company law should require firms to specify and implement whatever purposes they deem appropriate'); Colin Mayer, *Prosperity: Better Business Makes the Greater Good* (1st edn, OUP 2021) 40, 109.

[7] Claudine Gartenberg, Andrea Prat, and George Serafeim, 'Corporate Purpose and Financial Performance' (2019) 30(1) Organization Science 1, 26.

[8] The British Academy, 'Principles for Purposeful Business' www.thebritishacademy.ac.uk/publications/future-of-the-corporation-principles-for-purposeful-business/.

worthy social goal. How, if at all, does this impact a project whose goal is to 'restate' rent law?

## II. The Restatement of Corporate Governance's Description of the 'Objective' of a Corporation

In January 2019, the Council of the American Law Institute approved the initiation of a Restatement of the Law of Corporate Governance, and asked me to head the project as the 'Reporter'.[9] The goal of a Restatement is to 'to recapitulate the law as it presently exists' at the same time as there is an 'impulse to reformulate it, thereby rendering it clearer and more coherent while subtly transforming it in the process'.[10] In doing so, Restatements are 'analytical, critical and constructive'.[11] While they 'resemble codifications more than mere compilations of the pronouncements of judges', they are not proposed statutes and must 'reflect the flexibility and capacity for development and growth of the common law'.[12] As a result, a 'Restatement thus assumes the perspective of a common-law court, attentive to and respectful of precedent, but not bound by precedent that is inappropriate or inconsistent with the law as a whole'.[13]

The section that most directly intersects with the 'corporate purpose' debate is section 2.01 on the 'Objective of a Corporation', approved by the ALI Council and the ALI membership at the May 2022 annual meeting. Section 2.01 describes the 'objective' of a corporation as follows:[14]

> § 2.01. The Objective of a Corporation
> (a) The objective of a corporation is to enhance the economic value of the corporation, within the boundaries of the law;
>   (1) in common-law jurisdictions: for the benefit of the corporation's shareholders. In doing so, a corporation may consider:
>     (a) the interests of the corporation's employees;
>     (b) the desirability of fostering the corporation's business relationships with suppliers, customers, and others;
>     (c) the impact of the corporation's operations on the community and the environment; and
>     (d) ethical considerations related to the responsible conduct of business;

---

[9] Professor Jill Fisch (University of Pennsylvania Law School) and Professor Marcel Kahan (NYU Law School) were the original Associate Reporters. Professor Elisabeth de Fontenay recently joined the team after Professor Fisch stepped down in 2023.
[10] American Law Institute, 'Capturing the Voice of the American Law Institute' (rev 2015) 4 www.ali.org/media/filer_public/65/25/6525b3d0-0ac1-4dba-b2bb-5b0eb022fd55/stylemanual.pdf.
[11] ibid.
[12] ibid 5.
[13] ibid.
[14] Restatement of Corporate Governance § 2.01 (American Law Institute Tentative Draft No 1, 2022).

(2) in stakeholder jurisdictions: for the benefit of the corporation's shareholders and/or, to the extent permitted by state law, for the benefit of employees, creditors, suppliers, customers, or communities in which offices or other establishments of the corporation are located.

(b) A corporation, in the conduct of its business, may devote a reasonable amount of resources to public-welfare, humanitarian, educational, and philanthropic purposes, whether or not doing so enhances the economic value of the corporation.

How did the ALI come to this version? First, it is important to realize that, as with the common law subjects of Restatements, corporate law in the United States is state law, not federal law. There are thus, to some degree, fifty different versions of corporate law in the United States. There are two main approaches to answering the question 'for whom is the corporate managed?' (Let me note here that this may or may not be the same question raised by the 'corporate purpose' debate, but it is clearly related to it.)

The traditional or common law approach is a version of 'shareholder primacy' and set forth in section 2.01(a)(1): 'The objective of a corporation is to enhance the economic value of the corporation, within the boundaries of the law, for the benefit of the corporation's shareholders.'

Traditional jurisdictions like Delaware do not explicitly define the objective of the corporation. The priority and distinctiveness of shareholder interests emerges in several ways. For example, a director or officer is considered 'interested' in a transaction or conduct only when he or she receives 'a direct or indirect benefit (or suffers a detriment) as a result of, or from, the transaction or conduct when the benefit (or detriment) is not generally shared pro rata according to the number of shares held'.[15] The fact that a director or officer who holds shares is not considered interested when the director or officer receives a benefit that is shared pro rata according to the number of shares held illustrates how the priority of shareholder interests is part of the deep structure of corporate law. As a result, the decision by directors who are also shareholders to pay a dividend is not considered an interested transaction and typically is not subject to heightened scrutiny because shareholders receive dividends on a pro rata basis.

Shareholder priority also emerges from the basic corporate statutes in which only shareholders have the power to elect directors and to approve an amendment of the certificate of incorporation, mergers, a sale of all or substantially all the assets, or a dissolution. When shares are sufficiently concentrated for shareholders to act collectively, this assignment of voting rights creates a power structure in which shareholder interests are primary.

Finally, when the interests of shareholders diverge from the interests of other participants in the firm, for example, preferred shareholders and bondholders, courts in common law jurisdictions have consistently held that shareholder interests must be given priority. At the same time, the board of directors has wide discretion to take into

---

[15] Restatement of Corporate Governance (n 14) § 1.23.

account the interests of non-shareholder constituencies as it deems appropriate, and such decisions are protected by the business judgment rule.

During the 'takeover wars' of the 1980s, and in response to Delaware case law affirming 'shareholder primacy' in the context of sales of control, including the well-known *Revlon* case, many states adopted 'constituency' statutes designed to give boards of directors more flexibility in considering the interests of non-shareholder constituencies or stakeholders. Because of the variation among constituency statutes and additional variations introduced by judicial interpretation, it is best to think of the 'stakeholder' approach as a range of approaches.

The statutes can be divided into three principal types: 'modified shareholder primacy' statutes that make clear that a board *must* consider the best interests of shareholders and *may* consider other interests; the 'level playing-field' statutes that list the factors a board *may* consider and lists the interests of shareholders as one of a number of interests without an indication of any priority; and 'strong form level playing-field' statutes that contain language making it clear that a board may totally sublimate some of the listed factors to others. At present, no state makes the consideration of non-shareholder interests mandatory, although one state, Connecticut, did so until 2010.

While the history of stakeholder statutes makes clear that they were intended to grant boards of directors more discretion in selling the company than Delaware was thought to provide, the extent to which they were intended to change the basic economic objective is unclear. Subsequent case law development has not generally clarified the scope of the expanded discretion provided to boards of directors. This class of approaches is restated in section 2.01(a)(2).

More recently, with the enactment of 'benefit corporation' statutes in thirty-four states, the organizational options have expanded. When an entity is organized as a benefit corporation that follows the model benefit corporation legislation, its board of directors is required to 'consider the effects of any action or inaction upon' shareholders, employees, customers, communities, the environment, and its identified public benefit purposes, and 'need not give priority to a particular interest or factor'.[16] In many states, a corporation may become a benefit corporation by means of a simple amendment to the certificate of incorporation, so long as the heading in the certificate of incorporation includes the words 'public benefit corporation' or 'PBC'.[17] The benefit corporation form, although still in its early years, is growing in use, especially among new companies. It is likely to become a primary channel for opting out of, or tailoring, both the common law form and the stakeholder form of the corporation. Because benefit corporations are such a new enterprise form, and there is minimal case law interpreting their provisions, the Restatement is not 'restating' them.[18] They are, however, important in understanding the full range of alternative enterprise forms.

---

[16] Model Benefit Corporation Legislation § 301. See also DGCL § 362.
[17] DGCL § 362; Model Benefit Corporation Legislation § 104.
[18] In addition, there are a variety of non-corporate enterprise forms that are available (and beyond the scope of the Restatement of Corporate Governance (n 14)). The most common is the 'limited liability company' or 'LLC' and the 'limited partnership', both of which permit nearly unlimited modification. Finally, there are some newer forms designed specifically for 'social enterprises' including the 'low-profit limited liability company' or

## III. What Is 'Corporate Purpose'?

If the above is an accurate description of the legal 'state of play', how does it relate to the debate over 'corporate purpose'?

I touched on this before but let me elaborate here. First, there is a descriptive claim or conjecture that businesses which are organized around a 'corporate purpose', understood as 'a concrete goal or objective for the firm that reaches beyond profit maximization',[19] outperform firms that directly focus on maximizing profits or 'total shareholder return' or some similar measure. I think of this as the 'Fink conjecture', after Larry Fink's 2019 letter to CEOs in which he stated that:

> Purpose is not a mere tagline or marketing campaign; it is a company's fundamental reason for being—what it does every day to create value for its stakeholders. *Purpose is not the sole pursuit of profits but the animating force for achieving them. Profits are in no way inconsistent with purpose—in fact, profits and purpose are inextricably linked.* Profits are essential if a company is to effectively serve all of its stakeholders over time—not only shareholders, but also employees, customers, and communities. Similarly, when a company truly understands and expresses its purpose, it functions with the focus and strategic discipline that drive long-term profitability. Purpose unifies management, employees, and communities. It drives ethical behaviour and creates an essential check on actions that go against the best interests of stakeholders. Purpose guides culture, provides a framework for consistent decision-making, and, ultimately, helps sustain long-term financial returns for the shareholders of your company.[20]

This is a plausible claim about how best to manage large businesses. It is also a claim that the phrase 'corporate purpose' does not adequately capture. If correct, it is correct for enterprises that are organized as LLCs or LPs or even general partnerships and not as corporations. As such, it is really a claim about the importance of a 'business purpose' and not of a 'corporate purpose'. Indeed, it is a claim about how best to manage businesses and not, in itself, a claim about the law at all.

There is a second, more normative, use of the term 'corporate purpose'. When Larry Fink says that '[s]ociety is demanding that companies, both public and private, serve a social purpose',[21] he is referring to a social and political demand that large business enterprises behave in a socially responsible manner. This is a statement about what used to be known as 'corporate social responsibility'. Like the descriptive use of the term

---

L3C (adopted in eight states); the 'benefit limited liability company', or the BLLC (adopted in five states); and the 'social purpose corporation' or SPC (offered in four states).

[19] Gartenberg, Prat, and Serafeim (n 7) 26.
[20] Larry Fink, 'Larry Fink's 2019 Letter to CEOs: Purpose & Profit' www.blackrock.com/americas-offshore/en/2019-larry-fink-ceo-letter (emphasis in the original). See also Mayer (n 6).
[21] Fink (n 1).

'corporate purpose', it too applies to all significant business enterprises and not just to those that are organized as corporations.

## IV. The Link between the 'Objective of a Corporation' and 'Corporate Purpose'

With this conceptual clarification, we can ask a central question: what is the link, if any, between the Restatement's 'objective of a corporation' and what I will now refer to as 'business purpose'?[22] What should the link be?

There are, it seems to me, two sorts of answers to this question: a public law answer and a private law answer. Let me start with the public law answer. For those convinced that 'business purpose' is essential for business success and/or for social and political legitimacy, there is a temptation to interpret (or reform) corporate law to impose a legal requirement for firms to adopt a legally enforceable 'business purpose'. Thus, for example, Colin Mayer argues for a requirement that corporations set out a specific 'corporate purpose' in their constitutive documents:[23]

> [Corporate Law] should [require] companies to articulate their purposes, incorporate them in their articles of association, and require them to demonstrate how their ownership, governance, values, culture, leadership, measurement, incentives, and performance uphold and promote their purposes.

To my eyes, this proposal is badly misconceived. First, while it strikes me as plausible that, for some firms, organizing around a central articulated purpose will lead to superior performance, there is simply insufficient evidence to support a claim that this is true of all firms. Secondly, if 'business purpose' does, in fact, lead to superior performance, then one would expect firms in competitive markets to organize around a common purpose spontaneously. Thirdly, the history, perverse effects on third parties, and ineffectiveness of the ultra vires doctrine should make any corporate scholar think twice about reviving it in this form.[24] Finally, whatever the virtues of Professor Mayer's proposal, it is not current law in any jurisdiction and thus inappropriate for a Restatement.

There is a second, 'private law' approach that provides a more promising and interesting analysis of the link between 'corporate objective' and 'business purpose'. As noted above, the law provides a wide menu of organizational forms including corporations (with somewhat different characteristics depending on the jurisdictions),

---

[22] I address these issues at greater length in Edward B Rock, 'Business Purpose and the Objective of the Corporation' in Elizabeth Pollman and Robert Thompson (eds), *Research Handbook on Corporate Purpose and Personhood* (Edward Elgar Publishing 2021).
[23] Mayer (n 6) 225.
[24] For a brief overview of the problems it created see Paul Davies and Sarah Worthington, *Gower: Principles of Modern Company Law* (10th edn, Sweet & Maxwell 2016) section 7-29.

general partnerships, limited partnerships, LLCs, and others. Much of the law relating to these different forms clarifies their precise characteristics.

Each of these forms has characteristics that make the form appropriate for some sort of enterprises while inappropriate for others. Thus, for example, all partners in a general partnership are jointly and severally liable for the debts of the partnership. By contrast, in the corporation, shareholders' liability is limited to the amounts that they have invested in the firm. These enterprise forms create very different governance structures. The joint and several liability of general partners creates a structure in which partners have to monitor each other's behaviour in order to protect themselves. By contrast, the limited liability of shareholders in the corporation substantially reduces shareholders' incentives to monitor the managers. There is a large literature that tries to understand the link between organizational form and enterprise type, including the ways in which the characteristics of a particular form can facilitate or undermine business success.

Approaching the question from this perspective immediately opens up a very interesting question. Assuming that Larry Fink is correct that (some) purpose-oriented firms outperform firms that prioritize profit maximization, what is the best organizational form for those firms? Should they be organized as traditional corporations with the 'shareholder primacy' objective? Should they be organized in a 'constituency' jurisdiction that gives the board greater discretion to balance the interests of different stakeholders? Or should they be organized as 'benefit corporations' in which board consideration of stakeholder interests is mandatory? Or should they use some other enterprise form such as an LLC?

The importance of this question demonstrates that my complaint about the ambiguity of the term 'corporate purpose' is not merely pedantic. Rather, it emerges from a private law view of business law. On this view, business law provides a variety of tools that private parties may use in ordering their affairs. These tools include contracts, agency relationships, and a whole menu of enterprise forms. The tools themselves are neutral as to many of the most important social controversies, to the chagrin of many. Moreover, the tools are used in a wide range of situations. Over the decades, the same basic corporate form has been used for everything from small privately held businesses, to wholly owned subsidiaries, to mutual companies, and to the largest publicly held firms.

For generations, contract law has been attacked as being insufficiently attentive to differences in bargaining power or wealth. Similarly, corporate law has been attacked for being insufficiently attentive to the social responsibility of corporations or, more recently, environmental concerns. The standard response of traditionalists is that contract law and corporate law have a narrow set of goals and that overloading either with additional demands will fail to advance those goals while undermining their traditional usefulness.

The value of the traditional approach can be seen when one takes seriously the hypothesized link between 'purpose' and 'performance'. If, for example, as some have argued, the path by which purpose leads to superior performance runs primarily through its galvanizing effect on middle management, then the traditional corporate form may be perfectly adequate. After all, 'superior performance' benefits shareholders. By contrast, if the link between purpose and performance requires enforceable commitments to key stakeholders, then the optimal form might be the benefit corporation, unless enforceable contracts provide sufficient protection. When one conflates 'corporate purpose' and the 'objective of a corporation', one cannot even ask this question.

As one goes down this route, it becomes more and more likely that there is no single answer. Even accepting that, for some firms, a strong purpose will lead to superior performance, the channels will probably vary from firm to firm. A 'one size fits all' answer like Colin Mayer proposes is unlikely to be appropriate, even for all purpose-driven firms.

This private law approach emphasizes the importance of clear descriptions of the characteristics of different enterprise forms so that business planners can accurately select the form best suited to their needs. From this perspective, the task of the Restatement should be accurately to describe the characteristics of the corporate form as it exists in traditional jurisdictions like Delaware and as it has been modified in other states through the adoption of 'constituency' statutes. This is largely a technocratic exercise rather than a normative one.

This approach is agnostic on the important questions raised by the 'corporate purpose' debate. It will not answer the management question of how to build great companies. Likewise, it takes no position on the political question of the social obligations of large business enterprises. But correctly describing the characteristics of the corporate form under current law is still an important and useful goal for a Restatement of the Law of Corporate Governance. After all, neither the ALI nor the Reporters nor the members of the ALI who will vote on whether to approve the text of the Restatement have the responsibility for managing large enterprises or the authority to legislate the social obligations of business.

## V. The US Discussion of Corporate Purpose

This conceptual framework may be useful in understanding the US debate. First, there is a debate over the legal characteristics of the corporate form. I have argued above that, in traditional jurisdictions, the corporate form is best understood as a form with 'shareholder primacy'. Others disagree.[25] Some argue that, while shareholders predominate as a matter of *realpolitik*, the law does not require any sort of shareholder primacy. Others argue that, while in specific and rare 'end game' situations like the sale of a corporation for cash, Delaware law requires that the interests of shareholders predominate, in normal, day to day, situations, the board has great discretion to further the interests of non-shareholder constituencies, a discretion protected by the business

---

[25] For a sense of the various arguments made in a voluminous literature see Lynn Stout, *The Shareholder Value Myth: How Putting Shareholders First Harms Investors, Corporations and the Public* (Berrett-Koehler 2010); Cynthia Williams, 'Corporate Social Responsibility and Corporate Governance' in Jeffrey N Gordon and Wolf-Georg Ringe (eds), *Oxford Handbook of Corporate Law and Governance* (1st edn, OUP 2018).

judgment rule. Still others point to the states that have adopted 'constituency statutes' as comprising a numerical majority and thus providing a better expression of 'U.S. law'.

These are interesting legal questions on which reasonable people may differ. For what it is worth, Delaware judges clearly believe that Delaware law includes a 'shareholder primacy' principle alongside great discretion given to the board of directors and protected by the business judgment rule.

There is also a debate among managers and management scholars on how best to manage large business enterprises. For this debate, the legal characteristics of the corporate form are relatively unimportant, except insofar as someone might think (incorrectly) that sound management practices that increase firm value by treating stakeholders well are impermissible under current law. Here, the Restatement can be helpful in clarifying that, on the contrary, such management practices are entirely permissible.

Finally, there is a lively political debate over the social responsibility of big business. For this debate, the law enters in various ways. For some, 'shareholder primacy' is an attractive target of disdain.[26] For others, 'the law' should mandate that large businesses act in a socially responsible manner.

Each of us has our own political views, and the traditional description of the objective of a corporation in section 2.01 is completely consistent with believing that a carbon tax is the only policy intervention that stands a chance of mitigating climate change, or that large businesses have social responsibilities beyond making money for their shareholders.

## VI. Shareholder-driven ESG Activism

There is an additional debate that intersects with the 'corporate purpose' discussion and existing corporate law. For many, political dysfunction and legislative gridlock has rendered the political branches incapable of responding to the most pressing crises of our time. Despite overwhelming evidence of anthropocentric climate change, Congress has proved itself incapable of enacting even so basic a response as a carbon tax. Despite increasing economic inequality that undermines the democratic legitimacy of our market economy, the only tax legislation that ever passes cuts taxes and exacerbates inequality. Despite clear evidence that ordinary workers have lost out from globalization, even the most basic protection of workers' rights to organize do not stand a chance of enactment.

Given this political failure, some have pushed for a shareholder-driven activism around ESG. This can take various forms. One approach is to use non-binding shareholder proposals to put pressure on corporate boards to pay more attention to carbon

---

[26] See eg Marco Rubio, 'American Investment in the 21st Century: Project for Strong Labor Markets and National Development 22' (15 May 2019) www.rubio.senate.gov/public/_cache/files/94fcb79e-eedd-4496-a262-7091647563e6/B68DE3EF858700E482305C9ED26AEC72.5.14.2019.-final-project-report-american-investment.pdf.

emissions or human resource issues.[27] And, even more recently, shareholder proposals to change 'corporate purpose' have proliferated.[28] At the other extreme, some argue that the 'universal owners' who control increasing percentages of public companies should use their collective power to force companies to internalize externalities rather than focusing on increasing the value of the firm.[29]

Precatory shareholder proposals raise few corporate law questions and have been a common way for shareholders and non-shareholders to raise issues of concern. Individual shareholders can vote their shares as they like. Institutional asset owners and asset managers face a more complex decision, as they typically owe fiduciary and contractual duties to their beneficiaries. The success of shareholder proposals vary but have clearly been responsible for some significant changes in corporate governance, including the disappearance of staggered boards and increased focus on ESG concerns.

More robust forms of ESG activism pose more significant issues, especially when they involve trade-offs among portfolio companies. Madison Condon provides an interesting hypothetical that nicely crystallizes the issues posed. ExxonMobil and Chevron are each responsible for approximately 1 per cent of annual global carbon emissions. In light of the effects of climate change on the firms in its portfolio, Condon claims that BlackRock has a financial interest in forcing Exxon and Chevron to reduce their carbon emissions by 40 per cent, even if doing so would reduce stock price by 20 per cent because the benefit to other firms in BlackRock's portfolio would substantially offset the losses on their holdings of Exxon and Chevron.[30]

Assuming this were true, this sort of robust climate activism raises substantial corporate law issues under the duty of loyalty.[31] Exxon and Chevron directors owe a duty of loyalty to their companies, a duty that requires them to prioritize the corporation's interests over any personal interests, financial or political. For a director to sacrifice Exxon's or Chevron's interests at the behest of a large shareholder and for the benefit of that shareholder's other investments is a prima facie violation of those duties. Similarly, to the extent that BlackRock teamed up with other large shareholders to force Exxon to do so, the BlackRock team could become a controller of Exxon with resulting fiduciary duties to Exxon and its shareholders as a group.

## VII. The Golden Thread: Corporate Law's Single Firm Focus

The debate over corporate purpose, like shareholder proposals on ESG and shareholder-driven climate activism, often share a common goal, namely for

---

[27] For an overview see Georgeson, '2021 Annual Corporate Governance Review', 17–22 https://www.georgeson.com/us/news-insights/annual-corporate-governance-review.
[28] Jill Fisch, 'Purpose Proposals' (2022) 1 University of Chicago Business Law Review 113.
[29] See eg Frederick H Alexander, 'The Benefit Stance: Responsible Ownership in the Twenty-First Century' (2020) 36 Oxford Review of Economic Policy 341, 356. See generally The Shareholder Commons, 'Creating Guardrails to Protect our Common Interest' https://theshareholdercommons.com/.
[30] Madison Condon, 'Externalities and the Common Owner' (2020) 95 Washington Law Review 1.
[31] Marcel Kahan and Edward Rock, 'Systemic Stewardship with Tradeoffs' (2023) 48 Journal of Corporation Law 497.

corporations to prioritize social goals over promoting the value of individual firms. In doing so, these efforts run headlong into a deep and abiding feature of corporate law, namely, its 'single firm focus'.[32] Directors are elected by shareholders of a particular corporation to oversee the business and affairs of that corporation, and owe fiduciary duties to that corporation. Managers, like directors, owe duties to their particular firm, and, moreover, are typically compensated based on the performance of 'their' firm. Conflicts of interest are defined with regard to a given firm.

While directors and officers owe their loyalty to the particular firm in which they serve, shareholders' interests will often be heterogeneous. Some, like managers who are incentivized with stock options, will be substantially overweight in the stock of the company. Others, like index funds, will be widely diversified with portfolio interests that may diverge from the interests of any particular portfolio company and its undiversified shareholders. Some investors may be 'underweight' relative to a benchmark portfolio and thus have a financial incentive that rewards a decline in firm value. Some will interact with the firm in a variety of ways (as creditors, suppliers, customers, or employees) and may weight those other interests more heavily than their interests as shareholders. Others will care more about non-investment interests (eg the state of the environment) than they do about their investments.

Corporate law's traditional response to the heterogeneity of shareholders' actual interests is subtle. First, by defining the duty of loyalty as owed to a specific firm, corporate law limits the consideration of shareholders' other interests. Secondly, while traditional corporate law makes clear that the promotion of the value of the firm is 'for the benefit of the shareholders', as distinct from other stakeholders, it defines 'shareholders' interest' as the interests that shareholders have in common, qua shareholders. For example, in the seminal *Revlon* case, the court held that the board breached its fiduciary duties in erecting barriers to a higher cash offer in favour of a lower offer that protected the creditor interests of a group of shareholders who had tendered their shares into an earlier exchange offer.[33] This constructed notion of 'shareholder interest'—a definition that, to a first approximation, is the residuum of the firm's cash flows—means that the duty of the board to promote the value of the corporation is for the benefit of the shareholder interest and not for the benefit of the actual shareholders. The advantage of this approach is that it reduces heterogeneity of interests (indeed, defines it away) and thus avoids the higher decision costs that would accompany any attempt to satisfy shareholders' actual interests or preferences.[34]

This feature of corporate law is often overlooked. In recent papers, Oliver Hart and Luigi Zingales have argued that the board should promote the welfare of the actual shareholders even when those interests are not homogeneous and even when doing so

---

[32] ibid.
[33] *Revlon Inc v MacAndrews & Forbes Holdings Inc* 506 A2d 173 (Del 1986).
[34] Bengt Holmstrom, 'Session III: Corporate Purpose and the Theory of the Firm' (IESE ECGI Conference on Corporate Purpose, Spring 2021) 33 Journal of Applied Corporate Finance 60, 62–63.

does not promote the value of the corporation.[35] This departs from current corporate law in two ways. First, as described above, corporate law is focused on the firm. The directors' duty is to promote the value of this particular corporation. Doing so will benefit this particularly group of shareholders but it will only do so indirectly. The statement that a corporation should maximize shareholder value is shorthand for a longer, more correct, statement, namely that when share value is an accurate proxy for firm value, promoting share value will promote firm value. Shareholder 'welfare', as understood by Hart and Zingales, is clearly *not* a proxy for firm value. Secondly, the notion of shareholder interest that is relevant is not the actual interests of a particular group of shareholders but this abstract notion of the 'shareholders' interest', as contrasted with an equally abstract notion of the 'creditors' interest'.

While the single firm focus of corporate law is fundamental, the board has a great deal of discretion in making decisions for the firm, and those decisions are largely protected by the business judgment rule. This means that the board will be able to take seriously the interests of employees or the environment or the interests of communities in which the firm operates so long as they believe that paying attention to these interests is rationally related to long-term firm value. Directors thus have substantial discretion to prefer non-shareholder interests over shareholder interests without incurring legal risk.

However, the concentration of shareholdings in the hands of institutional investors and hedge funds constrains the board's ability to depart from a focus on shareholder value. Similarly, the widespread use of equity linked compensation aligns the interests of managers with shareholders, an alignment that likewise will limit a typical board's appetite for substantial departures from shareholder value.

In light of this, the traditional corporate law rules, as reflected in the Restatement, do not precisely preclude boards from pursuing the social good at the expense of firm value, but they certainly make it more difficult. First, the 'ideology' of the boardroom—directors' self-understanding of their social role—is affected by the basic legal and market ground rules of corporate governance. For better or for worse, in the decades since the 1980s, boards have come to understand that they work for the shareholders. Secondly, the current structure of shareholdings means that shareholders with a focus on maximizing firm value have a realistic chance of being able to redirect firms that lose sight of shareholder value.

## VIII. Conclusion

The Restatement of Corporate Governance stands in a complex relationship with the current debate over 'corporate purpose' and will probably leave all combatants dissatisfied. On the one hand, against those who would impose an obligation on corporations

---

[35] Oliver Hart and Luigi Zingales, 'Companies Should Maximize Shareholder Welfare Not Market Value' (2017) 2 Journal of Law and Financial Accounting 247; Oliver Hart and Luigi Zingales, 'The New Corporate Governance' (2022) 1 University of Chicago Business Law Review 195.

to adopt a legally enforceable corporate purpose that gives weight to non-shareholder interests even when those interests diverge from shareholder interests, the Restatement makes clear that this is not the rule either in the traditional common law jurisdictions like Delaware or in the states that rejected Delaware's shareholder primacy by adopting 'constituency' statutes. On the other hand, against those who would impose upon directors a duty to maximize stock price, the Restatement makes it clear that directors' discretion is far broader than any such maxim would permit, a discretion that permits directors to take seriously the interests of all stakeholders as they work to promote the value of the corporation.

Finally, those who would recruit corporate governance to address challenges such as climate change and inequality will be frustrated. The traditional model of corporate governance, a model that the Restatement seeks to capture, views corporate law as narrowly focused on defining and enforcing a particular enterprise form that, as it happens, has proved to be well-suited to generating wealth over the last 150 years. The argument for the social value of that form, however, substantially depends on other areas of law fulfilling their roles, with, inter alia, environmental externalities controlled by environmental law, inequality redressed through the tax system, and employees' interests protected by labour law. The existing structure of corporate governance is simply not well suited to redress regulatory failure.

# 7
# ESG Regulation, CSR, and Corporate Purpose

## A UK Perspective

*Irene-marié Esser and Iain MacNeil*[*]

## I. Introduction

The 2030 Agenda for Sustainable Development,[1] adopted by all United Nations member states in 2015, provides a shared blueprint for peace and prosperity for people and the planet. It makes provision for seventeen sustainable development goals (SDGs), which are an urgent call for action by all countries—developed and developing—in a global partnership. In December 2019, the European Commission presented the European green deal, a growth strategy aiming to make Europe the first climate-neutral continent by 2050. The UN Guiding Principles on Business and Human Rights 2011 provide a bridge between the SDGs and human rights by setting out the respective responsibilities of states and companies. This is all in an effort to have more sustainable companies, in the context of the environmental, social, and governance (ESG) focus that has emerged in recent years.

Sustainability is a key theme in corporate and financial law.[2] It has many strands but one of the key overarching themes is a focus on how corporate governance and financial regulation might contribute to resolving or mitigating externalities. Corporate governance and financial regulation have a role to play in the transition to a sustainable

---

[*] This chapter draws on research by the authors conducted during the last five years with a focus on their empirical work on non-financial and strategic reporting requirements applicable in the UK, workforce engagement, and a proposed ESG entity model. For an overview of their projects see https://www.gla.ac.uk/schools/law/research/groups/corporate-and-financial/impact/#consultations,financeandsocialjusticeproject,environmental%2Csocialandgovernance(esg). All internet sources were last accessed on 15 January 2024.

[1] United Nations, 'Transforming our World: The 2030 Agenda for Sustainable Development' https://sdgs.un.org/2030agenda.

[2] Sustainability and sustainable development are on the agenda not only in corporate governance, but across the board. In 2018, the OECD published the Policy Note on Sustainability: OECD, 'Better Business for 2030: Putting the SDGs at the Core' (2018). The note explores ways in which the private sector can contribute to the SDGs by putting them at the centre of decision-making and provides examples of companies that have integrated the SDGs in their strategies. The 1987 Brundtland Report famously defined sustainability as 'development that meets the needs of the present without compromising the ability of future generations to meet their own needs'. UN, *Report of the World Commission on Environment and Development: Our Common Future* (1987) https://digitallibrary.un.org/record/139811?ln=en. Bruner argues that promoting sustainable corporate governance requires reforming fundamental attributes of the corporation that encourage excessive risk-taking and externalization of costs. Christopher M Bruner, 'Corporate Governance Reform and the Sustainability Imperative' (2022) 131(4) Yale Law Journal 1217, 1224.

economic model, especially in a global context. This is already happening through voluntary action driven by global guidelines, policies, and principles, as well as national, self-regulatory codes of best practice. Some of these soft law recommendations are also starting to be framed as harder obligations mandating responsible behaviour from companies through, for example, reporting requirements. For example, the UK is now making it mandatory for Britain's largest businesses to disclose their climate-related risks and opportunities, in line with the Taskforce on Climate-related Financial Disclosures (TCFD) recommendations.[3] In March 2021, the European Parliament also approved an outline proposal for the EU Directive on Mandatory Human Rights, Environmental and Good Governance Due Diligence,[4] now continuing through the legislative process.

In this chapter we will provide an overview of the ESG regulatory framework in the UK with a focus on directors' duties, non-financial reporting, and stakeholder engagement. We will also consider corporate purpose in this context and look at various proposals and the way forward.

We argued above that, on the one hand, ESG is focused on risk and return in terms of portfolio investment; in other words, it is a technique to improve returns by derisking the portfolio. Corporate social responsibility (CSR), on the other hand, is more focused on the ethical dimension of corporate behaviour—in the context of sustainability, internalizing the externalities linked to corporate activities. The shift in focus over time from CSR to ESG has probably diluted board accountability as the ESG model means the board effectively cedes responsibility for initiating CSR actions to investors. This also carries implications for the integration of CSR or ESG with operational activity, as investors lack the information and expertise to make operational decisions on ESG or CSR implementation.[5] In the next section we explore these issues in the context of the UK corporate law regime.

## II. UK Regulatory Position

### 1. Directors' Duties

In the UK, the duty of a director to promote the success of the company for the benefit of its members as a whole, but with reference to other factors embedding some form of stakeholder protection, is codified in section 172 of the Companies Act 2006 (CA 2006). Even so, the consensus view is that the UK corporate governance system is one characterized by shareholder primacy and the shareholders are the ultimate beneficiaries

---

[3] See https://www.fsb-tcfd.org/. The UK government has already signalled its intention to implement the ISSB standards, which build on the TCFD approach; see https://www.fca.org.uk/news/news-stories/fca-welcomes-launch-issb-standards#:~:text=The%20UK%20Government%20also%20recently,to%20reference%20the%20ISSB%20standards.

[4] Proposal for a Directive on Corporate Sustainability Due Diligence COM(2022) 71.

[5] Iain MacNeil and Irene-marié Esser, 'From a Financial to an Entity Model of ESG' (2022) 23(1) European Business Organization Law Review 9.

of directors' duties.[6] The consideration of non-shareholders' interests is of secondary importance and is subordinated to the interests of shareholders—confirming the supremacy of shareholders' interests.[7] Stakeholders have some protection through disclosure and reporting requirements and the latest Corporate Governance Code 2018 makes provision for various stakeholder engagement mechanisms. It is well-known that section 172 attracted, and still attracts, a great deal of criticism, principally because it does not adequately provide for some form of stakeholder protection.[8]

The discretion available to directors under section 172 is related to the 'proper purposes' rule in section 171 of the CA 2006 since all powers must be exercised in a proper manner. In determining proper purpose reference can be made to the CA 2006 and the articles of association and so in principle it is open to shareholders to define purpose through adjustment of the articles.[9] While there are (mainly) historical examples of this occurring with reference to so-called 'objects clauses',[10] it has generally not occurred with reference to stakeholder interests. Thus, despite its potential role, the proper purposes rule remains rather marginalized in the context of the delimitation of directors' powers to consider stakeholder interests. That observation remains true with respect to both the potential facilitative role of the rule (permitting ESG actions) as well as its constraining role (preventing ESG actions) as the absence of purpose provisions in articles is matched by an absence of reported cases challenging ESG actions by company boards in the UK.[11]

Nor have the boundaries of section 172 been adequately determined by the courts, although that might well be expected in a phase of evolutionary development linked to stakeholder interests. However, section 172 was recently referred to in the case of *BTI*

---

[6] Andrew Keay, 'Moving towards Stakeholderism? Enlightened Shareholder Value, Constituency Statutes and More: Much Ado about Little?' (2011) 22(1) European Business Law Review 1, 33–36; Fraser Dobbie, 'Codification of Directors' Duties: An Act to Follow?' (2008) 11 Trinity College Law Review 1, 18–19.

[7] CA 2006 (c 46) Commentary on s 172, Explanatory Note 325 www.legislation.gov.uk/ukpga/2006/46/notes/division/6/2.

[8] See Parker Hood, 'Directors' Duties under the Companies Act 2006: Clarity or Confusion?' (2013) 13(1) Journal of Corporate Law Studies 15; Lady Justice Arden, 'Companies Act 2006 (UK): A New Approach to Directors' Duties' (2007) 81 Australian Law Journal 162; *Richmond Pharmacology Ltd v Chester Overseas Ltd* [2014] EWHC 2692 (Ch), paras 66–68 (Stephen Jourdan QC); *Re Southern Countries Fresh Foods Ltd* [2008] EWHC 2810 (Ch) para. 53 (Mr Justice Warren). See also: Deirdre Ahern, 'Directors' Duties, Dry Ink and the Accessibility Agenda' (2012) 128 Law Quarterly Review 114, 132. Referring to the *Re West Coast Capital (Lios) Ltd* [2008] CSOH 72 decision, Lynch doubts whether s 172 CA will be discussed in courts: 'it seems that s.172 really is nothing more than a restatement of the previous law, and deserves the almost dismissive judicial treatment that it has received': Elaine Lynch, 'Section 172: A Ground-breaking Reform of Director's Duties, or the Emperor's New Clothes?' (2012) 33(7) Company Lawyer 196, 202.

[9] The CA 2006 adopts a 'delegated' approach to the delimitation of directors' powers whereby control ultimately rests with the shareholders, albeit that the default articles provide directors with 'all the powers of the company'.

[10] See Iain MacNeil and Irene-marié Esser, 'The Elusive Purpose of Corporate Purpose' (2023) https://papers.ssrn.com/sol3/papers.cfm?abstract_id=4523037. See also Iain MacNeil and Irene-marié Esser, 'Corporate Purpose as a Conduit for Sustainability in Corporate Governance' in Marta Santos Silva and others (eds), *Routledge Handbook of Private Law and Sustainability* (Routledge 2024).

[11] There are, however, some cases addressing failure to act. A recent case has challenged failure to act with respect to climate change on the part of the Universities Superannuation Scheme, the largest pension fund in the UK: see *McGaughey v USSL* [2022] EWHC 1233 (Ch) and on appeal [2023] EWCA Civ 873. In both instances the claim was dismissed, albeit mainly because it did not meet the standards required for a derivative action. The Court of Appeal left open the possibility of a direct action based on breach of trust. A case has also been brought by ClientEarth against the board of Shell plc alleging breach of directors' duties for failing to adopt and implement an energy transition strategy that aligns with the Paris Agreement: see https://www.clientearth.org/latest/press-office/press/clientearth-files-climate-risk-lawsuit-against-shell-s-board-with-support-from-institutional-investors/. Both cases are framed as derivative actions, the former under the common law and the latter under the CA 2006.

*2014 LLC v Sequana SA & Ors*[12] on the nature, scope, and contents of directors' duties with regard to creditors, when a company is nearing insolvency. In that context, the Supreme Court considered the duty of directors to act, in good faith, for the benefit of the company and what that means. In other words, who are the ultimate beneficiaries of the duty to act in good faith? Even though this case focused primarily on the point in time when directors should consider the interests of creditors, which may be different from those of the shareholders, it also provides a confirmation by the Court of shareholder primacy.[13]

Referencing the common law, Lord Reed stated that the director's fiduciary duty to act in good faith in the interests of the company means the interests of its members as a whole (paragraphs 11, 17, and 21). With respect to section 172 of the Companies Act 2006 (where this has now been codified) the court held that since this duty is focused on promoting the success of the company 'for the benefit of its members as a whole', it is clear that, although the duty is owed to the company, the shareholders are the intended beneficiaries of that duty. The court did refer to the secondary importance of other considerations that directors need to take into account under section 172 but held that the primary duty in section 172 remains focused on promoting the success of the company for the benefit of its members (paragraph 67). To that extent, 'the common law approach of shareholder primacy is carried forward into the 2006 Act' (paragraph 65). It seems clear to us that the court's approach confirmed shareholder primacy as the position under the common law but also under the codified section 172(1).[14] In this chapter, we will consider whether reform[15] to section 172 is the best approach or whether stakeholders can be protected through procedural mechanisms like due diligence, non-financial reporting, and engagement mechanisms. We will also look at the role of purpose in this context.

Also relevant in this context is the 'soft law' represented by the UK Corporate Governance Code. The first principle of the Code under the first section 'Board Leadership and Company Purpose', provides that: 'A successful company is led by an effective and entrepreneurial board, whose role is to promote the long-term sustainable success of the company, generating value for shareholders and contributing to wider society.'

That provision, read alongside comments in the introduction to the Code, indicates that its focus has moved considerably towards recognizing the significance of stakeholder interests in successful companies by comparison with the sole focus on shareholders in early versions of the Code.[16] We move on in section 3 below to evaluate

---

[12] [2022] UKSC 25.
[13] See for elaboration on this aspect https://blogs.law.ox.ac.uk/oblb/blog-post/2022/12/shareholder-primacy-and-corporate-purpose.
[14] See generally on this https://blogs.law.ox.ac.uk/oblb/blog-post/2022/12/shareholder-primacy-and-corporate-purpose.
[15] Such as the proposed Better Business Act https://betterbusinessact.org/.
[16] See further on the history of the UK Code and its approach with a comparative perspective Iain MacNeil and Irene-marié Esser, 'The Emergence of Comply or Explain as a Global Model for Corporate Governance Code' (2022) 33(1) European Business Law Review 1.

how the most specific provision of the Code (on workforce engagement) has worked in practice and later consider what further measures might usefully be adopted in the Code.

## 2. Non-financial Reporting

Through the process of reporting companies disclose the various risks that they face, especially with regard to the social dimension and the environment. Non-financial reporting has risen in significance in recent years as the role of stakeholders who are not shareholders has been recognized in corporate governance frameworks. This plays an important role in providing transparency for investors and other stakeholders and, in general, encourages development of a responsible approach to business.[17]

In this context, the role of materiality as a threshold for disclosure plays a key role. Single materiality requires disclosure by reference to the impact on the company (and by implication shareholders) whereas double materiality requires disclosure by reference to the external impact of corporate activities, and in particular environmental and social impacts. The EU's Non-Financial Reporting Directive (NFRD)[18] led the way in the global development of reporting based on the double-materiality perspective. In the UK, according to the CA 2006, the directors of a company must prepare a strategic report for each financial year of the company.[19] Strategic reporting introduced enhanced disclosure requirements with regard to non-financial information in the UK. Although the emphasis on section 172 CA 2006 (the duty to promote the success of the company) in the relevant statutory provisions is a welcome development, the strategic report requirement raises questions about the effectiveness of non-financial reporting and the market's ability to evaluate the performance of the disclosing company.

We evaluated and analysed the impact of the strategic report of a quoted company on shareholders and especially other stakeholders (eg employees, customers, suppliers, environmental agencies, social, community, and human rights bodies) in the context of section 172 of the CA 2006.[20] We scrutinized the strategic reports of the FTSE 100

---

[17] There is also evidence that engagement by investors with companies on environmental, social, and governance (ESG) issues can create shareholder value. See PRI, 'How ESG Engagement Creates Value for Investors and Companies' (2018) https://www.unpri.org/research/how-esg-engagement-creates-value-for-investors-and-companies/3054.article. At the same time, an empirical study shows that companies disclosing the widest range of socially responsible policies are more likely to experience ethics controversies. See Gerald T Garvey and others, 'A Pitfall in Ethical Investing: ESG Disclosures Reveal Vulnerabilities, Not Virtues' (19 September 2016) https://ssrn.com/abstract=2840629 or http://dx.doi.org/10.2139/ssrn.2840629.
[18] Directive 2014/95 [2014] OJ L330/1.
[19] See CA 2006, s 414A(1) and the exception for small companies (s 414A(2)). The provisions of the EU NFRD were implemented in the UK via the provisions of the CA 2006 and related regulations.
[20] I-M Esser, I MacNeil, and K Chalaczkiewicz-Ladna, 'Engaging Stakeholders in Corporate Decision-making through Strategic Reporting: An Empirical Study of FTSE 100 Companies (Part 1)' (2018) 29(5) European Business Law Review 729, I-M Esser, I MacNeil, and K Chalaczkiewicz-Ladna, 'Engaging Stakeholders in Corporate Decision-making through Strategic Reporting: An Empirical Study of FTSE 100 Companies (Part 2)' (2020) 31(2) European Business Law Review 209. See also other studies eg FRC, *Review of Corporate Governance Reporting* (November 2021) 18–19 https://www.frc.org.uk/getattachment/b0a0959e-d7fe-4bcd-b842-353f705462c3/FRC-Review-of-Corporate-Governance-Reporting_November-2021.pdf.

companies (from 2015 and 2016).[21] The following issues, and the extent to which they are addressed in the strategic reports of selected companies, were considered:

- the role and objective of the strategic report and how this is explained;
- the description of the company's strategy and business model;
- review of the company's business and the principal risks and uncertainties facing the company;
- whether the information in the strategic report has a forward-looking orientation;
- whose interests are taken into consideration during decision-making, in particular, whether the report considers: (i) environmental matters; (ii) the interests of the company's employees; and (iii) social, community, and human rights issues;
- when the report does not contain information specified above, whether the company explains and highlights this;
- gender diversity on the board; and
- quality and transparency of reporting.

With regard to the quality of non-financial reporting and the extent that non-financial reporting facilitates stakeholder engagement in corporate decision-making, we found that compliance with NFR requirements is very high, amounting even to super or over-compliance. We also evaluated the quality of non-financial reporting through a series of interviews with stakeholders to determine whether the current regulatory framework on non-financial reporting in the UK informs stakeholders adequately so as to facilitate effective engagement in corporate decision-making. Some interesting things were observed, for example, that, according to the participants, the main reasons for disclosing non-financial information are purely compliance, while genuine interest in ESG matters is at the bottom of the list.[22] Participants observed that disclosure of non-financial information is not enough, and stakeholder engagement and participation methods are needed. We argued that even though disclosure is important, as it provides information and can have an impact on the reputation of a company, it is often not sufficient on its own. It is only one mechanism to protect stakeholders, and its aim is to keep them informed. For proper engagement, much more is needed.

## 3. Stakeholder Engagement

The emphasis on strengthening stakeholders' engagement during corporate decision-making processes through improved reporting remains firmly in the spotlight not only

---

[21] Esser, MacNeil, and Chalaczkiewicz-Ladna (Part 1) (n 20). See relatedly https://blogs.law.ox.ac.uk/business-law-blog/blog/2017/10/corporate-decision-making-through-strategic-reporting-empirical-study.

[22] However, it has been noted that financial motivations pushed companies to reduce GHG emissions following the introduction of standardized GHG emissions disclosure in the UK strategic report. See Valentin Jouvenot and Philipp Krueger, 'Mandatory Corporate Carbon Disclosure: Evidence from a Natural Experiment' (8 August 2019) https://ssrn.com/abstract=3434490, http://dx.doi.org/10.2139/ssrn.3434490.

in the UK, but also in other jurisdictions.[23] Workers, especially, play an important role in companies, even though their direct involvement in corporate governance processes seems invisible or marginal. While shareholder primacy has been justified by the argument that shareholder interests are equivalent to those of the company, the interests of company workers are closely aligned with those of the company and the company's long-term success. Arguably, the role of workers can be crucial in addressing new challenges faced by companies and in implementing initiatives within the framework of corporate sustainability.

In 2018, the Corporate Governance Code introduced for the first time—through Provision 5—workforce engagement tools. This provision states that one or a combination of the following methods should be used: (i) a director appointed from the workforce; (ii) a formal workforce advisory panel; (iii) a designated non-executive director. If the board has not chosen one or more of these methods, it should explain what alternative arrangements are in place and why it considers them effective.

The requirement to adopt one of three options for workforce engagement specified in Provision 5 of the Corporate Governance Code is an important development in terms of integrating stakeholder interests into board decision-making, resulting in better stakeholder engagement. Unlike much of the history of the Code, in which the soft law provisions of the Code have generally run ahead of hard law, there is a clear link between the workforce engagement provision and the stakeholder focus on non-financial reporting, which has been implemented through hard law, albeit with selective adoption of the 'comply or explain' technique that was pioneered by the Corporate Governance Code.

We view Provision 5 of the Code as a key stage in the evolution of the Corporate Governance Code in terms of integrating stakeholder interests into board decision-making. First, at a high level, the key statutory provision providing for integration of stakeholder interests (s 172 CA 2006) is focused on outcome as it specifies that the board should consider the relevant stakeholder interests. But this provision provides no process for engagement with stakeholders nor integration of their interests. In that sense, the outcome can be compared to that of the archetypal 'black box': we trust it to produce the right outcome, but we cannot verify how it has been reached. The move to Provision 5 indicates that the 'black box' model of board-decision making is no longer fit for purpose as it is replaced by a more explicit process for the integration of a (limited) set of stakeholder interests, focused on a more precise form of control. While this approach is not entirely new—one could view the introduction and evolution over time of independent directors and board committees as representing a similar trend for the representation of shareholder interests—it is a first in the UK in connection with the integration of stakeholder interests.

---

[23] For instance, in a recent study the European Commission identified stakeholder involvement as one of the factors contributing to company sustainability and helping to tackle short-termism. See European Commission, *Study on Directors' Duties and Sustainable Corporate Governance: Final Report* (July 2020) https://op.europa.eu/en/publication-detail/-/publication/e47928a2-d20b-11ea-adf7-01aa75ed71a1/language-en.

Secondly, the shift towards specifying process also represents a move away from the reliance on disclosure as the primary regulatory technique that has been evident in the development of stakeholder interests through non-financial reporting. That shift can be rationalized on the basis that, while disclosure can inform stakeholders, it does not provide an engagement opportunity with corporate decision-making. In that sense, Provision 5 fills a clear gap, especially for one set of stakeholders (workers). Whether it represents the start of a broader shift towards specifying a process for stakeholder engagement remains to be seen, but it seems at least plausible to posit that Provision 5 will provide a test case as to whether process may eventually trump reliance on disclosure as the primary regulatory technique or at least operate in tandem.

We view the Provision 5 workforce engagement tools as *one* of the available channels leading towards our proposed ESG entity model (a model that locates accountability more clearly with the board, focusing on internal decision-making), with the aim of making suggestions on how to improve stakeholder participation in corporate governance. Provision 5 is not only a stakeholder empowerment tool but can be seen more broadly as the start of a process of experimentation to determine the best ways to engage all stakeholders in board decision-making. Moreover, Provision 5 can provide an effective model for the development of the social dimension of sustainability, which to date has attracted less attention in the ESG model of sustainability.[24]

The location of Provision 5 in the Corporate Governance Code means that it is not a classic experiment (as it has already been institutionalized), but its flexibility does arguably allow it to operate in that way. This means that Provision 5 models could evolve over time and influence engagement by other stakeholders. Alternatively, it could also help to explain an end point in which the experiment had failed and direct regulatory action was necessary—the experimentation paradigm would let us track the Provision 5 data over time and report the results of the ongoing experiment without pressure to reach a clear outcome before the experiment itself supported such an approach.

In an earlier project,[25] we evaluated the early stages of the implementation of Provision 5 by FTSE 100 companies in 2019, the first year that the Corporate Governance Code was in force. This analysis was conducted in the context of the 'outcome versus control' and 'process versus disclosure' themes outlined above. We presented empirical evidence on the options selected by companies, the rationale for adoption, overlap with pre-existing techniques, and the role of the 'comply or explain'

---

[24] See generally on ESG MAL Agudelo, L Jóhannsdóttir, and B Davídsdóttir, 'A Literature Review of the History and Evolution of Corporate Social Responsibility' (2019) 4(1) International Journal of Corporate Social Responsibility 1 doi.org/10.1186/s40991-018-0039-y; Elizabeth Pollman, 'Corporate Social Responsibility, ESG, and Compliance' (2021) Faculty Scholarship at Penn Carey Law 2568 https://scholarship.law.upenn.edu/faculty_scholarship/2568.

[25] K Chalaczkiewicz-Ladna, I-M Esser, and I MacNeil, 'Workforce Engagement and the UK Corporate Governance Code' in A Martínez-Echevarría y García de Dueñas (ed), *Corporate Governance, Sustainability and Reputation* (Thomson Reuters Aranzadi 2021) https://papers.ssrn.com/sol3/papers.cfm?abstract_id=3834387. See https://blogs.law.ox.ac.uk/business-law-blog/blog/2021/06/workforce-engagement-and-uk-corporate-governance-code and https://blogs.law.ox.ac.uk/oblb/blog-post/2023/01/workforce-engagement-mechanisms-uk-way-towards-more-sustainable-companies. See also Deloitte, 'Hearing the Stakeholder Voice: Effective Stakeholder Engagement for Better Decision-Making' (September 2018) 6 https://www2.deloitte.com/content/dam/Deloitte/uk/Documents/risk/deloitte-uk-risk-hearing-the-stakeholder-voice.pdf.

approach in facilitating the development of alternative models. We also considered the quality of disclosure, linked to Provision 5, and the manner in which disclosure and process work together to produce real impact on board decision-making in the context of workers' interests.

We argued that workers' engagement and participation in corporate decision-making is a critical missing element of the UK's corporate governance system and therefore implementation of Provision 5 engagement tools and the creation of an effective engagement strategy are of paramount importance. While Provision 5 provides the process for the anticipated outcome—participation during decision-making—this outcome is not yet visible and, at least for now, Provision 5 achieves the same result as mere disclosure. We concluded that on their own even well-functioning workforce engagement tools are unlikely to improve the standards of workforce engagement, and a more integrated ('bundled' or 'packaged') approach to workforce engagement and participation is required, encompassing both corporate and labour law.

## 4. Corporate Purpose

Corporate purpose has emerged as a key focal point in the debate on how corporate governance might contribute to sustainability and was addressed in our proposed entity model of ESG, discussed below, and elaborated in a later contribution.[26] Corporate purpose can be viewed as a form of direct control over the operation of a business or alternatively as an outcome that is driven by other elements of the legal framework. The former view was clearly present in the past when the objects clause in company law defined purpose by reference to the scope of the business and limited the powers of the directors so as to protect shareholders and creditors from the risks of diversification into broader activities.[27] That restriction has now gone, but corporate purpose has been revitalized as a concept by reference to sustainability considerations, encompassing the idea that the interests of stakeholders other than shareholders (eg employees, consumers) should be considered in corporate decision-making. That approach is reflected in the so-called 'enlightened shareholder value' model of corporate governance in section 172 of the Companies Act 2006 but it is generally accepted that in practice corporate decision-making remains focused on shareholder interests, even though the law provides some flexibility to consider other stakeholders.

Many proposals address corporate purpose directly on the basis that it is a variable that could be directly adjusted. An alternative view is that it is an outcome that depends on other variables for its calibration. On that view, constituent elements such as capital, profit and governance are key drivers of purpose and more amenable to adjustment

---

[26] See MacNeil and Esser, 'The Elusive Purpose of Corporate Purpose' (n 10). See also MacNeil and Esser, 'Corporate Purpose as a Conduit for Sustainability in Corporate Governance' (n 10).
[27] P Davies, 'Shareholder Voice and Corporate Purpose: The Purposeless of Mandatory Corporate Purpose Statements' European Corporate Governance Institute Law Working Paper No 666/2022 https://ssrn.com/abstract=4285770.

through recognized legal techniques than the more amorphous concept of purpose. This could in principle be done in two ways: by founders selecting a legal entity in which the purpose provided by law fits their vision for the business; or by founders/owners adjusting purpose within an entity that is already established.

Following this approach, we start by distinguishing three different contexts in which the concept of corporate purpose has played a foundational role in the framing of the law. The first relates to entity selection, where corporate purpose represents a division between commercially focused entities and those with a more social orientation. The second relates to shareholder and creditor protection in the transactional context and emerged from concerns that directors might use their powers to expose shareholders and creditors to risks that went beyond the business for which the company was established. The third, focused more on the contemporary debate around purpose, is the role of corporate purpose in stakeholder protection. While the third instance dominates contemporary discourse, the other two instances remain relevant in terms of understanding purpose as a legal technique and how it might contribute to stakeholder protection.

Entity selection options have expanded over time in recognition of the fact that founders can have very different objectives and modes of operation. They range from entities such as partnerships with a purely commercial focus at one end of the spectrum to charities with an exclusively public benefit focus at the other end. In the middle are entities that can mix commercial and social or public benefit objectives such as community enterprise companies and (generally to a lesser degree) commercial companies. In the United States, there is an even wider range of options, including the public benefit corporation. At the global level, B-corp certification provides a model for business with a social purpose that links to the local legal framework for establishing companies.

While entity selection potentially provides a mechanism to integrate ethics into a business, the evolution of ESG has drawn attention to the challenge of adjusting the purpose of commercial companies. Business leaders, policy-makers, and academics have all addressed this issue and there is a proliferation of proposals and solutions. But profit in the conventional sense tends to remain to the fore and draws attention to the centrality of that concept as a driver of corporate purpose and a constraint on change.

In the light of the embedded nature of corporate purpose and its linkage to the key levers of capital, profit and governance, adjustment of those levers in commercial entities may be the only option for significant change. The extent to which that can occur within the exiting legal framework in the UK is variable: partnerships (including LLPs) offer some scope to adjust governance, less so profit; companies already have some flexibility in their governance and so the board of directors could exercise it so as to change corporate purpose incrementally (more fundamental change would probably require shareholder approval or adjustment of the articles of association).

While we make the case for indirect adjustment (via the levers), considerable attention has focused on direct adjustment of purpose, for example, through a provision in a company's articles of association or a 'say on purpose' resolution at annual general meetings (along the lines of the 'say on pay' process already in place).[28] Proponents view this as a method of direct intervention to change corporate purpose. We are less convinced by this approach and, in that context, take heed of the fate of the (historic) objects clause which was rendered irrelevant over time as broadly drafted clauses circumvented its objective.

Corporate purpose is intrinsically linked to the debate relating to sustainable companies and better stakeholder protection but there are potential challenges in this context, not least how to define corporate purpose. The concept of purpose as something that goes beyond the goal of profit was evident in the definition proposed by the British Academy Future of the Corporation programme which characterized corporate purpose as 'Producing profitable solutions for problems of people and planet, not profiting from producing problems for either'.[29]

Davies[30] refers to corporate purpose in the context of directors' duties and identifies the often-problematic framing of purpose within a shareholder-orientated company law framework. In that context, commentators are not always in agreement when it comes to (1) the potential for setting a corporate purpose encompassing broader, sustainable goals within the current legal framework; and (2) the interaction with the codified directors' duty in section 172 of the Companies Act 2006. Under a shareholder primacy approach, it is therefore unclear to what extent directors could set a corporate purpose, through strategy and policies, which has the potential to deviate from shareholder value.

Edmans, in his book *Grow the Pie*,[31] argues that it is clear that companies should serve wider society, but what is not clear is how they should do that. He argues that one needs an approach where companies can create both profit for investors and value for society. However, without profits, shareholders would not finance companies and companies would not finance investors. Any reform to businesses that ignores the role of profit in society is unlikely to be implemented. So, a solution is needed that will work for both business and society. In that sense he recognizes that traditional economic incentives cannot alone lead to sustainable outcomes, but he relies on market-led initiatives rather than a regulatory solution. Edmans proposes a 'grow the pie' mentality focusing on creating value for society, which can, but will not necessarily, lead to profit maximization over the long term. Under the pie-growing mentality, a company's primary objective is social value rather than profits. Edmans provides various examples where this approach ended up more profitable than if profits were the end goal. That's because it enables many investments to be made by the company, which ended up delivering substantial long-term pay-offs. But since these pay-offs could not have been forecast from the outset, the projects might never have been approved under a traditional shareholder value framework.

---

[28] See eg Colin Mayer, *Prosperity: Better Business Makes the Greater Good* (OUP 2018).
[29] See British Academy, 'Principles for Purposeful Businesses' https://www.thebritishacademy.ac.uk/publications/future-of-the-corporation-principles-for-purposeful-business.
[30] Davies (n 27).
[31] A Edmans, *Grow the Pie: How Great Companies Deliver Both Purpose and Profit* (CUP 2021).

The FRC Report (April 2022)[32] claims that, while companies need to take into account the interests of a broad range of stakeholders, it is only through sustained growth and healthy profits that can they have sufficient resources for redistribution and 'doing good'. According to the report, purpose should not become an aim on its own but should be underpinned by ethics, 'it should serve as a "moral compass" through which innovation and profitability are pursued'. Detail on what this should entail and how it should link to the current company law framework is however missing.

Mayer[33] argues that profit must be derivative from solving a problem; it should not create or produce a problem. He proposes rethinking corporate purpose by identifying or determining purpose and then implementing it and this is something that the board should oversee. Barby and others[34] suggest that this process can be supported by changes to the role of capital and profit by comparison with the conventional model, focusing on the need to value and report on human, social and natural capital. They propose a three-stage approach via 'Motives, Metrics and Money', arguing that both enterprise cost and social valuation approaches should be available for this purpose. The former would be modified to incorporate negative externalities as costs and positive externalities as investments. The latter would aim to measure impacts and value them for inclusion in the reported accounts by reference to metrics related to non-material and non-financial assets and liabilities.

Davies[35] argues that section 172 Companies of the Act 2006 should not be seen as an obstacle when directors want to set sustainable policies as it is only policies with no benefit to shareholders over the long term which are really ruled out. It gives a wide discretion to the board over the setting of policies and, even though it refers to the members as ultimate beneficiaries, it does not restrict the setting of a corporate purpose that benefits stakeholders, other than just shareholders. It actually puts corporate purpose at the heart of directors' duties. Davies therefore does not propose to reform section 172 but instead evaluates mandatory and voluntary purpose provisions (as proposed by Mayer) and especially whether the adoption of a stated purpose should be mandatory for (at least large) companies and that the chosen purpose should be required to contain a social or communal element. Davies argues that such a proposal is not desirable as a mandatory rule as a broad purpose requirement will be either (largely) ineffective or (largely) unnecessary. To be effective, substantial changes in corporate law would be needed (which would downgrade the governance rights of shareholders significantly) or a change in the investment goals of shareholders.

It is clear, therefore, that commentators hold diverse views on setting a corporate purpose encompassing broader, sustainable goals within the current legal framework. The Better Business Act (BBA)[36] initiative proposes to change business behaviour

---

[32] See https://media.frc.org.uk/documents/FRC-In-Focus-Corporate-Purpose_April-2022.pdf. This report followed on from a previous report on culture, which argued that it is important to consider culture with ESG and corporate purpose, as they are interlinked.
[33] Mayer (n 28) 201.
[34] C Barby and others, 'Measuring Purpose: An Integrated Framework' https://papers.ssrn.com/sol3/papers.cfm?abstract_id=3771892.
[35] Davies (n 27).
[36] See n 15 above.

through reform of directors' duties. It proposes law reform to ensure that businesses are legally responsible for benefiting workers, customers, communities, and the environment while delivering profit. Under this initiative the BBA would change the default position of shareholder primacy for all companies so that directors would be empowered to advance the interests of their shareholders alongside those of wider society and the environment. In situations where a director has to choose between the company's intention to create positive social or environmental impacts and the interests of shareholders, the directors would no longer be compelled to default to prioritizing shareholders. It is however stated that this Act would not create new rights for stakeholders. The position would remain the same that the directors owe their duties only to the company, and only the company, or a shareholder(s) acting on behalf of the company, can take action against a director for a breach of their duty. It therefore remains unclear how this would improve the position of stakeholders and how it is different from the current position.

## III. Aligning ESG with UK Corporate Law: An Entity Model of ESG

### 1. Context

We argued above that ESG investing evolved over time from the earlier concept of CSR. The process of evolution moved the focus from the external impact of corporate activities (CSR) to the risk and return implications for financial investors of failing to address ESG issues in their portfolio selection and corporate engagement. The bridge between the two approaches was the framing of sustainability in the early part of the millennium as an overarching concept that could be mapped onto the supply of capital and the techniques employed by institutional investors. The financial model of ESG investing is now the standard approach around the world and is reflected in ESG ratings, codes, guidance, and regulatory rules. It focuses on the role of capital and investors in driving change in sustainability practices and pays much less attention to the role of board decision-making and directors' fiduciary duties.[37]

CSR evolved with a clear focus on ethical responsibility and accountability, albeit that the 'business case' for CSR shifted the focus to 'doing well by doing good' as the potential for CSR to improve performance became clearer over time. In contrast, ESG was motivated by concerns over the risk and return implications for investors arising from its three constituents. That difference in approach is fundamental even if ESG and CSR

---

[37] Fiduciary duty was mentioned as a potential constraint in the UNEP-led Principles for Responsible Investment (2005) but that was a reference to the fiduciary duty of asset owners and managers to their clients. That formulation of fiduciary duty differs in many jurisdictions from corporate fiduciary duty (owed by directors): see MacNeil and Esser (n 5).

are often assimilated in academic discourse and can overlap in their objectives. The differences can be explained with reference to the *transmission channel, focus, implementation, metrics, and reporting*.

The *transmission channel* for CSR and ESG differs. CSR developed on the basis that corporate entities and their boards would lead on the framing and implementation of CSR policies. ESG, in contrast, was based on the premise that the supply of finance would be the primary driver of behavioural change and that investors would be the agents of change. Engagement with the board is an important element of ESG, but it is framed in a context that prioritizes shareholder interests and marginalizes stakeholders. In the case of CSR, the prioritization of the board as the transmission channel means that implementation is linked more directly with operations than in the case of ESG, which focuses on the supply of capital. The CSR approach provides a more detailed and contextual understanding of the operational environment as directors will generally be better informed on those issues than shareholders and better able to integrate and balance CSR issues with other elements of board oversight. *Implementation* in the case of ESG is through the investment process, with the launch of the Principles for Responsible Investment (PRI) in 2006 representing a catalyst in the movement towards ESG. While there is sometimes reference to the 'measurement of CSR' or to *metrics* relevant to CSR, it is far less common compared to ESG. Metrics are usually aimed at ESG factors and relevant to investors when making portfolio choices. To date, the lack of an objective standard for evaluating the sustainability characteristics of investment projects, products and portfolios has been a major problem and has led to allegations of so-called 'greenwashing'. Recent initiatives such as the EU Taxonomy Regulation[38] aim to resolve that issue. The development of *reporting* frameworks linked to ESG was a key factor in the movement from CSR to ESG. In the EU, the NFRD focused on corporate disclosure, although it could be viewed as neutral as between CSR and ESG as transmission mechanisms. More broadly, the development of reporting frameworks encompassed a variety of different techniques that combined reliance on private initiatives with public endorsement through regulatory frameworks. Developments at the global (eg the Global Reporting Initiative (GRI) and the TCFD), as well as sectoral levels (eg the Green Bond Principles) were more clearly aligned with ESG as the dominant paradigm. The EU's 2018 sustainability strategy set out a clear pathway for developing the financial model of ESG. This was followed through with the 2019 Regulation[39] requiring disclosure from financial firms to inform investors about the sustainability characteristics of their products and portfolios. The more recent Taxonomy Regulation has established a framework to evaluate the sustainability characteristics of portfolio companies.

---

[38] Regulation (EU) 2020/852 on the establishment of a framework to facilitate sustainable investment [2020] OJ L198/13.
[39] Regulation (EU) 2019/2088 on sustainability-related disclosures in the financial services sector [2019] OJ L317/1.

## 2. An Entity Model of ESG Aligned with the UK Regulatory Framework

The move from a financial/ESG model to an entity model can thus be explained as follows (see Table 7.1 below), with various adjustments mechanisms in place, through hard law as well as soft law:

The underlying premise of the financial model is that there is no clear or consistent obligation to implement sustainability at the entity/operational level. Once that constraint is overcome, it is no longer necessary to use the financial channel to drive ESG as all funding can only be channelled to entities that comply with such an obligation.

Table 7.1 Adjustment of financial model to an entity model of ESG.

|  | Financial Model | Adjustment mechanism | Entity Model |
| --- | --- | --- | --- |
| Focus | Portfolio risk and return, linked to metrics, benchmarks and indices. | Regulatory intervention focused on corporate responsibility, stakeholder integration and remuneration. | Internalize externalities via stakeholder integration. Link ESG to remuneration and sustainability strategy. |
| Channel | Institutional investors and the investment chain | *Law reform*: duty of due diligence, stakeholder committee, *Soft law*: CG Codes *Voluntarism*: purpose provision in articles and 'say on purpose' | Corporate entities via board decision-making. |
| Implementation | Integration into portfolio selection and engagement. | Broader scope (beyond capital markets) and focus on systemic risks. Residual role for 'stewardship'. | Operational focus in ESG implementation linked to 'real world' effects. |
| Metrics | Multiple, with different custodians, scope, and legal effect. Limited verification. Ratings add another layer of complexity. | Standardize and integrate with NFR and the sustainability strategy linked to the duty of due diligence. | Metrics become more focused on operational decision-making. Financial market indices and benchmarks transmit the entity model. |
| Reporting | Two levels of disclosure: corporate and financial channels. Mainly through five sustainability frameworks (GRI, CDSB, IIRC, SASB, CDP).[a] | Less reliance on reporting/disclosure as the transmission mechanism for ESG. | Align ESG reporting obligations with NFR. Financial channel disclosure then focused on narrower principal–agent issues in the investment chain. |

[a] The sustainability reporting frameworks shown in brackets are: Global Reporting Initiative (GRI), Climate Disclosure Standards Board (CDSB), International Integrated Reporting Council (IIRC), Sustainability Accounting Standards Board (SASB), Carbon Disclosure Project (CDP).

Thus, the financial model in its current form is an interim market driven solution, which responds to legal risk and is a precursor to a more systematic approach at the entity level.[40] This approach would also mitigate greenwashing as it would remain a risk mainly at the corporate level and not have two potential layers as in the financial model (ie greenwashing by companies and financial firms, respectively).

## 3. The Entity Model and Corporate Purpose

Our entity model of ESG encompassed the role of corporate purpose in the transition to sustainability. By referencing the older model of CSR it focuses more on the role of the board and operational decision-making by comparison with the financial model of ESG that is more focused on portfolio selection and stewardship. The entity approach allows for the contextual calibration of purpose by reference to the operational context whereas the financial model of ESG is generally less able to do that—eg investment and stewardship policies are more generic and do not respond precisely to context.

In the context of the entity model, we would propose the following definition: 'Corporate purpose is the articulation of how a company's business model links to its environmental and social responsibilities.' This would link well with our claim that the entity model aligns better with the old CSR model and does not require reform of directors' duties or even adjustment of the articles but, as outlined above, could be facilitated by reforms in the governance process and due diligence. While those elements align it with the approach of the International Sustainability Standards Board (ISSB),[41] our approach differs in the sense that it aims for a more prominent role for stakeholder interests in corporate decision-making and reporting (double rather than single materiality). We also see a more prominent role for entity selection in resolving the tensions implicit in the standard corporate model.

On the basis that we favour implementation techniques for corporate purpose that generally fall within the (typically broad) powers delegated to the board in the UK, we propose that the board should be responsible for articulating corporate purpose. That is linked to favouring evolutionary as opposed to transformative change, as the latter would probably have to involve shareholders more directly.[42] It is also aligned with the approach of the UK Corporate Governance Code, which provides in Principle B that the board should establish the company's purpose. This is not to say that shareholders would necessarily be excluded. Routine engagement with shareholders would help to define the acceptable boundaries of any shift in purpose, while

---

[40] See MacNeil and Esser (n 5), arguing that legal risk was a significant factor in the global shift from CSR to ESG.

[41] See https://www.ifrs.org/projects/completed-projects/2023/general-sustainability-related-disclosures/#final-stage.

[42] See MacNeil and Esser, 'The Elusive Purpose of Corporate Purpose' (n 10). See also MacNeil and Esser, 'Corporate Purpose as a Conduit for Sustainability in Corporate Governance' (n 10).

shareholder resolutions provide a more formal mechanism for driving change in corporate strategy.[43]

In the context of the approach we propose, in which variables other than purpose (ie capital, profit, and governance) are adjusted, we are of the view that mandatory, or even voluntary, purpose statements or amendments to the articles are perhaps not the best way forward. It is likely, as argued by Davies, that such mandatory purpose provisions could be circumvented (eg by broad drafting techniques) and would not therefore represent a reliable technique for changing the balance in board decision-making as between commercial factors (prioritizing shareholder interests) and other factors (such as environmental and social).[44]

Adjustments to purpose are likely to involve changes to the role of capital, profit, and governance by comparison with the conventional model. We address the last aspect by reference to our proposal for a stakeholder committee and a due diligence obligation linked to board decision-making. We envisage a stakeholder committee along the lines of the South African social and ethics committee that could represent stakeholder interests and lead to more informed decision-making by the board.[45] Due diligence obligations are now familiar in several EU countries and an EU proposal is currently in the legislative process.[46] The first two levers of purpose (capital and profit) are more problematic and less amenable to explicit adjustment in a model that envisages evolutionary change. But they are amenable to adjustment through strategic decisions made by the board in terms of balancing shareholder and stakeholder interests in the context of issues such as supply chain management, dividend policy, and employee profit-sharing.

## 4. Corporate Purpose and Related Issues

Corporate purpose as a legal concept gives effect to different objectives in different contexts. We noted that purpose has been used: to differentiate commercial entities from those with social purposes; to protect shareholders and creditors from transactions in which directors attempted to diversify the scope of the business defined by the constitution; to specify the objectives for which directors could validly exercise powers delegated to them; and to specify whose interests are relevant for board decision-making. While the last aspect dominates current discourse, we note the potential for the first to take a more prominent role in the current debate in the light of expansion in the options for entity selection.

---

[43] For a comparative analysis of the role of shareholder resolutions in various jurisdictions see Sofie Cools, 'Climate Proposals: ESG Shareholder Activism Sidestepping Board Authority' in Thilo Kuntz (ed), *Research Handbook on Environmental, Social, and Corporate Governance* (Edward Elgar 2024), noting the relative ease of bringing ESG-focused shareholder resolutions in the UK.
[44] See Davies (n 27).
[45] See I-M Esser and I MacNeil, 'Disclosure and Engagement: Stakeholder Participation Mechanisms' (2019) 30(2) European Business Law Review 201, 218.
[46] See n 4 above.

In recent times, attention has focused in particular on the role of purpose in the context of sustainability and stakeholder protection. But even in that context its meaning and potential for changing corporate behaviour remains unclear. That is reflected in proposals to change corporate purpose extending across a wide spectrum from incremental to transformative: some proposals involve legislative change while others claim that meaningful change is possible within the current legal framework or soft law codes; some focus on the board of directors as the agents of change while others view the board as trapped in a paradigm of shareholder primacy that necessitates mandatory regulatory intervention; and some view shareholders as potential agents of change through stewardship and the sustainability preferences of underlying investors.

What does seem clear is that the role of corporate purpose in driving change is contingent on parallel developments related to sustainability in adjacent domains. In the EU and UK context, developments linked to sustainability such as non-financial reporting, financial market and product disclosures, and due diligence are particularly relevant. To the extent that they incentivize or require corporate strategy and behaviour to become more sustainable, they potentially limit the burden that falls onto corporate purpose as a driver of change. In that sense, the movement towards sustainability can be seen as shared across the corporate and financial/investment channels that we highlighted in previous research. It also encompasses the global evolution of stewardship by institutional investors, which we have previously characterized as an accelerator of the rise of the salience of ESG as a driver of corporate governance. Moreover, in accordance with the evolution of EU policy, it seems likely that mandatory and market-led actions need to move in tandem, at least if global rather than just national or regional change is envisaged.

The emergence of corporate purpose draws attention to the need to adjust board-decision-making and corporate strategy to adapt to sustainability at the operational level, rather than relying on the more indirect effects that may transmitted through the financial investor channel. In that sense it aligns very clearly with our earlier entity model of ESG, which drew attention to the limitations of the financial channel and the benefits of focusing more clearly on entities. In particular we focused on the limited scope of the financial model (such as the exclusion of banking from the relevant EU regulatory framework) and its questionable links to 'real world' impact.[47] In this section we elaborated on the role of corporate purpose in that model, focusing on the case for adjusting the levers of purpose rather than purpose itself and arguing that incremental change is more realistic than transformational change. Against that background, it will be interesting to observe how corporate purpose evolves in the years ahead and how far law can be a driver of change.

---

[47] See MacNeil and Esser (n 5).

## IV. Conclusion

Our analysis of the regulatory framework linked to ESG suggests that the UK corporate law framework is relatively open to the possibility that company boards might shift their strategy to adopt more sustainable solutions. This is made possible primarily by the discretion granted to boards to consider stakeholder interests within the context of the 'enlightened shareholder value' model that prevails in the UK. It would certainly be the case where a shift would carry benefits for shareholders such as a rise in the share price linked to managing risks associated with climate change. But in the case of more difficult decisions which carry long-term costs rather than benefits, it would seem less likely in practice that a board could favour stakeholder interests over shareholders without formal or informal shareholder approval for such action. Formal approval might be in the form of purpose provisions in the articles of association (rare) or shareholder resolutions (more common), while informal approval might be the result of engagement with shareholders.

Although much academic debate has recently focused on the adoption of explicit corporate purpose provisions in articles of association, there has not been much take-up of the idea in practice. While voluntary provisions may have a role to play, we are sceptical about the benefits of such provisions being mandated in law. We see evolutionary and indirect change as a more likely outcome than explicit transformation of corporate purpose through law reform.

We concluded by linking the UK framework to our earlier entity model of ESG, which was framed as a conceptual approach that could be adapted to any jurisdiction. Implicit in the entity model is the proposition that, by comparison with the dominant financial model, it would extend the scope of sustainability initiatives and link more directly to 'real world' impact and the earlier focus on ethics under CSR. But with the financial model of ESG now in the ascendancy, even with concerns over its reliability as an investing framework, it probably remains a serious challenge for the entity model to gain any traction.

# 8
# ESG and the Ethical Dimension

*Christine Osterloh-Konrad\**

## I. Introduction

For several years now, the discussion on the responsibility of business for social and environmental concerns has been gaining more and more ground. Focusing first on the concept of 'corporate social responsibility',[1] it then shifted to the acronym of ESG;[2] as of late, the concept of 'corporate purpose' has emerged as the new centre of the debate.[3] The attractiveness of the latter stems from the fact that it promises a more holistic approach to the topic than the other two alternatives, as may be illustrated by the following quote from the final report of the Future of the Corporate programme of the British Academy: 'The issue is not whether to promote the interests of shareholders *or* stakeholders but how to do both.'[4] The report centres on the idea that the purpose of business is 'creating profitable solutions for problems of people and planet, and not profiting from creating problems'.[5] To implement this idea, the legal framework shall be changed accordingly, aligning the private purpose of corporations with their social purposes and concentrating on a company's individual purpose as the 'guiding star' of its board.

The impetus to transform traditional capitalism and to strengthen business's commitment to the greater good is driven by several serious concerns. Globalization makes the limits of direct legal regulation more and more visible; a narrow focus on shareholder wealth maximization is considered deeply unsatisfactory; put more generally, there exists a great unease with a business world where all action seems motivated by financial concerns.

---

[*] All internet sources were last accessed on 24 January 2024.

[1] cf Archie B Carroll, 'A History of Corporate Social Responsibility: Concepts and Practices' in Andrew Crane and others (eds), *The Oxford Handbook of Corporate Social Responsibility* (OUP 2008); Markus Kitzmueller and Jay Shimshack, 'Economic Perspectives on Corporate Social Responsibility' (2012) 50 Journal of Economic Literature 51.

[2] cf UN Global Compact, 'Who Cares Wins: Connecting Financial Markets to a Changing World – Recommendations by the financial industry to better integrate environmental, social and governance issues in financial analysis, asset management and securities brokerage' (2004) www.unepfi.org/fileadmin/events/2004/stocks/who_cares_wins_global_compact_2004.pdf.

[3] Arguably most prominently promoted by Colin Mayer, *Prosperity: Better Business Makes the Greater Good* (OUP 2019).

[4] The British Academy, *Policy & Practice for Purposeful Business: The Final Report of the Future of the Corporation Programme* (2021) 21 www.thebritishacademy.ac.uk/publications/policy-and-practice-for-purposeful-business/.

[5] ibid 6.

This discussion has many connections with the fields of morality and ethics, although it is primarily led by lawyers, economists, and experts in business administration, not by philosophers. Against this background, the aim of the following text is to link it to the fields of individual and social ethics by expressing some critical considerations inspired by legal philosophy. First, what might be called the personhood theory of the corporation will be discussed (section II). Then, the focus will shift from the alleged virtue of corporations to the virtue of managers (section III). The next part of the chapter will be on the law and morality-divide and about why mandatory ESG reporting as pushed forward by European regulators obscures the boundary between those two sets of norms (section IV). The chapter will finish with some critical remarks on a certain type of ESG rhetoric (section V) and a few words on the function corporate purpose might, irrespective of all legitimate criticism, indeed fulfil (section VI).

## II. Corporations as Moral Agents?

At least some parts of the CSR, ESG, and corporate purpose literature put forward the idea that corporations should be treated as moral agents in their own right, just in the way humans are.[6] If *we* have personal values and purposes to our lives, why should business entities be any different? If *we* can behave virtuously, why shouldn't the same be true for artificial entities endowed with legal personality?[7]

Behind this 'personhood theory' of the corporation, a basic philosophical attitude can be discerned that places the whole above its parts. Such an attitude sees in a purposeful association of individuals more than a vehicle drawing its justification from each individual's interests. In the history of ideas, this attitude can be found especially with regard to the state.[8] Significantly, however, it is also present in corporate law theory, for example in the writings of the influential nineteenth century German author Otto von Gierke.[9] In one of his books, he formulates the commandment: 'Love the whole more than yourself.'[10] For him, a community is more than a means to the ends of its members; likewise, a corporate legal entity is a whole that has a higher value than its shareholders. If this is the case, then the will of this whole must be something other than the aggregated will of the individuals; it must be a kind of *volonté générale*. Under this perspective, the whole becomes an autonomous person in the true sense, ie a person to whom moral imperatives can reasonably be addressed.

---

[6] cf Michael J Phillips, 'Corporate Moral Personhood and Three Conceptions of the Corporation' (1992) 2 Business Ethics Quarterly 435; Aditi Gowri, 'On Corporate Virtue' (2007) 70 Journal of Business Ethics 391.
[7] For an elaborate concept of the virtuous corporation see Geoff Moore, 'Corporate Character: Modern Virtue Ethics and the Virtuous Corporation' (2005) 15 Business Ethics Quarterly 659.
[8] cf Jean-Jacques Rousseau, *Du contrat social* (first published 1762, Flammarion 2011); Georg Wilhelm Friedrich Hegel, *Grundlinien der Philosophie des Rechts* (first published 1820, Suhrkamp 2004).
[9] Otto Gierke, *Das Wesen der menschlichen Verbände* (Duncker & Humblot 1902).
[10] ibid 32.

Ultimately, however, this view turns the legal person into a mystical person. *Persona mystica* is, in fact, an old term for legal entities,[11] but it is a term which has fallen into oblivion, and rightly so. Private law knows nothing about mysticism. The best way to understand legal entities is to reduce them to their function as instruments for the common pursuit of a purpose set by human beings.[12] It is from this purpose that they draw their justification. This purpose may lie in the realization of profit through entrepreneurial activity, or in the promotion of some common good, or in both; in any case, it is defined by human beings. It is only the human being, not the legal entity, who is able to set his or her own ends. With regard to this capacity to moral autonomy, human beings and legal entities differ fundamentally from one another. And it is this autonomy alone which can be the basis for an attribution of the term 'virtue'.

If, in contrast, one equates human beings and legal entities from a moral point of view, one must, for example, consequently consider the board of directors to be entitled to even make substantial donations without reputational effect. Then, however, one must consider the question of managerial discretion for this type of decision. Is the board entitled to decide at its own will whether *Médecins sans Frontières* or Amnesty International should be supported? It seems to be common ground that the board must not pursue personal preferences when making this kind of choice.[13] But what is there to rely on, instead? There must be some guiding principle for the decision to take; but, unfortunately, the legal entity itself has no moral compass to guide it.[14] References in the literature to consulting additional bodies or to the need for a collective decision by the board and for its members to disregard purely private interests are merely crutches. They obscure the real problem. A legal entity itself has no free will and therefore simply cannot act virtuously.

A similar problem arises when it comes to the amount of such donations.[15] Here, there is a consensus that the long-term viability of the company must not be jeopardized.[16] Mostly, it is also assumed that donations must be in reasonable proportion to the company's profit situation.[17] But where does this criterion result from? Apparently,

---

[11] Ernst Kantorowicz, *The King's Two Bodies* (first published 1957, PUP 2016) 202; Thomas Raiser, 'Der Begriff der juristischen Person. Eine Neubesinnung' (1999) 199 Archiv für die civilistische Praxis 104, 109.

[12] For two early, particularly straightforward accounts of this view of the corporation, see Friedrich Carl von Savigny, *System des heutigen Römischen Rechts*, vol 2 (Veit 1840) 235–41; Bernhard Windscheid, *Pandektenrecht*, vol 1 (Julius Buddeus 1862) 105.

[13] Hans-Joachim Mertens, 'Zur Auslegung und zum Verhältnis von § 76 Abs. 1 und § 58 AktG im Hinblick auf uneigennützige soziale Aktivitäten der Aktiengesellschaft' in Hans Havermann (ed), *Bilanz- und Konzernrecht: Festschrift zum 65. Geburtstag von Dr. Dr. h.c. Reinhard Goerdeler* (IdW 1987) 349, 357; Harm Peter Westermann, 'Gesellschaftliche Verantwortung des Unternehmens als Gesellschaftsrechtsproblem' (1990) Zeitschrift für Wirtschaftsrecht 771, 775; Holger Fleischer, 'Unternehmensspenden und Leitungsermessen des Vorstands im Aktienrecht' (2001) Die Aktiengesellschaft 171, 178.

[14] Therefore, it is convincing to tie charitable corporate behaviour to shareholders' preferences. cf Oliver Hart and Luigi Zingales, 'Companies Should Maximize Shareholder Welfare Not Market Value' (2017) 2 Journal of Law, Finance, and Accounting 247.

[15] cf Martin Vorderwülbecke, 'Die Spendenkompetenz der Geschäftsführung' Betriebs-Berater (1989) 505, 508.

[16] Mertens (n 13) 356; Olaf Müller-Michaels and Wiebke Ringel, 'Muss sich Ethik lohnen? Wider die ökonomistische Rechtfertigung von Corporate Social Responsibility' (2011) Die Aktiengesellschaft 101, 109.

[17] Mertens (n 13) 360; Fleischer (n 13) 177; Müller-Michaels and Ringel (n 16) 110; Jochen Vetter, 'Geschäftsleiterpflichten zwischen Legalität und Legitimität: Muss sich Ethik lohnen?' (2018) Zeitschrift für Unternehmens- und Gesellschaftsrecht 338, 369.

a legal entity is supposed to act virtuously, but not to become a Mother Teresa. But why not?

These difficulties in justifying restrictions on the decision-making power of the directors of a virtuous corporation point to another difficulty inherent to the personhood theory of the corporation which has often been elaborated on in corporate law literature.

The more diverse the goals to which a board feels committed, the fewer concrete guidance can be drawn from them.[18] At the same time, decisions already taken can hardly be reviewed in retrospect to determine whether they were in conformity with fiduciary duties or not, as it is difficult to evaluate actions in multidimensional decision-making situations. After all, there will almost always be one or another reason that spoke in favour of the actual decision. Ambiguous objectives therefore lead to a wide leeway for action. At the same time, however, they invite to selfish behaviour. In the academic literature on the principle-agent conflict, this problem is sometimes summarized with the biblical saying: 'No one can serve two masters.'[19]

Therefore, the fear that a commitment of the public company to the common good would, in practice, above all result in a far-reaching release of directors from any control cannot be dismissed out of hand. Against this background, it is not surprising that the CEO who was largely responsible for the famous corporate purpose statement of the Business Roundtable at times felt, according to his own statement, like Thomas Jefferson formulating the Declaration of Independence.[20]

To sum up, the idea that legal entities may be subject to similar moral expectations as human beings must firmly be rejected. As the US Supreme Court puts it: 'A corporation is simply a form of organization used by human beings to achieve desired ends.'[21] Corporations lack moral autonomy; therefore, corporations cannot behave virtuously—only humans can.

If there is nothing about the common good or a specific non-profit purpose in their articles of association, corporations are therefore not obliged to the common good for moral reasons. If there is such a thing as 'virtue' in a corporation's actions, it consists in fulfilling the purpose of the corporation, which is to serve as efficiently as possible. To achieve this objective, it is much more helpful to give its directors clear guidelines than to confront them with a multidimensional optimization problem in which they have to consider the common good as well as various concerns of all kinds of stakeholders.

The concept of corporate purpose may be used as a shortcut to denominate the common purpose the relevant constituencies want to achieve by the corporate form. But the concept is deeply problematic if its usage leads to a wholly-fledged moral personification of the corporation because, in formulating moral imperatives for

---

[18] cf Jens-Hinrich Binder, ch 11 in this present volume.
[19] José María Gonzàlez-Gonzàlez and others, '"The Future of an Illusion": A Paradox of CSR' (2019) 32 Journal of Organizational Change Management 2, 6.
[20] cf David Gelles and David Yaffe-Bellany, 'Shareholder Value Is No Longer Everything, Top CEOs Say' *The New York Times* (19 August 2019).
[21] *Hobby Lobby Stores Inc* 573 US 682, 706 (2014).

corporations, fiduciary duties in the principal-agent relationship within the corporation risk to be ignored.

## III. Moral Behaviour and Fiduciary Duties

Nevertheless, there is a legitimate concern behind the idea that firms should be treated as moral agents. Proponents of this view are often worried that the strictly instrumental view of the firm referred to above, at least if combined with a strong taste for shareholder primacy, might lead to situations where the directors of the firm are legally bound to take a course of action which maximizes shareholder value even though it causes great damage to stakeholders, society, or the environment. It might seem that, under the paradigm of shareholder value, even 1$ more of shareholder value trumps any detriment to others. Many authors apparently consider an obligation of the company to the common good necessary in order to justify that directors are entitled to virtue in their decisions on behalf of the company.

But even if directors were, in principle, legally obliged to pursue shareholder value, this consequence would not follow, as the law leaves room for autonomous virtuous action even where someone acts as a representative or trustee.

Even if someone exerts a certain legal function for the benefit of others, he or she remains a human being capable of moral autonomy. Directors of a corporation may, in their function, primarily be obliged to the shareholders; at the same time, however, they are moral persons in the true sense of the word. A manager does not lay down his conscience in the anteroom of his office.

Any liberal society depends on people exercising their freedom in an at least remotely virtuous manner; otherwise, peaceful coexistence will not succeed. Therefore, society cannot do without a legally undetermined sphere of responsible action. This dependence of responsibility on autonomy makes any attempt to institutionalize ethics in companies through legal interventions and detailed guidelines highly questionable. One might say: The free market needs the honourable merchant.

This is not a question of moral responsibility of legal entities (which, in fact, they do not have); it is about human beings acting as morally autonomous persons.[22] Parts of the current discussion on ESG suffer from a fundamental confusion of levels. The debate often focuses on the moral behaviour of legal artefacts, although it should actually centre on the moral behaviour of the human beings acting on behalf of these artefacts.

These different categories are somewhat obscured if the behaviour of managers is analysed primarily from the perspective of economic models that reduce them to rational utility maximizer. If, for example, the relationship between shareholders and board members is viewed through the lens of the principal-agent theory, attention is primarily drawn to the question which incentive mechanisms will lead board members

---

[22] A similar argument is made by Lutz Strohn, 'Moral im Geschäftsleben: verdrängt durch das Recht' (2016) 180 Zeitschrift fur das gesamte Handelsrecht und Wirtschaftsrecht 2, 5.

to act in the interests of the shareholders while pursuing their own interests. This type of consideration is important and helpful; for when designing the law, it must be borne in mind that people do not simply shed their egoism when they take on a fiduciary legal function. But neither should one lose sight of the existence of moral intuitions of those same people.[23] Above all, law should not demand that directors suppress these intuitions in every case where they cannot be converted into financial benefits for shareholders.

Any liberal legal system must leave room for individual moral behaviour.[24] Therefore, corporate law should—and will—never force a moral agent to behave amorally. It is, therefore, not convincing to argue that corporate law imposes a duty on managers to maximize profits in the interest of shareholders at all possible costs.

This line of reasoning is consistent with the findings of an empirical study about managerial decision-making showing that, in their everyday decision-making, directors act primarily according to their own personal values, seemingly regardless of whether their corporate law environment follows a more shareholder- or a more stakeholder-oriented approach.[25] If directors consider a certain course of action the right thing to do, they will simply follow it—and rationalize it in conformity with the particular legal framework they operate within.

But where, one might object, does this approach leave the interests of other constituencies? Is the board of directors not once again given unrestricted freedom to realize its own moral standards with other people's money?

First, shareholders have the power to choose more or less scrupulous managers depending on their own moral preferences: in the monistic system through the election of the management body; in the dualistic system indirectly through the election of the supervisory body, which in turn appoints the board of directors. Moreover, any individual investor can make his investment decision dependent on how virtuous managers tend to behave.

Secondly, and most importantly, saying that, even in the case of fiduciary activities, there is still some leeway for following one's own moral intuitions is by no means saying that there are no limits to the realization of individual moral tastes. Indeed, some limits are set by the function in which an individual acts. The law does not require her to fulfil this function in an unscrupulous manner; but neither does it give her the freedom to transgress the limits of this function in order to freely realize her moral inclinations.

By way of example, one can hardly deny the director of a company the right to offer financial support to the needy family of a long-suffering, deceased employee. Nor can it be demanded of him to contract with the one supplier who offers the lowest prices if this supplier is notorious for inhumane production conditions. In both cases, the manager

---

[23] For an in-depth analysis of crowding out-problems which might arise if the law treats people as thoroughly selfish, see Bruno S Frey, 'A Constitution for Knaves Crowds Out Civic Virtues' (1997) 107 The Economic Journal 1043; for an even broader perspective of crowding out by legal rules, see Emad H Atiq, 'Why Motives Matter: Reframing the Crowding Out Effect of Legal Incentives' (2014) 123 Yale Law Journal 1070.

[24] cf Vetter (n 17) 349.

[25] René B Adams, Amir N Licht, and Lilach Sagiv, 'Shareholders and Stakeholders: How Do Directors Decide?' (2011) 32 Strategic Management Journal 1331.

fulfils the function assigned to him even if he does not follow the profit-maximizing course of action. He is managing the affairs of the corporation. It is a completely different question whether he is allowed to donate the corporation's money for charitable purposes as he sees fit; with such a decision, he places himself outside the function assigned to him, at least if the specific donation is not justifiable by reputational concerns.

The leeway left to the individual to act virtuously even in the exercise of fiduciary activities does not cover every conceivable moral conviction. Fiduciary duties are not eliminated by postulating some leeway for self-responsible moral action. To take the example of tax minimization: from the board's obligation to maximize after-tax profits, one can infer a duty to take advantage of obvious opportunities for tax optimization.[26] However, directors are not obliged to engage in highly complex aggressive tax planning which might produce tax advantages that were clearly not intended by the legislator.

## IV. Mandatory ESG Reporting and the Law-Morality Divide

Another troublesome feature of the legal trend towards ESG concerns a regulatory course of action the European legislator, in contrast to its US counterpart, has resolutely embarked on: mandatory ESG reporting.[27] From a legal philosophy perspective, this type of regulation is problematic because it tends to obscure the line between morality and the law; that is because, at least partly, mandatory ESG reporting amounts to the state instrumentalizing public moral resentment.

The relationship between law and morality is a fundamental topic in the philosophy of law. At its origin lies the distinction between two types of ought propositions: legal norms and moral norms. A moral norm can generally be described as any norm that evaluates a certain human behaviour as right or wrong and prescribes or forbids it accordingly. Legal norms are characterized by three special features concerning their origin, their validity, and their enforcement. They are created by institutions authorized to do so, such as parliaments; they are legally binding; and they can be enforced by the authorities, who respond to violations with sanctions.

The distinction between legal and moral norms leads to the classic question of whether or to what extent law requires an extra-legal justification, that is, a foundation in morality, in order to be valid.[28] It also leads to the equally notorious problem of the validity of unjust statutory law.[29]

---

[26] Wolfgang Schön, 'Vorstandspflichten und Steuerplanung' in Gerd Krieger, Marcus Lutter, and Karsten Schmidt (eds), *Festschrift für Michael Hoffmann-Becking zum 70. Geburtstag* (CH Beck 2013) 1085, 1090.
[27] As last amended by the so-called Corporate Sustainability Reporting Directive (Directive (EU) 2022/2464 of the European Parliament and of the Council of 14 December 2022 amending Regulation (EU) No 537/2014, Directive 2004/109/EC, Directive 2006/43/EC and Directive 2013/34/EU, as regards corporate sustainability reporting [2022] OJ L322/15 (16 December 2022).
[28] As, arguably, most prominently formulated by *Augustinus* in the following quote: 'Justice being taken away, then, what are kingdoms but great robberies?' See Augustinus, *De civitate dei* (written 413–26, Modern Library 1950) IV. 4.
[29] cf Gustav Radbruch, *Gesetzliches Unrecht und übergesetzliches Recht (Statutory Injustice and Suprastatutory Law)* (first published 1946, Nomos 2002).

But the issue of 'law and morality' has more aspects to it than these famous questions. For example, the observation that law *can*, at least, incorporate moral standards is automatically followed by the question to what extent it should do so. Is the fact that a certain behaviour is considered immoral a sufficient justification for threatening it with legal punishment? This question is often discussed under the heading 'legal moralism'.[30] If one asks the arguably most famous German legal philosopher, Immanuel Kant, the answer is clearly 'no'. For Kant, morality is primarily about the interior of the human being, about his or her motives (which is why 'nothing in the world—indeed nothing even beyond the world—can possibly be conceived which could be called good without qualification except a good will'[31]). Law, on the other hand, is concerned with defining the outer spheres of personal freedom.[32] Law is interested in actions, not in motives.

As far as moral discourse is concerned, law therefore has an enabling function. By creating and maintaining spaces of freedom, it makes room for a debate about right and wrong in which people with the most diverse backgrounds and beliefs can talk to each other without having to fear sanctions for expressing their opinions.

Having in mind this enabling function is central to the question of legal moralism. For it makes two things very clear: first, that, in any even remotely liberal society, law must necessarily cover much less types of behaviour than morality; and, secondly, that law and morality differ from each other in yet another crucial aspect concerning the legitimacy of any claim to objectivity they might make.

Morality is an inherently subjective matter. The source of moral judgement lies in the individual. Even though someone may personally be convinced that there are universally valid moral standards, he still cannot be sure that, in a dispute about their content, he is the one who has got them right, not his counterpart.

Thus, the conviction of universal moral values conflicts with the respect for the other as a moral person on an equal footing with oneself. This tension between believing in universal moral standards and realizing that no individual can claim privileged access to them cannot be resolved.[33] It is precisely because of this tension that morality is something deeply subjective. Everyone may search for moral commandments within his own conscience and act according to them; but no one is entitled to impose them on others. Certainly majority opinions on moral standards may emerge in society. However, a merely factual majority alone does not make a moral norm binding for everyone.

---

[30] John Stanton-Ife, 'The Limits of Law' in *The Stanford Encyclopedia of Philosophy* (Spring edn, 2022) https://plato.stanford.edu/entries/law-limits/.

[31] Immanuel Kant, *Grundlegung zur Metaphysik der Sitten* (first published 1785, wbg 1968) 18.

[32] Immanuel Kant, *Metaphysik der Sitten* (first published 1797, Suhrkamp 1997) 337 (Einleitung in die Rechtslehre § B).

[33] This is why, according to Friedrich A Hayek, in the context of social justice, 'the choice open to us is not between a system in which everybody will get what he deserves according to some absolute and universal standard of right, and one where the individual shares are determined partly by accident or good or ill chance, but between a system where it is the will of a few persons that decides who is to get what, and one where it depends at least partly on the ability and enterprise of the people concerned and partly on unforeseeable circumstances'. See Friedrich A Hayek, *The Road to Serfdom* (first published 1944, Institute of Economic Affairs 2005) 134.

Law, on the other hand, is something inherently objective. It contains norms that apply to all members of a society; the recognition of their validity is based on the fact that they are set by an institution to which this particular society attributes the competence of law-making. Legal positivists such as Hans Kelsen and H.L.A. Hart have long pondered how the law-specific nature of validity can be explained in a theoretically satisfactory way.[34] Fortunately, in the particular context of ESG, it is not necessary to look for an ultimate justification. It is sufficient to point out that legal norms have a kind of objectivity that moral norms lack—and that this kind of objectivity does not stem from their content, but from their process of creation.

Therefore, law not only enables the moral discourse, but it may also relieve it, namely when a particular social norm is transferred from the moral to the legal sphere. When a certain type of behaviour is legally and no longer only morally required, the participants in the moral discourse can almost stop discussing it; at least, the moral discussion loses a great deal of its relevance because sceptics do no longer have to be convinced, but only need to be reminded of their effective legal obligations.

Thus, the institutional process of law-making in the democratic state, by which rules are incorporated in law, is a way out of the tension between universal moral convictions and the respect for the other as a moral being. The democratic formation of a majority in an orderly process lends ought-propositions a form of objectivity that moral intuitions may never claim. Citizens recognize the objective validity of norms that have gone through this process precisely *because* they have gone through it, not due to their content.

Due to this subjectivity-objectivity divide, the separation of law and morality is one of the great achievements of modern liberal legal systems. Everyone is allowed to behave as they wish unless they violate legal norms. Everyone else, of course, has the right to criticize the actions of his fellow human beings as violations of moral norms or even to denounce it publicly. Thereby, he can initiate a discussion on whether the behaviour in question should continue to be tolerated or should be forbidden by law.

However, the state itself may not make use of these naming and shaming mechanisms. It must remain neutral towards actions that could be classified as 'morally undesirable' but are nevertheless legal. This is because, when relying on pressure through moral condemnation by the public to discourage certain actions, the state undermines the very mechanism which serves to transform subjective moral standards into objective norms.

Therefore, any instrumentalization of public reputational pressure by the government is illegitimate. This insight causes considerable unease with mandatory ESG reporting. That many types of behaviour are open to moral evaluation does not mean that legal institutions are entitled to make use of public moral resentment. Law is neither meant nor able to enforce morality.

---

[34] cf Hans Kelsen, *Reine Rechtslehre* (first published 1934, Mohr Siebeck 2008); HLA Hart, *The Concept of Law* (OUP 1961).

## V. Brave New World

Behind some of the corporate purpose rhetoric, there seems to be a fundamental desire for unanimity. In statements like the following from the Business Roundtable: 'Each of our stakeholders is essential. We commit to deliver value to all of them',[35] as well as in the initial quotes from the British Academy report, seems to be latent a vision of a world where all conflicts of interests disappear, corporations turn into benevolent social planners, and mankind strives in unison for the common good.

This is a vision which, in a more generalized form, has been prominent in political philosophy at all times (eg in Rousseau's *volonté générale*). Its attraction stems from the fact that conflicts are, in general, difficult to endure. In addition, we naturally tend to generalize our personal ideas about what is good and what is evil, and we would be enormously relieved if the tension between the claim to general validity of our personal convictions and the respect for other moral beings with different convictions were to be resolved by pure harmony.

However, it is a dangerous vision. It can lead to a dismissive, if not discriminatory, attitude towards anyone who denies the possibility of converging interests or brings forward considerations which are not compatible with current mainstream ideas. After all, such a person not only expresses a different opinion but threatens the whole enterprise of collective harmony; he fits into the whole picture only if he is not taken seriously because he is considered to be on a lower level of understanding. Therefore, if this vision is pursued to its extreme, it tends to turn into totalitarianism.

## VI. Concluding Remarks

All these considerations lead to a rather sceptical perspective on the potential and the appropriateness of an ambitious concept of corporate purpose.

Defining a corporate purpose can be helpful as a voluntary instrument to promote the objectives of those involved in the company. With a carefully designed statement of corporate purpose, a company might successfully signal priorities to customers, potential employees, and investors. In turn, those constituencies can adjust their behaviour according to whether their personal preferences match with these priorities.

To fulfil this instrumental function, vague phrases, as frequently encountered at present, are not helpful; the purpose of a corporation should be concrete. Ideally, it should also be connected, as far as possible, with publicly available metrics set by the corporation itself. This would make it easier to assess whether and to what extent the company is achieving the goals it has set for itself.

In contrast, current attempts to define universal ESG metrics to make the ESG performance of different firms comparable with the aim of encouraging companies to put

---

[35] Business Roundtable, 'Statement on the Purpose of a Corporation' (2019) https://opportunity.businessroundtable.org/ourcommitment/.

their efforts at the service of some common good are rightly countered with scepticism. After all, assessing the overall benefit of a particular course of action for 'people and planet'[36] is often incredibly difficult, due to the world's complexity and the variety of individuals' preferences. In fact, the enormous difficulties we sometimes face when we try to assign moral values to our actions is another reason for the size of the gap between law and morality. Law only sets minimum standards; it cannot do otherwise.

---

[36] The British Academy (n 4) 6.

# 9
# Corporate Purpose in the United States 1800–2000

*Harwell Wells**

## I. Introduction

Over the past few years, the issue of 'corporate purpose' has moved to the centre of debates over the business corporation.[1] These debates, at least in the United States, have tended to fall along a few now-familiar lines: should the corporation's purpose be solely to benefit shareholders, or should corporations be run to benefit other groups as well? Once chosen, how should these purposes be pursued, and how can we measure whether they have been met? And, given possibly competing claims on the corporation, who should have a voice in choosing the corporation's ends—shareholders, or managers, or should a wider array of stakeholders also be heard?

Today's debates may be new, but the question of corporate purpose is not. Over the last two centuries Americans have considered and reconsidered the purposes for which corporations can be created and the ends they should pursue. Often these disputes are about the law—over when and why the state should create or recognize particular business corporations and how they should be governed—but they have frequently spilled into politics and even culture, with debates in different arenas running in parallel, overlapping, or even at cross-purposes. This chapter aims to provide a selective historical overview of the United States' debates over corporate purpose, emphasizing that 'corporate purpose' has always been questioned and in dispute; even in eras when one understanding of the business corporation's purpose has been dominant, there have been dissenting voices pushing to rework the institution. Furthermore, accounts of the corporation's purpose have rarely been neutral. In the debates discussed here the disputants have often had normative goals, sketching out as much an idealized or

---

* My thanks to the editors of this volume and participants at the Conference on Public Corporations held at the University of Tübingen for useful comments and suggestions, and the Temple University James E. Beasley School of Law for research support. This chapter draws on my earlier work, particularly 'Corporation Law Is Dead' (n 71 below) and 'The Cycles of Corporate Social Responsibility' (n 57 below). All internet sources were last accessed on 15 January 2024.

[1] L Fink, 'Profits & Purpose' (BlackRock 2019 Letter to CEOs) https://www.blackrock.com/americas-offshore/en/2019-larry-fink-ceo-letter; JE Fisch and SD Solomon, 'Should Corporations Have a Purpose?' (2021) 99 Texas Law Review 1309; E Pollman and RB Thompson, 'Corporate Purpose and Personhood: An Introduction' in E Pollman and RB Thompson (eds), *Research Handbook on Corporate Purpose and Personhood* (Edward Elgar Publishing 2021).

hoped-for version of the corporation as a presently-existing one. Even the terms have changed. As we shall see, the debates over corporation's purpose have not always used the phrase 'corporate purpose', even though they have turned on the question of who the corporation should serve.

A comprehensive history of corporate purpose would be a history of the American corporation—too big a subject for a small chapter. So this chapter focuses on four episodes that occurred between the middle of the nineteenth century and the end of the twentieth, each illustrating a different way the concept of corporate purpose was formulated and, equally important, deployed. It begins with a piece of legal machinery, the corporate purpose clause, an artefact of nineteenth century corporation law that required every corporation have a specific purpose spelled out in its charter, and the ultra vires doctrine which empowered shareholders to hold the corporation and its managers to that purpose. It then moves into the twentieth century, when the dominance of the giant business corporation and the separation of ownership and control created new possibilities for corporate purpose. In 1932, the corporate law scholars Adolf A. Berle and Merrick Dodd engaged in a debate over the corporation's purpose that laid down the lines along which the debates have since been waged: should corporations be run solely to benefit shareholders, or should managers seek to benefit other groups—'other constituencies'—as well? Shifting focus, the chapter then moves into the post-Second World War era and broadens its scope to examine not only academic debates over corporate governance, but public and management perceptions of who corporations should be run for. The final episode occurred a few decades later, when economic and political changes led to the triumph of a view of corporate purpose that focused almost exclusively on the shareholder. Parts of this story may be familiar to readers; what this chapter emphasizes is the ways that debates over corporate purpose, which one might think would be limited to the discourses of business and law, have been unavoidably intertwined with and shaped by larger social, political, and economic developments in the United States.

## II. Purpose in the Nineteenth Century

From the start corporations in America had to have a purpose.[2] Between the beginning of the nineteenth century and the US Civil War, a period when the corporate form became attractive to for-profit enterprises, corporations were usually formed by special acts of state legislatures which spelled out a corporation's purpose in its charter.[3] In 1818, to give one example, the Pennsylvania legislature chartered the Lehigh Coal Company with the purpose of 'making a road from the river to the [coal] mines, and

---

[2] DB Guenther, 'Of Bodies Politic and Pecuniary: A Brief History of Corporate Purpose' (2019) 9 Michigan Business and Entrepreneurial Law Review 1, 15–25.

[3] SP Hamill, 'From Special Privilege to General Utility: A Continuation of Willard Hurst's Study of Corporations' (1999) 49 American University Law Review 81; E Hilt, 'Early American Corporations and the State' in N Lamoreaux and WJ Novak (eds), *Corporations and American Democracy* (HUP 2017).

of bringing coal to market by the means of navigation'.[4] Narrow purpose clauses were a product of the belief that corporations were created by the state to provide some public benefit. As Angell and Ames' *Treatise on the Law of Private Corporations*, the first treatise on US corporation law, put it, a 'public benefit is deemed a sufficient consideration of a grant of corporate privileges'.[5] The earliest corporations were typically chartered to supply some public good the state was unable or unwilling to provide, which helps explain why banks, turnpike, bridge, and canal companies often predominated among early corporations.[6] That does not mean, however, that early corporations were akin to public utilities. Business corporations, even those providing public benefit, had owners who intended to profit from them.[7] As one early incorporator said: '[C]orporations were considered by us all a money making business'.[8] Nor were corporations' purposes always limited to providing well-defined public goods. While before 1830 most corporations were those providing transportation infrastructure, with financial infrastructure such as banks close behind, the historian Robert Wright found almost 700 manufacturing firms received state charters during that period.[9] At least some charters had only loose ties to the public benefit; in 1790 the charter of the New-York Manufacturing Company spoke of its purpose to 'furnish[] employment for the honest and industrious poor',[10] while in 1809 the Albany Manufacturing Society was chartered for the 'laudable purpose of extending the manufactory of cotton and wood'.[11] That there were not more manufacturing corporations may be chalked up to the fact that most manufacturing during these decades was small-scale and organizers did not need the particular benefits offered by the corporate form (eg capital lock-in, asset partitioning).[12]

In this era a corporation's purpose was both empowering and limiting. Literally empowering, inasmuch as a corporation's purpose justified its legislative creation and was the source of whatever powers it possessed. But purpose also limited, for a corporation was not empowered to engage in activities other than those to fulfil its stated, and usually narrow, purpose. According to Angell and Ames, it was a 'tacit condition of a grant of incorporation that the grantees shall act for the end or design for which they

---

[4] M Blair, 'Locking in Capital: What Corporate Law Achieved for Business Organizers in the Nineteenth Century' (2003) 51 UCLA Law Review 387, 417.

[5] JK Angell and S Ames, *A Treatise on the Law of Private Corporations Aggregate* (Hillard, Gray, Little & Wilkins 1832) 7.

[6] JW Cadman Jr, *The Corporation in New Jersey: Business and Politics* (HUP 1949) 206.

[7] Some paid dividends (see eg Cadman (n 6) 320), while others were akin to cooperatives whose member-owners benefit from low prices. See H Hansmann and M Pargendler, 'The Evolution of Shareholder Voting Rights: The Separation of Ownership from Consumption' (2014) 123 Yale Law Journal 946.

[8] RE Wright, *Corporation Nation* (University of Pennsylvania Press 2014) 85 (quoting early corporation promoter Elkanha Watson); Angell and Ames (n 5) 7–8 ('The object in creating a corporation is, in fact, to gain the union ... of several persons for the successful promotion of some design of general utility, though the corporation may, at the same time be established for the advantage of those who are members of it').

[9] Wright (n 8) 62.

[10] Hilt (n 3) 41.

[11] E Pollman, 'The History and Revival of the Corporate Purpose Clause' (2021) 99 Texas Law Review 1423, 1435.

[12] Blair (n 4); H Hansmann, R Kraakman, and R Squire, 'Law and the Rise of the Firm' (2006) 119 Harvard Law Review 1333.

were incorporated'.[13] While purpose clauses may have had more than one function—as Elizabeth Pollman has pointed out, they could also serve a coordinating function among investors—they were both a publicly imposed and privately agreed-to limit upon a corporation's act.[14] Initially, enforcement of this 'tacit condition' was left to a state's attorney general, who could use the writ of *quo warranto* and seek to have a corporation dissolved if it exceeded its chartered purpose, as when in New York an insurance company lost its charter after offering banking services.[15] By the 1830s, however, state enforcement began to wane, as the growing number of business corporations, and the view they were chiefly vehicles for their organizers, made state involvement in their operations less central.[16]

In place of public enforcement, private enforcement arose via the ultra vires doctrine, which still prohibited a corporation from acts that were contrary to its charter but could be invoked by individual shareholders.[17] This turned corporate purpose from a public tool of state control into a private tool for intra-corporate struggle. In a period when derivative litigation and corporate fiduciary duties were still taking shape, ultra vires was a prime weapon for shareholders challenging controllers' decisions. When shareholders concluded that managers were engaged in fraud, or aggrandizement by committing the corporation to act beyond its chartered purpose, they alleged the acts were *ultra vires*. While the precise number of such suits filed cannot be measured, by the late 1870s and 1880s treatises hundreds of pages long were published dealing with the topic.[18] Particular cases almost always show minority shareholders trying to rein in management (typically controlling shareholders). Courts parsed charters to answer such questions as whether a corporation chartered to run a hotel could sell its hotel and use the proceeds to purchase another one (yes),[19] whether a corporation formed to manufacturer iron could go into the milling business (no),[20] or whether a coal mining and transportation company could buy a steamboat to transport coal (no).[21] While there were occasional *quo warranto* cases filed by attorneys general even late in the century,[22] the predominance of ultra vires was a sign of the changing role of the purpose clause and the increasingly private nature of the corporation itself.

---

[13] Angell and Ames (n 5) 163.
[14] Pollman (n 11) 1425.
[15] *People ex rel Attorney General v Utica Insurance Co* 15 Johns 358 (NY 1818). See also EM Dodd, *American Business Corporations to 1860* (HUP 1954) 57–61; H Hovenkamp, *Enterprise and American Law 1836–1937* (HUP 1991) 56–64.
[16] JW Hurst, *The Legitimacy of the Business Corporation* (University Press of Virginia 1970) 51–58.
[17] K Greenfield, 'Ultra Vires Lives! A Stakeholder Analysis of Corporate Illegality' (2001) 87 Virginia Law Review 1279, 1302–10. Formally, ultra vires asserted that 'an act by the directors of a corporation, though done with the consent of all the stockholders, if not within the purposes for which it was created' by the state was unenforceable. G.H.W., 'Ultra Vires' (1878) 6 Central Law Journal 2, 3.
[18] See eg R Reese, *The True Doctrine of the Law of Ultra Vires in the Law of Corporations* (TH Flood 1897); GW Field, *The Doctrine of Ultra Vires* (Mills 1881).
[19] *Freeman v Sea View Hotel Co* 40 A 219 (NJ Ch 1898).
[20] *Cherokee Iron Co v Jones* 52 Ga 276 (1874).
[21] *Calloway v Clark* 32 Mo 305 (1862).
[22] *Quo warranto* was used by several state attorney generals to challenge corporations' participation in business trusts, notably Standard Oil, in the late nineteenth century. *State v Standard Oil Co* 30 NE 279 (Ohio 1892) (trust creates monopoly so ultra vires as against public policy); Hovenkamp (n 15) 249.

Ultra vires litigation dwindled by the end of the century. One reason was that such claims were increasingly made not by aggrieved shareholders but by corporations themselves to escape contractual obligations (essentially, corporations claimed they should not be held to contracts validly entered into but exceeding their corporate purpose).[23] It also reflected changing views of the corporation. Older views that the corporation was created by the state via incorporation were replaced by views that corporations were created by their founders and only subsequently acknowledged by the state, moving the corporation's locus from the state to its owners.[24] Methods of incorporation reflected this as well, as (special) incorporation by act of the legislature was replaced by (general) incorporation which simply required filing of documents with the state and made the corporate form available to all.[25] Finally, state-imposed limits on the corporate form eroded. Nineteenth century corporation statutes were inflexible, for instance imposing minimum and maximum limits on capital and requiring unanimous shareholder approval of fundamental transactions. At the end of the century, these were slowly superseded by 'enabling' statutes which gave organizers much greater flexibility in arranging the internal operations of their firms.[26] The *laissez-faire* philosophy of the enabling statutes reached corporate purpose; by the 1890s, it was possible for corporations in some states to be chartered for 'any lawful purpose'.[27]

## III. The Origins of the Modern Debate

The twentieth century would produce very different ideas of corporate purpose as it grappled with a different kind of business corporation. Beginning with the railroads in the 1870s and accelerating with the 'great merger movement' at the turn of the century, large corporations with operations crossing state lines swiftly came to dominate the nation's economy.[28] During these decades, issues of corporate purpose were eclipsed by fears of corporate power—particularly giant corporations' monopoly power.[29] National policy concerning corporations came to focus on competition law—'antitrust'—which targeted only corporations alleged to be engaged in unfair competition or seeking monopolies. Corporation law itself continued along a path of increasing flexibility and largely abandoned its regulatory aspect; while not every state changed its corporation statute, the 'internal affairs doctrine', and Supreme Court decisions, made it easy for

---

[23] Greenfield (n 17) 1310–13.
[24] D Millon, 'Theories of the Corporation' [1990] Duke Law Journal 201, 205–25.
[25] JL Hennessey and JJ Wallis, 'Corporations and Organization in the United States after 1840' in N Lamoreaux and WJ Novak (eds), *Corporations and American Democracy* (HUP 2017) 78–85.
[26] EM Dodd Jr, 'Statutory Developments in Business Corporation Law, 1886–1936' (1936) 50 Harvard Law Review 27; WB Rutledge Jr, 'Significant Trends in Modern Incorporation Statutes' (1937) 22 Washington University Law Quarterly 305.
[27] LM Friedman, *A History of American Law* (3rd edn, Simon & Schuster 2005) 396.
[28] AD Chandler Jr, *Scale and Scope: The Dynamics of Industrial Capitalism* (HUP 1994).
[29] GA Mark, 'The Corporate Economy: Ideologies of Regulation and Antitrust, 1920–2000' in M Grossberg and C Tomlins (eds), *The Cambridge History of Law in America*, vol 3 (CUP 2008) 619.

corporations to organize in states whose laws placed fewer limits on their activities.[30] Corporate externalities were left to other bodies of law. There were occasionally radical proposals to revivify corporation law's regulatory functions by, for instance, requiring large corporations to gain a Federal charter or license, but these aimed not at reinvigorating public purpose but at encouraging competition, limiting financial fraud, and publicizing corporate accounts.[31] There was still public concern over the giant corporations (henceforward simply referred to as 'corporations') but there was no longer opposition to the corporate form in general, a form by then often used by smaller firms that once would have been partnerships.[32]

Here we find the roots of a very different discourse over corporate purpose, as Americans' worries came to focus on large corporations possessing significant political, social, and economic power, with fears that such behemoths would dominate the communities in which they were based and overwhelm legal controls placed on them. Public opinion began to demand more from corporations than just efficiency. In response, the historian Roland Marchand showed, many corporations after the turn of the century began a 'quest for purpose and legitimacy' to remedy the corporation's 'perceived lack of a conscience'.[33] Corporations, according to Marchand, sought to portray themselves as 'something more than just a money-making machine', promoting instead images and metaphors that would depict the corporation as akin to natural persons with an ethical compass.[34] To communicate their new image, corporations turned to the new field of public relations to create a human face for the faceless corporation and to suggest they were imbued with ethical purpose. Different corporations took different approaches; AT&T's advertisements highlighted its dispersed shareholder population to claim it was actually a 'democracy', while General Motors, advised by PR guru Bruce Barton, used 'kinship and community metaphors' in its advertising and public pronouncements, all to assert that they were not merely businesses but should be regarded as more like neighbours.[35] Just as people and communities could have purposes beyond profit, corporate image-makers asserted, so could corporations.

The notion that corporations could have purposes beyond profit spread widely during the 1920s. Many corporate leaders embraced notions of 'business statesmanship', and insisted that that they were not just business leaders but 'public trustees', governing their firms with at least one eye towards public benefit.[36] 'Progressive' business leaders like GE's Gerald Swope highlighted their firms' 'welfare capitalist' policies which offered workers profit-sharing and pensions, claiming this as further evidence

---

[30] D Crane, 'The Dissociation of Incorporation and Regulation in the Progressive Era and the New Deal' in N Lamoreaux and WJ Novak (eds), *Corporations and American Democracy* (HUP 2017) 109; C McCurdy, 'The Knight Sugar Decision and the Modernization of American Corporate Law' (1979) 53 Business History Review 304.

[31] G Kolko, *The Triumph of Conservatism: A Reinterpretation of American History 1900–1916* (Free Press 1963) 172–77; M Sklar, *The Corporate Reconstruction of American Capitalism 1890–1916* (CUP 1983) 191–203.

[32] Hurst (n 16) 62–74.

[33] R Marchand, *Creating the Corporate Soul: The Rise of Public Relations and Corporate Imagery in American Big Business* (CUP 1998) 3, 7.

[34] ibid 165.

[35] ibid 131.

[36] ibid 164.

that corporations were being run to benefit workers, retirees, and their communities as well as shareholder. A number of reasons were adduced for this change, but one frequently cited was the spread of shareholding, the implication being that as corporations gained more small shareholders managers would become more conscious of their obligations to run the corporation responsibly. As the philanthropist Robert Brookings put it, the 'widespread diffusion of ownership and the increasing sense of responsibility to management to all the interested parties point to a satisfactory solution of "the industrial problem"'.[37] The point is not that corporations were really being run differently—at least there is not much evidence of that—but rather that the public began to expect more of the nation's large corporations, and that these public expectations, and corporation's responses, fed into the new discourse over corporate purpose.

Given this, it's somewhat surprising to realize that the famous case of *Dodge v Ford Motor Co.*, today seen as announcing that the corporation's purpose was to seek profits for shareholders, was decided at this time.[38] The facts are straightforward. After many years of rapid growth and paying rich dividends, Ford Motor Co., under the thumb of Henry Ford, ceased paying special dividends for reasons both practical (to fund expansion) and malicious (to harm minority shareholders). When the decision was challenged by those minority shareholders, the Dodge brothers, Henry Ford bull-headedly told a court that the firm was retaining earnings because he wanted to operate it for general public benefit. The Michigan Supreme Court slapped this down, famously stating that 'a business corporation is organized and carried on primarily for the profit of its stockholders'.[39] In decades to come, the case would be cited as evidence that a corporation's purpose was to benefit shareholders—which is indeed what the court said. But this reading is incomplete. It overlooks the debates over corporate purpose which were flourishing elsewhere—debates which would reach very different conclusions. It treats *Dodge v Ford* as set in stone, as though the pronouncement of one state court in 1919 settled the legal issue of corporate purpose once and for all, ignoring how later cases revisited the question of corporate purpose.[40] And it also ignores the way that *Dodge v Ford* was a backward-looking case. Ford Motor Company was of course one of America's great corporations, but it differed in one important way from the corporations that would dominate the United States in the century to come. Ford was closely held, with a handful of shareholders.[41] The twentieth century's debates over corporate purpose would revolve around a different kind of entity: the publicly traded corporation marked by the separation of ownership and control.

By the early 1930s, observers had identified two related developments beyond mere growth fundamentally changing the American corporation: the dispersal of share

---

[37] R Brookings, *Industrial Ownership: Economic and Social Significance* (Ayer 1925) 14; see also J Ott, *When Wall Street Met Main Street: The Quest for an Investors' Democracy* (HUP 2011).
[38] 170 NW 668 (Mich 1919).
[39] ibid 684.
[40] See eg *AP Smith Manufacturing Co v Barlow* 98 A2d 581 (NJ 1953); *Shlensky v Wright* 237 NE2d 776 (Ill App 1968); LA Stout, 'Why We Should Stop Teaching Dodge v Ford' (2008) 3 Virginia Law & Business Review 164.
[41] MT Henderson, 'The Story of Dodge v Ford Motor Co: Everything Old Is New Again' in JM Ramseyer (ed), *Corporate Law Stories* (Foundation Press 2009).

ownership and the movement of corporate control to managers lacking a major ownership stake, labelled the 'separation of ownership and control' by Adolf A. Berle and Gardiner Means in *The Modern Corporation and Private Property* (1932).[42] Starting in the 1910s, a growing number of Americans began buying common stock, resulting in corporations with a large number of small shareholders but no dominant one. By 1920, for instance, AT&T, the Pennsylvania Railroad, and US Steel each had more than 100,000 shareholders.[43] As no shareholder had a controlling or even major stake, power in these corporations gravitated to managers insulated from shareholders' demands, and ownership of the corporation was separated from control of it.

The separation of ownership and control was a necessary precondition for modern debates over corporate purpose, at least as they took shape in the United States. So long as a corporation was owned by a small number of shareholders, there was little question it would be run for their benefit, if only because those shareholders would choose, or be, the managers. While early American corporation law envisioned public benefit from incorporation, that public benefit depended on the private gains sought by the corporation's owners. As ownership fragmented, however, shareholders were unable to mobilize and control of corporate operations shifted to managers. Initially, this raised the familiar fear that managers would run corporations to benefit not shareholders but themselves, and a few corporate law scholars in the 1920s, notably Berle and Harvard's William Z. Ripley, analysed the way that changes in ownership and the law had made it easier for managers to manipulate the corporate structure and divert economic benefits from shareholders into their own pockets.[44] But lurking in the split between ownership and control was another possibility: if managers were able to run the corporation for their own benefit rather than that of shareholders, could managers also run the corporation for the benefit of yet other groups?

This idea runs through the modern American debates over corporate purpose, and as a legal issue it was most clearly formulated in 1932 when Merrick Dodd, a corporate law scholar at the Harvard Law School, connected dispersed shareholding and managerial autonomy to new public expectations of corporations and the growing movement for business statesmanship in his *Harvard Law Review* article 'For Whom Are Corporate Managers Trustees?'.[45] Dodd opened by observing that managers had over the past few decades been freed 'from any substantial supervision by stockholders by reason of the difficulty which the modern stockholder has in discovering what is going on and taking effective measures even if he has discovered it'.[46] To remedy this, some proposed new legal mechanisms to yoke managers more tightly to shareholder interests—Berle for instance had argued just a year before that managers' powers should be treated as 'powers

---

[42] AA Berle and GC Means, *The Modern Corporation and Private Property* (Macmillan 1932). Berle and Means distinguished between management and 'control' and acknowledged that management did not always control large corporations, but their readers tended to miss this point.
[43] ibid 55.
[44] WZ Ripley, *Main Street and Wall Street* (Little, Brown 1927); AA Berle, 'Non-Voting Stock and Bankers' Control' (1926) 39 Harvard Law Review 673.
[45] EM Dodd, 'For Whom Are Corporate Managers Trustees?' (1932) 45 Harvard Law Review 1145.
[46] ibid 1147.

in trust' for shareholders, and that courts should police managers' exercise of those powers whenever used to shareholders' detriment.[47] Dodd went the opposite direction, and argued that the growing distance between managers from shareholders was less a problem than an opportunity.

As Dodd saw it, accepting at face value the claims of 'business statesmen', corporate managers had begun to treat their corporations as having a 'social service as well as a profit-making function'.[48] As shareholders became absentee owners, with less involvement or stake in the corporation, managers' loyalty to them frayed while their ties to other groups, such as workers, grew. Citing examples such as GE's Swope, the best-known advocate of corporate welfare capitalism, Dodd argued that a few visionary corporate leaders had developed 'a sense of social responsibility toward employees, consumers, and the general public'.[49] While the law did not yet incorporate this new managerial attitude, it was catching up, and he pointed to railroad and public utility regulation to show that corporate property now had a public aspect, rather than being the concern of shareholders alone. Behind these specific developments Dodd discerned a larger shift in 'public opinion with regard to the obligations of business to the community'.[50] Although the exact mechanisms were not spelled out, he hinted that public pressure would lead managers 'to adopt and disseminate the view that they are guardians of all the interests which the corporation affects and not merely servants of its absentee owners'.[51] Given this, he argued, the law should follow, and treat managers' duties as owed not to shareholders but the corporation itself, a move that would enable them to 'employ [the corporation's] funds in a manner appropriate to a person ... with a sense of social responsibility without thereby being guilty of a breach of trust'.[52] Although Dodd did not use the terms, here was a fully-stated theory of corporate purpose at odds with shareholder-centred version of *Dodge v Ford*: managers should owe duties to the corporation itself, and be trusted to distribute its benefits to different groups as though the corporation was an autonomous person 'with a sense of social responsibility'.

A counterblast quickly came from an unexpected party, Adolf A. Berle. In 'For Whom Are Corporate Managers Trustees: A Note', also published in 1932 in the *Harvard Law Review*, Berle defended the idea that managers should owe duties solely to shareholders, drawing on his experience as a Wall Street lawyer during the 1920s to mock the idea that corporate managers would live up to the statesmanship Dodd wished to thrust upon them.[53] Berle's reasoning was simple: managers freed of stringent duties to shareholders would not serve others but themselves. Whatever Dodd might think, Berle wrote, while managers of giant corporations might appear 'more as princes and ministers that as promoters or merchants', it was foolish to believe they would run their corporations for the benefit of employees, consumers, or the general public.[54]

[47] AA Berle Jr, 'Corporate Powers as Powers in Trust' (1931) 44 Harvard Law Review 1049.
[48] ibid 1148.
[49] ibid 1160.
[50] ibid 1153.
[51] ibid 1157.
[52] ibid 1161.
[53] AA Berle Jr, 'For Whom Are Corporate Managers Trustees: A Note' (1932) 45 Harvard Law Review 1365.
[54] ibid 1367.

The manager 'does not now think of himself as a prince, he does not now assume responsibilities to his community; ... his lawyers do not advise him in terms of social responsibility'.[55] Were Dodd's proposals adopted, Berle quipped, corporate property would be 'simply handed over ... to the present administrators with a pious wish that something nice ... come out of it'.[56] Much of the corporate purpose discourse over the rest of the century would simply repeat one side or the other of the Berle-Dodd debate.[57]

Were we to stop here, the battle lines would be clear, with Dodd sunnily pushing to let management run corporations to benefit multiple constituencies and Berle throwing cold water on the whole idea. But a further wrinkle appeared when, even as the Berle-Dodd debate was underway, Berle and Means' *The Modern Corporation and Private Property* was published. This work gave yet another account of the possibilities for the modern corporation, one seemingly at odds with what Berle had just written *contra* Dodd. For the most part *The Modern Corporation* rigorously set out how the dispersion of share ownership and legal changes had split ownership and control in many large publicly traded corporations, depicting this as an ongoing and accelerating historical process. But here an unexpected observation appeared. At their book's tail end, Berle and Dodd speculated that, as ownership and control continued to diverge, '[i]t is conceivable ... that the 'control' of the great corporation should develop into a purely neutral technocracy, balancing a variety of claims by various interest groups in the community and assigning to each a portion of the income stream on the basis of public policy rather than private cupidity'.[58] In short, historical development might eventually produce a corporation run to benefit multiple groups, just as Dodd had claimed was happening. The main difference between the two sides was that Dodd saw this as occurring in the present, while Berle and Means placed it in a hoped-for future.

After almost a century the Berle-Dodd debate remains relevant to contemporary debates over corporate purpose, not least because rarely have the two sides to the shareholder-versus-stakeholder controversy been so clearly set out. When debates over corporate purpose resurfaced after the Second World War, however, they took a surprising turn, with many observers arguing the debates were over and an unexpected side had won.

## IV. Corporate Purpose at Mid-century

Writing in 1954, Berle revisited his debate with Dodd. In 1932, he recalled, he argued that 'corporate powers were powers in trust for shareholders, while Professor Dodd had argued these powers were held in trust for the entire community'. Twenty years

---

[55] ibid.
[56] ibid 1368.
[57] CAH Wells, 'The Cycles of Corporate Social Responsibility: An Historical Retrospective for the Twenty-First Century' (2002) 51 Kansas Law Review 77.
[58] Berle and Means (n 42) 312.

on, Berle concluded that he had been wrong, and the argument settled 'squarely ... in favour of Dodd's contention'.[59]

A view of corporate purpose that had seemed radical in the 1930s had become a commonplace in the 1950s. As Berle now saw it, while American corporations still had obligations to shareholders, those shareholders 'no longer hold the center of the corporate stage',[60] and management was now obligated to run their firms as trustees for the benefit of the 'entire community'.[61] As evidence he pointed to legal changes allowing corporate boards to direct part of their profits to 'schools, colleges, hospitals', as well as social and economic changes that had made corporations (at least the ones we now call Berle-Means corporations) central institutions of American life and 'the conscience carriers of twentieth century American society'.[62] Berle was not alone in this conclusion; as we shall see, many managers agreed.

To understand why this expansive view of corporate purpose won so much support at mid-century, we should pause to sketch out the political and economic developments behind it. In the aftermath of the Second World War, the United States and its large corporations dominated the world economy, and the United States enjoyed a period of robust economic growth—growth that was widely distributed.[63] Despite how it is remembered, this was not simply an era of unchecked corporate power. Large corporations, small business, strong unions, and an active and interventionist Federal government all jostled in the political arena, creating a polity of 'countervailing powers' as the economist John Kenneth Galbraith put it, in which corporations' power was partially offset by that of other organized groups.[64] Workers won new benefits and rising wages, for instance, due less to managerial beneficence than strong, broad-based unions willing to strike. The 1950 agreement between General Motors and the United Auto Workers is illustrative of this. The agreement gave workers higher wages, cost-of-living adjustments, and health and pension benefits, all of which soon became industry standards, but was only reached after a bitter, months-long strike.[65] The Federal government's power was also significant and sometimes used against business interests, as when in 1952 President Truman seized the steel mills in an attempt to maintain wartime production.[66] As the historian Howard Brick summed up the era, 'US capitalism settled into roughly a "corporatist" form: corporate power was secured in the economic sphere by tactical compromise with representatives of labor and by a measure of collaboration with a government

---

[59] AA Berle Jr, *The Twentieth Century Capitalist Revolution* (Harcourt Brace 1954) 169.
[60] ibid 170.
[61] ibid 169.
[62] ibid 182.
[63] T Piketty and E Saez, 'Income Inequality in the United States, 1913–1998' (2003) 118 The Quarterly Journal of Economics 1, 7.
[64] JK Galbraith, *American Capitalism: The Concept of Countervailing Power* (Houghton Mifflin 1952); B Cheffins, 'Corporate Governance and Countervailing Power' (2018) 74 Business Lawyer 1, 15–20.
[65] N Lichtenstein, *State of the Union: A Century of American Labor* (PUP 2013) 123.
[66] *Youngstown Sheet & Tube v Sawyer* 343 US 579, 582–84 (1952) (holding the President's attempt to seize the steel mills unconstitutional).

that was opened to a relatively wide range of organized interests emerging from a democratic public'.[67]

Even if their power was not unlimited, it was a good time for corporate managers, enjoying as they did unprecedented legitimacy and stability. In the wake of the Second World War, overseas competition was almost non-existent for many firms, while at home 'in many sectors of the American economy ... oligopoly prevailed and with it, competitive practices that downplayed short-term price competition'.[68] This was the heyday of 'managerial capitalism', with salaried managers often spending their entire careers at one firm, facing relatively few constraints on their decisions from shareholders, directors, or competitors, and enjoying an enviable 'reputation for propriety'.[69] Mechanisms that would in a few decades prod CEOs to focus relentlessly on shareholders' interests, such as active institutional investors, boards dominated by independent directors, or the market for corporate control, were almost non-existent.[70] Given this, a mad scramble to maximize profits seemed no longer required nor even attractive.

Americans' views of corporate purpose had made an unusual pivot since the 1930s. While Dodd had identified a few visionary leaders whom he believed were running their corporations with a sense of 'social responsibility', and Berle and Means thought a managerial elite that could 'balance a variety of claims by various interest groups' could evolve in the future, many in the 1950s concluded that managers were *now* running corporations to benefit diverse constituencies.[71] We should distinguish this view from mere managerialism, which is simply a descriptive term for a system in which large corporations are run by managers with little involvement from owners.[72] In the expanded view which attracted many adherents in the 1950—elsewhere I have called it 'heroic managerialism'—corporate leaders rejected the assumption that corporations were run solely to benefit shareholders.[73] In 1951, *Fortune* magazine published a special issue called 'USA: The Permanent Revolution' announcing this shift, featuring a quotation from Frank Abrams, chairman of Standard Oil, who described his role as to 'conduct the affairs of the enterprise in such a way as to maintain *an equitable and working balance among the claims of the various directly interested group* – stockholders, employees, customers, and the public at large'.[74] He was not an outlier, but stating what had become generally believed by the 'corporate liberals' who ran many large firms. A 1956 survey of corporate leaders' public pronouncements by four distinguished social scientists,

---

[67] H Brick, *Transcending Capitalism: Visions of a New Society in Modern American Thought* (Cornell UP 2006) 250–51.
[68] L Galambos, 'The U.S. Corporate Economy in the Twentieth Century' in SL Engerman and R Gallman, *The Cambridge Economic History of the United States*, vol 3 (CUP 2008) 927.
[69] BR Cheffins, *The Public Company Transformed* (OUP 2019) 65.
[70] ibid 70–72, 79–80.
[71] H Wells, 'Corporation Law Is Dead: Heroic Managerialism, Legal Change, and the Puzzle of Corporation Law at the Height of the American Century' (2013) 15 University of Pennsylvania Journal Business Law 305.
[72] AF Conard, 'Beyond Managerialism: Investor Capitalism?' (1988) 22 University of Michigan Journal of Law Reform 117, 121–22.
[73] Wells (n 71).
[74] J Delton, *Rethinking the 1950s: How Anticommunism and the Cold War Made America Liberal* (CUP 2013) 68 (quotation from *Fortune* Magazine, 'USA: The Permanent Revolution').

*The American Business Creed* (that business had a 'creed' was itself telling), found that most no longer voiced the belief that an owner had 'the right to use his property just the way he pleases', but instead had adopted 'the belief that ownership carries social obligations, and that a manager is a trustee not only for the owner but for society as a whole'.[75] (To be sure, the authors also identified a 'classical' strand of business thought that rejected this conclusion, but depicted it as the minority view.) Managers could point to workers' rising wages and company-provided health benefits and pensions, as well as increased corporate charitable contributions, as solid evidence of a corporate transformation. So widespread were such claims that, in 1958, one acerbic commentator in the *Harvard Business Review* would complain that it was no longer 'fashionable for the corporation to take gleeful pride in making money. What *is* fashionable is for the corporation to show that it is a great innovator; more specifically, a great public benefactor; and, very particularly, that it exists "to serve the public"'.[76]

No single cause can fully explain why this view won so much support. Certainly, CEOs' relative freedom from external and internal corporate pressures, mentioned above, made it safer for them to assert they were not guided solely by shareholder interests. Claims they were directing corporate profits to serve other constituencies may also have been making a virtue of necessity, as it allowed them to take credit for actions they were forced to take anyway, such as raising wages of unionized employees. Income taxes were extremely high, making it hard for managers to divert corporate funds into their own pockets through higher compensation.[77] Given that many industries were highly regulated, claiming to operate in the public interest may also have been good politics. Finally, in a development both important and tough to quantify, a powerful social consensus lay behind managers' claims. It is an exaggeration to see the 1950s as a repressive era for most Americans, but the United States did enjoy an unusual degree of social cohesion during the decade, produced by the aftermath of the Second World War, shared economic growth, and the Cold War.[78] Communism in particular challenged the 'free enterprise system', and one response was to insist that system benefited all Americans, rather than only the wealthy—which meshed with managers' claims they were governing corporations to benefit the entire community.[79] The existence of a widely shared consensus over social goals may have made it easier for corporate managers to decide how to distribute their beneficence (if indeed they did).[80] When this consensus fell apart in later decades, it was no longer so easy to reach agreement about who the corporation should serve, or how it should go about this.

---

[75] FX Sutton and others, *The American Business Creed* (HUP 1956) 32–34.
[76] T Levitt, 'The Dangers of Corporate Social Responsibility' (1958) 36 Harvard Business Review 41, 42
[77] SA Bank, BR Cheffins, and H Wells, 'Executive Pay: What Worked?' (2016) 42 Journal of Corporation Law 61, 73–80.
[78] This is not to say all groups enjoyed prosperity equally; certainly, African-Americans suffered under this consensus.
[79] Delton (n 74); *AP Smith Manufacturing Co v Barlow* (n 40) 585–87.
[80] James Nelson and Elizabeth Sepper, 'Adolf Berle's Corporate Conscience' (2021) 45 Seattle University Law Review 27.

A more difficult question is whether managers actually ran corporations for the benefit of constituencies beyond shareholders. Scholars studying corporations in the 1950s believed managers sought reasonable profits, rather than maximum profits, and it was in the 1950s that the organizational psychologist Herbert Simon developed the idea of 'satisficing' to describe managerial behaviour in firms.[81] But managers still pursued profits; as one historian put it, '[p]rofit was still the light at the end of the corporate tunnel, but the tunnel stretched on for years'.[82] Nor did managers abandon shareholders; dividends were regularly paid, and the *American Business Creed* study reported that firms offered a variety of justifications for returning profits to shareholders. The best we can say is that managers claimed that their actions were taken to benefit groups beyond shareholders.[83]

The new view of corporate purpose did not sweep all before it. A central field remained largely untouched: corporate law itself. While many senior managers, and from what we can tell the public, believed that corporations should be governed with a sense of civic responsibility, neither corporate operations nor law changed to give groups other than shareholders a real role in governance or a legally enforceable claim on corporate management. In 1945–46, the United Auto Workers went on strike at General Motors for 113 days, demanding that workers be given 'say over investment and production decisions', but they lost.[84] Managerial capitalism, it appeared, meant power for managers, and worker participation was a non-starter. At the margins the law did erode shareholders' rights, but that chiefly resulted in more freedom for managers. Statutory and case law changes, for instance, made it harder to file derivative suits challenging corporate decisions,[85] and easier for managers to make charitable donations unconnected to corporate benefit, but more radical change in the law was never seriously considered.[86] A handful of scholars could point to these developments, especially the charitable contributions cases, and argue that corporations now had legal obligations to non-shareholder constituencies, but their evidence was thin.[87] At the end of the 1950s Yale Law School Dean Eugene Rostow, a sharp critic of stakeholder rhetoric, pointed out that law books still said 'that the board of directors owes a single-minded duty of unswerving loyalty to the stockholders'.[88] Writing in 1970, the legal historian Willard Hurst summed up the gap between the hopes of some proponents of heroic managerialism and the reality of corporate law when he wrote that, for all the claims of managerialism, 'the law added no definition of standards or rules to spell out for what

---

[81] J Levy, *Ages of American Capitalism* (Random House 2021) (citing Herbert Simon, 'A Behavioral Model of Rational Choice' (1955) 69 The Quarterly Journal of Economics 99); EV Rostow, 'To Whom and for What Ends Is Corporate Management Responsible?' in C Kaysen (ed), *The Corporation in Modern Society* (HUP 1959) 65.

[82] Levy (n 81) 527.

[83] Sutton and others (n 75) 80–88.

[84] Levy (n 81) 473–75.

[85] Mark (n 29) 636; Dalia Tsuk Mitchell, 'Status Bound: The Twentieth Century Evolution of Directors' Liability' (2009) 5 New York University Journal of Law & Business 63, 116–20.

[86] Wells (n 71) 29–31.

[87] MA de Capriles, 'Fifteen-Year Survey of Corporate Developments 1949–1955' (1959) 13 Vanderbilt Law Review 1, 12; WB Katz, 'The Philosophy of Mid-Century Corporation Statutes' (1958) 23 Law & Contemporary Problems 177, 188.

[88] Rostow (n 81) 63.

purposes or by what means management might properly make decisions other than in the interests of shareholders'.[89]

Thus, the mid-century's divided idea of corporate purpose. Managers of large corporations claimed they were running them as trustees for the 'institution' and balancing the demands of various constituencies, but the result was not enforceable legal duties to those other groups but instead slightly weakened duties to shareholders. Corporation law was largely unchanged, with shareholders still the indispensable actors in the legal drama. When this dissonance was noted, commentators simply observed that the corporation was simultaneously profit-seeking—presumably for shareholders—and socially beneficent, without much wondering whether the two goals were compatible. In 1956, the British corporate law scholar L.C.B. Gower, then visiting at the Harvard Law School, wrote in the *Harvard Law Review* that *Dodge v Ford* should be read to hold that while managers could not ignore shareholder interests they need not consider 'the interests of stockholders alone', an interesting reading that left aside the question of how competing interests should be balanced.[90] Almost a decade later the legal scholar David Ruder, later chairman of the SEC, could observe both that it was the 'normal obligation that the corporation is operated for the purpose of making profit' and that '[a]lthough some businessmen still cling to the notion that the business of the corporation is solely to make profits, their position is not a popular one'.[91] These statements are prime illustrations of the mid-century consensus that downplayed conflict between social groups and made it easy to believe that shareholder and societal interests were largely harmonious and could usually be reconciled. In 1952, after all, when GM's president Charles Wilson was nominated to be Secretary of Defense, he responded to a question about possible conflicts of interest by saying that he could not conceive of a situation where the corporation's interests would be opposed to the government's, because 'what was good for our country was good for General Motors, and vice versa'.[92]

This would not last. Ideas of corporate purpose grow out of and are bound with larger views about society and politics, and as American society changed over the next decade so, slowly, did views corporate purpose. In the 1960s, the broad social consensus of the previous decade collapsed in the face of the civil rights struggle, new social movements, and the Vietnam War, which revealed deep divisions in the nation. This did not immediately kill the idea of a socially responsible corporation; in the more tumultuous late 1960s and 1970s corporations continued to express the view that they could fulfil social responsibilities; to use a cliché, during these decades they insisted they were a part of the solution rather than part of the problem. In 1968, a major industry group, the National Association of Manufacturers, boasted of the 'growing effort of industry to help resolve basic social problems',[93] while two years later *Business Week*

[89] Hurst (n 16) 107.
[90] LCB Gower, 'Corporate Control: The Battle for the Berkeley' (1956) 68 Harvard Law Review 1176, 1191–92.
[91] DS Ruder, 'Public Obligations of Private Corporations' (1965) 114 University of Pennsylvania Law Review 209.
[92] 'Charles E. Wilson' in BI Kaufman and D Kaufman (eds), *Historical Dictionary of the Eisenhower Era* (Scarecrow Press 2009) 251.
[93] Wells (n 57) 112.

magazine would write that a corporate executive could 'no longer ... live a cloistered life behind the walls of private enterprise, concerning himself solely with turning out a product and a profit ... [because] tenacious demonstrators and persistent consumers are insisting that he do something about ... minority rights and the environment'.[94] As late as the early 1980s another lobbying group, the Business Roundtable, would announce that 'managers are expected to serve the public interest as well as private profit', with its chair explaining that '[t]he simple theory that management can get along by considering only the shareholder has been left behind'.[95] What the 1960s did kill was widespread faith in enlightened management. No longer were managers seen as 'business statesmen' to be trusted to run the corporation for social benefit; instead outside groups began to believe they would need to pressure management to change corporate policies in order to produce social benefit.

At the end of the 1960s we find for the first time significant mobilization by outside groups demanding that corporations fulfil social obligations.[96] Activists discovered that, under US corporate and securities laws, they could acquire a few shares in a corporation and then use their rights as shareholders to lobby for non-shareholder interests.[97] Starting in 1968, activist shareholders used the SEC's shareholder proposal rule (Rule 14a-8), to pressure corporations into ending activities such as selling napalm to the United States military.[98] (That corporations were being asked to oppose a war being waged by the US government itself shows the disappearance of the 1950s consensus.) A few also proposed changing corporate law to give non-shareholder groups a real voice in corporate governance, as when consumer advocate Ralph Nader pushed for corporations to have 'public interest' directors appointed by the government and charged with representing non-shareholder constituencies.[99]

The best-known attempt by activist shareholders to reform the corporation was 1970's 'Campaign GM', when a group inspired by Nader tried to turn GM into a corporation answerable to groups beyond shareholders. As Nader put it, the goal was to provide 'a new definition of the corporation's constituency', a call for an expansive corporate purpose if ever there was one.[100] Campaign GM sought shareholder approval for a slate of changes that would have, among other things, amended GM's charter so that none of its activities would 'be implemented in a manner ... detrimental to the public health, safety, or welfare' and created a shareholder committee charged with recommending how GM could 'achieve a proper balance between the rights and interests of shareholders, employees, consumers, and the general public'.[101] After a legal

---

[94] ibid.
[95] B Cheffins, 'Stop Blaming Milton Friedman!' (2021) 98 Washington University Law Review 1607, 1626.
[96] L Talner, *Origins of Shareholder Activism* (Investor Responsibility Research Center 1983).
[97] H Wells, 'A Long View of Shareholder Power: From the Antebellum Corporation to the Twenty-First Century' (2015) 67 Florida Law Review 1033, 1077–79.
[98] S Haan, 'Civil Rights and Shareholder Activism: SEC v Medical Committee for Human Rights' (2019) 76 Washington & Lee Law Review 1167.
[99] R Nader, M Green, and J Seligman, *Taming the Giant Corporation* (WW Norton 1976) 124; AF Conard, 'Reflections on Public Interest Directors' (1977) 75 Michigan Law Review 941.
[100] DE Schwartz, 'The Public-Interest Proxy Contest: Reflections on Campaign GM' (1971) 69 Michigan Law Review 419, 425.
[101] ibid 534–35.

fight, the car maker agreed to put two proposals before shareholders, one calling for public interest directors. Both lost overwhelmingly, gaining less than 3 per cent of the vote. Even institutional investors perceived as liberal, such as Harvard University, the Rockefeller Foundation, and TIAA-CREF, voted against them.[102] Campaign GM seems a capstone to (or headstone for) three decades of responsibility rhetoric; while corporate managers were happy to claim they governed corporations to benefit society and not just shareholders, they fiercely opposed any attempt to have a duty to do so imposed on them, and shareholders when given the chance likewise rejected any attempts to remake the corporation.

## V. Back to Shareholders

American views of the purpose of the corporation would shift sharply over the next decade, as the belief that corporations should be run almost completely to benefit shareholders became widely accepted, eclipsing the idea that the corporation should pursue social purposes beyond shareholder interest.[103] When exactly this change occurred is impossible to say but it was well underway by the early 1980s.

As no single cause can fully explain the rise of the view of the corporation as having a social purpose beyond serving shareholders, no single cause can explain its demise. Politically, as mentioned above, the social consensus of the 1950s unravelled rapidly at the end of the 1960s, as the Vietnam debacle, social upheaval, and later political scandals undermined any easy faith in government and society's 'best and the brightest'.[104] In the corporate realm, business changes and stumbles produced a loss of faith in established management. One early cause was the appearance of conglomerates in the 1960s. These shifting configurations of unrelated businesses, rapidly assembled and disassembled by financial wizards, took the spotlight away from traditional corporate managers and made large corporation appear less as stable social institutions that could be assigned social responsibilities and more like a fluid assemblage 'in constant cyclical evolution'.[105] Conglomerates' collapse at the end of the decade did not restore confidence in either old or new management. High-profile corporate scandals, beginning with the collapse of the Penn Central railroad in 1970 and continuing with revelations of overseas and domestic bribery in the mid-1970s, further undermined any residual faith in 'corporate statesmen' and provided an early impetus for the corporate governance movement which would push to impose tighter controls on managers in the next few decades.[106] Another change, perhaps not fully appreciated at the time, was the slow

---

[102] ibid 503–507.
[103] Cheffins (n 95) 1628–31; L Stout, *The Shareholder Value Myth* (Berrett Koehler 2012) 18–19.
[104] D Halberstam, *The Best and the Brightest* (Random House 1972).
[105] CS Maier, *In Search of Stability: Explorations in Historical Political Economy* (CUP 1987) 69.
[106] JN Gordon, 'The Rise of Independent Directors in the United States 1950–2005: Of Shareholder Value and Stock Market Prices' (2007) 59 Stanford Law Review 1465, 1514–18; M Pargendler, 'The Corporate Governance Obsession' (2016) 42 Journal of Corporate Law 359.

return of shareholder power starting with the growth of institutional investors, who would become influential in the 1980s.[107]

Corporations' problems were only one facet of problems facing the American economy. Readily apparent by the early 1970s was the rapid erosion of many American industries and slowing economic growth, soon joined by rising inflation. Foreign competition hammered industries such as auto and steel, leading to closure of many plants in the nation's industrial heartland and producing a 'rust belt' of deindustrializing cities in the north-east and mid-west.[108] The massive shock produced by the Arab Oil Embargo in 1973 did not help.[109]

These economic and political developments sowed the ground for intellectual change, particularly for the resurgence of the view that corporations existed chiefly to serve shareholders. In 1970, Milton Friedman published his iconic essay 'The Social Responsibility of Business Is to Increase Its Profits' in the *New York Times* magazine. A blunt challenge to the prevailing wisdom, it opened by targeting businessmen, apparently not needing further identification, who 'declaim that business is not concerned 'merely' with profit but also with promoting desirable 'social' ends'. Against this view Friedman argued that executives were mere agents for the corporation's owners, its shareholders, and money spent on social problems was money misappropriated from them.[110] A few years later the economists Michael Jensen and William Meckling made a similar argument in 'The Theory of the Firm', an article that put the 'agency costs' generated by managers' deviation from stockholders' interests at the centre of their analysis.[111] As should be clear, these authors did not invent the idea that management's job was to serve shareholders. Their work was important, however, because they offered readers trying to understand recent economic ills a simple diagnosis: corporations were in trouble because managers had misunderstood their role, which was not to benefit society but to create value for shareholders.[112] There was also a corollary, usually unstated: once managers began to run the corporation for the sole benefit of shareholders, the nation's economic performance would improve.

Corporate purpose was put in in the public eye at the end of the 1970s when a vigorous market for corporate control emerged in the United States.[113] During the

---

[107] BS Black, 'Agents Watching Agents: The Promise of Institutional Investor Voice' (1992) 39 UCLA Law Review 811; M Gelter, 'The Pension System and the Rise of Shareholder Primacy' (2013) 43 Seton Hall Law Review 909, 954.

[108] Levy (n 81) 544–51.

[109] M Jacobs, *Panic at the Pump: The Energy Crisis and the Transformation of American Politics in the 1970s* (Hill and Wang 2016).

[110] M Friedman, 'The Social Responsibility of Business is to Increase its Profits' *New York Times* (17 September 1970) SM 17.

[111] MC Jensen and WH Meckling, 'Theory of the Firm: Managerial Behavior, Agency Costs, and Ownership Structure' (1976) 3 Journal of Financial Economics 305. Both Friedman and Jensen & Meckling used 'agent' in its economic sense; under American law corporate directors and officers are not agents of the shareholders; S Bainbridge, *Corporate Law* (4th edn Foundation Press 2020) 95–97.

[112] Friedman was a brilliant publicist who found a wide audience for his ideas; cf A Bergin, *The Great Persuasion: Reinventing Free Markets Since the Depression* (HUP 2012) 186–97. Jensen and Meckling's work had a huge impact as it was widely disseminated in academia and business schools, especially after Jensen began teaching at the Harvard Business School; by the late 1980s two-thirds of Harvard MBA students took his elective before graduating; cf R Khurana, *From Higher Aims to Hired Hands: The Social Transformation of American Business Schools and the Unfulfilled Promise of Management as a Profession* (PUP 2007) 317–22.

[113] Cheffins (n 69) 162–72.

1980s, more than a quarter of Fortune 500 corporations were subject to takeover attempts.[114] In takeovers, 'corporate raiders' took advantage of newly available pools of funds, and the willingness of many institutional investors to listen to their pitches, to launch tender offers designed to oust management and open corporations up to radical reengineering—often meaning massive lay-offs. They played out in the popular press as morality tales, with 'takeover artists' such as T. Boone Pickens claiming that they were championing shareholders neglected by complacent managers, while management frequently pitched opposition to takeovers as defending not only shareholders, but also workers, communities dependent on corporate operations, and the corporation as an institution.[115] Takeovers thus put the question of corporate purpose—of who corporations should be run *for*—on the national agenda. As Rakesh Khurana described it, '[t]he social and political context that had favored managerialism since the Progressive Era ... was rapidly dismantled during the 1980s'.[116]

Because takeover battles involved complicated legal manoeuvres, with boards adopting new legal tools such as the 'poison pill' to thwart insurgents, the question of managerial discretion and control soon became an issue for the courts, specifically the courts of Delaware, legal home of most of the nation's largest corporations.[117] While shareholder interest had always held pride of place in corporation law, how this interest was to be achieved was for management to decide. Before the 1980s, the law granted managers great discretion in choosing how to react to a takeover attempt: 'under the business judgment rule the prevailing approach upheld ... defensive maneuvers of all types and magnitudes ... on a showing that the bidder would likely operate the target company in a manner that diverged from the course followed or recommended by the incumbent management'.[118] During the 1980s, however, new legal devices to block takeovers invited new scrutiny by the courts, and one question facing Delaware's courts was whose interests a board could consider when deciding whether to block a takeover.

Boards' duties were owed to the 'corporation and its shareholders'—but did boards have discretion when making decisions to consider other constituencies as well? For a brief moment, Delaware's courts suggested that they did. In 1985's *Unocal v Mesa Petroleum*, the Delaware Supreme Court announced that directors, in weighing whether to adopt anti-takeover measures, could take into account the takeover bid's potential 'effect on the corporate enterprise... [including] the impact on 'constituencies' other than shareholders (ie creditors, customers, employees, and perhaps the community generally)'.[119] This brought a moment of hope to those who believed corporations

---

[114] N Lemann, *Transaction Man: The Rise of the Deal and the Decline of the American Dream* (Farrar Strauss Giroux 2019) 116.

[115] Bryan Burrough and John Helyar, *Barbarians at the Gate: The Fall of RJR Nabisco* (Harper & Row 1990); Connie Bruck, *The Predators' Ball: The Inside Story of Drexel Burnham and the Rise of the Junk Bond Raiders* (Penguin Books 1989).

[116] Khurana (n 112) 302.

[117] David Yosifon, 'The Law of Corporate Purpose' (2013) 10 Berkeley Business Law Journal 181, 188 ('Delaware's jurisprudence on corporate purpose was most pointedly developed in a series of hostile takeover cases from the 1980s').

[118] James D Cox and Thomas Lee Hazen, *Corporations* (2d edn, Aspen Publishers 2003) 649.

[119] *Unocal Corp v Mesa Petroleum Co* 493 A2d 946, 955 (Del 1985).

had obligations to 'other constituencies'. It was however dashed a year later in the *Revlon* decision, which held that when a 'bust-up' of the corporation was inevitable a board's duty was solely to 'obtain the highest price for the benefit of the stockholders', and also walked back *Unocal*'s holding to make clear that a board could only 'have regard for various constituencies in discharging its responsibilities ... provided there are rationally related benefits accruing to stockholders'.[120] Later decisions still left directors great discretion in deciding what was in stockholders' best interests, empowering them for instance to block an offer in favour of pursing a long-term strategy favoured by the board, but nowhere was there a hint that shareholder interests could be weighed against the interests of non-shareholder constituencies.[121] Under Delaware law, a corporation's purpose was to benefit shareholders.[122]

One counter-trend deserves mention, 'corporate constituency' statutes, although on closer examination they reveal not a split in corporation law but the dominance of shareholder value as corporate purpose, even if not strictly imposed by law. Beginning in the mid-1980s, a number of states (although not Delaware)[123] altered their corporation statutes to allow directors, when making decisions, to take into account non-shareholder constituencies.[124] Pennsylvania's act, for example, states that 'directors shall not be required, in considering the best interests of the corporation or the effects of any action, to regard ... the interests of any particular group affected by such action as a dominant or controlling interest or factor'.[125] These statutes were a direct response to hostile takeovers and were often passed after vigorous lobbying by labour and management, each seeking to preserve their jobs.[126] But these last-gasp attempts to write the presumptions of managerial capitalism into corporation law had little success. None of the statutes had meaningful enforcement mechanisms—no one was given the right to sue a board for not considering another constituency in making a decision—and the statutes were rarely invoked even when a hostile takeover loomed.[127] As one observer noted two decades after most of the acts were passed, 'there is no evidence that constituency statutes have had any effect on director behavior'.[128]

This last comment is significant, as it reminds us that the widespread acceptance of the view that a corporation's purpose was to serve shareholders may have been enabled

---

[120] *Revlon Inc v McAndrews & Forbes Holdings Inc* 506 A2d 173, 182 (Del 1986).
[121] *Paramount Communications, Inc. v Time Inc* 571 A2d 1140 (Del 1989) (broadening definition of 'threat' to which board can respond with defensive tactics).
[122] *eBay Domestic Holdings v Newmark* 16 A3d 1, 34 (Del Ch 2010) (a business plan that 'eschews stockholder wealth maximization' violates Delaware law).
[123] Delaware did adopt an anti-takeover measure in 1988, but it did not mention other constituencies. Del Code Ann tit 8 § 203 (2022); Guhan Subramanian, Steven Herscovici, and Brian Barbatta, 'Is Delaware's Takeover Statute Unconstitutional? Evidence from 1988–2008' (2010) 65 Business Lawyer 685, 686–88.
[124] Eric Orts, 'Beyond Shareholders: Interpreting Corporate Constituency Statutes' (1992) 61 George Washington Law Review 16, 16–26.
[125] Pa Cons Stat §15.515(b) (2022).
[126] Orts (n 124) 25; Jonathan D Springer, 'Corporate Constituency Statutes: Hollow Hopes and False Fears' [1999] Annual Survey of American Law 85, 96.
[127] John W Cioffi, *Public Law and Private Power: Corporate Governance Reform in the Age of Finance Capitalism* (Cornell UP 2010) 87; Springer (n 126) 108 (finding only eleven cases invoking the statutes between 1985 and 1999).
[128] Julian Velasco, 'The Fundamental Rights of the Shareholder' (2006) 40 UC Davis Law Review 407, 464.

by the law but was not produced by it. Disappearance of a national social consensus, widespread loss of faith in 'corporate statesmen', evidence that American corporations were losing against overseas competition, economic stagnation, the rise of institutional investors, financial innovation that gave life to a market for corporate control—all these developments outside the law undermined the mid-century consensus that managers could be trusted to run corporations to benefit multiple groups long before the hostile takeover boom and its resulting jurisprudence. Of course, the fact that the law never fully embraced the view that managers could run corporations to benefit other constituencies made the shift easier; when hard cases arose in the 1980s requiring courts to answer squarely whether corporations should be run for shareholder benefit alone, or whether boards could trade off shareholder benefit to help other groups, the answer from the nation's leading business court was well rooted in existing law: shareholder benefit should prevail. The political and economic conditions that once made a different conclusion plausible were long gone.

By the 1990s there was little opposition to the view that the corporation's purpose was to produce 'shareholder value', a term that 'took on a talismanic quality' during that decade.[129] While the free enterprise system as a whole was still justified by its ability to produce widespread prosperity and freedom, a corporation's success was to be judged more narrowly, by the economic benefit it provided its shareholders (however that benefit was described).[130] This assumption appeared in unexpected places. When, for example, high executive compensation was publicly attacked in the 1980s, one might have expected the complaints to be about resulting income inequality and its undesirable societal consequences, but instead the protests targeted the disconnect between executive pay and shareholder benefit. The solution was widespread adoption of 'pay for performance', an approach written into tax law in 1993 by a Democratic president and Congress—a requirement that in turn focused executives even more tightly on shareholder value and tended to produce even higher compensation.[131] When union pension funds became activist investors in the 1990s, their main goal was most often not improved working conditions for members but 'to maximize return on capital'.[132] By 1997, when the Business Roundtable announced that 'the principal objective of a business enterprise is to generate economic returns to its owners', it received almost no media attention, as it was merely stating what had become the conventional wisdom.[133]

---

[129] Cheffins (n 69) 240.

[130] This did not mean that there remained no disagreements about how corporations should be run, but rather that even those who disagreed strongly shared a common starting-point: that the corporation's ultimate goal was to benefit its shareholders. Disputes remained vigorous as to how that benefit was to be achieved and measured; cf. JM Fried, 'The Uneasy Case for Favoring Long-Term Shareholders' (2013) 124 Yale Law Journal 1554; JB Heaton, 'The "Long Term" in Corporate Law' (2013) 72 Business Lawyer 353.

[131] H Wells, 'U.S. Executive Compensation in Historical Perspective' in RS Thomas and JG Hill (eds), *Research Handbook on Executive Pay* (Edward Elgar Publishing 2012).

[132] SJ Schwab and RS Thomas, 'Realigning Corporate Governance: Shareholder Activism by Labor Unions' (1998) 96 Michigan Law Review 1018, 1019–20.

[133] Business Roundtable, *Statement on Corporate Governance* (1997). No contemporaneous article reporting on the Roundtable's revised statement appeared in the *New York Times*, the *Wall Street Journal*, or the *Washington Post*.

## VI. Conclusion

By 2000, so widely accepted was the view that the purpose of the corporation, particularly in corporate law, is to increase shareholder wealth that two eminent legal scholars could publish an article entitled 'The End of Corporate Law' in which they asserted that '[t]here is no longer any serious competitor to the view that corporate law should principally strive to increase long-term shareholder value'.[134] At the time, they might have been right. Two decades on, however, this no longer seems true, with developments (in the United States) ranging from the new benefit corporations,[135] to revived proposals for Federal incorporation with stakeholder mandates,[136] to the swift rise of ESG ('environmental, social, and governance') investing,[137] to giant institutional investors' insistence that corporations strive to make a positive impact on society,[138] each of which in different ways challenge the single-minded pursuit of shareholder value and hearken back to the old debates considered here.

This should not surprise us. This chapter shows that, over the past two centuries, corporate purpose has been the subject of recurrent debates in the United States, admittedly under different terms and in different ways, and that questions about corporations' purpose have always been inescapably intertwined not only with changes in business, but with larger economic, political, social, intellectual, and even cultural developments. Corporate purpose—what we ask of corporations and who they should serve—shifts along with changes in all these fields, as corporations are perceived as wielding more or less power over Americans, as trust in their leaders waxes and wanes, as they succeed or fail along a variety of measures, and as trust in other American institutions grows or, lately, falters.

---

[134] H Hansmann and R Kraakman, 'The End of History for Corporate Law' (2000) 89 Georgetown Law Journal 439, 439.
[135] MJ Loewenstein, 'Benefit Corporations: A Challenge in Corporate Governance' (2013) 68 Business Lawyer 1007.
[136] Accountable Capitalism Act, s 3348, 115th Cong (2018).
[137] 'Special Report ESG Investing' *The Economist* (23 June 2022).
[138] Fink (n 1).

# 10
# Corporate Purpose and the Blurred Boundaries of Internal and External Governance

*Ann M. Lipton*[*]

## I. Introduction

From 1887 to 1927, Arthur Conan Doyle published a series of stories about Sherlock Holmes, the world's greatest detective, and his companion, Dr John Watson. The stories were written in the first person, from Watson's point of view, as he chronicled the adventures of his extraordinary friend. Today, when Sherlock Holmes fans analyse the series, they frequently characterize themselves as adopting either a 'Watsonian' or a 'Doylist' perspective.[1] A 'Watsonian' perspective assumes that John Watson was a living person describing the world around him. With this premise, fans attempt to flesh out the 'facts' that underly his (potentially unreliable) narration. A Watsonian might, for example, try to identify how characters behaved when Watson was not present to witness them; inconsistencies across stories—such as differing accounts of Watson's marital status—are attributed to Watson's own dissembling, for his own reasons.[2] A fan adopting a 'Doylist' perspective, by contrast, analyses the stories for what they are: works of fiction by the real-life Arthur Conan Doyle. From this perspective, inconsistencies are attributed to the fact that the stories were published over a forty-year period, and Doyle may have lost track of what he had written earlier.

Neither approach is *wrong*; they are both valid ways to think about the text. But unless one shifts perspective, a Watsonian and a Doylist will never be able to have a coherent conversation; they are, quite literally, inhabiting different universes.

Debates about corporate purpose sometimes have the flavour of a Watsonian talking to a Doylist, although in this case, the Watsonians are those who are arguing from within the corporation, with respect to how corporate executives should understand their duties (or at the very least, how they should be incentivized to behave with respect to those duties), while the Doylists are arguing from outside the corporation, from the point of view of society writ large, with respect to the ultimate reasons that a

---

[*] All internet sources were last accessed on 15 January 2024.
[1] See LM Dee, 'Watsonian vs. Doylist: An Overview' (19 April 2016) https://lmdee.wordpress.com/2016/04/19/watsonian-vs-doylist-an-overview/; Peter Clines, 'Elementary' (27 September 2018) http://thoth-amon.blogspot.com/2018/09/elementary.html.
[2] See eg B Keefauver, 'Counting Watson's Wives' (9 March 2002) www.johnwhatsonsociety.com/counting-watsons-wives/.

polity charters corporations and formally recognizes their existence. Thus, when Larry Fink declared in 2018 that 'Companies must benefit all of their stakeholders, including shareholders, employees, customers, and the communities in which they operate,'[3] his statement was heralded as a challenge[4] to Milton Friedman's famous 1970 declaration that the 'social responsibility of business is to increase its profits'.[5] But, read correctly, the two essays are entirely reconcilable, with Friedman's a Watsonian statement of individual managerial motivation, and Fink's a Doylist statement of the corporation's role in society as whole. Indeed, Friedman was explicit that corporations should act to benefit communities when doing so would cause the corporation to prosper,[6] whereas Fink was explicit that corporations would not prosper unless they acted to benefit their communities.[7]

In fact, as I argue below, there is widespread agreement on the Doylist proposition that the corporation's purpose is to serve society; most disputes concern how to design the regulatory system so as to effectuate that purpose. And that is where the Watsonian perspective comes in. Shareholder primacists argue that corporations fulfil their essential function best when managers act solely to maximize shareholder wealth; stakeholderists contend that managers should take into account a broader array of social concerns. As this chapter will demonstrate, however, even in the shareholder primacists' view, internal corporate processes must be sufficiently developed to be able to respond to societally created rewards and punishments for pro- and anti-social behaviour, necessitating some degree of outward-lookingness in design. The system viewed as a whole, then, is one where corporate governance is continually adjusted according to societal needs, regardless of whether one formally adopts a stakeholderist or a shareholder primacist position.

## II. The Great Debate

Corporations are fundamentally legal creations, by which I mean, they exist because of legal rules that recognize them as distinct entities and treat them differently from other forms of economic activity.[8] The typical attributes of a corporation—independent legal personality, indefinite life, tradable shares, asset partitioning, and centralized

---

[3] L Fink, 'Larry Fink's 2018 Letter to CEOs: A Sense of Purpose' www.blackrock.com/corporate/investor-relations/2018-larry-fink-ceo-letter.

[4] See eg AR Sorkin, 'BlackRock's Message: Contribute to Society, or Risk Losing Our Support' *The New York Times* (15 January 2018) www.nytimes.com/2018/01/15/business/dealbook/blackrock-laurence-fink-letter.html.

[5] M Friedman, 'The Social Responsibility of Business is to Increase its Profits' *The New York Times Magazine* (13 September 1970).

[6] ibid ('it may well be in the long-run interest of a corporation that is a major employer in a small community to devote resources to providing amenities to that community or to improving its government').

[7] Fink (n 3) ('Without a sense of purpose, no company ... can achieve its full potential ... It will succumb to short-term pressures to distribute earnings, and, in the process, sacrifice investments in employee development, innovation, and capital expenditures that are necessary for long-term growth ... And ultimately, that company will provide subpar returns to the investors').

[8] E Rock, 'For Whom is the Corporation Managed in 2020? The Debate Over Corporate Purpose' (2021) 76 Business Lawyer 363, 370 (describing the corporation as a 'durable and useful invention').

management[9]—require a legal infrastructure capable of enforcing the rights of dispersed shareholders,[10] and willing to distinguish between the pool of assets available to entity creditors from those available to creditors of the entity's investors.[11] Nothing requires that states develop such infrastructure and they have not always done so historically.[12] States choose to recognize corporations (and other limited liability business entities) because of the societal benefits that flow from this type of economic ordering, namely to deploy large amounts of capital productively, to encourage ingenuity, to enable economic expansion, and to facilitate entrepreneurial self-expression. In that sense, then, from the Doylist perspective, the purpose of the corporation as a state-sponsored institution is to benefit the community overall.

The problem is that corporations are, by their nature, powerful. They are designed to combine the resources of countless investors, employees, creditors, and suppliers, and—under the direction of a handful of managers—redeploy these resources in particular, coordinated fashion. As a result, corporations are capable of bringing great innovations to society, but they are also capable of doing tremendous harm, such as when their products turn out to be unexpectedly dangerous,[13] or are misused by malefactors,[14] or even when the byproducts of their production processes result in catastrophe.[15] The question then becomes one of how best to structure the legal rules that govern the corporation, in order to ensure that their benefits are maximized and their harms minimized.[16]

In general, the debate begins by distinguishing between *corporate law*—which has been loosely defined as 'the set of rules that defines the decision making structure of corporations'[17] and dictate the corporation's internal functioning—from regulatory,

---

[9] See ibid.

[10] T Zhang and J Morley, 'The Modern State and the Rise of the Business Corporation' (2022) 132 Yale Law Journal 1970.

[11] MM Blair, 'Locking in Capital: What Corporate Law Achieved for Business Organizers in the Nineteenth Century' (2003) 51 UCLA Law Review 387; MM Blair, 'How Trustees of Dartmouth College v. Woodward Clarified Corporate Law' https://papers.ssrn.com/sol3/papers.cfm?abstract_id=3830603; H Hansmann, R Kraakman, and R Squire, 'Law and the Rise of the Firm' (2006) 119 Harvard Law Review 1335.

[12] Hansmann, Kraakman, and Squire (n 11); Zhang and Morley (n 10).

[13] See eg ED Lawrence, 'GM Settles Deadly Ignition Switch Cases for $120 Million' *USA Today* (20 October 2017) www.usatoday.com/story/money/cars/2017/10/20/gm-settles-deadly-ignition-switch-cases-120-million/777831001/.

[14] P Mozur, 'A Genocide Incited on Facebook, With Posts From Myanmar's Military' *The New York Times* (15 October 2018) www.nytimes.com/2018/10/15/technology/myanmar-facebook-genocide.html.

[15] EP Dalesio, 'Duke Energy Sued for 2014 Coal Ash Spill Environmental Harm' *AP News* (18 July 2019) https://apnews.com/article/d669e8e278ca47e4997088d0f798e583.

[16] RM Green, 'Shareholders as Stakeholders: Changing Metaphors of Corporate Governance' (1993) 50 Washington & Lee Law Review 1409, 1421 (debates about whether corporate managers should serve shareholders exclusively 'take ... place on the plane of public policy. The question concerns which model of corporate governance makes most sense and best serves all of our needs in a modern business environment'); LA Bebchuk, 'Federalism and the Corporation: The Desirable Limits on State Competition in Corporate Law' (1992) 105 Harvard Law Review 1435, 1442 ('Consider a given corporate law issue that implicates not only the interests of shareholders, but also those of third parties. From the perspective of efficiency, the socially desirable rule is the one that maximizes the aggregate wealth of society's members'); H Hansmann and R Kraakman, 'The End of History for Corporate Law' (2001) 89 Georgetown Law Journal 439, 441 ('All thoughtful people believe that corporate enterprise should be organized and operated to serve the interests of society as a whole, and that the interests of shareholders deserve no greater weight in this social calculus than do the interests of any other members of society'; debates about corporate purpose concern 'the best means to this end (that is, the pursuit of aggregate social welfare)').

[17] DG Smith, 'Response: The Dystopian Potential of Corporate Law' (2008) 57 Emory Law Journal 985, 990; see also EW Orts, 'The Complexity and Legitimacy of Corporate Law' (1993) 50 Washington & Lee Law Review 1565,

or external, law, namely the set of legal rules (environmental, consumer protection, employment) that constrain the behaviours that corporations may undertake in their business dealings. In the United States, corporate law is generally described as imposed by the chartering state, and also federally, through a system of securities regulation; external laws are also imposed federally, or by the states in which the corporation conducts its business.

All commentators agree that corporations should be governed by external law (although, of course, they may have different policy preferences as to the content of those laws),[18] so the divide typically runs between those who go further by arguing that *corporate law* rules should also be structured to ensure that the entity's decision-making processes exhibit due regard for constituencies beyond the equity investors, ie stakeholderists, and those who argue that corporate internal decision-making should be designed solely to maximize the wealth of the equity investors, ie shareholder primacists.[19] It is the debate over these corporate law rules that constitutes the Watsonian viewpoint, ie purpose as viewed from within the corporate form.

Under the stakeholderist view, business leaders should have the freedom, if not the obligation, to maximize the value of the enterprise for all of its constituents; they should balance profit-seeking with an effort to protect the environment, elevate employees, provide valuable goods and services to customers, pay appropriate taxes, and so on.[20] Although these ideas have often been associated with progressive commentators and the politically liberal concept of 'corporate social responsibility',[21] they have also been characterized as 'radically libertarian' because, depending on how they are deployed (more on that below) they suggest that internal corporate decision-making can replace external regulation.[22] It is hardly surprising, then, that the Business Roundtable adopted a statement in 2019 purportedly committing to deliver value to 'all' corporate stakeholders, including customers, employees, suppliers and—last on the list – shareholders;[23] indeed, the head of MSCI recently argued that it advocated for

---

1578 ff ('Corporate law, like most law, is primarily about the rule-oriented structuring of social power, and it is specifically about the rules that structure the organization of economic power. Corporate law is primarily concerned with business, that is, the structure of economic power in the form of its institutions and processes').

[18] K Greenfield, 'Proposition: Saving the World with Corporate Law' (2008) 57 Emory Law Journal 948, 963.

[19] Compare, eg Greenfield (n 18) with Smith (n 17). I have previously argued that 'shareholder primacy' can mean either shareholder wealth maximization or shareholder choice, and that these may not be the same thing. See AM Lipton, 'What We Talk About When We Talk about Shareholder Primacy' (2019) 69 Case Western Reserve Law Review 863. For the purposes of this chapter, however, I use the term shareholder primacy to mean the pursuit of profit to maximize shareholder wealth, unless otherwise indicated.

[20] See eg D Yosifon, *Corporate Friction* (CUP 2018) 177; E Elhauge, 'Sacrificing Corporate Profits in the Public Interest' (2005) 80 New York University Law Review 733.

[21] KY Testy, 'Linking Progressive Corporate Law with Progressive Social Movements' (2002) 76 Tulane Law Review 1227.

[22] JR Macey, 'ESG Investing: Why Here? Why Now?' (2022) 19 Berkeley Business Law Journal 258, 271; see also LA Bebchuk and R Tallarita, 'The Illusory Promise of Stakeholder Governance' (2020) 106 Cornell Law Review 91, 171 (arguing that a focus on 'stakeholderism' will reduce more rigorous regulatory reform); M Gatti and CD Ondersma, 'Stakeholder Syndrome: Does Stakeholderism Derail Effective Protections for Weaker Constituencies?' (2021) 100 North Carolina Law Review 167.

[23] Business Roundtable, 'Statement on the Purpose of a Corporation' (19 August 2019) https://system.businessroundtable.org/app/uploads/sites/5/2023/02/WSJ_BRT_POC_Ad.pdf. Under pressure, the Business Roundtable clarified that of course businesses' first responsibility is to deliver value to shareholders; it only meant

socially responsible investing in order to 'protect capitalism. Otherwise, government intervention is going to come, socialist ideas are going to come'.[24] Even as far back as 1932, the argument that corporate leaders should serve as stewards of the economy was advanced as a substitute for a strong external regulatory framework.[25]

On the other side of the debate, it is argued that the societal benefits that flow from use of the corporate form are best realized by what Mariana Pargendler has described as 'modularity',[26] namely, by sharply distinguishing regulation of corporate behaviour from the regulations that concern entity structure, the latter of which should encourage managers solely to pursue profits on shareholders' behalf. On this view, corporate managers lack democratic legitimacy to serve as society's saviours,[27] and because there is no mechanism for evaluating their progress toward that goal, conferring upon managers a roving commission to do good will ultimately result in lack of accountability to any constituency at all.[28] Instead, these commentators argue that government should use external regulation to make it *expensive* for corporations to engage in destructive behaviour. If misbehaving corporations have to pay fines or criminal penalties, or lose employees and customers, or lose access to government contracts and other regulatory privileges,[29] the shareholder's interest in profit, and the societal interest in productive economic development, will naturally align, without tasking corporate managers with making controversial political judgments.[30] Corporations, competing in a free market for customers, employees, and investment capital will ultimately choose to structure themselves in a manner that most efficiently combines profit-seeking with prosocial behaviour.[31]

---

that 'for corporations to be successful, durable and return value to shareholders, they must consider the interests and meet the fair expectations of a wide range of stakeholders in addition to shareholders'; Business Roundtable, 'Redefined Purpose of a Corporation: Welcoming the Debate' (25 August 2019) https://bizroundtable.medium.com/redefined-purpose-of-a-corporation-welcoming-the-debate-8f03176f7ad8.

[24] C Simpson, A Rathi, and S Kishan, 'The ESG Mirage' *Bloomberg* (9 December 2021) www.bloomberg.com/graphics/2021-what-is-esg-investing-msci-ratings-focus-on-corporate-bottom-line/; see also Martin Lipton, 'Stakeholder Corporate Governance Business Roundtable and Council of Institutional Investors' (21 August 2019) https://corpgov.law.harvard.edu/2019/08/21/stakeholder-corporate-governance-business-roundtable-and-council-of-institutional-investors/ ('The failure to recognize the existential threats of inequality and climate change, not only to business corporations but also to asset managers, institutional investors and all shareholders, will invariably lead to legislation that will regulate not only corporations but also investors and take from them the ability to use their voting power to influence the corporations in which they invest').

[25] See WW Bratton and ML Wachter, 'Shareholder Primacy's Corporatist Origins' (2008) 34 Journal of Corporation Law 99, 125 ff.

[26] M Pargendler, 'Controlling Shareholders in the 21st Century: Complicating Corporate Governance Beyond Agency Costs' (2020) 45 Journal of Corporation Law 953.

[27] See eg Friedman (n 5) ('Here the businessman—self-selected or appointed directly or indirectly by stockholders—is to be simultaneously legislator, executive and jurist. He is to decide whom to tax by how much and for what purpose, and he is to spend the proceeds—all this guided only by general exhortations from on high to restrain inflation, improve the environment, fight poverty and so on and on').

[28] SM Bainbridge, 'Director Primacy: The Means and Ends of Corporate Governance' (2003) 97 Northwestern University Law Review 547, 581; Macey (n 22) 283; Bebchuk and Tallarita (n 22) 165.

[29] See eg 17 CFR § 230.507 (disqualifying bad actors from taking advantage of certain Securities Act exemptions); 42 CFR § 1001.601 (disqualifying bad actors from participating in federal health care programmes).

[30] FH Easterbrook and DR Fischel, *The Economic Structure of Corporate Law* (HUP 1991) 37–39.

[31] See C Williams, 'Corporate Compliance with the Law in an Era of Efficiency' (1998) 76 North Carolina Law Review 1265 (describing this view); SJ Griffith, 'Corporate Governance in an Era of Compliance' (2016) 57 Willliam & Mary Law Review 2075, 2135 ff.

What is notable, then, is that whatever side of the argument one takes, even when one adopts the narrower, within-entity Watsonian perspective, corporate law is necessarily deployed in service of societal interests more broadly. Either the corporation's internal processes should directly encourage corporate prosociality, or they should encourage profit seeking *in service of* a greater theory of prosociality.

## III. Corporations Are Designed to Benefit Multiple Constituencies

Within the corporation, shareholders—the equity investors—are granted the right to vote for directors, and for certain fundamental transformations, such as mergers, dissolutions, and charter amendments.[32] Directors are tasked with managing the business affairs of the corporation,[33] and in modern corporations, they typically delegate that authority to the Chief Executive Officer.[34] Because shareholders are the only corporate constituency with formal governance rights, it is typically asserted that corporations are ultimately designed to accommodate only the equity investors.[35]

That said, it is important to remember that for the earliest business corporations, there was no distinction between corporate law and external regulation; the corporate charter was the 'technique par excellence for state regulation of economic activity'.[36] Businesses operated locally, almost entirely within the boundaries of their chartering state, and states granted charters on a case by case basis through special acts of the legislature. The precise boundaries of each corporation's permissible behaviour—such as its duration, its capitalization, the scope of its business activities, and the prices it could charge—were specified therein.[37] In this manner, states assured themselves that each corporation was *not* designed only to respond to the providers of capital; instead, it was designed to respond to the community's needs, and to protect other stakeholders such as creditors and customers.

Eventually, however, economic growth and technological improvements made it both possible and necessary for businesses to operate across state lines, and chartering states had little interest in limiting the activities of companies whose business would be conducted elsewhere.[38] Beginning in the late 1800s, corporate regulation was decoupled from the grant of the charter and instead hived out into what we now think of as external regulation. Instead of regulating corporations by defining their permissible

---

[32] Del Code tit 8, §§ 102(a)(4), 211, 251, 275.
[33] ibid § 141.
[34] OS Simmons, 'Forgotten Gatekeepers: Executive Search Firms and Corporate Governance' (2019) 54 Wake Forest Law Review 807, 818.
[35] See eg LE Strine Jr, 'Our Continuing Struggle with the Idea that For-Profit Corporations Seek Profit' (2012) 47 Wake Forest Law Review 135, 153.
[36] M Pargendler, 'Veil Peeking: The Corporation as a Nexus for Regulation' (2021) 169 University of Pennsylvania Law Review 717.
[37] F Tung, 'Before Competition: Origins of the Internal Affairs Doctrine' (2006) 32 Journal of Corporation Law 33.
[38] ibid.

activities within corporate governing documents, states regulated corporate behaviour within their territory, such as by limiting workers' hours, regulating worker pay, and the like. Corporations also came to be regulated federally, with antitrust law to limit market and political power, bankruptcy protection for creditors, labour law for employees, and securities law for investors.[39] After this evolution, corporate law consisted only those aspects of business functioning that had not been moved into other areas.

Those areas, however, frequently operate not merely by dictating permissible corporate behaviour, but by altering the corporate decision-making process. For example, a wide swathe of 'external' corporate regulation mandates that corporations adopt various decision-making procedures. Regulatory agencies might require that the company inspect equipment on a particular schedule, create specific methods for handling hazardous materials, accidents, or complaints, and adopt layers of internal supervisory review. Reports establishing that these procedures have been developed and followed may be submitted to the relevant agency, which may then request revisions to those procedures.[40] Participation in government programmes, such as Medicare, may also be conditioned on adopting specific decision-making and documentation procedures[41]; in the highly regulated bank industry, an examiner may work full time at the bank's offices, monitoring the bank's legal compliance and business practices.[42] Corporations can also minimize the penalties they incur for misbehaviour if they create internal procedures for preventing and remedying problems, either ex ante,[43] or ex post,[44] so long as those procedures meet government requirements (and those requirements can be extraordinarily detailed, dictating the responsibilities of particular corporate personnel, the reporting hierarchy, and the like[45]). Regulators frequently require that compliance programmes be overseen by the corporate board of directors, or its equivalent in a non-corporate entity,[46] and may even demand reform of compensation practices to alter employee incentives, thereby explicitly harnessing the organs of the corporate form to serve non-shareholder constituencies.[47] In some cases of corporate wrongdoing, regulators even impose corporate monitors—outside parties who oversee

---

[39] DJH Greenwood, 'Democracy and Delaware: The Mysterious Race to the Bottom/Top' (2005) 23 Yale Law & Policy Review 381; JW Hurst, *The Legitimacy of the Business Corporation in the Law of the United States 1780–1970* (The University of Virginia Press 1970); E Pollman, 'Constitutionalizing Corporate Law' (2016) 69 Vanderbilt Law Review 639; LE Ribstein and EA O'Hara, 'Corporations and the Market for Law' (2008) University of Illinois Law Review 661, 694; A Winkler, 'Corporate Law or the Law of Business?' (2004) 67 Law & Contemporary Problems 109.

[40] V Root, 'The Compliance Process' (2019) 94 Indiana Law Journal 203, 213 ff; JA Fanto, 'The Governing Authority's Responsibilities in Compliance and Risk Management' (2018) 90 Temple Law Review 699, 707f; R Van Loo, 'Regulatory Monitors: Policing Firms in the Compliance Era' (2019) 119 Columbia Law Review 369, 399 ff.

[41] M Bullard, 'Caremark's Irrelevance' (2013) 10 Berkeley Business Law Journal 15, 38.

[42] Congressional Research Service, 'Bank Supervision by Federal Regulators: Overview and Policy Issues' (28 December 2020) https://sgp.fas.org/crs/misc/R46648.pdf.

[43] *Faragher v City of Boca Raton* 524 US 775, 807 (1998); US Sentencing Guidelines Manual § 8B2.1 (US Sentencing Commission 2016).

[44] J Arlen and M Kahan, 'Corporate Governance Regulation Through Non-Prosecution' (2017) 84 University of Chicago Law Review 323.

[45] Bullard (n 41) 37.

[46] Fanto (n 40) 711; Griffith (n 31) 2089.

[47] Griffith (n 31) 2089, 2109; S Jarvis, 'DOJ Tackling Voluntary Self-Disclosure In M&A, Official Says' *Law360* (21 September 2023) www.law360.com/securities/articles/1724493.

the corporation's efforts to overhaul its internal compliance systems—for years-long periods.[48] Even corporations that have not been accused of wrongdoing may copy reforms imposed on their peers in expectation that doing so will win them more favourable government treatment in the future.[49]

Aside from the compliance function, corporations may be required to include employees in their decision-making processes via labour law's imposition of good faith bargaining requirements.[50] Corporations are prohibited from using decision-making processes that employ certain criteria, such as race or gender.[51] Antitrust laws directly limit corporate structure, not only by preventing mergers that would grant a single entity too much market power, but also by blocking overlapping directors and common ownership among competing enterprises.[52] This is why Adam Winkler has argued that the stakeholder vision of the corporation has not been vanquished; it has simply moved into 'the law of business'.[53] Or, to put the point more bluntly, to the extent the argument is that 'corporate law' is, descriptively, designed to encourage shareholder wealth maximization, it begins by defining out of the category of 'corporate law' all of the mandatory corporate decision-making rules that are *not* designed to encourage wealth maximization but instead exist to protect non-shareholders.

The category of rules widely understood to encompass 'corporate law' also contain aspects that can only be explained as outer limits on the boundaries of permissible profit-seeking activities. For example, demonstrating that the privilege to do business in the corporate form is conditional on providing net benefits to society, states will *withdraw* the protection of limited liability when shareholders abuse it with respect to their dealings with third parties. This concept, known as 'veil-piercing', is usually decided by reference to the chartering state's law (although a minority of jurisdictions use ordinary choice of law analysis),[54] suggesting that the grant of the charter itself retains some of its original regulatory character.

Similarly, although corporate capitalization and dividend policy are obviously of concern to investors, creditors in particular have an interest in ensuring that corporations do not make distributions that threaten their solvency. As a result, states typically impose minimum capitalization requirements, and prohibit payment of dividends that would render the company insolvent.[55] This, too, operates less as a protection of shareholders than a form of regulation for the benefit of third parties by the chartering state.

---

[48] See V Root Martinez, 'Modern-Day Monitorships' (2016) 33 Yale Journal on Regulation 109, 127–30.
[49] Griffith (n 31) 2089, 2090, 2109.
[50] Winkler (n 39) 130 ff.
[51] 42 USC § 2000e–2.
[52] 15 USC §§ 18, 19. Additionally, although it has been said that corporate law operates by making 'corporate managers strongly accountable to shareholder interests and, at least in direct terms, only to those interests', Hansmann and Kraakman (n 16) 441 state that individual corporate managers may be punished with monetary penalties or even imprisonment if they violate the duties imposed by environmental law, health law, and the like, all created to protect non-shareholders. See JS Nelson, 'The Corporate Conspiracy Vacuum' (2015) 37 Cardozo Law Review 249, 283–90.
[53] Winkler (n 39).
[54] GS Crespi, 'Choice of Law in Veil Piercing Litigation: Why Courts Should Discard the Internal Affairs Rule and Embrace General Choice of Law Principles' (2008) 64 New York University Annual Survey of American Law 85.
[55] See eg Del Code tit 8, §§ 154, 160, 174.

Additionally, the fiduciaries duties of corporate managers typically include the duty to obey the law,[56] even when legal violations would maximize value; as one Delaware court put it, 'Delaware law does not charter law breakers'.[57] That position is difficult to square with the notion that corporate law is designed to promote shareholder interests,[58] but it makes perfect sense if the grant of a corporate charter carries with it responsibilities to the public.

Finally, most states grant corporate directors the power to resist hostile takeover offers, even when the acquirer would pay a significant premium above the corporation's standalone value. Although these are often defended as mechanisms to protect shareholders from manipulative or deceptive acquisition tactics,[59] it is widely understood that their true purpose is to protect employees, incumbent managers, and local communities from the economic upheaval associated with corporate buyouts.[60]

To be sure, many shareholder primacists would argue that these regulations of the corporate form—intended for the benefit of non-shareholders—are fundamentally *misguided*. Sean Griffith, for example, observes that the compliance function redirects the firm toward a stakeholder orientation, and argues that government should not involve itself in internal firm procedures[61]; Stephen Bainbridge has recommended that veil-piercing be abolished,[62] while both he and Charles Korsmo have objected to fiduciary duties against law-breaking,[63] and disputes about the legitimacy of takeover defences go back decades.[64] Those objections notwithstanding, simply as a descriptive matter, there have been few or no historical periods where corporate structure—or even the structure of more modern entities, such as limited liability companies (LLCs) s – have been entirely designed around the interests of equity investors, without state-imposed regard for other constituencies.

## IV. Shareholder Primacy Is One Option for a Governmentally Mandated Design to Benefit All Stakeholders

Given the above, it might be more accurate to say that shareholder primacists adopt the following set of arguments. First, the social benefits of the corporate form are best

---

[56] See eg *Marchand v Barnhill* 212 A3d 805 (Del 2019); E Pollman, 'Corporate Oversight and Disobedience' (2019) 72 Vanderbilt Law Review 2013.
[57] *In re Massey Energy Co* WL 2176479 at *20 (Del Ch 2011).
[58] K Greenfield, 'Ultra Vires Lives! A Stakeholder Analysis of Corporate Illegality (With Notes on How Corporate Law Could Reinforce International Law Norms)' (2001) 87 Virginia Law Review 1279, 1292.
[59] See eg *Unitrin Inc v American General Corp* 651 A2d 1361 (1995).
[60] AR Palmiter, 'The CTS Gambit: Stanching the Federalization of Corporate Law' (1991) 69 Washington University Law Quarterly 445; J Coffee, 'Shareholders Versus Managers: The Strain in the Corporate Web' (1986) 85 Michigan Law Review 1.
[61] Griffith (n 31) 2134–36.
[62] S Bainbridge, 'Abolishing Veil Piercing' (2001) 26 Journal of Corporation Law 479.
[63] SM Bainbridge, 'Don't Compound the Caremark Mistake by Extending it to ESG Oversight' (2022) 77 Business Lawyer 651; CR Korsmo, 'Illegality and the Business Judgment Rule' in Sean Griffith and others (eds), *Research Handbook on Representative Shareholder Litigation* (Edward Elgar Publishing 2018).
[64] See M Lipton, 'Pills, Polls, and Professors Redux' (2002) 69 University of Chicago Law Review 1037 (describing the history of the debate).

achieved when managers are incentivized to advance shareholder interests exclusively, and shareholder interests are aligned with the interests of society as a whole; second, shareholder interests should be made to align with those of society by making it difficult for corporations to profit when they deviate from society's interests; third, the law that pertains to ensuring that managers advance shareholder interests is what we categorize as 'corporate law',[65] while the law that imposes costs on corporations for deviating from the best interests of society is what we categorize as 'external' law.

Even that more mild formulation has its problems, both theoretically and in practical application. In order to work, the corporation has (1) to endure costly penalties for antisocial behaviour; (2) those penalties, and their causes, have to be known to investors; and (3) investors have to have sufficient power to discourage further rule-breaking, either via capital allocation decisions or via the selection of new managers. Finally, and critically, the latter two rules have to be in place *as a function of corporate law*, which is to say, for the benefit of investors, rather than having been put in place for the benefit of other constituencies, in order to render the two realms conceptually separable.

### 1. Corporate Procedure Must Be Regulated to Satisfy the First Condition

The first problem—which has been extensively discussed—is that a purely wealth-maximizing corporation is heavily incentivized to use its power to undermine any regulatory system that would stand in the way of profit-seeking.[66] In purely financial terms, the returns corporations earn from lobbying may far exceed any returns they would earn from productive investment;[67] corporate managers whose sole remit is to maximize profits will rationally choose to undermine regulations rather than comply with them if doing so is likely to generate greater returns for shareholders. Because corporations, by definition, are able to accumulate massive amounts of capital, their lobbying is usually effective; thus, a clean division between corporate and external law carries with it the seeds of its own destruction. Managers tasked with maximizing

---

[65] J Fisch and SD Solomon, 'Centros, California's "Women on Boards" Statute and the Scope of Regulatory Competition' (2019) 20 European Business Organization Law Review 493; J Armour and others, 'Foundations of Corporate Law' in R Kraakman and others (eds), *The Anatomy of Corporate Law: A Comparative and Functional Approach* (3rd edn, OUP 2017)('the use of legal rules for purposes other than increasing the value of the firm is the boundary separating corporate from other areas of law').

[66] LE Strine Jr and N Walter, 'Conservative Collision Course? The Tension Between Conservative Corporate Law Theory and Citizens United' (2015) 100 Cornell Law Review 335; JE Fisch, 'The "Bad Man" Goes to Washington: The Effect of Political Influence on Corporate Duty' (2006) 75 Fordham Law Review 1593; DG Yosifon, 'The Public Choice Problem in Corporate Law: Corporate Social Responsibility After Citizens United' (2011) 89 North Carolina Law Review 1197; FA Gevurtz, 'The Complex Dualisms of Corporations and Democracy' (2022) 14 Northeastern University Law Review 365.

[67] A Blumberg, 'Forget Stocks Or Bonds, Invest in a Lobbyist' *NPR* (6 January 2012) www.npr.org/sections/money/2012/01/06/144737864/forget-stocks-or-bonds-invest-in-a-lobbyist; James Bessen, 'Lobbyists Are Behind the Rise in Corporate Profits' *Harvard Business Review* (26 May 2016) https://hbr.org/2016/05/lobbyists-are-behind-the-rise-in-corporate-profits; Matthew D Hill and others, 'Determinants and Effects of Corporate Lobbying' (2013) 42 Financial Management 931.

profits are also obligated to use the political power of the corporation to undermine the very external law on which the system depends.

Corporations' wealth and power has a secondary effect, namely, the ability to evade sanction by hiding responsibility for misdeeds through layers of impenetrable bureaucracy.[68] If corporations can use their sheer size and complexity to delay or avoid penalties, a system of regulatory sanction will only be effective if the few penalties that ultimately are imposed are especially large and severe, in order to make law-breaking appear unprofitable from an ex ante perspective. This is often not how the regulatory system currently works, however,[69] and many regulations generally impose compensatory penalties rather than punitive ones.[70] Even when enhanced penalties are available, judges may be reluctant to mete them out,[71] and some corporations may be 'too big to jail', that is, too essential to lock out of the economic system via the most severe sanctions.[72]

These dynamics are part of what necessitate the compliance function, namely, government involvement with corporate internal procedure. Standardized and transparent decision-making allow regulators to gain insight into whether and how corporate wrongdoing has occurred, which facilitates regulators' ability to impose penalties for misconduct.[73] Thus, government control over internal corporate organs becomes a necessary aspect of the regime for aligning shareholder interests with those of society as a whole.

## 2. Investors Must Receive 'Overdisclosures' to Satisfy the Second Condition

The second problem concerns the necessity of publicity. Today, there are increasing calls for corporations to disclose matters pertaining to their social performance, under such labels as 'ESG' (environmental, social, governance) or 'sustainability' reporting.[74] Such disclosure is, in fact, a necessary aspect of shareholder primacy, because shareholder primacy itself is justified (from a Doylist perspective) on the grounds that external regulation will cause misbehaving corporations to incur societal wrath, rendering them less profitable. The theory is that companies that are at risk of reputational or legal sanction will have a higher cost of capital, and will reform (or be forced by

---

[68] JS Nelson, 'Paper Dragon Thieves' (2017) 105 Georgetown Law Journal 871.
[69] R Shapira, 'The Challenge of Holding Big Business Accountable' (2022) 44 Cardozo Law Review 203.
[70] See eg SF Befort, 'Labor and Employment Law at the Millennium: A Historical Review and Critical Assessment' (2002) 43 Boston College Law Review 351, 371–75 (discussing inadequate remedies under the NLRA).
[71] R Chopra and LM Khan, 'The Case for "Unfair Methods of Competition" Rulemaking' (2020) 87 University of Chicago Law Review 357, 371; MS Popofsky, 'The Section 2 Debate: Should Lenity Play A Role?' (2010) 7 Rutgers Business Law Journal 1, 10.
[72] Shapira (n 69).
[73] J Arlen and R Kraakman, 'Controlling Corporate Misconduct: An Analysis of Corporate Liability Regimes' (1997) 72 New York University Law Review 687, 699–701; Shapira (n 69).
[74] AM Lipton, 'Not Everything is About Investors: The Case for Mandatory Stakeholder Disclosure' (2020) 37 Yale Journal on Regulation 499, 527.

voting shareholders to reform) their practices. It follows that investors need to know of corporations' prosocial and antisocial practices, so that they can value their securities accordingly.

That said, when companies disclose potential risks so that investors can make informed decisions, other constituencies—customers, employees, regulators, and the like—can more readily impose penalties for antisocial behaviour,[75] which ultimately changes the risk profile of the firm. For example, companies may be required to disclose the racial make-up of their workforces so that investors can determine if they are at risk of employment discrimination litigation, but those disclosures may also alert regulators and plaintiffs' lawyers as to the existence of employment discrimination in the first place, thereby making litigation more likely. Similarly, companies may be required to disclose their carbon emissions so that investors can become aware of any transition risks they may experience as regulators impose limits on greenhouse gases, but those disclosures may also be used by regulators to determine which sectors require greater oversight. This is not necessarily a *problem*; it may ultimately be better for society if such disclosures are required,[76] but it highlights the difficulty of distinguishing between law for investors and law for everyone else. In many cases, investors—as pure profit seekers—may prefer that they be kept *uninformed* of potential risks, if disclosure itself has the effect of elevating risk levels,[77] but to accommodate investor preferences in this regard would (like the problem of political lobbying) undermine the very system meant to align investor preferences with the preferences of the broader society.

### 3. Investors Must Be Regulated to Satisfy the Third Condition

The final problem concerns investor power. If shareholders have sufficient influence over managerial behaviour, they can theoretically force corporations to behave with more consideration for non-shareholder constituencies (presumably, when doing so would be more profitable for the firm). In practice, however, shareholder influence has been associated with the precise opposite. In recent years, as shareholders have gained more power within the corporate form (both due to regulatory interventions, and due to greater institutionalization of the shareholder base),[78] shareholder returns have

---

[75] ibid 532.
[76] Lipton (n 74).
[77] It has frequently been observed that current investors in a firm may prefer to be kept uninformed of negative information, in order to maintain stock at inflated prices. See eg JC Spindler, 'Optimal Deterrence When Shareholders Desire Fraud' (2019) 107 Georgetown Law Journal 1071; J Fried, 'The Uneasy Case for Favoring Long-Term Shareholders' (2015) 124 Yale Law Journal 1554; see also *Water Island Event-Driven Fund v Tribune Media Co* 39 F 4th 402, 407-08 (7th Cir 2022) (denying securities fraud claim in part by observing that had full disclosure been made, it would have alerted antitrust regulators of problems, thereby harming the investors who claimed to have been defrauded by concealment).
[78] See RJ Gilson and JN Gordon, 'The Agency Costs of Agency Capitalism: Activist Investors and the Revaluation of Governance Rights' (2013) 113 Columbia Law Review 863; JC Coffee and D Palia, 'The Wolf at the Door: The Impact of Hedge Fund Activism on Corporate Governance' (2016) 1 Annals of Corporate Governance 1.

increased and wages have fallen.[79] Hedge fund activism in particular has become associated with generating returns to shareholders at the expense of other constituencies,[80] and leveraged buyouts are famous for showering profits on investors while decreasing employment and product quality.[81]

It is precisely for this reason that numerous scholars have argued that it is detrimental to corporations to increase shareholder power, because shareholders have a distorted, short-term outlook that blinds them to the profit potential of less cost-cutting, more investment in employees, and more innovative research.[82] In other words, there are significant trade-offs. The shareholder power that is necessary to ensure that the incentives of corporate managers are aligned with societal dictates can be used to derail that same project, harming non-shareholder constituencies in the process.

To those who subscribe to the view that corporations should be designed to maximize shareholder wealth, one response is to perceive these corporate deviations from societal welfare as representing a market failure, whereby shareholders simply do not have the informational tools necessary to price securities for the long-term alignment of corporate value with societal value. Thus, they propose interventions such as requiring that earnings be reported on a semi-annual rather than quarterly basis, or that corporations report more information regarding their social performance,[83] while social reporting, as described above, may have less an effect of *informing* investors than actually *increasing* firm vulnerability.[84] There have also been various proposals that investors be incentivized for long-term capital allocation with tax incentives, additional voting power, or greater cash flow rights.[85] Even assuming that investors need economic incentives to take actions that—by hypothesis—are already wealth maximizing,[86] these

---

[79] C Ingraham, 'The Race for Shareholder Profits Has Left Workers in the Dust, According to New Research' *The Washington Post* (25 February 2019) www.washingtonpost.com/us-policy/2019/02/25/race-shareholder-profits-has-left-workers-dust-according-new-research/; A Falato, H Kim, and T von Wachter, 'Shareholder Power and the Decline of Labor' https://papers.ssrn.com/sol3/papers.cfm?abstract_id=4153096.

[80] AC Baker, 'The Effects of Hedge Fund Activism' https://andrewcbaker.netlify.app/publication/baker_jmp/; A Agrawal and Y Lim, 'Where Do Shareholder Gains in Hedge Fund Activism Come From? Evidence from Employee Pension Plans' (2022) 57 Journal of Financial &Quantitative Analysis 2140; A Falato, H Kim, and T von Wachter, 'Shareholder Power and the Decline of Labor' www.nber.org/papers/w30203.

[81] See eg LA Bebchuk, K Kastiel, and R Tallarita, 'For Whom Corporate Leaders Bargain' (2021) 94 Southern California Law Review 1467, 1495–98; D Folkenflik, '"Vulture" Fund Alden Global, Known for Slashing Newsrooms, Buys Tribune Papers' *NPR* (21 May 2021) www.npr.org/2021/05/21/998730863/vulture-fund-alden-global-kno0wn-for-slashing-newsrooms-buys-tribune-papers; M Ewens, A Gupta, and ST Howell, 'Local Journalism Under Private Equity Ownership'(February 2022), www.nber.org/system/files/working_papers/w29 743/w29743.pdf; K Taggart and others, 'Profit, Pain, and Private Equity' *Buzzfeed News* (25 April 2022) www.buzzfeednews.com/article/kendalltaggart/kkr-brightspring-disability-private-equity-abuse; H Vogell, 'When Private Equity Becomes Your Landlord' *ProPublica* (7 February 2022) www.propublica.org/article/when-private-equity-becomes-your-landlord; D Scott, 'Private equity ownership is killing people at nursing homes' *Vox* (22 February 2021) www.vox.com/policy-and-politics/22295461/nursing-home-deaths-private-equity-firms.

[82] Z Goshen and RS Steel, 'Barbarians Inside the Gates: Raiders, Activists, and the Risk of Mistargeting' (2022) 132 Yale Law Journal 411; WW Bratton and ML Wachter, 'The Case Against Shareholder Empowerment' (2010) 158 University of Pennsylvania Law Review 653.

[83] Of course, these necessarily have drawbacks: infrequent reporting may only render stock more volatile and give trading advantages to insiders see Knowledge at Wharton, 'Should Companies Abandon Quarterly Earnings Reports?' (27 August 2018) https://knowledge.wharton.upenn.edu/article/ending-quarterly-reporting/.

[84] Other kinds of informational deficiencies, as well, may only be curable with disclosure of additional information to the point that might be detrimental to the disclosing firm. See Bratton and Wachter (n 82).

[85] Fried (n 77) 1572–75.

[86] The evidence that 'short-termism' does, in fact, prevent corporations from taking long-term wealth maximizing actions is somewhat mixed. See eg L Cunningham, 'The Case for Empowering Quality Shareholders'

too have drawbacks. They might end up benefiting insiders, leading to entrenchment, and benefiting index funds,[87] who are frequently criticized as having insufficient or conflicted incentives when exercising their voting power.[88]

Which is likely why the next level intervention is to regulate the *shareholders themselves* to ensure they advocate for the 'proper' corporate policies. As I have written elsewhere,[89] powerful shareholders are almost always institutions, such as hedge funds, mutual funds, and pension funds, and they are just as much legal constructs as the corporations in which they invest. Thus, their incentives and their legal obligations can be manipulated to ensure they play their correct role in influencing corporate behaviour, however 'correct' is conceived.

Unsurprisingly, then, that role has been a significant site of contention. The SEC, which has jurisdiction over investment companies, has encouraged mutual funds to exercise oversight over their portfolio companies as part of their fiduciary duties to their own investors.[90] The Department of Labor, which oversees retirement funds, has done the same with respect to pension plans within its jurisdiction, in order to protect plan beneficiaries.[91] (Significantly, the Labor Department's regulatory jurisdiction is normally treated as 'external', ie for the benefit of workers rather than shareholders). An entire ecosystem of advisory services has sprung up to assist institutional shareholders in discharging these duties, and the SEC has intervened to regulate these services, as well.[92]

One particular point of dispute has been whether, and to what extent, institutional investors may consider the social behaviour of corporations in which they invest as part of the valuation process; although such considerations are, quite literally, *necessary* for shareholder primacy to work, many shareholder primacists suspect that institutions use their voting power to express the preferences of the institutions' managers rather than to protect the financial interests of their beneficiaries.[93] As a result, legislation has been proposed to require that mutual funds offer the option of 'pass through' voting, whereby investors in those funds would instruct the fund how to vote their pro rata share of the funds' holdings.[94] Probably in response, some of the largest asset managers

---

(2020) 46 Brigham Young University Law Review 1, 31–35; MJ Roe, 'Stock Market Short-Termism: What the Empirical Evidence Tells Policymakers' (2022) 7 Journal of Law and Financial Accounting 1.

[87] MJ Roe and FC Venezze, 'Will Loyalty Shares Do Much for Corporate Short-Termism?' (2021) 76 Business Lawyer 467.
[88] See eg LA Cunningham and others, 'Proposal on Climate-Related Disclosures for Investors', Letter to the United States Securities and Exchange Commission (25 April 2022); L Bebchuk and S Hirst, 'Index Funds and the Future of Corporate Governance: Theory, Evidence, and Policy' (2019) 119 Columbia Law Review 2029.
[89] AM Lipton, 'Beyond Internal and External: A Taxonomy of Mechanisms for Regulating Corporate Conduct' [2020] Wisconsin Law Review 657, 684–87
[90] See AM Lipton, 'Family Loyalty: Mutual Fund Voting and Fiduciary Obligation' (2017) 19 Tennessee Journal of Business Law 175.
[91] ibid.
[92] United States Securities and Exchange Commission, Proxy Voting Advice, Release No 34-95266 (July 13, 2022).
[93] See eg LA Cunningham and others, 'Proposal on Climate-Related Disclosures for Investors' Letter to the United States Securities and Exchange Commission (25 April 2022).
[94] A Au-Yeung, 'Lawmakers Seek to Curb Voting Power of BlackRock, Vanguard and Other Big Asset Managers' The Wall Street Journal (18 May 2022) www.wsj.com/articles/lawmakers-seek-to-curb-voting-power-of-blackrock-vanguard-and-other-big-asset-managers-11652875481.

have begun voluntarily to offer versions of pass through voting in certain funds[95]—heralding an industry shift that could dilute mutual funds' power to influence corporate managers across the board.[96] Meanwhile, with respect to pension plans, different administrations have been more or less receptive to the notion that these investors should consider the social behaviour of corporations in which they invest as part of the valuation process, leading to shifts in position with each new president.[97] Some commentators have become so concerned that shareholders are voting the 'wrong' way that they have sought to *reduce* particular types of shareholder voice within the corporate polity, while amplifying the voices of others types of shareholders.[98]

These debates inject corporate commentators into some of the most hot-button political issues of our time,[99] and that's because even the (Watsonian) shareholder wealth maximization norm is, at its core, an argument from a (Doylist) perspective about how firms can best serve society, and many shareholder primacists take evidence that the *latter* is lacking as proof that the *former* is not being effectuated. So, back to the drawing board: if firms are not appropriately serving society, the corporate governance rules must be adjusted.[100]

Taking a further step back, the nature of the institutions that hold America's equities are also a product of regulatory intervention, and that intervention dictates both shareholders' interests and their timelines for achieving returns. For example, the adoption of the Employee Retirement Income Security Act in 1974 and section 401(k) of the Internal Revenue Code had the effect of encouraging employers to shift workers' retirement assets from pension plans to mutual funds.[101] This matters because pension plans, which cater to defined pools of employees who typically elect at least some board members, are more likely to involve themselves actively in corporate governance issues and to treat labour policy as a financial consideration relevant to the health of the plan.[102] Mutual funds, by contrast, have a much broader and more diverse investor

---

[95] 'Empowering everyday investors through proxy voting choice' Vanguard (1 February 2023) https://advisors.vanguard.com/insights/article/empowering-everyday-investors-through-proxy-voting-choice; BlackRock, 'Voting Choice FAQ' (April 2023) www.blackrock.com/corporate/literature/publication/voting-choice-faqs.pdf.

[96] JE Fisch, 'The Uncertain Stewardship Potential of Index Funds' in D Katelouzou and DW Puchniak (eds), *Global Shareholder Stewardship: Complexities, Challenges and Possibilities* (CUP 2022). But cf JE Fisch and J Schwartz, 'Corporate Democracy and the Intermediary Voting Dilemma' (2023) 102 Texas Law Review 1 (suggesting alternatives to pure pass-through voting that might preserve institutions' bargaining power within the corporate form).

[97] Lipton (n 19) 889–90. Several states have also threatened to withdraw business from financial institutions and asset managers that consider corporate social behavior as part of the investment process. See eg Shelly Hagan, 'Texas Asks 19 Finance Firms for Details on Fossil-Fuel Stances' *Bloomberg* (16 March 2022) www.bloomberg.com/news/articles/2022-03-16/texas-queries-19-finance-firms-on-details-of-fossil-fuel-stances, and they have accused asset managers of violating their fiduciary duties to pension funds for incorporating climate change considerations into their investment and voting processes see Mark Brnovich and others (A-G), Letter to Laurence D Fink, CEO BlackRock Inc (4 August 2022).

[98] Cunningham (n 86); DS Lund, 'The Case Against Passive Shareholder Voting' (2018) 43 Journal of Corporation Law 493; SJ Griffith and DS Lund, 'Conflicted Mutual Fund Voting in Corporate Law' (2019) 99 Boston University Law Review 1151.

[99] See eg JM Fried, 'Will Nasdaq's Diversity Rules Harm Investors?' https://papers.ssrn.com/sol3/papers.cfm?abstract_id=3812642; Sean J Griffith, 'What's "Controversial" About ESG? A Theory of Compelled Commercial Speech under the First Amendment' (2023) 101 Nebraska Law Review 976; C Brummer and LE Strine Jr, 'Duty and Diversity' (2022) 75 Vanderbilt Law Review 1.

[100] M Pargendler, 'The Corporate Governance Obsession' (2016) 42 Journal of Corporation Law 359.

[101] M Gelter, 'The Pension System and the Rise of Shareholder Primacy' (2013) 43 Seton Hall Law Review 909.

[102] DH Webber, *The Rise of the Working Class Shareholder: Labor's Last Best Weapon* (HUP 2018).

base who have little say in their governance, and thus are both less likely to take an interventionist stance with respect to corporate governance, and less likely to favour labour in their consideration of corporate policy.[103] Meanwhile, both mutual funds, and pension plans, are required to diversify their holdings, which may encourage a certain indifference to the degree of risk assumed by each firm in their portfolio.[104]

Similarly, changes to the securities laws—and, in particular, alterations to the rules governing private investment funds—have fuelled the rise of new types of investors whose incentives are shaped by the regulatory environment that created them. In 1996, Congress gave the green light for private funds to raise unlimited amounts of capital, without becoming subject to registration under either the Securities Act or the Investment Company Act, so long as their own investors consist solely of persons with significant assets.[105] At the same time, Congress and the SEC also made it easier for operating companies to raise capital while remaining private, so long as they mostly limit their investor base to these newly supercharged private funds.[106] The result is the very opposite of an attempt to cultivate the kind of long-term investment ecosystem where companies build wealth by balancing the interests of multiple constituencies, because the illiquid nature of the funding vehicles (necessitated by their private, non-tradable status) encourages a short-termist orientation in search of a quick payout. The result has been that one particular category of investor—wealthy, institutional, private, illiquid, risk-seeking, and with limited ability to express negative sentiment[107]—has come to dominate the private markets.[108] These investors, whose very existence is a product of the regulatory scheme, prefer businesses that, in keeping with their short-termist orientation, exhibit rapid growth (often in search of monopoly profits).[109] Due to the high-risk nature of their strategy, private funds invest in multiple firms in the

---

[103] ibid; see also Y Nili and K Kastiel, 'The Giant Shadow of Corporate Gadflies' (2021) 94 Southern California Law Review 569.

[104] DJH Greenwood, 'Fictional Shareholders: For Whom Are Corporate Managers Trustees, Revisited' (1996) 69 Southern California Law Review 1021, 1073–75; JE Fisch, 'The Mess at Morgan: Risk, Incentives and Shareholder Empowerment' (2015) 83 University of Cincinnati Law Review 651, 668.

[105] E de Fontenay, 'The Deregulation of Private Capital and the Decline of the Public Company' (2017) 68 Hastings Law Journal 445, 467–68; 15 USC §§ 80a-3(c)(7), 80a-2(a)(51).

[106] By statute and SEC rule, companies may raise capital and remain private so long as they only seek investment from wealthy investors, and so long as they do not have more than 2,000 shareholders, excluding employees. See de Fontenay (n 105) 467–69. Thus, companies are incentivized to seek capital from small numbers of very wealthy funds – which, due to the changes to the Investment Company Act, are now in abundant supply.

[107] JM Fried and JN Gordon, 'The Valuation and Governance Bubbles of Silicon Valley' *The CLS Blue Sky Blog* (10 October 2019) http://clsbluesky.law.columbia.edu/2019/10/10/the-valuation-and-governance-bubbles-of-silicon-valley/.

[108] See JS Fan, 'The Landscape of Startup Governance in the Founder-Friendly Era' (2022) 18 New York University Journal of Law & Business 317, 329–30; E Aguirre, 'Money or Mission: Uncovering Venture Capital Barriers to Social Startup Success' (unpublished draft, on file with the author) ('It is quite rare for a startup to achieve longterm viability without securing VC'); R Winkler, 'The Failed Promise of Online Mental Health Treatment' *The Wall Street Journal* (18 December 2022) www.wsj.com/articles/the-failed-promise-of-online-mental-health-treatment-11671390353 ('When you put venture capital money into this mixture, it really pushes people to take risks').

[109] Fan (n 108); B Broughman and M Wansley, 'Risk-Seeking Governance' (2023) 76 Vanderbilt Law Review 1299, 1306; E Ongweso Jr, 'How One Billionaire With a 300-Year Plan Fueled the Popping Tech Bubble' *Vice* (2 June 2022) www.vice.com/en/article/4awkjw/how-one-billionaire-with-a-300-year-plan-fueled-the-popping-tech-bubble; M Stoller, 'An Economy of Overfed Middlemen' *BIG by Matt Stoller* (19 July 2022) www.thebignewsletter.com/p/a-moat-trajectory ('venture capitalists are now promoting investment models based on explicit violation of antitrust laws').

expectation that most will fail but a few will become outsized hits;[110] and recently they have favoured 'gig' or 'platform' business models that avoid labour costs.[111] That means that start-up businesses have to restructure themselves around these preferences; sometimes under threat that funds would otherwise invest in their competitors and drive them out of the market.[112] That business model, however, has resulted in a string of failed companies around the globe, wreaking havoc on the lives of small entrepreneurs, labourers, and customers, and potentially even crowding out more productive business models.[113] The regulatory reforms also enabled the rise of giant private equity firms and hedge funds, both of which, as described above, tend to goose shareholder profits with wealth transfers from other constituencies.

A host of other regulatory choices affect firm structure in various ways. For example, distinction between passive and active investor is important in terms of regulatory burdens under the antitrust laws and the securities laws, both of which require additional disclosures or transactional delays for shareholders who fall into the 'active' category.[114] As a result, large mutual fund complexes are required to minimize their involvement with corporate governance in order to stay on the correct side of the line, which may include alterations to procedures for determining how to vote in contested corporate matters.[115]

In sum, the shareholder primacist view depends on an empowered shareholder base that is motivated to align corporate behaviour with societal mores, but in today's system, shareholder power and shareholder motivations exist by virtue of governmental intervention. Investors' preferences and their capital allocation decisions—on particular timelines, with particular business models—are not a natural, pre-existing feature of the landscape, but are shaped by regulatory choices. And unless regulators act with blinders on, they must try to anticipate the allocative consequences of their decisions and direct capital in a manner that benefits society overall. All of which demonstrates that a distinction between the law that purports to adopt a Watsonian focus on

---

[110] B Zider, 'How Venture Capital Works' *Harvard Business Review* (November-December 1998) https://hbr.org/1998/11/how-venture-capital-works; RP Bartlett, 'Venture Capital, Agency Costs, and the False Dichotomy of the Corporation' (2006) 54 UCLA Law Review 37.

[111] N Popper, V Goel, and A Harindranath, 'The SoftBank Effect: How $100 Billion Left Workers in a Hole' *The New York Times* (12 November 2019) www.nytimes.com/2019/11/12/technology/softbank-startups.html; E Ongweso Jr, 'How One Billionaire With a 300-Year Plan Fueled the Popping Tech Bubble' *Vice* (2 June 2022) www.vice.com/en/article/4awkjw/how-one-billionaire-with-a-300-year-plan-fueled-the-popping-tech-bubble.

[112] S Kolhatkar, 'WeWork's Downfall and a Reckoning for SoftBank' *The New Yorker* (14 November 2019) www.newyorker.com/business/currency/weworks-downfall-and-a-reckoning-for-softbank; N Crooks, 'Ray Dalio Says the 'World Has Gone Mad' With So Much Free Money' *Bloomberg* (5 November 2019) www.bloomberg.com/news/articles/2019-11-05/ray-dalio-says-the-world-has-gone-mad-with-so-much-free-money.

[113] N Popper, V Goel and A Harindranath, 'The SoftBank Effect: How $100 Billion Left Workers in a Hole' *The New York Times* (12 November 2019) www.nytimes.com/2019/11/12/technology/softbank-startups.html R Roy, 'Doordash and Pizza Arbitrage' *Margins* (17 May 2020) www.readmargins.com/p/doordash-and-pizza-arbitrage. See also Aguirre (n 108) (arguing that the VC investment model may be incompatible with seeking social benefits beyond profit); R Winkler, 'Startup Cerebral Soared on Easy Adderall Prescriptions. That Was Its Undoing' *The Wall Street Journal* (8 June 2022) www.wsj.com/articles/cerebral-adderall-adhd-prescribe-11654705250 describing one tragically failed start-up following the VC model).

[114] JD Morley, 'Too Big to Be Activist' (2019) 92 Southern California Law Review 1407, 1425; 16 CFR § 802.9.

[115] AM Lipton, 'A Most Ingenious Paradox: Competition vs. Coordination in Mutual Fund Policy' (2021) 71 Case Western Reserve Law Review 1275, 1284 n 57.

internal firm governance, and the law that Doylistically addresses the role of the firm in society, is nearly impossible to maintain.

## V. The Stakeholderist Side of the Coin

Stakeholderists offer various critiques of shareholder primacy. Among these are that shareholder primacy assumes corporate behaviour should be entirely dictated by price—the price the corporation has to pay, versus the profits it can make, for antisocial behaviour—when, in fact, some values should not be treated as mere prices.[116] Another is that laws cannot impose a price on all forms of antisocial conduct; although to some extent social sanctions can fill in the gaps,[117] without an internal sense of morality, external pressures are unlikely to control corporate behaviour fully.[118] But the line of critique I highlight here is that shareholder primacy itself requires pervasive governmental tinkering within the corporate form in order to ensure that it operates as intended, namely, to generate the expected societal benefits. As a result, it not only fails as an exercise in private ordering, but it also obscures the role that regulation actually plays in structuring economic activity, thereby making governmental action less visible to everyone except corporate insiders. Or, as William Bratton put it, 'The problem lies instead with shareholder primacy itself, which claims that shareholder power assures certain efficient outcomes and then goes into denial when it turns out that real world shareholders do not have the incentive profile needed to bring those outcomes about.'[119] Stakeholderists argue that it would be more transparent, and more effective, if the corporate governance was redesigned to promote greater consideration of the interests of non-shareholder constituencies.

That leaves open a number of questions regarding how the stakeholder model can be implemented successfully. As described above, one method is to reduce shareholder power in order to give corporate managers the discretion to make socially conscious decisions,[120] a position predictably favoured by business leaders.[121] Corporate managers rarely offer any concrete commitments to promote stakeholder interests, however.[122]

Others have proposed that restrictions on corporate behaviour, or prosocial commitments, be built into the corporate form via its organizational documents.[123]

---

[116] C Williams, 'Corporate Compliance with the Law in the Era of Efficiency' (1998) 76 North Carolina Law Review 1265.
[117] See HA Sale, 'Corporate Purpose and Social License' (2021) 94 Southern California Law Review 785.
[118] Elhauge (n 20).
[119] WW Bratton, 'Shareholder Primacy versus Shareholder Accountability' 33 https://papers.ssrn.com/sol3/papers.cfm?abstract_id=4431055.
[120] ibid; MM Blair and LA Stout, 'A Team Production Theory of Corporate Law' (1999) 85 Virginia Law Review 247.
[121] See eg M Lipton, 'The New Paradigm A Roadmap for an Implicit Corporate Governance Partnership Between Corporations and Investors to Achieve Sustainable Long-Term Investment and Growth' International Business Council of the World Economic Forum (2 September 2016) www.wlrk.com/webdocs/wlrknew/AttorneyPubs/WLRK.25960.16.pdf.
[122] LA Bebchuk and R Tallarita, 'Will Corporations Deliver Value to All Stakeholders?' (2022) 75 Vanderbilt Law Review 1031; Strine (n 35).
[123] ST Omarova, 'The "Franchise" View of the Corporation: Purpose, Personality, Public Policy' in E Pollman and R Thompson (eds), *Research Handbook on Corporate Purpose and Personhood* (Edward Elgar Publishing

This idea hearkens back to the earliest days of the business corporation, when regulatory limits on corporate activity were effectuated through the grant of a charter. But whether limits on corporate activity are identified in a charter, or in an applicable statute or regulation, the limit still has to be enforced, and the sticking point is always expecting a judge to, ex post, decide when the limits have been exceeded (not to mention additional questions like identifying the appropriate plaintiff, venue, and remedy).

Another alternative is for shareholders themselves to promote stakeholderism, via socially responsible or impact investing.[124] Theoretically, shareholders could choose to sacrifice some portion of potential returns in favour of benefiting other constituencies. The main obstacle here is similar to the one above: the institutional shareholders who dominate today's markets may be legally *prohibited* from sacrificing returns in favour of social benefits,[125] and even if they were not, the rules surrounding their creation tend to select for particular types of profit-seeking. So, for example, one idea has been for shareholders to choose to invest in companies organized as 'benefit' corporations, in which incorporators pledge to balance profit-seeking with social goals.[126] But the benefit corporation form currently has very few mechanisms for ensuring that managers adhere to their promises. Thus, in public markets, they are likely to be subject to the same pressures to maximize profits as any other company.[127]

As a result, there have been a number of proposals to reshape the shareholder base, such as by giving institutions greater freedom to pursue social goals,[128] or by promoting retail investor voice on the assumption that they are more likely than institutions to temper profit-seeking with humanitarian preferences.[129] These proposals raise questions about practicality and effectiveness; for example, it may be just as difficult to ensure that institutions balance multiple social goals as it is to ensure that corporations do.[130] Retail shareholders may be too dispersed, uninformed, or distracted to monitor corporate behaviour effectively, and, as above, if institutional investors 'pass through'

---

2021); CD Mayer, 'The Future of the Corporation and the Economics of Purpose' (2020) 58 Journal of Management Studies 887; Accountable Capitalism Act, 2018.

[124] This is distinct from ESG investing, which is a somewhat malleable concept but is often a mechanism for identifying companies that will ultimately underperform because of the social risks they pose. When ESG is used as a tool for maximizing shareholder returns, it fits neatly within the shareholder primacist framework described in section II. By contrast, socially responsible investing, as that term is used here, refers to an intentional choice by shareholders to sacrifice some return to themselves in order to benefit non-shareholder constituencies. See generally,- AM Lipton, 'ESG Investing, or, If You Can't Beat 'Em, Join 'Em' in Elizabeth Pollman and Robert Thompson (eds), *Research Handbook on Corporate Purpose and Personhood* (Edward Elgar Publishing 2021).

[125] Lipton (n 74) 533.

[126] A Aguirre, 'Beyond Profit' (2021) 54 UC Davis Law Review 2077, 2101–104.

[127] ibid 2113–14; Strine (n 35) 149–51.

[128] See eg N Atkinson, 'If Not the Index Funds, Then Who?' (2020) 17 Berkeley Business Law Journal 44; Scott Hirst, 'Social Responsibility Resolutions' (2018) 43 Journal of Corporation Law 217.

[129] C Griffin, 'Environmental and Social Voting at Index Funds' (2020) 44 Delaware Journal of Corporation Law 167; S Hirst, 'Social Responsibility Resolutions' (2018) 43 Journal of Corporation Law 217, 237–38; SA Gramitto Ricci and CM Sautter, 'Harnessing the Collective Power of Retail Investors' in Christopher M Bruner and Marc Moore (eds), *A Research Agenda for Corporate Law* (Edward Elgar Publishing 2023) 207; JE Fisch, 'GameStop and the Reemergence of the Retail Investor' (2022) 102 Boston University Law Review 1799; J Taub, 'Able But Not Willing: The Failure of Mutual Fund Advisers to Advocate for Shareholders' Rights' (2009) 34 Journal of Corporation Law 843.

[130] Fisch (n 96).

votes to their own investor base, regardless of the preferences of those voters, the resulting deconcentration of voting power may ultimately weaken shareholder voices across the board.[131]

Another possibility could be to lean into the ways in which the regulatory framework has created multiple types of shareholders, and further encourage the development of, essentially, different equity constituencies, with different timelines, social preferences, diversification levels, and the like, much like the separation of powers was intended to function in the U.S. political sphere.[132]

For example, there are already attempts to create private equity funds tailored to modestly wealthy individuals;[133] properly regulated, these funds would presumably have different business models and incentives from their institutionally-focused cousins. Others have proposed employee-only vehicles with the power to vote shares on their beneficiaries' behalf.[134] There have been stirrings of ideas for issuing stock compensation to gig workers;[135] one could imagine regulated vehicles established to accommodate their interests, as well. Meanwhile, with the SEC's attempt to bring order to the ESG space,[136] additional funds could be created with more tightly focused social mandates. Each group of shareholders, with different priorities, would have to find common ground in order to wield power effectively, ideally balancing the pursuit of profit against other social values.[137] This vision is not unlike one promoted by Edward Rock and Marcel Kahan, who argue that, in proxy contests, boards should promote a 'deliberative' election process that channels decision-making through neutral, informed, institutional shareholders,[138] with one major difference being that retail investors could also be included as a constituency, taking advantage of technological mechanisms that may make it easier for them to participate in corporate governance.[139]

That said, the fundamental problem with these options is that they rely on shareholders—the capital class—to make determinations as to the best interest of society as a whole and voluntarily effectuate them. Not only are shareholders unrepresentative

---

[131] ibid.

[132] cf *West Virginia v Environmental Protection Agency* 142 S Ct 2587, 2618 (2022) (Gorsuch, J concurring) ('By effectively requiring a broad consensus to pass legislation, the Constitution sought to ensure that any new laws would enjoy wide social acceptance, profit from input by an array of different perspectives during their consideration ... The need for compromise inherent in this design also sought to protect minorities by ensuring that their votes would often decide the fate of proposed legislation—allowing them to wield real power alongside the majority').

[133] See M Gottfried, 'Blackstone, Other Large Private-Equity Firms Turn Attention to Vast Retail Market' *The Wall Street Journal* (7 June 2022) www.wsj.com/articles/blackstone-other-large-private-equity-firms-turn-attention-to-vast-retail-market-11654603201.

[134] B Sanders, 'Corporate Accountability and Democracy' (2020) https://berniesanders.com/issues/corporate-accountability-and-democracy/; Jonathan Ford, 'Labour Takes Aim at Shareholder Capitalism' *Financial Times* (3 September 2019) www.ft.com/content/f4d9c1a8-ca48-11e9-a1f4-3669401ba76f.

[135] M Price, 'U.S. Tech Firms Can Compensate Gig-Workers with Equity under SEC Proposal' *Reuters* (24 November 2020) www.reuters.com/article/us-usa-sec-tech-idUKKBN2842TL.

[136] United States Securities and Exchange Commission, 'SEC Proposes to Enhance Disclosures by Certain Investment Advisers and Investment Companies About ESG Investment Practices' (25 May 2022) www.sec.gov/news/press-release/2022-92.

[137] Lipton (n 89) 689–92.

[138] M Kahan and E Rock, 'Anti-Activist Poison Pills' (2019) 99 Boston University Law Review 915, 942.

[139] See Gramitto Ricci and Sautter (129).

of the broader society,[140] but to rely on shareholders in this manner is simply to reconstitute shareholder primacy in a different form,[141] with the same problem of a 'submerged' state attempting to alter corporate behaviour obliquely by altering the legal obligations and voice of equity investors.[142] In other words, the stakeholder proposals look like the B-side of the shareholder primacist proposals: they seek greater or lesser shareholder power within the corporate form, they move the lever one way or another in terms of institutional shareholder obligations, they promote retail investor voice—all of which only solidifies the basic critique of shareholder primacy, namely, that it is a government-mandated form of corporate organization in service of a particular social vision.

## VI. Rethinking the Form

Several stakeholderists have proposed fundamental redesigns of the corporate form to promote greater non-shareholder voice. One option is the co-determination model, which would allow employees to vote for corporate directors alongside shareholders.[143] Senators Elizabeth Warren and Tammy Baldwin have each offered legislation along these lines.[144] There have also been arguments that certain consumers should play a role in governance.[145] Typically, these positions are accompanied by economic analysis to demonstrate that there is no necessary reason that shareholders should be the only voting constituency, and that, by including other constituents within the firm structure, firm performance may be enhanced (by, for example, introducing new sources of knowledge into the governance process).[146]

For that reason, the co-determination proposal of Jens Dammann and Horst Eidenmüller is striking in that it makes precisely the opposite argument. These authors contend that co-determination introduces *inefficiencies* into the boardroom, because employees—with their own heterogeneous interests—will make it more difficult for corporations to decide on a course of action, including any course of action that undermines democratic institutions via use of the corporation's lobbying power.[147] In other words, it is very difficult for corporations to intervene aggressively in politics when labour as well as capital participate in decision-making. These authors view the benefits

---

[140] Lipton (n 124).
[141] J Velasco, 'Shareholder Primacy in Benefit Corporations' in Arthur B Laby and Jacob Hale Russell (eds), *Fiduciary Obligations in Business* (CUP 2021).
[142] cf S Mettler, *The Submerged State: How Invisible Government Policies Undermine American Democracy* (University of Chicago Press 2011).
[143] See eg GM Hayden and MT Bodie, 'The Corporation Reborn: From Shareholder Primacy to Shared Governance' (2019) 61 Boston College Law Review 2419; SE (Summer) Kim, 'Dynamic Corporate Residual Claimants: A Multicriteria Assessment' (2021) 25 Chapman Law Review 67.
[144] See Accountable Capitalism Act 2018; Reward Work Act 2018.
[145] SE (Summer) Kim, 'Consumer Primacy: A Dynamic Model of Corporate Governance for Consumer-Centric Business' [2022] Utah Law Review 235; DG Yosifon, 'The Consumer Interest in Corporate Law' (2009) 43 UC Davis Law Review 253.
[146] Hayden and Bodie (n 143) 2458–62; Kim (n 145) 257–64; Yosifon (n 145) 308.
[147] See J Dammann and H Eidenmüller, 'Corporate Law and the Democratic State' [2022] University of Illinois Law Review 963, 992–93.

that co-determination offers in terms of democratic stability to be worth any reductions in firm value that may ensue.[148]

As Dammann and Eidenmüller recognize,[149] this is the intuition behind the political separation of powers: the US Constitution fashions the polity into different interest groups, partly to ensure widespread agreement on any course of action, but also because it introduces friction into the law-making process.[150] The high level of procedural complexity necessary for the federal government to act ultimately impedes the exercise of any governmental power at all, which functions as a structural limitation against governmental abuse.

There is nothing unusual about transferring this insight to the corporate realm. In the pre-Industrial era, procedural limitations on corporate action, such as unanimity requirements for shareholder voting, were used to limit corporate power;[151] in the modern day, as I have argued elsewhere, it is very likely that demands for independent boards, or separation of the chair and CEO roles, or shareholder approval of political spending, are at least as much about inhibiting corporate power via the introduction of procedural friction as they are about controlling agency costs.[152] The value of proposals such as carving the shareholder base into different constituencies—or permitting non-shareholder constituencies, such as employees and consumers, to play a role in selecting board members—may ultimately lie less in their substantive influence over corporate decision-making than in their ability to render corporate decision-making more *cumbersome*, which itself impedes the dangerous accumulation of corporate power.[153]

## VII. Conclusion

Shareholder primacy and stakeholderism both posit that corporations exist to benefit society as a whole; they simply differ as to how best to bring about that result. That means that even under a shareholder primacist view, the corporation is a multistakeholder entity, and—as its real-world behaviour proves less than optimal—its design must be modified accordingly. The result is that it is impossible to preserve corporate governance as a purely investor-oriented space; the rest of society inevitably intrudes.

---

[148] ibid 999.
[149] ibid 975–76.
[150] See Lipton (n 89) 673–77.
[151] ibid.
[152] ibid.
[153] ibid.

# 11
# Leading Wherever They Want? CSR, ESG, and Directors' Duties

*Jens-Hinrich Binder**

## I. Introduction

The global trend towards incentivizing corporations (and their directors) to integrate social and environmental concerns in their business operations and in their interaction with stakeholders[1] clearly has the potential to trigger far-reaching ramifications for the legal position of corporate directors vis-à-vis their company (and, indeed, its shareholders). Some jurisdictions have long recognized a (limited) right of corporate directors to take into account, and cater for, stakeholder interests when exercising their business judgment, whereas others have followed a strict concept of shareholder orientation. While fundamental differences continue to exist in principle, converging standards relating, in particular, to reporting practices on corporate social responsibility (CSR) and environmental, social and governance (ESG) issues appear to have been closing the conceptual gap between jurisdictions on both sides of the Atlantic.[2]

---

* I would like to thank Mr Johannes Koch for valuable research assistance. I would also like to thank participants at the conference 'The Public Company: How 'Public' Is It?', organized at Eberhard-Karls-University on 23 and 24 June 2022, where a first version of this chapter was presented, and seminars at the University of North Carolina at Chapel Hill Law School, the London School of Economics and Political Science, and University of Cambridge Faculties of Law for numerous insightful comments. Special thanks to Patrick Corrigan, Edward Rock, Christine Osterloh-Konrad, Louise Gullifer, David Kershaw, Amir Licht, Yaron Nili, Felix Steffek, Eva Micheler, Niamh Moloney, Jo Braithwaite, Sarah Paterson, Eva Micheler, Philipp Paech, and Roy Shapira for very helpful input. All internet sources were last accessed on 10 January 2024.

[1] To quote the definition developed in European Commission, 'Green Paper: Promoting a European framework for Corporate Social Responsibility' COM(2001) 366 final (18 July 2001) para 20: 'Most definitions of corporate social responsibility describe it as a concept whereby companies integrate social and environmental concerns in their business operations and in their interaction with their stakeholders on a voluntary basis.'

[2] Despite (or perhaps because of) an abundant literature, the exact meaning of, and delineation between, the concepts of 'corporate purpose', 'corporate social responsibility' and 'environmental, social and governance' issues (ESG) still remains somewhat obscure. At the same time, the question whether—and if so, to what extent—stakeholder considerations can and should be accepted to be integral in the economic and societal functions of corporations clearly is a common denominator. Given this chapter's focus on practical consequences in terms of directors' duties, not on the ideological and doctrinal foundations, the concepts will therefore be treated—admittedly in gross simplification—not as identical, but still as emanations of essentially similar approaches to the (re-)interpretation of fundamental principles of corporate law and corporate governance: approaches that may aptly be referred to as taking a 'stakeholderist' (as opposed to shareholder-oriented) view of public corporations. cf R Eccles, C Mayer, and J Stroehle, 'The Difference Between Purpose and Sustainability (aka ESG)', Harvard Law School Forum on Corporate Governance (20 August 2021) https://corpgov.law.harvard.edu/2021/08/20/the-difference-between-purpose-and-sustainability-aka-esg. For the origins of the broader concept of ESG cf UN Global Compact, 'Who Cares Wins: Connecting Financial Markets to a Changing World: Recommendations to better integrate environmental, social and governance issues in financial analysis, asset management and securities

Notably, the range of relevant stakeholders, across all dimensions of the debate, goes far beyond traditional interpretations of that term (and, indeed, of whose interests may have to be protected by law). While traditional concepts, by and large, would have been confined to a corporation's creditors and workforce, relevant stakeholder groups, for the purposes of the current debate, include essentially all individuals (even remotely) affected by the impact of the corporation's commercial activities, irrespective of the legal nature of that relationship. Within the European Union, recent legislative initiatives will reinforce a trend towards the regulation of corporate behaviour in the interest of stakeholders. These go beyond mere external regulation in that they directly change, or impact on, corporate governance structures—and come with additional duties for corporate directors in this regard. In the United States, by contrast, the legislator or, indeed, regulatory bodies for a long time refrained from imposing specific ESG-related obligations on corporations and their boards and kept public interest regulation outside the realm of general corporate law,[3] while the draft Restatement of the Law, Corporate Governance, expressly recognizes the legality of the inclusion of specific stakeholder concerns in corporate decisions to a limited extent, but no positive obligations in that regard.[4]

From a European perspective, in view of a steadily growing body of relevant laws and regulations, it is certainly tempting to interpret what has been aptly termed

---

brokerage Recommendations by the financial industry to better integrate environmental, social and governance issues in analysis, asset management and securities brokerage' (2004) https://www.unepfi.org/fileadmin/events/2004/stocks/who_cares_wins_global_compact_2004.pdf. By contrast, the term CSR has a much longer tradition and can be traced back to the 1950s. cf HR Bowen, *Social Responsibilities of the Businessman* (University of Iowa Press 1953). For further discussion cf eg AB Carroll, 'A History of Corporate Social Responsibility: Concepts and Practices' in A Crane and others (eds), *The Oxford Handbook of Corporate Social Responsibility* (OUP 2008) 19; Klaus J Hopt, Chapter 2 in this volume; D Melé, 'Corporate Social Responsibility Theories' in *The Oxford Handbook of Corporate Social Responsibility*, ibid, 47; WG Ringe, 'Investor-led Sustainability in Corporate Governance' (2022) 7(2) Annals of Corporate Governance 2, 7–13; MJ Roe, 'Corporate Purpose and Corporate Competition' (2021) 99 Washington University Law Review 223, 232–36. Specifically on the concept(s) of corporate purpose cf eg JE Fisch and SD Solomon, 'Should Corporations Have a Purpose?' (2021) 99 Texas Law Review 1309; AN Licht, 'Varieties of Shareholderism: Three Views of the Corporate Purpose Cathedral' in E Pollman and R Thompson (eds), *Research Handbook on Corporate Purpose and Personhood* (Edward Elgar Publishing 2021) 387; E Pollman, 'The History and Revival of the Corporate Purpose Clause'(2021) 99 Texas Law Review 1423; H Spamann and J Fisher, ch 3 in this volume. The concept of 'corporate purpose' as a catchword for a broader stakeholder orientation has been promoted, in particular, by Colin Mayer. see Colin Mayer, *Prosperity: Better Business Makes the Greater Good* (OUP 2018); Colin Mayer, 'The Future of the Corporation and the Economics of Purpose' (2021) 53 Journal of Management Studies 887; Colin Mayer, 'What is Wrong with Corporate Law? The Purpose of Law and the Law of Purpose' ECGI Law Working Paper 649/2022 http://ssrn.com/abstract_id=4136836. For a useful, albeit already outdated, survey of the abundant literature see D Burand and A Tucker, 'Legal Literature Review of Social Entrepreneurship and Impact Investing (2007–2017): Doing Good by Doing Business' (2019) 11 William & Mary Business Law Review 1.

[3] On June 2022 the Securities Exchange Commission (SEC) published proposed amendments to its rules under the Securities Act of 1933 and the Securities Exchange Act of 1934 requiring corporations to provide certain climate-related information in their registration statements and annual reports. See https://www.sec.gov/rules/proposed/2022/33-11042.pdf. Following a host of controversial comments on this proposal (https://www.sec.gov/comments/s7-10-22/s71022.htm), the final rule was adopted only on 6 March 2024 (see https://www.federalregister.gov/documents/2024/03/28/2024-05137/the-enhancement-and-standardization-of-climate-rela ted-disclosures-for-investors). For a critical analysis of that move see eg PG Mahoney and JD Mahoney, 'The New Separation of Ownership and Control: Institutional Investors and ESG' (2021) 2 Columbia Business Law Review 841.

[4] For a detailed analysis see American Law Institute (ALI), 'Restatement of the Law, Corporate Governance: Tentative Draft No. 1' (April 2022) 25–58.

'stakeholderism'[5]—claims promoting an increasing role of stakeholder interests in the formation of business decisions in a broad sense, including positive obligations of corporate directors to that effect—as a *regulatory* trend, reflecting a number of complex policy movements that have been triggered and promoted by influential stakeholder groups, prominent academics, and, ultimately, implemented and enforced by the European legislator responding to public and academic pressure. Indeed, it has been stated that the responsibility of corporations for the protection of stakeholder interests is, and should be, to a large extent a *voluntary* matter, driven, not least, by the insight that greater awareness for stakeholder interests contributes not only to the public good but also creates more beneficial investment and business environments that would ultimately also enhance the individual prosperity of each particular firm.[6] At the same time, it is evident that the European Union in particular has been asserting its ambition to reinforce (perceived) market trends to that effect through public regulation, whose potential—particularly where coupled with effective sanctions—as a source of new obligations that may result in substantial changes to residual incentive structures of corporate directors can hardly be overestimated.

Indeed, awareness of the broader societal implications of corporate behaviour has, for a long time already, translated into demand for 'sustainable' products and investment opportunities on the part of consumers and private investors irrespective of the existence of applicable laws and regulations, and independently from their emergence. As evidenced, for example, by a host of providers of ESG ratings (applying a vast range of highly diverse criteria),[7] but also by a growing number of industry-driven standards in the field, the growing influence of 'stakeholderism' certainly has resulted from market pressure (through direct or indirect, collective investment) as well as from legal and/or regulatory influence[8]—and can thus be interpreted *both* as a 'bottom-up' phenomenon *and* as 'top-down' regulation. Likewise, the most prominent expression by corporate directors in support of stakeholder orientation published so far—the 2019 (re)Statement on the Purpose of a Corporation issued by the 'Business Roundtable' (an association of chief executive officers of major US companies)[9]—can be perceived as a reaction to market pressure. This holds true irrespective of whether that statement

---

[5] See eg LA Bebchuk and R Tallarita, 'The Illusory Promise of Stakeholder Governance' (2020) 91 Cornell Law Review 106.

[6] cf, characteristically, European Commission (n 1) para 21: 'Being socially responsible means not only fulfilling legal expectations, but also going beyond compliance and investing "more" into human capital, the environment and the relations with stakeholders. The experience with investment in environmentally responsible technologies and business practice suggests that going beyond legal compliance can contribute to a company's competitiveness. Going beyond basic legal obligations in the social area, e.g. training, working conditions, management-employee relations, can also have a direct impact on productivity. It opens a way of managing change and of reconciling social development with improved competitiveness.'

[7] On ESG ratings see eg F Berg, JF Kölbel, and R Rigobon, 'Aggregate Confusion: The Divergence of ESG Ratings' (2022) 26 Review of Finance 1315; M Billio and others, 'Inside ESG Ratings: (Dis)agreement and performance' (2021) 28 Corporate Social Responsibility and Environmental Management 1426.

[8] For examples cf eg V Harper Ho and S Kim Park, 'ESG Disclosure in Comparative Perspective: Optimizing Private Ordering in Public Reporting' (2019) 41 University of Pennsylvania Journal of International Law 249, 293–94; Mahoney and Mahoney (n 3) 842–54.

[9] Business Roundtable, 'Statement on the Purpose of a Corporation' https://s3.amazonaws.com/brt.org/May-2022BRTStatementonthePurposeofaCorporationwithSignatures.pdf (19 August 2019).

should be interpreted as reflecting a genuine commitment to an increased protection of stakeholder interests[10]—or rather as an inconsequential public-relations statement, intended to 'deflect regulatory pressure (on environmental, labor, privacy, and other pressing issues) by introducing hopes that corporations would address concerns about stakeholders on their own without the need for government intervention',[11] ultimately serving the private interests of corporate directors and reducing shareholder control.[12] And it holds true irrespective of whether or not investor-driven initiatives promoting increased protection of stakeholder interests have actually been effective.[13]

Given the intensity of the debate, the sheer number and the diversity of actors involved, and the dynamic evolution of relevant standards and performance criteria by supranational organizations, international standard-setters as well as by industry and investor organizations, it is, at the same time, striking and hardly surprising that the results, as far as their implications for the legal position of corporate directors are concerned, remain rather obscure. Both from an investors' perspective *and* measured against public policy objectives, a host of empirical studies[14] appear to suggest that, for all the seemingly consistent support of stakeholder-orientation as a guiding principle of modern corporate governance and market-based investment, the causal link between adherence to relevant standards (whatever they may be) and the outcome in terms of both relevant stakeholder interests and the profitability of firms remains obscure. From a directors' perspective, this has resulted in growing uncertainty as to the implications in terms of the overall orientation of their obligations vis-à-vis firms and shareholders. Essentially, this uncertainty boils down to four interrelated questions. Is it within the powers of corporate directors to cater for stakeholder interests in their business decisions? If so—what are the limits? And are there any *positive* obligations in this regard? Above all—have market trends and/or new regulatory requirements

---

[10] cf reviewing initial press coverage and the subsequent discussion eg LA Bebchuk and R Tallarita, 'Will Corporations Deliver Value to All Stakeholders?' (2022) 75 Vanderbilt Law Review 1031, 1034–35. See also EB Rock, 'For Whom Is the Corporation Managed in 2020? The Debate over Corporate Purpose' (2021) 76 Business Lawyer 363, 364–67.

[11] Bebchuk and R Tallarita (n 10) 1042.

[12] ibid. See also Bebchuk and R Tallarita (n 5); LA Bebchuk and R Tallarita, 'The Perils and Questionable Promise of ESG-Based Compensation' (2022) 48 Journal of Corporation Law 37, 42–43.

[13] For sceptical assessments in this regard cf eg P Brest, RJ Gilson, and MA Wolfson, 'How Investors Can (and Can't) Create Social Value' (2018) 44 Journal of Corporation Law 205; JR Macey, 'ESG Investing: Why Here? Why Now?' (2022) 19 Berkeley Business Law Journal 258. For a decidedly more optimistic view cf Ringe (n 2); see also M Becht, A Pajuste, and A Toniolo, 'Voice Through Divestment' ECGI Finance Working Paper 900/2023 https://ssrn.com/abstract=4386469 (arguing that the divestment movement in relation to producers of fossil fuels actually *has* had a visible impact on relevant stock prices). Specifically on the impact of institutional investors in this regard, cf A Dyck and others, 'Do Institutional Investors Drive Corporate Social Responsibility? International Evidence' (2019) 131 Journal of Financial Economics 693.

[14] Reflecting the intensity of the debate and the wide-spread support of stakeholder orientation in international fora, empirical studies addressing a wide range of assumptions and implications can be counted by the hundreds. Results so far have been controversial and inconclusive. For examples cf eg CE Bannier, Y Bofinger, and B Rock, 'Doing Safe by Doing Good: ESG Investing and Corporate Social Responsibility in the U.S. and Europe' (2023) 32 European Accounting Review 1; P Krüger, 'Corporate Goodness and Shareholder Wealth' (2015) 115 Journal of Financial Economics 304; A Ferrell, H Liang, and L Renneboog, 'Socially Responsible Firms' (2016) 122 Journal of Financial Economics 585; and cf, reviewing the available empirical literature, HB Christensen, L Hail, and C Leuz, 'Mandatory CSR and Sustainability Reporting: Economic Analysis and Literature Review' (2021) 26 Review of Accounting Studies 1176; G Friede, T Busch, and A Bassen, 'ESG and financial performance: aggregated evidence from more than 2000 empirical studies' (2015) 5 Journal of Sustainable Finance & Investment 210.

changed the traditional orientation of (fiduciary) duties of corporate directors to their firms?

Against this backdrop, the present chapter, focusing on listed (publicly held) companies, contributes to the emerging academic debate on the purpose of corporations and directors' duties in the light of a growing body of CSR- and ESG-related obligations in two fundamental respects. First, reviewing that debate in the light of the established controversy on the role of stakeholder interests in corporate governance more generally, it seeks to explore the dimension of potential implications on existing concepts of directors' (fiduciary) duties. Secondly, it examines how corporate directors, facing both existing and incoming regulatory requirements on the one hand and market pressure demanding increasing commitment to stakeholder concerns on the other hand, can be expected to respond, including by exploiting their discretionary powers through active participation in self-regulatory initiatives, in order to influence the interpretation of obligations they are expected to comply with. In this regard, the chapter critically examines the role of self-regulation and its potential to provide remedies to the residual uncertainties as to the legal position of corporate directors in an environment characterized by growing stakeholder orientation. It argues that, while self-regulatory initiatives on the part of market participants could, in principle, prove more effective than regulatory initiatives driven by national legislators and supra-national standard setters, their impact on both the economic performance of corporations and the protection of stakeholder interests could nonetheless be problematic, in view of potential difficulties to define and delineate the boundaries of 'sustainable' corporate behaviour—and in view of residual incentives to misuse the power of self-regulation for self-serving motives. The chapter thus ties in with a prominent critique of 'stakeholderism' in corporate law as inadequate and, indeed, potentially outright counterproductive.[15]

All in all, the chapter thus seeks to help improve understanding of (a) the substantive content of new stakeholder-oriented directors' duties (if any) in the light of established principles of corporate law, and (b) potential implications for the constitutional balance between shareholders and management of public corporations and the associated incentive structure of corporate directors. Throughout the chapter, the perspective is predominantly a European one: focusing on European regulatory trends and their implications on the constitutions of European companies, while the broader international context and comparative outlook on the situation in US law will be addressed where appropriate.

The remainder of the chapter is organized as follows. In order to prepare the ground for the subsequent legal analysis of the European regulatory framework, section II below recounts the historic evolution of shareholder orientation and stakeholder orientation as diverging paradigms for the interpretation and execution of corporate directors in different legal systems. As directors' duties, in the changing environment of increasing stakeholder orientation, are shaped by a dynamic interplay between established fundamental principles, an ever-growing number of relevant international

---

[15] For some of the most prominent critiques so far see Bebchuk and Tallarita (n 5); Bebchuk and Tallarita (n 10).

standards, their implementation by national and (within Europe) supra-national legislators and, last not least, market forces, section III then turns to an analysis of how exactly relevant norms and standards should be expected to work. On this basis, section IV discusses how corporate directors, in view of the regulatory framework and the incentive structure associated with it, may be expected to respond. Section V concludes.

## II. Stakeholderism versus Shareholderism: The Backdrop in Traditional Corporate Law Doctrine

### 1. New Stakeholderism and Established Principles of Corporate Governance: Where Are the Differences and What Is Actually New?

Whether conceived of as a market-driven phenomenon, triggered and fuelled by widespread concerns about the environmental and social implications of business activities among consumers and investors, or, alternatively, as a regulatory trend, the impact and implications of 'stakeholderism' within the meaning roughly defined above cannot be assessed without taking into account the broader legal environment and, in particular, doctrinal differences in terms of the orientation of directors' duties across different jurisdictions. Over time, jurisdictions have developed diverging concepts of the fundamental objectives to be pursued in corporate decisions. At first sight, the claim that corporate directors are—or should be—required to take into account and, indeed, protect stakeholder interests when exercising their business judgment (whether as a result of general fiduciary duties or otherwise) will be perceived to be more controversial within the context of a corporate law framework that traditionally adheres to strict shareholder orientation than within a setting where the protection of stakeholder interests has been recognized as part of the responsibilities of corporate directors.

On closer inspection, however, the traditional conceptual approaches appear to differ gradually rather than fundamentally, and their implications for the assessment of CSR- or ESG-related policies and business decisions may therefore be less dramatic than would appear at first sight. Indeed, the growing influence of 'stakeholderism', in particular following the 2019 statement of the Business Roundtable,[16] has been perceived as a deviation from the fundamental principle of shareholder orientation long established in the majority of US corporate laws and mainstream US corporate law doctrine.[17] At the same time, it has been pointed out that the doctrine of strict shareholder supremacy, while widely recognized in corporate law theory, has been contested repeatedly ever since the seminal debate on the fundamental nature of directors'

---

[16] See n 9 and accompanying text.
[17] See also n 10 and accompanying text. For the majority view advocating strict shareholder orientation see eg FH Easterbrook and D Fischel, *The Economic Structure of Corporate Law* (HUP 1996) 37–38. However, for a broader restatement from a comparative perspective see also J Armour and others, 'What Is Corporate Law?' in Reinier Kraakman and others (eds), *The Anatomy of Corporate Law* (3rd edn, OUP 2017) 1, 22–24.

fiduciary duties between Professors Merrick Dodd and Adolph Berle in the early 1930s.[18] Moreover, it has been argued that US case law reality, applying state corporation laws generally respecting a substantial margin of appreciation under the different emanations of the 'business judgment rule', appears *not* to have followed an overly restrictive concept of shareholder orientation, and *not* to prohibit outright a broader interpretation of directors' duties that would include the recognition of stakeholder implications of business decisions.[19] By contrast, even jurisdictions where corporate directors are *not* subject to a formal standard of shareholder wealth maximization tend to uphold the notion that the economic welfare of the company should be the guiding objective to be pursued in all business decisions, and that the protection of stakeholder interests is permissible only if and to the extent compatible with that fundamental objective.[20]

If the rough sketch developed above holds true, different jurisdictions, while adhering to different conceptual interpretations of the fundamental orientation of directors' duties, can be said to reach not entirely dissimilar results when evaluating business decisions taken with stakeholders' interests in mind. Irrespective of the doctrinal gap between stakeholder and shareholder orientation as guiding principles, the pursuit of stakeholder interests by corporate directors, arguably, can be said to be consistent with established standards of corporate law if (and only if) *and* to the extent that it does respect the ultimate supremacy of the profitability of the company (and, thus, the investors' interest in maximizing their returns), which must not be jeopardized even in systems allowing for broader stakeholder orientation.[21]

Seen in this light, the true difference between shareholder and stakeholder orientation in terms of evaluating stakeholder-oriented business decisions may be found in different *modes of operationalization* rather than in different normative outcomes (that is to say, different substantive standards as to whether stakeholder concerns may motivate business decisions). Taking shareholder-oriented US corporate laws, as they have emerged since the 1930s, as an example, it appears that, for all the doctrinal commitment to a strict form of shareholder orientation as a guiding principle, a director determined (for whatever motive) to cater for specific stakeholder interests when

---

[18] See on the one hand AA Berle, 'Corporate Powers as Powers in Trust' (1931) 44 Harvard Law Review 1049; and AA Berle, 'For Whom Corporate Managers *Are* Trustees: A Note' (1932) 45 Harvard Law Review 1365(arguing in support of strict shareholder orientation, the recognition of shareholders as the sole beneficiaries of directors' in the exercise of their fiduciary powers, and, consequently, against broad discretion for directors to cater for stakeholder interests) and, on the other hand, EM Dodd Jr, 'For Whom Are Corporate Managers Trustees?' (1932) 45 Harvard Law Review 1145.

[19] See eg L Johnson, 'Corporate Law and the History of Corporate Social Responsibility' in H Wells (ed), *Research Handbook on the History of Corporate and Company Law* (Edward Elgar Publishing 2018), 570, 584–85; L Johnson, 'Relating Fiduciary Duties to Corporate Personhood and Corporate Purpose' in DG Smith and A Gold (eds), *Research Handbook on Fiduciary Law* (Edward Elgar Publishing 2016) 260. For an in-depth analysis of the diverse positions adopted by different US jurisdictions in this regard see also ALI (n 4) 28–29, 51–58, emphasizing (at 52) that 'shareholderist' jurisdictions tend to apply a stricter reasonableness test than 'stakeholderist' jurisdictions in relation to 'the utilization of corporate resources for public welfare, humanitarian, educational, or philanthropic purposes' rather than prohibiting them outright.

[20] For a good comparative analysis see eg C Gerner-Beuerle and M Schillig, *Comparative Company Law* (OUP 2019) 249–73. For the divergent positions in US corporate laws, cf ALI (n 4) and Armour and others (n 17).

[21] For an instructive comparison of stakeholder- and shareholder-oriented jurisdictions in the United States with regard to specific decisions cf ALI (n 4) 31–46.

making business decisions will not be hindered from doing so other than in exceptional circumstances, where relevant activities do not have positive implications for the corporation at all. This is so because courts will probably accept the argument that such decisions, based on the information available at the relevant time, could reasonably be regarded to be in the long-term interest of the corporation.[22] While applying a shareholder-oriented approach, relevant jurisdictions, in other words, appear to mollify the rigidity of that principle at the operational level; that is, when defining the margin of discretion granted under the business judgment rule. Under this approach, the scope for protection of stakeholder interests might be restricted as a matter of principle, but such protection ultimately will be granted—to some extent, subject to limitations—in the course of operationalization. German corporate law, to use a contrasting example, would be more flexible at the level of doctrinal principle, while restricting excessive discretion at the operational level, ie when applying the German adaptation of the business judgment rule.[23] According to the prevailing interpretation of these principles, the substantive content of business decisions remains within the discretion of directors, but the (profitability) interest of the corporation generally prevails.[24]

Indeed, '*normative* outcomes' within the meaning used above (referring to the normative standards by which specific decisions are being measured in legal practice) should not be confused with the substantive *economic* outcomes (referring to the de facto orientation of business decisions). Within a system expressly committed to the principle of shareholder supremacy, decisions may conceivably turn out to be geared more towards maximizing immediate financial returns than in a system favouring a broader stakeholder orientation, as business decisions will be oriented along that general principle, even if the standard of judicial review applied to individual business decisions may ultimately be similar in both settings.[25] In other words, even if the standard is relaxed in the course of operationalization in individual lawsuits (by respecting a certain margin of discretion for business judgments generally), requiring directors to adhere to a principle of strict shareholder orientation could result in different incentives—and, indeed, different substantive outcomes—than providing them with a margin of discretion with regard to the balance between shareholder and stakeholder interests in the first place. One possible explanation for that assumption could be found in the expressive function of the overarching normative objective.[26] Precisely because

---

[22] For a similar conclusion see CA Williams, 'Corporate Social Responsibility and Corporate Governance' in J Gordon and WG Ringe (eds), *Oxford Handbook of Corporate Law and Governance* (OUP 2018) 634, 672–74.

[23] To be found in s 93(1), sentence 2 of the Stock Corporation Act, whereby duties will not be deemed to have been breached in circumstances 'in which the member of the management board, in taking an entrepreneurial decision, was within their rights to reasonably assume that they were acting on the basis of adequate information and in the best interests of the company' (official translation of the Act https://www.gesetze-im-internet.de/englisch_aktg/englisch_aktg.html#p0536).

[24] Reviewing the academic literature and relevant case law see generally J Koch, *Aktiengesetz* (17th edn, CH Beck 2023), Commentary on § 76 Aktiengesetz (German Stock Corporation Act) paras 33–34, 36.

[25] This may, in fact, explain at least part of the controversial policy debate about the shareholder/stakeholder dichotomy in both law and economics.

[26] On the 'expressive' function of norms cf generally eg CR Sunstein, 'On the Expressive Function of Law' (1996) 144 University of Pennsylvania Law Review 2021; MD Adler, 'Expressive Theories of Law: A Skeptical Overview'

the shareholder supremacy paradigm could be interpreted as a signal that *any* decision other than one clearly favouring the maximization of shareholder wealth would not be consistent with the overall doctrine, it raises the stakes for the defence, or justification, of decisions whose economic impact cannot, or not easily, be explained as compliant with that objective, while deviations from that may appear more acceptable under a system where the balance of shareholder and stakeholder interests is left to the discretion of corporate directors in the first place.

Whether or not these assumptions hold true, remains a matter of speculation, of course, and the alternative assumption that the substantive content of business decisions might reflect general societal values rather than applicable normative standards is equally plausible, in which case the formulation of the standard as such—and, indeed, adjustments to that standard—would not matter much. It is perhaps worth noting, in this context, that the introduction of the concept of 'enlightened shareholder value' through section 172(1) of the UK Companies Act 2006, marking a doctrinal shift from a more shareholder-oriented paradigm, does not appear to have had a measurable impact in terms of actual substantive outcomes.[27] Against this backdrop, it is probably fair to conclude that the actual relevance of the fundamental doctrinal concept is as difficult to establish empirically as the notion that the application of the doctrine of pure shareholder orientation, in itself, should be condemned as harmful to the public good, as has been argued repeatedly by the advocates of CSR and the 'corporate purpose' movement.[28] In the absence of a detailed comparison of substantive solutions for specific scenarios (involving, for example, measures to protect the environment, support of workers' interests beyond working-place safety, support of minority groups, political donations, etc.), which would be outside the scope of the present chapter, a reliable assessment of the full dimension of similarities and differences between 'shareholderist' and 'stakeholderist' jurisdiction is impossible. For present purposes, however, it is sufficient to conclude that neither corporate law systems applying a shareholder supremacy standard nor those allowing for a greater role of stakeholder concerns can be said to prohibit the advancement of stakeholder interests *a limine*.[29]

---

(2000) 148 University of Pennsylvania Law Review 1363; ES Adler and RH Pildes, 'Expressive Theories of Law: A General Restatement' (2000) 148 University of Pennsylvania Law Review 1503; specifically in the context of directors' duties cf JC Lipson, 'The Expressive Functions of Directors' Duties to Creditors' (2007) 12 Stanford Journal of Law, Business, and Finance 224. An illustrative case in point is the argument that Delaware corporate law in general and its fiduciary directors' duties in particular ought the be interpreted as a narrative shaping corporate behaviour; cf EB Rock, 'Saints and Sinners: How Does Delaware Corporate Law Work?' (2010) 44 UCLA Law Review 1009.

[27] See section II.2.b) above, nn 38–39 and accompanying text.
[28] See eg the programmatic book by L Stout, *The Shareholder Value Myth: How Putting Shareholders First Harms Investors, Corporations, and the Public* (Barrett-Koehler 2010). And see Mayer, *Prosperity* (n 2); A Edmans, *Grow the Pie: How Great Companies Deliver Both Purpose and Profit* (CUP 2020).
[29] In the words of Edward Rock: 'While shareholder primacy is the best description of the (default) legal characteristics of the corporate form, one should not think that the [principle] will decide more than it decides': see Rock (n 10) 375.

## 2. Some Implications

The foregoing analysis, if correct, arguably holds a number of important implications for present purposes, which may considerably improve our understanding of the issues involved.

a) Explaining the US conundrum: why are stakeholder concerns (apparently) so prominent in a system of strict shareholder orientation?

For a start, the considerations above may help to understand what could be described as the US conundrum, that is, the somewhat puzzling question why even those US jurisdictions which adhere to the principle of strict shareholder orientation, to date, appear to have been rather tolerant of declarations of commitment to the protection of stakeholder interests—as reflected, for example, in the 2019 statement promulgated by the Business Roundtable, but also in countless individual statements on the advancement of stakeholder interests in the operations of public corporations. If the principle of shareholder orientation were as strictly upheld in legal practice as some of its advocates seem to suggest, it would undoubtedly leave no room for the reinterpretation of the corporate purpose as reflected in that prominent display of 'stakeholderism', and any director promoting that view might be expected to be reigned in by liability lawsuits before long. At the same time, the above analysis could help to understand why the *actual* impact of such commitments for the relevant stakeholder groups, despite all the fanfare associated with their announcement, appears to have been limited so far.[30] *If* the decision whether and to what extent business decisions should cater for stakeholder interests is left to the discretion of directors, one should not wonder that such discretion also allows directors to fall short of their own commitments to further the public good.

However, while general principles of US corporate laws—irrespective of the relevant jurisdiction's fundamental orientation as 'shareholderist' or 'stakeholderist'—thus appear to *facilitate* the inclusion of stakeholder concerns into corporate decision-making, none of the considerations above actually explain *why* stakeholder orientation has come to feature so prominently in contemporary US corporate law debates. In the absence of regulatory requirements to take into account specific stakeholder interests or, at least, disclose information on relevant strategies and activities, the increasing trend to cater for such interests—and to promote a reorientation of established standards of conduct in this regard—certainly cannot be explained on the grounds of compliance needs. As laws and regulations do not (yet) provide any specific substantive and/or disclosure obligations relating to CSR or ESG matters, the *failure* to expand the scope of corporate decisions beyond (long-term) profit maximization certainly would

---

[30] According to recent studies, corporations whose CEOs participated in the Business Roundtable's 2019 statement have failed to adopt any changes to existing corporate documents and business models. See LA Bebchuk and R Tallarita, 'Will Corporations Deliver Value to All Stakeholders?' (2022) 75 Vanderbilt Law Review 1031; LA Bebchuk, K Kastiel, and R Tallarita, 'Stakeholder Capitalism in the Time of COVID' (2023) Yale 40 Journal on Regulation 60.

not carry any sanctions by law. Instead, the recent trend towards 'stakeholderism', as discussed above,[31] probably has to be interpreted as reflecting a combination of market pressure, exercised, inter alia, by investor demand, market pressure, activist shareholders, and, perhaps, the desire to *avoid* specific regulation on the part of corporate boards.[32]

Against this backdrop, the current situation in US corporate law debate should be read as evidence that the impact of 'stakeholderism' on the actual governance of relevant firms in general, and its implications on directors' duties in particular, cannot meaningfully be assessed without regard to the *general* corporate governance framework established in relevant jurisdictions.[33] In this regard, it is worth noting that specific voting proposals submitted by activist shareholders, advocating environmental and/or social stakeholder interests, appear to have played a significant role as drivers of the debate in publicly held US corporations in recent years.[34] Irrespective of whether or not such initiatives were ultimately successful, their very existence—and thus, the existence of a shareholder voting system which facilitates the submission and promotion of shareholder proposals in the way established in US corporations generally—arguably has been instrumental for the promotion of CSR- or ESG-related matters in recent years, and has played a formative role for the incentive structure of corporate directors as a result. In an environment like this, where 'stakeholderism' can be characterized as a 'bottom-up' phenomenon, the implications of relevant initiatives on the legal position of directors inevitably will look very different from an environment where relevant *positive* obligations are imposed by laws and regulations, not least because directors' liability as a potential sanction will hardly play a role.

b) Understanding the full dimension: what is actually new?

Even more importantly, the findings developed above may be useful in facilitating a better understanding of the full dimension of the recent trend towards enhanced stakeholder orientation generally, particularly in jurisdictions where—like in the European Union—this trend is driven, to a large extent, by mandatory legislation and regulation. If corporate laws world-wide, irrespective of the underlying doctrinal background, have been tolerant of the advancement of stakeholder interests to the extent that such advancement could reasonably be argued to be broadly consistent with the overarching objective of (long-term) profitability, growing awareness of stakeholder implications of business decisions and corporate behaviour among corporate directors cannot, as such, be interpreted as a deviation from, or in conflict with, established principles. Nor is it inconsistent with such principles if such growing awareness results in specific corporate decisions that would have been hardly conceivable, say, a decade or so

---

[31] See nn 8–13 above and accompanying text.

[32] For an insightful discussion of potential means of enforcement of ESG standards cf R Shapira, 'Mission Critical ESG and the Scope of Director Oversight Duties' (2022) 2 Columbia Business Law Review 734.

[33] For a very general analysis in this respect see also AK Buchholtz, JA Brown, and KM Shabana, 'Corporate Governance and Corporate Social Responsibility' in A Crane and others (eds), *The Oxford Handbook of Corporate Social Responsibility* (OUP 2008) 327, 334–36.

[34] cf sources cited in n 8 above.

ago, always provided that that decision, directly or indirectly, is ultimately motivated by enhancing the profitability of the company in the long term. Relevant examples may include measures to reduce environmental consequences of business activities beyond the absolute minimum, or to improve labour relations beyond mandatory legal requirements, funding programs to protect the interests of specific minority groups, or donations to philanthropic organizations.[35]

A particularly clear-cut case, in this regard, is business decisions motivated by demand-side pressure. Imagine, for example, that the management of a major clothing retailer decides to substitute their existing suppliers in emerging markets, in the face of increased pressure by human rights groups pointing to hazardous working conditions and/or specific requests or complaints by a growing number of customers, and to enter into contracts with other suppliers who produce according to higher standards. The decision to use such more expensive sources, irrespective of its immediate effect on the corporation's revenues, is likely to be upheld also within a system of strict shareholder orientation, as courts would respect the business judgment that such a move ultimately will be in the corporate interest.[36] By contrast, claims that stakeholder concerns should—always or in specific scenarios—prevail over, or rank on par with, the conflicting interest in maximizing the profitability of the corporation clearly are inconsistent both with corporate law systems adhering to the principle of shareholder supremacy *and* with those systems that have traditionally allowed for some discretion to directors to balance shareholder and stakeholder interests already at the normative level.

Against this backdrop, it would be misleading to conclude, as has been suggested,[37] that recent claims for enhanced 'stakeholderism' were entirely consistent with established principles of corporate law. While it is certainly true that corporate law standards will usually require the directors to take into account all (foreseeably) relevant implications of business decisions, including for stakeholders, such obligations— again, irrespective of the doctrinal background—thus far appear to have been focused on those implications that are actually relevant to the financial position of the company. This is entirely consistent with the notion of 'enlightened shareholder value', a concept first developed in two papers by Michael Jensen on the trade-offs between value maximization and the role of stakeholder interests published in 2002 and 2010[38]

---

[35] For similar conclusions from a US perspective (with a focus on Delaware law) see Rock (n 10) 375–76.
[36] Reaching a similar conclusion for specific scenarios see ALI (n 4) 31–33; Rock (n 10).
[37] See prominently C Mayer, 'Shareholderism versus Stakeholderism: A Misconceived Contradiction. A Comment on "The Illusory Promise of Stakeholder Governance" by Lucian Bebchuk and Roberto Tallarita' (2021) 106 Cornell Law Review 1860.
[38] MC Jensen, 'Value Maximization, Stakeholder Theory, and the Corporate Objective Function' (2002) 12 Business Ethics Quarterly 235 and (2010) 22 Journal of Applied Corporate Finance 32, respectively. For a discussion of the concept in the present context see also G Ferrarini, 'Redefining Corporate Purpose: Sustainability as a Game Changer' in D Busch, G Ferrarini, and S Grünewald (eds), *Sustainable Finance in Europe* (Palgrave Macmillan 2021) 85, 88–91, 96–108; V Harper Ho, '"Enlightened Shareholder Value": Corporate Governance Beyond the Shareholder-Stakeholder Divide' (2010) 36 Journal of Corporation Law 59. For a critical analysis from a US perspective cf DS Lund, 'Enlightened shareholder value, stakeholderism, and the quest for managerial accountability' in E Pollman and RB Thompson (eds), *Research Handbook on Corporate Purpose and Personhood* (Edward Elgar Publishing 2021)

and incorporated into the UK Companies Act 2006[39] on the recommendation of the Company Law Review Committee on the basis of a comprehensive evaluation of English case law and academic contributions.[40] According to established standards, a corporate director would thus not just be prohibited, as a rule, to attach greater weight to *stakeholder* interests than to the financial interests of his or her corporation when preparing and taking business decisions. Moreover, corporate directors, under this standard, would *not* be subject to a *positive* obligation (*qua* fiduciary or other duties rooted in corporate law) to take specific steps to protect such interests if and to the extent that these interests could not reasonably be argued to have an impact on the corporation's financial position.

To illustrate the point yet further, *refraining* from potentially lucrative business opportunities involving potentially abusive or otherwise detrimental labour conditions in other parts of the world may be a perfectly defensible decision under the applicable standard of care and in recognition of the wide margin of discretion under modern business judgment rules (eg in view of potentially adverse reactions by consumers or stakeholder initiatives which may come with a reputational damage).[41]

A *positive* obligation *not to use* such business opportunities, by contrast, has *not* been recognized under traditional concepts so far, regardless of the relevant doctrinal background. Likewise, *positive* obligations to systematically explore and assess such implications on an ongoing basis—including with regard to implications not just of their own company's activities, but also of activities of suppliers in a value chain[42]—or to take organizational steps to obtain and process relevant information, or liaise with, potentially affected stakeholders would go beyond what can be described as established principles of law in *any* traditional doctrinal background. Imposing such *positive* duties on corporate directors would deviate from established principles of law, irrespective of whether compliance with such duties would come with measurable costs for their respective corporation.

---

[39] See UK Companies Act, s 172(1), whereby '[a] director of a company must act in the way he considers, in good faith, would be *most likely to promote the success of the company for the benefit of its members as a whole*, and *in doing so have regard* (amongst other matters) to (a) the likely consequences of any decision in the long term, (b) the *interests of the company's employees*, (c) the need to foster the company's business relationships with suppliers, customers and others, (d) the *impact of the company's operations on the community and the environment*, (e) the desirability of the company maintaining a reputation for high standards of business conduct, and (f) the need to act fairly as between members of the company' (emphasis added). For critical (and controversial) evaluations of this provision see eg N Grier, 'Enlightened shareholder value: did directors deliver?' (2014) 2 Juridical Review 95; A Keay, 'Having Regard for Stakeholders in Practising Enlightened Shareholder Value' (2019) 19 Oxford University Commonwealth Law Journal 118; A Keay and H Zhang, 'An Analysis of Enlightened Shareholder Value in Light of Ex Post Opportunism and Incomplete Law' (2011) 8 European Company and Financial Law Review 445; R Williams, 'Enlightened Shareholder Value in UK Company Law' (2012) 35 UNSW Law Journal 360.

[40] Company Law Review Steering Group, *Modern Company Law for a Competitive Economy: Developing the Framework* (Department of Trade and Industry 2000) chs 2, 3.

[41] On the (potential and actual) role of consumer demand cf NC Smith, 'Consumers as Drivers of Corporate Social Responsibility' in A Crane and others (eds), *The Oxford Handbook of Corporate Social Responsibility* (OUP 2008) 281.

[42] For a modern statutory version of such obligations under the incoming European Corporate Governance Due Diligence Directive see section III.2 above.

c) Understanding the nature of stakeholder-related directors' duties

Importantly, and related to the foregoing, the differences between stakeholder- and shareholder oriented concepts of directors' duties are, to some extent, balanced out by a feature common to both. As discussed above, both concepts promoting a (nominally) strict shareholder orientation and those allowing for a greater role of stakeholder interests in the formation of business decisions have always been, by and large, permissive, not restrictive. Across jurisdictions, the definition of directors' duties has served to delineate the limits of what office holders can do, while their *general* obligation to exercise these powers in a way beneficial to the company has never been questioned. Directors' duties, in both corporate law systems to date, have consisted of general duties of care (fiduciary duties) rather than specific obligations with a prescriptive positive content. Exceptions—for example, a duty to file for bankruptcy proceedings in the interest of the company's creditors once statutory triggers such as balance-sheet insolvency or illiquidity are met—do exist, of course, but they have been limited in scope and generally been the outcome of a 'sedimentation' of findings established in successive cases into statutory law.[43] Generally speaking, corporate directors, irrespective of the doctrinal orientation of their respective jurisdiction, have been subjected to a general standard of care, by which individual decisions would be measured if contested (for example in liability actions), while the specific content of business decisions (in whatever context) has been left to their discretion. While public law regulation, addressing the respective company (which directors are, of course, bound to comply with) is perfectly consistent with this regime, the incorporation of public interest concerns *into* the corporate law (fiduciary) duties of directors is not.

This regulatory concept can be explained on the grounds of the historic emanation of such duties in fiduciary law. Traditionally, across a wide range of jurisdictions at least (and not just in common law jurisdictions), the role of corporate directors and their obligations vis-à-vis the company itself, its shareholders and, to some extent, external stakeholders such as creditors, has been conceived as fiduciary in nature.[44] Just as with other types of fiduciaries, the law would measure their activities by general standards of care derived from established principles of fiduciary law, which provide for restrictions for certain types of decisions (eg decisions motivated by conflicts of interests on the part of directors, or other decisions clearly incompatible with the interests of the beneficiary), but otherwise do not interfere with the fiduciary's discretion. Evidently, both the treatment of stakeholder interests in jurisdictions following the shareholder supremacy approach discussed above and the role of such interests in jurisdictions traditionally allowing for a broader stakeholder orientation are perfectly consistent with

---

[43] For a comparative analysis of the evolution of directors' duties in different corporate law regimes cf JH Binder, *Regulierungsinstrumente und Regulierungsstrategien im Kapitalgesellschaftsrecht* (Mohr Siebeck 2012) 506–37.

[44] ibid. For an in-depth analysis of US and English corporate law in this regard cf D Kershaw, *The Foundations of Anglo-American Corporate Fiduciary Law* (CUP 2018) 23–133; similarly, also including Australian law see JG Hill and M Conaglen, 'Directors' Duties and Legal Safe Harbours: A Comparative Analysis' in DG Smith and A Gold (eds), *Research Handbook on Fiduciary Law* (Edward Elgar Publishing 2016) 305; and see JG Hill, 'Corporations, Directors' Duties and the Public/Private Divide' in AB Laby and JH Russell (eds), *Fiduciary Obligations in Business* (CUP 2021) 285.

this tradition. As discussed above, *both* doctrinal backgrounds, for all their conceptual differences, allow for, and respect, a certain margin of discretion also with regard to the advancement of stakeholder interests through business decisions, while *both* have traditionally refrained from prescribing any specific normative content in this regard.

If the above analysis is true, claims for *enhanced* 'stakeholderism' and, specifically, for positive obligations—contrary to what has been argued in the existing literature[45]— cannot be described as consistent with established principles of corporate law from a functional perspective, or, to be more precise, from a *modal* perspective. *Positive* obligations to cater for stakeholder interests (in whatever form and however they may be enforced) as part of directors' duties under corporate law do not just deviate from the established substantive content of directors' duties; they also deviate from the traditional regulatory mode, adding entirely new *prescriptive* content and thus new exceptions to the general principle that directors' duties have traditionally been largely permissive, with only a few restrictive elements. Against this backdrop, claims for enhanced 'stakeholderism' reflect an understanding of the role of corporate law that fundamentally deviates from traditional interpretations, whereby directors are, by and large, free to define and implement business decisions as they think fit, within a very broad corridor, subject to only a limited range of restrictions established in the interest of the company, its shareholders and, to some extent, its creditors. Claims to the effect that corporate directors should *generally* be aware of a wide range of stakeholder interests, and should take measures—including by organizational arrangements—to protect them on an ongoing basis, by contrast, are effectively *regulatory* in nature; imposing such duties would mean no less than changing the established role of the law—and the very nature of directors' duties as they have evolved over the centuries.

As a consequence, in traditional systems of corporate law, whatever their doctrinal origins and orientation, it is perfectly legal (and, indeed, necessary) for corporate directors to respond to changing patterns in investor or consumer preferences which have an impact on the respective business models and, thus, its ultimate viability. Frontrunning such changes, in accordance with personal preferences, by promoting policies irrespective of their impact on the long-term profitability is not. In other words: The promotion of stakeholder interests as an objective separate from pursuing the long-term profitability of corporations would be entirely inconsistent with established principles.

d) Understanding the impact of 'stakeholderism' for 'stakeholderist' jurisdictions

Finally, all of the above considerations are also helpful in that they facilitate a better understanding of the (potential) impact of claims for enhanced stakeholder orientation in those jurisdictions which have traditionally rejected the concept of strict shareholder supremacy, and more open to the advancement of stakeholder interests in business decisions. German corporate law provides ample illustration in this regard. The concept of *strict* shareholder supremacy, which has also been advocated occasionally in

---

[45] See Mayer (n 37).

German academic literature,[46] has never been accepted as the guiding principle for the interpretation and application of general fiduciary duties of corporate directors, and the standard of care for the evaluation of business decisions has been defined so as also to include the protection of stakeholder interests.[47] However, irrespective of this doctrinal background, the surge in CSR-related (reporting) obligations has met with substantial criticism amongst German scholars, and the notion that, as a consequence, the traditional orientation of directors' duties ought to be reinterpreted so as to include *positive* obligations to cater for stakeholder interests under the German *Aktiengesetz* (the Stock Corporation Act)[48] has been largely rejected by the majority of legal scholars and has not been recognized in case law either.[49]

In view of the foregoing, the reasons are not difficult to understand. As discussed above, 'stakeholderist' jurisdictions, to use that misleading term again, traditionally may have taken a broader perspective as far as the role of stakeholder interests in the formation of business decisions (and, ultimately, in the definition of the purposes of company law more generally)[50] is concerned, but have *not* gone as far as to comprehensively subordinate the financial success of the company to any such external interests. As a consequence, the imposition of *positive* obligations to cater for stakeholder concerns inevitably has to be interpreted as a deviation from established practices also in such jurisdictions. This conclusion is, effectively, also reflected in the European Commission's recent consultation on the further development of European company law in order to enhance the sustainability of corporate governance arrangements, carried out between 2020 and 2021, which had solicited the respondents' views on whether companies environmental and social responsibilities should be bolstered through express and specific directors' obligations to that effect imposed by EU legislation[51]—thereby recognizing that the introduction of new obligations in the field would deviate from established concepts of corporate law and governance.

---

[46] cf eg PO Mülbert, 'Marktwertmaximierung als Unternehmensziel der Aktiengesellschaft' in G Crezelius, H Hirte, and K Vieweg (eds), *Festschrift für Volker Röhricht zum 65. Geburtstag* (Verlag Dr Otto Schmidt 2005) 421; see also C Kuhner, 'Unternehmensinteresse vs. Shareholder Value als Leitmaxime kapitalmarktorientierter Aktiengesellschaften' (2004) 33 Zeitschrift für Unternehmens- und Gesellschaftsrecht 244.

[47] See n 25 and accompanying text.

[48] For suggestions to that effect see eg Peter Hommelhoff, 'Nichtfinanzielle Ziele in Unternehmen von öffentlichem Interesse: Die Revolution über das Bilanzrecht' in Reinhard Bork and others (eds), *Festschrift für Bruno Kübler zum 70. Geburtstag* (CH Beck 2015) 291; Peter Hommelhoff, 'Nichtfinanzielle Unternehmensziele im Unionsrecht — Zwanzig Bemerkungen zum Kommissionsvorschlag für die Novellierung der 4. und 7. Bilanzrichtlinie vom April 2013' in Burkhard Boemke and others (eds), *Festschrift für Gerrick Frhr. von Hoyningen-Huene zum 70. Geburtstag* (CH Beck 2014) 137.

[49] For a comprehensive recent review of the literature and relevant case law see eg Koch (n 24) paras 35–35g.

[50] cf in this regard Armour and others (n 17) 23–24.

[51] For details see https://ec.europa.eu/info/law/better-regulation/have-your-say/initiatives/12548-Sustainable-corporate-governance/public-consultation_en. For critical analysis see G Ferrarini, M Siri, and S Zhu, 'The EU Sustainable Governance Consultation and the Missing Link to Soft Law' ECGI Law Working Paper 576/2021 https://ssrn.com/abstract=3823186. See also, analysing specific policy options in this respect, European Commission, 'Study on directors' duties and sustainable corporate governance: Final Report' (2020) 61–69. For a forceful critique of the study cf MJ Roe and others, 'The Sustainable Corporate Governance Initiative in Europe' (2021) 38 Yale Journal on Regulation 133.

## III. Which Duties? Emerging Obligations in the Light of Statutory Frameworks and International Standards—A European Perspective on a Global Trend

Against the backdrop developed above, the following section continues to explore the dimension of stakeholder-related directors' obligations by identifying specific prescriptive duties and analysing their functional characteristics. The section examines, first, the current position in European corporate law and incoming challenges (section 1 below) and, subsequently, relevant international standards (section 2 below), which have been incorporated by reference in a number of relevant obligations under European law. Adopting a functional perspective, the remainder of the section then analyses key characteristics of the relevant obligations under both regimes, and discusses potential implications for the addressees.

### 1. European Corporate and Non-financial Reporting Law

Within European Union law, specific prescriptive norms requiring the advancement of stakeholder interests have so far been limited to reporting obligations relating to issues of CSR, which, to date, continue to be prescribed mainly by what has become known as the Non-Financial Reporting Directive (NFRD) of 2014.[52] Even prior to the adoption of that instrument, European regulation of corporate accounting principles, going back to a Commission recommendation of 2001,[53] had required companies to disclose information relating to 'environmental and social aspects' as part of the management report in their annual accounts, but only to the extent 'necessary and for an understanding of the company's development, performance or position.'[54] In comparison with these earlier requirements, which continue to apply but have not been specified

---

[52] Directive 2014/95/EU of the European Parliament and of the Council of 22 October 2014 amending Directive 2013/34/EU as regards disclosure of non-financial and diversity information by certain large undertakings and groups [2014] OJ L330/1 (15 November 2014).

[53] Commission Recommendation of 30 May 2001 on the recognition, measurement and disclosure of environmental issues in the annual accounts and annual reports of companies [2001] OJ L156/33 (13 June 2001).

[54] See Directive 2003/51/EC of the European Parliament and of the Council of 18 June 2003 amending Directives 78/660/EEC, 83/349/EEC, 86/635/EEC and 91/674/EEC on the annual and consolidated accounts of certain types of companies, banks and other financial institutions and insurance undertakings [2003] OJ L178/16 (17 July 2003) recital 9: 'The annual report and the consolidated annual report are important elements of financial reporting. Enhancement, in line with current best practice, of the existing requirement for these to present a fair review of the development of the business and of its position, in a manner consistent with the size and complexity of the business, is necessary to promote greater consistency and give additional guidance concerning the information a "fair review" is expected to contain. The information should not be restricted to the financial aspects of the company's business. It is expected that, where appropriate, this should lead to an analysis of environmental and social aspects necessary for an understanding of the company's development, performance or position.' The new reporting requirements were then laid down in art 1(14) of Directive 2003/51/EC, amending Article 46 of the Fourth Council Directive 78/660/EEC of 25 July 1978 … on the annual accounts of certain types of companies [1978] OJ L222/11 (14 August 1978), as well as Article 2(10) of Directive 2003/51/EC, amending Article 36(1) of the Seventh Council Directive 83/349/EEC of 13 June 1983 based on Article 54(3)(g) of the Treaty on consolidated accounts [1983] OJ L193/1 (18 July 1983).

any further as such,[55] the 2014 NFRD went a substantial step further by requiring large listed companies (and certain financial intermediaries)[56] to include in the annual management report

> [a] non-financial statement containing information to the extent necessary for an understanding of the undertaking's development, performance, position and impact of its activity, relating to, as a minimum, environmental, social, and employee matters, respect for human rights, anti-corruption and bribery matters, including:
> (a) a brief description of the undertaking's business model;
> (b) a description of the policies pursued by the undertaking in relation to those matters, including due diligence processes implemented;
> (c) the outcome of those policies;
> (d) the principal risks related to those matters linked to the undertaking's operations including, where relevant and proportionate, its business relationships, products or services which are likely to cause adverse impacts in those areas, and how the undertaking manages those risks;
> (e) non-financial key performance indicators relevant to the particular business.[57]

Significantly, when reporting pursuant to that provision, 'undertakings may rely on national, Union-based or international frameworks, and if they do so, undertakings shall specify which frameworks they have relied upon'.[58] While refraining from defining any specific substantive duties in this regard, European law, through this latter provision, effectively referred to CSR standards promulgated by a wide range of international bodies, including, for example, European agencies, but also the United Nations (UN), the OECD, or the International Organization for Standardization.[59]

---

[55] See now art 19(1) subpara (3) of Directive 2013/34/EU of the European Parliament and of the Council of 26 June 2013 on the annual financial statements, consolidated financial statements and related reports of certain types of undertakings [2013] OJ L182/19 (29 June 2013).

[56] In the words of art 19a(1) of Directive 2013/34/EU as amended by Directive 2014/95/EU: 'large undertakings which are public-interest entities exceeding on their balance sheet dates the criterion of the average number of 500 employees'. 'Large undertakings' within that meaning are defined by art 3(4) of Directive 2013/34/EU as 'undertakings which on their balance sheet dates exceed at least two of the three following criteria: (a) balance sheet total: EUR 20 000 000; (b) net turnover: EUR 40 000 000; (c) average number of employees during the financial year: 250'. 'Public-interest entities', as defined by art 2(1) of Directive 2013/34/EU, are 'undertakings within the scope of Article 1 [which, in turn, is defined by reference to two Annexes of the Directive] which are: (a) governed by the law of a Member State and whose transferable securities are admitted to trading on a regulated market of any Member State; (b) credit institutions; (c) insurance undertakings; or designated by Member States as public-interest entities, for instance undertakings that are of significant public relevance because of the nature of their business, their size or the number of their employees'.

[57] Directive 2013/34/EU, art 19a(1) subpara (1), as introduced by art 1(1) of the CSR Directive.

[58] Directive 2013/34/EU, art 19a(1) subpara (5), as introduced by art 1(1) of the CSR Directive.

[59] CSR Directive, recital 9: 'In providing this information, undertakings which are subject to this Directive may rely on national frameworks, Union-based frameworks such as the Eco-Management and Audit Scheme (EMAS), or international frameworks such as the United Nations (UN) Global Compact, the Guiding Principles on Business and Human Rights implementing the UN 'Protect, Respect and Remedy' Framework, the Organisation for Economic Co-operation and Development (OECD) Guidelines for Multinational Enterprises, the International Organisation for Standardisation's ISO 26000, the International Labour Organisation's Tripartite Declaration of principles concerning multinational enterprises and social policy, the Global Reporting Initiative, or other recognised international frameworks.' By the same token, recital 11 also expressly refers to the influence of UN work in the field: 'Paragraph 47 of the outcome document of the United Nations Rio+20 conference, entitled "The Future We Want", recognises the importance of corporate sustainability reporting and encourages undertakings, where

Corresponding requirements were introduced for the consolidated annual accounts of corporate groups.[60] The European Commission, using its mandate under Article 2 of the CSR Directive, has promulgated non-binding complementary guidelines on non-financial reporting generally (in 2017),[61] as well as on specific aspects on reporting climate-related information (in 2019),[62] which reconfirm the general strategy to implement relevant international standards as part of the European law approach to CSR reporting.

Based on a Commission Proposal released in 2021,[63] which in turn reflects the Commission's ambitious agenda first published in 2011 and subsequently adjusted and expanded in scope in 2019/20,[64] the 2014 Directive has now been amended by a new Corporate Sustainability Reporting Directive (CSRD) of 2022.[65] Under the revised regime, the scope of application of CSR reporting requirements is far wider than under the 2014 CSR regime,[66] and has been extended to 'sustainability matters' more generally.[67] Moreover, the new Directive establishes a new framework for the development of 'sustainability reporting standards', whereby the European Commission will be empowered to adopt delegated legislation on reporting standards relating to environmental, social and governance factors. It will do so in consultation with the European Financial Reporting Advisory Group (EFRAG), an expert body established in 2001 to assist the European Commission in relation to the adaptation of international financial reporting standards.[68] Moreover, statutory audit requirements have also been expanded, in order to activate the (private sector) auditors as enforcers of relevant requirements.[69] All in all, the reformed regime develops its predecessor into a rather comprehensive set of new requirements, both substantive and procedural in nature,

appropriate, to consider integrating sustainability information into their reporting cycle. It also encourages industry, interested governments and relevant stakeholders with the support of the United Nations system, as appropriate, to develop models for best practice, and facilitate action for the integration of financial and non-financial information, taking into account experiences from already existing frameworks.'

[60] Directive 2013/34/EU, art 29a, as introduced by art 1(3) of the CSR Directive.
[61] European Commission, 'Communication from the Commission: Guidelines on non-financial reporting (methodology for non-financial reporting)' (2017/C/215/01) [2017] OJ C215/1 (5 July 2017).
[62] European Commission, 'Communication from the Commission: Guidelines on non-financial reporting: Supplement on reporting climate-related information' (2019/C 209/01) [2019] OJ C209/1 (20 June 2019).
[63] European Commission, 'Proposal for a Directive of the European Parliament and of the Council amending Directive 2013/34/EU, Directive 2004/109/EC, Directive 2006/43/EC and Regulation (EU) No 537/2014, as regards corporate sustainability reporting' COM(2021) 189 final (21 April 2021).
[64] See European Commission, 'Communication from the Commission to the European Parliament, the Council, the European Economic and Social Committee and the Committee of the Regions: A renewed EU strategy 2011–14 for Corporate Social Responsibility, COM(2011) 681 final (25 October 2011); European Commission and High Representative of the Union for Foreign Affairs and Security Policy, 'Joint Communication to the European Parliament and the Council: EU Action Plan on Human Rights and Democracy 2020–2024' (25 March 2020), JOIN(2020) 5 final; see also European Commission, 'Reflection Paper: Towards a Sustainable Europe by 2020'. Note that, in this context, the focus of specific measures to date has been primarily on the protection of global climate.
[65] Directive (EU) 2022/2464 of the European Parliament and of the Council of 14 December 2022 amending Regulation (EU) No 537/2014, Directive 2004/109/EC, Directive 2006/43/EC and Directive 2013/34/EU, as regards corporate sustainability reporting [2022] OJ L322/15 (16 December 2022).
[66] ibid, introducing a revised art 19a into Directive 2013/34/EU, whereby the scope would extend to 'large undertakings' generally as well as also to listed small and medium-sized companies.
[67] ibid. 'Sustainability matters are defined, in a broad sense as "environmental, social and human rights, and governance factors". cf Directive 2013/34/EU, art 1(2)(17), as introduced by Directive (EU) 2022/2464.
[68] ibid arts 29b, 29c (on 'corporate sustainability reporting standards' and 'corporate sustainability reporting standards for SMEs', respectively).
[69] ibid arts 26a, 27a, 28a, 36a.

much more detailed—and far wider in scope. The new regime also marks the shift from the traditional CSR focus to the broader concept of ESG, covering a considerably wider range of relevant issues.[70] From a functional perspective, however, the new Directive does not deviate from the established strategy of *indirect*, procedural regulation through the imposition and enforcement of reporting requirements, compliance with which will be based on a variety of international standards at the discretion of corporate management. Specifically, it does *not* impose any substantive duties of care with regard to individual stakeholder interests.

Taken together, European CSR and ESG law, as it currently stands, can thus be described as following a *procedural* rather than a substantive concept of *indirect* regulation. Rather than imposing more or less specific substantive requirements, large listed (and certain other) companies have been required merely to assess the implications of their business activities on certain stakeholder interests, adopt (unspecified) 'policies' in relation to such interests, and include relevant information in their annual accounts, and they may do so by way of reference to accepted international standards (which, as

---

[70] cf ibid art 29b(2): The sustainability reporting standards shall ensure the quality of reported information, by requiring that it is understandable, relevant, verifiable, comparable and represented in a faithful manner.

The sustainability reporting standards shall, taking into account the subject matter of a particular sustainability reporting standard:
  (a) specify the information that undertakings are to disclose about the following environmental factors:
      (i) climate change mitigation, including as regards scope 1, scope 2 and, where relevant, scope 3 greenhouse gas emissions;
      (ii) climate change adaptation;
      (iii) water and marine resources;
      (iv) resource use and the circular economy;
      (v) pollution;
      (vi) biodiversity and ecosystems;
  (b) specify the information that undertakings are to disclose about the following social and human rights factors:
      (i) equal treatment and opportunities for all, including gender equality and equal pay for work of equal value, training and skills development, the employment and inclusion of people with disabilities, measures against violence and harassment in the workplace, and diversity;
      (ii) working conditions, including secure employment, working time, adequate wages, social dialogue, freedom of association, existence of works councils, collective bargaining, including the proportion of workers covered by collective agreements, the information, consultation and participation rights of workers, work-life balance, and health and safety;
      (iii) respect for the human rights, fundamental freedoms, democratic principles and standards established in the International Bill of Human Rights and other core UN human rights conventions, including the UN Convention on the Rights of Persons with Disabilities, the UN Declaration on the Rights of Indigenous Peoples, the International Labour Organization's Declaration on Fundamental Principles and Rights at Work and the fundamental conventions of the International Labour Organization, the European Convention for the protection of Human Rights and Fundamental Freedoms, the European Social Charter, and the Charter of Fundamental Rights of the European Union;
  (c) specify the information that undertakings are to disclose about the following governance factors:
      (i) the role of the undertaking's administrative, management and supervisory bodies with regard to sustainability matters, and their composition, as well as their expertise and skills in relation to fulfilling that role or the access such bodies have to such expertise and skills;
      (ii) the main features of the undertaking's internal control and risk management systems, in relation to the sustainability reporting and decision-making process;
      (iii) business ethics and corporate culture, including anti-corruption and anti-bribery, the protection of whistleblowers and animal welfare;
      (iv) activities and commitments of the undertaking related to exerting its political influence, including its lobbying activities;
      (v) the management and quality of relationships with customers, suppliers and communities affected by the activities of the undertaking, including payment practices, especially with regard to late payment to small and medium-sized undertakings.

shall be discussed further below, do not define any specific positive obligations either). By requiring and enforcing transparency in this respect, the (reformed) CSR Reporting Directive clearly reflects the expectation that rising investor (and stakeholder) awareness of relevant policies would create market pressure and, by gearing investment towards companies with more sustainable business models, indirectly force management to adjust their behaviour accordingly.[71]

The actual impact of such requirements, however, remains as obscure as the incentives associated with them. As will have become clear from the wording of the relevant obligations, corporate directors retain a substantial margin of discretion not just with regard to the identification of relevant stakeholder interests and corresponding risks, but also to the development and substantive content of policies adopted to address them—as well as in relation to the content and granularity of the mandatory report. Although the new framework for the development of harmonized non-financial reporting standards certainly can be expected to drive the further convergence of market practices in this regard and (along with other legislative activities) may ultimately accomplish a higher level of standardization of relevant information, the core obligation essentially remains a duty to disclose intentions and policies rather than a duty to adopt specific measures for the protection of stakeholder interests with no real sanction other than the ultimate judgment of investors—whether or not these may ultimately turn out to appreciate the disclosed information and adjust their investments accordingly.[72]

## 2. New Horizons? Incoming Corporate Sustainability Due Diligence Legislation

The legislative self-restraint in terms of positive substantive duties may come to an end, however, with yet another Commission proposal adopted, namely the Corporate Sustainability Due Diligence Directive (CSDDD).[73] With this proposal, the final version of which has just been formally adopted, the European Commission, following up on international standards[74] and earlier legislation in a number of Member States,[75] proposed the introduction of substantive CSR due diligence obligations for certain corporations above certain quantitative thresholds.[76] The proposal first envisaged an

---

[71] For a comparative perspective on the European approach cf also Harper Ho and Park (n 8) 302–306.
[72] For the available empirical evidence see the sources cited in n 14 above.
[73] European Commission, Proposal for a Directive of the European Parliament and of the Council on Corporate Sustainability Due Diligence and amending Directive (EU) 2019/1937 COM(2022) 71 final (23 February 2022). As of 5 July 2024, the final version of the Directive has been adopted as Directive (EU) 2024/1760 of the European Parliament and of the Council of 13 June 2024 on corporate sustainability due diligence ( … ), OJ L 5 July 2024.
[74] See ibid 1–2.
[75] For an analysis of the general background see eg A Pietrancosta, 'Codification in Company Law of General CSR Requirements: Pioneering Recent French Reforms and EU Perspectives' ECGI Law Working Paper No 639/2022 (October 2022) 9–13, 21–22 https://ssrn.com/abstract=4083398. On the European Commission's preparatory study (n 71) see also MJ Roe and others, 'The Sustainable Corporate Governance Initiative in Europe' (2021) 38 Yale Journal on Regulation 133.
[76] For details see Commission Proposal (n 73) art 2a in conjunction with art 3(a): certain types of corporations with more than 500 employees on average and a net worldwide turnover of more than €150 million irrespective of their business activities or, alternatively, more than 250 employees and a net worldwide turnover of more than

obligation to 'integrate due diligence into all ... corporate policies and [to] have in place a due diligence policy'.[77] While this duty, which survived in a slightly revised form until the end of the legislative process, remains rather vaguely defined and does not prescribe specific substantive elements, corporations, under the Directive, will also be obliged to 'take appropriate measures to identify actual and potential adverse human rights impacts and adverse environmental impacts arising from their own operations or those of their subsidiaries and, where related to their value chains, from their established business relationships',[78] including consultations with potentially affected stakeholder groups in this context.[79] Moreover, corporations will also be required to take specific action in order 'to prevent, or where prevention is not possible or not immediately possible, adequately mitigate potential adverse human rights impacts and adverse environmental impacts that have been, or should have been, identified'[80] in the process just mentioned, and to bring to an end or 'neutralise' adverse effects in due course.[81] In addition to these obligations and complementing them, companies will be required to establish complaints procedures for aggrieved stakeholders,[82] to carry out periodic self-assessments with regard to their compliance,[83] and regularly to report on due diligence matters (if they are not subject to the reporting requirements under the NFRD).[84] Significantly, the draft Directive also provides for a rather complex sanctions and enforcement regime, including monitoring obligations for designated authorities in each Member State,[85] the obligation for Member States to provide for effective sanctions in their national laws,[86] and, above all, civil liability to aggrieved parties for breaches of specific due diligence obligations.[87] Going even further, Article 25 of the original Commission Draft then anticipated a rather fundamental amendment of existing company legislation by requiring that:

> 1. Member States shall ensure that, when fulfilling their duty to act in the best interest of the company, directors of companies ... *take into account the consequences of their decisions for sustainability matters*, including, where applicable, human rights, climate change and environmental consequences, including in the short, medium and long term [and]

---

€40 million, if at least 50 per cent of this turnover is generated in one or more designated sectors (eg manufacture of textiles, agriculture, fisheries, food products, extraction of mineral resources). In the final version of the Directive, the thresholds were raised to companies with more than 1,000 employees and a net world turnover of more than €450 million, without modifications for specific sectors.

[77] ibid art 5(1).
[78] ibid art 6(1), now art 8(1) of the final Directive.
[79] ibid art 6(4), see now art 13 of the final Directive.
[80] ibid art 7(1), now art 10(1) of the final Directive. This obligation is then specified further in the subsequent paragraphs, which provide for specific steps and required investments in this regard.
[81] ibid art 8, now art 11 of the final version of the Directive.
[82] ibid art 9, now art 14 of the final version of the Directive.
[83] ibid art 10, now art 15 of the final version of the Directive.
[84] ibid art 11, now art 16 of the final version of the Directive.
[85] ibid arts 17–19, cf now arts 24–27 of the final version of the Directive.
[86] ibid art 20, see now art 27 of the final version of the Directive.
[87] ibid art 22, see now art 29 of the final version of the Directive.

2. Member States shall ensure that their laws, regulations and administrative provisions providing for a breach of directors' duties apply also to the provisions of this Article.

Last but not least, Article 26 of the initial Proposal then required corporate directors to be personally responsible for compliance with due diligence duties. Interestingly, neither Article 25 nor Article 26 has survived the legislative process and was deleted in response to substantial criticism from individual Member States.

Measured against the *status quo ante* in European law, whose focus—as discussed above—has been on reporting obligations but left it to corporations and their directors to determine the substance of their engagement for stakeholder interests (if any), the new Directive clearly marks a drastic shift in the underlying regulatory paradigm. Addressees will be required to take specific and potentially costly steps with potentially detrimental effects on firms' profits. Although the restatement of directors' duties in Article 25 of the original Draft has been dropped from the table, directors of corporations falling within the Directive's scope of application would still, to some extent, be provided with a new compass: a new standard measure for corporate decision-making that will profoundly change their fiduciary duty towards the firm and, ultimately, the shareholders as beneficial owners, whether or not they consent.[88]

At the same time, it is striking that, for all its granularity, the new Directive still remains vague as to how exactly directors will be expected to behave, and could aptly be described as a rather peculiar arrangement of highly prescriptive obligations in vaguely defined terms. Key concepts determining the relevant obligations, such as 'appropriate measures', '(severe) adverse impacts', or the 'effectiveness' of policies and measures, have taken the form of general principles, which have to be interpreted and specified further in the course of application by addressees, the newly assigned national supervisory authorities, and, ultimately, the courts. Indeed, relevant obligations have been specified, to some extent, in the Annexes to the Directive, including by way of reference to specific international standards and agreements.[89] Nonetheless, as these standards themselves tend to be defined vaguely and focus on general principles and procedural standards rather than specific rules,[90] the resulting legal uncertainty can still be expected to be substantial.[91] It will be aggravated further by the fact that the relevant interests—environmental and social interests alike—may conflict and be difficult to balance, let alone reconcile, in the circumstances of each particular case.[92] Given, further, the uncertainties associated with (diverging national) requirements for the

---

[88] For further analysis see Pietrancosta (n 74) 56–57 (noting differences between European jurisdictions in this regard).

[89] See European Commission (n 73) Annex I.

[90] For further discussion see eg JH Binder, 'Neue Vielfalt der Regelgeber und Regelungstechniken im Gesellschafts- und Kapitalmarktrecht unter Einschluss des Bilanzrechts' (2022) Zeitschrift für Unternehmens- und Gesellschaftsrecht 502, 512–13.

[91] For further analysis see Pietrancosta (n 74) 29–37.

[92] cf eg AA Gözlügöl, 'The Clash of "E" and "S" of ESG: Just Transition on the Path to Net Zero and the Implications for Sustainable Corporate Governance and Finance' (2022) 15 Journal of World Energy Law & Business 1 (discussing potential conflicts between environmental and social interests in this regard).

assertion of civil liability as sanctions for (alleged) breaches of obligations under the new regime,[93] the challenges for directors seeking orientation can hardly be underestimated. Whether or not (and when) a consistent interpretation of these standards can be expected to emerge is as uncertain as the actual effectiveness in terms of greater awareness of stakeholder interests—and, indeed, in terms of substantial improvements with regard to their protection.

### 3. Europe and the Broader Picture: Parallels, Differences, and Substantive Outcomes

At first sight, European legislation may appear well in line with broader international trends towards greater awareness for stakeholder interests in corporate decision-making. This impression is certainly reinforced by the fact that already within the present framework of CSR- and ESG-related reporting obligations, but in particular under the Corporate Sustainability Due Diligence Directive, specific obligations refer to, and to some extent, effectively incorporate relevant standards promulgated by a broad range of international standard setters. Nonetheless, the European law approach to promoting stakeholder interests clearly stands out at least in one important respect.[94] Taken together, both under the existing (and recently reformed) framework governing disclosure of non-financial information and, in particular, under the incoming regime to be established by the CSDDD, it presents itself as distinctively regulatory in nature. Within this context, legal requirements for corporate decision-making—unlike under established principles of corporate governance—are regulated *not* primarily in the interest of the firm and its shareholders, but in order to *instrumentalize* them in the public interest. In stark contrast to the situation in US markets, business decisions and firm behaviour with regard to CSR- or ESG-related matters, under the European approach, will be motivated to an important degree *not* by *actual* demand for relevant policies, in response to *actual* investor and/or consumer pressure, but by compliance needs perceived or real. In the absence of effective representation of shareholders in corporate decision-making, the decision to invest or disinvest (directly or indirectly, through ESG-oriented funds) is essentially the only transmission mechanism for investors' ESG preferences. As noted above, CSR reporting obligations are meant to incentivize, and reinforce, market pressure by investors expressing their ESG preferences, but it remains uncertain whether or not this effect has been accomplished as intended, as a causal link between compliance with applicable standards and stock prices appears difficult to establish.[95] Indeed, it remains an open question whether or not legislative intervention is justifiable or even necessary in order to improve the standardization of relevant information and, thus, the comparability of investment opportunities in

---

[93] See also ibid 45–46.
[94] For a comparative analysis CF Harper Ho and Park (n 8).
[95] But see Becht, Pajuste, and Toniolo (n 13).

a setting where the markets themselves have failed to accomplish just that[96], and this chapter does not offer a final verdict in this respect. Arguably, however, there are solid reasons to assume that the instrumentalization of disclosure standards in order to incentivize investors and/or consumers in the form established within the EU, for the reasons stated above, has not been overly successful.

## IV. How Will They Respond? The Reorientation of Directors' Duties and Their Implications in the Real World

While actual outcomes—in terms of investor preferences and, ultimately, the economic outcome of existing and incoming regulation—are difficult to predict, some observations are nonetheless possible already on the basis of the above functional analysis. First and foremost, in a system characterized by prescriptive positive obligations, directors' incentives are likely to differ fundamentally from those in system where activist shareholders constitute the main driver. If strategic as well as individual business decisions with implications for the position of stakeholders will be made less in response to specific initiatives by investors or, for that matter, perceived investor preferences reflected in the stock price, but motivated by prescriptive regulatory obligations, the substantive content of such decisions can be expected to reflect, in addition to other motives, a strong desire to comply with such obligations (just) to the extent necessary to avoid sanctions. To put it differently, while directors facing pressure by activist investors may ask whether, and to what extent, they are entitled to act accordingly without risking a breach of fiduciary obligations geared towards ensuring the profitability of the firm, directors facing a complex set of prescriptive ESG reporting obligations are likely to do whatever they perceive to be necessary in order to be able to demonstrate compliance with these obligations, regardless of what their general obligation towards the firm may be, and regardless of actual substantive outcomes.

The substantive *economic* outcome of relevant decisions may look very different in these two scenarios, especially where—as has been diagnosed above both with regard to the existing European framework of CSR reporting obligations *and* with regard to the incoming Due Diligence Directive—the relevant obligations have been drafted in a way that leaves a substantial margin of discretion for management decisions. Business decisions driven by specific investor demand, for example, made upon successful votes in shareholder meetings, or motivated by changes in consumer behaviour, can be expected to take a rather specific form: by implementing new business models, specific activities, or strategies—or by adjusting, or giving up, old ones. As noted above, in the absence of regulatory intervention, whether or not firms will move towards more sustainable business models will depend, to a large extent, on actual investors' or consumers' preferences—in other words, on who invests in a firm, or who is willing (and

---

[96] For a detailed argument to that effect cf eg V Harper Ho, 'Modernising ESG Disclosure' [2022] University of Illinois Law Review 277; and see Park (n 8).

on what conditions) to purchase its products or services. While it remains dubious whether changes driven by investor demand come with actual benefits in terms of increased 'stakeholder value' also in these circumstances, the scope for decisions motivated exclusively by the directors' own judgment appears to be more limited in the absence of specific regulatory requirements. By contrast, if and to the extent relevant objectives are defined in vague principles rather than specific, rules-based targets, the operationalization and, thus, also the further specification of relevant objectives falls to corporate directors in the first place. Against this backdrop, legal uncertainty as to the substantive content, unwelcome though it may appear at first sight, may ultimately turn out to allow rather welcome room for manoeuvre: a 'new area of managerialism', with ever more limited control for managerial discretion.[97]

The legislative technique employed in the applicable EU legislation is of particular interest in this context. As noted above, relevant obligations thus far have refrained from imposing specific positive duties other than reporting obligations. The overall regulatory strategy can be described as procedural in nature, aiming at incentivizing market pressure on corporate decisions and incorporating international best practice standards which, in turn, rely heavily on broad principles rather than specific substantive rules. Against this backdrop, it may appear tempting to describe the regulatory approach as 'principles-based'—and thus benefiting from perceived advantages that have long been associated with this type of regulation. Unlike rules which define the required (or prohibited) behaviour in clear-cut terms, but thus provide ample room for what has been aptly described as 'compliant non-compliance'[98] (compliance in form, but avoiding the legislative intention in substance), principles-based regulation is widely believed to be more effective, in that it defines a broad standard of conduct which will be interpreted—and adjusted to address relevant behaviour—flexibly in the circumstances and thus reduces the scope for norm evasion.[99] At first sight, the vague nature of relevant standards could thus be interpreted as beneficial and, indeed, as particularly effective in view of the highly diverse range of activities covered. On closer inspection, however, things may well turn out rather differently. As part of the established framework of non-financial reporting, vaguely defined concepts inevitably facilitate a wide range of potential interpretations.[100] As discussed above, this is so particularly if potentially conflicting stakeholder interests are treated indiscriminately. With no ultimate arbiter at hand, and in the absence of binding further standardization, information on individual policies and measures based on, and responding to such concepts

---

[97] cf Bebchuk and Tallarita (n 12) 43 (summarizing critical analyses in US corporate law doctrine): '[Critics] worry that relying on managerial discretion and corporate leaders' pledges to serve stakeholders would not produce significant benefits for stakeholders; rather, it would harm stakeholders by worsening the economic performance of the company and by creating illusory and distracting hopes for stakeholder welfare.' But for a more positive assessment (based on empirical studies) see also Ferrell, Liang, and Renneboog (n 14) 585.

[98] J Braithwaite, 'Rules and Principles: A Theory of Legal Certainty' (2002) 27 Australian Journal of Legal Philosophy 47, 55–56.

[99] See generally Binder (n 42) 174–202 (discussing the respective functional characteristics within the context of corporate law).

[100] It is therefore hardly surprising that the introduction of s 172(1) of the UK Companies Act, which provides for a rather wider duty to take into account different stakeholder interests, does not appear to have triggered meaningful changes in business decisions: cf Grier (n 39).

and standards—unlike traditional forms of principles-based standards—are unlikely to promote actual best practice, and probably will give rise to confusing, incoherent signals instead. With corporate directors unable to establish with certainty what the expected conduct will be, creative and self-serving interpretations of relevant expectations are likely to abound. Absent comparable, standardized parameters with which investors could distinguish between firms (provided they have an actual interest to do so), a meaningful market response cannot happen. The established, procedural form of indirect regulation based on vaguely defined parameter thus may well fail on a number of grounds—and ultimately prove counterproductive.

If, then, the concept of indirect, procedural regulation based on vaguely defined standards is unlikely to yield meaningful results—will this be any different following introduction of substantive duties by the new Corporate Sustainability Due Diligent Directive? Indeed, as discussed above, the range of prescriptive duties stipulated by that instrument is as wide as the proposed range of enforcement mechanisms in private and administrative law.[101] Nonetheless, as also mentioned above, management decisions will continue to be measured by their compliance with international best practice to a considerable extent also under the new regime, so that vaguely defined concepts will continue to play a role as benchmarks for firm behaviour. Moreover, the causality between specific acts or omissions on the one hand and specific disadvantages and/or losses caused to the detriment of stakeholders on the other hand will also continue to be difficult to establish, so that the existence of new enforcement regimes as such may have a limited impact.

If legal uncertainty regarding the substantive standards is at the heart of the problems diagnosed above, one potential reaction by corporate directors could well turn out to be deliberate attempts to influence the very standards they are expected to comply with. One possible avenue towards this could be the participation in organized lobbying, including in self-regulatory organizations promoting the development of specific ESG standards. As has been observed elsewhere,[102] there is at least some evidence that industry organizations are already moving into this direction. While substantive outcomes remain difficult to assess also in this regard, there are reasons to doubt whether this should be welcomed. Indeed, self-regulation can provide a commendable, flexible, and effective alternative to state interference in circumstances where standardization of market practices is required in order to reign in externalities. Generally speaking, self-regulation can be more beneficial than state regulation in such circumstances, in that it facilitates the development, and ongoing improvement, bespoke solutions, based on the intimate knowledge of business practices and business needs and the swift and effective adaptation of relevant standards to changing circumstances. At first sight, given the dynamically emerging understanding of the implications of a wide range of different business activities on social or environmental stakeholder interests, these

---

[101] See section III.2.
[102] See eg W Schön, '"Nachhaltigkeit" in der Unternehmensberichterstattung' (2022) Zeitschrift für die gesamte Privatrechtswissenschaft 208, 240–41.

advantages could certainly commend self-regulation as an alternative in the area of CSR and ESG. However, while directors may be expected to have strong incentives to structure relevant standards in a way that maximizes discretion and to reduce the risk of either liability or regulatory intervention, they are perhaps not the best guardians of relevant public interests in the first place.[103] And as actual preferences of investors with regard to ESG matters are difficult to determine and relevant parameters for regulating ESG-related decisions both difficult to calibrate and difficult to measure, it is indeed questionable whether a further standardization of 'best practice' through self-regulatory initiatives can be expected to yield meaningful results. As a result, self-regulatory initiatives, rather than promoting greater standardization of best practice in a way that could actually enhance, and thus leverage investor-driven demand for more sustainable business initiatives, potentially could be exploited as a strategy to avoid *both* public regulation *and* the application of traditional restrictions on business decisions. While European law can hardly be said to have accomplished its objectives thus far, the fact that it has taken a sceptical stance with regard to self-regulation in the field, as such, therefore does not come as a surprise.

## V. Conclusions

As evidenced, not least, by a comparison between corresponding developments in the United States on the one hand and the European Union on the other, convergence with regard to the promotion of CSR- or ESG-related matters in corporate laws on both sides of the Atlantic has taken place only in a rather superficial sense. While it has taken a decidedly regulatory form within the EU, regulatory intervention has only very recently commenced in the United States, leaving the relevant decisions mainly to corporations themselves—with (activist) shareholder initiatives as key drivers. Irrespective of this fundamental difference in context, the broader trend promoting positive directors' duties for the protection of stakeholder interests, which has been advocated both within the United States and in Europe, is inconsistent with both shareholder- and stakeholder-oriented corporate law doctrines. Addressing stakeholder concerns to the extent compatible with (long-term) profitability of firms has been consistent with 'shareholder-oriented' regimes in the past, whereas even 'stakeholder-oriented' doctrines traditionally have not gone as far as to recognize positive obligations in this respect. Specifically within the EU, the predominant regulatory strategy to date has aimed at the incentivization of investors to exercise market pressure on corporate strategies and business decisions, and thus can be characterized as indirect and procedural in nature. However, in the absence of (a) standardized information that would allow for discrimination in investment patterns and (b) reliable empirical evidence as to investors' real preferences, the potential to accomplish objectives remains dubious. As it is unclear if (a) investors care at all and (b), even if they did care, whether

---

[103] See eg Ferrarini, Siri, and Zhu (n 51) 9–12.

they could distinguish between different strategies on the basis of published information, expectations that investor preferences will ultimately trigger a move towards greater sustainability of business models and strategies may well prove premature and overly optimistic. In terms of substantive outcomes, the current and the incoming regulatory frameworks both fail to offer reliable and sufficient guidance for directors willing to comply and offer wide margins of discretion that could be exploited for manipulative ends. All in all, the resulting uncertainty and room for self-serving manoeuvre may well turn out to be outright counter-productive. While traditional barriers for corporate decisions inconsistent with the long-term profitability of the respective firm will be weakened, the risk of self-serving decisions, reflecting individual policy choices or outright egoistic management interests, is likely to increase. Substituting the (long-term) interest of the corporation with (potentially conflicting) stakeholder interests as the ultimate measure for corporate decision-making may thus do little to advance the latter—while coming with potentially damaging consequences for the former.

# 12
# Stewardship and ESG in Europe

*Guido Ferrarini and Michele Siri**

## I. Introduction

ESG is at the core of modern corporate governance, which in the view of many should promote not only the pursuit of profits, but also the environmental and social factors that are more relevant for the individual companies and for society in general.[1] Nonetheless, the discussion is still pending in academia and practice on whether and how the ESG orientation of corporate boards and managers should be enhanced.[2] Moreover, while adherence to ESG standards is recognized as a good practice internationally, it is less clear how managers and employees should be motivated to engage in ESG effectively. One possible answer is that compliance with ESG standards helps maximizing firm's value in the long-term and should therefore motivate the managers to take care of sustainability issues.[3] Another is that corporate purpose should extend beyond profits and include sustainability considerations to motivate employees properly.[4] Yet, agency problems may lead corporate managers to focus on short-term financial results, ignoring the adverse impacts of their firms on the environment and society[5] and possibly cheating investors and stakeholders through 'greenwashing'.

Therefore, the usual corporate governance mechanisms should intervene to promote true ESG focus of corporate management.[6] First, boards of directors should

---

* All internet sources were last accessed on 15 January 2024.

[1] On the history, use, and critique of the term ESG see E Pollman, 'The Making and Meaning of ESG' (31 October 2022) University of Pennsylvania Carey Law School ILE Research Paper 22–23. For an overview of corporate purpose from a comparative perspective see G Ferrarini, 'Corporate Purpose and Sustainability Due Diligence' in D Busch, G Ferrarini, and S Grünewald (eds), *Sustainable Finance in Europe* (2nd edn, Palgrave Macmillan 2024) 121; for critical analysis of the relevant concepts and trade-offs see G Ferrarini, 'Firm Value versus Social Value: Dealing with the Trade-offs' in K Alexander, M Gargantini, and M Siri (eds), *The Cambridge Handbook of EU Sustainable Finance* (CUP 2024).

[2] See from different perspectives the contributions in B Sjåfjell and C Bruner (eds), *The Cambridge Handbook of Corporate Law, Corporate Governance, and Sustainability* (CUP 2020); and in P Camara and F Morais, *The Palgrave Handbook of ESG and Corporate Governance* (Palgrave Macmillan 2022).

[3] The relevant concepts here are those of enlightened shareholder value (M Jensen, 'Value Maximization, Stakeholder Theory, and the Corporate Objective Function' (2002) 22 Journal of Applied Corporate Finance 32 and (2002) 12 Business Ethics Quarterly 235) and of shared value (M Porter and M Kramer, 'Creating Shared Value: How to Reinvent Capitalism and Unleash a Wave of Innovation and Growth' (2011) 89 Harvard Business Review 62).

[4] See C Mayer, *Prosperity: Better Business Makes the Greater Good* (OUP 2018); R Henderson, *Reimagining Capitalism: How Business Can Save the World* (Penguin Business 2020).

[5] See Henderson (n 4) 121 ff, underlining that managers are often led to short-termism by pressure from asset managers.

[6] See in general A Edmans, *Grow the Pie: How Great Companies Deliver Both Purpose and Profit* (CUP 2020) 97 ff.

exercise their monitoring role and direct corporate managers to take environmental and social factors into account in all corporate actions. To this effect, boards often link parts of executive remuneration to ESG parameters to incentivize the pursuit of sustainability targets by the managers.[7] Moreover, boards make sustainability goals explicit in their strategic plans and check proper execution of the same by the executives. Secondly, institutional investors and asset managers monitor the ESG performance of the investee companies in addition to financial performance. They include sustainability factors amongst those to consider in the management of their portfolios and engage companies on ESG issues. Furthermore, they consider the preferences of their clients, including retail investors, policy holders, and pensioners, who are the ultimate beneficiaries of their investments. To this end, institutions ask their clients to specify their ESG preferences and offer them financial products which cater to such preferences. Clearly, the clients' preferences may vary to the extent that some may not be interested in ESG matters, while others are pro-social investors to different degrees.

In this chapter, we analyse the role of soft law and hard law in promoting ESG stewardship by institutional investors and asset managers. First, we examine the rules and incentives that stimulate institutional investors to integrate sustainability risks of investee companies in portfolio management, monitor their evolution and engage with companies when needed. Secondly, we analyse the rules and incentives that lead institutional investors and intermediaries to identify their clients' preferences as to environmental and social sustainability and to tailor their offer of financial products suitably. In addition, we examine how disclosure rules react to information asymmetries between financial institutions and clients and reduce the risk of 'greenwashing' in the offer of financial products. Thirdly, we consider the more general policy implications, such as the impact of recent reforms on the sustainability of companies and of the wider EU economy.

Three main legal strategies are used globally to pursue ESG stewardship: stewardship codes; disclosure regulation; and fiduciary duties.[8] In this chapter, we compare these strategies focussing on the EU approach to ESG stewardship, which is mainly based on regulation. In section II, we introduce the three strategies from a comparative perspective. We briefly analyse the origins and practice of stewardship codes, and the main EU regulatory measures concerning ESG stewardship that we further examine throughout the chapter. In section III, we analyse the extent to which institutional investors are incentivized by EU disclosure regulation to take ESG matters into account when investing in corporate securities. To this end, we analyse the integration of sustainability risks in investment decisions and the recourse to impact investing under the SFDR. Moreover, we consider how institutional investors classify their investments

---

[7] L Bebchuk and R Tallarita, 'The Perils and Questionable Promise of ESG-Based Compensation' (2022) 48 Journal of Corporation Law 37; M dell'Erba and G Ferrarini, 'An Assessment of ESG & Executive Remuneration in Europe' (2024) European Business Organization Law Review (forthcoming).

[8] D Katelouzou and A Klettner, 'Sustainable Finance and Stewardship: Unlocking Stewardship's Sustainability Potential' in D Katelouzou and D Puchniak (eds), *Global Shareholder Stewardship: Complexities, Challenges and Possibilities* (CUP 2022) 16.

in practice based on the relevance attributed to ESG considerations and summarize the criteria followed by institutional investors and their asset managers in the selection of investments from an ESG perspective. Furthermore, we examine what type of information issuers make available to investors about their ESG profile through the non-financial disclosure required from them under EU harmonized requirements. Finally, we examine the Commission Delegated Directives on fiduciary duties and sustainability and draw some conclusions on institutional investors' incentives to analyse ESG data and preferences and take investment decisions based on them. In section IV, we focus on investor engagement in ESG matters and ask whether regulation and/or voluntary codes enhance the incentives to engage. In section IV, we draw some general conclusions.

## II. Main Legal Strategies

Stewardship codes opened the way to the policy discussion on stewardship activities of institutional investors and asset managers. More recently, they have also identified ESG issues as a core stewardship theme. Nonetheless, the EU approach to ESG stewardship has rapidly evolved from soft law to regulation especially for what concerns the disclosure of the activities of institutional investors. The motivation of disclosure duties is found in the information asymmetries which affect end-investors and in the risk of greenwashing that derives from such asymmetries.[9] Moreover, the latest trend of EU regulation focuses on fiduciary duties and on the behaviour of institutions and intermediaries towards their clients. In this section, we first analyse the origins and practice of stewardship codes and then introduce the main EU regulatory measures concerning ESG stewardship that we further examine throughout the chapter.

### 1. The Origins of Stewardship Codes

The UK Stewardship Code was the first document of this kind to be published. It was adopted by the Financial Reporting Council (FRC) just two years after the great financial crisis,[10] following a recommendation by Sir David Walker[11] and at the government's request.[12] Its purpose was 'to enhance the quality of engagement between institutional

---

[9] See A Pacces, 'Will the EU Taxonomy Regulation Foster Sustainable Corporate Governance?' (2021) 13(21) Sustainability 12316. ·

[10] Financial Reporting Council, 'The UK Stewardship Code' (July 2010). The Code's origins had deeper roots in the principles for the responsibilities of institutional investors, initially developed by the Institutional Shareholders' Committee in 1991.

[11] Walker Review, 'A Review of Corporate Governance in UK Banks and other financial institutions: Final Recommendations' National Archive UK (26 November 2009). Published for consultation on 16 July 2009, the Walker Review formulated thirty-nine recommendations to improve corporate governance.

[12] D Katelouzou and M Siems, 'The Global Diffusion of Stewardship Codes' (29 May 2020) European Corporate Governance Institute Law Working Paper No 526/2020, King's College London Dickson Poon School of Law Legal Studies Research Paper Series: Paper No 2020-41, LawFin Working Paper No 10 https://ssrn.com/abstract=3616798 or http://dx.doi.org/10.2139/ssrn.3616798.

investors and companies to help improve long-term returns to shareholders and the efficient exercise of governance responsibilities'. The Code was therefore grounded on the concept of responsible investment and the belief that institutional investors should exercise an active role in companies in view of curbing the short-term orientation of their managers. There was no specific reference to sustainability, a concept which was still at the margin of the corporate governance discussion and was mainly considered from the perspective of corporate social responsibility (CSR).

The Code reflected the UK approach to corporate governance, which already relied on a corporate governance code for listed companies since the Cadbury report was issued in 1992.[13] The experiment of the Stewardship Code was, however, deeply criticized in 2018 by the Kingman Review of the Financial Reporting Council, which concluded that the Code was 'not effective in practice'.[14] The FRC was criticized for focusing its monitoring efforts on assessing the quality of stewardship policies, which signatories to the Stewardship Code are required to produce, whilst passing lightly over the implementation of those policies by the asset owners and asset managers which signed up to the Code.[15] The Review concluded that if a change of focus towards outcomes and effectiveness 'cannot be achieved, and the Code remains simply a driver of boilerplate reporting, serious consideration should be given to its abolition'.[16] The tacit implication was that failure of the Code should result in the adoption of legislation targeting similar goals.

As a result, in 2020 the FRC radically revised the Code.[17] The new version presents two main differences to the first one.[18] First, the 'guidance' to the principles has been replaced by 'reporting expectations' designed to report in some detail what signatories have done by way of stewardship. Secondly, the 2020 Code contains a much broader concept of stewardship and of the techniques to further it by clearly moving away from an almost exclusive focus on engagement as the recommended version of stewardship.[19] Although engagement is still emphasized, it is only one of several recommended activities: 'Stewardship activities include investment decision-making, monitoring assets and service providers, engaging with issuers and holding them to account on material issues, collaborating with others, and exercising rights and responsibilities.'[20] As we shall see throughout this chapter, a similar concept of stewardship which includes not only engagement, but also investment and divestment activities and monitoring in

---

[13] See Report of the Committee on the Financial Aspects of Corporate Governance (1 December 1992) https://ecgi.global/sites/default/files//codes/documents/cadbury.pdf. The Committee was chaired by Sir Adrian Cadbury.

[14] See Independent Review of the Financial Reporting Council (FRC): Final Report by Sir John Kingman (2018) 7 ff https://assets.publishing.service.gov.uk/government/uploads/system/uploads/attachment_data/file/767387/frc-independent-review-final-report.pdf.

[15] P Davies, 'The UK Stewardship Code 2010–2020 from Saving the Company to Saving the Planet?' (12 March 2020) European Corporate Governance Institute Law Working Paper No 506/2020 https://ssrn.com/abstract=3553493 or http://dx.doi.org/10.2139/ssrn.3553493. A Reisberg, 'The UK Stewardship Code: On the Road to Nowhere?' (2015) 15(2) Journal of Corporate Law Studies 217.

[16] See n 13, 12.

[17] See FRC, 'UK Stewardship Code 2020' https://www.frc.org.uk/investors/uk-stewardship-code.

[18] Davies (n 15).

[19] ibid.

[20] 'UK Stewardship Code 2020' (n 17) 7.

general, is presently accepted also in jurisdictions like the EU which mainly follow a regulatory approach to sustainability.

The UK Stewardship Code is the prototype after which regulators and investors groups around the world have modelled their own private codes.[21] The principles of the UK Code have travelled with success especially in the former British colonial common law countries in Asia, in part due to the UK role as a leading exporter of legal concepts in corporate governance.[22] Nonetheless, the transplant of the UK Code principles also occurred in civil law countries, like Japan and Denmark, previous adaptation to the local context.[23] Generally, stewardship codes aim to ensure the long-term success of investee companies through enhanced investor monitoring and engagement with corporate management. In the EU, they are the result of market initiatives, save for the Danish Code which came out of a regulatory initiative.[24] Industry-led regulation is, to some extent, an expression of shared and collective identity, mediating between different demands of market operators. Moreover, the focus on investors' priorities contributes to a flexible and dynamic pattern tailored to the specificities of the case, rather than subject to inflexible and pre-defined criteria.[25]

Despite scholarly scepticism about the effectiveness of voluntary codes,[26] empirical studies support the view that stewardship codes improve investor monitoring over investee companies,[27] showing that the introduction of a code in a country may increase the value of firms with high institutional ownership. Indeed, stewardship codes encourage institutional investors to engage in monitoring to improve their reputation and attract new funds. Moreover, they easily adapt to the changing needs of financial markets, avoiding the long path to legislation. As a result, successive versions of the existing codes

---

[21] The stewardship codes around the globe emanate from three different types of bodies: regulators or quasi-regulators, industry participants, and investors. See J Hill, 'Good Activist/Bad Activist: The Rise of International Stewardship Codes' (2017) 41 Seattle University Law Review 497, 507, European Corporate Governance Institute (ECGI) Law Working Paper No 368/2017, Sydney Law School Research Paper 17/80 https://ssrn.com/abstract=3036357). Codes of regulatory origin are found in Denmark, Hong Kong, India, Kenya, Japan, Malaysia, Taiwan, and Thailand; codes issued by market participants are found in South Korea, South Africa, and Singapore; codes of the third type are found in Australia, Brazil, Canada, Italy, the Netherlands, Switzerland, and the United States. The third category includes the transnational codes, drafted by the International Corporate Governance Network (ICGN), whose members represent governance professionals from over forty-five countries, and the European Funds and Asset Management Association (EFAMA).

[22] B Cheffins, 'Corporate Governance Reform: Britain as an Exporter, Corporate Governance and the Reform of Company Law', Hume Papers on Public Policy, 8(1) (Edinburgh UP 2000) https://ssrn.com/abstract=215950 or http://dx.doi.org/10.2139/ssrn.215950.

[23] Katelouzou and Siems (n 12).

[24] Stewardship codes can be regarded as voluntary instruments created by multi-stakeholder groups and intended to resolve some of the tensions that the current situation presents. See Brian R Cheffins, 'The Stewardship Code's Achilles' Heel' (2 July 2010) University of Cambridge Faculty of Law Research Paper No 28/2011 https://ssrn.com/abstract=1837344 or http://dx.doi.org/10.2139/ssrn.1837344.

[25] See G Ringe, 'Investor-led Sustainability in Corporate Governance' (1 November 2021) European Corporate Governance Institute Law Working Paper No 615/2021 https://ssrn.com/abstract=3958960 or http://dx.doi.org/10.2139/ssrn.3958960.

[26] See Cheffins (n 24); P Brest, R Gilson, and M Wolfson, 'How Investors Can (and Can't) Create Social Value' (2018) 44 Journal of Corporation Law 205 https://scholarship.law.columbia.edu/faculty_scholarship/2098.

[27] See Y Shiraishi and others, 'Stewardship Code, Institutional Investors, and Firm Value: International Evidence' (14 January 2022) https://ssrn.com/abstract=3462453 or http://dx.doi.org/10.2139/ssrn.3462453. They show that the introduction of stewardship codes in thirteen countries increased the value of firms with high institutional ownership and mitigated the free cash flow problem of the portfolio firms with low investment opportunities.

have adjusted the scope and contents of stewardship activities. The inner dynamism and flexibility of soft law instruments allows them to respond to new challenges, especially concerning sustainability. In addition, 'comply or explain' permits the stewardship principles to remain mostly suitable and up to date, pre-empting a 'one-size-fits-all' approach.

## 2. ESG in European Stewardship Codes

Although stewardship codes support responsible investing and long-termism, the extent to which they specifically refer to ESG varies.[28] Some refer to 'environmental, social and governance' or 'ESG' or 'environment and social' factors in their text, while others are less specific.[29]

### a) The Danish Code and the Dutch Code

The Danish Stewardship Code refers to the aim 'to promote the companies' long-term value creation and thereby contribute to maximising long-term return for investors', while mentioning 'corporate social responsibility'.[30] The comment has been made by scholars that in countries like Denmark, where the law on ESG is relatively good and corporate governance is stakeholder-focused, the need for emphasizing ESG in stewardship codes is lower.[31]

The Dutch Stewardship Code instead emphasizes ESG factors. It provides that the 'stewardship policy should promote long-term value creation at Dutch listed investee companies'[32] and that, in doing so, 'it is critical to consider environmental (including climate change risks and opportunities), social and governance information (including board composition and diversity) besides financial information'. The Dutch Stewardship Code was developed by the institutional investor platform Eumedion[33] and several institutional investors and came into force in January 2019. It was clearly influenced by the Shareholder Rights Directive II (SRD II)[34] that introduced new transparency obligations for institutional investors to encourage long-term shareholder engagement between companies and investors.[35]

---

[28] See Katelouzou and Klettner (n 8) 18.
[29] On the ESG concept see Pollman (n 1).
[30] See the Committee on Corporate Governance, 'Stewardship Code' (November 2016) 3 ff https://www.ecgi.global/code/danish-stewardship-code-2016.
[31] See Katelouzou and Klettner (n 8) 21.
[32] See 'Dutch Stewardship Code 2018', Guidance Principle 2 https://www.eumedion.nl/nl/public/kennisbank/best-practices/2018-07-nederlandse-stewardship-code.pdf.
[33] Eumedion is an institutional investor's organization which promotes interests in the fields of corporate governance and sustainability. See https://en.eumedion.nl/About-Eumedion.html.
[34] Directive EU 2017/828 of the European Parliament and of the Council amending Directive 2007/36/EC as regards the encouragement of long-term shareholder engagement [2017] OJ L132/60 (20 May 2017).
[35] See C Van der Elst and A Lafarre, 'Shareholder Stewardship in the Netherlands: The Role of Institutional Investors in a Stakeholder Oriented Jurisdiction' (17 February 2020) European Corporate Governance Institute Law Working Paper 492/2020 https://ssrn.com/abstract=3539820 or http://dx.doi.org/10.2139/ssrn.3539820. The authors point out that the lobbying efforts of Eumedion (see n 33 above) led to the adoption of a qualified majority requirement of 75 per cent for remuneration policy resolutions in the new art 2:135a(2) of the Dutch Civil Code, providing institutional investors with a stronger tool to address pay issues in Dutch listed companies.

In the Netherlands, corporate law is stakeholder-oriented and focuses on long-term value creation, as recognized by Dutch scholarship, case law,[36] and the Dutch Corporate Governance Code.[37] The institutional investors are required to disclose publicly how they are accountable for those Dutch Corporate Governance Code provisions applicable to them[38] and may be fined by the Dutch Financial Supervisory Authority in the case of breach of this disclosure requirement. As proven empirically,[39] institutional investors show significantly higher opposition rates than other investors regarding voting items which could negatively affect shareholder rights (eg amendments to the articles of association or remuneration packages that contain insufficient or inappropriate incentives), while Eumedion members show even higher opposition rates than institutional investors in general. Therefore, many institutional investors take their engagement role seriously and play a significant role in pursing sustainable development goals and accelerating corporate ESG strategies.

b) The Italian Code

The Italian Stewardship code does not explicitly refer to either ESG or sustainability, while mentioning long-term value creation.[40] Specifically, Principle 3 of the Code states that 'Investment Management Companies should establish clear guidelines on when and how they will intervene with investee companies to protect and enhance value'[41] and that 'regular interaction with investee companies can help to protect and guarantee value in the long term'. Institutional investors are expected to engage with investee companies in relation to corporate governance matters and their approach to environmental and social issues. In addition, long-termism is a yardstick for the fiduciary duties of Investment Management Companies who should 'follow the investment

---

[36] See HR 29 May 2017, JOR 2017, 261 (Akzo Nobel), cited by Van der Elst and Lafarre (n 35). The case involved Dutch listed company AkzoNobel and US hedge fund Elliott Management Corp. AkzoNobel rejected three unsolicited friendly offers from the American Fortune 500 company PPG Industries in 2017, arguing that PPG did not make any serious commitments to AkzoNobel's stakeholders. Elliott requested to call a general meeting to remove AkzoNobel's chairman. Although the 10 per cent threshold required under Dutch law was met, the request was rejected by the company and Elliott started an inquiry procedure before the Enterprise Chamber to investigate the decisions taken by the company for the rejection of PPG's offers. The Enterprise Chamber held that there were no serious grounds to question the proper management of the company in adherence to the ruling stakeholder model.

[37] For the English version of the current Dutch Corporate Governance Code, issued in 2016, see https://www.mccg.nl/?page=4738. Principle 1.1 of the Code states: 'The management board is responsible for the continuity of the company and its affiliated enterprise. The management board focuses on long-term value creation for the company and its affiliated enterprise and takes into account the stakeholder interests that are relevant in this context. The supervisory board monitors the management board in this.'

[38] These provisions include one on the 'Publication of institutional investors' voting policy' (4.3.5) and another on the 'Report on the implementation of institutional investors' voting policy' (4.3.6).

[39] See Van der Elst and Lafarre (n 35).

[40] See the 'Italian Stewardship Principles for the Exercise of Administrative and Voting Rights in Listed Companies', 2016 https://www.assogestioni.it/articolo/principi-italiani-di-stewardship. They were adopted by Assogestioni, the Italian Asset Managers Association, in 2013 and subsequently revised in 2015 and 2016.

[41] See the following definition contained in Italian Stewardship principles: 'Investment Management Company: an Italian or foreign company that provides collective investment management and/or portfolio management services. If the Investment Management Company offers services other than the management of collective investment undertakings or portfolios, only the management of collective investment undertakings or portfolios shall be subject to these Principles; the other services provided are not affected. Self-managed SICAVs or similar entities are considered to be Investment Management Companies.'

strategy with long-term performance objectives indicated by the client/investor or reflected in the investment policies of collective investment undertakings'.[42]

Despite a long tradition of controlling shareholders and ownership concentration in listed companies,[43] the Italian financial market has lately experienced an increasingly active role of institutional investors in the governance of investee companies.[44] According to a recent study, activism is relatively more frequent in Italy than in the United States and the UK, where the number of engagements is, however, greater.[45] Indeed, Italian corporate law enhances activism through the mechanism of slate voting which allows for the appointment of independent directors by institutional investors.[46] Under the slate voting system, minority shareholders can appoint at least one director (generally independent) and one member of the statutory board of auditors.[47]

The submission of candidates to the board by institutional investors is a constructive form of engagement with investee companies and enhances the potential for monitoring. Also, the board approach to ESG issues could improve as a result, given that minority directors 'monitor investee companies on important issues, including strategy, financial and non-financial results as well as risks, capital structure, social and environmental impact and corporate governance'.[48] Moreover, the new version of the Italian Corporate Governance code sets the pursuit of 'the sustainable success of the company's business'[49] as the main goal of the board, which should generate value for shareholders and contribute to the wider society.

c) Non-EU countries

As to non-EU countries in Europe, the Swiss Stewardship Code[50] considers sustainability in the exercise of participation rights by institutional investors suggesting that they refer to the interest of their clients and adopt 'a long-term and sustainable

---

[42] See the Purpose of Principles in Italian Stewardship principles for the exercise of administrative and voting rights in listed companies (2020).

[43] See OECD, 'Capital Market Review of Italy 2020: Mapping Report' OECD Capital Market Series (2020) https://www.oecd.org/corporate/OECD-Capital-Market-Review-Italy.htm.

[44] See M Belcredi and L Enriques, 'Institutional Investor Activism in a Context of Concentrated Ownership and High Private Benefits of Control: The Case of Italy' in J Hill and R Thomas (eds), *Research Handbook on Shareholder Power* (Edward Elgar Publishing 2015) 383.

[45] See M Becht and others, 'Returns to Hedge Fund Activism: An International Study' (2017) 30 The Review of Financial Studies 2933.

[46] For detailed analysis see G Strampelli, 'Institutional Investor Stewardship in Italian Corporate Governance' in D Katelouzou and D Puchniak (eds), *Global Shareholder Stewardship* (CUP 2022) 130.

[47] Article 147-ter of the Consolidated Law on Finance (Testo Unico della Finanza, Legislative Decree 24 February 1998, n 58) states that shareholders holding a minimum threshold of shares can present lists of candidates for election to the management board and the board of statutory auditors. At least one member must be elected from the minority submitted slate, having obtained the largest number of votes. However, the shareholders who submit the minority slate must not be related in any way, either directly or indirectly, to the shareholders who voted on the list that received the largest number of votes.

[48] cf article 124-quinquies of the Consolidated Law on Finance (Testo Unico della Finanza, Legislative Decree 24 February 1998, n 58).

[49] See the 2020 version of the (Italian) Corporate Governance Code, approved in January 2020 https://www.borsaitaliana.it/comitato-corporate-governance/codice/2020eng.en.pdf.

[50] Swiss Association of Pension Fund Providers et al., 'Guidelines for institutional investors governing the exercising of participation rights in public limited companies', 2013 https://swissinvestorscode.ch/?lang=en.

approach, unless the relevant investment guidelines stipulate to the contrary'.[51] The Swiss Code concentrates more on beneficiaries and clients than on investee companies, which might be explained by considering that the Code was the result of cooperation between public authorities and investor associations.[52]

The UK Stewardship Code 2020 mentions ESG by stating that 'environmental, particularly climate change, and social factors, in addition to governance, have become material issues for investors to consider when making investment decisions and undertaking stewardship'.[53] Moreover, the Code refers to climate change as a type of systemic risk that institutional investors should identify and respond to. It also requires asset managers and asset owners to integrate and report material ESG factors in their investment and engagement activities and explain how their decisions serve best the views and needs of their clients/beneficiaries.[54]

## 3. EU Stewardship Regulation and ESG

The EU approach to ESG stewardship is grounded on regulation rather than voluntary codes, which however complement regulation in some countries. The following regulatory instruments are relevant to present purposes: (a) Regulation (EU) 2019/2088 on sustainability-related disclosures in the financial services sector (SFDR);[55] (b) Regulation (EU) 2020/852 on the establishment of a framework to facilitate sustainable investment, and amending Regulation (EU) 2019/2088 (Taxonomy Regulation);[56] and (c) the six Commission delegated acts, including three delegated Directives, concerning the sustainability risks and sustainability factors to be taken into account for Undertakings for Collective Investment in Transferable Securities (UCITS),[57] investment firms and product governance obligations,[58] and three delegated Regulations

---

[51] See Principle 2 of the Guidelines (n 50).
[52] See Hill (n 21). The Swiss Code has been published by the Government (Swiss Federal Office for Social Security), ASIP (Swiss Association of Pension Fund Providers), Swiss Federal Social Security Funds, economiesuisse (Swiss Business Federation), Ethos (Swiss Foundation for Sustainable Development), Swiss Bankers Association, and SwissHoldings (Federation of Industrial and Service Groups in Switzerland).
[53] See UK Stewardship Code (n 17) Introduction.
[54] ibid Principles 1, 5, and 7.
[55] Regulation (EU) 2019/2088 of the European Parliament and of the Council of 27 November 2019 on sustainability-related disclosures in the financial services sector [2019] OJ L317/1 (9 December 2019).
[56] Regulation (EU) 2020/852 of the European Parliament and of the Council of 18 June 2020 on the establishment of a framework to facilitate sustainable investment, and amending Regulation (EU) 2019/2088 [2020] OJ L198/13 (22 June 2020).
[57] Commission Delegated Directive (EU) 2021/1270 of 21 April 2021 amending Directive 2010/43/EU (Text with EEA relevance) as regards the sustainability risks and sustainability factors to be taken into account for Undertakings for Collective Investment in Transferable Securities (UCITS) [2021] OJ L277/141 (2 August 2021).
[58] Commission Delegated Regulation 2021/1256 of 21 April 2021 amending Delegated Regulation (EU) No 231/2013 as regards the integration of sustainability risks in the governance of insurance and reinsurance undertakings [2021] OJ L277/14 (2 August 2021); Commission Delegated Regulation (EU) 2021/1257 of 21 April 2021 amending Delegated Regulations (EU) 2017/2358 and (EU) 2017/2359 as regards the integration of sustainability factors, risks and preferences into the product oversight and governance requirements for insurance undertakings and insurance distributors and into the rules on conduct of business and investment advice for insurance-based investment products [2021] OJ L277/18 (2 August 2021).

concerning similar issues with reference to alternative investment fund managers (AIFMs),[59] insurance and reinsurance undertakings and insurance distributors.[60]

### a) Sustainable Finance Disclosure Regulation

The SFDR preamble argues that the Union is increasingly faced with the catastrophic and unpredictable consequences of climate change, resource depletion and other sustainability-related issues, so that urgent action is needed to mobilize capital not only through public policies but also by the financial services sector.[61] Therefore, financial market participants and financial advisers are required to disclose specific information regarding their approaches to the integration of sustainability risks and the consideration of adverse sustainability impacts. According to the preamble, divergent disclosure standards and market-based practices make it very difficult to compare different financial products, create an uneven playing field, and erect additional barriers within the internal market.[62] Such divergences could be confusing for end-investors and distort their investment decisions. There is also a risk that Member States adopt divergent national measures to ensure compliance with the Paris Agreement, which could create obstacles to the smooth functioning of the internal market. Furthermore, the lack of harmonized rules relating to transparency makes it difficult for end-investors to compare different financial products in different Member States effectively with respect to their ESG risks and sustainable investment objectives.

The SFDR aims to reduce information asymmetries in principal-agent relationships with regard to the integration of sustainability risks, the consideration of adverse sustainability impacts, the promotion of environmental or social characteristics, and of sustainable investment, by requiring financial market participants and financial advisers to make pre-contractual and ongoing disclosures to end-investors when they act as agents of those investors.[63] The SFDR maintains the requirements for financial market participants and financial advisers to act in the best interest of end-investors, including the requirement of conducting adequate due diligence prior to making investments.[64] However, in order to comply with their duties under those rules, financial market participants and financial advisers should integrate in their processes and should assess on a continuous basis not only all relevant financial risks, but also all relevant sustainability risks that might have a relevant material negative impact on the financial return of an investment or advice.

---

[59] Commission Delegated Regulation (EU) 2021/1255 amending Delegated Regulation (EU) No 231/2013 as regards the sustainability risks and sustainability factors to be taken into account by Alternative Investment Fund Managers [2021] OJ L277/11 (2 August 2021).

[60] Commission Delegated Regulation (EU) 2021/1256 (n 58); Commission Delegated Regulation (EU) 2021/1257 (n 58).

[61] See SFDR, 8th Considerandum. On the Directive in general see D Busch, 'Sustainability Disclosure in the EU Financial Sector' in D Busch, G Ferrarini, and S Grünewald (eds), *Sustainable Finance in Europe* (2nd edn, Palgrave Macmillan 2024) 563.

[62] See SFDR 9th Considerandum.

[63] ibid 10th Considerandum.

[64] ibid 12th Considerandum. These requirements are provided for in Directives 2009/65/EC, 2009/138/EC, 2011/61/EU, 2013/36/EU, 2014/65/ EU, (EU) 2016/97, (EU) 2016/2341, and Regulations (EU) No 345/2013 and (EU) No 346/2013, as well as in national law governing personal and individual pension products.

Yet, the open definition of 'sustainable investment' and the absence of an obligation to exclude harmful economic activities from financial products that have sustainable investment as their objective threaten the proper functioning of the disclosure regime.[65] Therefore, the European Commission launched in 2023 a public consultation to understand how the SFDR has been implemented and any potential shortcomings, including in its interaction with the other parts of the European framework for sustainable finance, and to explore possible options improving the framework.[66]

b) Taxonomy Regulation

The Taxonomy Regulation similarly aims at harmonizing the terminology and disclosure of sustainability.[67] The establishment of a unified classification system for sustainable activities is included in the 2018 Commission action plan on financing sustainable growth, which recognized that a shift of capital flows towards more sustainable activities had to be underpinned by a shared understanding of the environmental sustainability of activities and investments.[68] As argued in the preamble to the Taxonomy Regulation, clear guidance on activities that qualify as contributing to environmental objectives would help inform investors about the investments that fund environmentally sustainable economic activities.[69] Given the systemic nature of global environmental challenges, there is a need for a systemic approach to environmental sustainability that addresses growing negative trends, such as climate change, the loss of biodiversity, the global overconsumption of resources, food scarcity, ozone depletion, ocean acidification, the deterioration of the fresh water system, and land system change as well as the appearance of new threats, such as hazardous chemicals and their combined effects.[70]

In view of the scale and costs of the challenge, the financial system should be gradually adapted to support the sustainable functioning of the economy. According to the preamble, sustainable finance needs to become mainstream, and consideration needs to be given to the sustainability impact of financial products and services. Requirements for marketing financial products or corporate bonds as environmentally sustainable investments, including requirements set by Member States and the Union to allow financial market participants and issuers to use national labels, aim to enhance investor confidence and awareness of the environmental impact of those financial products or corporate bonds, and to address concerns about 'greenwashing'.[71]

---

[65] E Partiti, 'Addressing the Flaws of the Sustainable Finance Disclosure Regulation: Moving from Disclosures to Labelling and Sustainability Due Diligence' (21 February 2023) TILEC Discussion Paper No 2023-05 https://ssrn.com/abstract=4387626 or http://dx.doi.org/10.2139/ssrn.4387626.

[66] See https://finance.ec.europa.eu/news/financial-markets-commission-consults-sustainable-finance-disclosures-2023-09-14_en.

[67] See C Gortsos and D Kyriazis, 'The Taxonomy Regulation and Its Implementation' in D Busch, G Ferrarini, and S Grünewald (eds), *Sustainable Finance in Europe* (2nd edn, Palgrave Macmillan 2024) 351; Pacces (n 9).

[68] See EC Communication, 'Action Plan: Financing Sustainable Growth' COM/2018/097 final.

[69] See Taxonomy Regulation, 6th Considerandum.

[70] See Taxonomy Regulation, 7th Considerandum.

[71] In the context of the Taxonomy Regulation, greenwashing refers to the practice of gaining an unfair competitive advantage by marketing a financial product as environmentally friendly, when in fact basic environmental standards have not been met (11th Considerandum).

The criteria for determining whether an economic activity qualifies as environmentally sustainable should therefore be harmonized at Union level in order to remove barriers to the functioning of the internal market with regard to raising funds for sustainability projects, and to prevent the future emergence of barriers to such projects.[72]

With harmonization, economic operators should find it easier to raise funds across borders for their environmentally sustainable activities, as their businesses can be compared against uniform criteria. Harmonization therefore facilitates cross-border sustainable investment in the Union. The Taxonomy Regulation establishes the criteria for determining whether an economic activity qualifies as environmentally sustainable for the purposes of establishing the degree to which an investment can be defined as such. In this regard, an exhaustive list of environmental objectives is laid down. The six environmental objectives of the Taxonomy Regulation are: climate change mitigation; climate change adaptation; the sustainable use and protection of water and marine resources; the transition to a circular economy; pollution prevention and control; and the protection and restoration of biodiversity and ecosystems.[73]

c) Commission delegated acts

The way in which the fiduciary duties of institutional investors and of their asset managers are formulated and enforced is also important to promote sustainable business. As we explain in section III, paragraph 3, EU law clarifies that sustainability characteristics should be factored in by institutional investors, asset managers, insurance undertakings and intermediaries, and investment intermediaries when taking investment decisions. Moreover, sustainability factors should be considered in product governance determinations and in advisory activities taking into account clients' preferences as to sustainability.

## III. Investment Activities and ESG

In the present section, we enquire to what extent institutional investors are asked by EU regulation to take ESG matters into account when investing in corporate securities. In paragraph 1, we analyse the integration of sustainability risks in investment decisions and impact investing under the SFDR. Moreover, we consider how institutional investors classify their investments in practice based on the relevance attributed to ESG considerations. In paragraph 2, we summarize the criteria followed by institutional investors and their asset managers in the selection of investments from an ESG perspective. In addition, we examine what type of information issuers make available to investors about their ESG profile through the non-financial disclosure required from them under EU harmonized requirements. In paragraph 3, we examine the Commission Delegated Directives on fiduciary duties and sustainability and draw

---

[72] See Taxonomy Regulation, 12th Considerandum.
[73] See Taxonomy Regulation 23rd Considerandum.

some conclusions on institutional investors' incentives to analyse ESG data and preferences and take investment decisions based on them.

## 1. SFDR Requirements

Principle 1 of the Principles for Responsible Investment (PRI)[74] requires institutional investors to integrate sustainability risks into their investment decisions.[75] Consistently with international principles, Article 3(1) of the SFDR provides what follows: 'Financial market participants shall publish on their websites information about their policies on the integration of sustainability risks in their investment decision-making process.'[76] Article 6(1) of the SFDR further asks financial market participants 'to include descriptions of the following in pre-contractual disclosures: (a) the manner in which sustainability risks are integrated into their investment decisions; and (b) the results of the assessment of the likely impacts of sustainability risks on the returns of the financial products they make available'.

a) Sustainability risk

*Sustainability risk* is defined by Article 2(22) of the SFDR as 'an environmental, social or governance event or condition that, if it occurs, could cause an actual or a potential material negative impact on the value of the investment'. Therefore, sustainability risks are considered by the SFDR mainly as affecting the investment at issue, whose value may suffer a material negative impact if the risk materializes (internalized risk). Whether the environment or society are negatively impacted by the risks in question is not directly relevant: in other words, double materiality does not apply. However, *adverse impacts* (ie negative externalities) must be taken into account by financial market participants under Article 4 of the SFDR, requiring them to 'publish and maintain on their websites (a) where they consider principal adverse impacts of investment decisions on sustainability factors, a statement on due diligence policies with respect to those impacts, taking due account of their size, the nature and scale of their activities and the types of financial products they make available; or (b) where they do

---

[74] See https://www.unpri.org/about-us/what-are-the-principles-for-responsible-investment.
[75] Similarly, Principle 6 of the ICGN Global Stewardship Principles (https://www.icgn.org/icgn-global-stewardship-principles) states: 'Investors should promote the long-term performance and sustainable success of companies and should integrate material environmental, social and governance (ESG) factors in investment decision-making and stewardship activities.' Along similar lines, Principle 7 of the UK Stewardship Code provides: 'Signatories systematically integrate stewardship and investment, including material environmental, social and governance issues, and climate change, to fulfil their responsibilities.'
[76] Under art 2(1) of the SFDR, '"financial market participant" means: (a) an insurance undertaking which makes available an insurance-based investment product (IBIP); (b) an investment firm which provides portfolio management; (c) an institution for occupational retirement provision (IORP); (d) a manufacturer of a pension product; (e) an alternative investment fund manager (AIFM); (f) a pan-European personal pension product (PEPP) provider; (g) a manager of a qualifying venture capital fund registered in accordance with Article 14 of Regulation (EU) No 345/2013; (h) a manager of a qualifying social entrepreneurship fund registered in accordance with Article 15 of Regulation (EU) No 346/2013; (i) a management company of an undertaking for collective investment in transferable securities (UCITS management company); or (j) a credit institution which provides portfolio management.'

not consider adverse impacts of investment decisions on sustainability factors, clear reasons for why they do not do so, including, where relevant, information as to whether and when they intend to consider such adverse impacts'.

The provision just quoted refers to adverse impacts which have been originated by portfolio companies. Financial market participants should have due diligence policies in place to ascertain the nature and extent of such impacts and the measures adopted by the companies in question to reduce or eliminate the same. The relevant information will mainly be provided by the issuers in the sustainability disclosure concerning their adverse impacts and relevant due diligence policies. Financial market participants will conduct their due diligence activities mainly with regard to similar information checking the same on the basis of other information which is publicly available or privately available to them.

b) Impact investing

Impact investing is a noteworthy step in the evolution of responsible investing. It is a type of sustainable investing in which investment decisions are made to deliver positive financial returns and a benefit to society and to the environment at the same time. As noted by three scholarly experts, it is 'very difficult to create social value through one's investments while nonetheless earning risk-adjusted financial returns'.[77] However, the same scholars disagree with those who define impact investing to include only concessionary investments, that is to say investments in which financial concessions are made over time.[78] In their opinion, the definition of impact investing should be reserved to investors who seek social value creation rather than only value alignment. 'Value alignment' occurs when investors seek to align their investments with their social values, while 'value creation' happens when they seek to cause the investee companies to create more social value.[79]

Impact investing is considered by the SFDR mainly for information purposes regarding the due diligence policies adopted by financial market participants.

c) Special types of ESG investments

Articles 8 and 9 of the SFDR acknowledge that financial market participants may attach special importance to the sustainability of investee companies by envisaging two hypotheses. Article 8(1) refers to a financial product that '*promotes*, among other characteristics, *environmental* or *social characteristics*, or a combination of those characteristics'. In a similar case, 'provided that the companies in which the investments are made follow good governance practices, the information to be disclosed pursuant to Article 6(1) and (3) shall include the following: (a) information on how those characteristics are met; (b) if an index has been designated as a reference

---

[77] Brest, Gilson, and Wolfson (n 26) 209.
[78] ibid.
[79] ibid 206.

benchmark, information on whether and how this index is consistent with those characteristics'.[80]

Article 9(1) SFDR envisages a financial product that has *sustainable investment as its objective*. According to Article 2(17) SFDR, 'sustainable investment' means an investment in an economic activity that contributes either to an *environmental objective* or to a *social objective*. 'Environmental objectives' are defined by Article 9 of the Taxonomy Regulation as including: climate change mitigation; climate change adaptation; the sustainable use and protection of water and marine resources; the transition to a circular economy; pollution prevention and control; protection and restoration of biodiversity and ecosystems.[81] These objectives are measured by key resource efficiency indicators on the use of energy, renewable energy, raw materials, water and land; on the production of waste, and greenhouse gas emissions; or on its impact on biodiversity and the circular economy. The social objectives regard an investment in an economic activity that contributes to tackling inequality or that fosters social cohesion, social integration and labour relations, or an investment in human capital or economically or socially disadvantaged communities (Article 2(17) SFDR). In all cases, such investments should not significantly harm any of those objectives and the investee companies should follow good governance practices with respect to sound management structures, employee relations, remuneration of staff and tax compliance.

As to the environmental objectives, Article 9(3) specifies that a financial product can have a reduction in carbon emissions as its objective, in which case the information to be disclosed shall include the objective of low carbon emission exposure in view of achieving the long-term global warming objectives of the Paris Agreement.[82] Indeed, climate change has become one of the biggest sustainability issues for investment portfolios, as investors have become aware that greater climate variability and more frequent extreme weather events have negative impacts on businesses. Overall, the SFDR criteria for distinguishing between different types of financial products are rather vague, given that the promotion of environmental or social characteristics is not always neatly distinguishable from the pursuit of sustainable investment objectives. As noted above, one financial market participant classifies as Article 8 of the SFDR all investments the management of which integrates sustainability risks, while another defines Article 8 investments those targeting an internal sustainability score. Still another

---

[80] Under art 8(2), financial market participants shall include in the information to be disclosed pursuant to art 6(1) and (3) an indication of where the methodology used for the calculation of the index referred to in paragraph 1 of this article is to be found.

[81] Article 3 of the Taxonomy Regulation provides that: '[a]n economic activity shall qualify as environmentally sustainable where that economic activity: (a) contributes substantially to one or more of the environmental objectives set out in Article 9 in accordance with Articles 10 to 16; (b) does not significantly harm any of the environmental objectives set out in Article 9 in accordance with Article17; (c) is carried out in compliance with the minimum safeguards laid down in Article 18; and (d) complies with technical screening criteria that have been established by the Commission in accordance with Article10(3), 11(3), 12(2), 13(2), 14(2) or 15(2) of the same Regulation'.

[82] Article 9(3) further provides: 'By way of derogation from paragraph 2 of this Article, where no EU Climate Transition Benchmark or EU Paris-aligned Benchmark in accordance with Regulation (EU) 2016/1011 of the European Parliament and of the Council (20) is available, the information referred to in Article 6 shall include a detailed explanation of how the continued effort of attaining the objective of reducing carbon emissions is ensured in view of achieving the long-term global warming objectives of the Paris Agreement.'

considers all impact investments as Article 9 compliant. In the case of Article 9 financial products the principle of no harm to any sustainability objective must be complied with. However, this principle is not part of the definition of an Article 9 investment, rather assuming this definition as given.

As a result, financial market participants are given wide discretion as to the choice of the label to use for their financial products and will probably choose based on divergent criteria. The relative flexibility of the definitions was presumably intentional on the part of the EU legislator, given that the practice of sustainable investments is relatively new and difficult to standardize. However, the lack of standards may give rise to greenwashing if laxer criteria are applied by some participants in the definition of their financial products to make them appear more sustainable than they effectively are in practice.

## 2. Investment Criteria and Processes

Most institutional investors and asset managers today believe that the selection of companies with sustainable business models is important to maximize risk-adjusted returns to their clients over the long term. They regard ESG issues as important drivers of financial performance and investment returns and are committed to integrate them across their investment strategies. Moreover, ESG criteria help to identify companies which are effectively transitioning to new business models which are better suited to current economic and social environments.

a) Risk-related risks

ESG-related risks and opportunities are relevant both in the management of firms and in the selection of investments. Nevertheless, there is no universal definition of ESG-related risks, so that each company may define them based on its business model; internal and external environment; product or services mix; mission, vision, and core values.[83] ESG-related risks are not entirely new, to the extent that corporations and investors have been considering governance risks for many years, including those relating to financial accounting and reporting, board leadership and composition, anti-bribery and corruption, business ethics, and executive compensation.[84] However, the breadth of ESG-related risks has expanded rapidly over the last ten years. The World Economic Forum's Global Risks Report for 2021 highlighted that four of the top five risks by likelihood were environmental, including those concerning extreme weather events, climate action failure, human environmental damage, and biodiversity loss.[85]

---

[83] See Committee of Sponsoring Organizations of the Treadway Commission (COSO) and World Business Council for Sustainable Development (WBCSD), 'Enterprise Risk Management: Applying Enterprise Risk Management to Environmental, Social and Governance-related Risks' (October 2018) 1.

[84] ibid.

[85] World Economic Forum, 'Global Risks Report 2021' https://www3.weforum.org/docs/WEF_The_Global_Risks_Report_2021.pdf.

The following are examples of organizations that experienced extraordinary ESG-related impacts over the last decades.[86] Starting from the E (environmental factors), in 2010 BP's oil rig *Deepwater Horizon* exploded in Mexico, killing and injuring workers, and creating an environmental disaster; in 2013, millions of Volkswagen cars were recalled after the company admitted to falsifying emissions tests; in 2014, flooding in Thailand resulted in disruptions to automotive and technology supply chain networks; in 2015, the Samarco dam (Vale and BHP) collapse killed people and sent iron ore debris through south-eastern Brazil. Focusing on the S (social factors), in the 1980s Nestlé faced a boycott for misleading consumers as to baby milk formulae in emerging countries; in the 1990s Nike was accused of employing children and paying workers less than the minimum wage; in 2013, the Rana Plaza factory building in Bangladesh, used by more than twenty-five brands, collapsed killing more than 1,100 workers; in 2017, Wells Fargo created millions of accounts in the names of its clients without their permission; in 2018, Oxfam faced the alleged cover-up of a sexual harassment scandal in Haiti; in 2017, Uber faced a sexual harassment scandal leading to a #DeleteUber movement.

Most of these cases also concerned the G (governance factors) to the extent that either the E or the S failures (including human rights violation) had been caused or at least made possible by G weaknesses or failures. As a result, there is growing interest from investors in understanding how organizations identify and respond to ESG-related risks.[87] In the United States, for example, environmental and social proposals in the annual meetings of corporations have accounted for around half of all shareholder proposals submitted (the other types of proposals included board issues, anti-takeover and strategic themes, and executive compensation).[88]

The above comments briefly explain why sustainability risk integration is recommended to institutional investors by international best practices and is widely followed by these investors in the management of their portfolios. Moreover, the special categories of financial products examined in the previous paragraph may require the recourse to additional criteria for the selection of investments by institutional investors and asset managers. As illustrated in the previous paragraph, Article 8 of the SFDR refers to financial products that promote environmental or social characteristics, which must be indicated in the relevant disclosure document together with the reference benchmark (if any) which has been designated for the purpose of attaining those characteristics.[89] Article 9 refers to financial products which have a sustainable investment objective, ie an investment in an economic activity that contributes to an

---

[86] See COSO–WBCSD (n 83) 3.
[87] ibid.
[88] ibid.
[89] According to art 6 of the Taxonomy Regulation, where a financial product as referred to in art 8(1) of the SFDR promotes environmental characteristics, art 5 of the Taxonomy Regulation shall apply mutatis mutandis. Therefore, the information to be disclosed in accordance with arts 6(3) and 11(2) of the SFDR shall include the information on the environmental characteristic or characteristics to which the investment underlying the financial product contributes; and a description of how and to what extent the investments underlying the financial product are (if any) in economic activities that qualify as environmentally sustainable.

environmental or social objective, provided that the investment does not significantly harm any environmental or social objective and that the investee companies follow good governance practices. Therefore, financial market participants do additional and specific research in relation to the offer of Article 8 products—depending on the E and S characteristics that they promote—and Article 9 products with respect to their sustainability objectives.

To make an example, for impact investments they need information on the environmental and social impacts pursued, which they can collect on the basis of either corporate disclosure or other publicly available data on the positive and negative impacts of investee companies on the planet and people. Consequently, asset managers will have to run due diligence processes directed to establish negative impacts whose presence may lead to excluding given investments and positive ones which may be required for an investment to be selected by them. Moreover, they will scrutinize the information concerning the corporate governance of firms to ascertain whether they follow good practices with respect to sound management structures, employee relations, remuneration of staff and tax compliance.

b) Sustainability reporting by issuers

Sustainability reporting by issuers provides investors—as well as stakeholders and the public at large—with information on ESG issues and corporate sustainability in general that can be used in the activities and processes analysed in the previous paragraph. Under Article 19a of Directive 2013/34/EU, as recently modified by the Corporate Sustainability Reporting Directive (CSRD),[90] large undertakings, and small and medium-sized undertakings, except micro undertakings, which are public-interest entities shall include in the management report information necessary to understand the undertaking's impacts on sustainability matters, and information necessary to understand how sustainability matters affect the undertaking's development, performance, and position.

This information shall describe the undertaking's business model and strategy, including the opportunities for the undertaking related to sustainability matters and the plans to ensure that its business model and strategy are compatible with the transition to a sustainable economy. It shall also describe how the business model and strategy take account of the interests of stakeholders and of the impacts of the undertaking on sustainability matters, and how the strategy has been implemented with regard to sustainability matters. Moreover, the information should contain a description of

---

[90] See Directive (EU) 2022/2464 of the European Parliament and of the Council of 14 December 2022 amending Regulation (EU) No 537/2014, Directive 2004/109/EC, Directive 2006/43/EC and Directive 2013/34/EU, as regards corporate sustainability reporting [2022] OJ L322 (16 December 2022), usually referred to as the Corporate Sustainability Reporting Directive; Directive 2014/95/EU of the European Parliament and of the Council of 22 October 2014 amending Directive 2013/34/EU as regards disclosure of non-financial and diversity information by certain large undertakings and groups [2014] OJ L330/1 (15 November 2014). See also G Balp and G Strampelli, 'Institutional Investors as the Primary Users of Sustainability Reporting' in K Alexander, M Gargantini, and M Siri (eds), *The Cambridge Handbook of EU Sustainable Finance: Regulation, Supervision, and Governance* (CUP 2024).

the targets related to sustainability matters set by the undertaking, including absolute greenhouse gas emission reduction targets for at least 2030 and 2050, a description of the progress the undertaking has made towards achieving those targets, and a statement of whether the targets related to environmental factors are based on conclusive scientific evidence. Furthermore, a description should be given of the role of the administrative, management and supervisory bodies with regard to sustainability matters, and of their expertise and skills in relation to fulfilling that role, together with information about the existence of incentive schemes linked to sustainability matters which have been offered to members of the administrative, management and supervisory bodies. In addition, the due diligence process implemented by the undertaking with regard to sustainability matters should be described, in line with prospective EU requirements concerning the conduct of such process.

On 31 July 2023, the European Commission adopted the European Sustainability Reporting Standards (ESRS) for use by all companies subject to the CSRD, as foreseen by Articles 19(a)(4) and 29(b) of the Accounting Directive, as amended.[91] The standards cover the full range of environmental, social, and governance issues, including climate change, biodiversity, and human rights. They provide information for investors to understand the sustainability impact of the companies in which they invest. They also take account of discussions with the International Sustainability Standards Board (ISSB) and the Global Reporting Initiative (GRI) in order to ensure a very high degree of interoperability between EU and global standards and to prevent unnecessary double reporting by companies.[92] The ESRS were adopted by the Commission based on technical advice (draft standards) from EFRAG.[93] They take a 'double materiality' perspective, in the sense that they oblige companies to report both on their impacts on people and the environment, and on how social and environmental issues create financial risks and opportunities for the company.[94]

### 3. Fiduciary Duties and the Integration of Sustainability

The EU Commission has created further incentives for financial market participants to integrate sustainability risks in their investment activities and services through the enactment of the six delegated acts already cited.[95] Three of them regard the integration of sustainability factors into investment selection and risk management, while the other

---

[91] See Commission Delegated Regulation (EU) supplementing Directive 2013/34/EU of the European Parliament and of the Council as regards sustainability reporting standards https://finance.ec.europa.eu/regulation-and-supervision/financial-services-legislation/implementing-and-delegated-acts/corporate-sustainability-reporting-directive_en.
[92] See 'The Commission adopts the European Sustainability Reporting Standards' https://finance.ec.europa.eu/news/commission-adopts-european-sustainability-reporting-standards-2023-07-31_en.
[93] See the Commission's Questions and Answers on the ESRS https://ec.europa.eu/commission/presscorner/detail/en/qanda_23_4043.
[94] ibid.
[95] See section II.3.

three regard the integration of sustainability factors into product governance and rules of conduct.

a) Investment selection and risk management

Commission Delegated Directive 2021/1270 concerns the sustainability risks and sustainability factors to be taken into account for UCITS,[96] while Commission Delegated Regulation 2021/1255 concerns the same theme with reference to AIFMs.[97] These two acts specify the fiduciary duties owed by UCITS and their asset managers, and AIFMs to their clients with respect to the sustainability of the investments offered to them. The Delegated Directive modifies Article 4(1) of Directive 2010/43/EU on UCITS by adding a subparagraph providing, inter alia, that: 'Member States shall ensure that management companies take into account sustainability risks when complying with the requirements laid down in the first subparagraph' (Article 1 of the Commission Delegated Directive). Article 5a has also been added including the obligation for investment companies to integrate sustainability risks in the management of UCITS 'taking into account the nature, scale and complexity of the business of the investment companies'. Similar provisions are also found in the delegated Regulation concerning AIFMs.[98]

Commission Delegated Regulation 2021/1256 regards the integration of sustainability risks in the governance of insurance and reinsurance undertakings.[99] Its preamble states that insurance undertakings that disclose principal adverse impacts on sustainability factors in accordance with the SFDR should also adapt their processes, systems, and internal controls with respect to those disclosures.[100] In particular, the prudent person principle laid down in Article 132 of the Solvency II Directive[101] requires that insurance and reinsurance undertakings only invest in assets the risks of which they can identify, measure, monitor, manage, control, and report properly. The implementation of this principle requires that climate and environmental risks are effectively managed by insurance and reinsurance undertakings and that the latter reflect in their investment processes the sustainability preferences of their customers as taken into account in the product approval process.[102] The provisions of Delegated Regulation (EU) 2015/35 of 10 October 2014 supplementing the Solvency II Directive[103] have been modified accordingly by the Delegated Regulation 2021/1256 that we are specifically considering.

Commission Delegated Regulation (EU) 2021/1253 regards the integration of sustainability factors, risks, and preferences into the organizational requirements and

---

[96] Commission Delegated Directive (EU) 2021/1270 (n 57).
[97] See Commission Delegated Regulation (EU) 2021/1255 (n 59).
[98] ibid.
[99] ibid.
[100] See the 4th Considerandum.
[101] Directive 2009/138/EC of the European Parliament and of the Council of 25 November 2009 on the taking-up and pursuit of the business of Insurance and Reinsurance (Solvency II) [2009] OJ L335/1 (17 December 2009).
[102] See the 6th Considerandum of Commission Delegated Regulation 2021/1256 (n 58).
[103] See Commission Delegated Regulation (EU) 2015/35 of 10 October 2014 supplementing Directive 2009/138/EC of the European Parliament and of the Council on the taking-up and pursuit of the business of Insurance and Reinsurance (Solvency II) [2015] OJ L12/1 (17 January 2015).

INVESTMENT ACTIVITIES AND ESG 267

operating conditions for investment firms.[104] As stated in the preamble, investment firms should, when identifying conflicts of interest, include those conflicts that stem from the integration of the client's sustainability preferences.[105] Moreover, investment firms that provide investment advice and portfolio management should be able to recommend suitable financial instruments to their clients and potential clients and should therefore ask questions to identify a client's individual sustainability preferences.[106] Such recommendations should reflect both the financial objectives and sustainability preferences expressed by clients. Investment firms should therefore have in place appropriate arrangements to ensure that the inclusion of sustainability factors in the advisory process and portfolio management does not lead to mis-selling practices or to the misrepresentation of financial instruments or strategies as fulfilling sustainability preferences where they do not.[107]

The preamble still notes that financial instruments with various degrees of sustainability-related ambition have been developed so far. To enable clients or potential clients to take informed investment decisions in terms of sustainability, investment firms that provide investment advice and portfolio management services should explain the distinction between three types of financial instruments: (a) those that pursue, fully or in part, sustainable investments in economic activities that qualify as environmentally sustainable under Regulation (EU) 2020/852; (b) sustainable investments as defined in Article 2, point (17), of Regulation (EU) 2019/2088; (c) financial instruments that consider principal adverse impacts on sustainability factors that might be eligible for recommendation as meeting the individual sustainability preferences of clients.[108]

b) Integration of sustainability in product governance and rules of conduct
Commission Delegated Directive 2021/1269 amends Delegated Directive 2017/593 regarding the integration of sustainability factors into the product governance obligations.[109] As explained in the preamble, investment firms manufacturing and distributing financial instruments should consider sustainability factors in the product approval process of each financial instrument and in the other product governance and oversight arrangements for each financial instrument that is intended to be distributed to clients seeking financial instruments with a sustainability-related profile.[110] Moreover, considering that the target market should be set at a sufficient granular level, a general statement that a financial instrument has a sustainability-related profile should not be sufficient. Investment firms manufacturing and distributing financial

---

[104] Commission Delegated Regulation (EU) 2021/1253 of 21 April 2021 amending Delegated Regulation (EU) 2017/565 as regards the integration of sustainability factors, risks and preferences into certain organisational requirements and operating conditions for investment firms [2021] OJ L277/1 (2 August 2021).
[105] See the 4th Considerandum.
[106] See the 5th Considerandum.
[107] ibid.
[108] See the 6th Considerandum.
[109] Commission Delegated Directive (EU) 2021/1269 of 21 April 2021 amending Delegated Directive (EU) 2017/593 as regards the integration of sustainability factors into the product governance obligations [2021] OJ L277/137 (2 August 2021).
[110] See the 5th Considerandum.

instruments should rather specify to which group of clients with sustainability-related objectives the financial instrument is supposed to be distributed.

Commission Delegated Regulation (EU) 2021/1257 of 21 April 2021[111] concerns the integration of sustainability factors, risks, and preferences into the product oversight and governance requirements for insurance undertakings and insurance distributors. As explained in the preamble, insurance undertakings and insurance intermediaries manufacturing insurance products should consider sustainability factors in the product approval process of each insurance product and in the other product governance and oversight arrangements for each insurance product that is intended to be distributed to customers seeking insurance products with a sustainability-related profile.[112] Considering that the target market should be set at a sufficient granular level, the insurance undertaking or insurance intermediary manufacturing the insurance product should specify to which group of customers with specific sustainability-related objectives the insurance product is supposed to be distributed.[113]

Moreover, insurance intermediaries and insurance undertakings that provide advice on insurance-based investment products should be able to recommend suitable insurance-based investment products to their customers or potential customers and should therefore be able to ask questions to identify a customer's individual sustainability preferences. In accordance with the obligation to carry out distribution activities in accordance with the best interest of costumers, recommendations to customers or potential customers should reflect both the financial objectives and any sustainability preferences expressed by those customers.[114] The provisions of Delegated Regulation (EU) 2017/2358 and Delegated Regulation (EU) 2017/2358[115] have been amended accordingly by the Delegated Regulation 2021/1256 that we are specifically considering.

c) Assessment

EU regulation concerning sustainability disclosure is complemented by the provisions reviewed in this paragraph which foresee fiduciary duties and regulatory duties concerning the integration of sustainability by financial market participants. On one side, there are rules requiring the integration of sustainability in the selection of investments and in risk management processes of UCITS, asset managers, insurance undertakings, and intermediaries, and investment intermediaries. On the other side, sustainability factors must be considered in product governance processes and in portfolio management and advisory activities which must consider clients' preferences

---

[111] Commission Delegated Regulation (EU) 2021/1257 (n 58).
[112] See the 5th Considerandum.
[113] See the 6th Considerandum.
[114] See the 11th Considerandum.
[115] See Commission Delegated Regulation (EU) 2017/2358 of 21 September 2017 supplementing Directive (EU) 2016/97 of the European Parliament and of the Council with regard to product oversight and governance requirements for insurance undertakings and insurance distributors [2017] OJ L341/1 (20 December 2017); and Commission Delegated Regulation (EU) 2017/2359 of 21 September 2017 supplementing Directive (EU) 2016/97 of the European Parliament and of the Council with regard to information requirements and conduct of business rules applicable to the distribution of insurance-based investment products [2017] OJ L341/8 (20 December 2017).

as to sustainability. The two sides of regulation—disclosure and fiduciary/regulatory duties—complement each other in the sense that disclosure contributes to incentivizing performance by financial market participants of their fiduciary/regulatory duties, while the latter reinforce the quality of disclosure by assuring that adequate processes and activities stand behind the reports published by financial market participants. Overall, the regulation that we have been considering aims to reduce the agency costs between financial market participants and their clients/investors aligning the investment activities of the former with the latter's preferences as to sustainability.

## IV. Engagement Activities and ESG

In section I, we noted that the 2020 edition of the UK Stewardship Code refers to 'engaging with issuers and holding them to account on material issues, collaborating with others, and exercising rights and responsibilities'. At the same time, the UK Code considers engagement along other stewardship activities, such as investment decision-making and monitoring assets and service providers. Other stewardship codes in Europe follow a similar approach to stewardship reflecting a holistic view of the activities that institutional investors and asset managers perform in the interest of end-investors. In section II, we further considered how ESG issues are factored in by financial market participants when deciding on investments and divestments, and monitoring assets and service providers.

In this section, we focus on engagement concerning ESG matters and analyse the incentives of financial market participants to engage with issuers and exercise their rights and responsibilities in investee companies, keeping however in mind that the different aspects of stewardship can be a substitute one for another. Indeed, stewards' monitoring on ESG issues can lead either to formal or informal engagement with issuers or to divestment from the relevant company. In paragraph 1, we examine how the SRD II has tried to enhance the incentives to engagement by requiring publication of an engagement policy. We also examine similar requirements under the SFDR as implemented by a Commission Delegated Regulation with special regard to ESG engagement. In paragraph 2, we consider the limited incentives to engagement and ask whether ESG engagement will be different. In paragraph 3, we draw some conclusions.

### 1. Engagement Disclosure under SRD II and SFDR

The original Shareholder Rights Directive of 2007[116] was amended in 2017 by the SRD II[117] regarding the encouragement of long-term shareholder engagement.

---

[116] Directive 2007/36/EC of the European Parliament and of the Council of 11 July 2007 on the exercise of certain rights of shareholders in listed companies, [2007] OJ L184/17 (14 July 2007).

[117] Directive (EU) 2017/828 of the European Parliament and of the Council of 17 May 2017 amending Directive 2007/36/EC as regards the encouragement of long-term shareholder engagement [2017] OJ L132/1 (20 May 2017). For a definition of this Directive as a 'missed opportunity' see A Pacces, 'Shareholder Activism in the CMU'

As stated by new Article 1(1), the Directive establishes requirements in relation to the exercise of certain shareholder rights attached to voting shares in relation to general meetings of companies which have their registered office in a Member State and the shares of which are admitted to trading on a regulated market situated or operating within a Member State. It also establishes specific requirements to encourage shareholder engagement in the long term.

The preamble to the Directive claims that, in many cases before the financial crisis, shareholders supported managers' short-term risk taking. Moreover, the level of 'monitoring' of investee companies and engagement by institutional investors and asset managers was often inadequate and focused too much on short-term returns, which may lead to suboptimal corporate governance and performance.[118] Consequently, in a 2012 Communication[119] the Commission announced several actions in corporate governance to encourage long-term shareholder engagement and to enhance transparency between companies and investors. In the Commission's view, effective and sustainable shareholder engagement is one of the cornerstones of the corporate governance model of listed companies, which depends on checks and balances between the different organs and different stakeholders.[120] Greater involvement of shareholders in corporate governance is one of the levers that can help improve the financial and non-financial performance of companies including with regard ESG factors, as also argued in the Principles for Responsible Investment supported by the United Nations. In addition, greater involvement of all stakeholders in corporate governance is important to ensure a more long-term approach by listed companies.

Institutional investors and asset managers are often important shareholders of EU listed companies, so that they can play an important role in their corporate governance. However, the SRD II preamble claims that experience of the last years has shown that institutional investors and asset managers often do not engage with companies in which they hold shares, while evidence shows that capital markets frequently exert pressure on companies to perform in the short term.[121] Moreover, institutional investors and asset managers often are not transparent about their engagement policies and the implementation of the same. However, 'public disclosure of such information could have a positive impact on investor awareness, enable ultimate beneficiaries such as future pensioners optimize investment decisions, facilitate the dialogue between companies and their shareholders, encourage shareholder engagement and strengthen their accountability to stakeholders and to civil society'.[122]

---

in D Busch, E Avgouleas, and G Ferrarini (eds), *Capital Markets Union in Europe* (OUP 2018) 507, providing a critical analysis of the policy choices made by the EU legislator as to shareholder engagement.

[118] See the 2nd Considerandum.
[119] See Commission Communication of 12 December 2012, 'Action Plan: European company law and corporate governance: a modern legal framework for more engaged shareholders and sustainable companies' COM/2012/0740 final.
[120] See SRD II, 14th Considerandum.
[121] ibid 15th Considerandum.
[122] ibid 16th Considerandum.

As a result, new Article 3g(1) SRD on engagement policy provides that Member States shall ensure that institutional investors and asset managers either comply with the requirements set out in points (a) and (b) or publicly disclose a clear and reasoned explanation why they have chosen not to comply with one or more of those requirements. Under point (a), institutional investors and asset managers are required to develop and publicly disclose an engagement policy that describes how they integrate shareholder engagement in their investment strategy. The policy shall describe how they monitor investee companies on relevant matters, including strategy, financial and non-financial performance and risk, capital structure, social and environmental impact and corporate governance; conduct dialogues with investee companies, exercise voting rights and other rights attached to shares; cooperate with other shareholders, communicate with relevant stakeholders of the investee companies and manage actual and potential conflicts of interests in relation to their engagement. Under point (b), institutional investors and asset managers shall, on an annual basis, publicly disclose how their engagement policy has been implemented, including a general description of voting behaviour, an explanation of the most significant votes and the use of the services of proxy advisors. They shall publicly disclose how they have cast votes in the general meetings of companies in which they hold shares. Such disclosure may exclude votes that are insignificant due to the subject matter of the vote or the size of the holding in the company.[123]

Specific disclosure of sustainability engagement by financial market participants is required by Commission Delegated Regulation of 6 April 2022 supplementing the SFDR.[124] Under Article 8(1) of this Regulation, financial market participants shall provide in Table 1 of Annex I information as to their engagement policies including, where applicable, brief summaries of the engagement policies referred to in Article 3g of SRD II and brief summaries of any other engagement policies to reduce principal adverse impacts. Such brief summaries shall describe the indicators for adverse impacts considered in the relevant engagement policies and how those engagement policies will be adapted where there is no reduction of the principal adverse impacts over more than one period reported on.

---

[123] Article 3g(2) further provides that the information referred to in para 1 shall be available free of charge on the institutional investor's or asset manager's website. Where an asset manager implements the engagement policy, including voting, on behalf of an institutional investor, the institutional investor shall make a reference as to where such voting information has been published by the asset manager. Paragraph 3 specifies that conflicts of interests rules applicable to institutional investors and asset managers, including art 14 of Directive 2011/61/EU, point (b) of art 12(1) and point (d) of art 14(1) of Directive 2009/65/EC and the relevant implementing rules, and art 23 of Directive 2014/65/EU shall also apply with regard to engagement activities.

[124] See Commission Delegated Regulation (EU) 2022/1288 of 6 April 2022 supplementing the Regulation (EU) 2019/2088 of the European Parliament and of the Council with regard to regulatory technical standards specifying the details of the content and presentation of the information in relation to the principle of 'do no significant harm', specifying the content, methodologies and presentation of information in relation to sustainability indicators and adverse sustainability impacts, and the content and presentation of the information in relation to the promotion of environmental or social characteristics and sustainable investment objectives in pre-contractual documents, on websites and in periodic reports https://ec.europa.eu/finance/docs/level-2-measures/C_2022_1931_1_EN_ACT_part1_v6%20(1).pdf.

## 2. Limits of Engagement

The disclosure requirements examined in the previous paragraph react to the traditional passivity of institutional investors and asset managers, trying to stimulate their engagement both in general and with respect to ESG matters. Such passivity has been explained with various arguments mostly grounded on the lack of incentives to activism.[125] First, the market for asset managers is highly competitive and money goes to the managers offering higher returns, which do not necessarily depend on engagement with investee companies.[126] In addition, many funds track indices, so that superior returns only come from lowering distribution and management costs, while there is little interest for engagement.[127] Secondly, the costs of engagement are borne by the investors who engage, while the benefits are enjoyed by all shareholders in the company. This leads to rational apathy of investors (who do not engage because their private costs exceed their private benefits) and free riding of shareholders (who hope to benefit from the engagement of others). To the extent that the holdings of institutional investors have become more concentrated over the years and coordination amongst them has become easier, their rational apathy may gradually disappear.[128]

Thirdly, institutional investors typically earn commissions based on a percentage of assets under management, so that their dominant incentive is to increase their funds' size. This can be done through either marketing or better performance, with the link to fund performance being rather indirect.[129] Moreover, portfolio managers feel that engagement is generally a hard way to make money and prefer to walk away from a poor investment switching to a better one.[130] In addition, asset managers face a variety of conflicts of interests. For example, they may find it difficult to criticize a company while competing for the pension business of its employees; or, if they are part of a banking group, they may be pressured not to antagonize current or prospective clients by voting against the CEO's pay.[131]

One may wonder whether the incentives to engagement are stronger for institutional investors and asset managers with respect to the ESG characteristics of the investments offered. No doubt, also the market for the management of ESG investments is competitive, but competition does not necessarily depend on financial returns. The sustainability ratings of a given fund matter, to the extent that the end investors look at its ESG performance. Financial market participants will therefore also compete on ESG performance. Moreover, they will suffer less from rational apathy if they select the financial instruments in which to invest also based on sustainability considerations and

---

[125] See E Rock, 'Institutional Investors in Corporate Governance' in J Gordon and G Ringe (eds), *Oxford Handbook of Corporate Law and Governance* (OUP 2018) 363.
[126] ibid 373.
[127] ibid.
[128] ibid.
[129] ibid. Rock adds that money managers may have perverse incentives regarding activism. To the extent that funds depart from an index, but still compete with managers of similar funds, a fund's relative performance improves when 'underweighted' companies in their portfolio perform badly.
[130] ibid.
[131] ibid.

keep monitoring them from an ESG perspective. The private costs of their engagement could be lower as a result, particularly in the case of investments which pursue sustainability objectives and positive impacts. In addition, these costs may appear to be more justified if the relevant engagement shows a commitment of institutional investors and asset managers to ESG issues which are relevant to the end investors.

### 3. Is ESG Engagement More Likely?

To conclude, it is likely that the incentives for ESG engagement are greater than in the case of engagement related to financial performance, but only experience will show whether engagement in sustainability matters is more frequent and effective. We should also consider that environmental and social considerations may be relevant in terms of financial performance, so that engagement on them translates into a better financial performance of the company at issue.[132] The rules on disclosure examined in this paragraph may also contribute to enhance engagement to the extent that they rely on reputational incentives for financial market participants and allow better monitoring by the markets.

## V. Concluding Remarks

In this chapter, we have analysed the main regulatory strategies to promote ESG stewardship, namely voluntary codes, disclosure regulation, and fiduciary duties. While stewardship codes opened the discussion in this area, recent trends show that regulation of ESG stewardship is on the rise in the EU. Disclosure regulation addresses the information asymmetries between financial market participants and their clients and aims to prevent greenwashing. Fiduciary duties regulation is intended to clarify how sustainability factors and risks should be dealt with in investment selection and portfolio management as a prudential requirement for all types of financial products. Moreover, regulation specifies that sustainability preferences of clients should be considered both in product governance and in the assessment of suitability of financial products to end-investors.

As a result, investor protection stems both from stewardship disclosure by financial market participants and from regulation and supervision of their management and distribution activities. End-investors in all kinds of financial products should communicate their sustainability preferences to the relevant financial institution and make

---

[132] See A Dyck and others, 'Do Institutional Investors Drive Corporate Social Responsibility? International Evidence' (2019) 131 Journal of Financial Economics 693, showing that across forty-one countries, institutional ownership is positively associated with E&S performance with additional tests suggesting this relation is causal. See also G Balp and G Strampelli, 'Institutional Investor ESG Engagement: The European Experience' (2022) 23 European Business Organization Law Review 869 https://ssrn.com/abstract=4353703 or http://dx.doi.org/10.2139/ssrn.4353703.

their investments based on them. The suitability of such investments shall be assessed with reference to the clients' preferences, which are also classified to design the target market in product governance. To similar purposes, financial products are labelled under sustainability disclosure rules so that potential clients or investors can choose in an informed way according to their preferences. The supervision of disclosure should reduce the risk of greenwashing and the transactions costs relative to the selection of investments. However, supervision does not eliminate the risk of misrepresentation so that investor protection also depends on national rules concerning civil liability for false or misleading disclosure.

Overall, the legal framework concerning ESG stewardship is no doubt complex but also consistent with securities regulation and other parts of financial regulation such as insurance law. Sustainability is dealt with in ways that are not too different from those traditionally employed with respect to financial performance of investments and financial products in general. Indeed, recent reforms of fiduciary duties amend existing provisions simply integrating sustainability factors and risks into them. In all cases, the focus is on end-clients and their sustainability preferences. However, parts of the regulation do not strictly depend on those preferences but respond to prudential criteria which are applicable in all cases, such as the need for financial market participants to integrate sustainability risks into portfolio selection and risk management.

Regulatory policy serves not only the interests of end-investors and users of financial services, but also the economic and financial systems at large. The integration of sustainability in financial management should increase the resilience of the financial system and therefore reduce the risks to financial stability. Moreover, it should help the economy to reduce sustainability risks not only for enterprises but also for humanity by contributing, for instance, to reduce carbon emissions and therefore the impact of climate change. This justifies the choice of regulation made by the EU legislator given the public interest to enhance sustainability and the need to get both financial institutions and their clients involved in this extraordinary challenge. Nonetheless, the function of stewardship codes does not appear to be totally excluded by the rise of stewardship regulation in the EU. Rather, a rethink of the codes' function may be appropriate to the extent that they have ceased to be a substitute for regulation but could still be a complement of the latter, contributing to specify the regulatory principles and norms and to identify best practices in the relevant area of financial services.

# 13
# The French 'Duty of Vigilance' and the European Proposal on Companies' Due Diligence Duties

*Alain Pietrancosta**

## I. Introduction

This chapter focuses on the ongoing integration of CSR requirements into French company law. For a number of years, France has concentrated intensely on this topic of increasing interest to the rest of the world and has become for many an important CSR jurisprudential model.[1] Our CSR regimes continue to evolve, as this chapter reveals, inspiring ongoing national and international legislative work, leading in the short term to a proposal for a European directive, as part of the European Commission's action plan on financing sustainable growth, on corporate sustainability due diligence,[2] which could in turn, as a result of its worldwide application, become an international regulatory model.[3]

The French experience with what appears currently to be unique CSR provisions of French company law is accordingly interesting and, in several respects, revolutionary. For a number of years now, France has increasingly viewed itself as a global leader in CSR jurisprudence,[4] a forerunner hopefully providing an inspiring model for others to observe and perhaps follow.[5] This national ambition has manifested itself through two French company law reforms, intended to prevent companies' negative externalities or, simply put, harm to society. The first law, introduced in 2017, imposes an extensive so-called 'duty of vigilance' on large French corporations: a legally binding obligation to implement a proactive plan to prevent serious injury to human rights and fundamental freedoms, to the health and safety of people, and to the environment, which might result from company, subsidiary, supplier, and subcontractor activities throughout the

---

* All internet sources were last accessed on 10 January 2024.
[1] See European Parliament, 'Access to Legal Remedies for Victims of Coporate Human Rights Abuses in Third Countries' (February 2019) 109.
[2] Proposal for a Directive of the European Parliament and of the Council on Corporate Sustainability Due Diligence and amending Directive (EU) 2019/1937 COM(2022) 71 final, 2022/0051 (COD) (23 February 2022).
[3] Some may view it as a new illustration of the 'Brussels effect'. See A Bradford, *The Brussels Effect* (OUP 2020).
[4] For the 'white knight of CSR' see IM Barsan, 'Corporate Accountability: Non-Financial Disclosure and Liability—A French Perspective' (2017) 14 European Company and Financial Law Review 399.
[5] See 'Access to Legal Remedies for Victims of Coporate Human Rights Abuses in Third Countries' (n 1) 109.

world. A second piece of legislation, introduced in 2019, known as the 'PACTE law',[6] applicable to all companies registered in France, regardless of their form or size, imposed a broadly defined duty to take into consideration the social and environmental impacts of their activities, and also contains two optional provisions, introducing into French law two new concepts: the *raison d'être*—a company's fundamental reason for being—that a company may define in its bylaws; and the *société à mission* ('mission-driven company'), a new label, based on the B-corp model.

Thus, France has sought to distinguish itself as the first country in the world to experiment with such broad and general mandatory legal requirements. Needless to say, these two pieces of legislation have generated extraordinary international interest and have already become a reference point in ongoing national, European, and international legislative debates. Before briefly describing their respective contents, three general observations to provide some perspective and context for this evolution should be made.

First, these reforms reflect an important development from a regulatory viewpoint. CSR today no longer begins where the law ends.[7] In recent years, CSR norms, leaving the sphere of programmatic declarations, recommendatory principles, and experimental ethics, have made a remarkable breakthrough in legislation, particularly that applicable to companies.[8] Initially, to address CSR issues, legislators tended to favour disclosure. At first, voluntary, CSR disclosure regimes became mandatory for large companies.[9] France appears to be the first European country to introduce non-financial disclosure requirements for certain listed companies, with the Law of 15 May 2001 on new economic regulations (NREs).[10] On the climate front, the Law of 12 July 2010 on the national commitment to the environment requires large private and public entities to disclose at least every three years the amount of their greenhouse gas emissions, and describe the actions planned to reduce them.[11] The law of 17 August 2015 'for the energy transition and green growth' further obliged every company listed on a regulated market to include in its annual management report 'indications on the financial risks related to the effects of climate change and the presentation of the measures taken by the company to reduce them by implementing a low-carbon strategy in all the components of its activity'.[12] In the EU, the hardening or 'legalisation' of CSR is mainly[13] reflected in the European Directive of 22 October 2014 requiring disclosure

---

[6] Plan d'action pour la croissance et la transformation des entreprises.
[7] See CD Stone, *Where the Law Ends* (Harper & Row 1975).
[8] See C Bright and others, 'Toward a Corporate Duty for Lead Companies to Respect Human Rights in Their Global Value Chains?' (2020) 22(4) Business and Politics 667.
[9] G Berger-Walliser and Inara Scott, 'Redefining Corporate Social Responsibility in an Era of Globalization and Regulatory Hardening' (2018) 55(1) American Business Law Journal 167.
[10] See eg C Malecki, *Responsabilité sociale des entreprises: Perspectives de la gouvernance d'entreprise durable* (LGDJ 2014) margin no 127.
[11] Code de l'environnement, art L229-25, which, for private entities, applies to those with more than 500 employees. The decree n° 2022-982 of 1 July 2022 extended the disclosure obligation to scope 3 emissions.
[12] Code of Commerce, art L22-10-35.
[13] See the first references to the inclusion of 'non-financial key performance indicators' in the directive 2003/51/EC of 18 June 2003 on the annual and consolidated accounts of certain types of companies, banks and other financial institutions and insurance undertakings.

of non-financial and diversity information by large EU public-interest entities[14] (Non-Financial Reporting Directive or NFRD), supplemented by non-binding guidelines (2017), including the most recent ones (June 2019) on corporate climate-related information reporting.[15]

As announced in the 'Green Deal for Europe', the NFRD has been replaced by the Corporate Sustainability Reporting Directive (CSRD) of 14 December 2022 on the publication of sustainability information by companies.[16] The personal scope of the directive has been extended by significantly reversing the main criterion for application: the social and commercial dimension of the company replaces the listing on a regulated market. Gradually, by 2029, all 'large companies' in the EU within the meaning of the Accounting Directive (ie exceeding two of the following three criteria: 250 employees, €40 million turnover, €20 million balance sheet) will be covered, as well as 'public interest entity' small and medium-sized enterprises (SMEs). More unexpectedly, and in a departure from the ordinary rules governing the international application of company law, the CSRD will also apply to non-European companies with a significant European business (turnover in excess of €150 million) and a subsidiary or branch on EU territory. In total, the number of companies included would rise from 11,000 to 50,000, with the number of non-European entities estimated at more than 10,000.[17] The removal of listing as a prime criterion is worth noting, given the strong path dependence on the matter, associating public disclosure requirements with listed companies. However, this extension is likely to be a cause for concern for many small, medium-sized, and large companies, which have hitherto been spared.

In addition to extending its subjective scope, the CSRD modifies the objective scope and content of reporting obligations by proposing more precise and numerous requirements, in part in response to investors' increasing expectations and regulatory developments. The 'double materiality' of information is reflected in the requirement to include in the management report both how sustainability issues affect the company's performance (the outside-in perspective) and how the company itself impacts people and the environment (the inside-out perspective).

In the EU, one can also mention the recent Taxonomy Regulation[18] establishing the world's first ever 'green list'. The first building block of the 'Financing Sustainable Growth' action plan, the new regulation, which became effective in January 2022,

---

[14] The NFRD applied to large 'public-interest entities' (ie EU companies listed on an EU regulated market; listed or non-listed credit institutions, insurance undertakings, or any undertaking designated as such by Member States) with an average number of employees in excess of 500, and to public-interest entities that are parent companies of a large group with an average number of employees in excess of 500 on a consolidated basis.

[15] EU Guidelines on non-financial reporting: Supplement on reporting climate-related information, C/2019/4490 of June 2019.

[16] PE et Cons UE, dir no 2022/2464 (14 December 2022), modifiant le règlement (UE) no 537/2014 et les directives nos 2004/109/CE, 2006/43/CE et 2013/34/UE en ce qui concerne la publication d'informations en matière de durabilité par les entreprises [2022] OJ L322/15 (16 December 2022).

[17] VD Holger, 'At Least 10,000 Foreign Companies to Be Hit by EU Sustainability Rules' *The Wall Street Journal* (5 April 2023); the majority are from North America or the United Kingdom: 31 per cent from the United States, 13 per cent from Canada, and 11 per cent from the United Kingdom.

[18] Regulation (EU) 2020/852 of the European Parliament and of the Council of 18 June 2020 on the establishment of a framework to facilitate sustainable investment, and amending Regulation (EU) 2019/2088 [2020] OJ L198/13 (22 June 2020).

provides a classification system ('taxonomy') for sustainable economic activities that requires NFRD companies to disclose the extent to which their sales, investments, and/or expenditure are linked to activities defined in the EU taxonomy.[19] Likewise, financial market participants must now disclose the extent to which activities of their financial products funds meet the EU taxonomy criteria. The regulation thus makes it possible to share a common definition of sustainability and to reduce the risks of 'greenwashing'. The classification criteria were specified in a 349-page delegated regulation.[20]

Certain CSR promoters have questioned these reporting requirements, on the basis of alleged shortcomings, particularly that they are not very effective,[21] do not in many cases provide for sanctions for non-compliance, and do not require substantive due diligence.[22] They also come post facto.[23] Too harsh criticism runs the risk of ignoring the prevention, emulation, and sanctioning virtues, at least reputational, of disclosure requirements. Transparency does not merely reveal what exists: it often leads to changes in what exists. As Justice Brandeis famously noted: '[s]unlight is often the best disinfectant!' This change through disclosure requirements can be achieved by means of negative incentives, at least through fears of market reactions, but also by means of actual constraints, as reflected in the latest developments in transparency on sustainability issues. Obligations on companies to publicly disclose their sustainability strategies and due diligence policies therefore, in effect, require them to have some. In this context and perspective, transparency and substantive obligations are not so much alternatives to each other as complementary policies.

It is nonetheless clear that, reflecting experience with limitations on using reporting requirements, the second generation of CSR provisions is more substantive, utilising a priori or *ex ante* obligations designed to identify risks and prevent harm, to specifically protected human and/or environmental interests.[24] What was gained in terms of depth and sanctions, however, was lost in terms of scope: these later CSR legal provisions only targeted specific fields or issues, evidently selected on the basis of their perceived importance and social sensitivity.

---

[19] See Commission Delegated Regulation (EU) 2021/2178 of 6 July 2021 supplementing Regulation (EU) 2020/852 of the European Parliament and of the Council by specifying the content and presentation of information to be disclosed by undertakings subject to Articles 19a or 29a of Directive 2013/34/EU concerning environmentally sustainable economic activities, and specifying the methodology to comply with that disclosure obligation [2021] OJ L 443/9 (10 December 2021).

[20] Commission Delegated Regulation (EU) 2021/2139 of 4 June 2021 supplementing Regulation (EU) 2020/852 of the European Parliament and of the Council by establishing the technical screening criteria for determining the conditions under which an economic activity qualifies as contributing substantially to climate change mitigation or climate change adaptation and for determining whether that economic activity causes no significant harm to any of the other environmental objectives [2021] OJ L442/1 (9 December 2021).

[21] European Commission, 'Study on due diligence requirements through the supply chain' (January 2020) 247.

[22] ibid 154; C Macchi and C Bright, 'Hardening Soft Law: The Implementation of Human Rights Due Diligence Requirements in Domestic Legislation' in M Buscemi and others (eds), *Legal Sources in Business and Human Rights: Evolving Dynamics in International and European Law* (Brill 2020) 218.

[23] D Weber-Rey, 'Lost in Detail: Setting Priorities for Corporations in Challenging Times' in British Academy Review, 'Reforming Business for the 21st Century' (Autumn 2018) 15.

[24] On the interdependence of environmental protection measures and human rights, including those of future generations, see the very enlightening decision of the German Constitutional Court: BVerfG, Order of the First Senate of 24 March 2021; 1 BvR 2656/18.

# INTRODUCTION 279

Taking a further step in the legal escalation, a third generation of CSR provisions broadens many such substantive obligations, which become more horizontal, cross-sectoral and cross-issue. France, already an innovator in mandatory environmental disclosure regulation,[25] once again appears to lead the way, with this broader, more holistic approach. This new holistic approach has operated both objectively, with an extensive duty of vigilance, a substantive monitoring obligation, imposed on large stock corporations in 2017, and subjectively, with a duty imposed on all companies, regardless of their legal forms or sizes, in 2019 to take into consideration social and environmental issues. France has not only legally adopted the 2011 United Nations guiding principles on business and human rights (UNGPs), expressly including the health and safety of persons,[26] but has extended the diligence requirements to the protection of the environment, following OECD Guidelines. Such mandatory CSR laws reflect a tendency in France to use regulation as a policy instrument to react to crisis and to guide people's or companies' conduct more directly, rather than a particularly strong adherence to stakeholder theory. The French are also reputed to have some scepticism about markets, as now illustrated by a good number of opinion polls.[27]

Even if this idiosyncrasy explains the legal origin of the movement, it is unable to explain fully its dynamics and expansion. The political will behind the adoption of these new obligations, especially of the law on the duty of vigilance, has from the outset incorporated the idea that their effectiveness and efficiency would depend on their international appeal.[28] Thus, partly under the influence of the French government, encouraged by French companies willing to share the burden of such general obligations of vigilance with their worldwide competitors, the French approach has been used as a model by the European Commission, which has proposed to extend it to the entire European Union through a directive, under discussion for more two years.[29] This process started in January 2020, with a study on options for regulating due diligence requirements through the supply chain, which concluded that voluntary regimes across Europe had failed to change the way businesses managed their corporate governance responsibilities. As a consequence, in April 2020 the European Commission announced that it would introduce new company legislation on mandatory human rights and environmental due diligence. Reasons for support for a mandatory due diligence duty at the EU level 'include higher levels of implementation, access to remedies but also the levelling of the playing field, a single harmonized standard,

---

[25] France was the first European country to introduce non-financial reporting for certain large companies, with the Law of 15 May 2001 on new economic regulations (NREs) (art 116).
[26] See J Ruggie, 'Business and Human Rights: Towards Operationalizing the "Protect, Respect and Remedy" Framework' Report to the UN Human Rights Council, UN Doc A/HRC/11/13 (22 April 2009) § 71; J Bonnitcha and R McCorquodale, 'The Concept of "Due Diligence" in the UN Guiding Principles on Business and Human Rights' (2017) 28(3) European Journal of International Law 899.
[27] See 'Les Français champions du monde de l'anti-capitalisme' ['The French are world champions in anti-capitalism'] La Tribune (25 January 2011) https://www.latribune.fr/actualites/economie/20110125trib000595445/les-francais-champions-du-monde-de-l-anti-capitalisme.html.
[28] See T Sachs, 'La loi sur le devoir de vigilance des sociétés-mères et sociétés donneuses d'ordre: les ingrédients d'une corégulation' (2017) 6 Revue de droit du travail 380; P Pailot and D de Saint-Affrique, 'Loi sur le devoir de vigilance: éléments d'analyse d'une forme de juridicisation de la RSE' (2020) 24(2) Management International 109.
[29] European Commission (n 21).

and legal certainty'.[30] The European Commission issued this new legislative proposal on 23 February 2022,[31] described as 'real game changer in the way companies operate their business activities throughout their global supply chain'[32] or 'a watershed moment for human rights and the environment'.[33]

This directive proposal also contemplated to include provisions on directors' duties and sustainable corporate governance. The European Commission had already set out this idea in its 2018 Action Plan on Financing Sustainable Growth. Building on the work of the High-Level Expert Group on Sustainable Finance, the Commission stated that it would carry out analytical and consultative work with relevant stakeholders to assess: (i) the possible need to require corporate boards to develop and disclose a sustainability strategy, including appropriate due diligence throughout the supply chain, and measurable sustainability targets; and (ii) the possible need to clarify the rules according to which directors would be expected to act in the company's long-term interest. Following this path, in 2019, the Commission invited the European supervisory authorities to collect evidence of undue short-term pressure from capital markets on corporations[34] and commissioned EY to carry out a study on directors' duties and sustainable corporate governance, with the view of gathering evidence of a possible trend towards short-term shareholder value maximization by EU companies, of investigating the main factors contributing to this trend and of analysing how a possible reform of company law and board duties could contribute to greater accountability for sustainable value creation.

The EY report, dated July 2020, purported to provide evidence that there exists 'a trend for publicly listed companies within the EU to focus on short-term benefits of shareholders rather than on the long-term interests of the company'.[35] Data collected over the period from 1992 to 2018 allegedly indicates 'an upward trend in shareholder payouts, which increased fourfold, from less than 1% of revenues in 1992 to almost 4% in 2018. Moreover, the ratio of CAPEX and R&D investment to revenues has been declining since the beginning of the 21st century'. According to the report, corporate 'short-termism' finds its root, at least to some extent, in regulatory frameworks and market practices, which 'work together to promote a focus on short-term financial return rather than on long-term sustainable value creation'. Seven 'problem drivers' were identified: 1. Directors' duties and company's interest are interpreted narrowly and

---

[30] ibid 154.

[31] COM(2022) 71 final (n 2) In a Communication on Decent Work Worldwide, the EU Commission confirmed that it is preparing an additional legislative initiative to prohibit goods made with forced labour, including forced child labour, from the EU market, see Communication from the Commission to the European Parliament, the Council and the European Economic and Social Committee on decent work worldwide for a global just transition and a sustainable recovery COM(2022) 66 final (Brussels 23 February 2022).

[32] Didier Reynders, Commissioner for Justice.

[33] R Gardiner of *Global Witness* in Aoife White, A Nardelli, and S. Bodoni, 'Unethical Firms Risk Massive Bills in EU Supply-Chain Crackdown' *Bloomberg* (21 February 2022).

[34] See ESMA Report Undue short-term pressure on corporations (18 December 2019); EBA Report on undue short-term pressure from the financial sector on corporations (18 December 2019); EIOPA, Potential undue short-term pressure from financial markets on corporates: Investigation on European insurance and occupational pension sectors (18 December 2019).

[35] EY Final Report, 'Study on Directors' Duties and Sustainable Corporate Governance' (July 2020) https://ec.europa.eu/info/law/better-regulation/have-your-say/initiatives/12548-Sustainable-corporate-governance.

tend to favour the short-term maximization of shareholder value; 2. Growing pressures from investors with a short-term horizon contribute to increasing the boards' focus on short-term financial returns to shareholders at the expense of long-term value creation; 3. Companies lack a strategic perspective over sustainability and current practices fail effectively to identify and manage relevant sustainability risks and impacts; 4. Board remuneration structures incentivize the focus on short-term shareholder value rather than long-term value creation for the company; 5. The current board composition does not fully support a shift towards sustainability; 6. Current corporate governance frameworks and practices do not sufficiently voice the long-term interests of stakeholders; 7. Enforcement of the directors' duty to act in the long-term interest of a company is limited.

Rarely has a preliminary report to the European Commission raised as much criticism from the academia and business organizations. Criticism focused on the study's allegedly fundamental deficiencies in understanding capital market dynamics, company law and practices mischaracterizations, a subpar methodology and economic literature selection biases, all to satisfy the Commission's preconceptions.[36] Rather disturbingly, the Commission clearly did not take these criticisms into account in the questionnaire it submitted for public consultation a few days later,[37] whose equally reproachful wording reflected the initial biases to get the parties consulted to validate the Commission's preferred options.[38]

Fortunately, a number of opposing forces played their part. In the European Parliament ambitions had to be scaled back in order to secure a sufficient majority for a resolution asking the Commission to present a legislative proposal covering all EU listed and non-listed large undertakings and also non-EU companies operating in the EU market, 'to ensure that directors' duties cannot be misconstrued as amounting solely to the short-term maximization of shareholder value, but must instead include the long-term interest of the company and wider societal interests, as well as that of employees and other relevant stakeholders'.[39] At national level, in addition to the criticism of such an attack on the market economy and shareholders, many Member States denounced the inappropriateness, or even the illegality, of the European Commission's use of the climate issue to justify breaking the consensus on the principle of subsidiarity in corporate governance. This consensus is based on the

---

[36] See among others M Bianchi and M Milič, 'The Unconvincing Analysis and Conclusions of the Ernst & Young Study' *Oxford Business Law Blog* (13 October 2020); M.J Roe and others, 'The European Commission's Sustainable Corporate Governance Report: A Critique' *Oxford Business Law Blog* (20 October 2020); J Fried and C Wang, 'Short-Termism, Shareholder Payouts, and Investment in the EU' (October 2020) Harvard Business School; 'Levée de boucliers contre un rapport européen sur la gouvernance durable' *Les Échos* (21 October 2020); 'A Response from the Copenhagen Business School' *Oxford Business Law Blog* (26 October 2020); JC Coffee Jr, 'The European Commission Considers "Short-Termism" (and "What Do You Mean By That?")' *Oxford Business Law Blog* (17 November 2020); J Fried and C Wang, 'Le capitalisme durable menace la durabilité des entreprises' *Les Échos* (18 December 2020); A Pietrancosta in Aefinfo.fr (13 January 2021).
[37] See the Inception impact assessment (30 July 2020) Ares(2020)4034032.
[38] ECLE, EC Corporate Governance Initiative Series: Comment by the European Company Law Experts Group on the European Commission's Consultation Document 'Proposal for an Initiative on Sustainable Corporate Governance' *Oxford Business Law Blog* (9 December 2020).
[39] European Parliament resolution of 17 December 2020 on sustainable corporate governance (2020/2137(INI)), P9_TA(2020)0372.

idea that it is difficult to impose a meaningful common framework on corporate governance across the EU, for obvious reasons of different national regulations, traditions and cultures.

In the face of this resistance, the politically sensitive and strategic question arose as to whether there would be one or two proposals for a directive and, if there were only one, what would remain of the corporate governance component. The choice was finally made to introduce in the same text, in addition to general due diligence requirements and their subsequent specific duties, an Article 25 that defined a general duty of care for corporate directors and executives. This meant, as does the French model on which it is based, 'taking into consideration' the consequences of their decisions regarding sustainability matters, including human rights, climate change and environmental consequences. However, Article 25 did not survive the criticisms[40] and the various compromises that led to the final version of the directive.

A second observation is that we can only be struck by the use and co-option of company law for general social and environmental purposes, the consequent politicization of the role of companies, and the mix of genres and confusion arising between public and private goals.[41] Companies must bear the consequences of the commitments made by governments, in terms of protection of human rights or the environment.[42] As states and their governments are themselves bound by international standards of conduct that include prevention of various kinds of harm, they may try to minimize their non-compliance risks by passing their obligations of due diligence on to business enterprises. In environmental matters, states may even commit internationally and nationally to reach specific results,[43] some of which may require drastic changes whose burden is then largely passed on to companies, in the name of their contributing role.[44] Such 'privatization' of states' commitments reflects a policy choice to decentralize the means to achieve internationally defined global objectives or the states' role becomes reduced to imposing proactive duties on multinational enterprises commensurate to those enterprises' power and impact. As a matter of policy, this approach seeks to bridge the gap between the boundaries of national or regional legal requirements and the economic/social/environmental impacts of transnational firms. Technically, this may result in giving some direct effect to international agreements that do not by

---

[40] Adde, The proposed Due Diligence Directive should not cover the general duty of care of directors, ECLE, https://www.ecgi.global/publications/blog/the-proposed-due-diligence-directive-should-not-cover-the-general-duty-of-care-of.

[41] See T Levitt, 'The Dangers of Social Responsibility' (1958) 36(5) Harvard Business Review 41; in the same direction see RB Reich, *Supercapitalism: The Transformation of Business, Democracy and Everyday Life* (Knopf 2007).

[42] O Favereau and B Roger, *Penser l'entreprise: un nouvel horizon du politique* (éd. Paroles et silence 2015); O Favereau, 'Réformer l'entreprise' *Études* (2018/9) 55; T Sachs, 'Les dangers d'une dilution du devoir de vigilance dans la compliance' (2022) 6 Revue de Droit du Travail 352.

[43] See EU Regulation 2021/1119 of the European Parliament and of the Council of 30 June 2021 establishing the framework for achieving climate neutrality and amending Regulations (EC) No 401/2009 and (EU) 2018/1999 (European Climate Law) [2021] OJ L243/1 (9 July 2021); Regulation 2018/842 of the European Parliament and of the Council of 30 May 2018 on binding annual greenhouse gas emission reductions by Member States from 2021 to 2030 contributing to climate action to meet commitments under the Paris Agreement and amending Regulation (EU) No 525/2013 [2018] OJ L156/26 (19 June 2018).

[44] It is notable that the 2015 Paris Climate Agreement does not mention business enterprise once.

their terms seem to have such effect.[45] If, according to soft-law international standards, in particular the second pillar of the UNGPs, the corporate responsibility to respect human rights exists independently of the State duty to protect human rights, such decorrelation is indeed more difficult to conceive in hard law, which is expressed not in terms of abstract corporate responsibility, but in terms of specific legal duties. This result is in a sense realized indirectly, through specific prevention or remediation obligations which are often expressed as simple obligations of 'means', but which, depending on the case, may be similar to obligations of 'result' receiving a worldwide application, thus potentially conflicting with foreign national laws. By virtue of their mere legal or even economic attachment to the European Union, the companies concerned are thus made subject to mandatory international human rights and environmental norms of behaviour, from which they cannot depart by crossing borders. As it entails the substitution of a foreign legal system through obligations imposed on private operators for allegedly failing national states, these legal duties contain a certain proactive extraterritorial element that some would characterize as overreaching at least, and perhaps imperialistic.[46] Company law is used because of the significant influence it can have on business behaviour,[47] which optimists may view as reassuring and exciting, as company law is called to serve higher purposes, help solve what many consider monumental problems of our time and give effect to the highest human rights and environmental standards on a global scale. Those less optimistic may question, as a matter of public policy, the use and efficacy of these generalized precautionary measures intermediated by company leaders, rather than direct regulatory measures targeting specific social or environmental issues. This may even create an illusion that these issues are already appropriately taken care of and delay perhaps the necessary policy measures.[48] Some may also view this move as an attempt by big business to preempt more demanding and costly specific regulation. The flip side is that, since these legal provisions are formulated in a very general manner, they create a great deal of legal uncertainty for companies and have the additional disadvantage of fuelling criticism, disputes, and litigation under them. This vagueness often seems to reflect the origins of the approach to the current law in international human rights/environment oriented-soft regulation, which has not been subject to the necessary translation into language in hard law.

---

[45] On the lack of direct effect of the Paris Agreement, see Conseil d'État, 19 November 2020, No 427301, Commune de Grande-Synthe, Lebon, 406; Le « contrôle de la trajectoire » et la carence de l'État français à lutter contre les changements climatiques—Retour sur les décisions Grande-Synthe en passant par l'Affaire du siècle, AJDA 2021, 2115. Its content must, however, be 'taken into consideration in the interpretation of the provisions of national law', see Conseil d'État, decision of 1 July 2021.

[46] See J Lacroix and J-Y Pranchère, *Le procès des droits de l'homme: généalogie du scepticisme démocratique* (Éditions du Seuil 2016).

[47] United Nations, Guiding Principles on Business and Human Rights (2011) 6 https://www.ohchr.org/sites/default/files/Documents/Publications/GuidingPrinciplesBusinessHR_EN.pdf.

[48] See LA Bebchuk and R Tallarita, 'The Illusory Promise of Stakeholder Governance' (2020) 106 Cornell Law Review 91; LA Bebchuk and R Tallarita, 'Will Corporations Deliver Value to All Stakeholders?' (2022) 75 Vanderbilt Law Review 1031; E Strine, 'The Dangers of Denial: The Need for a Clear-Eyed Understanding of the Power and Accountability Structure Established by the Delaware General Corporation Law' (2015) 50 Wake Forest Law Review 761.

A *third* observation concerns the similarities and differences between the two laws in question. These laws share the values and articulate the requirements that are usually associated with responsible business conduct.[49] On the other hand they differ in spirit: the 2017 law on the duty of vigilance is a risk mitigation law. Even if it does so in an elaborate way, it basically expresses a no-harm duty; by contrast, the 2019 law aims to ensure the promotion of the common good by obliging managers to move towards a long-term alignment of what it assumes are common interests of shareholders and stakeholders. This is something in common with the draft EU directive. In addition to that they differ in scope. If the two laws only apply to French companies, the 2017 law covers the small circle of large joint-stock companies, whereas the 2019 law concerns all companies, regardless of their size or corporate form. Instead of instituting, as in France, a 'duty of vigilance' for some and an 'enlightened' company interest standard for all, the European Commission proposes to limit the CSDD scope to large EU companies and to extend due diligence requirements for large non-European companies.

As the issues related to the PACTE law are dealt with elsewhere,[50] this chapter will focus on the duty of vigilance, which the 2022 European proposal on the CSDD seeks to make more broadly applicable.

## II. The Genesis of the French 'Duty of Vigilance' and the Proposed European Generalization of 'Due Diligence Requirements'

### 1. In a Nutshell

The French corporate duty of vigilance law establishes a legally binding obligation for large French corporations to assess and mitigate the risks of serious harm to people and the environment. As a main requirement, such corporations are required to establish, implement, and publish in essence a 'vigilance plan'. This plan must include reasonable measures to identify risks and prevent serious harm to human rights and fundamental freedoms, the health and safety of persons and the environment, through their whole supply chain, meaning resulting from company, subsidiary, supplier, and subcontractor activities.

These harms are not legally defined. The law does not even say how these corporations should deal with different local legal requirements. In international situations, the basic principle is that group companies must comply with local law.[51] The new legal duty, however, requires companies to take steps to address relevant harms, regardless of whether they are permitted or prohibited by the laws of the countries where they take place.[52]

---

[49] See Stone (n 7).
[50] See also Alain Pietrancosta, '"Intérêt social" and "raison d'être": Thoughts about Two Core Provisions of the Business Growth and Transformation Action Plan (PACTE) Act that Amend Corporate Law' (November 2019) Annales des Mines: Réalités industrielles 55.
[51] See the 2018 OECD Due Diligence Guidance for Responsible Business Conduct (Comp ISO 26000), 'Guidance on Social Responsibility' 4.6 ff.
[52] European Commission (n 21) 266.

Civil liability would apply when companies default on their obligations, including the absence of a plan or faults in its implementation. 'Any interested parties—including affected people and communities—are empowered to hold companies accountable. They can require judicial authorities to order a company to establish, publish and implement a vigilance plan'.[53] Such parties may also bring civil liability lawsuits against companies and ask for compensation if the violation of these legal requirements has caused harm.

## 2. The Narrative

For many years, there have been documented abuses by transnational corporations, which allegedly demonstrate that the national and international legal frameworks or voluntary standards do not always allow for economic players to be held responsible when it comes to human rights or for payments of damages to be claimed wherever they may have occurred in the world,[54] and that a legally binding framework is necessary 'where achieving corporate accountability is hindered by: the complexity, scale and reach of corporate structures; the absence of a level playing-field; the legal and practical barriers faced by victims to access remedies;[55] or the lack of enforcement of existing standards especially concerning transnational corporations with a myriad of subsidiaries and suppliers' in multiple jurisdictions.

## 3. Counterpoint

Needless to say, the proposed reform has raised much criticism.[56] As for the main points of criticism, it was argued that:

(1) The major French groups have already been developing and implementing such vigilance strategies for many years. They are among the most compliant with international standards.[57]

---

[53] French Corporate Duty of Vigilance Law, Frequently Asked Questions, European Coalition for Corporate Justice (23 February 2017).

[54] See A Marx, C Bright, and J Wouters, 'Access to Legal Remedies for Victims of Corporate Human Rights Abuses in Third Countries' (2019) 107 http://www.europarl.europa.eu/RegData/etudes/STUD/2019/603475/EXPO_STU(2019)603475_EN.pdf.

[55] See Marx, Bright and Wouters (n 54); A Marx, C Bright, and J Wouters, 'Corporate Accountability Mechanisms in EU Member States for Human Rights Abuses in Third Countries' (2019) European Yearbook on Human Rights 157; OHCHR, 'Improving accountability and access to remedy for victims of business-related human rights abuse: the relevance of human rights due diligence to determinations of corporate liability' UN Doc A/HRC/38/20/Add.2 (1 June 2018) 19; European Commission (n 21) 228.

[56] See eg A Pietrancosta and É Boursican, 'Vigilance: un devoir à surveiller!' (2015) La Semaine Juridique: Edition Générale (JCP G) 553; D de Saint-Affrique, 'De l'opportunité de légiférer sur le devoir de vigilance: choix compassionnel pertinent ou inadapté?' La Semaine Juridique Entreprise et Affaires no 5 (2 février 2017) 1064; C Malecki, 'Le devoir de vigilance des sociétés mères et entreprises donneurs d'ordres: était-ce bien raisonnable?' (2017) Bulletin Joly Sociétés 298; A Reygrobellet, 'Devoir de vigilance ou risque d'insomnies?' (2017) 128 Revue Lamy Droit des affaires 35.

[57] See EcoVadis, 'Comparatif de la performance RSE des entreprises françaises avec celle des pays de l'OCDE et des BRICS' (Édition 2019).

(2) Voluntary CSR commitments already produce normative effects.
(3) No other country imposes such a broad obligation on its companies.
(4) Such a piece of legislation would impose both considerable and ill-defined obligations on French companies, thereby distorting international competition, creating major legal uncertainty, and seriously undermining the attractiveness of the French jurisdiction and territory without at the same time achieving the objectives of strengthening the protection of human rights, social rights, and the environment.
(5) This legislation does not only concern large companies: in practice, outsourcing companies will be led to impose on their subcontractors, primarily French SMEs.
(6) This law can have adverse effects on suppliers and subcontractors of French companies in emerging countries. Companies could be tempted to turn to less-risky global suppliers, to the detriment of the development of local businesses.[58]
(7) The broad legal standing granted to any interested person anywhere in the world to sue French companies dramatically increases the litigation risk for them.

## 4. Softening Amendments

Some of the above and other criticisms were taken into account with a softened, amended version. Thanks to a change in the national political environment, some of the bill's requirements were relaxed. In particular, the idea of creating a presumption of wrongdoing on the part of companies in the event of harm, a criminal offence or a class action mechanism were both abandoned. Other amendments were imposed by the French Constitutional Council. They mainly concern the imposition of new obligations, including civil penalties of €10 or €30 million for non-compliant companies, that were declared unconstitutional by the French Constitutional court in a decision dated 23 March 2017, ironically because they were found to be in violation of the French Declaration of human rights because of their lack of clarity.

## 5. Internationalization

As for the 'no-other-country' argument, the main promoters of the text took pride in it rather than circumspection in the hope that others will follow the French example. Following the well-known principle of self-fulfilling prophecy, France has since been playing a leading role in the adoption of international liability rules and presents itself

---

[58] See General Council of the Economy, 'Évaluation de la mise en œuvre de la loi n° 2017-399 du 27 mars 2017 relative au devoir de vigilance des sociétés mères et des entreprises donneuses d'ordre' (January 2020) rédigé par Mme A Duthilleul et M M de Jouvenel 38.

as a model.[59] At the national level, initiatives have indeed multiplied regarding due diligence requirements. According to the European Commission, they have been discussed or adopted in 13 countries, of which 11 are EU Member States. At the international level, a United Nations legally binding instrument to impose on transnational corporations due diligence requirements to prevent human rights violations, has been in preparation since 2014 and is still under discussion.[60]

## 6. Towards a European Directive

At the European level, the Commission's proposal on CSDD, published on 23 February 2022, is informed by and built on the French model. The two articles of the French Commercial Code are expanded to some thirty articles in the EU proposal, setting out the obligations of due diligence to be imposed on a wider range of companies, including non-European ones operating in Europe, regarding actual and potential human rights and environmental adverse impacts, with respect to their own operations, the operations of their subsidiaries and the value chain of operations carried out by entities with whom companies have established direct or indirect business relationships.

More innovative is the obligation for the largest EU and non-EU qualifying companies[61] to 'ensure' that their business models and strategies are 'compatible with the transition to a sustainable economy and with the limiting of global warming to 1.5°C in line with the Paris Agreement'.[62] This is a far cry from the French obligation to request large private entities or listed companies to disclose publicly the measures taken to reduce their carbon footprint.[63] While the European obligation is intended to provide a substantive basis for the disclosure requirement present in the forthcoming CSRD, a literal reading of its strict requirements contrasts with the means-based due diligence requirements. Indeed, it seems to lead to a meta-obligation with respect to climate impact results, exceeding what the Paris Agreement actually requires, which would condition the legal and economic survival of each subject company, without regard to its objective ability to reduce its emissions to specific levels, the materiality of such emissions on global climate change limitation targets, reinforced by the risk of circumvention (consisting for a qualifying company, for example, in merely selling its affected business to a non-qualifying company) or its otherwise positive contributions. Unsurprisingly, this provision has attracted much attention and criticism,[64] as

---

[59] See C Clerc, 'The French "Duty of Vigilance" Law: Lessons for an EU Directive on Due Diligence in Multinational Supply Chains, ETUI', The European Trade Union Institute, 15 January 2021 and Legislation of EU Supply Chain Due Diligence Act: Current Status, International Labor Brief (November 2021).
[60] Human Rights Council, 'Elaboration of an International Legally Binding Instrument on Transnational Corporations and Other Business Enterprises with Respect to Human Rights' (2014) A/HRC/Res 26/9.
[61] ie group 1 companies.
[62] CS3D Proposal, art 15.
[63] See n 4 above.
[64] See Response to the Proposal for a Directive on Corporate Sustainability Due Diligence by Nordic and Baltic Company Law Scholars, NORDIC & European COMPANY LAW, LSN Research Paper Series, No 22-01.

what could be an unconditioned 'death-penalty' sanction may appear disproportionate and therefore legally questionable with respect to the freedom of enterprise protected by the Charter of fundamental rights of the European Union and the many Member States' constitutions. Taking these criticisms into account, the final version of the directive has downgraded this obligation to an obligation of means (art 22).

## III. The French Vigilance and the European Diligence Compared

This comparison highlights the common inspiration of the French and European texts, but also the ambition of the European Commission to go beyond the French model in developing a more inclusive, elaborate, and better-enforced legal regime. These features will be verified through a comparison of their respective scope (section 1), content (section 2), and sanctions (section 3).

### 1. Personal scope

The French duty of vigilance applies to all types of commercial stock corporations registered in France. This restriction to only stock companies has been criticized as making little sense considering the purpose of the law.[65] In concrete terms, it allows certain companies, organized as other than stock companies to avoid this legal obligation. As some of the excluded companies are themselves limited liability ones, it appears that the French legislature did not conceive of the duty of vigilance as a condition to receiving the legal advantage of limited liability granted to shareholders.

A second condition is that, at the end of two consecutive financial years, at least 5,000 employees work for the company and its direct and indirect French-registered subsidiaries, or at least 10,000 employees work for the company and its direct and indirect French or foreign subsidiaries. Therefore, French subsidiary companies of foreign groups may fall within the scope of the law through their own French and foreign subsidiaries, and thus be required to establish a vigilance plan for their own value chains. An exemption exists for companies controlled by a company already covered.

Curiously, there is no official record of such companies. They are estimated to number around 250.[66] Perhaps influenced in turn by the European approach, a French parliamentary mission in February 2022 proposed redefining the scope of the French law by lowering the employee thresholds and introducing an alternative trigger linked

---

[65] In favour of an extension see General Council of the Economy (n 58) 20; Rapport Ass Nat no 5124 (24 February 2022) 45 ff.
[66] General Council of the Economy (n 58) 33. See also Terre solidaire and Sherpa, 'Le radar du devoir de vigilance. Identifier les entreprises soumises à la loi' (1st edn 2019, 2nd edn 2020, 3rd edn 2021).

to turnover.[67] This number is relatively low, compared to the thousands of companies, both European and non-European, potentially covered by the proposal for a European Corporate Sustainability Due Diligence directive. The Directive would, first, be applicable to EU companies that have more than 500 employees on average and a net worldwide turnover of more than €150 million; or more than 250 employees and a net worldwide turnover of more than €40 million, provided that at least 50 per cent of this net turnover was generated in one or more sensitive sectors. The final compromise raised these numbers to 1,000 employees and €450 million in turnover, with a gradually entry into force. Unlike the 2011 UNGPs and OECD Guidelines for Multinational Enterprises, which recommend their application to all companies 'regardless of their size, sector, location, ownership and structure', the European proposal follows the more restrictive French model, in particular regarding the legal forms or the size of companies, while including more legal forms and retaining much lower social thresholds (5–10 per cent of the French ones).

Conversely, moving away from the French regulatory model, referring to the domicile *and* place of economic operations of multinational enterprises,[68] the Directive would also be applicable to third-country companies of a comparable legal form with a net turnover of €150 million in the Union or of €40 million, provided that at least 50 per cent of their net worldwide turnover were generated in one or more of the above-mentioned sensitive sectors. Quantitative thresholds later set generally at €450 million in turnover. While an economic activity in Europe is not required for companies registered in the EU, for non-European companies the choice of a criterion related to turnover generated in Europe is rationalized by the fact that it ensures a sufficient territorial connection with the EU, which is necessary according to general EU law[69] and probably also to World Trade Organization (WTO) law.

As the French experience shows companies, particularly SMEs, that do not fall directly under the scope of the legislation are likely to feel as a practical matter its trickle-down effect as business partners or subsidiaries of the former ones. This trickle-down effect may materialize 'through contractual clauses included in B2B commercial contracts and other measures'.[70] In France, it has been estimated that '80% of French SMEs and midcaps (which are out of the French law's scope) are asked by their contractors on CSR issues, whether to sign a charter or a code of conduct, to declare themselves in conformity with the main social and environmental standards, to sign clauses in their contracts or to undergo an extra-financial audit'.[71]

---

[67] Rapport Ass Nat no 5124 (n 65) 57.
[68] See also the German and Norwegian due diligence acts, applicable to certain foreign companies operating in those countries.
[69] See CJCE (9 November 2000) *Ingmar* aff C-381/98 *Rec* p I-9305, EU:C:2000:605, Opinion AG Léger, ECLI:EU:C:2000:230.
[70] Commission Staff Working Document, Impact Assessment Report, Annex 5.
[71] Devoir de vigilance: les PME en première ligne, sans être assez accompagnées par les donneurs d'ordre, Novethic (16 January 2020) https://www.novethic.fr/actualite/entreprise-responsable/isr-rse/rse-et-devoir-de-vigilance-les-pme-en-premiere-ligne-sans-avoir-toujours-les-moyens-adequats-148094.html.

## 2. Substantive Requirements

a) French vigilance plans

Any company meeting the above-mentioned criteria is required to establish, effectively implement, and publish a 'vigilance plan'. This plan must include reasonable measures to identify risks and prevent serious harms with respect to 'human rights and fundamental freedoms, the health and safety of persons and the environment'.[72] These harms may result from company, subsidiary, supplier, and subcontractor activities. Here, subsidiaries are defined as companies that are under the exclusive control of the parent. Beyond subsidiaries, the law extends to subcontractors and suppliers, but only those with whom an 'established business relationship' is maintained if this relationship is related to the activities in question. Only 'serious harms' are addressed by the law and specifically intended to be prevented. The law does not define 'serious', although the term and concept appear commonly in French law, particularly in labour law, and French courts have a long experience in its interpretation.

As for the existence of harm to safety, health or the environment, a recurring question is the legal point of reference. In international situations, how should parent companies deal with different local legal requirements? The basic principle is that companies must comply with local law.[73] However, due diligence requires companies to take steps to address relevant harms regardless of whether they are permitted or prohibited by the laws of the countries where they take place.[74] Therefore, if local law is less prescriptive than French law, then there is typically a risk of severe harm. This risk must be identified and the company must consider whether it is possible to comply with a more prescriptive French or international standard[75] while still respecting local law. It is striking that this duty of vigilance exceeds the traditional framework of compliance, since it obliges companies to go beyond the mere requirement to comply with the applicable national laws and to apply higher standards internationally which are not even specified in the law. This deliberate ambiguity seems intended to avoid making the duty of vigilance a purely procedural obligation that would over time drift into merely a 'box-ticking' exercise.[76]

Another restriction comes from a requirement of 'reasonableness' of the measures contained in the plan, a standard that appears potentially to modulate the standard of vigilance. Reasonableness depends on the proportionality of the measures taken in

---

[72] According to an amendment introduced by the Law No 2021-1104 of 22 August 2021 *on combating climate change and strengthening resilience to its effects*, 'for companies producing or marketing products from agricultural or forestry operations, this plan includes, in particular, reasonable vigilance measures to identify the risks and prevent deforestation associated with the production and transport to France of imported goods and services'.

[73] See UNGPs (n 47) Guiding Principle 23; 2018 OECD Due Diligence Guidance for Responsible Business Conduct (n 51); General Council of the Economy (n 58) 42 Comp ISO 26000, Guidance on social responsibility, 4.6 ff.

[74] European Commission (n 21) 266.

[75] On the list of international human rights standards see ibid 222.

[76] See Rapport Ass Nat no 5124 (n 65) 38.

relation to the risks. Once again, the duty of vigilance is not cast as an unlimited requirement to prevent all harm. This implies in particular that the level of technical, human, and financial resources should be invested according to the seriousness of each risk.

b) Minimum content

The French vigilance plans must include at least five elements:

- a mapping that identifies, analyses, and ranks risks;
- an assessment procedure for subsidiaries, subcontractors, or suppliers with whom they have an established business relationship;
- appropriate actions to mitigate or prevent serious risks;
- a whistleblowing mechanism to issue alerts and obtain reports concerning such risks; and
- a system to monitor and evaluate the efficacy of these measures.

As we can see, the French duty of vigilance is more than a simple duty of care, ie a duty to do no harm, but includes a procedural requirement to take proactive and demonstrable steps. And it is not just a duty to *prevent* harm, which would only be breached if the company fails to prevent the harm.

As indicated by the Constitutional Council, the law does not require companies subject to the duty of vigilance to disclose publicly information relating to their industrial or commercial strategy, which makes it possible to consider that its provisions do not constitute a disproportionate infringement of the freedom of enterprise.

c) Elaboration of the plan

French law only provides that '[t]he plan should be elaborated in cooperation with the company's stakeholders, and where appropriate, as part of multiparty initiatives that exist in the subsidiaries or at a territorial level'. The law does not define these stakeholders,[77] nor does it specify how they should be associated. The law is not mandatory on this subject.[78] In practice, about a third of companies have reported in 2019 that they have discussed their vigilance plan with their stakeholders.

d) Public disclosure

The vigilance plans, as well as the reports on their implementation, are public and included in the company's annual report. This publication started in 2018, with the report covering 2017. A summary describing the implementation of the plan must also be published annually.

---

[77] See art 4 of law No 2012-1559 of 31 December 2012 on the creation of the Public Investment Bank.
[78] The law only mandates that the whistleblowing mechanism must be 'drawn up in consultation with the representative trade union organisations within the company'.

### e) European CS3D

While the 2022 Directive proposal follows the path opened by the French legal regime it is in many respects more elaborate, extensive, and ambitious, taking direct inspiration in the UNGPs,[79] the 2011 OECD Guidelines for Multinational Enterprises and the 2018 OECD Due Diligence Guidance for Responsible Business Conduct. Compared to the French system, the European proposal is much more specific and elaborate. It clearly attempts to respond to the criticisms levelled at it. Although it is far from certain that it will be sufficient to satisfy fully the need for the legal certainty, the attempt to do so is obviously welcome. It first manifests itself through the definition of key concepts. The proposal thus tries to minimize the use of imprecise and open-ended standards[80] and to describe specifically those with which companies must comply.

Thus, the notion of 'adverse environmental impact' is defined by reference to the violation of one of twelve prohibitions and obligations pursuant to specific international environmental conventions listed in the Annex of the CS3D (Part II).[81] The Paris Agreement is not included in the list at this stage, which may explain the existence of a separate article on climate change.[82] Similarly, an 'adverse human rights impact' results from the violation of one of 21 specific rights or prohibitions listed in the Annex (Part I).[83] Such impact is 'severe' if it is especially significant by its nature, affects a large number of people or a large area of the environment, or is irreversible and particularly difficult to remedy.[84]

A 'value chain' would be understood as encompassing 'activities related to the production of goods or the provision of services by a company, including the development of the product or the service and the use and disposal of the product as well as the related activities of upstream and downstream established business relationships of the company'.[85] If B-to-B relationships are surely covered, the reference made to the 'use' of the product creates an uncertainty as to the inclusion of end-clients in the value chain, particularly when they are not ordinary consumers, but powerful entities. In any case, this value chain has no territorial borders. The CS3D thus differs from ordinary international human rights conventions in requiring states to regulate the extraterritorial activities of companies domiciled in their territory and/or jurisdiction.[86] These standards of behaviour thus seem to operate as a jurisdictional trigger on EU companies making the regime applicable to them on a global basis. As in France, it seems that subsidiaries are covered even if they are not part of the value chain of their parent company because they do not contribute to the production of the goods and supply of services of the parent company; and that a parent company not otherwise subject to the proposal

---

[79] See the UNPs (n 47) 16 ff.
[80] See European Company Law Experts (ECLE), 'The European Parliament's Draft Directive on Corporate Due Diligence and Corporate Accountability' (2021) 66 Rivista Delle Società 276.
[81] CS3D Proposal, art 3(b).
[82] See ibid art 15 above.
[83] ibid art 3(c).
[84] ibid art 3(l).
[85] ibid art 3(g).
[86] See the UNGPs (n 47) Guiding Principle 2.

is only included if it is part of its subsidiary's value chain. In other words, if the value chain goes upstream and downstream, the chain of legally responsible companies only goes downstream.

Directly imported from French law, the Directive proposal introduces the 'novel and untested concept'[87] of an 'established business relationship'. A 'business relationship' refers to 'a relationship with a contractor, subcontractor or any other legal entities ("partner") (i) with whom the company has a commercial agreement or to whom the company provides financing, insurance or reinsurance, or (ii) that performs business operations related to the products or services of the company for or on behalf of the company'.[88] To qualify as an 'established' one, such a relationship, whether direct or indirect, is 'expected to be lasting, in view of its intensity or duration and … does not represent a negligible or merely ancillary part of the value chain'.[89] However, both the Council and the European Parliament have been critical of the concept, fearing that it would encourage ordering companies to multiply the number of very short-term contracts with their subcontractors in order to avoid the duty of care. Some Member States have proposed replacing it with a proportional approach based on risk, in line with the OECD's recommendations.

The notion of 'indirect' business relationship, on the other hand, is not defined. Its inclusion in the European text certainly entails the risk of a considerable extension of the scope of the duty of diligence and is currently the focus of criticism from business organizations. This inclusion of indirect business relationships will certainly disappoint those in France in particular, who were hoping that the European Directive would clarify and reduce the scope of the French duty of vigilance to companies belonging to the same group.

The clarification effort is also expressed at the operational level by the care taken to lay down, more precisely than French law does, the obligations to prevent, mitigate, or remediate risks or damage linked to potential or actual adverse impacts. Due diligence procedures are described step by step, almost like a *crescendo*, and formalized in companies' policies, some of which—prevention action plan; corrective action plan— would be developed 'in consultation with stakeholders'.[90]

Taking account of the criticisms levelled at the initial proposal, the final compromise has made a number of clarifications and reduced the scope of the new obligations. The concept of an established commercial relationship has disappeared; indirect commercial relationships are now defined and the chain of activity has been reduced, limiting downstream coverage to activities linked to distribution, transport or storage. On one major point, however, the proposal raises delicate problems that do not exist in French law, as a result of its application to certain non-EU companies. A clear distinction must indeed

---

[87] The EU Commission's Proposal for a Corporate Sustainability Due Diligence Directive Shift's Analysis (March 2022).
[88] UNGPs (n 47) § 13, art 3(e) Comp.
[89] ibid art 3(f).
[90] ibid art 7(2)(a) and 8(3)(b).

be made between the personal scope of the Directive and the territorial scope of the measures that the companies covered are required to take. While the former is by nature European, the latter is by nature global. As indicated in its impact assessment, the comparative advantage of the CS3D proposal on traditional EU environmental law lies in its application 'to the value chains outside the EU where up to 80–90% of the environmental harm may occur'.[91] A worldwide application of the directive to non-EU companies' value chains would, however, inevitably create international tensions and disputes.

## 3. Enforcement and Sanctions

a) French duty of vigilance: pre-emptive claims

Two different wrongdoings should be distinguished under French law. The first is a failure to establish, publish and maintain a plan in accordance with the law. Since the French duty of vigilance is framed as duty to conduct due diligence with respect to actual or potential harms, it is possible to bring a pre-emptive claim on the basis that the company is failing to meet the standard of due diligence required for actual or potential harms. In such a case, the company may be given formal notice to comply with its obligations. The proceedings may stop at this stage, in particular if the company concerned agrees to adopt the measures requested. Sometimes the formal notices are made public, which increases the pressure on the companies involved. If a company fails to comply with its obligations within a period of three months following the formal notice, the competent court may, at the request of any person proving an interest in acting, enjoin it to do so, where necessary under penalty. By early 2024, letters of formal notice have been issued and made public against eighteen companies, nine of which had been referred to the courts.[92] Most of these legal actions, brought by NGOs, trade unions, and public authorities, dealt with preliminary questions of judicial competence and admissibility. They underlined in particular the practical importance of the prior formal notice given to the company. When first asked to analyse the substance of a company's due diligence plan, however, trial judges largely met the plaintiffs' claims and showed their intention to fill in the legal gaps by providing necessary clarifications.[93]

---

[91] Commission Staff Working Document (n 70) 2.

[92] See Terre solidaire and Sherpa (n 66); S Brabant and E Savourey, 'All Eyes on France: French Vigilance Law First Enforcement Cases' *Current Cases and Trends* (24 January 2020) https://www.cambridge.org/core/blog/2020/01/24/all-eyes-on-france-french-vigilance-law-first-enforcement-cases-1-2-current-cases-and-trends/#_edn13; 'Loi sur le devoir de vigilance: Panorama des premières mises en demeure et des saisines des tribunaux (27 April 2020) https://www.cambridge.org/core/blog/2020/04/27/loi-sur-le-devoir-de-vigilance-panorama-des-premieres-mises-en-demeure-et-des-saisines-des-tribunaux/; E Savourey, 'Loi sur le devoir de vigilance: Les enjeux juridiques des mises en demeure et des saisines des tribunaux' (27 April 2020) https://www.cambridge.org/core/blog/2020/04/27/loi-sur-le-devoir-de-vigilance-les-enjeux-juridiques-des-mises-en-demeure-et-des-saisines-des-tribunau/; Rapport d'information sur le devoir de vigilance des entreprises en matière de durabilité no 1449, Assemblée nationale (28 juin 2023); Devoir de vigilance à la française, retour d'expériences et enseignements des contentieux, Cahiers de droit de l'entreprise n° 2, mars-avril 2024, 9.

[93] TJ Paris, 5 déc. 2023, n° 21/15827, Sud PTT c/ La Poste, JCP 2024, éd. G, 85, note J.-B. Barbiéri; B. Delmas, 'Prendre (enfin) le devoir de vigilance au sérieux', Bulletin Joly Travail, janv. 2024, n° BJT203c0; A. Oumedjkane,

The Law no 2021-1104 of 22 August 2021 'on combating climate change and strengthening resilience to its effects'[94] has added an optional sanction in the form of a possible exclusion of companies that do not comply with the obligation to adopt a vigilance plan from a public procurement process. This sanction is limited, however, to situations where the exclusion would not restrict competition or make it technically or economically difficult for the public authority to perform its public services.

b) French duty of vigilance: post-harm claims

A breach of the company's duties regarding its vigilance plan entails liability and requires the company to remedy any harm that the execution of these duties could have prevented. This is no more than the application of general tort law.[95] The Constitutional Council insisted on the fact that the liability incurred by infringers is an ordinary case of personal liability and not a new case of vicarious liability. Therefore, the burden of proof lies with the claimants to prove the breach of the duty of vigilance, harm, and a direct causal link between them;[96] only the victims of the infringements are allowed to file a liability suit; and companies could be sued for negligence. So far, only two civil liability cases—involving Casino and Yves Rocher—seem to have been filed and are pending.

If general tort law applies, one remains surprised, given the large number of places where faults could be committed and damage caused within the framework of global value chains, that the problem of international conflicts of laws is not dealt with. There is possible contradiction between this particular ground for liability of French parent companies and the international norms of conflict of laws, especially the Rome II Regulation.[97] Finally, a certain punitive effect on a company's reputation may come under the law through the possibility for the court to order the publication, dissemination or posting of its decision of a company's breach, according to the terms it specifies.

---

'Le tribunal judiciaire de Paris livre sa première interprétation de la loi relative au devoir de vigilance', JCP éd. Administrations et collectivités territoriales, n° 3, 22 janv. 2024; M. Tirel, 'Durabilité et devoir de vigilance', Dr. sociétés janv. 2024, com. n° 13; E. Valette et Ph. Métais, 'Devoir de vigilance: au-delà des difficultés procédurales, le fond enfin abordé', Option finance n° 1733, lundi 8 janv. 2024, 49; A. Dunoyer de Segonzac et K. Chaïb, 'Première condamnation sur le fondement du devoir de vigilance: quels enseignements en tirer?', JCP 2024, éd. G, 104; I. Grossi, 'Du nouveau sur les contours du devoir de vigilance', Lexbase N8323BZB; Bull. Joly Soc., mars 2024, 21, note E. Schlumberger.

[94] JORF no 196 of 24 August 2021, art 35(V); Public Procurement Code, art L2141-7-1.
[95] See A Danis-Fatôme and G Viney, 'La responsabilité civile dans la loi relative au devoir de vigilance des sociétés mères et des entreprises donneuses d'ordre' (2017) Recueil Dalloz 1610.
[96] In favour of a presumption of causality see ibid.
[97] Regulation (EC) No 864/2007 of 11 July 2007 regarding the conflict of laws on the law applicable to non-contractual obligations [2007] OJ L199/40 (31 July 2007). See Pietrancosta and Boursican (n 56) 553; H Muir-Watt, 'Devoir de vigilance et droit international privé' in S Brabant et E Savourey (eds), Dossier 'La loi relative au devoir de vigilance – une perspective pratique et multidimensionnelle', Supplement no 50 of the Revue Internationale de la Compliance et de l'Éthique des Affaires (Lexis Nexis Paris 2017); E Pataut, 'Le devoir de vigilance: Aspects de droit international privé' (2017) 10 Droit Social 833; O Boskovic, 'Brèves remarques sur le devoir de vigilance et le droit international privé' (2016) Recueil Dalloz 385.

### c) Application

NGOs drew up an initial assessment of the implementation of the 2017 law.[98] This unilateral assessment is unsurprisingly rather critical.[99] Basically, it seems that not all companies have met their obligation to publish a vigilance plan. At the beginning of 2019, 96 companies had published a vigilance plan or had publicly acknowledged that they were subject to the law. Clearly, not all companies have met their obligation. In 2020, the 'due diligence radar' counted 265 companies subject to the law, of which 72 companies did not appear to have published a due diligence plan; in 2021, the figures were 263 and 44 respectively.

When companies do comply, they sometimes face criticism for the content of their plans, particularly those which are short, which could be indicative of an insufficient consideration for the new legal requirements. Many plans also lack precision and contain gaps. The majority of them do not define the scope of the plan, notably with regard to suppliers and subcontractors.[100] Engaging with stakeholders in 2018 is explicitly mentioned by one in five companies: 'Very few companies stated that they have presented their plan to stakeholders. Where this has been done, it has been to employee representative bodies or external stakeholder committees that have already been established by the companies.'[101] This is, however, an ongoing process and progress is being made: 25 per cent of companies have set up dedicated steering committees; 35 per cent of companies mention the monitoring of the plan by Board Committees.

Finally, the first plans appear 'very heterogeneous, indicating that, faced with this new exercise, each company has applied this law with different stringency levels, with the majority of the plans still focusing on the risks for the companies rather than those for third parties or the environment'.[102] Most of the companies reviewed merely transpose their reporting practices or social liability commitments into their vigilance plans.[103] This has to do with the fact that the CSR or Sustainable Development departments are usually in charge of overseeing the approach within companies.

Others, however, have praised the effectiveness of the law and the change regarding sustainability matters it has triggered in such a short time in value chains. A public assessment of the Act showed that French multinationals apply the law correctly, being aware of the reputational consequences and legal risks that could arise from non-compliance with the duty of vigilance.[104] It underlines, however, that they

---

[98] See B&L and edh, 'Application of the Law on the Corporate Duty of Vigilance, Vigilance Plans 2018–2019, June 2019, and Vigilance Plans 2019–2020' (December 2020); Actionaid and others, 'The Law on Duty of Vigilance of Parent and Outsourcing Companies: Year 1: Companies Must Do Better' (February 2019); Sherpa, 'Vigilance Plans Reference Guidance' (2019); Terre solidaire and Sherpa (n 66).

[99] See Loi sur le devoir de vigilance: analyse des premiers plans de vigilance par EY (September 2018); P Barraud de Lagerie and others, 'Mise en œuvre de la Loi sur le devoir de vigilance: rapport sur les premiers plans adoptés par les entreprises' (November 2019); General Council of the Economy (n 58); Rapport Ass Nat no 5124 (n 65).

[100] Actionaid and others (n 98) 12.
[101] B&L and edh (n 98) 10.
[102] Actionaid and others (n 98) 10.
[103] ibid 15.
[104] See General Council of the Economy (n 58).

have an imperfect and non-standardized understanding of their vigilance duty. The European Commission also stressed how the French duty of vigilance had shown 'how—irrespective of personal scope—its impact trickles down the value chain and obligations are shifted on suppliers'.[105]

d) The CS3D enforcement regime

The European proposal is impressive in respect of the enforcement apparatus it puts in place. At the public level, the proposed system is based on national 'supervisory authorities'.[106] Each Member State would have to designate one or more authorities responsible for supervising compliance with human rights, environmental due diligence and combating climate change obligations.[107] Each of the supervisory authorities should have 'adequate powers and resources' to carry out its mission,[108] including the power to request information and conduct investigations.[109] The possibility for natural and legal persons to submit substantiated concerns to a supervisory authority is the functional equivalent of pre-emptive claims under French law. The inspections may, by exception, be carried out without prior warning where prior notification hinders their effectiveness; and on the territory of another Member State, with the assistance from the local supervisory authority. When a company fails to comply with national provisions adopted pursuant to the CS3D, including in cases where no harm is suffered, it is afforded 'an appropriate period of time to take remedial action, if such action is possible'.[110] Generally, all national supervisory authorities must have at least the power to order the cessation of infringements, abstention from any repetition of the relevant conduct and, where appropriate, remedial action proportionate to the infringement and necessary to bring it to an end; adopt interim measures to avoid the risk of severe and irreparable harm; and impose pecuniary sanctions. The sanctions provided for nationally would be effective, proportionate, and dissuasive.[111] Contrary to the French draft law on the duty of vigilance, the European proposal provides that sanctions imposed by the supervisory authorities must be based on the company's turnover, take into account the company's compliance and remedial efforts, and all be published.[112] Given the severity of penalties so calculated, it should be made clear whether natural persons, such as company directors, are covered by these provisions. The proposal adds that every person affected by a supervisory authority's legally binding decision 'has the right to an effective judicial remedy'.[113] Some will certainly consider that more specifications regarding the sanctioning power of the supervisory authorities would have helped ensure a better level playing-field within the EU. An additional disenfranchisement will

---

[105] Commission Staff Working Document (n 70) 27.
[106] Directive Proposal, art 17.
[107] With the exception therefore of the provisions on remuneration (ibid art 15(3)).
[108] ibid art 18(1).
[109] ibid art 19.
[110] ibid art 18(4).
[111] ibid art 20.
[112] ibid art 20.
[113] ibid art 18(7).

automatically attach to a sanction imposed on a company for failure to comply with the obligations of the Directive. This would consist of a ban for 'public support',[114] which is a drastic measure and could be considered a double jeopardy for the targeted company. Given its importance, one would have expected that the proposal would define clearly the term '*public support*', preferably perhaps in terms of its nature and duration.

As regards the jurisdiction of the supervisory authorities, the European proposal retains different criteria depending on whether the qualifying companies are European or non-European. The former are subject to the supervisory authority of the Member State in which they have their registered offices.[115] This criterion has the advantage to simplify identification, compared to the ones based on the companies' real seats or economic activities. It is also the one used to designate the 'Member State competent to regulate matters covered in this Directive', ie the applicable national law within the EU.[116] Things are different for non-EU companies. Since such companies do not have registered offices in the EU, the proposal tries to make a jurisdictional connection on the basis of a main structural criterion or, where this is non-existent or insufficient, a functional criterion. Thus, when the non-EU company has a branch in a Member State, it is supervised by the authority of that state. If a non-EU company does not have a branch in any Member State or has branches located in different Member States, the competent supervisory authority is that of the Member State in which it generated most of its net turnover in the European Union.[117] Regarding non-EU companies, one cannot help but notice that, contrary to what is provided for their European counterparts, the proposal does not designate which law is applicable to them. An analogy to EU companies and the existing international principle of mandatory law would suggest applying the law of the Member State of the supervisory authority.

e) Civil liability

The EU proposal sets out civil-liability rules to address the current divergences at national level.[118] According to the Commission, 'this fragmentation would lead to distortions of competition in the internal market'. In addition to the differences among general national liability regimes, the Commission refers to the contradictions among special diligence regimes, notably the French one, which includes a provision on civil liability, and the German *Sorgfaltspflichtengesetz*, which clarifies, that a violation of an obligation under the law does not give rise to any civil liability while general liability rules remain unaffected.

Following the French model,[119] the European proposal expressly chooses to impose civil liability on companies failing to comply with the diligence obligations,

---

[114] ibid art 24.
[115] ibid art 17(2).
[116] ibid art 2(4).
[117] ibid art 17(3).
[118] ibid art 22.
[119] For a comparison see A Danis-Fatôme, 'La responsabilité civile dans la proposition de directive européenne sur le devoir de vigilance' (2022) Recueil Dalloz 1107; I Barsan, Scope and private enforcement of corporate sustainability due diligence requirements – A comparative approach, ECCL, 1/2023, 31.

when, as a result of this failure, an adverse impact that should have been identified, prevented, mitigated, brought to an end or its extent minimized through the appropriate measures occurred and led to damage. In particular, it is stated that the civil liability of a company is 'without prejudice to the civil liability of its subsidiaries or of any direct and indirect business partners in the value chain'.[120] The fault and legal liability of a parent company do not therefore exclude those of its subsidiaries, any more than the liability of a subsidiary automatically imposes liability on its parent, a reality which may disappoint some supporters of the abolition of limited liability and the veil of legal personality in such circumstances. The creation of a due diligence obligation at the level of the parent company certainly exposes the latter to a direct action for damages by the possible victims of one of its subsidiaries, without however instituting group liability. The 2022 proposal held that the civil liability of a company for damages caused by an adverse impact arising as a result of the activities of an indirect partner with whom it has an established business relationship is limited to cases where 'it was unreasonable, in the circumstances of the case, to expect that the action actually taken, including as regards verifying compliance, would be adequate to prevent, mitigate, bring to an end or minimise the extent of the adverse impact'.[121] Understandably, a qualified fault was necessary here. This standard appeared, however, to be vague and prone to a significant retrospective bias, as courts are inherently called upon to rule ex post on the basis of actual damage caused, which could lead companies to seek more legislative clarity, predictability, and protection. The final compromise decided to exclude a company's civil liability for a damage caused only by its business partners in its chain of activities.[122] In order to improve claimants' access to justice, it provides, however, that Member States must ensure that: limitation periods for damages actions do not unduly hamper the bringing of actions for damages; costs of proceedings are not prohibitive; claimants can seek injunctive measures and authorize certain organizations to bring actions; and courts can order disclosure of evidence by companies when a claimant presents a reasoned justification containing reasonably available facts and evidence sufficient to support the plausibility of their claim for damages.

These civil liability rules are of a minimum nature, as their application does not prevent liability under Union or national stricter rules related to adverse human rights impacts or to adverse environmental impacts.[123] Of a minimum nature, these rules are, however, of 'overriding mandatory application in cases where the law applicable to claims to that effect is not the law of a Member State'.[124] Such mandatory application, called for in the European Parliament, would therefore trump the normal operation of conflict rules on non-contractual obligations set out in the Rome II European Regulation, which in principle designate the *lex loci damni*, unless, in case

---

[120] Directive Proposal, art 22(3).
[121] ibid art 22(2).
[122] ibid art 29(1).
[123] ibid art 22(4).
[124] ibid art 22(5).

of environmental damage, 'the person seeking compensation for damage chooses to base his or her claim on the law of the country in which the event giving rise to the damage occurred'.[125] Internationally, the European Union would thus be one of the most accessible territories to actions brought by victims of damage located outside its territory.

---

[125] Regulation (EC) No 864/2007 of the European Parliament and of the Council of 11 July 2007 on the law applicable to non-contractual obligations (Rome II) [2007] OJ L199/40 (31 July 2007), arts 4, 7. See O Boskovic, 'Les aspects de droit international privé du devoir de diligence et de la responsabilité des entreprises: bilan d'étape' (2022) Recueil Dalloz 185; Rapport sur le régime de responsabilité civile envisagé par la proposition de directive européenne sur le devoir de vigilance, Haut Comité Juridique de la Place Financière de Paris, 9 October 2023.

# 14
# Green Bonds and Their New Regulation in the EU

*Christoph Kumpan*\*

## I. Introduction

Currently, one of the most important—if not the most important—goal of most countries is to transform their economy into a sustainable one.[1] The EU and its Member States are particularly vocal about this transformation, with a special focus on environmental sustainability.[2] However, considerable efforts are needed to master such a seismic shift. In particular, substantial investments are needed to steer the economy onto a sustainable, environmentally friendly course. According to a 2018 estimate by the Intergovernmental Panel on Climate Change limiting warming to 1.5°C relative to pre-industrial levels by 2050 will require US$3.5 trillion annually in investment.[3] In the EU alone, €466 billion in annual investments are needed.[4]

Given such amounts, a successful transition to a low-carbon, climate friendly economy is unlikely without the help of private capital. Therefore, to master the transition to an environmentally sustainable economy private investments are needed. The transmission belts for the engagement of private investors and companies are 'green' financial instruments, in particular so-called green bonds. The former General Secretary of the United Nations, Ban Ki Moon, described the emergence of green bonds as 'one of the most significant developments in the financing of low-carbon, climate resilient investment opportunities'.[5]

---

\* All internet sources were last accessed on 25 June 2024.
[1] cf United Nations General Assembly 'Resolution adopted by the General Assembly on 25 September 2015, 70/1. Transforming our world: the 2030 Agenda for Sustainable Development' A/RES/70/1 (21 October 2015) https://undocs.org/en/A/RES/70/1.
[2] cf European Commission, 'A European Green Deal' https://commission.europa.eu/strategy-and-policy/priorities-2019-2024/european-green-deal_en.
[3] IPCC, 'Global Warming of 1.5°C. An IPCC Special Report on the impacts of global warming of 1.5°C above pre-industrial levels and related global greenhouse gas emission pathways, in the context of strengthening the global response to the threat of climate change, sustainable development, and efforts to eradicate poverty' (V Masson-Delmotte and others (eds), CUP 2018) 321.
[4] European Union, 'Contribution to the Green Deal and the Just Transition Scheme' https://investeu.europa.eu/contribution-green-deal-and-just-transition-scheme_en.
[5] Ban Ki Moon quoted in Climate Bonds Initiative, 'UN investment report confirms key role of green bonds in climate investment' (posted 12 October 2015) https://www.climatebonds.net/2015/10/un-investment-report-confirms-key-role-green-bonds-climate-investment. cf also OECD, 'Mobilising Bond Markets for a Low-Carbon Transition' (19 April 2017) 13 https://doi.org/10.1787/9789264272323-en.

The EU attaches great importance to green bonds, as well, and has now issued its own legal act for their regulation: Regulation (EU) 2023/2631 (EU Green Bonds Regulation).[6] A key aspect of enacting that regulation was—and still is—the uncertainty about what exactly is meant by 'green' or 'sustainable' when it comes to financial investments (section II.3). Nevertheless, the market for green bonds is growing strongly (section II.1), not least because of the benefits of such bonds (section II.2). While private standards for green bonds have prevailed so far (section III), the new Regulation (EU) 2023/2631 has now introduced a voluntarily applicable regulatory regime for green bonds (sections IV.1, IV.2) which will be critically examined (section IV.3).

## II. Green Bonds

Green bonds are debt instruments designed to raise capital for projects that are climate-related or strive for a positive environmental impact.[7] Like other bonds, green bonds are fixed-income financial instruments where the issuer borrows a fixed amount of capital for a certain period of time, pays interest to the bondholder during this time and repays the capital upon the bond's maturity.[8] Unlike conventional bonds, however, which are valued primarily according to the creditworthiness of their issuer and the interest offered, the characteristic feature of green bonds is the earmarked use of funds for 'green' projects.[9]

### 1. The Market for Green Bonds

The first climate awareness bond was issued by the European Investment Bank in 2007[10] and the first 'green bond' by the World Bank in 2008.[11] Since then the market

---

[6] Regulation (EU) 2023/2631 of the European Parliament and of the Council of 22 November 2023 on European Green Bonds and optional disclosures for bonds marketed as environmentally sustainable and for sustainability-linked bonds [2023] OJ L2023/2631 (30 November 2023).

[7] The World Bank 'What Are Green Bonds?' (2015) 23 https://documents1.worldbank.org/curated/en/400251468187810398/pdf/99662-REVISED-WB-Green-Bond-Box393208B-PUBLIC.pdf; OECD (n 5) 23; International Capital Market Association, 'Green Bond Principles: Voluntary Process Guidelines for Issuing Green Bonds' (June 2021, with June 2022 Appendix 1) 3 https://www.icmagroup.org/assets/documents/Sustainable-finance/2022-updates/Green-Bond-Principles-June-2022-060623.pdf; Lloyd Freeburn and Ian Ramsay, 'Green Bonds: Legal and Policy Issues' (2020) 15 Capital Markets Law Journal 418, 419; Gianfranco Gianfrate and Mattia Peri, 'The Green Advantage: Exploring the Convenience of Issuing Green Bonds' (2019) 219 Journal of Cleaner Production 127; Sergio Gilotta, 'Green Bonds: A Legal and Economic Analysis' (April 2023) 4 https://ssrn.com/abstract=4427927.

[8] OECD (n 5) 24.

[9] ibid 13; Freeburn and Ramsay (n 7) 419, 420; Gilotta (n 7) 5.

[10] European Investment Bank 'Climate Awareness Bonds' https://www.eib.org/en/investor-relations/cab/index.htm.

[11] The World Bank 'World Bank and SEB Partner with Scandinavian Institutional Investors to Finance "Green" Projects' (6 November 2008) https://www.worldbank.org/en/news/press-release/2008/11/06/world-bank-and-seb-partner-with-scandinavian-institutional-investors-to-finance-green-projects.

for green bonds has grown rapidly.[12] In 2021, green bond issues reached a total size of US$ 522.7 billion, an increase of 75 per cent compared to 2020.[13] In 2022 green bond issuance dropped to US$ 487.1 billion—however, in that year all categories of bonds experienced a decline in issuance due to difficult market conditions.[14] Looking at individual countries, China overtook the United States in 2022 as the biggest source of green debt, having issued an amount of US$85.4 billion.[15] The private sector was responsible for a bit more than half (54 per cent) of the volume of green bonds, a slight drop from 2021 levels.[16] In 2021, there were already 839 issuers from 58 countries,[17] which increased by a further 382 issuers in 2022.[18] While these amounts appear to be huge, compared to the global long-term bond market with an issuance value in 2022 of US$22.5 trillion and an outstanding amount of US$129.8 trillion, the market for green bonds is still rather small.[19]

## 2. Benefits of Green Bonds

The Technical Expert Group that laid the foundation for the EU Green Bonds Regulation sees the benefits of green bonds primarily in their impact on the environmental orientation of markets and issuing companies.[20] Due to green bonds markets, companies and investors would increasingly focus on green investments. Studies found that green bond issuers decreased the carbon intensity of their assets after issuing green bonds compared with conventional bond issuers.[21]

Green bonds would also increase the visibility of sustainable projects and thus contribute to the transition of companies. They would make green and environmental issues investable and have contributed to the expansion of green financing, as they enable investors to invest their money in sustainable projects and thereby get involved in environmental and climate protection via the capital market.

Moreover, issuers are given the opportunity specifically to request capital for sustainable investments and to promote their environmental credentials.[22] Thereby, they

---

[12] For an overview of the drivers of the market for green bonds see Anamaria Dan and Adriana Tiron-Tudor, 'The Determinants of Green Bond Issuance in the European Union' (2021) 14 Journal of Risk and Financial Management 446 https://doi.org/10.3390/jrfm14090446; Gilotta (n 7) 5–7.
[13] Climate Bonds Initiative, 'Sustainable Debt, Global State of the Market 2021' (2022) 6 https://www.climatebonds.net/resources/reports/sustainable-debt-global-state-market-2021.
[14] ibid 7; Sifma, '2023 Capital Markets Fact Book' (July 2023) 8 https://www.sifma.org/resources/research/factbook/.
[15] Climate Bonds Initiative (n 13) 7.
[16] ibid 9.
[17] ibid 8.
[18] ibid 8.
[19] Sifma (n 14) 8.
[20] EU Technical Expert Group on Sustainable Finance, 'Report on EU Green Bonds Standard' (June 2019) 19 ff https://finance.ec.europa.eu/system/files/2019-06/190618-sustainable-finance-teg-report-green-bond-standard_en.pdf.
[21] Serena Fatica and Roberto Panzica, 'Green Bonds as a Tool against Climate Change?' (2021) 30 Business Strategy and the Environment 2688; cf also Joao Leitao, Joaquim Ferreira, and Ernesto Santibanez-Gonzalez, 'Green Bonds, Sustainable Development and Environmental Policy in the European Union Carbon Market' (2021) 30 Business Strategy and the Environment 2077, 2087.
[22] Freeburn and Ramsay (n 7) 426.

have an opportunity to broaden their investor base and attract investors who are interested in sustainable investments and would not otherwise invest in bonds issued by the respective company.[23] A larger investor base leads to offerings being more likely to be oversubscribed and to smaller spreads.[24]

With regard to financial benefits of green bonds a study found statistically significant advantages for issuers when their bonds are labelled as green, as they have to pay less interest.[25] Another study found that investors react positively to the issuance of green bonds and that issuers improve their environmental performance post-issuance (ie higher environmental ratings, lower $CO_2$ emissions)—but only in those cases where green bonds have been certified by independent third parties.[26] Moreover, these companies would experience an increase in ownership by long-term and green investors.[27] However, other studies come to different results,[28] so the findings seem to be mixed.[29] More important factors influencing the pricing than just the 'greenness' of the financed project appear to be the type of issuer (for example supranational institutions, non-financial corporates), whether there is an external review of the green bonds, and the frequency of issuing green bonds.[30] Another study backed the finding that stock prices respond positively to green bond issuance.[31] However, it did not find a significant

---

[23] ibid.
[24] Climate Bonds Initiative, 'Green Bond Pricing in the Primary Market: July-December 2019, H2 (Q3-Q4) 2019' (March 2020) 3 https://www.climatebonds.net/files/reports/climate-bonds-pricing-report-h2-2019-310 320-final.pdf.
[25] See eg Malcolm Baker and others, 'Financing the Response to Climate Change: The Pricing and Ownership of U.S. Green Bonds' (12 October 2018) https://ssrn.com/abstract=3275327; Gianfrate and Peri (n 7) 128 ('on average ... 0.18% of the bond value'; see also the literature overview presented at 128); Olivier David Zerbib, 'The Effect of Pro-environmental Preferences on Bond Prices: Evidence from Green Bonds' (2019) 98 Journal of Banking & Finance 39; for similar results in China see Ran Zhang, Yanru Li, and Yingzuh Li, 'Green Bond Issuance and Corporate Cost of Capital' (2021) 69 Pacific-Basin Finance Journal 101626 ('green financing policies not only reduce the cost of debt but also lower the overall cost of capital of green bond issuers', 'average yield spread of green bonds is 24.9 basis points lower than that of non-green bonds').
[26] Caroline Flammer, 'Green Bonds: Effectiveness and Implication for Public Policy' (2020) Environmental and Energy Policy and the Economy 95 https://www.journals.uchicago.edu/doi/epdf/10.1086/706794; Caroline Flammer, 'Corporate Green Bonds' (2021) 142 Journal of Financial Economics 499; Ilia Kuchin and others, 'Does green bonds placement create value for firms?' (2019) National Research University Higher School of Economics, Basic Research Program Working Papers, Series: Science, Technology and Innovation, WP BRP 101/STI/2019, 17 https://wp.hse.ru/data/2019/10/30/1532092144/101STI2019.pdf; see also Samuel M Hartzmark and Abigail B Sussmann, 'Do Investors Value Sustainability? A Natural Experiment Examining Ranking and Fund Flows' (2019) ECGI Finance Working Paper No 565/2018 http://ssrn.com/abstract_id=3016092; Julia Kapraun and others, '(In)-Credibly Green: Which Bonds Trade at a Green Bond Premium?' (April 2021) https://ssrn.com/abstract=3347337 ('Investors are more likely to pay a premium for a Green bond, when it is certified as such by a third party').
[27] Flammer, 'Corporate Green Bonds' (n 26).
[28] David F Larcker and Edward M Watts, 'Where's the Greenium?' (2020) 69 Journal of Accounting and Economics 101312 ('greenium is essentially zero'); Flammer, 'Corporate Green Bonds' (n 26) 501 ('When comparing the yields of both, I find that the median difference is exactly zero and the average difference is small and statistically insignificant'); Dragon Yongjun Tang and Yupu Zhang, 'Do Shareholders Benefit from Green Bonds?' (2020) 61 Journal of Corporate Finance 101427, 2 ('if we compare yield spread within the same issuing firm in the same year, we do not find any significant pricing difference'); Kapraun and others (n 26) ('only certain types of bonds trade at a Green premium'). See also the studies referred to in Kuchin and others (n 26) 3–4.
[29] Nikos Maragopoulos, 'Towards a European Green Bond: A Commission's Proposal to Promote Sustainable Finance' (6 April 2022) EBI Working Paper Series 2022 No 103, 11 https://ssrn.com/abstract=3933766.
[30] Maragopoulos (n 29) 11.
[31] Tang and Zhang (n 28) 2. Generally about stock returns of carbon-efficient firms see Soh Young In, Ki Young Park, and Ashby Monk, 'Is "Being Green" Rewarded in the Market? An Empirical Investigation of Decarbonization and Stock Returns' (16 April 2019) https://ssrn.com/abstract=3020304.

premium for green bonds, suggesting that positive stock returns are not driven by the lower cost of debt. But the study found that 'institutional ownership, especially from domestic institutions, increases after the firm issues green bonds. Moreover, stock liquidity significantly improves upon the issuance of green bonds'.[32] Overall, the study concluded that the issuance of green bonds appears to be beneficial to existing shareholders of the issuing company.[33]

Green bonds are also considered less risky than conventional bonds because investors face fewer unaccounted environmental risks.[34] And they are regarded as less volatile than vanilla bonds because they are typically bought by more strategic, long-term institutional investors.[35]

## 3. Challenges for Green Bonds

While green bonds are heralded as the financial instruments to help solving the climate crisis, there are some issues that may hamper their success.

a) Competing standards—market fragmentation and investor confusion

One of the biggest hurdles for investors and issuers and, thus, the development of a global market for green bonds is the lack of a common framework for these financial instruments. This leads to uncertainty about what is considered 'green'. Beside general frameworks such as the popular Green Bond Principles[36] and the Climate Bonds Standard[37], there are various other approaches to regulating green bonds, such as those of Moody's Investor Services,[38] S&P Global Ratings Second Party Opinion,[39] DNV (Det Norske Veritas),[40] Institutional Shareholder Services,[41] or Morningstar Sustainalytics.[42] Moreover, countries like China and India have developed their own standards for sustainable financial products.

---

[32] Tang and Zhang (n 28) 3.
[33] ibid 22.
[34] Freeburn and Ramsay (n 7) 427.
[35] Louise Bowman, 'ESG: Green Bonds Have a Chicken and Egg Problem' (19 June 2019) https://www.euromoney.com/article/b1fxdsf5kpjxlg/esg-green-bonds-have-a-chicken-and-egg-problem, quoting Maxim Vydrine of Amundi.
[36] International Capital Market Association(n 7).
[37] Climate Bonds Initiative, Climate Bonds Standard Version 4.0 (April 2023) https://www.climatebonds.net/climate-bonds-standard-v4.
[38] Moody's, 'ESG & Climate Capabilities' https://sustainability.moodys.io/sustainability-esg-and-climate-capabilities. Moody's took over Vigeo Eiris https://ir.moodys.com/press-releases/news-details/2019/Moodys-Acquires-Majority-Stake-in-Vigeo-Eiris-a-Global-Leader-in-ESG-Assessments/default.aspx.
[39] S&P Global Ratings, Second Party Opinion https://www.spglobal.com/ratings/en/products-benefits/products/second-party-opinions, which uses the Shares of Green approach developed by CICERO, which sold its 'Shades of Green Business' to S&P Global in 2022 https://www.cicero.oslo.no/en/about.
[40] DNV, Second Party Opinion Service https://www.dnv.us/services/second-party-opinion-service-37202.
[41] ISS ESG https://www.issgovernance.com/esg/. ISS took over oekom research, a leading rating agency for sustainable financial products https://www.issgovernance.com/oekom-research-ag-join-institutional-shareholder-services/.
[42] Morningstar Sustainalytics https://www.sustainalytics.com.

An example of the variance of the meaning of sustainability is the classification of sustainability projects of airports.[43] If an airport operator were to issue a sustainable bond to support a carbon-neutral project, such as a zero-emissions airport building, it would be unclear how this project would be classified in terms of its sustainability. An airport building that produces no emissions could be classified as 'sustainable'. On the other hand, the building would support air travel, which is responsible for 2.5 per cent of global $CO_2$ emissions. Hence, it could be classified as 'not sustainable'.

In light of this situation, companies may find it difficult to determine whether a certain project is eligible for being classified as 'green' and whose standards to apply.[44] Thus, they might shy away from issuing green bonds to avoid reputational risks if their assessment of a bond's greenness is challenged. Those, that do not shy away, are confronted with different frameworks. That will probably lead to market fragmentation and confusion among investors and issuers. Since sustainable financial investments are based on trust,[45] and private investors cannot effectively monitor whether the financial intermediaries offering the products are actually investing sustainably, there is a danger that the functioning of the market for sustainable financial products will be impaired.

b) Limitations in assessing the sustainability of projects

Another impediment to the development of a larger market for green bonds is the often limited knowledge of market participants about green bonds. Assessing green investments and their impact on the environment is challenging. That can make it difficult for issuers to obtain good credit ratings for their bonds. Investors, on the other hand, face the problem that many bond issuers do not sufficiently assess the actual impact of their projects. Without transparency and/or reporting requirements it is difficult for them to obtain sufficient information. Second opinions might help, but their quality is sometimes questioned.

Moreover, in this context, the problem of 'greenwishing' may arise.[46] For example, when the airport operator considers whether his or her project is sustainable, he or she may be firmly convinced of its sustainability because of the efforts he or she has put into it, although objectively there is more to be said against it than for it. 'Greenwishing' is the first step towards greenwashing (see below).[47] The more clearly sustainability is defined or when an investment is to be considered sustainable, the greater the legal certainty in this respect and the less 'greenwishing' will occur.

c) Greenwashing

While the above mentioned problems arise rather unintentionally or due to a certain inability to gather information, so-called green washing is based on an intentional

---

[43] For this example see Freeburn and Ramsay (n 7) 419, 438.
[44] See also eg Gilotta (n 7) 17–18.
[45] Eckart Bueren, 'Sustainable Finance' (2019) Zeitschrift für Unternehmens- und Gesellschaftsrecht 813, 858.
[46] Duncan Austin, 'Greenwish: The Wishful Thinking Undermining the Ambition of Sustainable Business' (2019) https://preventablesurprises.com/wp-content/uploads/2019/07/2019-07-19-Greenwish-Essay.pdf.
[47] cf ibid 10 ('greenwish: a sort of greenwash gone meta').

action by issuers. Greenwashing describes the practice of misleading investors or giving them a false impression about how well an investment is aligned with its sustainability goals.[48] Such a practice undermines the confidence in green bonds and thus in the market. In Germany, a major case of potential green washing involved the investment firm DWS[49], a subsidiary of Deutsche Bank, which was blamed by its former head of sustainability to have committed green washing.[50]

d) Moral hazard

A closely related issue is that even if the money has been collected with the best of intentions, it might later be diverted to other projects[51] or the project no longer meets the 'green' requirements that applied when the bond was issued.[52] This issue is rooted in an information asymmetry between the issuers and the investors. Moreover, bondholders usually have no direct influence on the performance of the issuer and cannot enforce the issuer's pledge for green projects.[53] To mitigate this asymmetry issuers can obtain external reviews or third-party opinions for their green bonds. However, the various standards of the different reviewers usually deviate from each other as well, making it difficult for investors to compare the 'greenness' of different bonds. Moreover, such reviews have their own issues. Similar to rating agencies or auditors, external reviewers of green bonds face the risk of conflicts of interest. They may be inclined to give a better assessment than justified in order to keep the issuer as a client.[54]

## III. Self-regulation of Green Bonds

To counter these issues and provide a means for issuers to establish that their bonds are 'green' various voluntary standards for green bonds have been developed. The two main international standards are the Green Bond Principles[55] created by the

---

[48] Taxonomy Regulation, recital 11 sentence 3. On greenwashing and its drivers see eg ESMA, 'Progress Report on Greenwashing' (31 May 2023) ESMA30-1668416927-2498 https://www.esma.europa.eu/document/progress-report-greenwashing; Burim Ferati and Annabelle Meyer, '(K)eine grüne Märchenwelt? Fraud im ESG-Kontext' [2022] Corporate Compliance Zeitschrift 349, 353–55 (pressure and motivation; opportunity; justification). See also Gilotta (n 7) 13–17 (with suggestions for private regulation of greenwashing).

[49] Deutsche Gesellschaft für Wertpapiersparen.

[50] No author, 'Deutsche Bank's DWS and allegations of "greenwashing"' (10 July 2022) https://www.reuters.com/business/finance/deutsche-banks-dws-allegations-greenwashing-2022-06-09/.

[51] eg if the 'green' project for which the money was intended has been financed faster than expected.

[52] Freeburn and Ramsay (n 7) 440; Clarke Corke and Julie Myers, 'Green Bonds Series: Part 4: When 'Green' Bonds Go Brown' (17 October 2019) https://www.corrs.com.au/insights/green-bonds-series-part-4-when-green-bonds-go-brown ('green default'); Michael Pyka, 'The EU Green Bond Standard: A Plausible Response to the Deficiencies of the EU Green Bond Market?' (2023) 24 European Business Law Review 623, 630–34.

[53] Freeburn and Ramsay (n 7) 440; Stephen Kim Park, 'Investors as Regulators: Green Bonds and the Governance Challenges of the Sustainable Finance Revolution' (2018) 54 Stanford Journal of International Law 1, 13; Pyka (n 52) 631. Classifying the green pledge as a covenant which can be enforced by the bondholders see Gilotta (n 7) 9–10.

[54] For a comparison of the issues of green bond verifiers and credit rating agencies see Cristina M Banahan, 'The Bond Villains of Green Investment: Why an Unregulated Securities Market Needs Government to Lay Down the Law' (2019) 43 Vermont Law Review 842, 850–56.

[55] International Capital Market Association (n 7).

International Capital Market Association (ICMA) and the Climate Bonds Standard[56] established by the Climate Bonds Initiative.

## 1. Green Bond Principles

The Green Bond Principles are internationally recognized, voluntary guidelines that set out a structured approach for the issuance of green bonds and concrete requirements for transparency and disclosure. According to these principles there are four key aspects for a bond to be classified as 'green': (i) the proceeds of the bond must be used for green projects from a variety of categories (for example, renewable energies, energy efficiency, clean transport, environmentally friendly buildings), which have to be appropriately described in the legal documentation of the bond (use of proceeds);[57] (ii) the issuer of a green bond is expected to clearly communicate to investors the process for project evaluation and selection;[58] (iii) the net proceeds of the green bond, or an amount equal to these net proceeds, are to be separately accounted for and tracked, preferably verified by an auditor or other third-party;[59] and (iv) issuers have to make, and keep, up to date information on the use of proceeds to be renewed annually until full allocation, and on a timely basis in case of material developments.[60] Moreover, the Principles state that a Green Bond Framework should be established in which the alignment of the green bond with the four core components is explained.[61] Moreover, the Principles recommend that issuers ensure an external review to confirm the alignment of their bonds with the four core components.[62]

## 2. Climate Bonds Standard

The second major standard is the Climate Bonds Standard by the Climate Bonds Initiative.[63] It builds on the Green Bond Principles, however, it is much more detailed and contains more technical requirements and comes with a taxonomy for eligible projects and financial instruments. The Standard requires, for example, that an applying issuer includes and documents the nominated projects and assets associated with the green bond[64] and ensures that proceeds are not contaminated by environmentally inconsistent activities (ring-fence the proceeds).[65]

---

[56] Climate Bonds Initiative (n 37).
[57] International Capital Market Association (n 7) 4–5.
[58] ibid 5.
[59] ibid 6.
[60] ibid 6.
[61] ibid 7.
[62] ibid 7.
[63] Climate Bonds Initiative (n 37).
[64] ibid 13.
[65] ibid 17.

With its taxonomy, the Climate Bonds Standard provides more clarity as to which financial instruments and which projects are to be classified as 'green'.[66] It, thus, leads to more certainty for issuers and investors. Moreover, the certification process does not end after the issuance of the bonds. Instead post-issuance the issuer is required to submit annual update reports to the Climate Bonds Initiative in order to maintain certification.[67] This ensures, at least to a certain extent, that the collected funds are not diverted unexpectedly.

The documentation, communication and reporting requirements regarding the project, the use of the proceeds etc., especially the publication of the allocation reports and the impact reports, serve to solve the information asymmetry between the issuer und the investors. However, they also entail higher costs for issuers compared to conventional bonds, especially since external reviewers monitor these obligations.

## IV. EU Approach to Regulating Green Bonds

In order to emphasize the importance of green finance for the sustainable development of the internal market and to establish a uniform green bond standard in the EU, the EU has developed its own standards for green bonds in its new Regulation (EU) 2023/2631. This new regulation is embedded in a bundle of regulatory measures.[68]

### 1. Sustainability Regulation of the EU Financial Market

a) Action Plan 2018 and European Green Deal

The foundation was laid in the United Nations Paris Agreement of 12 December 2015[69] when the EU committed itself to bringing financial flows in line with a low-emission, climate change resilient development. In order to achieve the climate targets established in the Paris Agreement, it was agreed, among other things, to make 'finance flows consistent with a pathway towards low greenhouse gas emissions and climate-resilient development'.[70] Accordingly, in its Action Plan on Financing Sustainable Growth from March 2018,[71] the European Commission set the goal of

---

[66] Climate Bonds Initiative, 'Climated Bonds Taxonomy' (September 2021) https://www.climatebonds.net/files/files/Taxonomy/CBI_Taxonomy_Tables-08A%20%281%29.pdf.
[67] ibid 7. Climate Bonds Initiative (n 37) 18.
[68] On the need for a regulatory intervention see Banahan (n 54); Pyka (n 52).
[69] United Nations, Paris Agreement, Treaty Collection, ch XXVII 7 (2015) https://treaties.un.org/Pages/ViewDetails.aspx?src=IND&mtdsg_no=XXVII-7-d&chapter=27&clang=_en.
[70] ibid art 2(1)(c).
[71] European Commission, Communication from the Commission to the European Parliament, the European Council, the Council, the European Central Bank, the European Economic and Social Committee and the Committee of the Regions, Action Plan, Financing Sustainable Growth COM(2018) 97 final (Brussels, 8 March 2018) https://eur-lex.europa.eu/legal-content/EN/TXT/PDF/?uri=CELEX:52018DC0097. For comments on the Action Plan see eg Florian Möslein and Karsten Engsig Sorensen, 'The Commission's Action Plan for Financing Sustainable Growth and Its Corporate Governance Implications' (2018) 15 European Company Law 221.

creating 'sustainable finance' in the EU, in particular by redirecting capital flows towards sustainable investments and promoting transparency and long-termism in financial and economic activity.[72]

In 2019, the Commission transferred the envisioned approaches into its 'European Green Deal',[73] which aims to make the EU carbon-neutral by 2050 and reduce greenhouse gas emissions by at least 55 per cent from 1990 levels by 2030.[74] To achieve these goals, all sources of funding—public and private, national and multilateral—are to be aligned accordingly.[75] The European Commission estimates that the EU will need additional investments of around €350 billion per year this decade to meet the 2030 emissions reduction target alone, plus another €130 billion for other environmental goals.[76] Implementing these plans, the EU has already enacted the so-called Sustainable Finance Disclosure Regulation and the Taxonomy Regulation.

b) Sustainable Finance Disclosure Regulation

The Sustainable Finance Disclosure Regulation (SFDR),[77] supplemented by Delegated Regulation (EU) 2022/1288,[78] obliges financial market participants and financial advisors to disclose information on sustainable investments and the associated sustainability impacts and risks in connection with the financial products they offer. The purpose of the SFDR is to reduce information asymmetries between financial market participants and financial advisors on the one hand, and retail investors on the other, when incorporating sustainability risks and promoting environmental and social features of financial products, as well as when seeking sustainable investments.[79] This should counteract 'greenwashing' and enhance the communication to retail investors regarding the impact of strategies used by certain financial products to exclude investments based on environmental or social criteria.[80]

---

[72] COM(2018) 97 final (n 71) 2 ff.
[73] European Commission, Communication from the Commission to the European Parliament, the European Council, the Council, the European Economic and Social Committee and the Committee of the Regions, The European Green Deal COM(2019) 640 final (Brussels, 11 December 2019) https://eur-lex.europa.eu/resource.html?uri=cellar:b828d165-1c22-11ea-8c1f-01aa75ed71a1.0002.02/DOC_1&format=PDF.
[74] ibid 2, 4.
[75] ibid 15 ff.
[76] European Commission, Communication from the Commission to the European Parliament, the European Council, the Council, the European Economic and Social Committee and the Committee of the Regions, Strategy for Financing the Transition to a Sustainable Economy COM(2021) 390 final 1 (Strasbourg, 6 July 2021) https://eur-lex.europa.eu/resource.html?uri=cellar:9f5e7e95-df06-11eb-895a-01aa75ed71a1.0001.02/DOC_1&format=PDF.
[77] Regulation (EU) 2019/2088 of the European Parliament and of the Council of 27 November 2019 on sustainability related disclosures in the financial services sector [2019] OJ L317/1 (SFDR).
[78] Commission Delegated Regulation (EU) 2022/1288 of 6 April 2022 supplementing Regulation (EU) 2019/2088 of the European Parliament and of the Council with regard to regulatory technical standards specifying the details of the content and presentation of the information in relation to the principle of 'do no significant harm', specifying the content, methodologies and presentation of information in relation to sustainability indicators and adverse sustainability impacts, and the content and presentation of the information in relation to the promotion of environmental or social characteristics and sustainable investment objectives in pre-contractual documents, on websites and in periodic reports [2022] OJ L196/1.
[79] SFDR, recital 10; Commission Delegated Regulation (EU) 2022/1288 (n 78) recital 17 sentence 1.
[80] Commission Delegated Regulation (EU) 2022/1288 (n 78) recital 16; cf SFRD, recital 9.

### c) Taxonomy Regulation

The Taxonomy Regulation[81] is intended to create a uniform EU-wide classification system to determine whether economic activities can be deemed ecologically sustainable.[82] Moreover, additional transparency requirements for environmentally sustainable economic activities will be introduced to complement the requirements of the SFDR.[83] The aim is to steer private investments towards sustainable activities, strengthen investors' confidence in sustainable financial products and their awareness of the environmental impact of financial products, and prevent greenwashing.[84] However, the Taxonomy Regulation does not prohibit economic activities that do not meet the requirements of the Regulation, ie it does not force companies to act in an environmentally sustainable manner.[85] Nor does it oblige anyone to invest only in environmentally sustainable activities. Finally, private sustainability standards are still permissible, so that competition between different taxonomies remains possible.[86]

However, the Taxonomy Regulation only provides a framework for classifying ecologically sustainable economic activities. A more precise specification and classification of individual activities as ecologically sustainable is then provided in delegated regulations,[87] ie the Delegated Regulation (EU) 2021/2139 for establishing the requirement for the two climate objectives 'climate change mitigation' and 'climate change adaptation',[88] the Delegated Regulation (EU) 2021/2178,[89] the Delegated Regulation (EU) 2022/2014 which introduces nuclear energy and gas as Taxonomy aligned energy sources,[90] and the Delegated Regulation (EU) 2023/2486 establishing the requirements for the remaining environmental objectives.[91]

---

[81] Regulation (EU) 2020/852 of the European Parliament and of the Council of 18 June 2020 on the establishment of a framework to facilitate sustainable investment, and amending Regulation (EU) 2019/2088 [2020] OJ L198/13 (Taxonomy Regulation).

[82] cf ibid art 1(1).

[83] ibid arts 5 ff.

[84] ibid recital 11.

[85] The Taxonomy Regulation with its Delegated Regulations is designed (only) as a 'white list' of environmentally sustainable activities, not as a 'black list' of non-sustainable activities. See Christoph Kumpan and Robin Misterek, 'Nachhaltigkeitsrisiken von Kreditinstituten' (2023) 1 Zeitschrift für Bankrecht und Bankwirtschaft 8, 16.

[86] Eckart Bueren, 'Die EU-Taxonomie nachhaltiger Anlagen' (2020) 51 Wertpapier-Mitteilungen: Zeitschrift für Wirtschafts- und Bankrecht 1659, 1663.

[87] cf Taxonomy Regulation, art 19.

[88] Commission Delegated Regulation (EU) 2021/2139 of 4 June 2021 supplementing Regulation (EU) 2020/852 of the European Parliament and of the Council by establishing the technical screening criteria for determining the conditions under which an economic activity qualifies as contributing substantially to climate change mitigation or climate change adaptation and for determining whether that economic activity causes no significant harm to any of the other environmental objectives [2021] OJ L442/1.

[89] Commission Delegated Regulation (EU) 2021/2178 of 6 July 2021 supplementing Regulation (EU) 2020/852 of the European Parliament and of the Council by specifying the content and presentation of information to be disclosed by undertakings subject to Articles 19a or 29a of Directive 2013/34/EU concerning environmentally sustainable economic activities, and specifying the methodology to comply with that disclosure obligation [2021] OJ L443/9.

[90] Commission Delegated Regulation (EU) 2022/1214 of 9 March 2022 amending Delegated Regulation (EU) 2021/2139 as regards economic activities in certain energy sectors and Delegated Regulation (EU) 2021/2178 as regards specific public disclosures for those economic activities [2022] OJ L188/1.

[91] Commission Delegated Regulation (EU) 2023/2486 of 27 June 2023 supplementing Regulation (EU) 2020/852 of the European Parliament and of the Council by establishing the technical screening criteria for determining the conditions under which an economic activity qualifies as contributing substantially to the sustainable use and protection of water and marine resources, to the transition to a circular economy, to pollution prevention and

## 2. EU Green Bonds Regulation

a) Development of the EU Green Bonds Regulation

In July 2018, the European Commission established a Technical Expert Group on sustainable finance to assist in developing, among others, an EU Green Bonds Standard.[92] The Technical Expert Group published its report on an EU Green Bonds Standard in June 2019.[93] In January 2020, the European Commission announced the development of a green bond standard in its 'Sustainable European Investment Plan: European Green Deal Investment Plan'[94] and issued the corresponding legislative proposal in July 2021.[95] About eighteen months later, on 28 February 2023, the European Parliament and the Council reached a political agreement on the Commission's proposal[96] and on 10 May 2023, the trilogue of the Parliament, the Council, and the Commission ended with a compromise on the regulation. On 30 November 2023, the EU Green Bonds Regulation was published in the Official Journal of the EU as Regulation 2023/2631.[97]

b) The (perceived) need for an EU Green Bonds Regulation

The European Commission saw a need for a regulation on green bonds, since there were no harmonized rules for such bonds, making it difficult to compare bonds that are marketed as 'green' or 'sustainable'.[98] Moreover, the European Commission worried about a potential fragmentation of the internal market if Member States started to enact disparate national requirements.[99] Given the widespread use of the ICMA Green Bond Principles, which have become a kind of market standard, one might doubt the former. Hence, the danger of a fragmented internal market due to differing national regulations appeared to be questionable. On the other hand, the ICMA Green Bond Principles are so general and broad that a comparison of different green bonds which are based on the ICMA principles can be difficult.

---

control, or to the protection and restoration of biodiversity and ecosystems and for determining whether that economic activity causes no significant harm to any of the other environmental objectives and amending Delegated Regulation (EU) 2021/2178 as regards specific public disclosures for those economic activities [2023] OJ L2023/2486.

[92] European Commission, Technical expert group on sustainable finance (TEG) (13 June 2018) https://finance.ec.europa.eu/publications/technical-expert-group-sustainable-finance-teg_en.
[93] EU Technical Expert Group on Sustainable Finance (n 20). For an assessment see Rüdiger Veil, 'Europa auf dem Weg zu einem Green Bond Standard' (2020) 74 Zeitschrift für Wirtschafts- und Bankrecht 1093.
[94] European Commission, Communication from the Commission to the European Parliament, the European Council, the Council, the European Economic and Social Committee and the Committee of the Regions, Sustainable European Investment Plan, European Green Deal Investment Plan COM(2020) 21 final (Brussels 14 January 2020) 11 https://eur-lex.europa.eu/legal-content/EN/TXT/PDF/?uri=CELEX:52020DC0021.
[95] European Commission, 'Proposal for a Regulation of the European Parliament and of the Council on European green bonds' COM(2021) 391 final (6 July 2021) https://eur-lex.europa.eu/resource.html?uri=cellar:e77212e8-df07-11eb-895a-01aa75ed71a1.0001.02/DOC_1&format=PDF.
[96] European Commission, 'Sustainable Finance: Commission Welcomes Political Agreement on European Green Bond Standard' *Daily News* (1 March 2023) https://ec.europa.eu/commission/presscorner/detail/en/mex_23_1301.
[97] Regulation (EU) 2023/2631 (n 6).
[98] European Commission, Proposal (n 95) recital 6.
[99] ibid 5 and 6 (Explanatory Memorandum) and 16 (recital 5); EU Green Bonds Regulation, recitals 6 and 7; for a view critical of this argument see Pyka (n 52) 625–27.

The danger of greenwashing appears to be more real. At present, compliance with the ICMA Green Bonds Principles is not monitored by the authorities, their ecological standards are only rudimentarily defined, and the 'third party opinion' hardly leads to uniform standards, even though it does at least offer a certain degree of protection.

c) Overview of the EU Green Bonds Regulation

The EU Green Bonds Regulation '(a) lays down uniform requirements for issuers of bonds who wish to use the designation European Green Bond or EuGB for their bonds that are made available to investors in the Union; (b) establishes a system to register and supervise external reviewers of European Green Bonds; and (c) provides optional disclosure templates for bonds marketed as environmentally sustainable and sustainability-linked bonds in the Union' (Article 1). Thus, core elements of the EU Green Bonds Regulation are provisions on the use of proceeds, documentation, disclosure, and supervision.

The EU Green Bonds Regulation is closely linked to the Taxonomy Regulation (Regulation (EU) 2020/852), as it refers to the Taxonomy Regulation and its Delegated Acts for determining whether an economic activity qualifies as environmentally sustainable and thus as a suitable investment for the proceeds of an EU Green Bond.[100] The EU Green Bonds Regulation stipulates that the proceeds of a European Green Bond have to be (in principle only and fully) allocated according to the taxonomy requirements to certain investments such as fixed assets, capital and operating expenditures that fall under certain provision of Annex 1 to the Commission Delegated Regulation (EU) 2021/2178, financial assets—which, however, have to have been created no later than five years after the issuance of the European Green Bond, or assets and expenditures of households (Article 4).

Issuers are given some leeway ('flexibility pocket') in that 15 per cent of the proceeds can be allocated to taxonomy compliant economic activities for which there are no technical screening criteria yet or to activities 'in the context of international support reported in accordance with internationally agreed guidelines, criteria and reporting cycles' (Article 5(1)). In these cases the issuers have to provide information about the activities and the estimated percentage of the proceeds allocated to these activities in the factsheet of the green bond (Article 5(2)). Moreover, proceeds of one or more European Green Bonds may be used to finance a portfolio of taxonomy-compliant fixed assets or financial assets (so-called portfolio approach); in that case, however, the total value of the assets in the portfolio has to exceed the total value of the portfolio of outstanding European Green Bonds (Article 4(2)). Special restrictions apply to the allocation of proceeds from financial assets (Article 6).

---

[100] EU Green Bonds Regulation, art 2(3) ('"taxonomy requirements" means the criteria for environmentally sustainable economic activities set out in Article 3 of Regulation (EU) 2020/852'); EU Green Bonds Regulation, recital 11.

If the proceeds of a bond are used for capital or operating expenditures (Article 4(1) (b) or (c)) the issuer has to publish a capital expenditure (CapEx) plan that specifies a deadline when all these capital and operating expenditures shall be taxonomy aligned— before the green bond reaches maturity—which then has to be assessed by an external reviewer within sixty days of that date (Article 7). Since the technical screening criteria evolve and can be amended the regulation contains a grandfathering rule. For the allocation of the proceeds the technical screening criteria at the time of the issuance apply; if the technical screening criteria are amended after the issuance of a bond and the proceeds have not been allocated so far or they are covered by a CapEx plan and have not yet met the taxonomy requirements, the proceeds have to be allocated in alignment with the amended technical screening criteria within seven years after the amendment of the criteria (Article 8(1)).[101]

Moreover, the EU Green Bonds Regulation introduces various documentation and transparency provisions.[102] The Regulation requires the publication of a pre-issuance fact sheet the largest part of which should be dedicated to the intended allocation of the proceeds and which should be reviewed by an external reviewer (Article 10 and Annex I). Moreover, post-issuance the Regulation demands the publication of annual allocation reports (until the date of full allocation of the proceeds) and their reviews by an external reviewer (Article 11), and of an impact report after the full allocation of the proceeds and its (optional) review by an external reviewer (Article 12). In addition, issuing a European Green Bond requires the publication of a prospectus in accordance with the Prospectus Regulation[103] (Article 14(1)). Information in the factsheet can be incorporated by reference (Article 14(3)). Advice on incorporating sustainability-related information in prospectuses can be found in ESMA's public statement of 11 July 2023.[104] The factsheet, a pre-issuance review related to the factsheet, a link to a website with the prospectus, the allocation reports and the impact report and their respective reviews, and, where applicable, the CapEx plan have to be published on the issuer's website (Article 15(1)).

There is also a chapter on the conditions for securitization bonds (Articles 16–19) and provisions for optional disclosure templates (Articles 20–21). Finally, the Regulation also places particular emphasis on the regulation of external reviewers (Articles 22–43). They have to register with ESMA and are subject to detailed obligations regarding their organization, compliance, quality control, outsourcing, record keeping, conflicts of interest, and confidentiality.

---

[101] Criticizing such a limited grandfathering rule ICMA, Analysis of the Draft EuGB Regulation (8 July 2021) 3–4 https://www.icmagroup.org/assets/documents/Sustainable-finance/Responses/ICMA-analysis-of-the-EuGB-Regulation-080721.pdf. For a special grandfathering rule for the portfolio approach see art 8(2).

[102] On the value of increased disclosure by issuers of green bonds see Gilotta (n 7) 10–11.

[103] Regulation (EU) 2017/1129 of the European Parliament and of the Council of 14 June 2017 on the prospectus to be published when securities are offered to the public or admitted to trading on a regulated market, and repealing Directive 2003/71/EC [2017] OJ L168/12.

[104] ESMA, Public Statement: Sustainability disclosure in prospectuses, ESMA32-1399193447-441 (11 July 2023) https://www.esma.europa.eu/sites/default/files/2023-07/ESMA32-1399193447-441_Statement_on_sustainability_disclosure_in_prospectuses.pdf.

# 3. Assessment of the EU Green Bonds Regulation

### a) General assessment

The assessment of the new EU Green Bonds Regulation is mixed. The fact that its framework can be used voluntarily is—on the one hand—positive. On the other hand, voluntariness also means that the entire regulation may become meaningless if market participants turn to other, more suitable, or more convincing standards.

Moreover, the EU Green Bonds Regulation is not a globally developed standard and major markets for green bonds such as China or India have developed their own—partly more restrictive, partly more relaxed—standards. They are unlikely to replace their standards with the new EU provisions. Hence, the regulation will not solve the problem of a lack of a widely accepted common framework for green bonds.

On the positive side, the regulation follows appropriate concepts, for example by choosing transparency requirements for issuers. Equally welcome is the gatekeeper approach with regard to external reviewers. As information intermediaries, external reviewers are comparable to rating agencies and auditors. Accordingly, similar provisions appear to be appropriate.

### b) Taxonomy alignment

With regard to more legal certainty, the close link to the Taxonomy Regulation is meant to ensure that the need for clear sustainability criteria is met, as the new EU Green Bonds Regulation will provide more clarity with respect to which projects will be considered 'green'. While that is laudable, it has to be kept in mind that other standards, such as the Climate Bonds Standard, also come with a comprehensive taxonomy. In that regard it is interesting to read the Technical Expert Group's comment that the green bond market is a good example of a 'largely market driven and successful initiative addressing green challenges and climate change mitigation'. This statement of the Technical Expert Group appears to admit that there is no real reason for a regulatory intervention by the EU. Moreover, the regulatory structure of the EU Green Bonds Regulation together with the Taxonomy Regulation and its Delegated Regulations is complex and the mass and meticulous attention to detail of the Delegated Regulations, which appear to attempt to cover every aspect, could be a deterring factor for issuers and investors.

### c) Prospectus requirement

An important aspect of the new regulation is the prospectus requirement for EU Green Bonds. It increases transparency and improves the disciplining effect of liability, as issuers become subject to prospectus liability. This serves to protect investors. On the other hand, the prospectus requirement also means that smaller companies in particular, for whom the preparation of a prospectus involves a comparatively disproportionate effort, will tend to shy away from issuing green bonds. This runs counter to the goal of the Capital Markets Union, which is also being pursued by the European Commission, and which is intended to open up better financing opportunities for small and medium-sized enterprises. In addition, many new ideas are emerging in the sustainability sector and new companies are being formed as a result. These new companies would be predestined as issuers of green bonds. The prospectus requirement therefore leads to a restriction of competition in this sector in favour of established companies.

Moreover, the exemption from the prospectus requirement for green bonds issued or guaranteed by states (Article 14(2)) appears to be problematic. Significant information gaps can arise here, since, as recital 54 sentence 4 of the Prospectus Regulation states, '[e]nvironmental, social and governance circumstances can also constitute specific and material risks for the issuer and its securities and, in that case, should be disclosed'. Whether an information in the factsheet is sufficient in this case remains to be seen.

d) Factsheet

The relationship between factsheet and prospectus should be made clearer in the EU Green Bonds Regulation. Entries on the factsheet are likely to have—at least indirect— significance for the prospectus. Even if a factsheet is not to be classified as a prospectus itself, information in the factsheet will always have to appear in the prospectus, as well. Otherwise, the prospectus would have to be considered incomplete. In addition, the factsheet is likely to fall within the scope of Article 22 of the Prospectus Regulation, so that the requirements for advertising must also be complied with when drafting the factsheet.

e) External reviewers and supervision by state agencies

With regard to the regulation of external reviewers and the supervision by state agencies, the EU Green Bonds Regulation can be credited with sending a strong signal, as this prevents rogue reviewers from spreading and thus damaging investor confidence. The supervision by state authorities and the available sanctions enable tighter control and thus a containment of green washing both on the issuer as well as on the reviewer level, since not only are issuers regulated, but also the reviewers that monitor and verify the compliance of the issuers. This will increase investor confidence in green bonds and can thus counteract the possibility of a market failure due to a loss of confidence.

While the Climate Bonds Standard also stipulates that only 'approved verifiers' are allowed to check the issuers' compliance with the standards, they are supervised only by a private entity, the Climate Bonds Standards Board which is part of the Climate Bonds Initiative, and not by a state agency.

## V. Summary

Green bonds play a major role in the EU's plan to steer private finances towards more sustainable investments. They are debt instruments designed to raise capital for projects that are climate-related or strive for a positive environmental impact. The various standards used to assess green bonds led to uncertainty about what was meant by 'green' or 'sustainable' when it came to the investment of the funds raised by green bonds. Nevertheless, the market for green bonds is growing strongly.

While private standards for green bonds have prevailed until now, the EU has recently established its own voluntarily applicable regulatory regime for green bonds. Overall, the assessment of the EU Green Bonds Regulation is mostly positive. It solves the essential problem of greenwashing, but at the same time is only intended to be a voluntary framework. This approach gives issuers considerable flexibility and further enables competition with private standards; on the other hand, such a voluntary approach entails the danger that the regulation plunges into irrelevance if private standards are perceived to be more suitable. With its transparency- and gatekeeper-oriented regulation, the EU Green Bonds Regulation pursues a balanced approach. However, the prospectus requirement and the not yet entirely clear legal situation of the factsheet could prove problematic.

# 15
# ESG Demand-side Regulation—Governing the Shareholders

*Thilo Kuntz**

## I. Introduction

Corporate purpose, corporate social responsibility (CSR), sustainability, socially responsible investing, environmental, social, and corporate governance (ESG)—the debate about whether and to what extent the public corporation and, indeed, capital markets, must serve aims other than profit maximization is running at full throttle.[1] Sceptics may argue that 'we', the citizens and legal scholars of the twenty-first century, engage in nothing more than rehashing old debates.[2] In one way, this is certainly true. Purpose and the profit-orientation of corporations lay at the heart of debates about legislation on both sides of the Atlantic in the eighteenth and nineteenth centuries.[3] Employee representation has been debated in Germany since the nineteenth century.[4] And yet. What distinguishes the old wine from the new is the wave of regulatory interventions, especially in continental Europe, but not only there.

The European Commission (EU Commission) has drafted an ambitious project, the 'European Green Deal', and intends nothing less than to change the financial system into one supporting 'sustainable solutions'.[5] It aspires to embed sustainability into the

---

* The author thanks the participants of the conference on Corporate Purpose, CSR and ESG at Tubingen University in June 2022, participants of the International Fiduciary Law Workshop at Heinrich Heine University in Dusseldorf in June 2023, and Yasin Cetiner, Lukas Daub, Carsten Fedler, Alexander von Lützow, Robert Nies, and Ludwig Stimpel. Remaining errors are mine alone. All internet sources were last accessed on 10 January 2024.

[1] The meaning of these terms is far from clear. I will use ESG as a comprehensive term without claiming that it equates to CSR, sustainability, or encompasses everything and more inherent in the latter expressions. When I refer to 'ESG' in this chapter, I use it as shorthand for a concept aiming at more than traditional shareholder value unless otherwise indicated. In this respect, I follow the excellent piece on the issues lying behind the differing values by Laura T Starks, 'Sustainable Finance and ESG Issues: Value versus Values' (2023) 78 Journal of Finance 1837, 1838 fn 1.

[2] cf, for Germany: Gregor Bachmann, 'Zielsetzung und Governance von Unternehmen im Lichte der Klimaverantwortung' (2023) 187 Zeitschrift für das gesamte Handelsrecht und Wirtschaftsrecht 166, 170, 194.

[3] For the US see Harwell Wells (ch 9 in this volume); for Germany with a comparison to the US and the UK see Thilo Kuntz, 'Corporate Purpose: konzeptionelle Grundlagen, rechtshistorische und rechtsdogmatische Aspekte' (2022) 186 Zeitschrift für das gesamte Handelsrecht und Wirtschaftsrecht 166.

[4] See Thilo Kuntz, 'German Corporate Law in the 20th Century' in *Research Handbook on the History of Corporate and Company Law* (Edward Elgar Publishing 2018) 221–26, 230–32.

[5] European Commission, Communication from the Commission to the European Parliament, the European Council, the Council, The European Economic and Social Committee and the Committee of the Regions, The European Green Deal (11 December 2019) COM/2019/640 final, 2.

corporate governance framework[6] and redirect private investments into sustainable finance.[7] The UK Stewardship Code 2020 incorporates ESG norms, requiring signatories to consider, inter alia 'diversity … and workforce interests' and 'environmental and social issues, including climate change'.[8] In 2021, the UK government presented a 'Greening Finance' roadmap.[9] The US Securities and Exchange Commission (SEC) has published a hotly debated proposal for climate-change disclosure in 2022.[10] It also adopted new rules amending Form N-PX under the US Investment Company Act of 1940, enhancing the information requirements concerning proxy voting, forcing funds and investment managers to assign all their proxy votes to one or more of fourteen categories, a fair number of which refer to ESG.[11] California enacted several laws on climate disclosure subjecting major companies to provide public information on their greenhouse gas emissions and report on their climate-related financial risks.[12]

Taking its cue from these developments, this chapter proposes a novel vantage point and presents demand-side regulation as a new regulatory concept. If a regulator (in the broadest sense of the word) aims at implementing ESG-oriented decision-making in the structure of corporate governance, the regulatory strategy must include the shareholders and investors. When stockholders have to abide by norms mirroring those operating on the level of the corporate board, at least in theory, the incentives and investment aims of corporate directors and shareholders should align.

This approach fills a gap in the literature which, until now, has concentrated on the regulation of the corporate board and the question of whether and how the directors' fiduciary duties should entail stakeholder interests. Traditionally, scholars treat boards and board members as the suppliers of ESG-oriented decision making, despite obvious disadvantages. One issue is the well-known 'many-masters problem'.[13] Moreover, and perhaps more importantly, supply-side regulation fails to implement an effective incentive structure.[14] Considering that shareholders vote on members of the

---

[6] ibid 17.
[7] ibid 16.
[8] The Financial Reporting Council, 'The UK Stewardship Code 2020' (2020) 5 https://www.frc.org.uk/investors/uk-stewardship-code.
[9] https://www.gov.uk/government/publications/greening-finance-a-roadmap-to-sustainable-investing.
[10] Proposed Rule: The Enhancement and Standardization of Climate-Related Disclosures for Investors, https://www.sec.gov/rules/proposed/2022/33-11042.pdf. For an analysis see Lisa Fairfax, 'A Green Victory in the Midst of Potential Defeat? Concern and Optimism about the Impact of the SEC's Climate-Related Disclosure Rule' in Thilo Kuntz (ed), *Research Handbook on Environmental, Social, and Corporate Governance* (Edward Elgar Publishing 2024) ch 13.
[11] SEC, Release Nos 33-11131; 34-96206; IC-34745; File No S7-11-21, RIN 3235-AK67 https://www.sec.gov/news/press-release/2022-198.
[12] AB-1305 Voluntary carbon market disclosures https://leginfo.legislature.ca.gov/faces/billTextClient.xhtml?bill_id=202320240AB1305; SB-253 Climate Corporate Data Accountability Act https://leginfo.legislature.ca.gov/faces/billTextClient.xhtml?bill_id=202320240SB253; SB-261 Greenhouse gases: climate-related financial risk https://leginfo.legislature.ca.gov/faces/billTextClient.xhtml?bill_id=202320240SB261.
[13] For Germany see Thilo Kuntz, 'Regulierungsstrategien zur Durchsetzung von Gemeinwohlinteressen im Aktienrecht' in Stefan Grundmann and others (eds), *Festschrift für Klaus J Hopt zum 80. Geburtstag* (de Gruyter 2020) 654, 657; for the US see Frank H Easterbrook and Daniel R Fischel, *The Economic Structure of Corporate Law* (HUP 1991) 38; for France see Dominique Schmidt, 'La société et l'entreprise' (2017) 193 Recueil Dalloz 2380, 2383.
[14] For a recent critique see Lucian A Bebchuk and Roberto Tallarita, 'The Illusory Promise of Stakeholder Governance' (2022) 106 Cornell Law Review 91, 139–58.

board of directors, their demands set the norms a board maximizes. As long as shareholders measure return on their investment in monetary terms, supply-side regulation lacks teeth.

Major parts of the new laws and legal frameworks mentioned above already reflect the idea of demand-side regulation. Notwithstanding their far-reaching differences with respect to content and effect, they rest on a common denominator, namely the addressee. It is no longer the board of directors, the German *Vorstand*, or the French *conseil d'administration*, or a similar body managing the affairs of the public corporation or company, but rather the shareholders and investors. After decades of debating directors' duties vis-à-vis the corporation, stockholders, and society at large, this presents a major turn of events. Instead of focusing on the side offering managerial services in the interests of others, the new wave of regulatory activity concentrates on the demand side. Governing the shareholders holds the promise to change the incentive structure reigning over managerial decision-making. If the shareholders' interests no longer rest primarily on monetary aims as in the traditional world of 'shareholder value' in exchange for ESG values and criteria, directors may be more open to give ESG more weight—because their electorate does so, too.

This chapter offers a twofold contribution to the literature. It charts the territory and provides a description and analysis of legal instruments and regulatory strategies rule-makers already deploy for ESG demand-side regulation. Furthermore, it develops an analytical grid and evaluates promises and perils of the different ways to govern the shareholders. Notwithstanding the developments in the United States and the UK, it takes the recent EU regulations as its main frame of reference. They are by far more comprehensive and therefore may better serve as a model. Moreover, important parts have already been in force at least for a little while, so that the chapter may draw on early practical experiences and empirical studies. Additionally, the EU regulations have ramifications far beyond the EU's borders, in line with the EU Commission's ambition of world leadership in sustainability policy. According to recent estimates, more than 10,000 foreign companies will have to comply with EU sustainability rules alone, roughly one-third of them from the United States.[15]

Section II explains how demand-side regulation fits into the general scheme of corporate governance and explores basic strategies of demand-side regulation. A basic distinction can be drawn between direct and indirect demand-side regulation. Whereas the first type addresses shareholders and investors directly through ESG disclosure rules and requirements to commit to ESG, the second targets retail investors as a group and tweaks their revealed preferences towards ESG. In the EU, indirect demand-side regulation comes in the form of the rules on investment nudging retail investors into ESG products. Instead of narrowing down the number of eligible voting outcomes, it aims at letting only those into the corporate arena who—quite literally—subscribe to

---

[15] Dieter Holger, 'At Least 10,000 Foreign Companies to Be Hit by EU Sustainability Rules' *Wall Street Journal* (5 April 2023) https://www.wsj.com/articles/at-least-10-000-foreign-companies-to-be-hit-by-eu-sustainability-rules-307a1406.

ESG in the first place. If both institutional and retail investors lean towards ESG and publicly disclose related information, it becomes easier for boards of directors to discern their stockholders' preferences and to adapt corporate management accordingly. Moreover, it becomes easier for ESG-friendly shareholders to coordinate.

Section III describes and evaluates different approaches to direct demand-side regulation. While this approach holds promise because it forces institutional investors to commit to ESG publicly and vis-à-vis their beneficiaries, doubts remain. Considering the broad variety of sometimes diverging values and perspectives subsumed under the ESG rubric, navigating shareholders and investors towards this regulatory goal does not in itself alleviate the coordination problems within that group. In many instances, ESG-friendly shareholders pursue opposing aims, for example, workers owning stock and proponents of stricter environmental standards. Consequently, balancing and coordination problems remain.

Section IV focuses on indirect demand-side regulation and comes to similar conclusions. As mentioned above, indirect demand-side regulation tries to change the composition of the shareholder base by letting only those investors in who already express beliefs and attitudes in conformity with regulatory ESG goals. Surveying and analysing investors' preferences, according to recent EU regulation, falls to investment advisers. Asking for ESG preferences exploits the social desirability bias, that is, the tendency to act in conformity with prevailing legal and social norms, and nudges retail investors into the direction desired by the regulator. This promises to strengthen inflows into ESG funds and ESG-friendly voting of members and shareholders of institutional investors such as pension funds, even those not marketed as ESG-oriented. What remains open, however, is the extent to which this strategy really leads to ESG-friendly behaviour of ultimate beneficiaries and retail investors. Many empirical studies show that even those opting for an ESG product more often than not prefer pecuniary benefits once the investment is made. Consequently, the largest group of shareholders will still judge directors based on monetary gains. Given the lack of behavioural control and the ability of shareholders to choose those ESG aims closest to value maximization, indirect demand-side regulation is no panacea, nor does it completely solve the issues direct demand-side regulation encounters, especially the persisting degree of conflicting ESG goals and resulting difficulties to coordinate shareholders and the lack of behavioural control.

Section V concludes.

## II. Demand-side Regulation and Its Place in Corporate Governance

The traditional approach of promoting ESG, reigning supreme as a point of disagreement in corporate-law scholarship, focuses on the supply side, that is, boards of directors and their international equivalents, in Germany the management (or executive) board. Subsection 1 exposes its structural flaws bordering on the dysfunctional from a corporate governance point of view. Moreover, even if the members of corporate boards should be willing to pursue ESG-related goals and strategies and even if a significant part of the shareholders should play along, at least as a matter of first impression, managerial ESG-friendly decision-making suffers from several problems. A lack of information about concrete preferences, a coordination problem on the side of the stockholders, and the problem of aligning word—ESG talk—and deed—ESG-friendly stockholder voting. Subsection 2 argues that demand-side regulation may serve as a complement. Subjecting shareholders to disclosure rules helps producing information on their ESG preferences and thus to attenuate the information problem on the side of corporate directors. Additionally, stockholders themselves gain insight into their corporate siblings' leanings and may better coordinate their efforts in setting and implementing an ESG-friendly agenda. Pre-contractual disclosure of retail investors' preferences may help countering the mismatch between mere lip service and actual voting behaviour in ESG matters. Subsection 3 sketches out basic design options of ESG demand-side regulation.

## 1. The Problems of Supply-side Regulation

In one of the perennial debates of corporate governance, scholars argue about whether members of the board must or at least should include other interests than those of the shareholders and, if yes, to what extent.[16] According to the simplifying analytical apparatus typically brought to bear on the issue, the difference lies in 'shareholder value' versus 'stakeholder value'. The dividing line is stricter in theory than in practice, allowing for shades of grey. Many approaches somehow instruct boards to consider interests other than those of stockholders, be it 'enlightened shareholder value' of the UK variety,[17] the more demanding French standards requiring corporate directors to take stakeholder interests into account,[18] or the German model which arguably lies

---

[16] The literature is legion. I assume that readers are familiar with the gist of the debate and may easily access relevant material and will dispense with naming alibi contributions.

[17] See s 172(1) of the UK Companies Act 2006: 'A director of a company must act in the way he considers, in good faith, would be most likely to promote the success of the company for the benefit of its members as a whole, and in doing so have regard (amongst other matters) to—
  (a) the likely consequences of any decision in the long term,
  (b) the interests of the company's employees,
  (c) the need to foster the company's business relationships with suppliers, customers and others,
  (d) the impact of the company's operations on the community and the environment,
  (e) the desirability of the company maintaining a reputation for high standards of business conduct, and
  (f) the need to act fairly as between members of the company.' See https://www.legislation.gov.uk/ukpga/2006/46/section/172. On the meaning of 'enlightened shareholder value' and directors' duties in the UK see Paul Davies, Sarah Worthington, and Chris Hare (eds), *Gower: Principles of Modern Company Law* (11th edn, Sweet & Maxwell 2021) 10-026–10-028.

[18] See French Civil Code, art 1833(2): 'The company is managed in its own company's interest, taking into account the social and environmental concerns linked to its business' (the translation is mine; the original text reads: 'La société est gérée dans son intérêt social, en prenant en considération les enjeux sociaux et environnementaux de son activité.' See https://www.legifrance.gouv.fr/codes/article_lc/LEGIARTI00003

somewhere in between, at least as it is practiced.[19] The various versions of the law governing board members' fiduciary duties give rise to a set of well-known problems.

Stakeholder provisions cause the 'many masters problem' and ultimately create the risk that boards insulate themselves from liability.[20] They also do not address the problem of the incentives set by other parts of corporate law. If it is shareholders who vote in corporate directors, sue for damages, and decide on important issues of the corporate agenda, boards will probably act in the formers' interests whenever push comes to shove.[21] These problems have been subject to intense debate, so there is no need to go into them in more detail here. For now, it suffices to conclude that there are not many ties that bind a director wishing to play the corporate game to her advantage.

Observers may object to this bleak picture and argue that not all board members subscribe to the notorious shareholder capitalism of old, but instead turn towards 'doing well by doing good'[22] or at least to do what the law requires of them. Even Delaware, the most shareholderist jurisdiction of them all, allows directors to consider other constituencies as long as this promises to increase long-term shareholder value.[23] Only in a very few cases such as a sale, an inevitable break-up, or a change of control transaction, the board's duty shifts to realizing the highest immediate value for shareholders alone.[24] Consequently, Delaware law leaves enough of a wiggle room for corporate boards to include stakeholder interests in their day-to-day decision-making.[25] With a growing number of investors supporting some form of ESG,[26] one might argue that there is a more interesting question to be asked: are there any structural obstacles in establishing business strategies and decision-making if a corporate board decides to follow ESG norms and values? The same could be said for shareholders wishing for more than mere pecuniary gain[27] or for integrating ESG risks as a matter of adequate pricing in monetary terms, especially when it comes to climate risk.[28] Unfortunately,

---

8589931). On this provision and its background see Alain Pietrancosta, 'ESG Enhancements to Company Law: The French "PACTE" Law' in Thilo Kuntz (ed), *Research Handbook on Environmental, Social, and Corporate Governance* (Edward Elgar Publishing 2024) ch 2.

[19] See Christoph Seibt, 'Taking Stakeholder Interests Seriously: A Practitioner's View from Germany on Management Duties' in Thilo Kuntz (ed), *Research Handbook on Environmental, Social, and Corporate Governance* (Edward Elgar Publishing 2024) ch 1.

[20] See the sources cited in n 13.

[21] For a recent critique see Bebchuk and Tallarita (n 14).

[22] See eg Oliver Falck and Stephan Heblich, 'Corporate Social Responsibility: Doing Well by Doing Good' (2007) 50 Business Horizons 247.

[23] *In re Trados Inc Shareholder Litigation* 73 A3d 17, 36–37 (Del Ch 2013); *eBay Domestic Holdings Inc v Newmark* 16 A3d 1, 33 (Del Ch 2010).

[24] *Revlon Inc v MacAndrews & Forbes Holdings Inc* 506 A2d 173, 182 (Del 1986).

[25] ibid: 'A board may have regard for various constituencies in discharging its responsibilities, provided there are rationally related benefits accruing to the stockholders.'

[26] See section III.1.b)bb)(2) below.

[27] For studies suggesting that non-financial factors influence investment decisions see eg Samuel M Hartzmark and Abigail B Sussman, 'Do Investors Value Sustainability? A Natural Experiment Examining Ranking and Fund Flows' (2019) 74 Journal of Finance 2789; Florian Heeb and others, 'Do Investors Care about Impact?' (2023) 36 Review of Financial Studies 1737; Philipp Krueger, Zacharias Sautner, and Laura T Starks, 'The Importance of Climate Risks for Institutional Investors' (2020) 33 Review of Financial Studies 1067, 1085–86; Arno Riedl and Paul Smeets, 'Why Do Investors Hold Socially Responsible Mutual Funds?' (2017) 72 Journal of Finance 2505.

[28] See eg Patrick Bolton and Marcin Kacperczyk, 'Do Investors Care about Carbon Risk?' (2021) 142 Journal of Financial Economics 517; Patrick Bolton and Marcin Kacperczyk, 'Global Pricing of Carbon-Transition Risk'

the answer is yes. Corporate directors willing to build on ESG face three obstacles: (a) they suffer from a lack of information about shareholder preferences; (b) they have to grapple with coordination problems; and (c) issues of behavioural control. Letting shareholders vote on ESG matters is often not the solution (d).

a) Information problem

If the board of directors really is willing to transform their shareholders' preferences into managerial action, the board members have to figure out their electorate's inclinations.[29] Recent proposals to keep corporate decision-making centred on the board as a guardian of shareholder welfare against the perils of suboptimal outcomes when stockholders can trade[30] hinge on whether they know the post-trade stockholders' aims and wishes. Most stockholder communities include the whole spectrum from the most ardent defenders of the infamous creed that 'greed is good for you'[31] over run-of-the-mill ESG-friendly retirement savers who nonetheless favour return on investment over broader societal concerns to hard-nosed activists like the Oxfam America Activist Fund.[32] Whereas it often will be possible to identify the outspoken extremes, the majority typically gathers somewhere in between those positions without making personal commitments and investment aims explicit.[33] For directors who want to pursue ESG goals, this is difficult ground to tread. Not all ESG-friendly shareholders necessarily follow the same agenda. They value different aspects and sometimes want directors to achieve conflicting goals.[34] How do directors glean all the important information about these and other preferences? How do they find out whether shareholders want them to pursue conflicting goals?

This problem is mirrored on another level. Many retail investors do not hold stock in a corporation directly but buy shares (or their equivalent) in a mutual fund who holds the corporate stock and is the corporate shareholder in the legal sense. These retail investors have a hard time figuring out the preferences and decision-making processes on the fund level.[35] What is more important in this chapter, however, is the top-down perspective. Just as it is difficult for corporate directors to collect information about their

---

(2023) 78 Journal of Finance 3677. For a short survey over the empirical literature see Sebastian Steuer and Tobias H Tröger, 'The Role of Disclosure in Green Finance' (2022) 8 Journal of Financial Regulation 1, 24–26.

[29] Robert P Bartlett and Ryan Bubb, 'Corporate Social Responsibility through Shareholder Governance' (2023) 97 Southern California Law Review, ECGI Working Paper No 682/2023 https://www.ecgi.global/working-paper/corporate-social-responsibility-through-shareholder-governance.

[30] Doron Levit, Nadya Malenko, and Ernst Maug, 'Trading and Shareholder Democracy' (2023) 79 Journal of Finance 257.

[31] As coined by Michael Douglas' character Gordon Gekko in the movie *Wall Street*.

[32] See https://www.oxfamaction.org/take-action/.

[33] See Patrick Bolton and others, 'Investor Ideology' (2020) 137 Journal of Financial Economics 320, 321, noting that 'the ideology of most pension funds is to the left, while that of the largest mutual funds is to the right, and the funds voting in line with the proxy adviser ISS recommendations are squarely in the center'.

[34] This problem is acknowledged even by those who think that a corporation should be run with more sympathy to non-monetary aims of shareholders, for example, Oliver Hart and Luigi Zingales, 'Companies Should Maximize Shareholder Welfare Not Market Value' (2017) 2 Journal of Law, Finance, and Accounting 247, 250.

[35] Bartlett and Bubb (n 29) 40.

shareholders' preferences, it is equally hard for managers of mutual or pension funds to gain relevant data regarding their investors' ESG predispositions and desires.

The demand side's composite nature compounds the information problem. Information about preferences does not simply flow from the retail investors to the corporation with the institutional investors in between operating as mere conduits channelling data upstream. Not only is it difficult for institutional investors to procure relevant facts about their own beneficiaries. They also do not just pass on to corporate boards what they have learnt (which arguably would be illegal). Instead, board members can only guess at what basis institutional investors act on by indirect observation, that is, by evaluating past voting behaviour as an instance of revealed preferences or general structural features of funds such as a publicly advertised ESG-oriented investment strategy.

### b) Coordination problem

The information problem outlined above in subsection II.1.a) interlaces with another issue: in order to pursue their aims through voting, shareholders have to coordinate.[36] Even if it is not always necessary to achieve a majority to be successful in changing corporate policies, without at least support of others, activists' campaigns will fail. Higher support even in failed ES(G) campaigns predicts subsequent ES incidents and their effects on shareholder value.[37] To calculate chances of success and the likelihood to influence the board, stockholders need information about the ratio of ESG-friendly members of the shareholder side.[38] Moreover, the coalitions needed for reaching a majority typically are unstable, and therefore not useful as a dependable predictor of ESG-related voting outcomes. What is essential is a public focal point of reference shareholders may use independent of single events. This is far from trivial. Measuring or rating the performance of market actors like institutional investors according to ESG criteria is difficult because of a lack of clear criteria and widely diverging approaches.[39]

The problem becomes more pronounced considering the limited use of the price mechanism as the fundamental coordination mechanism for trading and evaluation on capital markets. Because of a feedback loop between trading and shareholder voting on contested issues, the outcome of shareholder voice depends on both the expected voting outcomes and expected trading *before* a shareholder meeting,[40] that is, on how much the composition of the stockholder side changes in light of shareholders buying or selling stock expecting certain proposal to be successful or decisions to be made.[41]

---

[36] On the importance of collaboration among investors with respect to ESG activism see Elroy Dimson, Oğuzhan Karakaş, and Xi Li, 'Active Ownership' (2015) 28 Review of Financial Studies 3226, 3240–42.
[37] Yazhou Ellen He, Bige Kahraman, and Michelle Lowry, 'ES Risks and Shareholder Voice' (2023) 36 Review of Financial Studies 4824.
[38] According to He and others (n 37) 4853, ES funds are 33 per cent more likely to vote for ES proposals.
[39] See Andreas Engert, 'ESG Ratings: Guiding a Movement in Search for Itself' in Thilo Kuntz (ed), *Research Handbook on Environmental, Social, and Corporate Governance* (Edward Elgar Publishing 2024) ch 14.
[40] On the feedback loop after shareholder meetings and contested proposals Sophia Zhengzi Li, Ernst Maug, and Miriam Schwartz-Ziv, 'When Shareholders Disagree: Trading after Shareholder Meetings' (2022) 35 Review of Financial Studies 1813.
[41] Levit and others (n 30) 26.

Contingent on how trading goes and whether the post-trading majority consists of ESG proponents or conventional investors, multiple equilibria can arise.[42] That is not only a problem for stockholder action, but also for corporate boards.[43]

c) Behavioural control

Whether and how shareholders may use information on ESG preferences to coordinate engagement strategies and voting hinges on an additional problem. Traditionally, shareholders have decided anonymously. They therefore might cast their vote diverging from opinions expressed publicly because they do not fear reputational losses or social sanctions for acting in a manner not appreciated by peers.[44] Institutional investors marketing themselves as ESG-oriented and supporting relevant norms and values does not equal ESG-friendly voting outcomes. This reinforces both the information problem on the side of corporate directors and the shareholders' coordination problem.

d) Why shareholder say on ESG is not the solution

In an influential contribution, Hart and Zingales propose to ask shareholders to vote on contentious issues more often.[45] Based on the assumption 'that in reality many investors are prosocial even though they are willing to hold the shares of tobacco or gun companies',[46] they suggest that corporate boards periodically call a shareholder vote on matters of social policy (in the broadest sense of the word).[47] This is, at best, a partial solution. Neither does it address the problems of shareholder coordination and behavioural control[48] nor is it possible to let stockholders permanently vote. Apart from practical problems to invite all the shareholders for a shareholders' meeting and increasing efficiency losses, the Hart and Zingales proposal runs counter to basic institutional arrangement of board authority in many modern corporate laws.[49] Additionally, an increasing frequency of shareholder voting on corporate policy has the potential to cause severe discord among stockholders due to diverging preferences, especially when they cast their ballot on politically charged subject matters.[50]

There is no need to dig deeper into this debate. For the purposes of the present chapter, it suffices to say that empowering stockholders with more rights to express a 'say on [x]' does not diminish the need for other solutions and regulatory approaches.

---

[42] ibid 26–29, 47.
[43] See text accompanying n 30 above.
[44] cf Bartlett and Bubb (n 29) 39.
[45] Hart and Zingales (n 34) 260–62.
[46] ibid 250.
[47] ibid 260–61.
[48] cf Bartlett and Bubb (n 29) 41.
[49] For a comparative analysis see Sofie Cools, 'Climate Proposals: ESG Shareholder Activism Sidestepping Board Authority' in Thilo Kuntz (ed), *Research Handbook on Environmental, Social, and Corporate Governance* (Edward Elgar Publishing 2024) ch 6.
[50] cf Bartlett and Bubb (n 29) 41.

## 2. Demand-side Regulation as a Complement

Taking into account the problems left by a regulatory approach centring on supply-side regulation and corporate boards, at least part of the solution could be a change of perspective and a turn to demand-side regulation as a complementary strategy. This means that, instead of concentrating on the board and its members, shareholders and investors become the object of attraction.[51] If the vast majority of shareholders embraced norms and values contributing to employee welfare, environmental concerns, and other aims of the ESG and sustainability movement, the three issues described above in section II.1 would lose at least part of their sting. First, the board of directors could implement ESG-friendly management strategies as a reflection of their shareholders' utility functions. Second, demand-side regulation could orchestrate shareholders preferences and voting patterns by excluding or at least crowding out more extreme forms of monetary value-maximization strategies. The obvious approach is disclosure regulation, a well-known tool of capital markets law. When it comes to ESG demand-side regulation, however, the traditional rationales of disclosure regulation with their emphasis on investor protection are incomplete. Sub-section b) provides the necessary supplementary rationalization and argues in favour of disclosure as a regulatory instrument. Empirical studies on the effects of mandatory disclosure on corporate behaviour strengthen the case for this approach also with respect to the problems of behavioural control and shareholder coordination (subsection c)). As a starting point, the notion of 'demand side' merits attention. As will be shown below, viewing it as the simple aggregate of the shareholders does not do it justice and would be oversimplifying (subsection a)).

### a) The notion of 'demand side'

There is not 'the' demand side. Rather, it comprises a broad variety of members. Shareholders are, of course, an important constituent. The term 'shareholder' requires disaggregation, however. In listed companies, institutional investors hold the lion's share of corporate stock. According to an OECD report, institutional investors, most importantly mutual funds, pension funds, and insurance companies, hold 41 per cent of the global market capitalization.[52] Institutional investors own 72 per cent of the 10,000 largest listed US companies' market capitalization and 38 per cent in Europe, where the public sector and strategic crossholdings play a larger role.[53] In all, 58.2 per cent of the shares in the German DAX40 are held by institutional investors.[54] Thus, an

---

[51] Leaving stakeholder empowerment aside in this paper.
[52] Adriana de la Cruz, Alejandra Medina, and Yung Tang, *Owners of the World's Listed Companies* (OECD Capital Market Series 2019) 5 www.oecd.org/corporate/Owners-of-the-Worlds-Listed-Companies.htm.
[53] De La Cruz et al. (n 52) at 11, Table 3.
[54] Standard and Poor's Global Market Intelligence and Deutsche Investor Relations Verband, *Who Owns the German DAX? The Ownership Structure of the German DAX in 2022* (2023) 8 https://www.dirk.org/wp-content/uploads/2023/06/DAX-Studie-Wem-gehoert-die-Deutschland-AG-10.0.pdf.

important middle layer exists between corporations and retail investors or 'ultimate' beneficiaries.

Institutional investors feature Janiform characteristics, however. As buyers of corporate stock, they resemble other shareholders in that they need information about an asset class and the investment target and its behaviour. Insofar, they populate the demand side. From the retail investors' perspective, however, they represent the supply side, selling shares, memberships, and investment products of their own. With respect to demand-side regulation, this dual role of institutional investors has to be kept in mind.

Of course, there are other actors like public investors, intermediaries, rating agencies, to name but a few. Considering the importance of institutional investors it suffices, however, to concentrate on institutional investors and their beneficiaries for the remainder of the chapter. Taking them as examples offers the chance to discuss basic issues of demand-side regulation—and to respect the word limit of this chapter.

b) Information and coordination through disclosure regulation

The medicine of choice to heal investors suffering from a shortage of information is mandatory disclosure. According to the vast majority of observers, the most important rationale underlying mandatory disclosure regimes is investor protection, both on primary and on secondary markets.[55] This certainly captures the needs of both institutional investors searching for standardized information about their investment targets and retail investors pondering whether the institutional investors they intend to give their money to, e.g., a mutual fund, are ESG friendly.[56] In essence, however, this type of disclosure is a kind of supply-side regulation. Those who wish to market their shares and products must disclose. From the perspective of demand-side regulation, however, this view is incomplete as it does not fully capture all market participants' informational needs. A closer look reveals two additional rationales grounding disclosure duties in the context of demand-side regulation.

First, corporate directors and institutional investors need to identify the ESG preferences of their shareholders. In light of the information problem identified above in section II.1.a), the managers of other people's money require data about the expectations of their constituents. Those that offer to pursue ESG-friendly business and investment strategies, willingly or because the law forces them to do so, depend on relevant information provided by those whose interests they purport to take into account in decision-making. If the broad investor base signals ESG friendliness, directors can at least be sure that they do not have to fear dismissal because of the mere fact of following ESG-oriented processes at all, even if they still must collect information about concrete preferences.

---

[55] For a survey see John Armour and others, *Principles of Financial Regulation* (OUP 2006) 161–67.
[56] See Steuer and Tröger (n 28) 31–44.

Additionally, if the broader regulatory environment, for example, the European 'Green Deal' and its legal offspring, aims at pushing market participants into the direction of ESG-oriented corporate governance, disclosing information about ESG also provides an incentive for corporate boards to adopt ESG-friendly strategies and procedures, at least if there is an overall trend in investor preferences. If the board members see that preferences change, the incentive structure will evolve concurrently, given the directors' interest in reelection, etc.[57]

Second, ESG-related disclosure duties serve the purpose of shareholder coordination. For institutional investors, proxy advisers, and other actors devising engagement strategies and considering the chances of success of ESG-related voting proposals, gathering data about shareholders' revealed preferences is a helpful tool. Disclosure helps other demand-side members to estimate the probability to accomplish an ESG-related goal through instruments like shareholder-initiated proxy proposals. Furthermore, potential buyers may use ESG disclosures by investors to evaluate their possible investment considering their own preferences and appraise whether the former and their own align or diverge. As a corollary, at least for bigger listed corporations with a publicly visible shareholder structure, the buyer of corporate stock can use the data of investor disclosure to assess whether the ESG policies of the corporation and those of the shareholder base match. All of this helps buyers to navigate the investment landscape and find opportunities to enter the market according to their own leanings and broader monetary and political goals. Consequently, investors with similar preferences should end up in similar investments. This attenuates the problem of diverging preferences as the chances increase that shareholders pursue the same or a similar agenda.

The regulatory approach depends on the actor on the demand side. For institutional investors and other professional players buying shares such as other corporations, it is relatively easy to extend extant disclosure duties to ESG-related information. Subjecting private individual retail investors to a comparably comprehensive disclosure regime simply would not be feasible. That does not mean, however, that disclosure is impossible. As demonstrated above in subsection II.2.a), retail investors are a negligible quantity when it comes to direct investment into corporate shares. Typically, they enter the stock market indirectly through an investment into mutual funds or pension funds, that is, institutional investors. When retail investors buy shares of financial actors like a mutual fund, either directly or by means of an intermediary such as a bank providing financial advice or an insurance broker, it is possible to have them disclose their ESG preferences at this stage.[58] This information then can be used on the level of the institutional investor and will be mirrored in this investor's behaviour and strategy, publicly available through regular capital market disclosure.[59]

---

[57] See above section II.1.a).
[58] Of course, there are legal limits to this; see section IV.2.b)bb) below.
[59] Depending on the depth of the information passed on to the institutional investors, see section IV.2.b) bb) below.

## c) Behavioural control and preference streamlining

Bringing shareholders to accept ESG as their North Star is a collective action problem. Scholars have long been heralding law, especially mandatory public law, as a powerful countervailing tool. From the perspective of game theory, some argue that '[o]nce [the players are] subject to a rule to which others are similarly subject, we can know that others will participate in the cooperative scheme put in place by the state'.[60] According to these scholars, '[w]e do not have to worry about free-riding or futility. This works because the public law rule is set out in advance of individual conduct to which it applies'.[61] Gone is the information problem because 'a mandatory rule issued by the state … gives us just the information we need when we need it'.[62] Observers prone to scepticism may be prone to argue, however, that, in the end, disclosure regulation produces words only. Consequently, they might question whether a regime concentrating on the public production of data on ESG translates into a change in attitude and action when push comes to shove. Put differently, at least as a matter of first impression, the problem of behavioural control set out in section II.1.c) above proves to be persistent and hard to overcome. As a true guru of ESG would perhaps say: 'Unity of thought, word, and deed is the underlying principle of true devotion and surrender'.[63] Without a change in the preferences of demand-side actors, the usefulness of disclosure regulation as an instrument of demand-side regulation remains dubious, endangering the enterprise as a whole. And yet, there is reason for hope.

Recent empirical studies indicate that mandatory non-financial disclosure affects corporate behaviour. The authors of an influential meta-study summarize 'that firms tend to expand and adjust CSR activities subject to disclosure requirements'.[64] Evidence can be found in studies on the effects of Californian supply-chain disclosure rules,[65] US disclosure duties related to mining activities,[66] and Chinese CSR stock-exchange reporting standards,[67] to name but a few.[68] Not only can the introduction of disclosure requirements induce improvements in ESG decision-making, the reverse is also true. A recent study shows how a reduction of mandatory disclosure burdens correlated with downgraded ESG activities.[69] Therefore, disclosure regulation may be expected to influence actual board practice and corporate policy and could at least temper the

---

[60] Aditi Bagchi, 'Law and the Moral Dynamics of Collective Action' (2022) 53 Seton Hall Law Review 149, 193.
[61] ibid.
[62] ibid.
[63] Guru Sathya Sai Baba, 'Unity of Thought, Word and Deed Is True Humanness' (2016) 59 Sanathana Sarathi 4, 6.
[64] Hans B Christensen, Luzi Hall, and Christian Leuz, 'Mandatory CSR and sustainability reporting: economic analysis and literature review' (2021) 26 Review of Accounting Studies 1176, 1215.
[65] See eg Guoman She, 'The Real Effects of Mandatory Nonfinancial Disclosure: Evidence from Supply Chain Transparency' (2022) 97 The Accounting Review 399.
[66] See eg Hans B Christensen and others, 'The Real Effects of Mandated Information on Social Responsibility in Financial Reports: Evidence from Mine-safety Records' (2017) 64 Journal of Accounting and Economics 284.
[67] Yi-Chun Chen, Mingyi Hung, and Yongxiang Wang, 'The Effect of Mandatory CSR Disclosure on Firm Profitability and Social Externalities: Evidence from China' (2018) 65 Journal of Accounting and Economics 169 (China).
[68] For further evidence see Christensen, Hall, and Leuz (n 64) 1213–15.
[69] Jewon Shin, 'How Reduced Mandatory Disclosure Impacts Corporate Social Responsibility: Evidence from the SEC's Reform of the Smaller Reporting Company Rule' (28 September 2023) Working Paper https://papers.ssrn.com/sol3/papers.cfm?abstract_id=4587249.

problem of behavioural control and the lack of alignment of word, deed, and thought on the level of institutional investors.

For stockholders, that makes coordination much easier. Effectively, a mandatory norm embossing a preference for ESG on investors excises strong shareholder value—understood as an opposite alternative—from the set of possible (legal) choices. Not only does this enable coherent and cohesive decision-making. Moreover, it provides an incentive for proponents of shareholder-value maximization either to stay in the system and adapt or to withdraw from asset classes falling in the ambit of mandatory ESG demand-side regulation and to concentrate on remaining opportunities for 'dirty' investment. Given that the number of those shrinks in a system of mandatory ESG demand-side regulation, it is likely that fewer and fewer investors will walk this path and, as a result, opt out of vast parts of the stock market, which also means that diversification becomes much harder to achieve.[70] Consequently, demand will contract, diminishing the attractiveness of offering 'dirty' investment opportunities.

Private retail investors, however, cannot be treated with the same ointment as they are not subject to rules enforcing public disclosure. There are two tools of indirect demand-side regulation with respect to private retail investors. First of all, they can be asked about their preferences in the pre-contractual stage. From a regulatory perspective, what is, and, according to EU supervisory bodies such as EIOPA[71] must be posed as a neutral question[72]—that is, whether the customer cares about sustainability/the environment/human rights/etc.—entails a subtle manipulation, exploiting the customer's social desirability bias. Respondents to survey questions will often not give an answer displaying their honest beliefs, attitudes, and personality traits, but rather skewed towards what they perceive as socially desirable in the eyes of others.[73] An inquiry about their willingness to do well by doing good most likely induces retail investors to affirm ESG-related values.[74] After all, who is not against child labour and for the environment and human rights? In the end, this is a different version of a well-known tool of regulation of capital markets, namely entry regulation. Moreover, it is tempting to ask how an insurance broker or other financial intermediaries ensures neutrality when their relevant professional organization professes to implement and follow an 'active, impact-oriented sustainability strategy'.[75]

---

[70] Because they cannot spread their investment over as many assets and asset classes anymore.

[71] EIOPA = European Insurance and Occupational Pensions Authority.

[72] See eg EIOPA, Guidance on the integration of sustainability preferences in the suitability assessment under the Insurance Distribution Directive (IDD) (2022), EIOPA-BOS-22-391, 20 July 2022, page 10: 'It is important that throughout the process, insurers and insurance intermediaries adopt a neutral and unbiased approach so as to not influence the customer's answers.' See https://www.eiopa.europa.eu/system/files/2022-07/guidance_on_integration_of_customers_sustainability_preferences_under_idd.pdf.

[73] The seminal work is Allen L Edwards, *The Social Desirability Variable in Personality Assessment and Research* (Dryden 1957); for a discussion of dimensions of social desirability bias see Delroy L Paulhus, 'Socially Desirable Responding: The Evolution of a Construct' in Henry I Braun, Douglas N Jackson, and David E Wiley (eds), *The Role of Constructs in Psychological and Educational Measurement* (Taylor & Francis 2002).

[74] See for impact investments Heeb and others (n 27) 1737: 'Our findings suggest that the [willingness to pay] for sustainable investments is primarily driven by an emotional, rather than a calculative, valuation of impact.' For more on the social-desirability bias and its problems see section IV.2b)aa) below.

[75] See eg the Bundesverband Deutscher Versicherungskaufleute eV (BVK), Checkliste: Nachhaltigkeit im Versicherungsvermittlerbetrieb (7 July 2022) 22, translated by the author from the original German: 'Der BVK

Entry regulation in the traditional sense relies on participation restrictions through mechanisms like licensing qualification requirements, controlled by public authorities and market organizations such as stock exchanges.[76] Institutions or individuals who wish to enter must apply for approval or they are blocked. Asking retail investors for ESG preferences has a similar effect, but relies on a different sorting mechanism. In light of the social desirability bias, instead of barring those with the 'wrong' ideas and wishes from entering the market, questioning retail investors shapes the structure of the demand side through a mechanism funnelling them into ESG by nudging them using a psychological bias, which is a more subtle strategy. Instead of blocking them, they are led through a different door.

The issue of behavioural control becomes less pronounced when demand-side regulation leads more investors with a predilection for ESG into the corporate arena. Granted, some of them secretly might wish for more 'doing well by doing bad'.[77] But if the tone is set by ESG as root note, it is highly unlikely that most shareholders suddenly push aggressively for managerial decision-making based on a more traditional framework of value maximization.[78] Consequently, it becomes less important whether they must consider social control and the game-theoretical issues of the behaviour of their fellows. Especially in jurisdictions obligating corporate boards to integrate stakeholder concerns into the decision-making process, fashioning sustainability-oriented shareholder duties dovetails nicely with directors' duties. As the directors are unable to uncover clandestine monetary-oriented motivations of their investor base, they will not risk working against preferences they regard as revealed given the regulatory background of ESG demand-side regulation, or so one might surmise. At least on a superficial level, demand and supply side match up, enabling directors to discard shareholder wealth maximization as the sole purpose of the corporation.

As a corollary, mandatory demand-side regulation softens the voting problem of an approach proposed by Hart and Zingales on shareholder voting.[79] In the Hart-Zingales model, stockholders can have a completely different set of motivations for investing in the first place. They allow for a shareholder value-driven investment choice, with ESG and relevant preferences playing out only afterwards. That limits the extent to which shareholders may be willing to deviate from this path and thus the force of 'say on [x]' as an instrument to implement ESG criteria into the managerial decision-making process.[80] Mandatory demand-side regulation works as an antidote because it constrains the set of choices available to shareholders and tilts voting outcomes towards ESG.

---

bekennt sich zu einer aktiven, impact-orientierten Nachhaltigkeits-Strategie' https://www.bvk.de/downloads/pressemitteilung/679/80cfea2c69b341523e6bdb44d64fd3e5/BVK_Checkliste_%20Nachhaltigkeit.pdf.

[76] See Armour and others (n 55) 74–76.
[77] cf Ye Cai, Hoje Jo, and Carrie Pan, 'Doing Well While Doing Bad? CSR in Controversial Industry Sectors' (2012) 108 Journal of Business Ethics 467.
[78] On the limits of this assumption see section IV.2.b)bb) below.
[79] See section II.1.d) above.
[80] Bartlett and Bubb (n 29) 37–42.

## 3. ESG Demand-side Regulation: Basic Design Options

Just like any other type of regulation, demand-side regulation can take many shapes and forms. For a more fine-grained analysis of the promises and perils of demand-side regulation, it is necessary to sketch basic design options which then can be discussed individually. One design option, already alluded to in section II.2 above, is the choice between direct and indirect demand-side regulation. *Direct* demand-side regulation focuses on the existing shareholders and their behaviour. It comprises a broad set of tools, reaching from publication and disclosure duties to guiding voting behaviour. *Indirect* demand-side regulation targets the composition of the demand side. Rather than prescribing certain goals or imposing disclosure rules, it herds more shareholders into the corporation with preferences reflecting those of the regulator. In contrast to direct regulation, the utility function of the investor stays intact. But indirect demand-side regulation ensures that only those investors become stockholders or fund members who accord ESG criteria a high rank in their order of preferences. Consequently, the preference scale of the shareholders as a whole swings towards ESG. Both direct and indirect demand-side regulation may come in various forms as regards their binding nature, ranging from mandatory law over default rules to 'soft law' recommendations.

## III. Direct Demand-side Regulation

In order to avoid mere abstract theorizing and to anchor the analysis in the legal real world, the following section relies on existing examples of legislation and normative frameworks. Section 1 analyses mandatory demand-side regulation, relying on the EU disclosure regime on sustainability-related investment activities, which is also of high relevance for US firms. Section 2 turns to voluntary demand-side regulation, with the UK Stewardship Code 2020 as an example.

### 1. Mandatory Demand-side Regulation

Subsection a) explains that the EU Sustainable Finance Disclosure Regulation (SFDR)[81] and the EU Taxonomy Regulation[82] establish mandatory disclosure duties for institutional investors or, more precisely, 'financial market participants'.[83] Their

---

[81] Regulation (EU) 2019/2088 of the European Parliament and of the Council of 27 November 2019 on sustainability-related disclosures in the financial services sector [2019] OJ L 317/1 (12 December 2019).

[82] Regulation (EU) 2020/852 of the European Parliament and of the Council of 18 June 2020 on the establishment of a framework to facilitate sustainable investment, and amending Regulation (EU) 2019/2088 [2020] OJ L198/13 (22 June 2020).

[83] These are by no means the only relevant normative frameworks relevant for institutional investors. To give just two examples, the prudential framework for investment firms established by Regulation (EU) 2019/2033 of the European Parliament and of the Council and Directive (EU) 2019/2034 of the European Parliament and of the Council contains provisions concerning the introduction of an ESG risk dimension in the Supervisory Review

consequences reach much further than merely making a public statement on ESG, however. Especially for institutional investors like investment funds, these disclosures entail a commitment as to how they will exercise their voting power—a commitment vis-à-vis their own investors who selected the fund because of its ESG orientation. US firms cannot view this without a shudder and a voyeur's interest. The SFDR covers US market participants offering products and services in the EU directly. BlackRock, to take one of the US-American 'big three',[84] has already published its SFDR statement on its website.[85] In a memo released in March 2021, BlackRock announced that 17 per cent of the €2 trillion (US$2.4 trillion) in assets it manages covered by new EU environmental, social and governance rules are classified as sustainable.[86] The firm announced that 70 per cent of the funds launched or repositioned in Europe in 2021 should meet the new threshold.[87] A more indirect effect of the SFDR will be what is known as the 'Brussels effect'.[88] In combination with the Taxonomy Regulation, the SFDR will most likely establish a comprehensive standard for ESG risk management and accountability in the investment sector.

This approach appears to solve both the information problem delineated above[89] and the coordination problem. Nevertheless, closer scrutiny reveals remaining problems, as will be explored in sub-section b).

a) EU sustainability disclosure and direct demand-side regulation

The SFDR[90] mandates that funds disclose how they incorporate sustainability in their investment decisions and advice at the entity and product levels and how they address adverse impacts of their investment advice and products on sustainability factors. It is very broad in scope and covers the vast majority of asset managers, investment-product providers, and financial advisers operating within in the EU.[91] 'Financial market participants' are subject to general requirements attaching to all, notwithstanding whether or not they pursue ESG objectives. They must disclose relevant information publicly on their websites and in regular reports and individually pre-contractually vis-à-vis retail investors. Additionally, the SFDR contains further specific disclosure

---

and Evaluation Process (SREP) by competent authorities, and contains ESG risk disclosure requirements for investment firms. As the text above is not concerned with the details of EU law, but with the general approach of demand-side regulation, this chapter does not delve into more detail as strictly necessary.

[84] BlackRock, Vanguard, State Street.
[85] BlackRock, *EU Entity Level Sustainability Risk Disclosure* https://www.blackrock.com/corporate/literature/continuous-disclosure-and-important-information/sfdr-sustainability-risk-statement.pdf; BlackRock, *EU Entity Level Principal Adverse Impacts Statement* https://www.blackrock.com/corporate/literature/continuous-disclosure-and-important-information/sfdr-principal-adverse-sustainability-impact-statement.pdf.
[86] See Simon Jessop, 'BlackRock says 17% of assets sustainable under EU rules: memo' *Reuters* (10 March 2021) https://www.reuters.com/article/us-blackrock-regulations-europe/blackrock-says-17-of-assets-sustainable-under-eu-rules-memo-idUSKBN2B20H1.
[87] ibid.
[88] Anu Bradford, *The Brussels Effect* (OUP 2020).
[89] See section II.1.a) above.
[90] See n 81 above.
[91] See the definition of 'financial market participant' in the SFDR (n 81) art 2.

obligations for different categories of financial market participants, depending on their ESG-orientation.

As part of the general requirements, according to Article 4(1), financial market participants have 'to publish and maintain on their websites ... where they consider principal adverse impacts of investment decisions on sustainability factors [and] a statement on due diligence policies with respect to those impacts'. Article 6(1) requires all financial market participants to include various information in pre-contractual disclosures, that is, the manner in which sustainability risks are integrated into their investment decisions and how they assess likely impacts of sustainability risks on their financial products. Pursuant to Article 7(1), they must include, inter alia, 'a clear and reasoned explanation of whether, and, if so, how a financial product considers principal adverse impacts on sustainability factors'.

Concerning the specific disclosure obligations, financial market participants fall into three basic categories, namely Article 6 SFDR (no ESG characteristics), Article 8 SFDR ('light green', that is, ESG characteristics but no sustainable investment), and Article 9 SFDR ('dark green', that is, sustainable). Under Article 6(1) SFDR, as already mentioned, all financial market participants must disclose whether they deem sustainability risks irrelevant for their investment decisions and concerning the returns of the financial products they make available. Should they think not, they 'shall include a clear and concise explanation of the reasons therefor' in their pre-contractual disclosures.[92] Moreover, Article 4(1)(b) SFDR forces them to publish this information on their website. Additional disclosure requirements flow from the Taxonomy Regulation. Should a financial market participant not consider the economic characteristics[93] of the financial products it makes available nor have a sustainable investment as objective, Article 7 of the Taxonomy Regulation forces them to disclose a statement that '[t]he investments underlying this financial product do not take into account the EU criteria for environmentally sustainable activities'.

Article 8 SFDR covers financial market participants promoting environmental or social characteristics without pursuing sustainable investment[94] and establishes disclosure duties expanding those of Article 6 SFDR. Pursuant to Article 8(1) SFDR, they must disclose information on how those characteristics are met and, if an index has been designated as a reference benchmark, information on whether and how this index is consistent with those characteristics.[95] Financial market participants with

---

[92] Article 7 SFDR builds on that and further states that these pre-contractual disclosures must be available in the manner required by EU law for different financial market actors see art 7(1) in connection with SFDR, art 6(3).

[93] As the Taxonomy Regulation covers only environmental sustainability (see art 1); it does not say anything about social characteristics.

[94] As defined in SFDR, art 2(17).

[95] The specific requirements are spelled out in Commission Delegated Regulation (EU) 2022/1288 of 6 April 2022 supplementing Regulation (EU) 2019/2088 of the European Parliament and of the Council with regard to regulatory technical standards, C/2022/1931 [2022] OJ L196/1 (25 July 2022). According to Annex II, art 8 funds must, inter alia, state which sustainability indicators they use, whether the financial product partially intends to make sustainable investments (and, if yes, how this contributes to the sustainability objectives), and what binding elements the investment strategy relies on.

sustainable investments as their objective and having an index designated as a reference benchmark must publish pursuant to Article 9 SFDR. Article 9(1) SFDR requires them to disclose information on how the designated index is aligned with that objective and an explanation as to why and how the designated index aligned with that objective differs from a broad market index.[96] Article 9 SFDR comes close to a sustainable finance mandate, restricting an investors' set of choices to firms with net-zero carbon emissions.[97] Articles 5 and 6 of the Taxonomy Regulation establish further disclosure duties for financial market participants within the ambit of Article 8 and 9 SFDR. Inter alia, they must disclose how and to what extent the investments underlying the financial product are in economic activities that qualify as environmentally sustainable under the Taxonomy Regulation.[98]

The European Commission has tied the SFDR disclosure rules with the extant framework on the transparency of financial market participants concerning the exercise of voting rights. According to Article 3g(1) of the EU Shareholder Rights Directive,[99] institutional investors and asset managers must 'develop and publicly disclose an engagement policy' which, inter alia, describes how they monitor 'social and environmental impact and corporate governance, ... exercise voting rights [and] ... cooperate with other shareholders'.[100] Additionally, they have to report on an annual basis 'how their engagement policy has been implemented, including a general description of voting behaviour, an explanation of the most significant votes and the use of the services of proxy advisers. They shall publicly disclose how they have cast votes in the general meetings of companies in which they hold shares'.[101] Building on this basis, the Commission mandates financial market participants to provide information on their website specifically concerning their engagement relating to economic characteristics or sustainability objectives.[102] Furthermore, they must publish summaries on their engagement in annual period reports.[103]

b) Promises and perils of mandatory direct demand-side regulation
aa) Promises of direct demand-side regulation
As already argued above in section II.2.c), introducing ESG-related disclosure duties has a strong potential to induce an increase in ESG-oriented conduct. This is not difficult to understand. Disclosure duties compel to commit to ESG. Yes, much of this may be 'greenwashing' or an exercise in wordplay and marketing games. But, as the empirical studies cited in section II.2.c) demonstrate, something appears to happen which

---

[96] Additionally, Annex III of the Commission Delegated Regulation (EU) 2022/1288 (n 95) sets out various specific information items to be used in pre-contractual disclosure.
[97] Harrison Hong, Neng Wang, and Jinqiang Yang, 'Welfare Consequences of Sustainable Finance' (2023) 36 Review of Financial Studies 4864.
[98] Taxonomy Regulation, art 5(1)(b).
[99] Directive 2007/36/EC of the European Parliament and of the Council of 11 July 2007 on the exercise of certain rights of shareholders in listed companies [2007] OJ L184/17 (14 July 2007).
[100] ibid s 3g(1)(a).
[101] ibid s 3g(1)(b).
[102] See Commission Delegated Regulation (EU) 2022/1288 (n 95) arts 35, 38.
[103] ibid art 8.

reaches deeper than that. With respect to institutional investors, inspecting the EU sustainability disclosure regime for 'financial market participants' outlined in section III.1.a) reveals two levels on which these demand-side actors must commit and how that fits into the idea of demand-side regulation, namely a commitment to the public at large (1) and to individual (retail) investors through pre-contractual disclosure (2).

**(1) Public commitment** First, financial market participants must declare publicly whether, how, and to what extent they adhere to ESG principles. Contrary to what the literature has dubbed 'peripheral commitments' to general standards without the force of law, such as being a signatory to the United Nations Principles of Reasonable Investment (PRI),[104] the EU mandatory disclosure regime forces financial market participants, inter alia, to profess which strategy they pursue as part of their binding declarations towards their investors in pre-contractual disclosure. This kind of binding core commitment has an effect on how funds manage their portfolio.[105] For financial market participants, disclosing reports and statements about their ESG policies under a normative framework such as the EU SFDR and the Taxonomy Regulation means much more than merely publicizing documents and information. Because the law exacts a relatively precise statement on core investment objectives from the financial market participants,[106] disclosure entails a commitment on how they exercise their discretion in creating, maintaining, and managing a portfolio. More importantly from demand-side regulation's perspective, they commit to an engagement and voting strategy vis-à-vis their own investors who selected the fund because of its ESG orientation.[107] These disclosures deliver a measuring rod other market actors and the public at large willingly use, both professional observers[108] and the press.[109] At least the financial market participants in the sense of the EU legislation can no longer vote hidden from the public eye. This addresses the problem of behavioural control resulting from anonymous voting described above.[110]

Recent empirical work and industry reports on the effects of the SFDR and the Taxonomy Regulation support these claims. EU funds affected by the new EU disclosure and transparency framework increased their ESG efforts more than non-EU funds outside EU law's ambit.[111] Concurrently, funds adjusted their labelling. One notable effect of the new EU disclosure regime has been to enlarge the supply of 'light green' opportunities and a reduction of the number of 'dark green' funds. Following a strict

---

[104] John R Nofsinger and Abhishek Varma, 'Keeping Promises? Mutual Funds' Investment Objectives and Impact of Carbon Risk Disclosures' (2023) 187 Journal of Business Ethics 493, 494. See https://www.unpri.org/.
[105] See Shane S Dikolli and others, 'Walk the Talk: ESG Mutual Fund Voting on Shareholder Proposals' (2022) 27 Review of Accounting Studies 864; Nofsinger and Varma (n 104) 501–12.
[106] See section III.1.a) above.
[107] See section III.1.a) above, text accompanying n 99.
[108] See eg https://www.morningstar.com/business/brands/esg.
[109] See eg Madison Darbyshire and Brooke Masters, 'Vanguard's Backing for Green and Social Proposals Falls to 2%' *Financial Times* (28 August 2023) https://www.ft.com/content/4313afe4-1fee-447d-b05b-0c8c38cfbff1.
[110] See section II.1.c).
[111] Martin G Becker, Fabio Martini, and Andreas Walter, 'The Power of ESG Transparency: The Effect of the New SFDR Sustainability Labels on Mutual Funds and Individual Investors' (2022) 47 Finance Research Letters 102708.

construal of the normative requirements for Article 9(1) SFDR funds with 'sustainable investment as its objective' in a 2022 guidance issued by the European Securities and Markets Authority (ESMA),[112] significantly more than 300 funds who had been touting themselves as Article 9 SFDR funds declassified and downgraded to Article 8 SFDR.[113] At the same time, however, inflows into the green funds has been significantly higher on a per-funds basis, while Article 6 SFDR funds begin losing the race.[114] Both early empirical studies and industry reports conclude that the new EU regime has significant effects and channels capital flows into funds geared towards EU 'greenness', with Article 9 SFDR funds receiving more money in relative terms.[115] Goldman Sachs reports clients having difficulty selling Article 6 SFDR (that is, conventional) funds and end-clients asking for redemptions of these funds.[116] Coincidentally, the support for 'E' and 'S' proposals by EU-based asset managers has gone up in from 2021 to 2022, whereas it stagnated in the UK and the United States.[117] While it may be true that the regime in its current form does not preclude 'greenwashing',[118] it nevertheless produces recognizable effects.

**(2) Commitment through pre-contractual disclosure** Second, through pre-contractual disclosure, the financial market participants bind themselves via contractual promise on the individual level of the retail investor. Sceptics might demur, arguing that this amounts to nothing, considering well-documented experiences with rational apathy of private non-professional contracting parties caused by an information overload due to detailed pre-contractual disclosures. Most retail investors will not completely read or understand these pre-contractual disclosures.[119] That does not preclude enforcement, however. Eventually, an industry of seasoned lawyers can be expected to develop a viable business model, constructed after those already tested in securities regulation and investment advice. Additionally, there are signs that the world is about

---

[112] Clarifications on the ESAs' draft RTS under SFDR (2022), JC 2022, 23 (2 June 2022) 6 no 19.

[113] European Fund and Asset Management Association, 'The SFDR Fund Market: State of Play' (2023) 12 Market Insights 1 4 https://www.efama.org/index.php/newsroom/news/efama-s-latest-market-insights-shows-fluctuations-sfdr-fund-market-and-makes-policy; see also Rahul Mahtani, 'SFDR Reclassification Tumult to Intensify amid the EU Revision' *Bloomberg Intelligence* (5 May 2023) https://www.bloomberg.com/professional/blog/sfdr-reclassification-tumult-to-intensify-amid-the-eu-revision/; for Germany see Nikolai Badenhoop and others, 'Quo Vadis Sustainable Funds? Sustainability and Taxonomy-aligned Disclosure in Germany under the SFDR' (August 2023) SAFE White Paper No 94 https://safe-frankfurt.de/de/policy-center/publikationen/detailsview/publicationname/quo-vadis-sustainable-funds-sustainability-and-taxonomy-aligned-disclosure-in-germany-under-the-sfdr.html.

[114] See Becker, Martini, and Walter (n 111); Bernd Scherer and Milot Hasaj, 'Greenlabelling: How Valuable Is the SFDR Art 9 Label?' (2023) 24 Journal of Asset Management 1; Goldman Sachs, 'SFDR, Two Years On: Trends and Anatomy of Article 8 & 9 Funds in 2023' (2023) https://www.goldmansachs.com/intelligence/pages/sfdr-two-years-on-trends-and-anatomy-of-article-8-and-9-funds-in-2023.html.

[115] ibid.

[116] Goldman Sachs (n 114) 8.

[117] ShareAction, *Voting Matters 2022* (2023 https://shareaction.org/reports/voting-matters-2022/general-findings#finding5.

[118] For SFDR, art 9 funds see Mark Chesney and Adrien-Paul Lambillon, 'How Green Is "Dark Green"? An Analysis of SFDR Article 9 Funds' (February 2023) Working Paper https://papers.ssrn.com/sol3/papers.cfm?abstract_id=4366889.

[119] cf Omri Ben-Shahar and Carl E Schneider, *More Than You Wanted to Know: The Failure of Mandated Disclosure* (PUP 2014) 55–118.

to witness a change of the tide even on the level of the individual consumer and retail investor when it comes to ESG. Sociologists and political scientists have been arguing for a while that the 'Millennial generation' is different from previous generations, not only in detail, but, for the first time over the course of several generations, with respect to core values.[120] Millennials widely accept that there is climate change and that the causes are anthropogenic.[121] On the whole and on average, they also espouse values related to human rights and social policies which traditionally have been ascribed to the political left, and readily demand them to be realized, often not through traditional means like voting, but by using other ways of engagement.[122] Corporate law scholars already start talking about the 'millennial corporation'.[123] Supported by activist institutions and partisan groups, they appear to be more likely to ask for a higher corporate accountability in ESG-related themes and goals, as is, one might add, the younger 'Generation Z',[124] as evinced by an Australian case.

In *McVeigh v Retail Employees Superannuation Pty Ltd*,[125] McVeigh, 'a 23 year old ecological landscaper',[126] supported by the activist Friends of the Earth Australia Inc, sued Retail Employees Superannuation Pty Ltd, an Australian superannuation fund with assets under management of more than AU$50 billion, for failure of providing him, as a fund member, information more specific than that published in the company's public disclosures, which would allow him to make an informed judgment about the management and financial condition of his Retail Employees Superannuation Pty Ltd product and about its investment performance.[127] Subsequently, McVeigh amended the case and alleged a breach of statutory and equitable fiduciary duties by not having a more developed climate change policy than indicated.[128] McVeigh and Retail Employees Superannuation Pty Ltd settled in 2020. Retail Employees Superannuation Pty Ltd committed, inter alia, to adapt the portfolio in conformity with the Paris Agreement and Paris-related climate policies and agreed to an extensive set of detailed disclosure duties.[129]

Furthermore, there are professional market participants with both interest, knowledge, and ability to parse the disclosure material provided by institutional investors. With the information 'financial market participants' must provide about their investment and the underlying assets, including benchmarks and methodologies,[130] it

---

[120] For the US see Stella M Rouse and Ashley D Ross, *The Politics of Millennials* (University of Michigan Press 2018) 3.
[121] ibid 149–72.
[122] ibid 173–223.
[123] Michal Barzuza, Quinn Curtis, and David Webber, 'The Millennial Corporation: Strong Stakeholders, Weak Managers' (2023) 28 Stanford Journal of Law, Business, and Finance 255.
[124] Just think of the participants of the 'Fridays for Future' movement.
[125] *McVeigh v Retail Employees Superannuation Pty Ltd* [2019] FCA 14. See https://jade.io/article/626880. For an analysis of the case see eg Esmeralda Colombo, 'From Bushfires to Misfires: Climate-related Financial Risk after McVeigh v. Retail Employees Superannuation Trust' (2022) 11 Transnational Environmental Law 173.
[126] *McVeigh* (n 125) no 15.
[127] ibid no 4.
[128] ibid no 7.
[129] See Colombo (n 125) 182. For press reports see eg Michael Slezak, 'Rest Super Fund Commits to Net-zero Emission Investments after Brisbane Man Sues' *ABC News* (2 November 2020) https://www.abc.net.au/news/2020-11-02/rest-super-commits-to-net-zero-emmissions/12840204.
[130] See SFDR, arts 8–11.

becomes easier for professional analysts and rating agencies to monitor their behaviour. Moreover, there are other institutional investors in need of green investments with the necessary know-how and incentives to hold their counterparty responsible. One prominent example is banks. Banks (and other financial institutions) have to make public their green asset ratio (GAR). According to Article 8(2) of the SFDR, banks have to disclose information on the proportion of the turnover and capital and operating expenditure (key-performance indicators or KPIs) of their activities related to assets or processes with environmentally sustainable economic activities. The European Commission expands on this provision in a delegated regulation and specifies the requirements of the SFDR duties.[131] Recital (5) of this delegated regulation crowns the GAR as the 'main key performance indicator'. It 'shows the proportion of exposures related to Taxonomy Regulation-aligned activities compared to the total assets of those credit institutions' and relates not only to debt investments, but also 'to their equity holdings to reflect the extent to which those institutions finance Taxonomy Regulation-aligned activities'.[132] If these banks buy shares offered by an investment fund, they have the incentive and monetary resources to analyse any disclosures and monitor these funds. The same is true for other institutional market actors, for example, asset managers.[133]

*bb) Perils of mandatory direct demand-side regulation*
Mandatory direct demand-side regulation does not overcome all the obstacles, however. The balancing problem persists (1), just like the issue of behavioural control (2), and the question of whether this kind of proxy voting—letting investors vote as a proxy for stakeholders—helps to defy the incentives of shareholders and corporate boards to act in favour of capital and monetary value-maximization strategies (3). Last, but not least, it is plagued by a problem afflicting general disclosure in securities regulation, namely boilerplate language (4).

**(1) Persistence of the balancing problem** First of all, the notorious balancing problem remains. Committing shareholders to ESG and sustainability does not solve the question of how much weight should be given to different interests and how to prioritize these interests under which circumstances. A well-known example is what happens if it were good for employees to keep the old factory when closing and substituting it with a new factory—with fewer job opportunities—would be preferable from an environmental point of view? Due to the lack of such a scheme of order, it remains for the various corporate actors to define and enforce their own preferences. This problem is

---

[131] Commission Delegated Regulation (EU) 2021/2178 of 6 July 2021 supplementing Regulation (EU) 2020/852 of the European Parliament and of the Council by specifying the content and presentation of information to be disclosed by undertakings subject to Articles 19a or 29a of Directive 2013/34/EU concerning environmentally sustainable economic activities, and specifying the methodology to comply with that disclosure obligation [2021] OJ L443/9 (10 December 2021).
[132] ibid recital (5).
[133] Which are also covered. See Commission Delegated Regulation (EU) 2021/2178 (n 131).

not specific to demand-side regulation but accompanies any kind of multipolar conception of duty. Establishing mandatory demand-side standards as a complement to supply-side analogues exacerbates the difficulties, however.

Diverging vantage points of the board and shareholders may lay the foundations for a conflict similar to the one between a stakeholderist board and stockowners holding fast to wealth-maximization. Combining the lack of a clear evaluative criterion such as shareholder wealth maximization and an obligation to take into account diverging and sometimes opposing interests leads towards the uncomfortable spot between a rock and a hard place. To illustrate by way of example, many shareholder ESG-proposals relate to environmental goals. Boards, however, have an incentive to put workers' interests ahead of other stakeholders as employee satisfaction is intimately tied to profitability and the survival of the business enterprise. Whose judgment should prevail and based on what normative criterion? In the end, it will fall upon the directors to decide.

**(2) Continuing disagreements among shareholders** The conflict on the vertical level between board and stockholders has a sibling on the horizontal plane. Shareholders come in many different flavours, even under a mandatory ESG model. Between environmental activists holding shares just to get a foot in the General Assembly's door, mutual funds pursuing investment strategies based on catholic investment principles, pension funds responsible for the retirement savings of employees, the run-of-the-mill hedge fund, and others, there is a great deal of room for disagreement even under a mandatory ESG regime. Committing to engagement and voting strategies under the EU disclosure regime[134] does not change the fact that the institutional investors' beneficiaries represent a heterogeneous group with diverging interests and different views on which aspects of ESG should be attributed weight and what that means when values and ordering schemes collide, even amongst those rallying to the ESG banner.[135]

A good example of what the future may hold is a recent pending suit against three New York pension funds for their investment policy by New York employees.[136] Just like Mr McVeigh in the Australian case sketched out above in subsection IIII.1.b)aa),[137] private non-professional investors sue powerful large institutional actors. Contrary to the Australian case, however, the New York pension fund beneficiaries want the trustee to deal less with ESG and climate change policy and more with maximizing returns. It is easy to imagine how these different ideologies and consumer investment strategies clash, especially when they are bound in the same investment object because the

---

[134] See section III.1.a)aa)(1) above.
[135] Investigating the 'ethical investor' see Robert H Berry and Fannie Yeung, 'Are Investors Willing to Sacrifice Cash for Morality?' (2013) 117 Journal of Business Ethics 477, 488–89.
[136] Saijel Kishan and Martin Z Braun, 'NYC Pension Funds Are Sued for Cutting Fossil-Fuel Stakes' *Bloomberg* (12 May 2023) https://www.bloomberg.com/news/articles/2023-05-12/nyc-pension-funds-are-sued-for-cutting-fossil-fuel-stake#xj4y7vzkg. Admittedly, the claimants sue the funds because of divesting fossil fuel assets. But this is a reverse engineering strategy.
[137] See text starting at n 125.

parties are all working for the same employer. Empirical research supports this hypothesis. ESG funds which are part of a family with non-ESG fund members have been found to support ES proposals only when the latter are highly unlikely to succeed and stand against ES proposals in situations where their own vote would be pivotal, consistent with family preferences.[138]

One could argue that disagreements between shareholders about strategy are nothing new and that majority voting solves the problem. That is true, but only to a certain extent. What is new is the loss of a focal point which any departure from needs justification. Shareholder-wealth maximization as the normatively enforced point of convergence made it easier to solve the collective-action problem on the side of shareholders. Current ESG regulation does not offer any substitute. Instead, it opens the door to push political conflict into the corporate arena. It is not only workers against the environment, just think of the catholic fund and the activists fighting for the rights of members of the LGBTQ+ community. Saving the world with corporate law[139] may therefore come with significant collateral damage. Corporate boards can no longer frame their decisions in a somewhat agnostic language whenever they explain which interests they took into account and how their solution caters to long-term shareholder value through the inclusion of certain aspects of ESG. If ESG is already the primary norm, directors will have to explain why they preferred one interest over another—and thus have to argue in a manner which until recently was reserved for politicians and activists.

Furthermore, the information and coordination problems sketched above remains.[140] Boards interested in parsing their shareholder base's preferences on a specific matter have to resort to 'say on [x]'. As this instrument does not consider prior motives for investing in a certain company at all, shareholder voting may be heavily skewed towards a limited number of ESG issues. Some investors might care more about the 'E', but not so much about the 'S',[141] others the 'S' over the 'E'.[142] As a result, these shareholders will forgo shareholder-value maximization only (at best) for those issues they regard as being associated with their specific preference[143] or covertly vote for pecuniary gain masked by an ESG aim close to it. Consequently, the board is left with the disincentives demand-side regulation is supposed to counter.[144] Empirical studies lend support to these conjectures about the retail investor base. Two points are worth

---

[138] Roni Michaely, Guillem Ordonez-Calafi, and Silvina Rubio, 'Mutual Funds' Strategic Voting on Environmental and Social Issues' (February 2023) ECGI Finance Working Paper No 774/2021 https://www.ecgi.global/sites/default/files/working_papers/documents/mutualfunds.pdf.

[139] See Kent Greenfield and D Gordon Smith, 'Debate: Saving the World With Corporate Law?' (2008) 57 Emory Law Journal 947.

[140] See section III.1.a) and b) above.

[141] For Poland see Janina Petelczyc, 'The Readiness for ESG among Retail Investors in Central and Eastern Europe. The Example of Poland' (2022) 23 Global Business Review 1299; for Sweden see Carl J Lagerkvist and others, 'Preferences for Sustainable and Responsible Equity Funds: A Choice Experiment with Swedish Private Investors' (2020) 28 Journal of Behavioral and Experimental Finance 100406.

[142] Blanca Pérez-Gladish, Karen Benson, and Robert Faff, 'Profiling socially responsible investors: Australian evidence' (2012) 37 Australian Journal of Management 189.

[143] cf Bartlett and Bubb (n 29) 23–24.

[144] See section II.1, 2.b) and c) above.

highlighted in the present context. The average retail investor's sustainability and ESG preferences vary wildly across countries, both in those which diverge in terms of social norms and culture,[145] but also in regional spaces with strong ties and common traditions, such as continental Europe.[146] Boards managing the affairs of a corporation with an international shareholder base deal can only assume that, perhaps, many of their stockholders consider ESG important.[147] But as soon as ESG values collide, the board is thrown back to its role as an umpire of a potentially divided electorate, choosing the smallest common denominator.

One might ponder whether these data about retail investors are important, because in the real world, most corporate shareholders are institutional investors.[148] For the latter group, however, the issue does not bear out differently. The only feasible way from a cost-benefit point of view is to exercise voting power in a way with the smallest potential for conflict with its own heterogeneous base of beneficiaries. In the end, the fund will operate as an umpire in the same manner as a corporate board.

**(3) Vagaries of shareholders as stakeholder proxy** Moreover, using shareholders as proxies for stakeholder interests remains dubious for other reasons. Although it may be easier for a regulator to harness shareholders than to include various stakeholder groups into corporate governance, shareholders are not 'the real thing'.[149] Many hold on to ESG only as long as it is economically viable and relegate it to second rank as soon as it hurts personal finances.[150] Just like the Monarchs in Henry James' story,[151] stockholders might prove rather inflexible and congregate at sustainability goals closest to the old shareholder wealth maximization norm.[152]

**(4) Boilerplate language and insufficient disclosure** Unsurprisingly, firms and other market actors subject to disclosure duties publish generic material which is not specific to them and their situation concerning ESG.[153] Boilerplate language does not further the needs of stakeholders[154] or those of others in search for information. Especially for non-professional investors, boilerplate language impairs decision-making.[155] As this problem is not confined to ESG disclosure, but troubles

---

[145] For Poland ('E') and Australia ('S') see the studies cited in n 141 and n 142.
[146] See Daniel Engler, Gunnar Gutsche, and Paul Smeets, 'Why Do Investors Pay Higher Fees for Sustainable Investments? An Experiment in Five European Countries' (2023) Working Paper https://papers.ssrn.com/sol3/papers.cfm?abstract_id=4379189.
[147] For more on this see section IV.2.b)bb) below.
[148] See above text at n 52.
[149] Henry James, 'The Real Thing' in Henry James, *Collected Stories*, vol 2 (Everyman's Library edn, 1999) 39.
[150] For more on this see section IV.2.b)bb) below.
[151] cf James (n 149).
[152] See Dorothy Lund and Elizabeth Pollman, 'The Corporate Governance Machine' (2021) 121 Columbia Law Review 2563, 2631–32.
[153] See Hans B Christensen, Luzi Hail, and Christian Leuz, 'Economic Analysis of Widespread Adoption of CSR and Sustainability Reporting Standards' (November 2018) Research Report to the Sustainability Accounting Standards Board (SASB) 120–22 https://papers.ssrn.com/sol3/papers.cfm?abstract_id=3315673.
[154] ibid.
[155] Ozlem Arikan, 'The Effect of Boilerplate Language on Nonprofessional Investors' Judgments' (2022) 52 Accounting and Business Research 417.

mandatory disclosure in securities regulation generally, it will not be dealt with more extensively here.

The boilerplate problem is not, however, a decisive argument against disclosure rules. Disclosure quality will vary with the quality of the underlying legal regulation. France is a good example. Already in 2001, it introduced a law on 'new economic regulations'[156] with Article 116(1) establishing a duty to publish an annual report 'on how the company takes into account the social and economic consequences of its activity'.[157] Due to a lack of more specific disclosure duties, the reports were largely narrative without a lot of detail.[158] With another law, the French legislator introduced stricter reporting standards.[159] They were, however, still not extensive and lacked a proper sanctioning mechanism. Unsurprisingly, disclosure quality was better, but still not good.[160] Arguably, the problem of boilerplate has its roots in failures of the legal framework.[161]

A problem related to boilerplate disclosure is the strategic limitation of disclosure by firms facing uncertainty about audience preferences. Mandatory norms enforce public disclosure. But they do not guarantee an optimal level of disclosure, both in terms of information depth and targeting. The more diverse the investing public and the more contrarian the investors' preferences are, the more likely it becomes that firms will choose silence over disclosure.[162] Paradoxically, enforcing public disclosure through mandatory law may cause a reduction of the level of public information.[163] This problem is salient in ESG disclosure, considering the extreme stances investors may take between sacrificing profit for non-pecuniary gains and emphasizing the priority of monetary return on investment[164] and that the impairment of price informativeness concerning financial pay-offs caused by the publication of non-financial information can lead to rising costs of capital.[165] Employing boilerplate language is one strategy to achieve silence despite being legally coerced to disclose data on ESG performance.

---

[156] Loi no 2001-420 du 15 mai 2001 relative aux nouvelles régulations économiques, Journal Officiel de la République française (JORF–Official Journal of the French Republic) no113 of 16 May 2001 https://www.legifrance.gouv.fr/jorf/id/JORFTEXT000000223114.

[157] ibid art 116(1): '[Le rapport] comprend également des informations, dont la liste est fixée par décret en Conseil d'Etat, sur la manière dont la société prend en compte les conséquences sociales et environnementales de son activité.'

[158] See eg Jacques Igalens, 'L'Analyse du Discours de la Responsabilité Sociale de l'Entreprise à Travers les Rapports Annuels de Developpement Durable d'Entreprise Françaises du CAC 40' (2006) 10 Revue Finance, Contrôle et Stratégie (Finance, Control and Strategy Review) 129.

[159] The so-called loi Grenelle II, LOI no 2010-788 du 12 juillet 2010 portant engagement national pour l'environnement, JORF n°0160 of 13 July 2010 https://www.loc.gov/item/global-legal-monitor/2010-08-12/france-law-on-national-commitment-for-the-environment/.

[160] See Jean-Noël Chauvey amd others, 'The Normativity and Legitimacy of CSR Disclosure: Evidence from France' (2015) 130 Journal of Business Ethics 789.

[161] On quality determinants with an eye on France see Fatma Baalouch, Salma D Ayadi, and Khaled Hussainey, 'A Study of the Determinants of Environmental Disclosure Quality: Evidence from French Listed Companies' (2019) 23 Journal of Management and Governance 939.

[162] Philip Bond and Yao Zeng, 'Silence Is Safest: Information Disclosure when the Audience's Preferences Are Uncertain' (2022) 145 Journal of Financial Economics 178.

[163] ibid 188.

[164] cf ibid 187.

[165] Itay Goldstein and others, 'On ESG Investing: Heterogeneous Preferences, Information, and Asset Prices' (28 June 2022) NBER Working Paper No 29839 () https://papers.ssrn.com/sol3/papers.cfm?abstract_id=4080653.

## 2. Voluntary Direct Demand-side Regulation

a) The UK Stewardship Code as an example

The UK Stewardship Code (UKSC) 'sets … stewardship standards for asset owners [that is, institutional investors] and asset managers, and for service providers that support them'.[166] Promulgated by the Financial Reporting Council, an executive non-departmental public body, sponsored by the UK Department of Business and Trade,[167] it 'comprises a set of 'apply and explain' principles for [the first two] and a separate set of principles for service providers'.[168]

As mentioned above,[169] the principles applicable to asset owners and asset managers pick up on ESG norms and standards. Investment service providers have to 'support clients' integration of stewardship and investment, taking into account material environmental, social and governance issues, and communicating what activities they have undertaken'.[170] As part of their duties to 'identify and respond to market-wide and systemic risks to promote a well-functioning financial system',[171] they have to consider account climate change.[172] Principle 11 asks, 'where necessary, [to] escalate stewardship activities to influence issuers'. Signatories of the UKSC must disclose their efforts and activities and should, for example, 'explain the expectations they have set for asset managers'.[173]

The UKSC is a voluntary framework, however. Rule 2.2.3 of the Financial Conduct Authority's[174] Conduct of Business Sources requires asset managers acting for professional clients[175] with a licence to operate in the UK to disclose whether they commit to the UKSC or not.[176] If not, they must explain their alternative investment strategy.[177] Contrary to the EU framework outlined in subsection 1, institutional investors and financial service providers do not even have to do that. There is no rule or instrument exercising pressure to become a signatory to the UKSC. Whereas the EU disclosure regime rests on a clear normative premise and exercises not only moral, but significant

---

[166] UK Stewardship Code (n 8) 4.
[167] https://www.gov.uk/government/organisations/financial-reporting-council.
[168] UK Stewardship Code (n 8) 4.
[169] See n 8 above and accompanying text.
[170] UK Stewardship Code (n 8) Principles for Investment Advisers, Principle 5.
[171] UK Stewardship Code (n 8) Principles for Investment Advisers, Principle 4.
[172] ibid 27.
[173] ibid 20.
[174] The Financial Conduct Authority is an independent public body responsible for a significant part of conduct and relevant prudential regulation in the UK. See https://www.fca.org.uk/about/what-we-do/the-fca.
[175] This is a simplified presentation of the definition of 'firm' in the sense of Financial Conduct Authority, 'Glossary "F"', in Financial Conduct Authority, Handbook of Rules and Guidance (9 June 2022) https://www.handbook.fca.org.uk/handbook/glossary/?starts-with=F.
[176] Financial Conduct Authority, FCA Release 19, *Conduct of Business Sourcebook* (1 May 2022) 29, Rule 2.2.3: 'A firm, other than a venture capital firm, which is managing investments for a professional client that is not a natural person must disclose clearly on its website, or if it does not have a website in another accessible form:
   (1) the nature of its commitment to the Financial Reporting Council's Stewardship Code; or
   (2) where it does not commit to the Code, its alternative investment strategy.'
[177] See text accompanying n 176.

regulatory pressure on all actors within its scope of application, even those deciding to stay 'conventional', the UKSC lacks comparative thrust.

b) Promises and perils of voluntary direct demand-side regulation
Considering its voluntary nature, the UKSC as an instrument of direct ESG demand-side appears promising because it is less intrusive than mandatory demand-side regulation. As far as the UKSC relies on voluntary disclosure, however, it is subject to the well-known critique of this type of regulatory instrument. There is no need to rehash this debate, readers can easily find literature on why mandatory disclosure rules are superior.[178]

Voluntary demand-side regulation is very likely a blunt blade. A general problem is the lack of a sanctioning mechanism. The UKSC is not tied to the listing rules of the London Stock Exchange.[179] Even to signatories to the UKSC or any other voluntary type of voluntary demand-side regulation, the framework does not entail consequences for a breach of promise. Investors are free to vote holding true to their real preferences, no strings attached. A shareholder thus should rationally typically expect others to vote for strategies maximizing monetary value, notwithstanding public ESG avowals of other stockholders. In game-theoretic parlance, defecting from ESG is the dominant strategy whenever it serves the shareholders' interests, creating a Nash equilibrium no player has an interest to break away from,[180] unless the stockholders have reason to believe that the number of 'true believers' is high enough to expect a change of outcome.[181]

From the vantage point of ESG regulation, this presents a major problem. As the philosophy of group agency demonstrates, coordination necessitates incentive compatibility.[182] '[I]ncentive compatibility requires the social mechanism to achieve a happy alignment between individually rational behavior on the one hand and the desired target property on the other.'[183] The 'desired target property' is an orientation towards ESG. Taking into account the incentives just described, instead of the 'happy alignment', a 'sad divergence' of individual goals and aspired outcome is the stable equilibrium. Because individual preferences determine how shareholders vote, an inextricable relation exists between preferences and conclusion. It is impossible to construct a decision-making procedure comprising the desired conclusion (that is, a conclusion against strong shareholder-value maximization) because the conclusion is necessarily relevant for the individual actors, contrary to, say, three judges presiding over a criminal case.[184] In the latter situation, it appears possible to unbundle the conclusion

---

[178] For an overview see eg Armour and others (n 55) 165–67.
[179] Arad Reisberg, 'The UK Stewardship Code: On the Road to Nowhere?' (2015) 15 Journal of Corporation Law Studies 217, 241.
[180] For a concise introduction to the Nash equilibrium see eg Emmanuel N Barron, *Game Theory* (2nd edn, Wiley 2013) 116–17.
[181] In this case, multiple equilibria can exist. See text accompanying nn 41–42 above.
[182] Christian List and Philip Pettit, *Group Agency* (OUP 2011) 105–106.
[183] List and Pettit (n 182) 106.
[184] ibid 112–14.

(prison or not) from voting on individual premises concerning the law. For shareholders, deciding whether to maximize dividend expectations or to protect a forest in a far-away country always implies a result impacting their individual interests. In other words, the decision-making procedure, however built, remains tied to the individual premises and preferences. Thus, individuals will always want the group to adopt their own attitudes.[185] Moreover, and again contrary to a jury or court decision, decisions of shareholders are not independent of the group agent. Typically, shareholders vote on proposals drafted by the board. These proposals are premise-based, governed by the expectations of the directors concerning shareholder preferences.

In sum, all of the three issues described above remain obstacles which, under a system of voluntary direct demand-side regulation, can prove hard to overcome, namely information problems both for corporate boards and retail investors buying fund products, cooperation problems, and the lack of sanction for behaviour deviating from ESG norms and standards. This is not to say that voluntary action has no role to play.[186] But, understood as an alternative to mandatory demand-side regulation, voluntary demand-side regulation is inferior.

## IV. Indirect Demand-side Regulation

Not all investors are bound to renounce profits in exchange for non-monetary utility they gain through investing in ESG funds. Until now, the law does not stop a retail investor from buying into a fund putting an emphasis on shale gas extraction ('fracking'), oil production, tobacco, weapons, and the pornographic industry. Although perhaps tempting for some proponents of ESG, outlawing these and other 'dirty' investments does not put an end to strategies oriented towards pecuniary growth, the investors' preference structure would remain untouched. Introducing a purely conclusion-based—that is, ESG-oriented—decision-making procedure provided no solution because unshackling the procedure from individual preferences proved to be impossible.[187] The only other way to unbundle undesirable individual attitudes and voting outcome is to change the preferences of the group's members.[188] As it is impossible for a democratic regulator to impose personal values on its human subjects they do not wish to adopt, direct demand-side regulation is not the suitable regulatory technique. Instead of aiming at the extant shareholder population, the regulator can try to funnel only those investors into the corporate arena who exhibit the desired preferences. This is indirect demand-side regulation. An example is the recent EU regulation of investment advice, which will be explored below (1), including its promises and perils (2) and its interplays with direct demand-side regulation (3).

---

[185] ibid 112.
[186] cf Lisa M Fairfax, 'Dynamic Disclosure: An Exposé on the Mythical Divide Between Voluntary and Mandatory ESG Disclosure' (2022) 101 Texas Law Review 273.
[187] See text starting at n 182 above.
[188] See List and Pettit (n 182) 113.

## 1. EU Regulation of Investment Advice as an Example

Until recently, the revised Markets for Financial Instruments Directive (MiFiD II)[189] contained a duty of investment advisers to 'act honestly, fairly and professionally in accordance with the best interests of its clients'.[190] The adviser had to 'obtain the necessary information regarding the client's or potential client's knowledge and experience in the [relevant] investment field … and his investment objectives including his risk tolerance'.[191] All that mattered was a client's need and his or her best interests. Investment advice was about helping the client find an asset class with the best return, taking into account the attitude towards risk and investment goal, such as long-term savings for retirement or short-term gain for anyone with enough money to spare for a limited time period. Should the client have been interested in ESG or a similar concept, she would have to ask for specific advice.

And then the European Commission stepped into the fray. As part of its efforts to transform the economy, the Commission promulgated two delegated regulations, one on investment advisers' duties,[192] the other on product oversight and governance requirements for insurance undertakings and insurance distributors and investment advice for insurance-based investment products.[193] These delegated regulations supplement MiFiD II.[194] They 'integrate … client's preferences in terms of sustainability as a top up to the suitability assessment'[195] and incorporate 'sustainability risks into the organisational requirements'.[196] Advisers have to ask for their clients' sustainability preference and recommend investments accordingly.[197] But this is not the end of it. Intractable clients insisting on a profit-only strategy are taken care of by the law. Advisers 'should explain to the clients … that the elements demonstrating the consideration of principal adverse impacts on sustainability factors might be relevant for various environmental, social, employee or governance matters, should allow for demonstrating that consideration and for showing the respective commitment to address principal adverse impacts over time, and might be represented by qualitative or quantitative indicators, including but not limited to those in accordance with the SFDR'.[198] In combination with the social desirability bias,[199] this is a powerful tool.

---

[189] Directive 2014/65/EU of the European Parliament and of the Council of 15 May 2014 on markets in financial instruments and amending Directive 2002/92/EC and Directive 2011/61/EU [2014] OJ L173/349 (12 June 2014) (MiFiD II).
[190] ibid art 24(1).
[191] ibid art 25(2).
[192] Commission Delegated Regulation (EU) 2021/1253 of 21 April 2021 amending Delegated Regulation (EU) 2017/565 as regards the integration of sustainability factors, risks and preferences into certain organisational requirements and operating conditions for investment firms, C/2021/2616 final.
[193] Commission Delegated Regulation (EU) 2021/1257 of 21 April 2021 amending Delegated Regulations (EU) 2017/2358 and (EU) 2017/2359 as regards the integration of sustainability factors, risks and preferences into the product oversight and governance requirements for insurance undertakings and insurance distributors and into the rules on conduct of business and investment advice for insurance-based investment products, C/2021/2614 final.
[194] See European Commission, Explanatory Memorandum to C(2021) 2616 final (n 192) 1.
[195] ibid.
[196] ibid 2.
[197] See Commission Delegated Regulation (n 192) art 1.
[198] European Commission, Explanatory Memorandum to C(2021) 2616 final (n 192) 2.
[199] See section II.2.c) above.

The European Commission is cognizant of the effects. Financial instruments 'that promote environmental or social characteristics without a proportion of sustainable investments or without a proportion of investments in taxonomy-compliant activities or where they do not consider principal adverse impacts will not be eligible for recommendation to the clients ... based on their individual sustainability preferences'.[200] Advisers have to 'prepare a report to the client that explains how the recommendation to the client meets his investment objectives, risk profile, capacity for loss bearing and sustainability preferences (ex-post information disclosure)'.[201] – Nudging with a club.

Not many retail investors will be able to duck the blow and consequently bow out of ESG investments. European demand for ESG funds will rise and most likely meet a growing supply, not only by European funds, but also by US-based funds. This is a big step towards altering the composition of shareholder assemblies, accelerating ESG-related shareholder activism. Instead of a majority of shareholders honing their shareholder-value affinities, most stockholders will expect the corporation—and, by extension, the board of directors—to address ESG issues and deliver more than just lip service. For better or worse, this tears down a wall critics of stakeholderist views of the corporation long have identified as a fundamental flaw of board-centric regulatory approaches, namely, that directors themselves do not have any incentive to really take stakeholder interests into account.[202] If shareholders change the utility function boards of directors have to cater to and evaluate directors' performance based on ESG factors, boards will have to adjust and at least pay homage to those stakeholder interests their stockholders want them to value.

## 2. Promises and Perils of Indirect Demand-side Regulation

Indirect demand-side regulation holds an obvious promise. Changing the composition of the set of shareholders and transforming the aggregate preferences from shareholder-value maximization to ESG should help to overcome the three problems sketched out above: gathering of information about shareholder preferences, shareholder coordination, and behavioural control.

### a) Promises of indirect demand-side regulation

If the vast majority of shareholders actually *acquire* ESG preferences as a result of public regulation, then the board of directors has no problem in figuring out which fiddle to play and what the relevant group is it has to cater to.[203] Institutional investors representing the retail investors' money and interests will also act in conformity with the regulator's wishes because this is the product they need to sell if they want to stay in business. There is no information gap. On a superficial level, the issues of shareholder coordination and behavioural control should lose their sting, too. A majority of

---

[200] European Commission, Explanatory Memorandum to C(2021) 2616 final (n 192) 5.
[201] ibid. See also the EIOPA Guidance mentioned in the text above at n 72.
[202] See Bebchuk and Tallarita (n 14).
[203] See section II.2.b), c) above.

stockholders prioritizing ESG over strong forms of shareholder-value maximization profit from a common denominator. Taking into account that investment advisers have to inquire about their clients' ESG preferences, these represent their 'real' attitudes so that there is no mismatch between the public expression of preferences and private voting behaviour, or so the European regulator apparently hopes.

Assuming that exploiting the social desirability bias works and consumers and other retail investors predominantly turn to ESG funds and ESG-related investment products,[204] the incentives of those offering funds and investment products will change concurrently. That has profound implications for the structure of the demand side. If institutional investors in their role as suppliers rationally must assume that most of their customers will buy ESG-oriented shares and fund memberships, they have a strong motivation to offer just that and set up (more) funds focusing on ESG. Should that bear out and the number of ESG funds grow, the composition of the demand side will change on the level of the institutional investors and also tilt towards ESG, perhaps not tomorrow, but in the long term.

An additional benefit of indirect demand-side regulation and the change it induces concerning the composition of the investor base consists in smoothing the preference structure. This helps in overcoming the problem of boilerplate language as a strategy of staying silent in the presence of uncertainty over audience preferences.[205] If the vast majority of retail investors consists of ESG proponents, institutional investors will publish more detailed and better targeted information on their ESG performance as they no longer have to fear significant backlash like the New York pension funds.[206] This, in turn, helps the demand-side to overcome their coordination problems and moreover provides a signal to corporations and corporate management about the wishes and values of an important fraction of their shareholders. The problem of multiple voting equilibria due to a heterogeneous stockholder base[207] also decreases since it becomes easier to predict voting outcomes and shareholder action in general.

b) Perils of indirect demand-side regulation

A closer look reveals persisting perils, however. Utilizing the social desirability bias to shepherd retail investors into ESG-oriented products does not necessarily equal an actual change of real personal preferences (aa). Moreover, they still enjoy freedom to vote without effective behavioural control, which means that shareholder and investor coordination remains an issue (bb).

*aa) Surveying preferences and the social desirability bias*

Above, the social desirability bias has been heralded as an instrument of navigating investors into ESG-oriented shares and investment products.[208] This bias entails a

---

[204] See section II.2.c) above.
[205] See section III.1.b)bb)(4) above.
[206] See text above accompanying n 136.
[207] See section II.1.b) above.
[208] See section II.2.c) above.

number of well-known problems, however. Asking investors about their preferences does not necessarily mean that they reveal their actual aims and attitudes, especially when they are nudged into one direction. Empirical studies demonstrate that a large part of the relevant population moves in a direction standing in stark contrast to preferences expressed in front of others. Such 'dark sides' of social desirability biases have been exposed in environmental psychology research[209] and in studies on racism,[210] two areas highly relevant for ESG.

Social scientists and marketing researchers employ a variety of techniques to attenuate the bias, such as anonymization and self-reporting, indirect questioning, and the use of a false polygraph (a so-called bogus pipeline).[211] These are probably not very useful in the context of investment advice. Anonymous self-reporting through a computer questionnaire and audio computer-assisted self-interviewing[212] may be viable in principle. The investment adviser must not be in the same room for the survey. In practice, it seems unlikely that advisers will deploy tools for debiasing, considering that the law does not require them to do so.

Not all hope is lost, however. Investment advice in the EU is heavily governed by legal norms. Norms in general, not only legal norms, are powerful determinants of what represents socially desirable behaviour and attitudes, and thus influence a respondent's behaviour.[213] ESG-focused investment advice is heavily loaded with norms expressly aiming at steering investors into ESG investment.[214] Not only that the interview is not neutral. If interviewees express a wish for other investment products, the adviser has to single out this attitude and address the consequences as negative for society and the environment.[215] Pressing investors like this has the likely consequence that not a few of them will refrain from investing in their preferred asset class in order to evade shaming and social stigma. Nevertheless, their true preferences remain unchanged. Although they buy ESG investment products, they vote for shareholder-value maximization whenever they want, or at least for the ESG proposal closest to monetary aims.[216] Additionally, investors without hard convictions and buying into ESG because 'it feels good' to be sustainable may still turn into Friedman philosophers, once they realize how ESG investing might affect performance and thus their retirement savings or other goals, just think about the suit against the New York pension funds.[217] It is a

---

[209] See eg Stepan Vesely and Christian A Klöckner, 'Social Desirability in Environmental Psychology Research: Three Meta-Analyses' (2020) 11 Frontiers in Psychology 1395.
[210] See eg Tobias H Stark and others, 'The Impact of Social Desirability Pressures on Whites' Endorsement of Racial Stereotypes: A Comparison Between Oral and ACASI Reports in a National Survey' (2022) 51 Social Methods and Research 605.
[211] For surveys see eg Ahmet Durmaz, İnci Dursun, and Ebru Tümer Kabadayi, 'Mitigating the Effects of Social Desirability Bias in Self-Report Surveys: Classical and New Techniques' in Mette L Baran and Janice E Jones (eds), *Applied Social Science Approaches to Mixed Methods Research* (IGI Global 2020) 146; Anton J Nederhof, 'Methods of Coping With Desirability Bias: A Review' (1985) 15 European Journal of Social Psychology 263, 264.
[212] See the description of the research set-up in Stark and others (n 210).
[213] Nederhof (n 211).
[214] See text above starting at n 192.
[215] See text above starting at n 196.
[216] See text above at n 143. For empirical data see text below starting at n 224.
[217] See text above at n 136.

bold assumption on the EU Commission's side that the general aspiration to do good in the world equals the concrete wish for ESG in investment decision-making.

*bb) The remaining problems of behavioural control and shareholder coordination*
Indirect demand-side regulation leaves retail investors where they always have been—in a place where they are able to vote behind the curtain, without effective behavioural control. The new EU regime introduced by the EU Commission most likely leaves enough room for shareholders to turn to traditional strategies of monetary gain and value maximization. Just as with direct demand-side regulation, stockholders can weigh ESG aims according to their proximity to shareholder value, making it very difficult to predict voting outcomes.[218] Moreover, even assuming that a significant number of investors will act at least with more emphasis on ESG, the fact remains that their individual preferences may diverge and thus lead to conflict when it comes to voting on decisions involving contrary aspects of ESG. Indirect demand-side regulation offers no better solution than direct demand-side regulation in that regard. Combining direct and indirect demand-side regulation does not help. Insofar, a regulatory square knot will not tie the ESG programme any tighter since both approaches lack precision and run into similar trouble.

Critics may rejoin that financial practice refutes these sceptic theoretical musings. Inflows into ESG funds continue to grow, perhaps not as impressive as a couple of years ago, but still following a significant positive trend.[219] Especially so-called Article 9 funds operating in the highest category of the EU SFRD transparency regime, that is, those funds pursuing sustainability objectives,[220] profit from significantly higher inflows compared to Article 8 or Article 6 funds on an inflow-per-fund basis.[221] Members of a Dutch pension fund opted for increasing sustainability investments out of non-monetary concerns[222] and, according to a well-known study, US mutual fund investors put a premium on sustainability.[223]

What many retail investors seem to care for *after* they transferred their money, however, is financial return, notwithstanding their ethical priors, leading researches to conclude that 'identifying ethical investors as those investors who hold an ethical portfolio is an inadequate approach'.[224] Recent studies maintain that US retail investors trade on ESG news only when they deem it financially material, not because the news are inconsistent with their non-pecuniary preferences,[225] and find that there is less portfolio reallocation and less growth in the number of investors in response to ESG press

---

[218] See section III.1.b)bb)(2) above, text at n 143.
[219] Becker and others (n 111).
[220] See above section III.1.a).
[221] See studies cited in n 114.
[222] Rob Bauer, Tobias Ruof, and Paul Smeets, 'Get Real! Individuals Prefer More Sustainable Investments' (2021) 34 Review of Financial Studies 3976.
[223] See eg Hartzmark and Sussman (n 27). For Dutch investors see Heeb and others (n 27).
[224] Berry and Young (n 135) 488.
[225] Qianqian Li, Edward M. Watts, and Christina Zhu, 'Retail Investors and ESG News' (26 September 2023) Working Paper https://papers.ssrn.com/sol3/papers.cfm?abstract_id=4384675.

releases when compared to non-ESG press releases.[226] Admittedly, these studies collate data on retail investors in general and not specifically on ESG investors. Yet it does not seem far-fetched to assume that the latter group is not an entirely different species once the investment decision is made. Various studies support this claim, showing again and again that ESG-oriented investors are, as the authors of one study put it, 'indeed fee and performance conscious' and 'although they have a social conscience ... financially aware',[227] and not only in the United States. European investors' willingness to pay higher fees for sustainable investments and to sacrifice profit for doing good is inversely correlated to financial literacy—the more financially literate investors are, the more sensitive to higher fees (compared to conventional investments) retail investors react.[228] Dutch investors are willing to pay more for sustainability compared to conventional investments, but this willingness to pay does not rise in correlation with higher impact.[229] They spend money for the 'warm glow' of engaging in a prosocial act, not for an optimal impact.[230] This dovetails with the impression that once an ESG investment is made, (even) retail investors change gears and calculate their return primarily in monetary terms, because, or so a cynic might argue, they had already done something for society writ large in buying into the ESG fund for a higher price. Moreover, investors' preferences vary over time and with the general economic environment. Whereas they seem to be willing to spend more money on ESG-related aims, they emphasize pecuniary returns on investment once the economy starts stalling.[231]

This problem is exacerbated because of the institutional investors' own preferences. Across industries and business models,[232] their emphasis is on the 'G', then the 'E', and finally the 'S', a recent study claims.[233] Considering the results of the various studies on their beneficiaries' behaviour, they do not have to fear a backlash; indeed, quite the contrary. Should the majority of their own investors continue to value ESG only as long as ESG-related decision-making also fosters financial success, it is likely that mutual funds and other professional players will support those ESG aims which happen to be aligned with pecuniary benefits. ESG proponents in the EU seem to have a counter-argument. With the new EU regime in place, investment advisers and financial and insurance brokers have to inquire about retail investors' ESG preferences. Theoretically, this information could be passed on to the fund or other institutions in which the retail investor is now a member or shareholder and then be used on the institutional level, as

---

[226] Austin Moss, James P Naughton, and Clare Wang, 'The Irrelevance of ESG Disclosure to Retail Investors: Evidence from Robinhood' (2023) 70 Management Science 2626.
[227] Pérez-Gladish, Benson, and Faff (n 142) 207.
[228] Catherine D'Hondt, Maxime Merli, and Tristan Roger, 'What Drives Retail Portfolio Exposure to ESG Factors?' (2022) 46 Finance Research Letters 102470; Engler, Gutsche, and Smeets (n 146).
[229] Heeb and others (n 27) 1748–58.
[230] ibid 1758–69.
[231] Ravi Bansal, Di (Andrew) Wu, and Amir Yaron, 'Socially Responsible Investing in Good and Bad Times' (2022) 35 Review of Financial Studies 2067; Eunyoung Cho, 'Time-varying Preferences for ESG Investments: Evidence from an Emerging Market' (2023) 31 Journal of Derivatives and Quantitative Studies 121; D'Hondt, Merli, and Roger (n 228).
[232] That is, private equity fund, venture capital fund, pension fund, etc.
[233] Joseph A McCahery, Paul C Pudschedl, and Martin Steindl, 'Institutional Investors, Alternative Asset Managers, and ESG Preferences' (2022) 23 European Business Organization Law Report 821.

has been argued above.[234] There is a limit to this, however. Advisers and brokers will probably not share personal data with a fund or other actors, both for legal reasons such as privacy laws and for business reasons.[235] What is passed on will be the decision to buy shares or units in a fund with a certain ESG profile, but not a detailed catalogue of data on specific issues for each and any buyer.

Notwithstanding these limitations, the approach discussed here has some merit, all the more so since direct demand-side regulation increases the chances that professional market actors adapt their strategies at least insofar as they must to comply with the EU transparency and disclosure regime. Whether is it is enough from the EU rule-maker's vantage point and the aim of entering the age of the 'green economy' remains to be seen.

## 3. The Interplay between Direct and Indirect Demand-Side Regulation

Direct and indirect demand-side regulation represents two sides of one coin. The EU direct demand-side regime rests on a 'comply or explain' approach. It is mandatory in that every financial market participant must opt into one of the three basic categories—conventional (Article 6 SFDR), 'light green' (Article 8 SFDR), or 'dark green' (Article 9 SFDR)—without being forced to declare themselves 'green'.[236] What the disclosure regime can do to a certain extent is mitigate the problem of 'greenwashing'. What it cannot do is change the basic choices of investors. Members of the demand side may invest into 'brown' or conventional funds according to their needs and predilections. This is where indirect demand-side regulation plays out—in funnelling retail investors into ESG investments, creating demand which, in turn, institutional investors can meet by offering better choice in this sector. The more retail investors buy into ESG funds, the more the demand side changes as a whole and tilts toward ESG.

## V. Conclusion

Demand-side regulation is a new tool regulators use in order to spread ESG-oriented corporate decision-making. Instead of addressing the corporate board and its international equivalents as a supplier of ESG-friendly management, demand-side regulation targets investors and shareholders. It comes in two basic flavours, indirect and direct demand-side regulation. Whereas the first attempts to let only those retail investors become stockholders or fund members who already espouse the correct beliefs

---

[234] See section II.2.b) above.
[235] Data about investors' preferences can be used, for example, for market research and marketing. Given the value of this information, it is not likely that brokers and similar actors will give it away lightly and on a regular basis.
[236] See section III.1.a) above.

and attitudes, the latter pushes professional market participants towards ESG through a double commitment, that is, to the public at large via disclosure and to individual investors through pre-contractual information. Taken together, as a matter of theory, this should change the preference structure of the demand side. The promise is clear: if the majority of shareholders want the corporate board to pursue ESG strategies, the directors lose the incentive to worship the idol of mammon because they must fear no longer retaliation through deposition. Whether this promise bears out remains to be seen.

First, ESG is far too broad a concept that it could determine outcomes and pave a single to road to corporate virtue. It comprises a broad variety of goals and values, many of them diverging and conflicting, not a few of them hard to reconcile when push comes to shove. Moreover, shareholders may pursue a decision-making strategy which aims at approximating ESG voting and value maximization by adopting those ESG goals which come closest to profit maximization. Given the lack of behavioural control, they do not have to fear any sanctions but increasing returns on their investment. Judging from extant empirical studies, indirect demand-side regulation in its current form will change the equation only slightly. Inquiring about investors' preferences suffers from the same issue any empirical survey has to cope with, namely the problem of a social desirability bias. Shareholders will most likely answer in a manner they perceive as being in line with social norms as expressed by the legal framework and transformed into a catalogue of questions asked by the investment adviser, but hold on to their true beliefs and attitudes once the investment decision has been made. At least for now, for most retail investors, including adherents to ESG, these beliefs and attitudes seem to lie more on the side of monetary gains. Nonetheless, over time, the recent EU regulation may crowd out the most ardent profit-maximization strategies.

In sum, there is a case for demand-side regulation to be made by those who want to transform the economy and cure corporate governance from several flaws of traditional supply-side approaches. If ESG as envisioned by the EU and others is supposed to work and implemented through corporate governance reform, demand-side regulation is an important regulatory strategy. Whether reforming corporate governance is the correct approach overall or whether public and administrative law would be better suited to address the pressing issues of our time is still subject to debate. Scholars have expressed substantial criticism which has to be taken seriously and dealt with—but elsewhere. This issue lies outside the scope of this chapter offering an analytical grid for a new regulatory strategy 'from the inside', that is, judged by its own aspirations.

# 16
# Sustainability and Competition Law

*Stefan Thomas*[*]

## I. Introduction

The debate about the consideration of sustainability in competition law has gained momentum in the EU and started to percolate into the United States recently.[1] Agencies have issued specific guidance (eg the EU Horizontal Guidelines, section 9;[2] the Austrian Antitrust Sustainability Guidelines;[3] and the UK Competition and Markets Authority draft guidance on environmental sustainability agreements[4]). In Austria, the legislator has even enacted a dedicated sustainability provision in the Austrian Cartel Act.[5] The Hellenic Competition Commission has started a 'sustainability sandbox' initiative inviting the industry to join a dialogue about concrete measures.[6]

The industry faces increasing pressure to consider sustainability agreements. The implementation of stricter sustainability standards (beyond what is required by law) can create a 'first mover disadvantage'[7] (eg when phasing out certain polluting product variant despite persisting consumer demand for such variant). Sustainability agreements between industry rivals may help overcome such conundrum. Establishing green industry standards can involve the sharing of competitively sensitive data, eg relating to production or distribution. Such exchange can amount to a concerted practice restrictive of competition. These are just two examples for situations in which rivals may engage in anticompetitive cooperation to implement a sustainability measure on the market.

---

[*] All internet sources were last accessed on 15 January 2024.
[1] Where some agencies take a critical stance towards specific sustainability considerations in the realm of antitrust, for example, the investigation of twenty-one state attorneys into some proxy firms' ESG practices under antitrust law see 'Attorney General Reyes Leads 21-State Challenge to Proxy Firms' ESG Practices' (17 January 2023) https://attorneygeneral.utah.gov/attorney-general-reyes-leads-21-state-challenge-to-proxy-firms-esg-practices/.
[2] European Commission, Guidelines on the applicability of Article 101 of the Treaty on the Functioning of the European Union to horizontal co-operation agreements [2023] OJ C259/1 https://eur-lex.europa.eu/legal-content/EN/TXT/?uri=uriserv%3AOJ.C_.2023.259.01.0001.01.ENG&toc=OJ%3AC%3A2023%3A259%3ATOC; see on the draft version of the guidelines Roman Inderst and Stefan Thomas, 'Sustainability Agreements in the European Commission's Draft Horizontal Guidelines' (2022) 13 Journal of European Competition Law & Practice 571.
[3] See www.bwb.gv.at/news/detail/bwb-veroeffentlicht-finale-leitlinien-fuer-unternehmen-zu-nachhaltigkeitskooperationen.
[4] See www.gov.uk/government/consultations/draft-guidance-on-environmental-sustainability-agreements.
[5] Austrian Cartel Act, art 2(1) subpara 2.
[6] See www.epant.gr/en/enimerosi/sandbox.html.
[7] European Commission (n 2) para 566.

Stefan Thomas, *Sustainability and Competition Law* In: *Corporate Purpose, CSR, and ESG*. Edited by: Jens-Hinrich Binder, Klaus J. Hopt, and Thilo Kuntz, Oxford University Press. © Jens-Hinrich Binder, Klaus J. Hopt, and Thilo Kuntz 2024.
DOI: 10.1093/oso/9780198912576.003.0016

An increasing number of cases with such a sustainability dimension reaches the agencies and courts (in the Netherlands: 'chicken of tomorrow';[8] in Germany: *Tierwohl*[9] and other cases;[10] a few EU cases[11] also exist). In the UK, some private plaintiffs even venture to rely on the antitrust laws to sue water sewage companies over their alleged breach of sustainability legislation arguing an abuse of a dominant position of such firms through their sustainability negligence.[12]

The current state of affairs is such that no clear EU-wide approach has emerged on how to reconcile sustainability with the posit of unimpeded competition. The Dutch agency pursues a transparent consumer welfare approach,[13] while the German *Bundeskartellamt* rather resorts to its 'intervention discretion' (*Einschreitermessen*) without committing to a certain metric.[14] The Commission, in its Horizontal Guidelines, generally subscribes to a consumer welfare metric, while at the same time allowing for a consideration of so-called 'collective benefits',[15] to the extent that the affected consumer group benefits from them,[16] even though this type of benefit does not correspond with an economic consumer rent derived from a contract.

The scholarly debate continues to explore a range of concepts.[17] Much of the writing focuses on finding legislative corroboration for the idea that sustainability is a goal of

---

[8] ACM, 'Welfare of Today's Chicken and That of the "Chicken of Tomorrow"' (13 August 2020) www.acm.nl/sites/default/files/documents/2020-08/welfare-of-todays-chicken-and-that-of-the-chicken-of-tomorrow.pdf; see on that Roman Inderst and Stefan Thomas, 'Prospective Welfare Analysis: Extending Willingness-To-Pay Assessment to Embrace Sustainability' (2022) 18 Journal of Competition Law & Economics 551.

[9] BKartA, press release of 28 September 2017, www.bundeskartellamt.de/SharedDocs/Publikation/DE/Pressemitteilungen/2017/28_09_2017_Tierwohl.pdf?__blob=publicationFile&v=2.

[10] BKartA, press release of 24 May 2022 [Catena X], www.bundeskartellamt.de/SharedDocs/Publikation/DE/Pressemitteilungen/2022/24_05_2022_Catena_X.pdf;jsessionid=45F22FEBA1683140704DBB6696ABACFA.1_cid389?__blob=publicationFile&v=2; BKartA, press release of 18 January 2022 [Prüfung Brancheninitiativen], www.bundeskartellamt.de/SharedDocs/Publikation/DE/Pressemitteilungen/2022/18_01_2022_Nachhaltigkeit.pdf?__blob=publicationFile&v=3; BKartA, press release of 13 June 2023 [Forum Nachhaltiger Kakao], www.bundeskartellamt.de/SharedDocs/Publikation/DE/Pressemitteilungen/2023/13_06_2023_Kakaoforum.pdf;jsessionid=FC1A91E8FF2D6A22C362350B8EF7626F.2_cid389?__blob=publicationFile&v=3.

[11] See eg *Consumer Detergents* (Case COMP/39579) Commission Decision C(2011) 2528 final; *Bayer/Monsanto* (Case M.8084) Commission Decision C(2018) 1709 final, paras 3019 and 3029; *Philips-Osram* (Case IV/34.252) Commission Decision 94/986/EC [1994] OJ L378/37, para 27; *DSD* (Case COMP/34.493 et al.) Commission Decision 2001/837/EC [2001] OJ L319/1; *CECED* (Case IV.F.1/36.718) Commission Decision 2000/475/EC [1999] OJ L187/47, para 56.

[12] See UK water sewage litigation https://www.businesswire.com/news/home/20221115005087/en/Fideres-Study-Believes-UK-Water-Companies-Potentially-in-Breach-of-Competition-Law-Over-Raw-Sewage-Spills; voicing objections against such a line of argumentation Roman Inderst and Stefan Thomas, 'Abuse of Dominance and Sustainability' (2023) 14 Journal of European Competition Law & Practice 48.

[13] ACM (n 8).

[14] BKartA, Background paper on public interest and competition law, www.bundeskartellamt.de/SharedDocs/Publikation/DE/Diskussions_Hintergrundpapier/AK_Kartellrecht_2020_Hintergrundpapier.pdf;jsessionid=576D124E4992D51AA08B4A3DE857125A.1_cid390?__blob=publicationFile&v=2.

[15] Meaning, in essence, such benefits, eg cleaner air, that are not already depicted in a specific willingness to pay in the relevant consumer group for this benefit.

[16] European Commission (n 2) paras 582 ff.

[17] Out of the vast amount of literature see Simon Holmes, 'Climate Change, Sustainability, and Competition Law' (2020) 8 Journal of Antitrust Enforcement 354, 377; Suzanne Kingston, 'Integrating Environmental Protection and EU Competition Law: Why Competition Isn't Special' (2010) 16 European Law Journal 780; Anna Gerbrandy, 'Solving a Sustainability-Deficit in European Competition Law' (2017) 40 World Competition 539, 554ff; Alexandra M Teorell, 'A Company's Guide to Environmental Action' (Master's Thesis, Lund University 2019) 18 ff https://lup.lub.lu.se/student-papers/search/publication/8976734; from the United States see Norman W Hawker and Thomas N Edmonds, 'Avoiding the Efficiency Trap: Resilience, Sustainability, and Antitrust' (2015) 60 Antitrust Bulletin 208, 220; Norman W Hawker and Thomas N Edmonds, 'Strategic Management Concepts for Antitrust: Cooperation, Stakeholders and Sustainability' (2014) 59 Antitrust Bulletin 769; Inara Scott, 'Antitrust

great importance, which can possibly trump economic efficiency in a competition assessment.[18] The deeper core of the problem, however, lies in the fact that individual consumption within a free market economy can cause harm to the environment (externalities), and that competition is supposed to cater to consumer demand irrespective of how reasonable or sustainable such demand is from a social perspective. The problem is that despite competition (or even due to competition), consumers get the chance to prefer their own benefit at the expense of the environment and of future generations. How does it reconcile with the competition paradigm if firms agree on countering such externalities?

The present paper will focus on this specific question. Other related questions must be left untouched, such as agreements or unilateral conduct that deprive consumers of more sustainable products, or merger effects on sustainability.

## II. The Externality Problem in Competition Law

### 1. The Notion of Externalities

For the purpose of this article, externalities are defined as those effects that consumption can have on other people or institutions, such as on the environment. To the extent that consumers are agnostic about the creation of such externalities, competition (and consequently antitrust enforcement) cannot remedy such effect. Restrictions of competition, however, possibly can.

### 2. The Role of Consumers' Willingness to Pay

Starting point for the legal analysis is to find an overarching concept for the assessment of the effects that a market-related measure can precipitate. This leads to the debate about the goals of antitrust. This paper is not the place to home in on all the diverging views, on the case law, and on the international policy developments in that regard. Rather, this analysis will rest on the consumer welfare paradigm. It is the recognized enforcement approach in the EU and the United States.

Against this backdrop, any measure can be assessed in the light of its implications on consumer rent. Consumer rent is the delta between the actual price and the consumer's willingness to pay (also 'reservation price').

---

and Socially Responsible Collaboration: A Chilling Combination?' (2016) 53 American Business Law Journal 97, 143; Ben Steinberg and Adam Mendel, 'US Antitrust Regulators Should Foster Climate Collaboration' (13 April 2021) www.robinskaplan.com/-/media/pdfs/publications/us-antitrust-regulators-should-foster-climate-collaboration.pdf?la=en. For further references see Roman Inderst and Stefan Thomas, 'Legal Design in Sustainable Antitrust' (2022) https://papers.ssrn.com/sol3/papers.cfm?abstract_id=4058367.

[18] See eg Holmes (n 17) 377.

Consumers may display an increased willingness to pay for a more sustainable product. The mitigation of externalities can thereby become a so-called 'non-use benefit' for the consumer to the extent that the consumer is willing to pay more for the sustainable product variant.[19] To the extent that such sustainability willingness to pay can be measured, an increase in price due to a sustainability agreement might, therefore, be offset by a concomitant consumer benefit, hence the legitimacy of the agreement under the cartel prohibition (see the efficiency defence in Article 101(3) of the Treaty on the Functioning of the European Union (TFEU)). This approach was followed by the Dutch agency in 'chicken for tomorrow' (although a defence was eventually denied based on the facts of the case),[20] and also the Commission recognizes that in its Horizontal Guidelines 2023.[21] Only if such increase in willingness to pay does not suffice (or cannot be measured) will there arise a conflict between consumer benefit and the mitigation of externalities through sustainability agreements. Those two scenarios must be clearly distinguished, since the legal implications are vastly different.

## 3. The Notion of Sustainability

The notion of sustainability is opaque. Some conceive of it in a broad manner, including, eg the fairness of wages and the respect for human rights in production (eg the Dutch agency[22] and the EU Commission[23]). Others define sustainability in a strictly environmental sense (eg the Austrian Sustainability Guidelines[24]). The conceptual problems, however, remain the same. As a matter of fact, any externality of consumption can produce the same questions in an antitrust framework irrespective how it is tagged or categorized.

It should be noted, however, that it can be difficult to determine scientifically whether a certain measure is sustainable or not. That is due to the difficulty of finding appropriate scientific gauges for the measurement of sustainability (or any other societal goal). Take, as an example, the weighting of diverging sustainability impacts (eg nuclear energy—zero carbon emission albeit production of nuclear waste—what is more important?). Also, the consumers' perceptions of sustainability can be non-consequentialist. The consumer might feel a certain measure to be sustainable even though the opposite is the case (eg buying an electric car that is rarely used so that—in comparison—a traditional combustion engine car would produce less $CO_2$ overall). Who defines sustainability? The intervention will return to these questions, but it is

---

[19] See eg Giles Atkinson and others, *Cost Benefit Analysis and the Environment* (OECD Publishing 2018) www.oecd-ilibrary.org/environment/cost-benefit-analysis-and-the-environment_9789264085169-en.
[20] ACM (n 8).
[21] European Commission (n 2) para 575.
[22] ACM Draft Guidelines, 'Sustainability Agreements: Opportunities within Competition Law' No 7, 27, 50 www.acm.nl/sites/default/files/documents/second-draft-version-guidelines-on-sustainability-agreements-oppurtunities-within-competition-law.pdf.
[23] European Commission (n 2) para 517.
[24] See n 3.

expedient to be clear about these implications of the notion of sustainability before elaborating further.

## 4. The Shortcomings of the 'Multi-Goal Approach'

Against this backdrop, some authors opt for a radical solution. They argue that, when there is a conflict between the protection of competition and a mitigation of environmental externalities, antitrust enforcement should prefer the latter over the former.[25] Effectively, this approach argues that sustainability is a goal that antitrust enforcement is supposed to pursue besides economic efficiency. The idea can therefore be referenced as a 'multi-goal approach'. This view is agnostic about the consumer welfare implications of a sustainability agreement so long as the agreement yields benefits for the environment.

Two problems arise, which is why this approach meets with objections. First, antitrust enforcement would eventually hinge on a balancing of consumer rent and the mitigation of externalities. There is no common unit of measurement, however, for such balancing. Effectively, this balancing is a normative exercise. Secondly, in view of the fact that the balancing is a normative exercise, it is questionable whether and to what extent an antitrust agency can claim to have a democratic legitimization to perform it on behalf of the entire society. Rather, one might find oneself inclined to argue that this matter is reserved for the legislator.[26]

## III. Integrating Externalities into the Consumer Welfare Paradigm

### 1. Reflective Willingness to Pay

Remaining within the traditional consumer welfare approach, the elicitation of consumers' willingness to pay for sustainability gains importance.[27] Yet antitrust analysis encounters challenges at this point, too.

When measuring consumers' willingness to pay, antitrust enforcement often focuses on so-called 'revealed preferences'. This means that the agency will look into actual payments being made by consumers for products at the point of sale. Those actual consumer choices are supposed to provide reliable information about the consumer's willingness to pay for certain product features, such as better sustainability.

---

[25] See eg Holmes (n 17) 377.
[26] On the underlying problems see Stefan Thomas, 'Normative Goals in Merger Control: Why Merger Control Should Not Attempt to Achieve "Better" Outcomes than Competition' in Ioannis Kokkoris and Claudia Lemus (eds), *Research Handbook on the Law and Economics of Competition Enforcement* (Edward Elgar Publishing 2022) 193–216.
[27] See on that Roman Inderst and Stefan Thomas, 'Integrating Benefits from Sustainability into the Competitive Assessment: How Can We Measure Them?' (2021) 12 Journal of European Competition Law & Practice 705 with further references.

Focusing on revealed preferences, however, implies that the consumer's willingness to pay will be measured in a specific purchasing context, eg at the supermarket counter. When it comes to the sustainability feature of the product, however, these concrete purchasing conditions can limit the extent to which the consumer is able to pay heed to the sustainability dimension of her purchase. Due to various constraints, which the consumer might face in such a concrete purchasing context, such as psychological stress, time constraints, distraction, etc., she might be biased towards neglecting the sustainability impact whilst putting greater weight on more salient features, such as price and quickness of availability.[28]

In 'Reflective Willingness to Pay' (2021),[29] Roman Inderst and I therefore argue in favour of more elaborate elicitation methods in willingness to pay analysis, inter alia borrowing from marketing science. We put forward a range of tests by which consumers can be provided more information and time to reflect upon the sustainability impact of their purchases when expressing their willingness to pay for a sustainability feature within the framework of a survey. To provide consumers with more time for reflection can yield sustainability-related willingness to pay measurements that exceed what could be read from revealed preferences.

This leads to the conceptual conundrum that one and the same person can express different willingness to pays depending on the circumstances in which she is being asked. To deal with such ambiguous data is a situation which is new to antitrust enforcement. Therefore, under such condition, the agency or court eventually needs to 'choose' between two (or more) diverging reservation prices when measuring the impact of the agreement on consumer rent.

In 'Reflective Willingness to Pay' (2021) we ultimately argue that, due to the legal endorsement which sustainability has received in the legal order, on the one hand the agency or court can rely on those reservation prices which put greater emphasis on sustainability. This approach is not tantamount to the multi-goal approach in that the consumer remains the ultimate arbiter when expressing her willingness to pay for the more sustainable variant. The agency is not allowed, on the other hand, to approve the sustainability agreement even though the actual price would rise more than what the highest reservation price for the more sustainable good would justify under the consumer welfare standard.

## 2. Prospective Willingness to Pay

When considering consumers' willingness to pay for sustainability, it is also necessary to behold the dimension of time. The consumption of an existing consumer generation can reduce the well-being of future consumers. Take, as an example, the extinction of

---

[28] See Roman Inderst and Stefan Thomas, 'Reflective Willingness to Pay: Preferences for Sustainable Consumption in a Consumer Welfare Analysis' (2021) 17 Journal of Competition Law & Economics 848.
[29] ibid.

an existing animal species through unsustainable fishing methods. While the current consumer generation might not feel inclined to pay more for a more sustainable fish product, a future generation of consumers might think differently in the face of a more direct exposure to the consequences of the previous consumption of others, and possibly due to better information and a change in the societal conviction about the importance of sustainability.

It can, therefore, become necessary to consider such a change in a future consumer generation's willingness to pay for sustainability when assessing a sustainability agreement if and to the extent that this agreement is necessary to prevent an irreversible harm to the environment.[30] It can be argued that, from a legal perspective, the notion of 'consumer' comprises future generations so that an intergenerational balancing of consumer rents can take place.[31] Conceptual problems remain, such as the measurement of future generations' change in willingness to pay and the discount rates to be applied when integrating rents from different points in time.[32] Nevertheless, the general posit remains that, in order to embrace consumers' willingness to pay fully, a prognosis of future changes in consumers' stances towards sustainability should be recognized to the extent that such information is obtainable.

## 3. Willingness to Pay and Social Norms

Consumers' willingness to pay can also be influenced by social norms about sustainable conduct. Economic research suggests that consumers tend to define their willingness to pay, inter alia, in relation to the social acceptance of their own purchasing behaviour.[33]

Understanding the interrelation between social norms and willingness to pay can, therefore, become important for the antitrust assessment of sustainability agreements.[34] In that regard, it can gain relevance that a sustainability agreement may, in itself, impact on a social norm about sustainable consumption, thereby yielding repercussions on consumers' willingness to pay for sustainability. The existence of the sustainability agreement—and its possible impact on social norms—should, consequently, be considered as a given when undertaking a counterfactual analysis.

It is important, however, to distinguish the recognition of the social norm from the question of whether the consumer would be willing to pay for a change in behaviour of others.

The social norms approach considers the implication of the agreement on the social norm as a given. The consumer is, then, being asked whether she would be willing to

---

[30] Inderst and Thomas (n 8).
[31] See ibid; Roman Inderst and Stefan Thomas, 'Nachhaltigkeit und Wettbewerb: Zu einer Reform des Wettbewerbsrechts für die Erreichung von Nachhaltigkeitszielen' SAFE Policy Letter No 94 (January 2022) 14 ff https://safe-frankfurt.de/fileadmin/user_upload/editor_common/Policy_Center/SAFE_Policy_Letter_94.pdf.
[32] See Inderst and Thomas (n 8).
[33] Roman Inderst, Felix Rhiel, and Stefan Thomas, 'Sustainability Agreements and Social Norms' (2022) 20 Zeitschrift für Wettbewerbsrecht (Journal of Competition Law) 225 with further references.
[34] ibid.

pay a premium for the more sustainable product, assuming that all other consumers will be willing to pay a higher price, too.

It would be unconvincing to argue, however, that antitrust enforcement should be concerned about whether the consumer would be willing to pay more in order to force other consumers to make the same contribution to sustainability.

The difference between both questions is the lack of conditionality within the social norms approach. Asking consumers about their willingness to pay for a change in behaviour of others would amount to a type of social choice exercise, which would lie outside the scope of what antitrust enforcement should look at. In a competition regime, the market outcome is shaped by the aggregation of individual consumer benefits, not by a voting process that results in a binding rule which can then be imposed on others.[35]

## 4. Individual Benefits and Collective Benefits

When considering consumer benefits as a result of the sustainability agreement, it is necessary to define the cohort of consumers that are exposed to harm and benefit in order to undertake the balancing. Sustainability agreements lead to the conceptual problem that the mitigation of externalities can affect a societal group that is larger than the consumers that are being affected by a price increase as a result of the sustainability agreement. Some antitrust agencies, nevertheless, argue that those externality benefits, which accrue to non-purchasers, can still be conceived of as a benefit that is recognizable within a consumer welfare approach.[36] The problem with this viewpoint, however, is that it appears to be difficult to define precisely the group of people the externality benefits of whom are recognizable.[37] Will environmental benefits, that accrue to people living outside the EU, justify a price increase within the EU? Could sustainability benefits occurring in France offset a consumer harm that results from higher prices being inflicted upon consumers in Germany? To date, no satisfactory answers have been given to these questions.[38]

The Commission, in its new Horizontal Guidelines, favours a limited recognition of collective benefits. While it rejects a recognition of benefits accruing to non-consumers, it shows openness to considering benefits that directly impact on the wellbeing of those consumers that also suffer from the economic detriment resulting from the agreement, eg through higher prices of the more sustainable good.[39] This approach, however, may become exposed to the objection that it is difficult to measure the relevance of this collective benefit in order to balance it against an

---

[35] See Roman Inderst and Stefan Thomas, 'The Scope and Limitations of Incorporating Externalities in Competition Analysis within a Consumer Welfare Approach' (2022) 45 World Competition 351.
[36] See eg European Commission (n 2) paras 582 ff.
[37] For a detailed discussion of the sustainability chapter of the draft guidelines see Inderst and Thomas (n 2).
[38] See Inderst and Thomas (n 27).
[39] European Commission (n 2) para 584.

economic consumer harm. The Commission's doctrine may, eventually, lead to the same conundrum as faced by the multi-goal approach addressed at the beginning of this article. What is more, the question arises why such collective benefits, accruing to the relevant consumer group, shall be considered in the first place, given the Commission's openness to recognizing consumers' willingness to pay for non-use benefits. If consumers are not willing to pay more for a mitigation of this specific externality, why would it be consistent with their welfare to recognize it as a (collective) benefit anyways?[40]

## IV. Reducing Externalities beyond the Consumer Welfare Paradigm

### 1. Practical and Conceptual Reasons to Transgress the Consumer Welfare Paradigm

In view of the above considerations, the consumer welfare paradigm can be seen as a powerful tool for reconciling sustainability goals with economic efficiency within the framework of an antitrust analysis. However, the question remains as to whether antitrust enforcement can transgress the limitations of the consumer welfare metric in order to embrace the mitigation of environmental externalities directly. Two reasons mandate reflections.

(1) Despite the power, which the consumer welfare analysis can have, it must be acknowledged that the elicitation methods and the extension of the consumer welfare analysis into the dimension of time are fraught with difficulties. On the one hand, the agency might struggle obtaining the relevant consumer data. Also, even if it is theoretically possible to undertake a fully-fledged reflective and prospective consumer welfare analysis, such procedure is costly and time consuming. The industry, on the other hand, must take quick decisions about their engagement in sustainability agreements. Such promptness will most often not be achievable with the elicitation methods outlined above.

(2) The legislator appears to be willing to transfer to a greater extent on the industry the mandate of developing and enforcing standards about sustainability autonomously. To the extent that this is the case, competitors face a problem: on the one hand, they are supposed to cater to the legislator's aim through collaboration, whilst on the other hand, it is unclear whether and to what extent consumers will appreciate such collaboration on sustainability standards. A concrete example for that can be found in the German Supply Chain Legislation

---

[40] Voicing objections against such 'soft paternalism' see Roman Inderst and Stefan Thomas, 'The Scope and Limitations of Incorporating Externalities in Competition Analysis within a Consumer Welfare Approach' (2022) 45 World Competition 351.

(*Lieferkettensorgfaltspflichtgesetz*).[41] There, the legislator explicitly encourages the industry to agree on supply chain standards, including on sustainability, and on methods to enforce them vis-à-vis their suppliers. In order to reconcile such collective measures with the antitrust laws, such supply chain agreements need to be justified either by a consumer welfare defence or through another type of antitrust exemption. The Supply Chain Legislation, however, remains silent to that end.

At this point, the European legal order poses a specific problem that does not exist anywhere else in the world. While any legislator is usually free (explicitly or implicitly) to provide exemptions from the antitrust laws in order to pursue goals outside economic efficiency, the European cartel provision is laid down in Article 101 TFEU. As a piece of primary legislation, the prohibition cannot be changed by way of secondary legislation or national Member State laws, unless there is a specific empowerment for such exemption under EU-law, which, however, only exists to a limited extent.[42] Also, it is highly unlikely that Article 101 TFEU itself will be amended by adding a sustainability exemption.

This provokes the question as to whether the primacy of Article 101 TFEU constrains the legislative leeway with respect to a greater accommodation of sustainability considerations through industry agreements. Are restrictive horizontal agreements within the realm of the German Supply Chain Legislation, after all, in breach of Articles 101 TFEU?[43]

## 2. Democratic Legitimization and the Primacy of EU Primary Legislation

The agencies have not yet developed a clear stance on this question. Rejecting a dedicated sustainability exemption seems to reconcile with the established adage that the cartel provision is agnostic about societal goals outside economic efficiency.[44] It is widely stated that the EU cartel provision does not entail a so-called 'rule of reason'.[45] While Article 101(3) TFEU allows for an economic efficiency defence, other societal

---

[41] Gesetz über die unternehmerischen Sorgfaltspflichten in Lieferketten of 16 July 2021, BGBl 2021 Teil I Nr 46 (22 July 2021) 2959.

[42] See Article 210a of its Common Market Organisation Regulation (Regulation (EU) No 1308/2013 of 17 December 2013 establishing a common organisation of the markets in agricultural products and repealing Council Regulations (EEC) No 922/72, (EEC) No 234/79, (EC) No 1037/2001 and (EC) No 1234/2007, OJ L347/671 https://eur-lex.europa.eu/legal-content/EN/TXT/?uri=CELEX%3A02013R1308-20211207), which is, however, by definition confined to the agricultural sector.

[43] See on the German Supply Chain Legislation Roman Inderst and Stefan Thomas, 'Legal Design in Sustainable Antitrust' (2022) 19–21 https://papers.ssrn.com/sol3/papers.cfm?abstract_id=4058367.

[44] Thomas (n 26) 193–216.

[45] Case 56 and 58/64 *Consten and Grundig v Commission* ECLI:EU:C:1966:41; Case T-29/92, *Vereniging van Samenwerkende Prijsregelende Organisaties in de Bouwnijverheid and others v Commission* ECLI:EU:T:1995:34, para 96; Case T-328/03 *O2 (Germany) v Commission* ECLI:EU:T:2006:116, paras 69 ff.

goals are commonly held as irrelevant under EU competition law. Article 210a of Regulation (EU) 1308/2013 (CMO Regulation; Common Market Organization) exempts certain sustainability agreements in the agricultural sector. Yet there is no overarching EU-sustainability exemption from the competition rules. In the absence of an explicit EU exemption for sustainability collaborations, horizontal agreements restrictive of competition would therefore be governed by Article 101 TFEU irrespective of their positive contribution to the environment.

However, closer scrutiny reveals that the EU jurisprudence does recognize implicit exemptions for restrictive agreements under certain circumstances outside the scope of Article 101(3) TFEU. The European Court of Justice has accepted in various judgments that agreements, which are ancillary to the pursuit of a legitimate main objective, can be exempt from Article 101 TFEU irrespective of any efficiency gains.[46] In *Wouters*, the Court of Justice decided that a decision by an association of undertakings restrictive of competition in relation to its members in the legal profession had the objective to 'ensure that the ultimate consumers of legal services and the sound administration of justice are provided with the necessary guarantees in relation to integrity and experience'.[47] The Court of Justice acknowledged that such decision was feasible under Dutch law about the professional conduct in the legal service industry. The Court of Justice moreover acknowledged that the measure contributed to ensuring a high quality of legal services in the Netherlands, which is, at the same time, a general policy goal that is also reflected in the overarching EU legislation in many ways. The Court of Justice therefore concluded that such restriction of competition was legitimate and did not fall within the scope of Article 101(1) TFEU irrespective of an increase in consumer welfare. A similar line of reasoning was provided in *Albany*,[48] which was about the exemption of collective bargaining on labour markets from the EU cartel prohibition.

There is an ongoing scholarly debate about how this line of jurisprudence maps onto the dogma that Article 101 TFEU does not entail a rule of reason.[49] The EU judicature has never elaborated deeply on the legal foundations of the *Wouters* doctrine. A convincing explanation can be seen in the court's willingness to support the pursuit of societal goals to the extent that they are at least indirectly recognized by the EU primary legislative order, and which, at the same time, have been explicitly taken up by the national legislator. To the extent that agreements restrictive of competition are being made in such legal embedment, Article 101 TFEU is not supposed to spoil the pursuit of the goal. The *Wouters* doctrine, therefore, is a matter of legal-systematic interpretation of the European legal order that creates a 'practical concordance' between diverging poles ('*praktische Konkordanz*').

One can rely on this argument, now, to put forward that the national legislator (or the EU secondary legislator) has the power to design so-called 'sustainability corridors'

---

[46] See Inderst and Thomas (n 43) 10–11.
[47] Case C-309/99 *Wouters and others v Algemene Raad van de Nederlandse Orde van Advocaten* ECLI:EU:C:2002:98, para 97.
[48] Case C-67/96 *Albany International BV v Stichting Bedrijfspensioenfonds Textielindustrie* ECLI:EU:C:1999:430.
[49] See on that Inderst and Thomas (n 43) 8 ff with further references.

in which the industry can then enter into horizontal agreements irrespective of a consumer welfare defence in order mitigate environmental externalities. In 'Legal Design in Sustainable Antitrust' (2022), Roman Inderst and I home in on methods of crafting such corridors in ways that allow assessing the necessity of the restrictive measure to attain a sustainability goal. We consider that this approach of legislative sustainability corridors can contribute to the solution of the sustainability problem in antitrust in several ways.

It allows the national legislator to contribute proactively to fostering sustainability. It bypasses the problems that would come along with the 'multi-goal approach'. Unlike the agency, which cannot claim about itself to have been bestowed with the authority for balancing sustainability against economic efficiency,[50] the legislator has such democratic legitimization. Moreover, the legislative definition of clear sustainability corridors increases the transparency of any antitrust measure taken in that regard. Also, the legislator can decide whether and to what extent non-consequentialist sustainability ideas might find endorsement or not. A measure is non-consequentialist if its effect on the overall goal of sustainability is questionable or even non-existent (such as, possibly, the contribution to climate protection of buying an electric vehicle which will be powered by fossil fuel-based electricity for the foreseeable future). Moreover, the existence of legislative sustainability corridors can provide the necessary robust guidance to the industry. It can bring legal certainty for day-to-day industry self-assessments without involving complex willingness to pay elicitations.

## V. Conclusions

Sustainability in competition law is not merely a scholarly debate. The transition to a greener economy has been embraced by public opinion, shareholders' perceptions, and the overall regulatory landscape. In contrast to established mechanisms, however, legislation bestows on firms, to an increasing extent, the task of shaping sustainability compromises thereby substituting for a lack of (clear) legislative regulation of externalities.

This leads to conceptual problems in terms of social choice theory and democratic legitimization of such business-driven approaches: how to ensure that firms do not impose de facto regulations that take away from consumers the ability to express their will about compromises between consumer welfare and externalities? Also, firms do not have any instruments to soften distributional implications of sustainability standards, eg by way of taxation and subsidization.

Can this be reason enough to deny the legitimacy of any sustainability claims under antitrust law? No, yet a cautionary approach is warranted.

---

[50] Thomas (n 26) 193–216; Stefan Thomas, 'Der Verbraucher und die Nachhaltigkeit im Kartellrecht' in Detlev Joost, Hartmut Oetker, and Marian Paschke (eds), *Festschrift für Franz Jürgen Säcker zum 80. Geburtstag* (CH Beck 2021) 342 ff.

1. To the extent that an increase in willingness to pay for the more sustainable variant, which is sufficient to offset any competitive harm, can be measured, an agreement can be justified under the standard consumer welfare doctrine.
2. It is necessary to behold the distinction between the individual willingness to pay for the consumer's own benefit as opposed to a consumer's 'willingness to pay for a change in the behaviour of others'. The latter is, actually, a matter of social choice rather than of individual market choices of consumers. In more concrete terms, the market outcome in an open competitive market order is shaped by the aggregate of individual benefits achieved by consumers in their contracts for themselves. The market outcome is, therefore, the accumulation of individual consumer welfare benefits. By making a contract, the consumer cannot impose restrictions on other consumers. The consumer can only incentivize firms to cater to her demands. In a political social choice process, eg in a political election, the voter can (directly or indirectly) vote on rules that will be binding on everybody. This distinction between 'market choice' and 'social choice' must be observed when undertaking a consumer welfare-oriented counterfactual analysis in an antitrust context.
3. The agency should not engage in a direct balancing of consumer welfare against a mitigation of externalities: the agency would lack a democratic legitimization, and such direct executive balancing would produce opaque reasoning.
4. A direct consideration of externality mitigation can take place where the legislator has created 'sustainability corridors' for firms. Such legislative sustainability corridors can exempt agreements from the EU cartel prohibition under the ancillary doctrine (the *Wouters* doctrine). Agencies and law-makers, however, are still reluctant to acknowledge this possibility.

# Index

*For the benefit of digital users, indexed terms that span two pages (e.g., 52–53) may, on occasion, appear on only one of those pages.*

Tables are indicated by an italic *t* following the page number.

Abrams, F. 184–85
abuse of dominant position 358
accountability 18
accounting law 8–9, 17–18, 105–6, 262
Adidas 19
adverse impacts 239–40
   environmental impact, concept of 292
agency costs 190, 216
Agenda for Sustainable Development (2030) 141
Ahern, K. R. 77–78
Akerlof, G. A. 40–41
Albany Manufacturing Society 174–75
alternative investment fund managers (AIFMs) 255–56, 259n.76, 266
alternative investment strategy 346–47
*American Business Creed* 184–85, 186
American Law Institute (ALI) 9, 29, 130
   Restatement of the Law of Corporate Governance xiv, 127, 129
Ames, S. 174–76
Amnesty International (AI) 163
Angell, J. K. 174–76
annual accounts 233–36
annual reports 43–44
antisocial behaviour 12–13, 206
anti-takeover/activist devices 71
antitrust law 5, 23–24, 52, 177–78, 358
appropriate measures 239–40
Arab Oil Embargo (1973) 190
asset managers 13–14
asset partitioning 174–75, 196–97
assets under management (AUM) 13–14
AT&T 179–80
Attorney General 5–6, 48–49, 53
auditing 5–6, 43–45, 53, 235–36
Australia 340
Austria
   Antitrust Sustainability Guidelines 357, 360
   Cartel Act 357
   stock exchange company law 25

baby milk formula 263
Bainbridge, S. 203
balancing problem 341–42
Baldwin, T. 215
Bangladesh 263
Bank for International Settlements (BIS) 84–85
banking services 175–76

bankruptcy 230
Barby, C. 152
Barton, B. 178
Basel Committee on Banking Supervision 22–23
Benchuk, L. A. 21, 76
behavioural control 327, 331–33, 353–55
behavioural economics 5–6, 52
Belgium 36–37
benefit corporation 131
benefit judgment rule 32–33, 52
Berle, A. A. 174, 179–82, 183, 184–85, 222–23
Bertelsmann 17–18
Better Business Act (BBA) 152–53
BHP 263
Biden, J. 7–8, 87
Biedenkopf Commission 120
Binder, J.-H. 13
biodiversity loss 257, 258, 261, 262
black box model 147
BlackRock 137, 334–35
board diversity, effects of 77
board elections 6–7, 70–71
board options 31
boilerplate reporting 250, 344–45, 351
Boone Pickens, T. 190–91
Bosch 17–18
BP 263
Brandeis, Justice 278
Bratton, W. 212
bribery 262
Brick, H. 183–84
British Academy 2–3, 17–18, 128
   Future of the Corporation programme 151, 161
Brookings, R. 178–79
burden of proof 295
business judgment rule 46–47, 66, 67, 116–18
business purpose 133
business relationship
   definition of 293
   indirect 293
Business Roundtable 187–88, 222–23
business statesmanship 178–79
*Business Week* magazine 187–88

Cadbury Report (1992) 250
Campaign GM 188–89
Canada 50–51

## 372  INDEX

capital expenditure (CapEx)  196n.7, 280–81, 314
capital lock-in  174–75
Capital Markets Union  315–16
capitalism  40–41, 183–84, 198–99
   enlightened  21–22
   ideological condemnation of  39–40
   managerial  184, 186–87
   stakeholder  20–21
Carbon Disclosure Project (CDP)  155t
carbon emissions  61, 274
carbon footprint  61
carbon neutrality  92–93
carbon tax  61, 136
care, duty of  293
Carlsberg  31
cash flow rights  207–8
Casino  295
catholic investment principles  342
CDR policy implementation  9–10
centralized management  196–97
Chandler, W.  29
Charter of fundamental rights of the EU  287–88
chemicals  257
Chevron  137
chief executive officers (CEOs)  19–20, 59–60, 66n.41, 73–74n.88, 81, 127, 132, 164, 184, 185, 200, 216, 219–20, 226n.30, 272
child labour  332
China  302–3, 305, 315, 331–32
choice of law  202
Christensen, H. B.  81
circular economy  258, 261
civil liability  34, 35–36, 273–74, 284–85, 295, 298–300
climate action failure  262
Climate Bonds Initiative  14–15, 301n.5, 307–9, 316
Climate Bonds Standard  14–15, 305, 307–9, 315, 316
climate change  5–6, 14, 37–39, 45–46, 50–51, 79–80, 87, 257, 258, 261, 274, 281–82, 287–88, 340
   disclosure  2–3, 7–8
   mitigation  311
climate disclosure
   laws on  319–20
   mandates  99n.118
   rules  4–5, 95, 96–97, 97–98n.104, 98
   standards  88, 92–93, 309
Climate Disclosure Standards Board (CDSB)  155t
climate disinformation campaigns  65
climate risk  86
code movement  5–6, 41–42, 53
co-determination  76, 119–24, 126, 215
   corporate policy impact  120–21
   laws, influence of  109–10
Cold War  185
collective benefits  358, 364–65
colonialism  1–2, 251
commercial sustainability ratings  80
Commission delegated acts  258
commitment
   contractual incompleteness  62–63
   corporate purpose and  62–65

common good before self-interest principle  8–9, 108
Common Market Organization (CMO)  366–67
communism  185
Companies Act 2006 (UK)  9–10, 43, 108, 142–43, 144, 149, 151, 225, 228–29, 242n.100, 323n.17
compensation
   damages  298–99
   equity-linked  139
   executive  262, 263
competition law
   sustainability and  16, 357–69
   *see also* consumer welfare approach; externality problem
compliance  41–42
   obligations  7–8
'comply and explain' approach  5–6, 23–24, 53, 118, 148–49, 251–52
concession system  52
Condon, M.  137
conflict of laws  295
constituency statutes  9, 29–30, 75–76, 135–36, 139–40, 192
consumer, concept of  363
consumer welfare approach  358, 361–65, 369
   collective benefits  364–65
   conceptual and practical rationale  365–66
   individual benefits  364–65
   prospective willingness to pay  362–63
   reducing externalities beyond  365–68
   reflective willingness to pay  361–62
   social norms and willingness to pay  363–64
control rights  17–18
coordination problems  15–16, 326–27
corporate bonds  257–58
corporate citizenship  1–2
corporate culture  40–41
corporate fiduciaries  66
corporate governance
   implications for  12–16
   objectives of  12–13
corporate law  200–1, 202, 203–4
   concept of  232
   definition of  197–98
   function of  204
   implications for  12–16
   principles of  231
   separation of  23–24
   theory  222–23
corporate procedure  204–5
corporate purpose
   commitment, as  62–65
   concept of  2–4, 74, 157
   definition of  6–7, 9–10, 127–28, 132–33
   empirics of  72–81
   great debate  196–200
   historical development (US)  11–12
   importance of  81
   irrelevance of  57–62
   mandatory vs optional  17–19
   movement  52, 225

proper 73–75
statement 74
theory of 57–62
US mid-century 182–89
Corporate Social Responsibility (CSR)
  business case of 153–54
  challenges 4–5
  concept of 153, 161, 198–99
  disclosure requirements 2–3
  ethical dimension 142
  focus 153–54, 155t
  historical activism 11–12
  implementation 153–54, 155t
  metrics 153–54, 155t
  reporting 153–54, 155t
  stakeholder value theories 20–21
  sustainability and 249–50
  transmission channel 153–54, 155t
corporate sustainability
  board members 39–40
  due diligence 33–39, 52, 275
  European Due Diligence Directive (2022) 36–39, 43–46, 288–89
  initiatives 81, 146–47
  reporting, importance of 234–35n.59
  see also Draft Directive on Corporate Sustainability Due Diligence (CS3D)
Corporate Sustainability Due Diligence Directive (CSDDD) 237–38, 240–41, 243
Corporate Sustainability Reporting Directive (CSRD) 2–3, 43–45, 84–85, 117, 167n.27, 235–36, 264, 265, 277, 287–88
corruption 262
cost, regulatory considerations 98–99
cost-of-living 183–84
Covid-19 pandemic 24–25
credence goods 62–63
CS3D enforcement regime 292–94, 297–98
CSR see Corporate Social Responsibility (CSR)
culture 72–73

Dammann, J. 215–16
dangerous products 197
Danone 19
Davies, P. 32–33, 151, 152, 157
Davos Manifesto (2020) 20–21
decarbonization 93
demand-side regulation 322–34
  basic design options 334
  complement, as a 328–33
  concept of 15–16
  direct 334–48, 355–56
  indirect 15–16, 334, 348–56
  mandatory 334–45
  notion of 328–29
  promises and perils of 337–45, 347–48
  voluntary 346–48
Denmark 251
  stewardship 13–14
Det Norske Veritas (DNV) 305

Deutsche Bank 306–7
Dimon, J. 19–20
Directors' duties 3–4, 9–10, 13, 217–45
  care, duty of 14
  corporate sustainability due diligence legislation 237–40
  European context 240–41
  international standards 233–41
  non-financial reporting law 233–37
  real world implications 241–44
  stakeholderism vs shareholderism 222–32
disclosure 5–6, 43–45, 53, 79–81
  climate risk 98–99
  corporate disclosure regulation 86–87
  EU sustainability 335–37
  information 7–8
  insufficient 344–45
  pre-contractual 339–41
  public 34, 291
  regulation 273, 329–30
  specialized 97
  standards 240–41
  stewardship 273–74
discretion
  intervention 358
  margin of 230–31, 237
discrimination
  employment 206
disinformation 65
Dittmar, A. K. 77–78
diversity, equity, and inclusion (DEI) 77–78, 92–93, 99, 100, 121–22, 252
dividend policy 157
Dodd, M. 11–12, 174, 180–83, 184–85, 222–23
Dodd-Berle debate 11–12
Dodge brothers 179
'doing well by doing good' 58–62
donations 67
double materiality standard 85–86, 277
DowDuPont 19
Doyle, A. C. 195–97
Draft Directive on Corporate Sustainability Due Diligence (CS3D) 4–6, 25n.59, 32, 33, 36–37, 45n.190, 47–48, 49, 52, 292–94
  enforcement regime 297–98
  due diligence 33–39, 52, 260, 275, 296
  European generalization of 284–88
  reforms 9–10
  requirements 3–4
DuPont 65
Dutch East India Company (VOC) 23–24

eBay 68
Eckbo, B. E. 77–78
economic theory 5–6, 52
  outcomes 224–25
  problems 28–29
Edmans, A. 18, 151
effectiveness of measures 239–40
Eidenmüller, H. 215–16

## 374    INDEX

electric vehicles  360–61, 368
employee, environmental, social, and governance (EESG)  21–22
employee co-determination  8–9, *see also* co-determination
employee profit-sharing  157
Employee Retirement and Income Security Act 1974 (ERISA)  90, 93, 209–10
Enacting Purpose Initiative  73
enforcement problems  39–51
enlightened shareholder value principle  43, 159, 225, 228–29, 323–24
enterprise law  5–6, 45–48, 53
   corporate organs, organization of the  46–48
   duties  46–48
   duties of the enterprise  45–46
   inside requirements  46–48
   outside requirements  45–46
   rights  46–48
entity maximization and sustainability model (EMS model)  18
environmental damage  50–51
environmental disasters  263
environmental groups  50–51
environmental law  3–4, 24, 140, 257
environmental problems  28
environmental, social, and governance (ESG)  1–2, 21–22, 83, 141, 145n.17, 194, 205–6, 217–18, 234, 235n.67, 259–60, 265, 319, 349
   anti-ESG backlash  4–5, 7–8, 93–95
   concept of  235–36
   corporate management  247–48
   definitions of  13–14
   demand-side decision-making  15–16
   disclosure rules  15–16
   engagement activities and  269–73
   engagement by investors, effectiveness of  13–14
   entity model of  9–10
   ethics and  10–11, 161–71
   EU Stewardship Regulation  255–58
   European stewardship codes  252–55
   federal challenges  93
   federal Regulation  85
   finance  9–10
   focus  153–54, 155t
   Global Disclosure Standards for Investment Products  90–91
   implementation  153–54, 155t
   integration, regulatory limits on  93–95
   investment activities and  258–69
   legislature, impact on  112–15
   mandatory disclosure  45
   mandatory reporting  10–11
   metrics  153–54, 155t
   movement  52
   options for regulation of  5–6
   reporting  153–54, 155t, 240–42
   risk integration  13–14
   scoping challenges  101
   shareholders  15–16
   social dimension of  100
   social goals  9
   standards  7–8
   state challenges  94–95
   state investment regulation  92–93
   stewardship  248–49
   stewardship and  13–14
   takeover fears  101–2
   transmission channel  153–54, 155t
   transnational context  7–8, 83–103
equity financing  63–64
equity investment  64–65
Ernst & Young (EY)  2–3, 124, 280–81
ESG *see* environmental, social, and governance (ESG)
Esser, I.-M.  9–10
ethics  152, 159, 161–71, 262
Eumedion  253
European Banking Authority (EBA)  49
European Central Bank (ECB)  49
European Commission (EC)  2–3, 36–38, 46–47, 116, 124, 232, 233–34, 257, 265–66, 279–80, 281–82, 286–87, 288, 309–10, 312, 315–16, 319–20, 321, 350
European Corporate Sustainability Due Diligence Directive (2022)  36–39, 43–46, 288–89
European Corporate Sustainability Reporting Directive (2022)  43–45
European Court of Justice (ECJ)  367
European Financial Reporting Advisory Group (EFRAG)  235–36, 265
European Green Deal  309–10, 319–20
European Network of Supervisory Authorities (ENSA)  49
European Parliament (EP)  281–82, 288–89, 293
European Proposal on Companies' Due Diligence Duties  14
European Securities and Markets Authority (ESMA)  49, 314, 338–39
European Sustainability Reporting Standards (ESRS)  84–85, 265
European Union (EU)
   accounting law  45–46
   enforcement approach  359
   ESG stewardship, approach to  248–49
   Green Deal  2–3
   Horizontal Guidelines  357
   investment advice, regulation of  348, 349–50
   primary law, primacy of  16, 366–68
   public interest  2–3
   public regulation  218–19
   sustainability disclosure  335–37
   US business  4–5
executive pay  6–7, 71–72
exploratory factor analysis  74–75
external governance  195–216
external regulation  65
externality problem  359–61
   consumers' willingness to pay, role of  359–60
   multi-goal approach, shortcomings of  361

# INDEX

notion of externality 359
sustainability, notion of 360–61
ExxonMobil 137

fair trade 58
fairness, wages 360
Federal Reserve Board (FRB) 7–8
federalism 95–96
Ferrarini, G. 13–14
fiduciary duties 3–4, 6–8, 15–16, 65–70, 75–76, 248–49
   moral behaviour and 165–67
   sustainability, integration of 265–69
fiduciary law, principles of 230–31
Financial Conduct Authority (FCA) 346–47
financial crisis (2007) 8–9, 111–12
financial institutions 22–23
financial investors 78
financial literacy 353–54
financial market participants 340–41
Financial Reporting Council (FRC) 19, 152, 249–51, 346
Financial Stability Oversight Council (FSOC) 91–92
fines 34
Fink, L. 127, 128–29, 132, 134
Fisher, J. 6–7
fishing 362–63
Fleischer, H. 32–33
food and beverage companies 19, 31
food scarcity 257
Ford Foundation 20–21
Ford Motor Company 179
Ford, H. 179
Fortune 100: Best Companies to Work For 74–75
Fortune 500 corporations 190–91
fossil fuels 59, 93, 368
fracking 348
France 24–25
   CAC 40 25
   company regulation 25
   *conseil d'administration* 321
   Constitutional Council 286, 295
   Constitutional Court 34
   Declaration of human rights 286
   Duty of Diligence Law (2017) 5–6, 14, 33–35, 36–37, 50–51, 52, 275–300
   enforcement and sanctions 294–300
   European diligence compared 288–300
   financial markets law 114–15
   *Loi Pacte* (2019) 5–6, 14, 31, 33–35, 52, 284
   minimum content 291–94
   personal scope 288–89
   plan elaboration 291
   *raison d'être* 275–76
   *société à mission* 32–33, 275–76
   softening amendments 286
   substantive requirements 290–94
   sustainability benefits 364
   vigilance plans 290–94
   yellow vest protests (2018) 59

free enterprise system 185
free market economy 358–59
freedom of speech 61
Friedman, M. 19–20, 57, 62, 190, 195–96
   legitimacy argument 58–60
Friends of the Earth 340
FTSE 100 companies 145–46, 148–49
fundamental freedoms 34
Future of the Corporation project 2–3

G20 Financial Stability Board 84–85, 88
gadflies 94
Galbraith, J. K. 183–84
game theory 333, 347
gas extraction 348
gender 77, 100, 202
   equality 77–78
   parity 70
   quotas 77–78, 92–93
   *see also* LGBTQ+ community
General Motors 178, 183–84, 186–87
Generation Z 339–40
Germany 105–26
   banking supervisory law 23
   business judgment rule 46–47
   CFOs, survey of 39–40
   civil liability 298
   company regulation 25
   Constitution 113, 123
   consumer prices 364
   Corporate Governance Code 41–42
   corporate law 223–24, 231–32
   DAX 40 25, 328–29
   employee participation 27, 47
   ESG and business policy 124–25
   Federal Constitutional Court 123
   Federal Ministry of Finance xiv
   Federal Ministry of Justice 111–12
   Federal Office of Economics and Export Control (BAFA) 35–36
   Federal Supreme Court 121
   greenwashing 306–7
   Hanseatic League 41–42
   industrial companies 17–18
   intervention discretion 358
   labour co-determination 119–24
   labour representation 47–48
   labour unions 47
   limited partnerships 123–24
   national socialism 107–8
   reform agenda 118–19
   *Regierungskommission* 111–12, 114
   regime development 119–20
   representative model 119–25
   stock corporation law (*Aktienrecht*) 8–9, 49–50, 105–9, 110–11, 231–32
   stock exchange company law 25
   Supply Chain Due Diligence Act (2021) 5–6, 35–37, 49
   supply chain legislation 365–66

Germany (*cont.*)
  tax scandal 40–41
  *Tierwohl* 358
  trustee model 106–19
  *Unternehmen an sich* debate 107–8
  value chain legislation 37–39
  *Vorstand* 321
  war economy 119–20
  Weimar Republic 107–8, 125
  World War II, reforms post- 108–9
Gierke, Otto von 162
gig economy 210–11
Gillian, S. L. 80–81
Glasgow Financial Alliance for Net Zero (GFANZ) 94–95
Global Reporting Initiative (GRI) 154, 155t, 234–35n.59, 265
global warming 287–88
globalization 136, 161
good faith 143–44
Google 19
governance arbitrageurs 94
Gower, L. C. B. 187
great merger movement 177–78
green asset ratio (GAR) 340–41
green bonds 301–17
  benefits of 303–5
  challenges for 14–15, 305–7
  competing standards 305–6
  development of 312
  EU regulatory approach 309–17
  external reviewers 316
  factsheet 316
  general assessment 315
  Green Bond Framework 308
  Green Bond principles 312–13
  Green Bonds Regulation 312–16
  Green Bonds Standard 312
  investor confusion 305–6
  market for 302–3
  market fragmentation 305–6
  moral hazard 307
  overview of 313–14
  perceived need for 312–13
  principles 308
  project sustainability 306
  prospectus requirement 315–16
  self-regulation of 307–9
  state agencies, supervision by 316
  summary 316–17
  taxonomy alignment 315
Green Deal (EU) 2–3, 14–15, 117, 277
green finance 4–5
green investment 14–15
Green Party 113
greenhouse gases (GHGs) 44n.178, 86–88, 92–93, 206, 261, 264–65, 276–77, 282n.43, 301n.3, 309–10, 319–20
greenwashing 14–15, 21–22, 40–41, 155–56, 248, 257–58, 277–78, 306–7, 337–39, 355

Griffith, S. 203
'grow the pie' mentality 151

Hail, L. 81
Haiti 263
hard law 13–14, 248, 282–83
harm 197, 282–85, 290, 295
  post-harm claims 295
Harper Ho, V. 7–8
Hart, H. L. A. 169
Hart, O. 19–20, 138–39, 327, 333
health and safety of persons 34
hedge fund activism 39–40, 78, 94, 206–7, 342
Hellenic Competition Commission 357
High-Level Expert Group on Sustainable Finance 280
historical foundations 10–12
Hopt, K. 5–6, 8–9, 105–6, 110
human rights 34, 38–39, 50–51, 105, 234, 282, 332, 360
  adverse impact 292
  organizations 228
  violations 35, 286–87
Hurst, W. 186–87

indefinite life 196–97
Inderst, R. 362, 367–68
index funds 78, 207–8
India 305, 315
indirect regulation, concept of 236–37
individual benefits 364–65
industrial problem 178–79
inflation 190
information problem 325–26
initiatives 81, 146–47
insolvency 26, 230
institutional investors 13–14, 21–22, 39–41
Institutional Shareholder Services 305
institutional underpinnings 65–72
insurance 266, 328–29
interested party, definition of 34
interests, balancing of 29–30
Intergovernmental Panel on Climate Change (IPCC) 301
internal affairs doctrine 177–78
internal governance 195–216
International Capital Market Association (ICMA) 90–91, 307–8
  Green Bond principles 312–13
International Financial Reporting Standards (IFRS) 84–85
International Integrated Reporting Council (IIRC) 155t
International Organization for Standardization (IOS) 234
International Organization of Securities Commissions (IOSCO) 84–85
International Sustainability Standards Board (ISSB) 84–86, 88, 92–93, 101–2, 142n.3, 156, 265
internationalization 286–87

investment
    activities 258–69
    criteria 13–14, 262–65
    ESG investments, special types of 260–62
    impact investing 13–14, 260
    processes 262–65
    product regulation and standards 90–91
    products 7–8
    selection 266–67
investors
    associations 21–22
    capital allocation decisions 12–13
    preferences 12–13, 15–16
    regulation 89–90, 206–12
Italy 24–25
    mandatory minority representation 47–48
    renaissance merchants 41–42
    stewardship 13–14

James, H. 344
Japan 251
Jefferson, T. 164
Jensen, M. 26–27, 56, 190, 228–29
JPMorgan Chase & Co 19–20
judicial review 49, 224–25

Kahan, M. 214
Kastiel, K. 76
Keay, A. 18
Kelsen, H. 169
key performance indicators (KPIs) 39–40, 234, 276n.13, 340–41
Khurana, R. 190–91
Ki Moon, B. 301
Kingman Review 250
Korsmo, C. 203
Kumpan, C. 14–15
Kuntz, T. 15–16, 23–24

labour law 8–9, 26, 105–6, 140
*laissez-faire* approach 177
land system change 257
law reform 155t
legal moralism 168, *see also* morality
legal personality 162, 196–97
legislation 31–33
    legislative options 29–30
Leuz, C. 81
LGBTQ+ community 343
limited liability companies (LLCs) 69n.57, 109–10, 120, 121, 131–32n.18, 132, 133–34, 203
limited liability partnerships (LLPs) 150
Lipton, A. M. 12–13
living wages 58
London Stock Exchange (LSE) 347
Luxembourg 36–37

MacNeil, I. 9–10
managerialism 190–91

capitalism 184, 186–87
    heroic 184–85, 186–87
mandatory purpose clauses 32–33
'many-masters' problem 320–21, 324
Marchand, R. 178
margin of appreciation 222–23
market capitalization 328–29
market choice 369
market discipline 5–6, 39–41, 53
Markets for Financial Instruments Directive (MiFiD II) 349
Mayer, C. 17–18, 45, 128, 133, 135, 152
Means, G. C. 179–80, 183, 184–85
Meckling, W. 190
*Médecins sans Frontières* 163
Medicare 201–2
members of Parliament (MPs) 108–9, 113, 120n.87
Mexico 263
Michelin 19
Millennial generation 339–40
Ministerial Instruction on the Licensing of Joint Stock Companies in Prussia (1845) 23–24
Moody's Investor Services 305
moral agents 10–11, 162–65
moral behaviour and fiduciary duties 165–67
moral hazard 14–15
morality 10–11, 167–69
Morningstar Sustainalytics 305
'most efficient operating' principle 5–6, 52
multi goals approach 368
    shortcomings of 361
multiple constituencies 200–3
mutual funds 89, 209–10, 328–29

Nader, R. 188–89
Names Rule amendments 91
Nasdaq 92–93
National Association of Manufacturers 187–88
national perspectives 6–10
National Securities Markets Improvement Act of 1996 (NSMIA) 96
Nestlé 263
Netherlands 41–42
    'chicken of tomorrow' 358
    climate change law 50–51
    due diligence legislation 36–37
    Dutch Financial Supervisory Authority 253
    services, quality of 367
    shipping and trade commerce 23–24
    stewardship 13–14
    tort law 4–5
new economic regulations (NREs) 276–77, 279n.25, 345
*New York Times* 190
New-York Manufacturing Company 174–75
Nike 263
'no-other-country' argument 286–87
nominal content 67–70
non-consequentialism 368

# 378  INDEX

non-financial reporting (NFR) 9–10, 142, 144, 146, 147, 148, 158, 242–43
   law 233–37
Non-Financial Reporting Directive (NFRD) 2–3, 13–14, 44, 145, 154, 233–34, 276–78
non-governmental organizations (NGOs) 7–8, 34n.118, 44, 88n.31, 124, 296
non-profit associations 50–51
non-use benefit 360
normative outcomes 224–25
Norway 77–78

objects clauses 143
ocean acidification 257
oil
   companies 65
   production 348
   rigs 263
operationalization, modes of 223–24
organizational psychology 186
Osterloh-Konrad, C. 10–11
overconsumption 257
overdisclosures 205–6
ownership 78–79
   common 78–79
   diffusion of 178–79
   dispersed 11–12
   rights 63
   social obligations and 184–85
   universal 78–79
Oxfam 263
   America Activist Fund 325
ozone depletion 257

*p*-hacking 73
Pargendler, M. 199
Paris Agreement 47–48, 83, 87, 117, 256, 261–62, 287–88, 292, 309–10, 340
Pennsylvania Railroad 179–80, 189–90
pensions 94, 178–79, 183–84, 208, 328–29, 342, 351
performance 79–81
personal liability 295
personhood theory 162
philanthropic organizations 227–28
philosophy 10–12
'pieconomics' 18
Pietrancosta, Alain 14
planetary boundaries 119, 126
platform business model 210–11
political lobbying 206
Pollman, E. 175–76
pollution 258
   prevention and control 261
pornography 348
portfolio approach 313
positive obligations 227, 228–29, 231, 232
pre-emptive claims 294–95
preference streamlining 331–33
principal-agent theory 26–27, 115, 116, 164–66
private bargaining 6–7
private enforcement 5–6, 49–51, 53
private enterprises 28–29

private equity 78
private interests 1–2
private law approach 9, 133–34
   mysticism and 163
product misuse 197
profit
   concept of 17–18
   maximisation 5–6, 52, 63, 128–29
Progressive Era 190–91
prosociality theory 200
proxy advisers 21–22
Prussia, Kingdom of 106–7
public benefit 23–24, 174–75, 178–79, 180
public benefit corporations (PBCs) 75, 76–77, 131, 150
public commitment 338–39
public companies
   concepts of 25
   purpose of 2–3
public corporation
   19th Century 23–24
   private corporation vs. 23–25
   retour of 24–25
public disclosure 291
public duties 1–2
public enforcement 5–6, 48–49, 53
public injunction 34
public interest entities (PIEs) 25, 277
public interests 1–2
public law approach 9, 23–24
public procurement 5–6, 48–49, 53
public support 297–98
public trustees 178–79
Purdue Pharma 65

*quo warranto*, writ of 175–76

race 77, 100, 202
rating agencies 21–22
reasonableness 290–91
regulated companies 22–23
Renaud, A. 107
renewable energy 261
reporting
   importance of 234–35n.59
   obligations 240–41
reservation price 359
return on assets (ROA) 74–75
returns 79–81
reverse causation 6–7
Rio+20 conference 234–35n.59
Ripley, W. Z. 180
risk
   management 39–40, 266–67
   risk-related 262–64
   sustainability 259–60
   systemic 91–92
Rock, E. 9, 17–18, 21, 25–26, 214
Rockefeller Foundation 188–89
Rome II Regulation 295, 298–99
Rostow, D. E. 186–87
Rousseau, J. J. 170

INDEX 379

Ruder, D. 187
rule of reason 366–67

S&P Global Ratings 305
sanctions 49, 63, 205–6, 218–19, 287–88, 294–300, 316, 356
   criminal 49
securities regulation 5, 23–24, 52
self-regulation 5–6, 39–41, 53
sexual harassment 263
shareholder interest, concept of 138–39
shareholder orientation
   concept of 217–18, 222–32, 244–45
   strict 226–27
shareholder primacy 63–65, 67, 130–31, 135–36, 143–44, 146–47, 157, 196, 203–15, 216
shareholder rights 89–90, 253
Shareholder Rights Directive II (SRD II) 13–14, 252, 269–70, 337
shareholder supremacy
   concept of 13
   doctrine of 222–23, 228, 231–32
shareholder value 3–4, 56, 62, 65–66, 67–68, 115–16, 193, 321
   concept 10–11, 19–20
   systems, pure or enlightened 29
   theory 51–52, 111, 115, 116–17
shareholder welfare 65–66
shareholderism 222–32
shareholders 19–23, 189–93
   coordination 353–55
   disagreements 342–44
   divergent interests of 27
   dividends 1–2
   ESG 327
   interests 21–22
   options for 31
   predatory 50–51
   primacy of 5–7, 9–10, 12–13, 29
   private enforcement by 49–51
   public interests vs 1–2
   shareholder/stakeholder distinction, unenforceability of 51, 66–67
   stakeholder proxy 344
   strict shareholder orientation 226–27
   ultimate risk-bearers 26
*Shell* case 50–51
Shiller, R. J. 40–41
short-term share-price maximisation 21, 29
Simon, H. 186
single materiality standard 85–86
Siri, M. 13–14
small and medium-sized enterprises (SMEs) 34n.117, 38–39, 117, 235n.66, 235n.68, 236n.70, 264, 277, 286, 289, 315–16
Smith, A. 57
social acts 66
social choice 369
Social Democratic Party (SDP) 47, 113
social desirability bias 15–16, 322, 351–53
social good 6–7
social norms approach 364

social problems 28–29
social purpose 57
social responsibility 184–85
social science 5–6, 25–29, 52
social welfare 56, 72
socialism 198–99
socially responsible investments (SRIs) 83, 94, 198–99, 213n.124
Societas Europaea 123–24
soft law 13–14, 85, 100–1, 144, 155, 155t, 248, 249
South African social and ethics committee 157
Spain 24–25
Spamann, H. 6–7
sportswear 19
stakeholderism 19–23, 65–66, 218–20, 222–23, 225, 226–27, 228–29, 231
   new 222–25
   shareholderism vs 222–32
   stakeholderist jurisdictions, impact of 231–32
stakeholders
   capitalism 20–21
   concerns, prominence 226–27
   directors' duties, nature of 230–31
   divergent interests of 27
   impacts on and contributions of 26
   interests 21–22, 26–27
   perspective of 212–15
   private enforcement by 49–51
   shareholder/stakeholder distinction, unenforceability of 66–67
   shareholders vs 51
   theory 279
   value theories 3–4, 20–21, 115–16, 323–24
Standard Oil 184–85
state agencies 5–6, 48–49, 53
state-owned enterprises (SOEs) 24–25
state responsibility 28–29
stewardship codes
   assessment 268–69
   codes, origins of 249–52
   Danish Code 252–53
   Dutch Code 252–53
   engagement activities and ESG 269–73
   engagement disclosure under SRD II and SFDR 269–71
   EU Stewardship Regulation 255–58
   European stewardship codes 252–55
   fiduciary duties 265–69
   function of 274
   investment activities 258–69
   investment selection 266–67
   Italian Code 253–54
   legal strategies 249–58
   likeliness of ESG engagement 273
   limits of engagement 272–73
   non-EU countries 254–55
   origins of 249–52
   product governance and sustainability 267–68
   risk management 266–67
   Swiss Stewardship Code 254–55
   *see also* UK Stewardship Code (UKSC)

stock exchange 21–22, 347
   company law 25
   reporting standards 331–32
stockholders, wealth maximisation 68
stock-market short-termism 78
strategic reports 43
Strine, Leo E. Jr. 21–22, 43–44
structural governance 70–72
structure 76–78
subsidiarity principle 281–82
substitution effects 60–62
supply chain management 157
supply-side regulation
   problems of 323–27
Sustainability Accounting Standards Board
     (SASB) 101–2, 155t
sustainability 79–81
   competition law and 16
   corridors 367–68, 369
   notion of 360–61
   preferences 266–67
   product governance 267–68
   reporting by issuers 264–65
   risk, adverse impacts of 259–60
   risk, definition of 259–60
   sandbox initiative 357
Sustainability Finance Disclosure Regulation
     (SFDR) 2–3, 13–15, 89, 90–91, 94–95, 248–49,
     255–57, 258–62, 263–64, 266, 269–71, 310, 311,
     334–37, 338–39, 340–41, 349, 355
Sustainability Regulation 309–11
   Action Plan 2018 309–10
   European Green Deal 309–10
   Sustainable Finance Disclosure Regulation
     (SFDR) 310
   Taxonomy Regulation 311
sustainable development 296, 301n.3, 309
   goals (SDGs) 86–87, 141, 253
sustainable finance 309–10
   investing 78, 79–80
   sourcing 58
Sweden 36–37
Switzerland
   stewardship 13–14
   stock exchange company law 25
Swope, G. 178–79, 181

tacit condition 175–76
takeover wars (1980s) 131
takeovers 190–91
Tallarita, R. 21, 76
Task Force for Climate-related Financial Disclosure
     (TCFD) 88, 92–93, 95, 99n.116, 101–2,
     101n.128, 141–42, 154
taxation 368
   incentives 207–8
   legislation 136, 140, 167
   transfer systems and 5–6, 52
Taxonomy Regulation (EU) 7–8, 13–15, 255–56,
     257–58, 277–78, 311, 336–37, 338–39, 340–41

Technical Expert Group 312, 315
Teflon 65
Thailand 263
theory of the firm 190
Thomas, S. 16, 362, 367–68
tobacco 348
*Tobin's Q* 74–75
tort law 295
totalitarianism 10–11, 170
trade unions 50–51, 121, 122
tradeable shares 196–97
traded emissions certificates 61
transnational context 6–10, 83–103
Treaty on the Functioning of the European Union
     (TFEU) 16, 360, 366–67
Truman, H. 183–84
Trump, D. 61
trustee model 8–9, 106–19
Truth Media 61
Twitter 61

Uber 263
UK Stewardship Code (UKSC) 13–14, 30n.85, 41–42,
     249–, 50–, 259n.75, 269, 319–20, 334, 346–47
*ultra vires* doctrine 11–12, 133, 176–77
Undertakings for Collective Investment in
   Transferable Securities (UCITS) 255–56,
   259n.76, 266, 268–69
United Airlines (UA) 70
United Auto Workers (UAW) 183–84, 186–87
United Kingdom (UK)
   activism 254
   antitrust laws 358
   community interest companies 32–33
   company law 228–29
   Competition and Markets Authority 357
   conceptual operation 2
   Corporate Governance Code (2018) 9–10, 19,
     41–42
   lightened shareholder value 29–30
   private vs public interests 1–2
   regulatory initiatives 5
   *see also* UK Stewardship Code (UKSC)
United Nations (UN) 84–85, 234, 286–87
   General Secretary 301
   Global Compact 234–35n.59
   member states 141
   Paris Agreement (2015) 309–10
   Rio+20 conference 234–35n.59
   system 234–35n.59
United Nations Guiding Principles on Business and
   Human Rights (UNGPs) 141, 279, 288–89, 292
United Nations Principles for Responsible Investment
   (UNPRI) 94–95, 153n.37, 154, 259, 270
United Nations Principles of Reasonable Investment
   (PRI) 338
United States (US)
   activism 254
   annual meetings 263
   antitrust law 24

# INDEX

benefit corporation 32–33
business judgement rule 67
Business Roundtable 3–4
capital markets 86, 98–99
capitalism 183–84
Civil War 174–75
conceptual operation 2
concession system 23–24
constituency states 29–30
constituency states 52
constituency statutes 75–76
Constitution 216
corporate governance 21–22, 135–36
corporate law 137–39, 197–98
corporate purpose 132–35, 182–89
corporate statesmen 192–93
Court of Appeals 92–93
CSR, concept of 2–3
Declaration of Independence 164
Department of Labor (DoL) 90, 99–100, 208
disclosure obligations 2–3
doctrines 110–11
economic theory 25–26
enforcement approach 359
ESG concept of 2–3
ESG mainstreaming 83–84
ESG Regulation, overview of 87–95
EU compliance 4–5
Federal Reserve 87
federalism 95–96
green debt 302–3
historical perspectives 173–94
institutional context for ESG regulation 95–102
military 188
modern debate, origins of 177–82
nineteenth century purpose 174–77
non-financial reporting 2–3
'objective' of corporations 129–31
politics 99–102
Principles of Corporate Governance 29–30, 52
private vs public interests 1–2
publications 184–85
regulatory initiatives 5
Restatements 9, 17–18, 127–40, 217–18
securities regulation 24
shareholder-driven ESG activism 136–37
shareholders 189–93
Supreme Court 29, 97–98, 164, 177–78
sustainable investment products 90–91
transnational context 7–8
Treasury 87
*see also* US Securities and Exchange Commission (SEC)

US Securities and Exchange Commission (SEC) 2–3, 4–5, 7–8, 22n.45, 43–44, 57n.8, 80n.118, 86n.18, 87–90, 91, 92–93, 95, 96–99, 100–2, 208, 210–11, 319–20
 rule-making authority 96–98
US Steel 179–80

Vale 263
value chains 292–93
veil-piercing 202
Veil, R. 8–9
Ventoruzzo, M. 32–33
vicarious liability 295
Vietnam War 187–88, 189–90
vigilance, duty of 14
Volkswagen 263
voluntarism 155*t*
voluntary codes 251–52
voting power 207–9

Walker, D. 20–21, 249–50
Warren, E. 215
waste production 261
water
 sewage companies 358
 systems 257, 258, 261
weapons 348
weather events 262
welfare capitalism 178–79
Wells Fargo 263
Wells, H. 11–12
willingness to pay (WTP) 16, 332n.74, 353–54, 358n.15, 359–60, 368, 369
 non-use benefits 364–65
 prospective 362–63
 reflective 361–62
 social norms and 363–64
Wilson, C. 187
Winkler, A. 202
women 70
workers' rights 136
World Bank 302–3
World Economic Forum Global Risks Report (2021) 262
World Trade Organization (WTO) 289
World War II, post-war reforms 108–10, 119–20, 174, 182, 183–84, 185
*Wouters* doctrine 367, 369
Wright, R. 174–75

Yves Rocher 295

Zingales, L. 19–20, 138–39, 327, 333